A SHAKESPEARE

Shakespeare DATABASE

H. Joachim Neuhaus   Marvin Spevack

A
SHAKESPEARE
THESAURUS

by MARVIN SPEVACK

2002
Georg Olms Verlag
Hildesheim · Zürich · New York

*

Die Deutsche Bibliothek - CIP-Einheitsaufnahme

Spevack, Marvin:
A Shakespeare thesaurus / by Marvin Spevack. -
Hildesheim ; Zürich ; New York : Olms, 2002
ISBN 3-487-09776-1

∞ ISO 9706
© Georg Olms Verlag AG, Hildesheim 2002
Unveränderter Neudruck der Auflage Hildesheim 1993
Alle Rechte vorbehalten
Die Rechte an den elektronisch gespeicherten Daten
verbleiben beim Projekt "Shakespeare Database"
© H. Joachim Neuhaus und Marvin Spevack
Printed in Germany
Gedruckt auf säurefreiem und alterungsbeständigem Papier
Textgestaltung: Prof. Dr. H. Joachim Neuhaus, Münster
Textschriften: Times (Linotype), Post Antiqua (H. Berthold AG)
Herstellung: Druckerei Lokay, 64348 Reinheim
ISBN 3-487-09776-1

To

GLORIA P. HERTZ
and the memory of
CHARLES HERTZ

Preface

If, as Edward Phillips says in the preface to his *New World of English Words* (1658), "the very Summe and Comprehension of all Learning in General, is chiefly reducible into these two grand Heads, *Words* and *Things*," then it is not surprising that dictionaries and similar lexica have always intended to present more than their rigid columns of information would seem to indicate, as may be seen in their insistence on terms like "world" — from John Florio's bilingual *Worlde of Wordes* (1598), whose title Phillips seems to inflect, to Johann Amos Comenius's *Orbis Sensualium Pictus* (tr. Charles Hoole, 1659), down the ages to *Webster's New World Dictionary* — or terms which amplify the simplex "world": general, comprehensive, unabridged, international, universal, and the like. This expansiveness is not a simple reflection of the growth of language as embodied in the development of dictionary entries from slim, glossarial word lists to extensive encyclopedic paragraphs. It makes quite clear that the dictionary purports to be a rendition of the world and that its aim is to teach "unskilfull persons" (etymologically understood, Robert Cawdrey's designation in 1604 for the target audience of his *Table Alphabeticall* still holds) to perceive and understand that world. The present work, which might also be called Shakespeare's world of words, is no exception. For its aim is to mirror the world which is to be derived from Shakespeare's idiolect, as well as to give an impression of the surrounding contemporary world since Shakespeare accounts for almost half of the recorded words of his time. The perspective is thus not solely personal or literary or linguistic but, importantly, historical, sociological, and cultural.

Organizing the words and things of the world is no simple matter. Lexicographers may be harmless drudges but the alphabetical structure they have adopted and favoured is not without a certain surrealistic cast. It may be easy to set up and of course to access, but its narrow columns and prefabricated formulas are uncanny: flat, abstract, almost ruthlessly democratic. Deficient quantitatively and qualitatively, isolated and atomized, the entries lack those meaningful contours for which neither their varying lengths nor the random usage markers nor the votes of experts' panels nor the occasional citations or illustrations can adequately compensate.

For the tradition of Comenius down to the present-day *English Duden: A Pictorial Dictionary*, the world is composed of scenes, a passing parade of things and activities. Although Comenius's presentation of the "visible world," of "things obvious to the senses," reflects a traditional hierarchical world view — it begins with a chapter or lesson on God, "the creator, so the Governor, and preserver of all things, which we call the world," and ends with the Last Judgement — the pictorial Duden, presenting a more extensive and secular series of pictures, is not inherently different. Nor are other more ingenious or complex systems — be they philosophical, like John Wilkins's tome *An Essay towards a Real Character and a Philosophical Language* (1668), or conceptual, like Rudolf Hallig and Walther von Wartburg's *Begriffssystem als Grundlage für die Lexikographie* (²1963), or eclectic, like the toweringly influential, well-nigh indestructible *Roget's Thesaurus* and its countless updates and mutations. For at their core dictionaries and especially thesauruses are interpretations, often reflecting quite personal and individual choices and perspectives, despite the pressures of lineal descent — that chain of dependencies which constitutes the evolution of dictionaries — the uniformity of formulas of definition, and the sameness of format. Indeed, the very selection of words to be included or of synonyms to be employed in the process of definition or the assignment of a word to one group and not another is proof enough of the particularity of lexicographical practice. In outline (whether the structure be alphabetical or conceptual) or in detail (the countless choices and decisions), a certain subjectivity is not only unavoidable, it is mandatory.

Not surprisingly, existing systems of classification cannot be simply or easily imposed upon the Shakespearean vocabulary. Roget's, the most obvious and developed, is at once too detailed and yet also insufficient. Too detailed in that the Shakespeare corpus may account for a healthy percentage of English, but it is not English per se. Its gaps in vocabulary are considerable: it lacks such common words as *agreeable, attack, bundle, caress, connect, effort, exert, explain, genuine, hesitate, intense, result, risk, timid,* among many others, useful both in themselves and as potential synonyms. Incomplete paradigms are common too: *appear* exists but not *disappear, disanimate* but not *animate,* the verb *gloom* but not the noun, *theoric* but not *theory.* Furthermore, existing systems are also insufficient in that linguistic processes, like compounding — to name but one morphological trait which plays so important a role in Shakespeare's creativity — are barely accounted for in a Roget or its clones, not to mention, of course, the uncharted, perhaps unchartable, splendours of his figurative language. Even the rudimentary things of the world — ships and sealing-wax, cabbages and kings — often receive inadequate focus. It would of course be interesting to compare Shakespeare and English, but the superimposition of the one upon the other might produce fairy gold since the inventories are so essentially different not only in semantics and grammar but indeed in emphases and quality.

A *Shakespeare Thesaurus* is admittedly an interpretation, one among others, and indebted to the thesaurus tradition. But it is less a universal anatomy than an attempt to describe the Shakespearean idiolect by classifying the vocabulary in an open and fair way: open, in that it prefers smaller units which allow for various and varying combinations and configurations; fair, in that it attempts to avoid what has been termed "instinctive associations" and such vagaries. It strives, in short, to strike a reasonable balance between what is suggested and what is feasible, to harmonize the responses of both the Shakespearean and the lexicographer. Accordingly, a pragmatic cycle of shuffling and filtering and reshuffling of the vocabulary has determined the classification: that is, the names were supplied after the groups began to take shape. When it was apparent, for example, that there was a defined and sizable number of words connected with ships, a group was constructed and titled. In fact, the preoccupation with ships seemed so detailed that further groups were necessary: parts of ships were numerous enough for further groups to be formed: for decks and oars, sails, masts, anchors, tackle, wracks, seamen, harbours, flood-gates, as well as a group dealing with navigation. A similar procedure was employed for most of the "things," the components of the physical universe, and for the "words," the abstracts, as well. An overview of the classification system is to be found on pp. XVII ff.

The system is unabashedly eclectic, since the Shakespearean context is responded to. The composition of individual groups is equally so, since size — that is, manageability and transparency — is an important factor in the avoidance of both fragmentation and diffuseness. There may, for example, be enough items for a group consisting of various kinds of knives or nails or hinges, but items

X

which would constitute a group of only a very few members — like mallets or saws or files — are integrated into the larger group called Other Tools. The same is true for the inclusion, in the same group as the base, of forms with prefixation and suffixation which may be too small in number (or elusive of classification) to constitute a group in themselves: e.g. negative, reversative or privative, pejorative and other prefixes, as in *unprepared* (under Readiness), *unhorse* (under Horse), *mishear* (under Hear), as well as denominal noun, noun/adjective, verb/noun, adjective/noun and other common productive suffixes, as in *doer, hopeful, inhabitant, sanity*. In the main, the individual groups are built around nouns, the dominant word class, and amplified by other word classes commonly derived from or associated with them. At times they are contrastive in character; occasionally, word-class semantics has been employed; sometimes, the scenic method of the pictorial Duden or the semantic field. To avoid unnecessary abstraction, the name of a group is generally that of the member most representative of all the members.

The interpretation of individual words, the designation of the members of what might be loosely called the taxonomic families, is obviously no simple matter. Adding to the customary unwieldiness of semantics is the fact that standard reference works like the *Oxford English Dictionary*, the Onions/Eagleson *Shakespeare Glossary* (an off-shoot of the *Shorter Oxford*), and Alexander Schmidt's *Shakespeare-Lexicon*, indispensable companions to the present work, employ dictionary definitions which cannot be adopted in toto in a classification. For one thing, the Oxford works do not always agree with Schmidt both in the number of meanings assigned to a word and even in the meanings themselves. Thus *layer-up* is defined by the *Shakespeare Glossary* as "storer, preserver," by Schmidt as "destroyer," in one of numerous examples. At times, the *Shakespeare Glossary* disagrees with its parent: it defines *by leisure* as "not at all," whereas the *Shorter Oxford* has "with deliberation"; it defines *transfix* as "remove," whereas the *Shorter Oxford* has "to pierce through with, or impale upon, a sharp-pointed instrument." More important is the tendency of such lexica toward extensive and imprecise synonymy, as in Schmidt's five definitions of the noun *spoil* and the Shakespeare Glossary's twelve of the verb *touch* or in the former's eight to the latter's ten definitions of the same word *nice*. A certain amount of fuzziness is of course almost endemic to semantics. But too often it leads to a diffuseness which militates against classification: where is the one instance of the noun *interchange* to be placed when the *Shakespeare Glossary* defines it as both "alternation, vicissitude"? where is *undoubted* to be placed when Schmidt and the *Shakespeare Glossary* detect a sense as "fearless," whereas the *Shorter Oxford* has "not called in question"? where is *well-graced* to be placed when both Schmidt and the *Shakespeare Glossary* define it as "popular"? What are the consequences for the classification when *woman-tired* is glossed as "henpecked" or *land-damn* as "to make hell on earth for (a person)"?

To these pitfalls must be added the inherent difficulties of recognition and thus classification: early or obsolescent meanings (e.g. *insult* meaning "exult"; *exalt*, "raise"; *crazy*, "shattered"; *reprisal*, "prize"; *imbecility*, "weakness"); specialized single usages of otherwise known words (*forbid* meaning "curse"; *read*, "teach"); homographic snares (*illness* meaning "badness", not "sickness"; *illustrious* meaning "full of" and also "lacking light"); semantic shifts resulting from changes of word class or morphological structure (e.g. *goat/goatish*); coined compounds, often hapax legomena, which defy literalness (*cream-faced, thrice-driven, fancy-sick*); octopus concepts (*grace, free, honest,* etc.); and perhaps most unwieldy of all, figurative and transferred uses. These obstacles must be dealt with individually, and to a degree subjectively, to be sure, and such decisions may at times be open to question, a situation which is admittedly unalterable however much it is stressed that the present work is not a Shakespeare dictionary or glossary intended to take on every possible sense of every single instance of every word. A step towards a semantic description, it does not define but attempts to classify by locating the core of each item and suggesting some of the main arteries.

Since that assignment is not uncomplicated, the attempt is always made to give the core sense — that is, the one closest to the etymon. If a rose is a rose is a rose, then *rose* is assigned to the family of flowers. Metaphorical uses are, in the main, resisted unless it is deemed they are clearly circumscribable and not items in a fairly nebulous spectrum of possibilities, like *rose* suggesting youthfulness or cheerfulness or loveliness and more. At times, however, when only the figurative sense is to be found in the Shakespearean context, it may be advisable to give the literal also, in order to stock the physical world: thus *hilding* is assigned to the group of horses as well as to that of strumpets and rogues; *nuthook* is found along with *hook* and *beadle*; *unchain* with *manacle* and *freedom*. At other times, when the concrete is absent, interpretation based on general consensus is necessary: *cloud-kissing* is assigned to Height; *cold-blooded* with *hard-hearted*. Often multiple assignments are necessary to demonstrate if not polysemy then at least the main possibilities. This holds true as well in cases where the difficulty of decision is extreme or critical opinion divided: thus *alacrity* is found along with *readiness* and *nimbleness, convent* with *summon* and *convenient*. In any event, since it is impossible to explain all decisions let it be said again that the yardstick has been applied with sobriety and flexibility and, given the dauntingly complex task, with respectful modesty.

To account for the entire spoken vocabulary, certain families not normally found in a work of this kind, and interesting in themselves, have been constituted. The largest section consists of the names of places and persons (the latter individualized, and as they are commonly called in the works) arranged so as to constitute what amounts to a map and pocket history, a mythology and onomasticon. Other groups include foreign words and familiar phrases, pseudo foreign words (including some of Pistol's puzzling constructions), malapropisms and similar blunders, oaths (restricted to those in which God and holy figures and symbols are invoked), salutations, numbers, anatomy compounds, and "small" word classes — articles, conjunctions, interjections, numerals, prepositions, pronouns, and some adverbs too difficult to integrate into other families. A small group of cruxes contains words most resistant to unequivocal interpretation. Special attention is given to such dominating interests as communication and motion, solidarity and warfare. Finally (and with considerable trepidation), an attempt has been made to include selected phrases and phrasal verbs — mainly those which are figurative and thus not self-evident — and a very few common syntagmas or fixed expressions. Both are extremely difficult areas, requiring a level of penetration beyond the scope of this work. Admittedly only hints, they may nevertheless be of interest in themselves and more important perhaps for their pointing up the complexities involved in capturing the Shakespearean idiolect.

A Note to the User

In the manner of a thesaurus this work consists of two parts: 37 main categories containing 897 subgroups and an alphabetical index to all the entries in the subgroups. These entries, it must be noted, are abstract concepts which resemble what are popularly known as dictionary headwords. They are given in standard British spelling except for oaths and certain phrases and expressions, which are given as in my Shakespeare concordances so as to preserve their identity and flavour. For each entry — and for the first time — a simplified word class is added in the customary abbreviation: adj., adv., art., conj., int., n., num., prep., pron., vb., as well as phr. vb. (phrasal verb). Following dictionary practice, homographs receive separate entries — e.g. three for the verb *baste*, two for the noun *calf*; raised numbers are used for homographs with the same word class found in the same group. Names, oaths and some expressions are not labelled since their group affiliation or orthography describes them adequately enough in a work of this kind. A play and/or exact act-scene-line location in the Riverside Shakespeare and my concordances is of necessity provided for malapropisms, for the differentiation of characters bearing the same first and/or surnames, and for the group of assumed names. In the treatment of names, pseudohistorical applies to characters derived from partially historical or legendary sources. The foreign words are normally those in foreign-language contexts only and are marked lat. (Latin), fr. (French), it. (Italian). A number of cross-references are supplied for key words in phrases which do not appear individually or are otherwise difficult to find in an alphabetical arrangement. For ease of reference the groups are printed in columns, the members alphabetically. At the end of each group the number of members is given.

The Shakespeare DATABASE

The classified inventory which this thesaurus presents is a small contribution to the daunting task of unravelling and penetrating Shakespeare and his time. Although "handmade," it is connected to a massive electronic database, utilizing mainly the lemmatization process of the database in which each word of the corpus is analysed as to wordform and lemma and assigned descriptive and analytical information. Drawing on my concordances and an extensive linguistic investigation of the Shakespeare corpus and Early Modern English, the database has been developed over the last ten years at the University of Münster by a team led by my colleague H. Joachim Neuhaus, who describes it thus:

The Shakespeare Database is organized according to current relational models. The design stresses the integration of editorial, linguistic, literary, and theatrical information by setting up seventeen database entities with well over a hundred attributes. Cardinality values for database entities range from 2,500 to over one million records per entity. Statistical and graphical data are included in the database. The simplified datastructure diagramme on the following page is meant to give a rough idea of the overall architecture of the Shakespeare Database. It shows the location of the thesaurus entity and its relation to other database entities and their respective data.

Besides standard query-languages various custom-made access methods are also supported. There are traditional, philological entry points, such as textual collation and editing with access to all copy-texts and variant readings. Electronic facsimile pages of early quarto and folio printings are accessible via play (act, scene, line, speech prefix) and word (lemma, wordform, morpheme) references. Linguistically oriented datastructures, such as word-formation down to the level of the morpheme, and inflection can be explored directly. Shakespeare's vocabulary is also accessible by means of etymological or chronological query strategies, including information on first occurrences in Early Modern English.

Since 1990 the Shakespeare Database project has been using a dedicated VAXstation™ cluster as a production platform. The database design and the user interface will be fully documented. For personal computer users there will be a self-contained Shakespeare Database CD-ROM product.

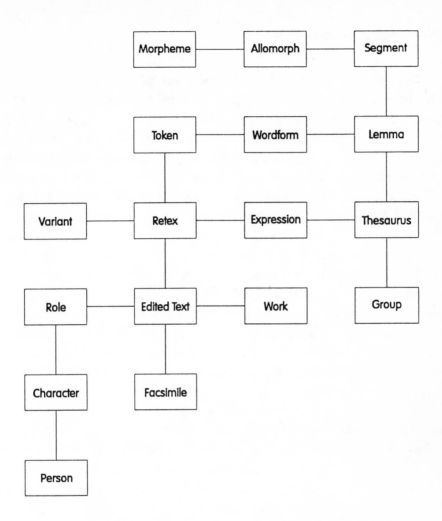

Shakespeare Database: entities and relations

The electronic database is a vehicle large and flexible enough to make available the structured totality of texts and grammar and various other literary, linguistic, and lexicographical perspectives necessary for complete interaction with the Shakespeare corpus.

Acknowledgements

Amassing the treasure which is a thesaurus takes many years and many hands and many skills. I am pleased to acknowledge the strong support, the engagement, and enthusiasm I have had from Shakespeareans, linguists, computer specialists, and organisations. Since listing them all would be tantamount to producing still another inventory, I hope it will be understood that if I mention only those who were with me over a considerable period of time I have by no means forgotten my debt to each and all who were there when needed. In the beginning I was helped by Hans-Jürgen Weckermann, Maria Rauschenberger, and Bernd Wuttke, who were involved in the setting up of the groups and the lemmatization process; by Peter Müller, who also outlined the ways the proper names were to be handled; and by Lydia Remke, for numerous tasks. Later, Sabine Ulrike Bückmann-de Villegas and Michael Hiltscher worked on the refinement of the groups. And throughout Marga Munkelt oversaw all stages with unswerving professionalism. For the not uncomplicated computational support I depended on the remarkable know-how of my colleague H. Joachim Neuhaus, whose command of the developments in linguistics and computer science enabled him to produce this book and effectively integrate its information into the electronic database. Gereon Franken and Peter Kollenbrandt were his able assistants. My thanks are also due to the Deutsche Forschungsgemeinschaft and Dr. Manfred Briegel for his concern and to the John Simon Guggenheim Memorial Foundation for providing me with a fellowship and thus the opportunity to think about what was to be done and how. Finally, yet foremost, Helga Spevack-Husmann was there from first to last, a learned, wise, and patient partner.

M. S.
August 1993

Classification System

08.35 tub
08.36 case
08.37 bag

09   food
09.01 appetite
09.02 feed
09.03 eat • drink
09.04 food • drink
09.05 cookery
09.06 salt • sugar
09.07 congeal
09.08 repast
09.09 pickle-herring
09.10 meat
09.11 sauce • porridge
09.12 pancake
09.13 bread • cake
09.14 butter
09.15 beer • wine
09.16 sweetmeat

10   clothing
10.01 attire
10.02 naked
10.03 cloth
10.04 leather
10.05 needlework
10.06 mantle
10.07 petticoat
10.08 sleeve
10.09 shoe • hose
10.10 hat
10.11 veil • mask
10.12 chaplet
10.13 belt
10.14 fan • glove
10.15 handkerchief
10.16 tape

10.17 fringe
10.18 ornament
10.19 gem
10.20 ring
10.21 brooch
10.22 perfume

11   basic manual acts
11.01 do
11.02 grasp
11.03 hit
11.04 press
11.05 cut
11.06 push
11.07 pull
11.08 break
11.09 rub
11.10 scratch
11.11 strip

12   sense perception
12.01 sight
12.02 show
12.03 semblance
12.04 colour
12.05 pale
12.06 spotted
12.07 hearing
12.08 sound
12.09 clangour
12.10 din
12.11 shout
12.12 whisper
12.13 neigh
12.14 bow-wow
12.15 touch
12.16 smell
12.17 taste

13   emotions
13.01 happiness
13.02 joy
13.03 smile
13.04 revelry
13.05 exult
13.06 rapture
13.07 (dis)pleasure
13.08 cheer(less)
13.09 seriousness
13.10 sorrow
13.11 lament
13.12 sob

14   qualities
14.01 goodness
14.02 love • hate
14.03 hope • despair
14.04 comfort
14.05 (in)constancy
14.06 (im)patience
14.07 humility
14.08 (un)gentle
14.09 lenity
14.10 moderation
14.11 liberality
14.12 (un)worthiness
14.13 (un)deserving
14.14 honesty
14.15 courtesy
14.16 honour
14.17 boldness
14.18 purity
14.19 chastity
14.20 beauty
14.21 spruce
14.22 badness
14.23 pride
14.24 ambition

14.25 braggardism
14.26 insolence
14.27 contempt
14.28 envy
14.29 anger
14.30 savageness
14.31 cruelty
14.32 hard-hearted
14.33 curstness
14.34 revenge
14.35 sternness
14.36 stubbornness
14.37 vehemence
14.38 uncontrolled
14.39 rashness
14.40 rudeness
14.41 levity
14.42 negligence
14.43 avarice
14.44 prodigality
14.45 corruption
14.46 fault
14.47 dishonour
14.48 desire
14.49 impurity
14.50 sensuality
14.51 fornication
14.52 fear
14.53 horror
14.54 ugliness

15   mind • thought
15.01 cognition
15.02 notion
15.03 mind
15.04 thought
15.05 logic
15.06 knowledge
15.07 memory

15.08 fantasy
15.09 amazement
15.10 wisdom
15.11 (in)discretion
15.12 foolishness
15.13 attempt
15.14 examination
15.15 search
15.16 surmise
15.17 choice
15.18 comparison
15.19 impartial
15.20 error • truth
15.21 (un)clear
15.22 (un)certainty
15.23 interpretation
15.24 belief
15.25 attribution
15.26 discovery
15.27 resolution
15.28 intention
15.29 motive
15.30 import
15.31 affair
15.32 circumstance

**16   socio-political
       structure**
16.01 commonwealth
16.02 government
16.03 statesman
16.04 senator
16.05 mayor
16.06 treasurer
16.07 council
16.08 assembly
16.09 council-house
16.10 edict
16.11 ruler

16.12 majesty
16.13 enthrone
16.14 ceremony
16.15 castle
16.16 heraldry
16.17 king
16.18 queen
16.19 duke
16.20 deputy
16.21 lord • lady
16.22 knight
16.23 ambassador
16.24 gentry
16.25 usher
16.26 attendant
16.27 household servant
16.28 bearer
16.29 servant
16.30 citizen
16.31 commoner
16.32 townsman

17   solidarity
17.01 attention
17.02 support
17.03 counsel
17.04 assistance
17.05 guide
17.06 protection
17.07 amendment
17.08 vigilance
17.09 agreement
17.10 (un)willingness
17.11 acknowledgement
17.12 affirmation
17.13 obligation
17.14 (dis)loyalty
17.15 (mis)trust
17.16 embrace • kiss

17.17 praise
17.18 encounter
17.19 salutation
17.20 hospitality
17.21 (in)gratitude

18 power
18.01 subjection
18.02 compulsion
18.03 (dis)obedience
18.04 supremacy
18.05 commandment
18.06 controlment
18.07 (ab)use
18.08 stifle
18.09 tame
18.10 permission
18.11 request
18.12 dependence
18.13 freedom
18.14 vassal
18.15 conspiracy
18.16 plot
18.17 enticement
18.18 instigation
18.19 deceit
18.20 flattery
18.21 rebellion

19 opposition
19.01 opposition
19.02 rival
19.03 menace
19.04 vexation
19.05 rejection
19.06 contradiction
19.07 debate
19.08 reproach
19.09 mockery
19.10 disparagement
19.11 quarrel
19.12 challenge
19.13 obstruction
19.14 negation
19.15 however
19.16 disorder
19.17 (un)rest
19.18 peril
19.19 avoid

20 warfare
20.01 combat
20.02 assault
20.03 foe
20.04 fighter
20.05 army • navy
20.06 officer
20.07 soldier
20.08 levy
20.09 camp
20.10 fortification
20.11 moat
20.12 armour
20.13 helmet
20.14 weapon
20.15 sword-hilt
20.16 gun
20.17 gunpowder
20.18 flag
20.19 booty
20.20 retreat
20.21 destruction
20.22 victory • defeat
20.23 peace

21 law
21.01 (un)justice
21.02 guilt • innocence
21.03 judgement
21.04 accusation
21.05 law court
21.06 testimony
21.07 privilegium
21.08 legacy
21.09 crime
21.10 murder
21.11 rape
21.12 thievery
21.13 punishment
21.14 prison
21.15 manacle
21.16 cudgel
21.17 gallows
21.18 hangman

22 trade • possession
22.01 trade
22.02 creditor • debtor
22.03 market
22.04 merchant
22.05 monger
22.06 money
22.07 price
22.08 payment
22.09 account
22.10 tax
22.11 pledge
22.12 contract
22.13 value
22.14 trifle
22.15 possession
22.16 keeping
22.17 chattel
22.18 estate
22.19 rich • poor
22.20 prosperity
22.21 beggar

XXII

27.04 archery
27.05 bear-baiting
27.06 games
27.07 gamester
27.08 toy
27.09 ball
27.10 sport terms
27.11 fisherman
27.12 falconer
27.13 forester
27.14 hunter
27.15 snare
27.16 horseman
27.17 bridle
27.18 saddle
27.19 curb

28 religion • superstition
28.01 religions
28.02 God
28.03 Abraham • Paul
28.04 Mars • Venus
28.05 spirits
28.06 mermaid
28.07 heaven • hell
28.08 worshipper
28.09 clergy
28.10 sermon
28.11 prayer
28.12 sacrament
28.13 holiness
28.14 saints
28.15 reverence
28.16 compassion
28.17 penitence
28.18 church
28.19 monastery
28.20 chantry
28.21 altar

28.22 pagan
28.23 irreligion
28.24 impiety
28.25 oaths
28.26 destiny
28.27 prognostication
28.28 sorcery

29 existence • relation
29.01 essence • matter
29.02 being
29.03 (un)natural
29.04 thing
29.05 indeed
29.06 pertain
29.07 proportion
29.08 pattern
29.09 rank
29.10 pre-eminence
29.11 foremost
29.12 extreme

30 manner
30.01 manner
30.02 disposition
30.03 behaviour
30.04 (im)possibility
30.05 (un)able
30.06 (un)skilful
30.07 preciseness
30.08 readiness
30.09 (un)aptness
30.10 easy • hard

31 quantity
31.01 quantity
31.02 quantor
31.03 all • nothing
31.04 full • empty

31.05 enough
31.06 load
31.07 count
31.08 numbers
31.09 pair
31.10 many • few
31.11 several
31.12 increase
31.13 decrease
31.14 swell
31.15 moreover
31.16 join
31.17 separation
31.18 mixture
31.19 stuff
31.20 excess
31.21 omission
31.22 cancel
31.23 equality
31.24 namely
31.25 difference
31.26 portion
31.27 heap
31.28 particle
31.29 drop
31.30 remnant
31.31 morsel
31.32 tatter
31.33 fragment
31.34 dreg
31.35 bunch
31.36 multitude
31.37 single
31.38 almost
31.39 weight
31.40 pint
31.41 scale
31.42 heavy • light

01.01
universe

---

creation, n.
monde, fr. n.
mundane, adj.
nature, n.
underworld, n.
universe, n.
world, n.
worldly, adj.
: 8

01.02
sky

---

caelum, lat. n.
celestial, adj.
ciel, fr. n.
cope, n.
element, n.
ensky, vb.
firmament, n.
heaven, n.
heavenly, adj.
horizon, n.
polus, lat. n.
roof, n.
sky, n.
skyey, adj.
skyish, adj.
welkin, n.
: 16

01.03
planet

---

aspect, n.
beneath world, n.
blazing star, n.
burning zone, n.
comet, n.
constellation, n.
crescent, n.
disaster, n.

disorb, vb.
Dragon's tail, n.
earth, n.
earthly, adj.
eclipse, n.
eclipse, vb.
equinoctial, n.
exhalation, n.
falling [star], n.
fixed star, n.
full moon, n.
globe, n.
globy, adj.
Guards, n.
half-moon, n.
heaven, n.
Hesperus
horn, n.
influence, n.
line, n.
lodestar, n.
lower world, n.
Mars
Mercury
meridian, n.
meteor, n.
middle earth, n.
moon, n.
moonish, adj.
new moon, n.
northern star, n.
north pole, n.
north star, n.
orb, n.
orbed continent, n.
planet, n.
planetary, adj.
pole, n.
polus, lat. n.
Saturn
seven stars, n.
shooting star, n.
sign, n.
Sol
sphere, n.

sphere, vb.
spherical, adj.
sphery, adj.
star, n.
star-like, adj.
starry, adj.
stelled, adj.
sun, n.
sunlike, adj.
sunny, adj.
tellus, lat. n.
terra, lat. n.
terre, fr. n.
terrene, adj.
terrestrial, adj.
under globe, n.
unsphere, vb.
unsunned, adj.
Venus
zenith, n.
zone, n.
: 74

01.04
zodiac

Aries
Bear
Bull
Cancer
Charles' wain, n.
Dragon
fiery Trigon, n.
Ram
Taurus
Ursa Major
Virgo
zodiac, n.
: 12

01.05
weather

---

climate, n.
climate, vb.

clime, n.
distemperature, n.
halcyons' days, n.
temperance, n.
temps, fr. n.
weather, n.
: 8

01.06
wind • storm

Aeolus
aer, lat. n.
aerial, adj.
air, n.
air, fr. n.
air, vb.
airless, adj.
airy, adj.
Aquilon
blast, n.
blastment, n.
blow, vb.
bluster, n.
bluster, vb.
blusterous, adj.
Boreas
drift-wind, n.
earthquake, n.
eastern wind, n.
east wind, n.
flaw, n.
four winds, n.
gale, n.
gust, n.
gusty, adj.
hurricano, n.
northeast wind, n.
north [wind], n.
overblow, vb.
sea-storm, n.
south, n.
south-west [wind], n.
south-wind, n.
storm, n.

storm, vb.
stormy, adj.
tempest, n.
tempestuous, adj.
weather, n.
west wind, n.
whiff, n.
whirlwind, n.
wind, n.
wind, vb.
wind-fanned, adj.
windy, adj.
Zephyr
: 47

01.07
thunder

bolt, n.
dread-bolted, adj.
lightning, n.
lightning-flash, n.
stone, n.
stones of sulphur, n.
sulphur, n.
sulphurous, adj.
thunder, n.
thunder, vb.
thunderbolt, n.
thunder-clap, n.
thunder-like, adj.
thunder-stone, n.
thunderstroke, n.
: 15

01.08
rain • snow

bow, n.
drizzle, vb.
flaw, n.
hail, n.
hail, vb.
hailstone, n.
Iris

overshower, vb.
oversnow, vb.
rain, n.
rain, vb.
rainbow, n.
rain-water, n.
rainy, adj.
shower, n.
shower, vb.
snow, n.
snow, vb.
snowball, n.
snow-broth, n.
snowy, adj.
water-gall, n.
: 22

01.09
cloud • vapour

cloud, n.
cloud, vb.
cloudiness, n.
cloudy, adj.
damp, n.
dew, n.
dew, vb.
dewdrop, n.
dew-dropping, adj.
dewy, adj.
encloud, vb.
exhale, vb.
field-dew, n.
fog, n.
foggy, adj.
fume, n.
fume, vb.
furnace, vb.
mist, n.
mist, vb.
mistful, adj.
mist-like, adj.
misty, adj.
morn-dew, n.
nubes, lat. n.

rack, n.
reek, n.
reek, vb.
reeky, adj.
smoke, n.
smoke, vb.
south-fog, n.
steam, n.
summer's cloud, n.
vaporous, adj.
vapour, n.
: 36

01.10
dry • wet

clamour-moistened,
adj.
damp, n.
dank, adj.
dankish, adj.
drought, n.
dry, adj.
dry, vb.
dryly, adv.
dryness, n.
ensear, vb.
humidity, n.
humorous, adj.
humour, n.
moist, adj.
moist, vb.
moisture, n.
oil-dried, adj.
parch, vb.
sear, vb.
sere, adj.
spongy, adj.
wash, vb.
water, vb.
watery, adj.
wet, adj.
wet, n.
wet, vb.
: 27

01.11
hot • cold

a-cold, adv.
ardour, n.
bask, vb.
bleak, adj.
chaud, fr. adj.
chill, adj.
chill, vb.
cold, adj.
cold, n.
coldly, adv.
coldness, n.
congeal, vb.
cool, adj.
cool, vb.
cull-cold, adj.
dead-cold, adj.
dissolve, vb.
easy-melting, adj.
freeze, vb.
freezing, n.
frost, n.
frosty, adj.
gelidus, lat. adj.
glowing-hot, adj.
heat, n.
heat, vb.
hissing-hot, adj.
hot, adj.
hot, n.
hotly, adv.
ice, n.
icicle, n.
icy, adj.
key-cold, adj.
lukewarm, adj.
melt, vb.
over-cool, vb.
raw, adj.
red-hot, adj.
scarce-cold, adj.
sultry, adj.
thaw, n.

thaw, vb.
warm, adj.
warm, vb.
warmth, n.
: 46

01.12
light • dark

appal, vb.
ashy, adj.
beacon, n.
beam, n.
bedim, vb.
bleach, vb.
blind, adj.
bright, adj.
brighten, vb.
brightest, n.
brightly, adv.
brightness, n.
bright-shining, adj.
burn, vb.
burnish, vb.
clear, adj.
clear, vb.
clearness, n.
clear-shining, adj.
clinquant, adj.
cloud, vb.
cloud-eclipsed, adj.
crisp, adj.
crystal, n.
crystalline, adj.
dark, adj.
dark, n.
dark, vb.
darken, vb.
darkling, adv.
darkly, adv.
darkness, n.
darksome, adj.
daughter-beamed,
  adj.
daylight, n.

deep-dark, adj.
dim, adj.
dim, vb.
dull, adj.
dusky, adj.
eclipse, n.
eclipse, vb.
enamel, vb.
enlighten, vb.
fade, vb.
fair, adj.
fiery, adj.
fire-eyed, adj.
flame, vb.
flash, n.
flash, vb.
flicker, vb.
flushing, n.
garish, adj.
gaudy, adj.
gild, vb.
gleam, n.
gleam, vb.
glimmer, n.
glimmer, vb.
glimpse, n.
glister, vb.
glitter, vb.
gloom, vb.
gloomy, adj.
gloss, n.
glow, n.
glow, vb.
illume, vb.
illuminate, vb.
illumine, vb.
illustrious, adj.
indistinct, adj.
indistinguishable,
  adj.
indistinguished, adj.
lack-lustre, n.
lamp, n.
light, adj.
light, n.

light, vb.
lighten, vb.
lightless, adj.
lightness, n.
lightning, n.
lustre, n.
lustrous, adj.
lux, lat. n.
moonbeam, n.
moonlight, n.
moonshine, n.
murk, adj.
murk, n.
murky, adj.
night, vb.
obscure, adj.
obscure, vb.
obscurely, adv.
obscurity, n.
orient, n.
outlustre, vb.
outshine, vb.
overcast, vb.
overshade, vb.
overshine, vb.
pitchy, adj.
polish, vb.
radiance, n.
radiant, adj.
reflect, vb.
reflection, n.
reflex, n.
reflex, vb.
relume, vb.
shade, n.
shade, vb.
shadow, n.
shadow, vb.
shadowy, adj.
shady, adj.
sheen, adj.
sheen, n.
shine, n.
shine, vb.
shiny, adj.

silver-bright, adj.
silverly, adv.
silver-shining, adj.
sparkle, vb.
starlight, n.
streak, n.
sun, n.
sunbeam, n.
sun-beamed, adj.
sun-bright, adj.
sunburn, vb.
sunny, adj.
sunshine, n.
taper-light, n.
thick, adj.
thicken, vb.
torch-light, n.
transparent, adj.
twilight, n.
twinkle, vb.
twire, vb.
umbra, lat. n.
umbrage, n.
undistinguishable,
  adj.
water, n.
white, adj.
: 150

01.13
fire

afire, adv.
ash, n.
ashy, adj.
bavin, n.
blaze, n.
blaze, vb.
bonfire, n.
brand, n.
bright-burning, adj.
burn, vb.
cauterize, vb.
chafe, vb.
cinder, n.

coal, n.
combustion, n.
combustious, adj.
country fire, n.
ember, n.
enkindle, vb.
ever-burning, adj.
feu, fr. n.
fiery, adj.
fire, n.
fire, vb.
fire-brand, n.
fire-work, n.
firing, n.
flame, n.
flame, vb.
flash, n.
fuel, n.
fume, n.
fume, vb.
furnace-burning, adj.
glow, n.
glow, vb.
heart-inflaming, adj.
hell-fire, n.
ignis, lat. n.
ignis fatuus
incense, vb.
inflame, vb.
kindle, vb.
new-enkindled, adj.
out-burn, vb.
reechy, adj.
relume, vb.
scald, vb.
scorch, vb.
sear, vb.
singe, vb.
smoke, n.
smoke, vb.
smoky, adj.
smother, n.
sooty, adj.
spark, n.
sparkle, n.

sparkle, vb.
sunburn, vb.
tinder, n.
tinder-like, adj.
trial-fire, n.
unburnt, adj.
unscorched, adj.
wild-fire, n.
: 66

01.14
water
---

billow, n.
brine, n.
brinish, adj.
bubble, n.
cataract, n.
confluence, n.
conflux, n.
currence, n.
current, n.
deluge, n.
eau, fr. n.
ebb, n.
ebb, vb.
eddy, n.
fleet, vb.
float, vb.
flood, n.
flow, n.
flow, vb.
fluent, adj.
fluently, adv.
flux, n.
fluxive, adj.
foam, n.
foam, vb.
foamy, adj.
froth, n.
froth, vb.
frothy, adj.
full-flowing, adj.
gulf, n.
inundation, n.

liquid, adj.
liquor, n.
main flood, n.
mantle, n.
ooze, vb.
overflow, n.
purl, vb.
recourse, n.
run, vb.
salt water, n.
sea-water, n.
sluice, vb.
stream, vb.
surge, n.
sweet water, n.
tide, n.
torrent, n.
trickle, vb.
trill, vb.
wash, n.
water, n.
water, vb.
water-flowing, adj.
waterish, adj.
watery, adj.
wave, n.
whirlpool, n.
: 59

01.15
sea

Adriatic, adj.
brine, n.
Channel, The
Charybdis
deep, n.
fall, n.
float, n.
flood, n.
Hellespont
Ionian Sea
main, n.
maritime, adj.
Mediterranean float, n.

Mediterraneum
Narrow Seas
Neptune
ocean, n.
Pontic Sea
Propontic [Sea]
salt-sea, n.
salt-waved, adj.
sea, n.
sea-like, adj.
sea-room, n.
sound, n.
South sea, n.
strait, n.
vast, n.
: 28

01.16
pool
---

bath, n.
brine-pit, n.
cistern, n.
fishpond, n.
fount, n.
fountain, n.
fresh, n.
lake, n.
Moorditch
plash, n.
pond, n.
pool, n.
puddle, n.
spring, n.
St. Gregory's well, n.
valley-fountain, n.
well, n.
: 17

01.17
river

Acheron
bourn, n.
brook, n.

channel, n.
Cocytus
creek, n.
Cydnus
Elbe
Euphrates
fresh-brook, n.
ice-brook, n.
Lethe
Lethied, adj.
Nile
Nilus
Po
river, n.
Saale
Severn
Simois
Somme
stream, n.
Stygian, adj.
stygius, lat. adj.
Styx
Thames
Tiber
Trent
Wye
: 29

01.18
effusion

bleed, vb.
broach, vb.
cast, vb.
dispunge, vb.
drain, vb.
draw, vb.
drivelling, adj.
drop, vb.
effuse, n.
effuse, vb.
effusion, n.
flux, n.
gum, n.
gush, vb.

imbrue, vb.
infuse, vb.
issue, vb.
lade, vb.
leak, vb.
leaky, adj.
new-shed, adj.
pour, vb.
rheum, n.
shed, vb.
silver-shedding, adj.
slaver, vb.
sluice, vb.
spill, vb.
spilth, n.
spit, vb.
spout, n.
spout, vb.
stream, vb.
sweat, n.
sweat, vb.
sweaty, adj.
swelter, vb.
tap, vb.
unstanched, adj.
vent, n.
void, vb.
: 41

01.19
dip

ale-washed, adj.
arrouse, vb.
aspersion, n.
bath, n.
bathe, vb.
bedabble, vb.
bedew, vb.
bedrench, vb.
bewet, vb.
blear, vb.
blood-drinking, adj.
dabble, vb.
dash, vb.

dew-bedabbled, adj.
dip, vb.
dive, vb.
drench, vb.
drop, vb.
drown, vb.
enew, vb.
ensteep, vb.
indrench, vb.
insteep, vb.
leach, vb.
mire, vb.
moisten, vb.
overflow, vb.
overwash, vb.
plunge, n.
plunge, vb.
sea-swallowed, adj.
sink, vb.
soak, vb.
souse, vb.
sprinkle, vb.
steep, vb.
submerge, vb.
swill, vb.
undrowned, adj.
wash, vb.
whelm, vb.
: 41

01.20
island

Albion
Bermudas
Britain
Canary
Candy
Colmekill
Crete
Cyprus
Delphos
England
Iceland
inch, n.

Ireland
island, n.
islander, n.
isle, n.
Isle of Man
Ithaca
Rhodes
Sardinia
Sicilia
Sicily
St. Colme's Inch
Tenedos
Thasos
Western Isles
: 26

01.21
fen • shore

Actium
aground, adv.
aland, adv.
ashore, adv.
bank, n.
bay, n.
beach, n.
beach, vb.
beachy, adj.
bog, n.
cape, n.
cliff, n.
coast, n.
dam, n.
Downs, The
embay, vb.
fen, n.
fenny, adj.
flat, n.
ford, n.
Goodwins
Goodwin Sands
headland, n.
Lincoln Washes
marsh, n.
moor, n.

promontory, n.
quagmire, n.
quicksand, n.
rivage, n.
Scylla
sea-bank, n.
sea-marge, n.
sea-side, n.
shallow, n.
shelf, n.
shelvy, adj.
shoal, n.
shore, n.
slough, n.
strand, n.
water side, n.
wharf, n.
 : 43

01.22
earth

continent, n.
earth, n.
earthly, adj.
earthy, adj.
ground, n.
land, n.
mother earth, n.
terrene, adj.
 : 8

01.23
soil

clay, n.
clod, n.
cloddy, adj.
dust, n.
dusty, adj.
earth, n.
earthen, adj.
earthly, adj.
earthy, adj.
ground, n.

land, n.
loam, n.
marl, n.
mould, n.
mouldy, adj.
overdust, vb.
sand, n.
sandy, adj.
soil, n.
umber, n.
winter-ground, vb.
 : 21

01.24
mud

bourbier, fr. n.
dirt, n.
filth, n.
grime, n.
mire, n.
miry, adj.
muck, n.
mud, n.
mud, vb.
muddy, adj.
muddy, vb.
ooze, n.
ooze, vb.
oozy, adj.
puddle, vb.
slime, n.
slimy, adj.
 : 17

01.25
stone

adamant, n.
alabaster, n.
coal, n.
craggy, adj.
crystal, n.
flint, n.
flinty, adj.

glass, n.
glass, vb.
glassy, adj.
glaze, vb.
gravel, n.
lapis, lat. n.
marble, n.
marble, vb.
mineral, n.
ore, n.
pebble, n.
pebbled, adj.
pebble stone, n.
rock, n.
rocky, adj.
sea-coal, n.
sea-salt, adj.
stone, n.
stony, adj.
touch, n.
touchstone, n.
whetstone, n.
 : 29

01.26
metal

argentine, adj.
brass, n.
brassy, adj.
braze, vb.
brazen, adj.
copper, n.
gold, n.
golden, adj.
iron, n.
latten, n.
lead, n.
leaden, adj.
metal, n.
metal of India, n.
ore, n.
pewter, n.
quicksilver, n.
silver, adj.

silver, n.
silverly, adv.
steel, n.
steel, vb.
steely, adj.
well-steeled, adj.
 : 24

01.27
hill • dale

Alps
Apennines
bank, n.
Birnam
bottom, n.
Caucasus
cliff, n.
dale, n.
down, n.
Dunsinane
enridged, adj.
Etna
head, n.
Helicon
hill, n.
hillock, n.
mole-hill, n.
mons, lat. n.
mount, n.
mountain, n.
mountainish, adj.
mountainous, adj.
Mount Misena
Olympus
Ossa
Pelion
Pillicock Hill
precipit, n.
Pyrenean, adj.
ridge, n.
steep, n.
Tarpeian, adj.
Taurus
vale, n.

7

01 the physical world • the elements

valley, n.
: 35

01.28
wood • field •
  garden
_____

acre, n.
afield, adv.
Arden
bed, n.
Birnam
Birnam Wood
Bosworth field, n.
brake, n.
broom-grove, n.
Burton Heath
champaign, n.
common, n.
coppice, n.
copse, n.
corn-field, n.
covert, n.
Dardan plains, n.

Datchet Mead
dispark, vb.
fallow, n.
feed, n.
feeding, n.
field, n.
fielded, adj.
flat, n.
forest, n.
garden, n.
Gaultree Forest
glade, n.
grass-plot, n.
green, n.
greensward, n.
greenwood, n.
grove, n.
headland, n.
heath, n.
hedge, n.
hedge, vb.
knot, n.
laund, n.
lea, n.

lily-bed, n.
linn-grove, n.
mead, n.
meadow, n.
Mile-end Green
orchard, n.
park, n.
park, vb.
park-ward, adv.
pasture, n.
patch, n.
petty-ward, adv.
plain, n.
plot, n.
purlieu, n.
Sarum Plain
St. George's Field
summer-field, n.
thicket, n.
turf, n.
turfy, adj.
vineyard, n.
warren, n.
weald, n.

wild, n.
wilderness, n.
Windsor Forest
wold, n.
wood, n.
woodland, n.
: 71

01.29
cave
_____

antre, n.
cave, n.
cavern, n.
den, n.
encave, vb.
hold, n.
hole, n.
mine, n.
mineral, n.
pit, n.
quarry, n.
: 11

02.01
tree • bush • twig

bark, n.
bark, vb.
barky, adj.
bavin, n.
bosky, adj.
bough, n.
branch, n.
branch, vb.
branchless, adj.
bush, n.
cork, n.
corky, adj.
disbranch, vb.
faggot, n.
fruit-tree, n.
graff, n.
grafter, n.
hawthorn bush, n.
hazel-twig, n.
knot, n.
lime-twig, n.
log, n.
lop, n.
love-spring, n.
olive-branch, n.
sapling, n.
scion, n.
sect, n.
shoot, n.
shrub, n.
slip, n.
sliver, n.
spray, n.
sprig, n.
spring, n.
stem, n.
stick, n.
stock, n.
thorn-bush, n.
top-branch, n.
tree, n.
trunk, n.
tuft, n.
twig, n.
twiggen, adj.
unshrubbed, adj.
wood, n.
wooden, adj.
: 48

02.02
oak • brier

ash, n.
aspen, adj.
bay, n.
bay-tree, n.
beech, n.
birch, n.
box-tree, n.
bramble, n.
brier, n.
cedar, n.
crab-tree, n.
cypress, n.
ebony, n.
eglantine, n.
elder, n.
elder-tree, n.
elm, n.
furze, n.
gorse, n.
hawthorn, n.
hazel, n.
heath, n.
Herne's oak, n.
holly, n.
ivy, n.
ivy-tod, n.
Jove's tree, n.
laurel, n.
linn, n.
long heath, n.
medlar, n.
mistletoe, n.
mountain pine, n.
mulberry, n.
myrtle, n.
oak, n.
oaken, adj.
olive, n.
olive-tree, n.
osier, n.
palm, n.
pine, n.
plane, n.
plum-tree, n.
pomegranate, n.
rosemary, n.
rue, n.
sycamore, n.
vine, n.
willow, n.
willow-tree, n.
yew, n.
: 52

02.03
sap

amber, n.
gum, n.
gum, vb.
juice, n.
love-juice, n.
precious-juiced, adj.
sap, n.
sapless, adj.
sappy, adj.
: 9

02.04
nettle • rush

bulrush, n.
bur, n.
clover, n.
cockle, n.
darnel, n.
dock, n.
fumitory, n.
furrow-weed, n.
grass, n.
hardock, n.
kecksy, n.
knot-grass, n.
moss, n.
moss, vb.
moss-grown, adj.
nettle, n.
reed, n.
reedy, adj.
rush, n.
rushy, adj.
sedge, n.
sedged, adj.
sedgy, adj.
spear-grass, n.
stinging nettle, n.
thistle, n.
toadstool, n.
vetch, n.
weed, n.
weeding, n.
weedy, adj.
: 31

02.05
plant

grassy, adj.
green, n.
herb, n.
herblet, n.
over-green, vb.
plant, n.
plant, vb.
root, vb.
short-grassed, adj.
vegetive, n.
verdour, n.
verdure, n.
: 12

02.06
bud • root

bell, n.
blade, n.
bladed, adj.
bud, n.
button, n.
cod, n.
honey-stalk, n.
insane root, n.
leaf, n.
leavy, adj.
peasecod, n.
prickle, n.
race, n.
rind, n.
root, n.
shallow-rooted, adj.
spine, n.
spur, n.
stalk, n.
thorn, n.
thorny, adj.
wood-leaf, n.
: 22

02.07
seed

fern-seed, n.
germen, n.
hempseed, n.
kernel, n.
nettle-seed, n.
seed, n.
: 6

02.08
flower

bloom, n.
blossom, n.
bridal flowers, n.
flower, n.

flower, vb.
flowered, adj.
floweret, n.
flowery, adj.
nosegay, n.
nose-herb, n.
posy, n.
: 11

02.09
rose

burnet, n.
canker, n.
canker-bloom, n.
canker-blossom, n.
carnation, n.
columbine, n.
cowslip, n.
crow-flower, n.
crown imperial, n.
cuckoo-bud, n.
cuckoo-flower, n.
Cupid's flower, n.
daffodil, n.
daisied, adj.
daisy, n.
damask rose, n.
dead men's fingers, n.
Dian's bud, n.
flag, n.
fleur-de-lis, n.
gillyflower, n.
harebell, n.
heartsease, n.
hip, n.
honeysuckle, n.
lady-smock, n.
lark's-heel, n.
lavender, n.
lily, n.
lily-bed, n.
long purple, n.
love-in-idleness, n.

mallow, n.
marigold, n.
mary-bud, n.
musk-rose, n.
narcissus, n.
oxlip, n.
pansy, n.
pink, n.
poppy, n.
primrose, n.
Provincial rose, n.
rose, n.
rosy, adj.
violet, n.
water-flower, n.
woodbine, n.
: 48

02.10
fruit • nut

berry, n.
cherry-stone, n.
fruit, n.
kernel, n.
nut, n.
nutshell, n.
rind, n.
stone, n.
: 8

02.11
walnut

acorn, n.
acorn-cup, n.
almond, n.
chestnut, n.
cup, n.
filbert, n.
hazel-nut, n.
pig-nut, n.
walnut, n.
walnut-shell, n.
: 10

02.12
strawberry

bilberry, n.
blackberry, n.
currant, n.
dew-berry, n.
gooseberry, n.
mulberry, n.
strawberry, n.
: 7

02.13
apple • grape

apple, n.
apple-john, n.
apricot, n.
cherry, n.
codling, n.
costard, n.
crab, n.
damson, n.
date, n.
fico, n.
fig, n.
grape, n.
leather-coat, n.
lemon, n.
medlar, n.
open-arse, n.
orange, n.
pear, n.
pippin, n.
plum, n.
pomegranate, n.
pomewater, n.
Poperinge pear, n.
prune, n.
quince, n.
raisins of the sun, n.
sweeting, n.
warden, n.
: 28

02.14
cabbage
————————————
bean, n.
cabbage, n.
leek, n.
lettuce, n.
locust, n.
mushroom, n.
onion, n.
parsnip, n.
pease, n.
pompion, n.
potato, n.
radish, n.
salad, n.
squash, n.
turnip, n.
wort, n.
: 16

02.15
grain
————————————
barley, n.

bran, n.
chaff, n.
chaffless, adj.
chaffy, adj.
corn, n.
ear, n.
grain, n.
grained, adj.
husk, n.
malt, n.
oat, n.
oaten, adj.
rice, n.
rye, n.
rye-straw, n.
shale, n.
sheave, vb.
straw, n.
strawy, adj.
stubble, n.
summer corn, n.
thatch, n.
wheat, n.
wheaten, adj.
: 25

02.16
parsley
————————————
caraway, n.
clove, n.
fennel, n.
garlic, n.
ginger, n.
marjoram, n.
mint, n.
mustard, n.
nutmeg, n.
parsley, n.
pepper, n.
peppercorn, n.
race, n.
saffron, n.
samphire, n.
savory, n.
Tewkesbury mustard,
   n.
thyme, n.
: 18

02.17
mandragora
————————————
aloe, n.
balm, n.
balsam, n.
balsamum, n.
camomile, n.
carduus benedictus
coloquintida, n.
eryngo, n.
herb of grace, n.
holy-thistle, n.
hyssop, n.
insane root, n.
mandragora, n.
mandrake, n.
plantain, n.
rhubarb, n.
senna, n.
simple, n.
wormwood, n.
: 19

03.01
animal

---

animal, n.
beast, n.
beastly, adj.
cub, n.
dam, n.
deer, n.
whelp, n.
  : 7

03.02
horse

Barbary
Barbary horse, n.
bay, n.
breeder, n.
Capilet
cheval, fr. n.
coach-fellow, n.
colt, n.
courser, n.
crop-ear, n.
Curtal
cut, n.
Cut
Dobbin
dun, n.
fill-horse, n.
filly, n.
filly foal, n.
foal, n.
fore-horse, n.
Galathe
Galloway nag, n.
gelding, n.
hackney, n.
hilding, n.
horse, n.
jade, n.
jennet, n.
long-tail, n.
malt-horse, n.

mare, n.
nag, n.
pack-horse, n.
palfrey, n.
post, n.
post-horse, n.
roan, n.
stalking-horse, n.
stallion, n.
steed, n.
sumpter, n.
Surrey
trotting-horse, n.
weed, n.
  : 44

03.03
ass

---

asinego, n.
ass, n.
mule, n.
  : 3

03.04
cattle

---

beef, n.
bull, n.
bull-calf, n.
bullock, n.
calf, n.
calf-like, adj.
cattle, n.
cow, n.
cowish, adj.
draught-ox, n.
heifer, n.
Manningtree ox, n.
milch-cow, n.
neat, n.
ox, n.
parish heifer, n.
pecus, lat. n.
steer, n.

town bull, n.
  : 19

03.05
sheep

---

bell-wether, n.
eanling, n.
ewe, n.
goat, n.
lamb, n.
mountain goat, n.
mutton, n.
ram, n.
sheep, n.
she-lamb, n.
wether, n.
  : 11

03.06
swine

Bartholomew
  boar-pig, n.
boar, n.
boarish, adj.
boar-pig, n.
farrow, n.
hog, n.
pig, n.
pig-like, adj.
sow, n.
swine, n.
swinish, adj.
tithe-pig, n.
truie, fr. n.
wild-boar, n.
  : 14

03.07
cat

---

cat, n.
cat-like, adj.
gib, n.

gib cat, n.
Graymalkin
kitten, n.
musk-cat, n.
ounce, n.
Purr
rat-catcher, n.
wild cat, n.
  : 11

03.08
dog

---

bandog, n.
beagle, n.
Belman
bitch, n.
Blanch
blood-hound, n.
Brabbler
brach, n.
canis, lat. n.
chien, fr. n.
Clowder
Crab
cur, n.
cur of Iceland, n.
currish, adj.
curtal dog, n.
cut, n.
ditch-dog, n.
dog, n.
dogged, adj.
Echo
Fury
greyhound, n.
Hector
Holdfast
hound, n.
hound of Sparta, n.
housekeeper, n.
hunter, n.
Iceland dog, n.
Jack-dog, n.
Lady

Lady Brach
long-tail, n.
lyam, n.
mastiff, n.
Merriman
mongrel, n.
mongrel bitch, n.
mongrel cur, n.
Mountain
night-dog, n.
puppy, n.
puppy-dog, n.
puppy greyhound, n.
Ringwood
sheep-biter, n.
shough, n.
Silver
Sowter
spaniel, n.
spaniel, vb.
spaniel-like, adj.
Spartan dog, n.
squirrel, n.
Sweetheart
Trey
Troilus
trundle-tail, n.
tyke, n.
Tyrant
watch-dog, n.
water-rug, n.
water-spaniel, n.
: 64

03.09
wolf

bitch-wolf, n.
demi-wolf, n.
hyena, n.
she-wolf, n.
wolf, n.
wolfish, adj.
: 6

03.10
fox

brock, n.
dog-fox, n.
ferret, n.
fitchew, n.
fox, n.
foxship, n.
otter, n.
polecat, n.
she-fox, n.
vixen, n.
weasel, n.
: 11

03.11
rat

bawd, n.
cony, n.
dormouse, n.
hare, n.
land-rat, n.
mole, n.
mouldwarp, n.
mouse, n.
rabbit, n.
rabbit-sucker, n.
rat, n.
squirrel, n.
Wat
water-rat, n.
: 14

03.12
hedgehog

hedgehog, n.
hedge-pig, n.
porcupine, n.
urchin, n.
: 4

03.13
deer

bribed-buck, n.
buck, n.
deer, n.
doe, n.
fawn, n.
hart, n.
hind, n.
horn, n.
horn-beast, n.
pricket, n.
rascal, n.
rascal-like, adj.
roe, n.
sore, n.
sorrel, n.
stag, n.
: 16

03.14
bear

bear, n.
bear-like, adj.
bear-whelp, n.
cub, n.
Sackerson
she-bear, n.
: 6

03.15
monkey

ape, n.
apish, adj.
babion, n.
baboon, n.
dog-ape, n.
jackanapes, n.
John ape, n.
marmoset, n.
monkey, n.
: 9

03.16
elephant • lion

camel, n.
catamountain, n.
elephant, n.
king of beasts, n.
leopard, n.
lion, n.
lioness, n.
mountain lioness, n.
panther, n.
pard, n.
rhinoceros, n.
tiger, n.
: 12

03.17
bird

bird, n.
brood, n.
feather, n.
fowl, n.
hatch, n.
summer-bird, n.
wild-fowl, n.
wood-bird, n.
: 8

03.18
nightingale

bird of peace, n.
bunting, n.
cuckoo, n.
cuckoo-bird, n.
dove, n.
dovelike, adj.
finch, n.
hedge-sparrow, n.
lapwing, n.
lark, n.
martlet, n.
night-bird, n.

nightingale, n.
ouzel, n.
ouzel cock, n.
Philip
Philomela
redbreast, n.
robin redbreast, n.
ruddock, n.
sparrow, n.
starling, n.
swallow, n.
throstle, n.
thrush, n.
turtle, n.
turtle-dove, n.
wagtail, n.
wren, n.
 : 29

03.19
chicken

biddy, n.
capon, n.
Chanticleer
chick, n.
chicken, n.
chuck, n.
cock, n.
cockerel, n.
craven, n.
goose, n.
hen, n.
March-chick, n.
Partlet, Dame
 : 13

03.20
pheasant

Barbary cock-pigeon,
 n.
barnacle, n.
cock, n.
Guinea hen, n.

partridge, n.
pheasant, n.
pheasant cock, n.
pigeon, n.
quail, n.
snipe, n.
turkey, n.
turkey-cock, n.
wild duck, n.
wild goose, n.
woodcock, n.
 : 15

03.21
swan

cormorant, n.
cygnet, n.
dive-dapper, n.
duck, n.
gosling, n.
gull, n.
halcyon, n.
heronsew, n.
mallard, n.
pelican, n.
swan, n.
swan-like, adj.
 : 12

03.22
hawk

aerie, n.
bird of prey, n.
buzzard, n.
eagle, n.
eyas, n.
eyas-musket, n.
falcon, n.
gripe, n.
haggard, n.
hawk, n.
Joan (2H6)
kite, n.

osprey, n.
puttock, n.
staniel, n.
tercel, n.
tercel-gentle, n.
vulture, n.
 : 18

03.23
owl • bat

bat, n.
batty, adj.
bird of night, n.
howlet, n.
night-owl, n.
owl, n.
rearmouse, n.
screech-owl, n.
 : 8

03.24
crow

carrion crow, n.
carrion kite, n.
chewet, n.
chough, n.
crow, n.
daw, n.
jay, n.
maggot-pie, n.
night-crow, n.
night-raven, n.
pie, n.
raven, n.
rook, n.
rooky, adj.
 : 14

03.25
peacock

noddy, n.
ostrich, n.

parakeet, n.
parrot, n.
peacock, n.
popinjay, n.
 : 6

03.26
fish

anchovy, n.
carp, n.
cod, n.
conger, n.
dace, n.
dog-fish, n.
dolphin, n.
dolphin-like, adj.
eel, n.
fish, n.
fishify, vb.
fish-like, adj.
gudgeon, n.
gurnard, n.
herring, n.
ling, n.
loach, n.
luce, n.
mackerel, n.
minnow, n.
pike, n.
pilchard, n.
porpoise, n.
salmon, n.
salt-fish, n.
shark, n.
shark, vb.
sprat, n.
tench, n.
trout, n.
whale, n.
 : 31

03 animals

03.27
oyster

cockle, n.
coral, n.
crab, n.
mussel, n.
oyster, n.
prawn, n.
shrimp, n.
sponge, n.
spongy, adj.
: 9

03.28
frog

frog, n.
newt, n.
paddock, n.
salamander, n.
tadpole, n.
toad, n.
wall-newt, n.
water[-newt], n.
: 8

03.29
serpent

adder, n.
alligator, n.
aspic, n.
blind-worm, n.
chameleon, n.
crocodile, n.
lizard, n.
serpent, n.
serpentine, adj.
serpent-like, adj.
snake, n.
snaky, adj.
tortoise, n.
viper, n.
viperous, adj.

worm, n.
: 16

03.30
vermin • spider

blood-sucker, n.
canker, n.
caterpillar, n.
grub, n.
horse-leech, n.
leech, n.
maggot, n.
scorpion, n.
slug, n.
snail, n.
spider, n.
spider-like, adj.
spinner, n.
vermin, n.
worm, n.
wormy, adj.
: 16

03.31
fly • louse

ant, n.
bee, n.
beetle, n.
blue-bottle, n.
breeze, n.
butterfly, n.
buzzard, n.
cricket, n.
drone, n.
drone-like, adj.
flea, n.
flesh-fly, n.
fly, n.
glow-worm, n.
gnat, n.
grasshopper, n.
honey-bee, n.
humble-bee, n.

lady-bird, n.
louse, n.
louse, vb.
mite, n.
moth, n.
mothy, adj.
night-fly, n.
nit, n.
pismire, n.
summer fly, n.
summer's fly, n.
tick, n.
wasp, n.
waspish, adj.
water-fly, n.
winter-cricket, n.
: 34

03.32
unicorn

Arabian bird, n.
Argus
basilisk, n.
bird of wonder, n.
boar of Thessaly, n.
Briareus
Centaur, n.
Cerberus
cockatrice, n.
dragon, n.
dragonish, adj.
dragon-like, adj.
fire-drake, n.
Gorgon
griffin, n.
harpy, n.
hell-hound, n.
hell-kite, n.
Hydra
Hydra-headed, adj.
land-fish, n.
leviathan, n.
Minotaur, n.
monster, n.

monster, vb.
monster-like, adj.
moon-calf, n.
Nemean lion, n.
Nessus
Pegasus
Phoenix
Phoenix-like, adj.
Sagittary
sea-monster, n.
Sphinx
Typhon
unicorn, n.
: 37

03.33
beak • horn

ass-head, n.
beak, n.
bill, n.
brow, n.
butt, n.
calf's-head, n.
comb, n.
combless, adj.
crest, n.
dewlap, n.
dew-lapped, adj.
dishorn, vb.
fang, n.
fanged, adj.
fangless, adj.
forked, adj.
head, n.
horn, n.
neb, n.
ox-head, n.
scythe-tusked, adj.
snout, n.
tush, n.
tusk, n.
urchin-snouted, adj.
: 25

03.34
fleece

---

bristle, n.
bristle, vb.
bristly, adj.
fell, n.
fetlock, n.
fleece, n.
fur, n.
fur, vb.
hair, n.
hairy, adj.
hide, n.
horsehair, n.
mane, n.
sable, n.
shag, adj.
wool, n.
woollen, adj.
woollen, n.
woolly, adj.
: 19

03.35
tail

---

bob-tail, n.
horse-tail, n.
red-tailed, adj.
scut, n.
tail, n.
: 5

03.36
feather

---

dove-feathered, adj.
dowl, n.
down, n.
down feather, n.
downy, adj.
feather, n.
feathered, adj.
fledge, adj.

lofty-plumed, adj.
moult, vb.
pinion, n.
plume, n.
plume, vb.
quill, n.
: 14

03.37
wing

---

clip-winged, adj.
eagle-winged, adj.
feather, n.
feathered, adj.
flight, n.
full-winged, adj.
strong-winged, adj.
wing, n.
winged, adj.
: 9

03.38
quill

---

prick, n.
quill, n.
sharp-quilled, adj.
sting, n.
stingless, adj.
: 5

03.39
shell

---

cockled, adj.
cockle-shell, n.
inshell, vb.
mussel-shell, n.
scale, n.
scaled, adj.
scaly, adj.
shard, n.
sharded, adj.
shell, n.

shelly, adj.
skin, n.
slough, n.
: 13

03.40
claw • hoof • fin

---

claw, n.
fin, n.
finless, adj.
finny, adj.
fore-foot, n.
gill, n.
hinder-leg, n.
hoof, n.
pastern, n.
paw, n.
round-hoofed, adj.
talon, n.
tawny-finned, adj.
: 13

03.41
tripe

---

calves'-gut, n.
catling, n.
chawdron, n.
maw, n.
tripe, n.
: 5

03.42
tallow

---

comb, n.
fat, adj.
grease, n.
grease, vb.
greasy, adj.
honeycomb, n.
keech, n.
liquor, vb.
oil, n.

oily, adj.
parmacety, n.
seam, n.
tallow, n.
unctious, adj.
wax, n.
waxen, adj.
: 16

03.43
dung

---

bully-stale, n.
cow-dung, n.
dung, n.
dungy, adj.
horse-piss, n.
ordure, n.
piss, vb.
purr, n.
stale, n.
urine, n.
: 10

03.44
egg

---

egg, n.
egg-shell, n.
finch-egg, n.
pigeon-egg, n.
pullet-sperm, n.
roe, n.
: 6

03.45
cobweb

---

cobweb, n.
film, n.
film, vb.
gossamer, n.
honey-dew, n.
spider web, n.
web, n. : 7

03.46
nest • kennel

---

aerie, n.
beehive, n.
burrow, n.
cabinet, n.
cage, n.
coop, vb.
crib, n.
crib, vb.
den, n.
dog-hole, n.
dovecot, n.
dovehouse, n.
encage, vb.
fishpond, n.
fold, n.

frank, n.
frank, vb.
hive, n.
hive, vb.
impound, vb.
kennel, n.
kennel, vb.
litter, n.
nest, n.
pen, n.
pen, vb.
perch, n.
pinfold, n.
pound, n.
pound, vb.
sheepcote, n.
stable, n.
stall, n.

stall, vb.
sty, n.
sty, vb.
unfold, vb.
unkennel, vb.
unroost, vb.
warren, n.
: 40

03.47
peck • graze

---

bare-gnawn, adj.
batten, vb.
begnaw, vb.
bill, vb.
bite, vb.
browse, vb.

canker-bit, adj.
chew, vb.
gnaw, vb.
graze, vb.
knap, vb.
mouse, vb.
mouse-eaten, adj.
munch, vb.
nibble, vb.
nibbler, n.
nip, vb.
peck, vb.
pinch, n.
pinch, vb.
sheep-biting, adj.
snap, vb.
: 22

04.01
mortal

———————————

body, n.
common man, n.
creature, n.
flesh, n.
flesh and blood, n.
head, n.
human, adj.
humanity, n.
liver, n.
man, n.
mankind, adj.
mankind, n.
microcosm, n.
mortal, adj.
mortal, n.
mortality, n.
mortally, adv.
mother's son, n.
one, n.
party, n.
person, n.
personage, n.
soul, n.
thing, n.
wight, n.
worldling, n.
  : 26

04.02
man

———————————

dan, n.
don, n.
eunuch, n.
father, n.
fellow, n.
goodman, n.
groom, n.
homme, fr. n.
homo, n.
homo, lat. n.
Jack

lord, n.
lordship, n.
male, adj.
male, n.
man, n.
man-entered, adj.
manfully, adv.
manhood, n.
manikin, n.
mankind, adj.
manlike, adj.
manly, adj.
mannish, adj.
masculine, adj.
master, n.
mastership, n.
merchant, n.
monsieur, n.
monsieur, fr. n.
nuncle, n.
seigneur, fr. n.
sex, n.
signor, n.
signor, it. n.
sir, n.
sirrah, n.
three-man, n.
Tom
unman, vb.
unmanned, adj.
vir, lat. n.
  : 42

04.03
boy • youth

———————————

bachelor, n.
bachelorship, n.
boy, n.
boy, vb.
boyish, adj.
child, n.
colt, n.
garçon, fr. n.
imp, n.

juvenal, n.
knave, n.
lad, n.
man-child, n.
princock, n.
son, n.
squire, n.
stripling, n.
swain, n.
wanton, n.
young, n.
younger, n.
youngest, n.
youngling, n.
youngster, n.
younker, n.
youth, n.
  : 26

04.04
rogue

———————————

besonian, n.
boor, n.
caitiff, adj.
caitiff, n.
Cataian, n.
coistrel, n.
companion, n.
costermonger, n.
coxcomb, n.
crack-hemp, n.
cullion, n.
cullionly, adj.
cut, n.
drumble, n.
dunghill, n.
filth, n.
harlot, n.
hilding, n.
jack, n.
jackanapes, n.
Jack-dog, n.
Jack sauce, n.
knave, n.

knavery, n.
knavish, adj.
land-rat, n.
loon, n.
losel, n.
micher, n.
miscreant, n.
miser, n.
patch, n.
peasant, n.
princock, n.
rag, n.
ragamuffin, n.
rampallion, n.
rascal, n.
rascally, adj.
rogue, n.
roguery, n.
rudesby, n.
scab, n.
scoundrel, n.
scroyle, n.
sheep-biter, n.
sheep-biting, adj.
sneak-up, n.
swain, n.
thief, n.
trash, n.
truant, adj.
tyke, n.
varlet, n.
varletto, n.
viliaco, n.
villain, n.
villain-like, adj.
villainous, adj.
villainous, n.
villainously, adv.
villain-slave, n.
villainy, n.
wagtail, n.
wen, n.
whipster, n.
whoreson, n.
wretch, n.   : 68

04.05
rustic
───────────
bacon, n.
boor, n.
boorish, n.
carl, n.
carlot, n.
chuff, n.
churl, n.
clown, n.
hind, n.
home-spun, n.
lob, n.
lout, n.
lubber, n.
lubberly, adj.
rustic, n.
 : 15

04.06
madcap
───────────
antic, adj.
antic, n.
antic, vb.
anticly, adv.
clown, n.
clownish, adj.
fool, n.
fool, vb.
foolery, n.
fooling, n.
friskin, n.
gamester, n.
idiot, n.
jest, n.
jest, vb.
jester, n.
jesting, n.
madcap, n.
motley, n.
out-jest, vb.
phantasime, n.
prank, n.

spark, n.
sport, n.
sport, vb.
sportful, adj.
sportive, adj.
trick, n.
tricksy, adj.
wag, n.
wit-cracker, n.
wit-snapper, n.
wittily, adv.
witty, adj.
zany, n.
 : 35

04.07
fop
───────────
barber-monger, n.
fangled, adj.
fashion-monger, n.
fashion-monging,
 adj.
finical, adj.
fop, n.
foppery, n.
foppish, adj.
newfangled, adj.
water-fly, n.
 : 10

04.08
cavalier
───────────
cabilero, n.
carpet-monger, n.
cavaleiro, n.
cavalery, n.
cavalier, n.
cavalleria, n.
chamberer, n.
gallant, adj.
gallant, n.
gallantly, adv.
gallantry, n.

guest-cavalier, n.
 : 12

04.09
woman
───────────
Amazon, n.
Amazonian, adj.
aunt, n.
country girl, n.
country maid, n.
country mistress, n.
dame, n.
dame, fr. n.
damosella, n.
damsel, n.
demoiselle, n.
demoiselle, fr. n.
effeminate, adj.
female, adj.
female, n.
feminine, adj.
Gill
goodwife, n.
gossip, n.
head lady, n.
Jill
kickie-wickie, n.
lady, n.
ladyship, n.
madam, n.
madame, fr. n.
madonna, n.
malkin, n.
matron, n.
mistress, n.
mistress-ship, n.
mother, n.
mulier, lat. n.
nymph, n.
sex, n.
she, n.
Tib
tithe-woman, n.
unsex, vb.

weaker vessel, n.
wench, n.
wenchless, adj.
wench-like, adj.
wife, n.
wifelike, adj.
woman, n.
woman, vb.
womanhood, n.
womanish, adj.
womankind, n.
womanly, adj.
womenkind, n.
 : 52

04.10
darling
───────────
calf, n.
chuck, n.
darling, n.
dear, n.
dove, n.
fair, n.
fondling, n.
heart, n.
honey, n.
joy, n.
lady-bird, n.
lamb, n.
lambkin, n.
leman, n.
minion, n.
mouse, n.
peat, n.
sweet, n.
sweet and twenty, n.
sweetest, n.
sweetheart, n.
sweeting, n.
true-love, n.
 : 23

04.11
crone

———————————

beldam, n.
crone, n.
hag, n.
haggish, adj.
scold, n.
shrew, n.
trot, n.
virago, n.
vixen, n.
witch[2], n.
Xantippe
 : 11

04.12
strumpet

———————————

aunt, n.
baggage, n.
Barbary hen, n.
blowze, n.
bona roba, n.
callet, n.
commoner, n.
courtesan, n.
customer, n.
dowdy, n.
doxy, n.
drab, n.
filth, n.
fitchew, n.
flirt-gill, n.
fustilarian, n.
gamester, n.
giglet, n.
giglet wench, n.
goose of Winchester,
 n.
Guinea hen, n.
hackney, n.
hare, n.
harlot, n.
harlotry, n.

hilding, n.
Hiren
hobby-horse, n.
housewife, n.
jade, n.
jay, n.
kite, n.
laced mutton, n.
land carrack, n.
lioness, n.
malkin, n.
minion, n.
minx, n.
nag, n.
pagan, n.
polecat, n.
prostitute, vb.
pucelle, n.
punk, n.
quail, n.
quean, n.
rampallion, n.
runnion, n.
skains-mate, n.
slut, n.
stale, n.
stewed prune, n.
strumpet, n.
Tib
tomboy, n.
trull, n.
wanton, n.
whore, n.
 : 58

04.13
somebody

———————————

alius, lat. n.
another, adj.
any, adj.
anybody, n.
anyone, n.
false-self, n.
in person, adv.

nobody, n.
one, n.
other, adj.
own, adj.
personal, adj.
personally, adv.
private, adj.
proper, adj.
properly, adv.
propre, fr. adj.
propriety, n.
self, adj.
self, n.
somebody, n.
someone, n.
unproper, adj.
whatever, adj.
whatsoever, adj.
 : 25

04.14
kindred

———————————

adopt, vb.
adoptedly, adv.
adoption, n.
adoptious, adj.
affined, adj.
affinity, n.
akin, adv.
ally, n.
ancestor, n.
ancestry, n.
birth, n.
blood, n.
breed, n.
breeding, n.
cater-cousin, n.
children's children,
 n.
consanguineous, adj.
consanguinity, n.
cousin, n.
cousin-german, n.
coz, n.

derivation, n.
derivative, n.
derive, vb.
descend, vb.
descending, n.
descent, n.
extract, adj.
familiar, adj.
family, n.
flesh, n.
flesh and blood, n.
forefather, n.
foregoer, n.
forerunner, n.
friend, n.
generation, n.
german, adj.
german, n.
great kinsman, n.
hag-seed, n.
half-blooded, adj.
heir, n.
house, n.
household, n.
increase, n.
issue, n.
issue, vb.
kin, n.
kind, n.
kindred, n.
kinsman, n.
kinswoman, n.
line, n.
lineal, adj.
lineally, adv.
name, n.
natural, adj.
near, adj.
nearest, n.
nearness, n.
next, n.
offspring, n.
parentage, n.
pedigree, n.
posterity, n.

predecessor, n.
progenitor, n.
progeny, n.
propinquity, n.
race, n.
seed, n.
sib, adj.
son, n.
stock, n.
strain, n.
succession, n.
successor, n.
tribe, n.
true-bred, adj.
true-derived, adj.
twin, n.
twin, vb.
unlineal, adj.
well-derived, adj.
  : 85

04.15
family

aunt, n.
aunt-mother, n.
baby-daughter, n.
bastard, n.
bastardly, adj.
bastardy, n.
beldam, n.
bowel, n.
brother, n.
brotherhood, n.
brother-in-law, n.
brother-like, adj.
brotherly, adj.
child, n.
child, vb.
cousin, n.
coz, n.
cub, n.
dad, n.
dam, n.
dame, n.

daughter, n.
daughter-in-law, n.
eldest-born, n.
family, n.
father, n.
father, vb.
father-in-law, n.
fatherly, adj.
filial, adj.
filius, lat. n.
fils, fr. n.
first-begotten, adj.
first-born, adj.
first-fruit, n.
firstling, n.
frater, lat. n.
fruit, n.
grandam, n.
grandchild, n.
grandfather, n.
grandmother, n.
grandsire, n.
great-grandfather, n.
great-grandsire, n.
great-uncle, n.
latter-born, n.
maid-child, n.
man-child, n.
mother, n.
nephew, n.
niece, n.
nuncle, n.
offspring, n.
parent, n.
pater, lat. n.
paternal, adj.
père, fr. n.
progenitor, n.
progeny, n.
sire, n.
sister, n.
sister, vb.
sisterly, adj.
son, n.
son-in-law, n.

stepdame, n.
stepmother, n.
twin-brother, n.
uncle, n.
uncle, vb.
uncle-father, n.
unfathered, adj.
unfilial, adj.
whelp, n.
  : 75

04.16
gossip

god-daughter, n.
godfather, n.
godson, n.
gossip, n.
gossip, vb.
gossip-like, adj.
  : 6

04.17
household

cotquean, n.
house, n.
household, n.
householder, n.
housekeeper, n.
housekeeping, n.
housewife, n.
housewifery, n.
  : 8

04.18
marriage

affiance, vb.
affy, vb.
assure, vb.
bed-mate, n.
bed-right, n.
bed-vow, n.
betroth, vb.

bigamy, n.
bridal, n.
bride, n.
bride, vb.
bridegroom, n.
combinate-husband,
  n.
contract, n.
contract, vb.
contracting, n.
contraction, n.
couple, n.
couple, vb.
court, vb.
courtier, n.
courtship, n.
divorce, n.
divorce, vb.
divorcement, n.
double-henned, adj.
dower, n.
dower, vb.
dowerless, adj.
dowry, n.
endow, vb.
espouse, vb.
fair-betrothed, adj.
fere, n.
goodman, n.
goodwife, n.
groom, n.
handfast, n.
husband, n.
husband, vb.
lady, n.
loose-wived, adj.
lord, n.
lordship, n.
love-suit, n.
make, n.
marriage, n.
marriage rite, n.
marry, vb.
match, n.
match, vb.

mate, n.
mate, vb.
new-married, adj.
new-trothed, adj.
noce, fr. n.
nuptial, adj.
nuptial, n.
pair, vb.
pre-contract, n.
promise, vb.
ring time, n.
singleness, n.
spousal, adj.
spousal, n.
spouse, n.
subcontract, vb.
suitor, n.
troth-plight, adj.
troth-plight, n.
union, n.
unmarried, adj.
unwed, adj.
unwooed, adj.
wed, vb.
wedding, n.
wedlock, n.
wife, n.
wifelike, adj.
wive, vb.
woman, n.
woo, vb.
wooer, n.
wooingly, adv.
: 84

04.19
child

babe, n.
baby, n.
bairn, n.
birth-child, n.
brat, n.
changeling, n.
child, n.

childish, adj.
childishly, adv.
childlike, adj.
crack, n.
cradle-babe, n.
fry, n.
infant, n.
infant-like, adj.
unchild, vb.
: 16

04.20
widow • orphan

dowager, n.
fatherless, adj.
husbandless, adj.
jointress, n.
maiden-widowed,
  adj.
makeless, adj.
orphan, n.
Princess Dowager, n.
pupil, n.
unfathered, adj.
widow, n.
widow, vb.
widower, n.
widowhood, n.
: 14

04.21
friend

amity, n.
backfriend, n.
befriend, vb.
bosom, vb.
bosom lover, n.
familiar, n.
familiarity, n.
familiarly, adv.
fellowship, n.
friend, n.
friend, vb.

friendless, adj.
friendliness, n.
friendly, adj.
friendship, n.
lover, n.
mouth-friend, n.
shoulder-clapper, n.
trencher-friend, n.
unfriended, adj.
unfriendly, adj.
unneighbourly, adj.
well-willer, n.
: 23

04.22
companion

accomplice, n.
acquaint, vb.
acquaintance, n.
alliance, n.
associate, n.
bawcock, n.
bedfellow, n.
besort, n.
brother, n.
brotherhood, n.
bully, n.
bully-rock, n.
colleague, vb.
co-mate, n.
communication, n.
companion, n.
companion, vb.
companionship, n.
company, n.
company, vb.
compeer, n.
compeer, vb.
competitor, n.
complice, n.
comrade, n.
confederacy, n.
confederate, adj.
confederate, n.

confederate, vb.
consort, n.
conversation, n.
converse, vb.
copartner, n.
copemate, n.
Corinthian, n.
corrival, n.
Ephesian, n.
familiar, adj.
federary, n.
fellow, n.
fellow, vb.
fellowly, adj.
fellowship, n.
gossip, n.
gossip, vb.
gossip-like, adj.
insociable, adj.
know, vb.
knowledge, n.
lad, n.
league, n.
league, vb.
lone, adj.
make, n.
makeless, adj.
mate, n.
merry man, n.
neighbour, n.
neighbourhood, n.
neighbourly, adj.
partake, vb.
partaker, n.
partner, n.
partner, vb.
party, n.
peer, n.
pew-fellow, n.
playfellow, n.
play-fere, n.
rival, n.
rivality, n.
schoolfellow, n.
skains-mate, n.

sociable, adj.
society, n.
sort, vb.
sworn brother, n.
Trojan, n.
troop, vb.
unacquainted, adj.
unneighbourly, adj.
vow-fellow, n.
well-acquainted, adj.
yoke-fellow, n.
: 84

04.23
stranger
―――――――――
alien, adj.

alien, n.
estrange, vb.
foreign, adj.
foreigner, n.
guest, n.
guestwise, adv.
mountain-foreigner,
n.
peregrinate, adj.
strange, adj.
strangely, adv.
strangeness, n.
stranger, n.
stranger, vb.
uncouth, adj.
: 15

04.24
solitary
―――――――――
alone, adv.
aloof, adv.
distance, n.
high-lone, adj.
insociable, adj.
inward, adj.
inward, n.
inwardness, n.
lone, adj.
loneliness, n.
lonely, adj.
monastic, adj.
privacy, n.
private, adj.

private, n.
privately, adv.
privy, adj.
reclusive, adj.
retirement, n.
secret, adj.
secret, n.
solitary, adj.
: 22

05.01
life • death

---

a-life, adv.
alive, adv.
book of life, n.
breathe, vb.
breathless, adj.
capital, adj.
cease, vb.
consummation, n.
darkness, n.
dead, adj.
dead, n.
dead-killing, adj.
deadly, adj.
deadly-handed, adj.
death, n.
death-darting, adj.
deathful, adj.
deathlike, adj.
decease, n.
decease, vb.
defunct, adj.
defunct, n.
defunction, n.
defunctive, adj.
depart, n.
depart, vb.
departure, n.
die, vb.
double-fatal, adj.
end, n.
ever-living, adj.
expire, vb.
fail, vb.
fatal, adj.
late-deceased, adj.
life, n.
lifeless, adj.
lifetime, n.
live, adj.
live, vb.
lively, adj.
lively, adv.

living, n.
long-lived, adj.
long-living, adj.
memento mori
mort, n.
mort, fr. n.
mortal, adj.
mortality, n.
mortal-living, adj.
mortally, adv.
mortify, vb.
outlive, vb.
overlive, vb.
pale-dead, adj.
pass, vb.
passing bell, n.
peace-parted, adj.
perish, vb.
predecease, vb.
quick, adj.
quick, n.
quicken, vb.
relive, vb.
requicken, vb.
resurrection, n.
revive, vb.
short-lived, adj.
starve, vb.
survive, vb.
survivor, n.
tender-dying, adj.
timely-parted, adj.
unlive, vb.
vie, fr. n.
vita, lat. n.
vital, adj.
vivant, fr. adj.
vivere, lat. vb.
vivre, fr. vb.
vivus, lat. adj.
    : 82

05.02
fertility • sterility

---

barren, adj.
barren, n.
barrenly, adv.
barrenness, n.
dry, adj.
fat, adj.
fatness, n.
fertile, adj.
fertility, n.
fructify, vb.
fruitful, adj.
fruitfully, adv.
fruitless, adj.
hungry, adj.
increaseful, adj.
issueless, adj.
lush, adj.
primy, adj.
sterile, adj.
sterility, n.
store, n.
unfruitful, adj.
unseminared, adj.
waste, adj.
    : 24

05.03
procreation

---

bastardize, vb.
bate-breeding, adj.
bed, vb.
beget, vb.
big, adj.
big-bellied, adj.
bolster, vb.
breed, vb.
breeder, n.
calve, vb.
child, vb.
conceive, vb.
conception, n.

conceptious, adj.
copulation, n.
copulative, n.
deed, n.
ean, vb.
eaning time, n.
engender, vb.
enwomb, vb.
father, vb.
foal, vb.
gender, vb.
generation, n.
generative, adj.
get, vb.
getter, n.
go, vb.
great-bellied, adj.
hatch, n.
hatch, vb.
heaven-bred, adj.
high-engendered, adj.
home-bred, adj.
ill-breeding, adj.
illegitimate, adj.
increase, n.
kindle, vb.
kitten, vb.
knot, vb.
know, vb.
knowledge, n.
leap, vb.
legitimate, adj.
legitimate, n.
legitimation, n.
litter, vb.
mad-bred, adj.
mell, vb.
misbeget, vb.
multiply, vb.
overteem, vb.
procreant, adj.
procreant, n.
procreation, n.
produce, vb.
propagate, vb.

propagation, n.
pullet-sperm, n.
put to, phr. vb.
quick, adj.
round, vb.
round-wombed, adj.
rut, vb.
rut-time, n.
sin-conceiving, adj.
sire, vb.
soldier-breeder, n.
spawn, vb.
still-breeding, adj.
teem, vb.
top, vb.
tread, vb.
true-begotten, adj.
true-bred, adj.
true-derived, adj.
tup, vb.
unbegotten, adj.
unbred, adj.
ungenitured, adj.
ungot, adj.
ungotten, adj.
unhatched, adj.
whelp, vb.
with child, adv.
  : 86

05.04
birth
——————————
abortive, adj.
abortive, n.
base-born, adj.
bawd-born, adj.
bear, vb.
birth, n.
brood, vb.
brooded, adj.
burden, n.
carry, vb.
childbed, n.
deliver, vb.

deliverance, n.
disclose, n.
disclose, vb.
ditch-delivered, adj.
fool-born, adj.
forest-born, adj.
hag-born, adj.
hedge-born, adj.
hell-born, adj.
high-born, adj.
labour, n.
labour, vb.
lie in, phr. vb.
mean-born, adj.
nativity, n.
new-born, adj.
new-delivered, adj.
now-born, adj.
regenerate, adj.
self-born, adj.
still-born, adj.
throe, vb.
true-born, adj.
twin-born, adj.
unborn, adj.
well-born, adj.
  : 38

05.05
nurse
——————————
cub-drawn, adj.
dry nurse, n.
feed, vb.
feeder, n.
foster, vb.
foster-nurse, n.
give suck, vb.
milk, vb.
nourice, n.
nourish, vb.
nourisher, n.
nourishment, n.
nurse, n.
nurse, vb.

nurse-like, adj.
nurser, n.
nursery, n.
nutriment, n.
suck, vb.
suckle, vb.
wean, vb.
  : 21

05.06
burial
——————————
bier, n.
burial, n.
burier, n.
bury, vb.
burying, n.
burying-place, n.
charnel-house, n.
churchyard, n.
coffin, n.
earth, vb.
embalm, vb.
enhearse, vb.
entomb, vb.
epitaph, n.
exequy, n.
funeral, n.
funeral bell, n.
grave, n.
grave, vb.
graveless, adj.
grave-maker, n.
grave-making, n.
gravestone, n.
hearse, n.
hearse, vb.
hic jacet
inter, vb.
inurn, vb.
lead, n.
monument, n.
monumental, adj.
mourning black, n.
mourning gown, n.

mourning weed, n.
obsequious, adj.
obsequiously, adv.
obsequy, n.
pyramid, n.
rake up, phr. vb.
sepulchre, n.
sepulchre, vb.
St. Katherine's
  churchyard, n.
stone, n.
storehouse, n.
tomb, n.
tomb, vb.
tombless, adj.
trophy, n.
unburied, adj.
unearth, vb.
urn, n.
  : 51

05.07
swathe • shroud
——————————
bearing-cloth, n.
cere, vb.
cerecloth, n.
cerement, n.
chrisom, n.
cloth, n.
cradle-clothes, n.
enswathe, vb.
sackcloth, n.
sheet, n.
shroud, n.
shroud, vb.
shrouding sheet, n.
swaddling-clothes, n.
swaddling-clouts, n.
swathe, n.
swathing-clothes, n.
winding-sheet, n.
  : 18

06.01
body

anatomy, n.
atomy, n.
bodiless, adj.
bodily, adj.
body, n.
body, vb.
bones, n.
bulk, n.
carcass, n.
carrion, n.
corporal, adj.
corporate, adj.
corpse, n.
corse, n.
flesh, n.
fleshly, adj.
incarnate, adj.
mummy, n.
organ, n.
tender-bodied, adj.
trunk, n.
unbodied, adj.
worm's-meat, n.
 : 23

06.02
head

bald-pate, n.
bald-pated, adj.
bare-headed, adj.
blockhead, n.
brain-pan, n.
costard, n.
crooked-pated, adj.
crown, n.
curled-pate, n.
death's face, n.
death's-head, n.
head, n.
headed, adj.
headless, adj.

head-piece, n.
hoary-headed, adj.
Hydra-headed, adj.
ill-headed, adj.
knot-pated, adj.
many-headed, adj.
mazard, n.
noddle, n.
noll, n.
pash, n.
pate, n.
periwig-pated, adj.
poll, n.
rug-headed, adj.
russet-pated, adj.
scalp, n.
sconce, n.
skull, n.
sleek-headed, adj.
smoothy-pate, n.
three-headed, adj.
top, n.
two-headed, adj.
 : 37

06.03
hair

bald, adj.
beard, n.
beard, vb.
bearded, adj.
beardless, adj.
black-haired, adj.
brow, n.
curl, n.
curled-pate, n.
elf-lock, n.
excrement, n.
eyebrow, n.
hair, n.
hairless, adj.
hairy, adj.
hard-haired, adj.
Lack-beard

lock, n.
mustachio, n.
periwig, n.
periwig-pated, adj.
scarce-bearded, adj.
shag-haired, adj.
top, n.
tress, n.
unhair, vb.
unhaired, adj.
valance, vb.
white-haired, adj.
wiry, adj.
 : 30

06.04
face

apple of eye, n.
baby-brow, n.
barefaced, adj.
beetle brow, n.
black-browed, adj.
black-eyed, adj.
black-faced, adj.
bloody-faced, adj.
blue eye, n.
blue-eyed, adj.
bridge, n.
broad-fronted, adj.
brow, n.
cheek, n.
cheek-rose, n.
chin, n.
coffer-lid, n.
cream-faced, adj.
dark-eyed, adj.
dimple, n.
dimple, vb.
ear, n.
eye, n.
eye-ball, n.
eyebrow, n.
eye-glass, n.
eyelid, n.

eyestring, n.
face, n.
fair-eyed, adj.
fair-faced, adj.
favour, n.
fire-eyed, adj.
flap-eared, adj.
forehead, n.
freckle-faced, adj.
front, n.
glass, n.
great-eyed, adj.
grey-eyed, adj.
grim-visaged, adj.
half-cheek, n.
hare-lip, n.
hollow-eyed, adj.
hook-nosed, adj.
humble-visaged, adj.
iris, n.
jowl, n.
labras, n.
lean-faced, adj.
lid, n.
lip, n.
malmsey-nose, n.
menton, fr. n.
narine, fr. n.
nose, n.
noseless, adj.
nostril, n.
pale-faced, adj.
pale-visaged, adj.
paper-faced, adj.
parti-eyed, adj.
penthouse lid, n.
prick-eared, adj.
red-faced, adj.
rose-cheeked, adj.
rose-lipped, adj.
round-faced, adj.
shag-eared, adj.
smooth-faced, adj.
sour-faced, adj.
tallow-face, n.

temple, n.
thick-lipped, adj.
thick-lips, n.
thin-faced, adj.
tripe-visaged, adj.
visage, n.
wall-eyed, adj.
whey-face, n.
white-faced, adj.
window, n.
windowed, adj.
wrinkle, n.
: 84

06.05
lineament

appearance, n.
aspect, n.
assemblance, n.
bent, n.
brow, n.
character, n.
cheer, n.
commixture, n.
complexion, n.
countenance, n.
face, n.
favour, n.
favour, vb.
feature, n.
feature, vb.
featureless, adj.
grim-looked, adj.
hard-favoured, adj.
ill-favoured, adj.
lean-looked, adj.
leer, n.
line, n.
lineament, n.
look, n.
outside, n.
outward, n.
person, n.
personage, n.

physiognomy, n.
red-looked, adj.
semblance, n.
swart-complexioned, adj.
thew, n.
visage, n.
visage, vb.
well-favoured, adj.
: 36

06.06
jaw

boneless, adj.
chap, n.
chap-fallen, adj.
chapless, adj.
flap-mouthed, adj.
flewed, adj.
gum, n.
jaw, n.
jaw, vb.
jaw-bone, n.
mouth, n.
mouth, vb.
palate, n.
roof, n.
sharp-toothed, adj.
stretch-mouthed, adj.
tongue, n.
tooth, n.
tooth, vb.
wide-chopped, adj.
: 20

06.07
neck

col, fr. n.
dewlap, n.
dew-lapped, adj.
gorge, n.
gorge, fr. n.
nape, n.

neck, n.
organ-pipe, n.
pipe, n.
strong-necked, adj.
throat, n.
weasand, n.
windpipe, n.
wry-necked, adj.
: 14

06.08
breast

bosom, n.
breast, n.
chest, n.
dug, n.
milk pap, n.
nipple, n.
pap, n.
teat, n.
udder, n.
unbosom, vb.
: 10

06.09
belly

belly, n.
groin, n.
lap, n.
loin, n.
midriff, n.
nave, n.
navel, n.
paunch, n.
rim, n.
waist, n.
womb, n.
womb, vb.
womby, adj.
: 13

06.10
back

back, n.
back, vb.
bow-back, n.
bunch-backed, adj.
chine, n.
crook-back, n.
horse-back, n.
shoulder, n.
shoulder-blade, n.
shoulder-bone, n.
withers, n.
: 11

06.11
flank

flank, n.
haunch, n.
hip, n.
red-hipped, adj.
side, n.
: 5

06.12
buttock

brawn-buttock, n.
bum, n.
buttock, n.
pin-buttock, n.
quatch-buttock, n.
rump, n.
tail, n.
: 7

06.13
cullion

cod-piece, n.
cullion, n.
dildo, n.
doucet, n.

open-arse, n.
pillicock, n.
pizzle, n.
stone, n.
tool, n.
unpaved, adj.
: 10

06.14
limb

artus, lat. n.
bone, n.
clean-timbered, adj.
good-limbed, adj.
joint, n.
limb, n.
limb-meal, adv.
member, n.
part, n.
short-jointed, adj.
strong-jointed, adj.
stump, n.
: 12

06.15
arm

arm, n.
bare-armed, adj.
bow-hand, n.
bras, fr. n.
coude, fr. n.
doigt, fr. n.
elbow, n.
finger, n.
finger-end, n.
fist, n.
forefinger, n.
hand, n.
hand, vb.
handed, adj.
handless, adj.
hard-handed, adj.
left hand, n.

little finger, n.
main, fr. n.
manual, adj.
manus, n.
manus, lat. n.
nail, n.
nieve, n.
ongle, fr. n.
palm, n.
picker, n.
right hand, n.
short-armed, adj.
ten commandments,
n.
thumb, n.
two-hand, n.
unhand, vb.
white-handed, adj.
wrist, n.
: 35

06.16
leg

ankle, n.
barefoot, adj.
calf, n.
crook-kneed, adj.
foot, n.
foot, vb.
fork, n.
forked, adj.
genou, fr. n.
ham, n.
heel, n.
knee, n.
leg, n.
legged, adj.
long-legged, adj.
nail, n.
near-legged, adj.
pied, fr. n.
plant, n.
shank, n.
shin, n.

short-legged, adj.
small, n.
sole, n.
thigh, n.
three-foot, n.
three-legged, adj.
tiptoe, n.
toe, n.
two-legged, adj.
: 30

06.17
blood • bone

artery, n.
bare-boned, adj.
bare-ribbed, adj.
big-boned, adj.
bladder, n.
blood, n.
bloodily, adv.
bloodless, adj.
bloody, adj.
bloody, vb.
blue-veined, adj.
bone, n.
bowel, n.
brain, n.
brained, adj.
brawn, n.
brawny, adj.
burly-boned, adj.
carved-bone, n.
chest, n.
collop, n.
cuore, it. n.
ear-wax, n.
entrail, n.
flesh, n.
gall, n.
gore, n.
gory, adj.
gut, n.
hamstring, n.
heart, n.

heart, vb.
heart-blood, n.
heart-string, n.
humour, n.
inward, n.
juice, n.
kidney, n.
life-blood, n.
liver, n.
liver-vein, n.
lung, n.
marrow, n.
marrowless, adj.
master-cord, n.
maw, n.
moisture, n.
nerve, n.
offal, n.
pia mater
pipe, n.
pulse, n.
raw-boned, adj.
reins, n.
rib, n.
rib, vb.
sanguis, lat. n.
sinew, n.
skin, n.
skin, vb.
spleen, n.
stomach, n.
string, n.
strong-ribbed, adj.
thew, n.
thick-ribbed, adj.
unbloodied, adj.
unheart, vb.
unnerve, vb.
unsinewed, adj.
vapour, n.
vein, n.
ventricle, n.
virgin-knot, n.
: 74

06.18
anatomy
compounds
_____
after-eye, vb.
Aguecheek
Agueface
baby-brow, n.
bald-pate, n.
bald-pated, adj.
bare-armed, adj.
bare-bone, n.
bare-boned, adj.
barefaced, adj.
barefoot, adj.
bare-headed, adj.
bare-ribbed, adj.
beetle-headed, adj.
big-bellied, adj.
big-boned, adj.
black-browed, adj.
black-eyed, adj.
black-faced, adj.
black-haired, adj.
blockhead, n.
bloody-faced, adj.
blue-eyed, adj.
blue-veined, adj.
boiled-brain, n.
bold-faced, adj.
bow-back, n.
bow-hand, n.
brawn-buttock, n.
brazen-face, n.
brazen-faced, adj.
break-neck, n.
broad-fronted, adj.
bunch-backed, adj.
burly-boned, adj.
carved-bone, n.
clay-brained, adj.
clip-winged, adj.
clod-poll, n.
close-tongued, adj.
cold-blooded, adj.

cold-hearted, adj.
cream-faced, adj.
crook-back, n.
crooked-pated, adj.
crook-kneed, adj.
cruel-hearted, adj.
curled-pate, n.
dark-eyed, adj.
deadly-handed, adj.
death's face, n.
death's-head, n.
deep-brained, adj.
deep-mouthed, adj.
dewlap, n.
dew-lapped, adj.
dizzy-eyed, adj.
dog-hearted, adj.
doughty-handed, adj.
dove-feathered, adj.
dry-foot, adv.
dull-brained, adj.
dull-eyed, adj.
eagle-winged, adj.
empty-hearted, adj.
even-handed, adj.
evil-eyed, adj.
faint-hearted, adj.
fair-eyed, adj.
fair-faced, adj.
false-faced, adj.
false-heart, n.
false-hearted, adj.
fat-brained, adj.
fat-guts, n.
fat-kidneyed, adj.
fiery-footed, adj.
fire-eyed, adj.
flap-eared, adj.
flap-mouthed, adj.
fleet-foot, n.
fleet-winged, adj.
flint-hearted, adj.
foul-faced, adj.
foul-mouthed, adj.
freckle-faced, adj.

free-footed, adj.
free-hearted, adj.
full-gorged, adj.
full-hearted, adj.
full-winged, adj.
gentle-hearted, adj.
glass-faced, adj.
good-faced, adj.
good-limbed, adj.
gorbellied, adj.
great-bellied, adj.
great-eyed, adj.
green-eyed, adj.
greybeard, n.
grey-eyed, adj.
grim-visaged, adj.
half-blooded, adj.
half-cheeked, adj.
half-face, n.
half-faced, adj.
hard-haired, adj.
hard-handed, adj.
hard-hearted, adj.
hare-brained, adj.
hare-lip, n.
hasty-footed, adj.
heart-blood, n.
heavy-headed, adj.
high-stomached, adj.
hoary-headed, adj.
hollow-eyed, adj.
hollow-hearted, adj.
honest-hearted, adj.
honey-mouthed, adj.
honey-tongued, adj.
hook-nosed, adj.
hot-blood, n.
hot-bloodied, adj.
humble-mouthed, adj.
humble-visaged, adj.
Hydra-headed, adj.
idle-headed, adj.
ill-faced, adj.
ill-headed, adj.

jolt head, n.
kind-hearted, adj.
knot-pated, adj.
knotty-pated, adj.
Lack-beard
lack-brain, n.
large-handed, adj.
leaden-footed, adj.
lean-faced, adj.
lewd-tongued, adj.
life-blood, n.
lightfoot, adj.
light-heeled, adj.
light-winged, adj.
lily-livered, adj.
lofty-plumed, adj.
loggerhead, n.
loggerheaded, adj.
long-legged, adj.
long-tongued, adj.
loose-bodied, adj.
mad-brain, n.
mad-brained, adj.
mad-headed, adj.
maiden-hearted, adj.
maiden-tongued, adj.
malmsey-nose, n.
many-headed, adj.
marble-breasted, adj.
marble-hearted, adj.
merry-hearted, adj.
milk-livered, adj.
narrow-mouthed, adj.
near-legged, adj.
nimble-footed, adj.
nimble-pinioned, n.
old-faced, adj.
onion-eyed, adj.
open-arse, n.
open-eyed, adj.
pale-faced, adj.
pale-hearted, adj.
pale-visaged, adj.
paper-faced, adj.
parti-eyed, adj.

periwig-pated, adj.
pigeon-livered, adj.
pin-buttock, n.
pitiful-hearted, adj.
prick-eared, adj.
proud-hearted, adj.
puppy-headed, adj.
quatch-buttock, n.
quick-eyed, adj.
raw-boned, adj.
red-eyed, adj.
red-faced, adj.
red-hipped, adj.
red-nose, n.
rose-cheeked, adj.
rose-lipped, adj.
round-faced, adj.
round-hoofed, adj.
round-wombed, adj.
rug-headed, adj.
russet-pated, adj.
sad-eyed, adj.
sad-faced, adj.
sad-hearted, adj.
scarce-bearded, adj.
scythe-tusked, adj.
shag-eared, adj.
shag-haired, adj.
shallow-hearted, adj.
shamefaced, adj.
sharp-quilled, adj.
sharp-toothed, adj.
short-armed, adj.
short-jointed, adj.
short-legged, adj.
shrill-gorged, adj.
shrill-tongued, adj.
single-soled, adj.
sleek-headed, adj.
slow-winged, adj.
smooth-faced, adj.
smooth-tongue, n.
smoothy-pate, n.
sober-blooded, adj.
soft-hearted, adj.

sour-eyed, adj.
sour-faced, adj.
stony-hearted, adj.
stout-hearted, adj.
stretch-mouthed, adj.
strong-framed, adj.
strong-hearted, adj.
strong-jointed, adj.
strong-necked, adj.
strong-ribbed, adj.
strong-winged, adj.
swag-bellied, adj.
sweet-faced, adj.
swift-footed, adj.
swift-winged, adj.
tallow-face, n.
tawny-finned, adj.
tender-bodied, adj.
tender-hearted, adj.
tender-hefted, adj.
thick-eyed, adj.
thick-lipped, adj.
thick-lips, n.
thick-ribbed, adj.
thickskin, n.
thin-faced, adj.
three-foot, n.
three-headed, adj.
three-legged, adj.
ticklebrain, n.
tiger-footed, adj.
treble-sinewed, adj.
tripe-visaged, adj.
true-hearted, adj.
trumpet-tongued, adj.
two-hand, n.
two-headed, adj.
two-legged, adj.
urchin-snouted, adj.
venomed-mouthed,
  adj.
wall-eyed, adj.
waspish-headed, adj.
weak-hearted, adj.
whey-face, n.

whitebeard, n.
white-bearded, adj.
white-faced, adj.
white-haired, adj.
white-handed, adj.
white-livered, adj.
wide-chopped, adj.
wry-necked, adj.
young-eyed, adj.
  : 273

06.19
breath
———————

blast, n.
blow, vb.
break wind, vb.
breath, n.
breathe, vb.
breather, n.
breathless, adj.
cough, n.
cough, vb.
gasp, n.
gasp, vb.
hawk, vb.
hem, vb.
inspire, vb.
long-winded, adj.
lust-breathed, adj.
neeze, vb.
pant, n.
pant, vb.
pantingly, adv.
puff, n.
puff, vb.
pursy, adj.
short-winded, adj.
sigh, n.
sigh, vb.
snore, n.
snore, vb.
snort, vb.
snuff, vb.
suspiration, n.

suspire, vb.
unbreathed, adj.
well-breathed, adj.
wheeze, vb.
wind, n.
  : 36

06.20
excrement
———————

belch, vb.
cast, vb.
cast (heave) the
  gorge, vb.
chamber-lye, n.
disgorge, vb.
excrement, n.
leak, vb.
make water, vb.
piss, vb.
puke, vb.
purgative, adj.
purge, vb.
siege, n.
sweat, n.
sweat, vb.
sweaty, adj.
urine, n.
vomissement, fr. n.
vomit, n.
vomit, vb.
water, n.
  : 21

06.21
sleep
———————

arouse, vb.
asleep, adv.
awake, adj.
awake, vb.
awaken, vb.
dormouse, n.
dream, n.
dream, vb.

dreamer, n.
drowse, vb.
drowsily, adv.
drowsiness, n.
drowsy, adj.
dullness, n.
entrance, vb.
gentle-sleeping, adj.
heaviness, n.
heavy-headed, adj.

nap, n.
nap, vb.
night-waking, adj.
outsleep, vb.
repose, n.
rest, n.
rouse, vb.
sleep, n.
sleep, vb.
sleeper, n.

sleepy, adj.
slumber, n.
slumber, vb.
slumbery, adj.
still-waking, adj.
stir, vb.
trance, n.
trance, vb.
undreamed, adj.
up-roused, adj.

wake, n.
wake, vb.
waken, vb.
watch, n.
watch, vb.
watcher, n.
watchful, adj.
: 45

07.01
health
_____

formal, adj.
fresh, adj.
freshly, adv.
freshness, n.
health, n.
healthful, adj.
health-giving, adj.
healthsome, adj.
healthy, adj.
heart-whole, adj.
liking, n.
perfect, adj.
safe, adj.
sanity, n.
sound, adj.
soundness, n.
weal, n.
welfare, n.
well, adv.
well-breathed, adj.
well-conditioned, adj.
well-liking, adj.
whole, adj.
wholesome, adj.
wholesome-profitable
  adj.
  : 25

07.02
vigour
_____

ability, n.
able, adj.
active, adj.
actively, adv.
activity, n.
amain, adv.
armipotent, adj.
big, adj.
bonny, adj.
brazen, adj.
by the head and

shoulders, adv.
deeply, adv.
emphasis, n.
fiery, adj.
flush, adj.
force, n.
force, fr. n.
forceful, adj.
forcible, adj.
forcibly, adv.
fortitude, n.
forza, it. n.
fresh, adj.
freshly, adv.
heart-deep, adj.
hey-day, n.
in blood, adv.
life, n.
lustihood, n.
lusty, adj.
mainly, adv.
mettle, n.
might, n.
mightful, adj.
mightily, adv.
mighty, adj.
multipotent, adj.
nature, n.
nervy, adj.
pith, n.
pithy, adj.
potency, n.
potent, adj.
potent, n.
potential, adj.
potently, adv.
power, n.
powerful, adj.
powerfully, adv.
pride, n.
profound, adj.
profoundly, adv.
proud, adj.
proudly, adv.
puissance, n.

puissant, adj.
puissant, fr. adj.
robustious, adj.
sinew, vb.
sinewy, adj.
sound, adj.
soundest, n.
soundly, adv.
spirit, vb.
stout, adj.
stoutly, adv.
strength, n.
strengthen, vb.
strong, adj.
strong, n.
strongest, n.
strongly, adv.
sturdy, adj.
swinge, n.
thew, n.
thrice-puissant, adj.
tight, adj.
tightly, adv.
treble-sinewed, adj.
validity, n.
verdour, n.
verdure, n.
vigour, n.
violent, adj.
violent, vb.
violently, adv.
virtuous, adj.
  : 87

07.03
weariness
_____

a-weary, adv.
day-wearied, adj.
dog-weary, adj.
dull, vb.
dully, adv.
emboss, vb.
fatigate, adj.
flat, adj.

fordo, vb.
forspend, vb.
forweary, vb.
jade, vb.
journey-bated, adj.
life-weary, adj.
never-lust-wearied,
  adj.
outbreathed, adj.
over-labour, vb.
overteem, vb.
shotten, adj.
sur-reined, adj.
tediosity, n.
tedious, adj.
tediously, adv.
tediousness, n.
tire, vb.
toil, vb.
untirable, adj.
untired, adj.
unwappered, adj.
unwearied, adj.
wappened, adj.
war-wearied, adj.
war-worn, adj.
wave-worn, adj.
wearily, adj.
weariness, n.
wearisome, adj.
weary, adj.
weary, vb.
woe-wearied, adj.
world-wearied, adj.
  : 41

07.04
weakness
_____

abate, vb.
allay, n.
allay, vb.
bate, vb.
break, vb.
brittle, adj.

craze, vb.
crazy, adj.
dash, vb.
debile, adj.
debility, n.
deficient, adj.
effeminate, adj.
enfeeble, vb.
fail, vb.
faint, adj.
faint, vb.
faintly, adv.
faintness, n.
feeble, adj.
feeble, n.
feeble, vb.
feebleness, n.
feebly, adv.
fever-weakened, adj.
foil, vb.
forceless, adj.
fragile, adj.
frail, adj.
frailty, n.
frustrate, adj.
frustrate, vb.
imbecility, n.
impair, vb.
impotence, n.
impotent, adj.
infirmity, n.
milky, adj.
pall, vb.
pigeon-livered, adj.
pithless, adj.
poor, adj.
poorest, n.
powerless, adj.
quail, vb.
sick, adj.
sickly, adj.
sickly, adv.
small, adj.
soft-hearted, adj.
softness, n.

strengthless, adj.
toast-and-butter, n.
undermine, vb.
unfirm, adj.
unman, vb.
unmanly, adj.
unmanned, adj.
unnerve, vb.
unsinewed, adj.
untimbered, adj.
weak, adj.
weak, n.
weaken, vb.
weaker, n.
weakest, n.
weak-hinged, adj.
weakling, n.
weakly, adv.
weak-made, adj.
weakness, n.
: 71

07.05
decay
————————
addle, n.
beauty-waning, adj.
begnaw, vb.
blast, vb.
canker, n.
canker, vb.
canker-bit, adj.
carrion, n.
cling, vb.
confound, vb.
consume, vb.
corky, adj.
corrosive, adj.
corrupt, vb.
corruption, n.
craze, vb.
crumble, vb.
decay, n.
decay, vb.
decayer, n.

declension, n.
decline, vb.
decrepit, adj.
dirt-rotten, adj.
droop, vb.
dry, vb.
fade, vb.
fall, vb.
fester, vb.
finewed, adj.
foul, adj.
foul, n.
fret, vb.
fretful, adj.
fust, vb.
fusty, adj.
gnaw, vb.
hoar, adj.
hoar, vb.
languish, n.
languish, vb.
languishing, n.
languishment, n.
languor, n.
marrow-eating, adj.
mildew, vb.
mouldy, adj.
mouse-eaten, adj.
musty, adj.
napless, adj.
out at elbow, adv.
out at heels, adv.
outwear, vb.
over-rank, adj.
overwear, vb.
over-weather, vb.
pall, vb.
peak, vb.
pine, vb.
putrefy, vb.
rank, adj.
rankly, adv.
rot, n.
rot, vb.
rotten, adj.

rottenness, n.
ruin, n.
ruin, vb.
ruinate, vb.
ruinous, adj.
sag, vb.
sap-consuming, adj.
sere, adj.
shrink, vb.
shrivel, vb.
slack, vb.
spend, vb.
stale, adj.
stale, vb.
staleness, n.
threadbare, adj.
time-bewasted, adj.
waste, n.
waste, vb.
wasteful, adj.
wear, vb.
weather-bitten, adj.
wither, vb.
worm-eaten, adj.
worn-out, adj.
wrinkle, vb.
writhled, adj.
: 92

07.06
sickness
————————
attaint, adj.
attaint, n.
attaint, vb.
contagion, n.
contagious, adj.
corruption, n.
crafty-sick, adj.
disease, n.
disease, vb.
distemper, n.
distemperature, n.
evil, n.
fancy-sick, adj.

green, adj.
ill, adj.
indispose, vb.
infect, adj.
infect, vb.
infection, n.
infectious, adj.
infectiously, adv.
infirm, adj.
infirmity, n.
lay up, phr. vb.
lion-sick, adj.
lovesick, adj.
malady, n.
malignant, adj.
passion, n.
relapse, n.
sea-sick, adj.
sick, adj.
sick, n.
sick, vb.
sicken, vb.
sick-fallen, adj.
sickliness, n.
sickly, adj.
sickly, adv.
sickly, vb.
sickness, n.
thought-sick, adj.
unwholesome, adj.
unwholesome, n.
 : 44

07.07
plague
—————————
pestiferous, adj.
pestilence, n.
pestilent, adj.
plague, n.
plaguy, adj.
red murrain, n.
red pestilence, n.
red-plague, n.
unplagued, adj.   : 9

07.08
fit
—————————
apoplex, vb.
apoplexy, n.
choler, n.
convulsion, n.
cramp, n.
emportment, n.
epilepsy, n.
epileptic, adj.
falling sickness, n.
fit, n.
fit, vb.
fitful, adj.
shaking fever, n.
spleen, n.
sprawl, vb.
start, n.
tremor cordis
 : 17

07.09
fever
—————————
ague, n.
ague, vb.
fever, n.
fever, vb.
feverous, adj.
hectic, n.
quotidian, n.
quotidian tertian
 : 8

07.10
gout
—————————
colic, n.
dropsied, adj.
dropsy, n.
gout, n.
gouty, adj.
green-sickness, n.
jaundice, n.

king's evil, n.
palsy, n.
palsy, vb.
sciatica, n.
 : 11

07.11
leprosy
—————————
hoar leprosy, n.
lazar, n.
lazar-like, adj.
leper, n.
leprosy, n.
leprous, adj.
 : 6

07.12
rheum
—————————
catarrh, n.
cold, n.
consumption, n.
phthisic, n.
pleurisy, n.
rheum, n.
rheumatic, adj.
rheumy, adj.
 : 8

07.13
pox
—————————
French crown, n.
goose of Winchester,
 n.
gravel, n.
Neapolitan
 bone-ache, n.
pocky, adj.
pox, n.
sweat, n.
Winchester goose, n.
 : 8

07.14
queasiness
—————————
dizzy, adj.
dizzy, vb.
dizzy-eyed, adj.
dozy, vb.
faint, adj.
faint, vb.
giddily, adv.
giddy, adj.
light, adj.
lightness, n.
qualm, n.
qualmish, adj.
queasiness, n.
queasy, adj.
staggers, n.
stomach-qualmed,
 adj.
swoon, vb.
 : 17

07.15
itch
—————————
itch, n.
itch, vb.
serpigo, n.
tetter, n.
tetter, vb.
 : 5

07.16
sore
—————————
blain, n.
blister, n.
blister, vb.
boil, n.
botchy, adj.
bubukle, n.
bump, n.
canker, n.
carbuncle, n.

core, n.
corn, n.
death-token, n.
fester, vb.
fistula, n.
gall, n.
gall, vb.
gangrene, vb.
impostume, n.
kibe, n.
knob, n.
mangy, adj.
measles, n.
pearl, n.
pin and web, n.
plague-sore, n.
quat, n.
rankle, vb.
roinish, adj.
scab, n.
scald, adj.
scall, adj.
scurvy, adj.
sore, adj.
sore, n.
token, n.
tokened, adj.
ulcer, n.
ulcerous, adj.
wart, n.
wen, n.
whelk, n.
  : 41

07.17
ache

ache, n.
ache, vb.
agony, n.
ail, vb.
bone-ache, n.
feeling-painful, adj.
grief, n.
heart-sore, adj.

hell-pain, n.
labour, n.
labour, vb.
pain, n.
pain, vb.
painful, adj.
painfully, adv.
pang, n.
pang, vb.
pinch, n.
pinch, vb.
side-stitch, n.
smart, adj.
smart, n.
smart, vb.
sore, adj.
sorry, adj.
stitch, n.
suffer, vb.
sufferance, n.
throe, n.
throe, vb.
toothache, n.
torment, vb.
tormenta, vb.
tormente, vb.
unaching, adj.
unpanged, adj.
wring, vb.
  : 37

07.18
wound

all-hurting, adj.
back-wounding, adj.
black and blue, adj.
blemish, vb.
bruise, n.
bruise, vb.
cicatrice, n.
contusion, n.
crest-wounding, adj.
damage, n.
damage, vb.

deep-wounded, adj.
disable, vb.
disaster, vb.
endamage, vb.
endamagement, n.
gall, vb.
gash, n.
hurt, n.
hurt, vb.
hurtless, adj.
impair, vb.
injure, vb.
injurer, n.
injurious, adj.
injury, n.
injury, vb.
invulnerable, adj.
love-wounded, adj.
maim, n.
maim, vb.
mar, vb.
merchant-marring,
  adj.
nip, vb.
rupture, n.
scar, n.
scar, vb.
scathe, n.
scathe, vb.
scatheful, adj.
scotch, n.
scratch, n.
shoulder-shotten, adj.
sore, n.
unbruised, adj.
ungalled, adj.
unhurtful, adj.
unscarred, adj.
unscratched, adj.
unvulnerable, adj.
vulnerable, adj.
wipe, n.
wonder-wounded,
  adj.
wound, n.

wound, vb.
wounding, n.
woundless, adj.
  : 57

07.19
glanders

bots, n.
farcy, n.
glanders, n.
lampas, n.
mose, vb.
murrain, n.
spavin, n.
staggers, n.
stringhalt, n.
vives, n.
windgall, n.
yellows, n.
  : 12

07.20
madness

bemad, vb.
bestraught, adj.
brainsick, adj.
brain-sickly, adv.
disinsanity, n.
distract, adj.
distract, vb.
distraction, n.
fanatical, adj.
frantic, adj.
franticly, adv.
frenzy, n.
fury, n.
hysterica passio
informal, adj.
insane, adj.
insanie, n.
lunacy, n.
lunatic, adj.
lunatic, n.

lune, n.
mad, adj.
mad, n.
mad, vb.
mad-brain, n.
mad-brained, adj.
mad-headed, adj.
madly, adv.
madman, n.
madness, n.
madwoman, n.
March hare, n.
midsummer madness,
  n.
moody-mad, adj.
mother, n.
non-come, n.
passion, n.
rage, n.
rave, vb.
stark mad, adj.
wood, adj.
  : 41

**07.21
cripple**
─────────────
bunch-backed, adj.
cripple, n.
cripple, vb.
crook-back, n.
crutch, n.
deformity, n.
disable, vb.
founder, vb.
halt, n.
halt, vb.
hip, vb.
hox, vb.
lame, adj.
larne, n.
lame, vb.
lamely, adv.
lameness, n.
limp, vb.

maim, n.
maim, vb.
  : 20

**07.22
physician**
─────────────
Aesculapius
apothecary, n.
artist, n.
body-curer, n.
bully-doctor, n.
Castalion-King-
  Urinal, n.
chirurgeonly, adj.
curer, n.
doctor, n.
doctor of physic, n.
empiric, n.
empiricutic, adj.
Galen
Hippocrates
leech, n.
medicine, n.
medicus, lat. n.
midwife, n.
mountebank, n.
Paracelsus
physician, n.
pothecary, n.
practiser, n.
purger, n.
surgeon, n.
surgery, n.
tooth-drawer, n.
  : 27

**07.23
hospital**
─────────────
alms-house, n.
Bedlam
hospital, n.
spittle, n.
spittle-house, n.   : 5

**07.24
medicine • cure**
─────────────
aloe, n.
antidote, n.
appliance, n.
application, n.
balm, n.
balm, vb.
balmy, adj.
balsam, n.
balsamum, n.
carduus benedictus
cataplasm, n.
cauterize, vb.
clyster-pipe, n.
coloquintida, n.
compound, n.
confection, n.
conserve, n.
cordial, adj.
cordial, n.
corrosive, n.
cure, n.
cure, vb.
cureless, adj.
diet, n.
diet, vb.
dieter, n.
drench, n.
drug, n.
drug, vb.
embalm, vb.
heal, vb.
help, n.
help, vb.
holy-thistle, n.
horse-drench, n.
incision, n.
incurable, adj.
infusion, n.
medicinable, adj.
medicinal, adj.
medicine, n.
medicine, vb.

mineral, n.
mixture, n.
mummy, n.
new-healed, adj.
past-cure, n.
physic, n.
physic, vb.
physical, adj.
pill, n.
plantain, n.
plaster, n.
potion, n.
poultice, n.
prescription, n.
preservative, n.
purgation, n.
purgative, adj.
purge, n.
receipt, n.
recover, vb.
recovery, n.
recure, vb.
relief, n.
remediate, adj.
remedy, n.
remedy, vb.
restoration, n.
restorative, n.
restore, vb.
rhubarb, n.
rue, n.
salve, n.
salve^1, vb.
salve^2, vb.
search, vb.
senna, n.
simple, n.
sleeping potion, n.
syrup, n.
tent, n.
tent, vb.
tub, n.
tub-fast, n.
unction, n.
uncurable, adj.

unrecuring, adj.
untented, adj.
: 89

07.25
poison
_____
aconitum., lat. n.

bane, n.
bane, vb.
contagion, n.
empoison, vb.
envenom, vb.
hebenon, n.
hemlock, n.
life-poisoning, adj.

outvenom, vb.
poison, n.
poison, vb.
poisonous, adj.
potion, n.
ratsbane, n.
venom, n.
venom, vb.

venomed-mouthed,
    adj.
venomous, adj.
: 19

08.01
house

Belmont
bridehouse, n.
building, n.
casa, it. n.
cote, n.
cottage, n.
crib, n.
dwelling, n.
dwelling-house, n.
dwelling-place, n.
edifice, n.
fabric, n.
farm, n.
farm-house, n.
grange, n.
habitation, n.
hall, n.
haunt, n.
home, adv.
home, n.
homeward, adv.
homewards, adv.
host, n.
house, n.
hovel, n.
inn, n.
Kate-hall
lodging, n.
maison, fr. n.
manor, n.
manor-house, n.
mansion, n.
mansionry, n.
place, n.
residence, n.
roof, n.
Rose
seat, n.
shelter, n.
summer-house, n.
tenement, n.
 : 41

08.02
lodge

arbour, n.
bower, n.
bower, vb.
garden-house, n.
lodge, n.
lodging, n.
penthouse, n.
penthouse-like, adj.
tent, vb.
tented, adj.
 : 10

08.03
storehouse

armoury, n.
barn, n.
barn, vb.
buttery, n.
buttery-bar, n.
cellar, n.
cellarage, n.
confectionary, n.
garner, n.
larder, n.
pantry, n.
storehouse, n.
 : 12

08.04
inhabit

bestow, vb.
billet, vb.
cabin, vb.
camp, vb.
cave, vb.
cave-keeper, n.
cave-keeping, adj.
chamber, vb.
climate, vb.
confiner, n.

depopulate, vb.
desert, adj.
desolate, adj.
dishabit, vb.
dwell, vb.
dweller, n.
encamp, vb.
garrison, vb.
harbour, n.
harbour, vb.
host, vb.
house, vb.
houseless, adj.
hovel, vb.
ill-inhabited, adj.
inhabit, vb.
inhabitable, adj.
inhabitant, n.
keep, vb.
kennel, vb.
lie, vb.
lodge, vb.
lodger, n.
pavilion, vb.
people, vb.
quarter, vb.
reside, vb.
resident, adj.
sojourner, n.
stall, vb.
stow, vb.
tenant, n.
tenantless, adj.
tent, vb.
unhoused, adj.
uninhabitable, adj.
unpeople, vb.
unpeopled, adj.
untent, vb.
 : 49

08.05
roof

chimney, n.

chimney-top, n.
eaves, n.
house-eaves, n.
lead, n.
roof, n.
roof, vb.
thatch, n.
thatch, vb.
tile, n.
unroof, vb.
 : 11

08.06
steeple

belfry, n.
lantern, n.
spire, n.
steeple, n.
 : 4

08.07
vane

cock, n.
vane, n.
weathercock, n.
 : 3

08.08
wall

abbey wall, n.
bescreen, vb.
brick, n.
brick-wall, n.
buttress, n.
city wall, n.
corner-stone, n.
fights, n.
frieze, n.
immure, n.
masonry, n.
mure, n.
out-wall, n.

partition, n.
prison wall, n.
screen, n.
wall, n.
wall, vb.
  : 18

08.09
arch

---

arch, n.
arch, vb.
bay, n.
vault, n.
vaultage, n.
vaulted, adj.
vaulty, adj.
  : 7

08.10
window

---

bay window, n.
casement, n.
chamber-window, n.
church-window, n.
clerestory, n.
grate, n.
lattice, n.
loop, n.
looped, adj.
loop-hole, n.
portage, n.
red-lattice, n.
sight-hole, n.
window, n.
window, vb.
windowed, adj.
  : 16

08.11
entry

---

abbey-gate, n.
Antenorides

back-door, n.
chamber-door, n.
Chetas
church-door, n.
city-gate, n.
city port, n.
counter-gate, n.
court-gate, n.
Dardan
door, n.
entrance, n.
entry, n.
gate, n.
hatch, n.
Helias
hell-gate, n.
North gate, n.
opening, n.
palace gate, n.
park-gate, n.
Pompey's Porch
porch, n.
port, n.
portal, n.
portcullis, vb.
postern, n.
prison gate, n.
six-gated, adj.
threshold, n.
Timbria
town gate, n.
Troien
  : 34

08.12
lock

---

bar, n.
belock, vb.
bolt, n.
bolt, vb.
key, n.
keyhole, n.
latch, n.
lock, n.

lock, vb.
picklock, n.
spring, n.
staple, n.
strong-barred, adj.
ten-times-barred-up,
  adj.
unbar, vb.
unbolt, vb.
unlock, vb.
ward, n.
  : 18

08.13
floor

---

base, n.
basis, n.
floor, n.
foundation, n.
gallery, n.
pavement, n.
strong-based, adj.
unpaved, adj.
  : 8

08.14
platform

---

platform, n.
pulpit, n.
scaffold, n.
scaffoldage, n.
scene, n.
stage, n.
tribunal, n.
  : 7

08.15
stair

---

degree, n.
footstep, n.
grece, n.
ladder, n.

ladder-tackle, n.
round, n.
scale, n.
stair, n.
stair-work, n.
step, n.
stile, n.
tackled stair, n.
  : 12

08.16
sewer

---

bench-hole, n.
chamber-pot, n.
channel, n.
close-stool, n.
conduit, n.
draught, n.
evil, n.
jakes, n.
kennel, n.
Pissing-conduit, n.
sewer, n.
shore, n.
sink, n.
stool, n.
  : 14

08.17
rooms

---

bedchamber, n.
bedroom, n.
bridal chamber, n.
Bunch of Grapes
by-room, n.
cabin, n.
cabinet, n.
cell, n.
chamber, n.
closet, n.
confectionary, n.
court of guard, n.
cubiculo, n.

dark room, n.
dining-chamber, n.
Dolphin chamber, n.
fat room, n.
garret, n.
great chamber, n.
Half-moon
hall, n.
Jerusalem
kitchen, n.
lobby, n.
nursery, n.
office, n.
open room, n.
parlour, n.
pastry, n.
Pomegranate
presence, n.
privy chamber, n.
privy-kitchen, n.
room, n.
study, n.
tiring-house, n.
vault, n.
vaultage, n.
voiding lobby, n.
wardrobe, n.
[Westminster] Hall
 : 41

08.18
hearth

---

andiron, n.
bellows, n.
chimney, n.
chimney-piece, n.
chimney-top, n.
fire-shovel, n.
forge, n.
furnace, n.
furnace, vb.
hearth, n.
kiln-hole, n.
lime-kiln, n.

oven, n.
warming-pan, n.
 : 14

08.19
plank

---

bar, n.
beam, n.
block, n.
board, n.
buttery-bar, n.
hard-timbered, adj.
hovel-post, n.
lath, n.
panel, n.
planch, vb.
plank, n.
rail, n.
shelf, n.
table, n.
timber, n.
timber, vb.
untimbered, adj.
wainscot, n.
 : 18

08.20
table

---

board, n.
desk, n.
dresser, n.
table, n.
 : 4

08.21
chair

---

barber's chair, n.
bench, n.
bench, vb.
chair, n.
chair of state, n.
church-bench, n.

close-stool, n.
disbench, vb.
disseat, vb.
drooping chair, n.
footstool, n.
form, n.
joint-stool, n.
pew, n.
public chair, n.
seat, n.
see, n.
siege, n.
stool, n.
three-foot stool, n.
three-legged stool, n.
throne, n.
 : 22

08.22
bed

---

abed, adv.
bed, n.
bed, vb.
bed of Ware, n.
bedrid, adj.
bedward, adv.
bridal bed, n.
bride-bed, n.
childbed, n.
couch, n.
cradle, n.
cradle, vb.
day-bed, n.
death's-bed, n.
down-bed, n.
feather-bed, n.
field-bed, n.
litter, n.
love-bed, n.
marriage-bed, n.
pallet, n.
standing-bed, n.
truckle-bed, n.
wedding-bed, n. : 24

08.23
curtain

---

arras, n.
bed-hanger, n.
chamber-hanging, n.
curtain, n.
curtain, vb.
hanging, n.
painted cloth, n.
tapestry, n.
tent, n.
 : 9

08.24
blanket

---

bed-clothes, n.
blanket, n.
blanket, vb.
canopy, n.
carpet, n.
counterpoint, n.
coverlet, n.
mattress, n.
over-canopy, vb.
quilt, n.
sheet, vb.
wedding-sheet, n.
 : 12

08.25
cushion

---

bolster, n.
bolster, vb.
cushion, n.
down pillow, n.
pillow, n.
 : 5

08.26
mirror

---

burning-glass, n.

glass, n.
glass-faced, adj.
looking-glass, n.
mirror, n.
mirror, vb.
perspective, n.
perspectively, adv.
stone, n.
: 9

08.27
torch

brand, n.
candle, n.
candle-case, n.
candle-mine, n.
candlestick, n.
candle-waster, n.
canstick, n.
cresset, n.
flax, n.
lamp, n.
lantern, n.
link, n.
night-taper, n.
rush-candle, n.
snuff, n.
taper, n.
taper-light, n.
torch, n.
torcher, n.
torch-light, n.
torch-staff, n.
travelling lamp, n.
wedding torch, n.
wick, n.
: 24

08.28
cupboard

closet, n.
court-cupboard, n.
cupboard, vb.

press, n.
: 4

08.29
receptacle

bucket, n.
censer, n.
flask, n.
horn, n.
receipt, n.
receptacle, n.
vessel, n.
: 7

08.30
dish

china, n.
clack-dish, n.
dish, n.
fruit-dish, n.
mess, n.
paten, n.
plate, n.
porringer, n.
saucer, n.
trencher, n.
trenchering, n.
: 11

08.31
cup

bowl, n.
can, n.
cannikin, n.
chalice, n.
chaliced, adj.
cup, n.
cup, vb.
glass, n.
goblet, n.
jack, n.
pint-pot, n.

pottle, n.
pottle-pot, n.
quart, n.
standing-bowl, n.
stoup, n.
: 16

08.32
pot

cauldron, n.
chamber-pot, n.
jordan, n.
pot, n.
quart pot, n.
skillet, n.
stew, n.
warming-pan, n.
water-pot, n.
: 9

08.33
bottle

alembic, n.
bombard, n.
bottle, n.
bottled, adj.
ear, n.
ewer, n.
flagon, n.
jug, n.
pitcher, n.
urinal, n.
urn, n.
vial, n.
: 12

08.34
basket

alms-basket, n.
basket, n.
buck-basket, n.
cage, n.

maund, n.
pannier, n.
: 6

08.35
tub

basin, n.
bucket, n.
font, n.
pail, n.
powdering-tub, n.
tallow-catch, n.
trough, n.
tub, n.
: 8

08.36
case

boîte, fr. n.
bolting-hutch, n.
bowcase, n.
box, n.
candle-case, n.
case, n.
case, vb.
cask, n.
casket, n.
casket, vb.
chest, n.
coffer, n.
coffin, n.
lead, n.
lute-case, n.
penner, n.
pepper-box, n.
pouncet-box, n.
tinderbox, n.
trunk, n.
: 20

08.37
bag
_____

bag, n.
budget, n.
cloak-bag, n.

halfpenny purse, n.
honey-bag, n.
impeticos, vb.
mail, n.
money-bag, n.
pocket, n.

pocket, vb.
poke, n.
pouch, n.
purse, n.
purse, vb.
sack, n.

satchel, n.
scrip, n.
Spanish-pouch, n.
wallet, n.
woolsack, n.
: 20

09.01
appetite

a-hungry, adv.
appetite, n.
batten, vb.
belly-pinched, adj.
cloy, vb.
cloyless, adj.
cloyment, n.
cormorant, n.
disedge, vb.
dry, adj.
empty, adj.
englut, vb.
epicure, n.
epicurean, adj.
epicurism, n.
famine, n.
famish, vb.
fare, vb.
fast, n.
fast, vb.
fast-lost, adj.
fat, vb.
feed, vb.
fill, vb.
forage, vb.
full, adj.
full-acorned, adj.
full-fed, adj.
full-gorged, adj.
glut, vb.
glutton, n.
glutton, vb.
glutton-like, adj.
gluttonous, adj.
gluttony, n.
gorge, vb.
gormandize, vb.
greedily, adv.
greediness, n.
half-supped, adj.
hunger, n.
hunger, vb.
hungerly, adj.
hunger-starve, vb.
hungry, adj.
hungry-starved, adj.
insatiate, adj.
lust-dieted, adj.
never-cloying, adj.
never-surfeited, adj.
overcloy, vb.
overeat, vb.
over-feed, vb.
overgorge, vb.
pine, vb.
raven, vb.
ravenous, adj.
ravin, n.
repletion, n.
sate, vb.
satiate, adj.
satiety, n.
sharp, adj.
sharp-looking, adj.
stanch, vb.
stanchless, adj.
starve, vb.
starveling, n.
still-pining, adj.
stomach, n.
surfeit, n.
surfeit, vb.
surfeiter, n.
surfeit-taking, adj.
thirst, n.
thirst, vb.
thirsty, adj.
unfed, adj.
unsatiate, adj.
unstanched, adj.
: 80

09.02
feed

after-nourishment, n.
alere, lat. vb.
bacon-fed, adj.
bean-fed, adj.
board, vb.
cater, vb.
caudle, vb.
diet, vb.
dish, vb.
feed, vb.
kitchen, vb.
line, vb.
nourish, vb.
nourisher, n.
nourishment, n.
nutriment, n.
over-feed, vb.
rump-fed, adj.
victual, vb.
: 19

09.03
eat • drink

ale-washed, adj.
all-eating, adj.
bait, vb.
banquet, vb.
beest-eating, adj.
blood-consuming, adj.
blood-drinking, adj.
blood-sucking, adj.
bloodthirsty, adj.
break bread, vb.
carouse, n.
carouse, vb.
consume, vb.
consumer, n.
convive, vb.
crush, vb.
devour, vb.
devourer, n.
diet, vb.
digest, vb.
digestion, n.
dine, vb.
diner, fr. vb.
drain, vb.
draught, n.
drink, n.
drink, vb.
drink health, vb.
drinking, n.
drown, vb.
drunkard, n.
drunkenly, adv.
drunkenness, n.
eat, vb.
eater, n.
fap, adj.
fare, vb.
feast, vb.
feast-won, adj.
feeder, n.
flap-dragon, vb.
flesh, vb.
fluster, vb.
garlic-eater, n.
glut, vb.
health, n.
intoxicate, vb.
lap, vb.
lick, vb.
malt-worm, n.
mess, n.
mouth, vb.
play off, phr. vb.
pork-eater, n.
pot, vb.
potable, adj.
quaff, vb.
repast, vb.
rouse, n.
serve, vb.
sip, vb.
sponge, n.
spoon, n.
spread, vb.
suck, vb.
sup, vb.
swallow, vb.

swill, vb.
swine-drunk, adj.
taste, n.
taste, vb.
tipple, vb.
tipsy, adj.
tosspot, n.
touch, vb.
trencher-man, n.
wassail, n.
water, vb.
: 78

09.04
food • drink

alms-drink, n.
beverage, n.
bread, n.
by-drinking, n.
cate, n.
cheer, n.
dainty, adj.
dainty, n.
delicate, n.
diet, n.
dish, n.
drink, n.
food, n.
kickshaws, n.
meat, n.
potation, n.
provision, n.
sustenance, n.
viand, n.
victual, n.
: 20

09.05
cookery

bake, vb.
baste, vb.
bespice, vb.
boil, vb.

brew, vb.
broil, vb.
churn, vb.
cook, vb.
cookery, n.
coquere, lat. vb.
decoct, vb.
doughy, adj.
fry, vb.
ill-roasted, adj.
impaste, vb.
keel, vb.
leaven, vb.
mash, vb.
over-leaven, vb.
overroast, vb.
preserve, vb.
roast, vb.
season, vb.
seethe, vb.
souse, vb.
spice, vb.
stew, vb.
toast, vb.
unbaked, adj.
: 29

09.06
salt • sugar

barm, n.
eisell, n.
flour, n.
mace, n.
meal, n.
mealy, adj.
pickle, n.
salt, adj.
salt, n.
season, n.
spice, n.
spicery, n.
sugar, n.
sugar-candy, n.
vinegar, n.

yeast, n.
yeasty, adj.
: 17

09.07
congeal

cake, vb.
candy, vb.
coagulate, adj.
congeal, vb.
congealment, n.
cream, vb.
curd, vb.
curdy, adj.
curdy, vb.
jelly, n.
posset, vb.
slab, adj.
thick, vb.
uncandied, adj.
: 14

09.08
repast

bait, n.
banquet, n.
breakfast, n.
bridal dinner, n.
dinner, n.
entertainment, n.
feast, n.
fish-meal, n.
half-supped, adj.
meal, n.
ordinary, n.
pittance, n.
recreation, n.
repast, n.
repasture, n.
service, n.
supper, n.
: 17

09.09
pickle-herring

caviar, n.
fish, n.
fish-meal, n.
pickle-herring, n.
poor John, n.
red herring, n.
salt-fish, n.
stock-fish, n.
white herring, n.
: 9

09.10
meat

bacon, n.
bake-meat, n.
beef, n.
brawn, n.
bull-beef, n.
carbonado, n.
chine, n.
flesh, n.
gammon, n.
meat, n.
mutton, n.
neat's foot, n.
neat's tongue, n.
ox-beef, n.
pettitoes, n.
pork, n.
rasher, n.
roast, n.
roast meat, n.
spoon-meat, n.
tripe, n.
veal, n.
venison, n.
: 23

09.11
sauce • porridge

broth, n.
gravy, n.
gruel, n.
hell-broth, n.
plum-broth, n.
plum-porridge, n.
porridge, n.
sauce, n.
sauce, vb.
saucy, adj.
stewed prune, n.
: 11

09.12
pancake

flapjack, n.
hodge-pudding, n.
pancake, n.
pudding, n.
: 4

09.13
bread • cake

apple-tart, n.
bake-meat, n.
batch, n.
biscuit, n.
bread, n.
brown bread, n.
cake, n.
cobloaf, n.
coffin, n.
crumb, n.
crust, n.
crust, vb.
crusty, adj.
custard-coffin, n.
dough, n.
doughy, adj.
gingerbread, n.
halfpenny loaf, n.
leaven, n.
loaf, n.
paste, n.
pasty, n.
pepper-gingerbread, n.
pie, n.
sop, n.
toast, n.
toast-and-butter, n.
wafer-cake, n.
white bread, n.
: 29

09.14
butter

Banbury cheese
butter, n.
butter, vb.
cheese, n.
cheese-paring, n.
cream, n.
curd, n.
egg, n.
milk, n.
salt-butter, n.
skim, vb.
skim-milk, n.
whey, n.
: 13

09.15
beer • wine

ale, n.
aqua-vitae, n.
barley-broth, n.
bastard, n.
beer, n.
bottle-ale, n.
brewage, n.
brown bastard, n.
canary, n.
caudle, n.
caudle, vb.
charneco, n.
claret wine, n.
double beer, n.
liquor, n.
Madeira, n.
malmsey, n.
metheglin, n.
muscatel, n.
nectar, n.
pipe-wine, n.
posset, n.
Rhenish, n.
sack, n.
sherris, n.
sherris-sack, n.
small beer, n.
ticklebrain, n.
wassail, n.
white bastard, n.
wine, n.
wort, n.
: 32

09.16
sweetmeat

candy, n.
candy, vb.
caraway, n.
conserve, n.
conserve, vb.
custard, n.
custard-coffin, n.
flap-dragon, n.
fool, n.
honey, n.
jelly, n.
junket, n.
kissing-comfit, n.
marchpane, n.
sweet, n.
sweetmeat, n.
: 16

10.01
attire

accoutre, vb.
accoutrement, n.
apparel, n.
apparel, vb.
array, n.
array, vb.
attire, n.
attire, vb.
bear, vb.
bride-habited, adj.
caparison, vb.
clad, adj.
cloth, n.
clothe, vb.
clothes, n.
cover, vb.
cut, n.
deck, vb.
discase, vb.
disguise, n.
dismantle, vb.
disrobe, vb.
divest, vb.
doff, vb.
don, vb.
dress, n.
dress, vb.
dressing, n.
enfold, vb.
enfolding, n.
enrobe, vb.
equipage, n.
flaunt, n.
furniture, n.
garb, n.
garment, n.
garnish, n.
garnish, vb.
gear, n.
habiliment, n.
habit, n.
habit, vb.

harness, vb.
invest, vb.
investment, n.
jollity, n.
lack-linen, n.
livery, n.
livery, vb.
mailed, adj.
mourning black, n.
mourning weed, n.
muffle, vb.
ornament, n.
pall, vb.
perk, vb.
prank, vb.
prick, vb.
rag, n.
raiment, n.
robe, n.
robe, vb.
suit, n.
suit, vb.
tire, n.
tire, vb.
trick, vb.
trim, n.
unbraced, adj.
uncase, vb.
undeck, vb.
undress, vb.
unready, adj.
untruss, vb.
vestment, n.
vesture, n.
wardrobe, n.
wear, n.
wear, vb.
wearer, n.
wearing, n.
wedding garment, n.
weed, n.
well-apparelled, adj.
  : 84

10.02
naked

bare, adj.
bare, n.
barely, adv.
bareness, n.
naked, adj.
nakedness, n.
stark-naked, adj.
thin, adj.
unbuttoned, adj.
uncover, vb.
uncovered, adj.
  : 11

10.03
cloth

bombast, n.
buck, n.
buckram, n.
cambric, n.
camlet, n.
canvas, n.
cloth, n.
clout, n.
cypress, n.
diaper, n.
dowlas, n.
durance, n.
everlasting, n.
felt, n.
flannel, n.
flap, n.
flax, n.
flaxen, adj.
frieze, n.
fustian, n.
hemp, n.
hempen, adj.
Holland
jean, n.
Kendal green, n.
kersey, n.

lack-linen, n.
lawn, n.
linen, n.
linsey-woolsey, n.
lockram, n.
nap, n.
napless, adj.
pile, n.
pile, vb.
russet, adj.
sackcloth, n.
sarsenet, n.
satin, n.
say, n.
serge, n.
silk, n.
silken, adj.
snipt-taffeta, n.
taffeta, n.
three-pile, n.
three-piled, adj.
tinsel, n.
tissue, n.
velure, n.
velvet, n.
woolward, adj.
  : 52

10.04
leather

buff, n.
calf-skin, n.
cheverel, n.
dog-skin, n.
dog's-leather, n.
eel-skin, n.
fox[-skin], n.
lambskin, n.
leather, n.
leathern, adj.
neat's leather, n.
sheepskin, n.
sow-skin, n.
  : 13

10.05
needlework

beam, n.
bone, n.
bottom, n.
bottom, vb.
clew, n.
embroider, vb.
embroidery, n.
knit, n.
knit, vb.
knotty, adj.
lace, n.
lace, vb.
needle, n.
needlework, n.
sampler, n.
seamy, adj.
skein, n.
sleave, n.
sleaved, adj.
sleave-silk, n.
spot, n.
spot, vb.
square, n.
staple, n.
stitchery, n.
string, n.
thimble, n.
thread, n.
thread, vb.
threaden, adj.
thrum, n.
thrum, vb.
twine, n.
unclew, vb.
unknit, vb.
unthread, vb.
Venice gold, n.
web, n.
window-bar, n.
woof, n.
yarn, n.
: 41

10.06
mantle

cape, n.
cassock, n.
cloak, n.
cloak, vb.
coat, n.
filthy-mantled, adj.
fire-robed, adj.
frock, n.
gaberdine, n.
gown, n.
grey-coated, adj.
jack, n.
jerkin, n.
mantle, n.
mantle, vb.
motley, n.
mourning gown, n.
night-gown, n.
pall, vb.
palliament, n.
parti-coated, adj.
riding-robe, n.
riding-suit, n.
robe, n.
robe, fr. n.
robe, vb.
sea-gown, n.
silken-coated, adj.
skin-coat, n.
sober-suited, adj.
stole, n.
surplice, n.
tawny-coat, n.
three-suited, adj.
toga, n.
toged, adj.
uncape, vb.
wailing robe, n.
wearing gown, n.
wedding gown, n.
: 40

10.07
petticoat

apron, n.
bases, n.
doublet, n.
farthingale, n.
foreskirt, n.
great-belly doublet,
  n.
half-kirtle, n.
kirtle, n.
petticoat, n.
placket, n.
shirt, n.
skirted, adj.
smock, n.
stomacher, n.
thin-bellied doublet,
  n.
: 15

10.08
sleeve

cuff, n.
down sleeve, n.
side sleeve, n.
sleeve, n.
sleeve-hand, n.
sleeveless, adj.
trunk sleeve, n.
: 7

10.09
shoe • hose

boot, n.
boot, vb.
boot-hose, n.
breech, n.
breech, vb.
brogue, n.
buskined, adj.
caddis, n.

caddis-garter, n.
chopine, n.
cod-piece, n.
cross-gartered, adj.
cross-gartering, n.
dancing shoe, n.
French hose, n.
French slop, n.
garter, n.
garter, vb.
gaskin, n.
heel, n.
high shoe, n.
hose, n.
netherstock, n.
overleather, n.
pantaloon, n.
puke-stocking, n.
pump, n.
round hose, n.
sandal shoon, n.
shoe, n.
shoeing-horn, n.
shoetie, n.
single-soled, adj.
slipper, n.
slippered, adj.
slipshod, adj.
slop, n.
sock, n.
sole, n.
stock, n.
stocking, n.
strap, n.
strosser, n.
unbreeched, adj.
ungartered, adj.
worsted-stocking, n.
: 46

10.10
hat

bare-headed, adj.
biggin, n.

block, n.
blue-cap, n.
bonnet, n.
bonnet, vb.
cap, n.
cap, vb.
cockle hat, n.
coif, n.
copataine hat, n.
corner-cap, n.
coxcomb, n.
cucullus, lat. n.
fool's head, n.
hat, n.
hive, n.
hood, n.
hood, vb.
kerchief, n.
Monmouth cap, n.
night-cap, n.
off-cap, vb.
porringer, n.
sea-cap, n.
ship-tire, n.
statute-cap, n.
tire, n.
tire-valiant, n.
turban, n.
turbaned, adj.
unbonneted, adj.
uncover, vb.
 : 33

10.11
veil • mask

collar, n.
dismask, vb.
immask, vb.
mask, n.
mask, vb.
moble, vb.
muffle, vb.
muffler, n.
over-veil, vb.

rebato, n.
ruff, n.
scarf, n.
scarf, vb.
tawdry lace, n.
unmask, vb.
unveil, vb.
veil, n.
veil, vb.
visor, n.
vizard, n.
vizard, vb.
vizard-like, adj.
wimple, vb.
 : 23

10.12
chaplet

brow-bound, adj.
chaplet, n.
circle, n.
circuit, n.
coronation, n.
coronet, n.
crants, n.
crown, n.
crown, vb.
crownet, n.
diadem, n.
fillet, n.
frontlet, n.
garland, n.
new-crowned, adj.
rigol, n.
thrice-crowned, adj.
uncrown, vb.
verge, n.
wreath, n.
 : 20

10.13
belt

baldric, n.

belt, n.
buckle, n.
centure, n.
clasp, n.
engird, vb.
engirt, vb.
gird, vb.
girdle, n.
girdle, vb.
girt, vb.
girth, n.
hanger, n.
unbuckle, vb.
unclasp, vb.
ungird, vb.
waist, n.
 : 17

10.14
fan • glove

fan, n.
fan, vb.
glove, n.
glove, vb.
 : 4

10.15
handkerchief

cloth, n.
handkerchief, n.
napkin, n.
 : 3

10.16
tape

band, n.
cord, n.
corded, adj.
inkle, n.
lace, n.
line, n.
point, n.

ribbon, n.
shoetie, n.
string, vb.
stringless, adj.
tape, n.
twist, n.
unbanded, adj.
unlace, vb.
 : 15

10.17
fringe

face, vb.
fringe, n.
fringe, vb.
guard, n.
guard, vb.
hem, vb.
line, vb.
lining, n.
list, n.
skirt, n.
underbear, vb.
unseam, vb.
valance, n.
valance, vb.
velvet-guard, n.
 : 15

10.18
ornament

adorn, vb.
adorning, n.
adornment, n.
become, vb.
bedeck, vb.
betrim, vb.
boss, vb.
branch, vb.
brave, adj.
bravery, n.
bugle, n.
button, n.

caparison, n.
cost, n.
deck, vb.
device, n.
dressing, n.
embellish, vb.
enamel, vb.
enchase, vb.
engild, vb.
enrich, vb.
facing, n.
flourish, n.
flourish, vb.
fret, vb.
furbish, vb.
garnish, vb.
gaud, vb.
gaudy, adj.
gayness, n.
gild, vb.
gilt, n.
grace, vb.
inlay, vb.
lace, vb.
ornament, n.
outbrave, vb.
parcel-gilt, adj.
pearl, n.
perk, vb.
pink, vb.
polish, vb.
prank, vb.
prick, vb.
pride, n.

prune, vb.
silver, vb.
spangle, vb.
spot, n.
stud, vb.
trap, vb.
trapping, n.
trick, vb.
trim, vb.
trinket, n.
undeck, vb.
unpinked, adj.
untrim, vb.
unvarnished, adj.
varnish, n.
varnish, vb.
 : 62

10.19
gem

───────────────

agate, n.
agate-stone, n.
amber, n.
carbuncle, n.
carbuncled, adj.
chrysolite, n.
diamond, n.
emerald, n.
foil, n.
gem, n.
horn, n.
ivory, n.
jet, n.

jetted, adj.
jewel, n.
jewel-like, adj.
opal, n.
pearl, n.
pearly, adj.
rich-jewelled, adj.
ruby, n.
sapphire, n.
stone, n.
turquoise, n.
union, n.
whale's bone, n.
 : 26

10.20
ring

───────────────

agate-ring, n.
circle, n.
hoop, n.
horn-ring, n.
joint-ring, n.
ring, n.
seal-ring, n.
thumb-ring, n.
wedding-ring, n.
 : 9

10.21
brooch

───────────────

aglet, n.
bead, n.

beaded, adj.
bracelet, n.
brooch, n.
brooch, vb.
bugle-bracelet, n.
button, n.
carcanet, n.
chain, n.
crystal-button, n.
medal, n.
necklace, n.
ouch, n.
periapt, n.
pin, n.
spangle, vb.
stud, n.
tassel, n.
trinket, n.
unbutton, vb.
 : 21

10.22
perfume

───────────────

civet, n.
musk, n.
perfume, n.
perfume, vb.
pomander, n.
rose-water, n.
 : 6

11.01
do

accomplish, vb.
accomplishment, n.
achieve, vb.
achievement, n.
achiever, n.
act, n.
act, vb.
action, n.
action-taking, adj.
actor, n.
actual, adj.
acture, n.
ado, n.
agent, n.
alms-deed, n.
bring, vb.
busily, adv.
business, n.
busy, adj.
busy, vb.
carry, vb.
cause, vb.
causer, n.
coact, vb.
coactive, adj.
commit, vb.
create, adj.
create, vb.
creation, n.
deal, vb.
dealing, n.
deed, n.
deed-achieving, adj.
deedless, adj.
discharge, n.
discharge, vb.
dispatch, n.
dispatch, vb.
do, vb.
doer, n.
doing, n.
effect, n.

effect, vb.
effectual, adj.
effectually, adv.
enact, n.
enact, vb.
enacture, n.
execute, vb.
execution, n.
executor, n.
exercise, n.
exercise, vb.
exigere, lat. vb.
exploit, n.
facere, lat. vb.
fact, n.
faire, fr. vb.
feat, n.
fulfil, vb.
function, n.
gest, n.
half-achieved, adj.
handle, vb.
harm-doing, n.
have at, phr. vb.
have to, phr. vb.
have with, phr. vb.
ill-dealing, adj.
ill-doing, n.
incur, vb.
keep, vb.
love-feat, n.
love-performing, adj.
make, vb.
maker, n.
manage, vb.
manager, n.
mover, n.
new-made, adj.
non-performance, n.
occupy, vb.
office, n.
office, vb.
official, adj.
operance, n.
operant, adj.

operate, vb.
operation, n.
operative, adj.
over-handle, vb.
part-created, adj.
perfect, vb.
perfection, n.
perform, vb.
performance, n.
performer, n.
practic, adj.
practice, n.
practise, vb.
practiser, n.
proceeding, n.
repeat, vb.
repetition, n.
self-doing, adj.
serve, vb.
thought-executing,
　adj.
treat, vb.
unacted, adj.
unactive, adj.
undeeded, adj.
undergo, vb.
undertake, vb.
undertaking, n.
undo, vb.
undone, adj.
uneffectual, adj.
unexecuted, adj.
unhandled, adj.
unmade, adj.
unmake, vb.
use, vb.
weak-made, adj.
well-dealing, adj.
well-doing, adj.
widow-maker, n.
work, n.
work, vb.
working, n.
: 129

11.02
grasp

apprehend, vb.
apprehension, n.
arrest, n.
arrest, vb.
attach, vb.
capere, lat. vb.
catch, n.
catch, vb.
claw, vb.
clutch, n.
clutch, vb.
distrain, vb.
encroach, vb.
extend, vb.
extent, n.
fang, vb.
fetch in, phr. vb.
fist, vb.
foot, vb.
get, vb.
grapple, vb.
grasp, n.
grasp, vb.
gripe, n.
gripe, vb.
guts-griping, n.
handle, n.
hent, vb.
hold, n.
holdfast, vb.
lapse, vb.
latch, vb.
large-handed, adj.
long-usurped, adj.
new-taken, adj.
occupare, lat. vb.
over-wrestle, vb.
possess, vb.
prendre, fr. vb.
preoccupy, vb.
reach, vb.
rest, vb.

resume, vb.
seize, vb.
seizure, n.
shark, vb.
snapper-up, n.
snatch, n.
snatch, vb.
surprise, vb.
take, vb.
taker, n.
taking, n.
uncaught, adj.
usurp, vb.
usurpation, n.
usurper, n.
usurpingly, adv.
whipstock, n.
wrestle, vb.
: 60

11.03
hit

bandy, vb.
bang, n.
bang, vb.
baste, vb.
bastinado, n.
batter, vb.
battery, n.
beat, vb.
bethump, vb.
blast, vb.
blow, n.
bob, n.
bob, vb.
bold-beating, adj.
box, n.
breech, vb.
buffet, n.
buffet, vb.
butt, vb.
clap, vb.
cudgel, vb.
cuff, n.

cuff, vb.
dash, n.
dash, vb.
dint, n.
dry baste, vb.
dry-beat, vb.
elbow, vb.
feeze, vb.
fidius, vb.
fillip, vb.
firk, vb.
fist, vb.
foot, vb.
frush, vb.
glance, vb.
grief-shot, adj.
hammer, vb.
have at, phr. vb.
heart-struck, adj.
hit, n.
hit, vb.
hurtle, vb.
jostle, vb.
jowl, vb.
kick, vb.
knap, vb.
knock, n.
knock, vb.
lash, n.
lash, vb.
lay about, phr. vb.
lay on, phr. vb.
lodge, vb.
maul, vb.
outstrike, vb.
over-beat, vb.
overscutch, vb.
pash, vb.
pelt, vb.
pepper, vb.
prat, vb.
pun, vb.
rap, vb.
rash, vb.
scour, vb.

scourge, vb.
shoot, vb.
shoulder-clapper, n.
smite, vb.
smoke, vb.
spurn, n.
spurn, vb.
stamp, n.
stamp, vb.
stone, vb.
storm-beaten, adj.
strike, n.
strike, vb.
striker, n.
stripe, n.
stroke, n.
swinge, vb.
take, vb.
tap, n.
thrash, vb.
thump, vb.
thwack, vb.
touch, n.
touch, vb.
truncheon, vb.
unbattered, adj.
undinted, adj.
unwhipt, adj.
weather-beaten, adj.
whip, vb.
whipper, n.
whipping cheer, n.
yerk, vb.
: 100

11.04
press

crush, vb.
dint, n.
downtrod, adj.
downtrodden, adj.
grind, vb.
gripe, vb.
impress, n.

impress, vb.
impression, n.
impressure, n.
imprimere, lat. vb.
imprint, n.
imprint, vb.
indent, n.
indent, vb.
knead, vb.
nip, vb.
oppress, vb.
oppression, n.
pinch, n.
pinch, vb.
press, vb.
pressure, n.
print, n.
print, vb.
printless, adj.
seal, vb.
sneap, vb.
squeeze, vb.
stamp, n.
stamp, vb.
trample, vb.
unpressed, adj.
vice, vb.
wring, vb.
: 35

11.05
cut

abroach, adv.
anatomize, vb.
barber, vb.
bore, vb.
bread-chipper, n.
broach, vb.
carbonado, vb.
carve, vb.
chip, vb.
chop, n.
chop, vb.
circumcise, vb.

cleave, vb.
clip, vb.
clipper, n.
couper, fr. vb.
crop, vb.
cut, n.
cut, vb.
dismember, vb.
draw, vb.
empierce, vb.
engrave, vb.
enter, vb.
entrench, vb.
fell, vb.
flesh, vb.
fleshment, n.
forked, adj.
furrow, vb.
gash, n.
gash, vb.
geld, vb.
glib, vb.
goad, vb.
gore, vb.
grained, adj.
grave, vb.
gutter, vb.
hack, n.
hack, vb.
haggle, vb.
heart-pierced, adj.
hew, vb.
hox, vb.
impenetrable, adj.
incision, n.
intrenchant, adj.
lance, vb.
lop, vb.
mammock, vb.
mangle, vb.
mince, vb.
nick, vb.
nip, n.
notch, vb.
oak-cleaving, adj.

pare, vb.
paring, n.
paunch, vb.
penetrable, adj.
penetrate, vb.
penetrative, adj.
pick, vb.
pierce, vb.
pink, vb.
poach, vb.
point, vb.
prick, vb.
prune, vb.
punch, vb.
quarter, vb.
rase, vb.
raze, vb.
razorable, adj.
rend, vb.
rent, n.
rift, vb.
rip, vb.
rive, vb.
rough-hew, vb.
run, vb.
saw, vb.
scissor, vb.
scorch, vb.
score, vb.
scotch, n.
scotch, vb.
scythe, vb.
search, vb.
shave, vb.
shear, vb.
sheathe, vb.
side-piercing, adj.
slash, n.
slash, vb.
slice, vb.
slish, n.
slit, vb.
sliver, vb.
snip, n.
spay, vb.

spit, vb.
spleet, vb.
split, vb.
spur, vb.
stab, n.
stab, vb.
stick, vb.
sting, vb.
strike, vb.
tame, vb.
tap, vb.
tatter, vb.
tear, vb.
tire, vb.
top, vb.
transfix, vb.
trench, vb.
trenchant, adj.
ungored, adj.
unhacked, adj.
unhatched, adj.
unpinked, adj.
unpruned, adj.
unrip, vb.
unscissored, adj.
unshorn, adj.
unwedgeable, adj.
wasp-stung, adj.
wedge, vb.
woman-tired, adj.
worry, vb.
: 133

11.06
push

bear, vb.
crowd, vb.
drive, vb.
huddle, vb.
jostle, vb.
jut, vb.
nuzzle, vb.
press, vb.
push, n.

push, vb.
put, vb.
rack, vb.
ram, vb.
rush, vb.
shoulder, vb.
shove, vb.
thrice-driven, adj.
thrust, n.
thrust, vb.
tilt, vb.
wedge, vb.
: 21

11.07
pull

attract, vb.
attraction, n.
bare-picked, adj.
choice-drawn, adj.
deep-drawing, adj.
deep-fetched, adj.
deracinate, vb.
displant, vb.
disroot, vb.
dove-drawn, adj.
drag, vb.
draught, n.
draw, vb.
exhale, vb.
exhaust, vb.
extirp, vb.
extirpate, vb.
extort, vb.
extract, vb.
fen-sucked, adj.
fetch, vb.
gather, vb.
hale, vb.
head-lugged, adj.
lug, vb.
over-wrest, vb.
pick, vb.
pluck, vb.

plucker-down, n.
plume-plucked, adj.
pull, n.
pull, vb.
puller-down, n.
rase, vb.
recollect, vb.
self-drawing, adj.
sowl, vb.
spread, vb.
stretch, vb.
stretched-out, adj.
touse, vb.
tow, vb.
trail, vb.
tug, vb.
tweak, vb.
uncropped, adj.
unpicked, adj.
unplucked, adj.
unroot, vb.
unsheathe, vb.
unsheathed, adj.
weeder-out, n.
wrench, n.
wrench, vb.
wrest, vb.
wring, vb.
  : 56

11.08
break

before-breach, n.
breach, n.
break, n.
break, vb.
breaker, n.
brokenly, adv.
burst, vb.
care-crazed, adj.
crack, vb.
craze, vb.
flaw, vb.
fracted, adj.
horse-back-breaker,
  n.
mammock, vb.
rib-breaking, n.
rupture, n.
shatter, vb.
shiver, vb.
split, vb.
unbroken, adj.
  : 20

11.09
rub

anoint, vb.

balm, vb.
brush, vb.
burnish, vb.
comb, vb.
coy, vb.
file, vb.
furbish, vb.
grind, vb.
polish, vb.
rub, vb.
salve[1], vb.
scour, vb.
scrape, vb.
streak, vb.
stroke, vb.
sweep, vb.
unpolished, adj.
unscoured, adj.
unswept, adj.
unwiped, adj.
whet, vb.
wipe, vb.
  : 23

11.10
scratch

clapperclaw, vb.
clapper-de-claw, vb.
claw, vb.

cloy, vb.
grate, vb.
rake, vb.
scrape, vb.
scratch, n.
scratch, vb.
unraked, adj.
unscratched, adj.
  : 11

11.11
strip

bare, vb.
bark, vb.
case, vb.
flay, vb.
glean, vb.
peel, vb.
pill, vb.
poll, vb.
sheel, vb.
strip, vb.
uncase, vb.
  : 11

12.01
sight

after-eye, vb.
all-seeing, adj.
appear, vb.
appearance, n.
aspect, n.
bedazzle, vb.
behold, vb.
beholder, n.
bend, n.
bisson, adj.
blind, adj.
blind, n.
blind, vb.
blindfold, adj.
blindly, adv.
blindman, n.
blindness, n.
by-peeping, adj.
conspectuity, n.
dare, vb.
dazzle, vb.
descry, n.
descry, vb.
discern, vb.
dizzy-eyed, adj.
dull-eyed, adj.
eagle-sighted, adj.
earnest-gaping, adj.
espy, vb.
ever-blinded, adj.
eye, n.
eye, vb.
eye-beam, n.
eye-glance, n.
eyeless, adj.
eyesight, n.
eye to eye, adv.
eye-wink, n.
gape, vb.
gaze, n.
gaze, vb.
gazer, n.

glance, n.
glance, vb.
glare, vb.
glass eye, n.
glass-gazing, adj.
glaze, vb.
gravel-blind, adj.
half-sight, n.
hoodwink, vb.
invised, adj.
invisible, adj.
ken, n.
ken, vb.
leer, n.
leer, vb.
lo, vb.
look, n.
look, vb.
looker-on, n.
mortal-staring, adj.
muffle, vb.
observation, n.
observe, vb.
ocular, adj.
oeillade, n.
outlook, vb.
outstare, vb.
over-eye, vb.
overglance, vb.
overlook, vb.
overpeer, vb.
overstare, vb.
over-view, n.
peep, vb.
peer, vb.
perceive, vb.
pore, vb.
purblind, adj.
quick-eyed, adj.
regard, n.
regard, vb.
respect, n.
respicere, lat. vb.
re-survey, vb.
review, vb.

sad-beholding, adj.
sand-blind, adj.
see, vb.
show, n.
sight, n.
sighted, adj.
sightless, adj.
sightly, adj.
sour-eyed, adj.
spectacle, n.
spectacled, adj.
spectatorship, n.
speculation, n.
speculative, adj.
spy, n.
spy, vb.
squinny, vb.
stare, n.
stare, vb.
staring, n.
steadfast-gazing, adj.
still-gazing, adj.
still-peering, adj.
supervise, n.
supervise, vb.
supervisor, n.
survey, n.
survey, vb.
thick-eyed, adj.
thick-sighted, adj.
under-peep, vb.
undescried, adj.
undiscernible, adj.
unnoted, adj.
unperceived, adj.
unseeing, adj.
unseen, adj.
unwitnessed, adj.
vedere, it. vb.
videre, lat. vb.
view, n.
view, vb.
viewless, adj.
visible, adj.
visibly, adv.

vision, n.
voir, fr. vb.
wall-eyed, adj.
wink, vb.
: 136

12.02
show

air, vb.
apparent, adj.
apparently, adv.
appearance, n.
big-looked, adj.
demonstrable, adj.
demonstrate, vb.
demonstration, n.
demonstrative, adj.
discover, vb.
display, vb.
evident, adj.
exhibit, vb.
exhibiter, n.
extern, n.
figure, vb.
foreshow, vb.
give, vb.
give out, phr. vb.
high-peering, adj.
look, vb.
manifest, adj.
manifest, vb.
muster, vb.
new-appearing, adj.
open, adj.
openly, adv.
openness, n.
ostent, n.
ostentare, lat. vb.
ostentation, n.
palpable, adj.
plane, vb.
present, vb.
presentation, n.
product, vb.

project, vb.
prospect, n.
refigure, vb.
regard, n.
remonstrance, n.
represent, vb.
sad-beholding, adj.
seld-shown, adj.
sharp-looking, adj.
show, n.
show, vb.
sight, n.
spectacle, n.
spectare, lat. vb.
unhidden, adj.
unshown, adj.
urchin-show, n.
view, n.
: 54

12.03
semblance

affect, vb.
affectation, n.
ape, n.
apish, adj.
apparent, adj.
apparition, n.
appear, vb.
appearance, n.
assume, vb.
belike, adv.
beseem, vb.
beseeming, n.
borrow, vb.
colour, n.
compliment, n.
copy, n.
counterfeit, n.
counterfeit, vb.
country form, n.
disliken, vb.
dissemble, vb.
dissembler, n.

effect, n.
effigies, n.
fashion, n.
follow, vb.
form, n.
gloss, n.
idea, n.
ill-seeming, adj.
image, n.
imitari, lat. vb.
imitate, vb.
imitation, n.
like, adj.
like, adv.
like, vb.
likelihood, n.
likely, adj.
likeness, n.
livery, n.
look, n.
look, vb.
methinks, vb.
model, n.
module, n.
personate, vb.
picture, n.
presentation, n.
prospect, n.
resemblance, n.
resemble, vb.
seem, vb.
seemer, n.
seeming, adj.
seeming, n.
seemingly, adv.
semblable, adj.
semblable, fr. adj.
semblable, n.
semblably, adv.
semblance, n.
semblative, adj.
shade, n.
shadow, n.
shape, n.
sign, n.

so-seeming, adj.
summer-seeming,
  adj.
think, vb.
twin, n.
twin, vb.
umbrage, n.
unseeming, adj.
well-seeming, adj.
: 75

12.04
colour

amber-coloured, adj.
auburn, adj.
auburn, n.
azure, adj.
azure, vb.
bay, adj.
bepaint, vb.
black, adj.
black, n.
blackness, n.
bloody, adj.
blue, adj.
blue, n.
bluish, adj.
brinded, adj.
brown, adj.
brown, n.
browny, adj.
cain-coloured, adj.
carnation, n.
cast, n.
chestnut, n.
coal-black, adj.
colour, n.
colour, vb.
colourable, adj.
coral, n.
crimson, adj.
crimson, n.
crimson, vb.
damask, n.

damask, vb.
deep-green, adj.
discolour, vb.
divers-coloured, adj.
dun, adj.
dun-coloured, adj.
dye, n.
dye, vb.
ebon, n.
ebon-coloured, adj.
encrimson, vb.
fallow, adj.
flame-coloured, adj.
freestone-coloured,
  adj.
French-crown-colour,
  n.
frosty, adj.
grain, vb.
grass-green, adj.
green, adj.
green, n.
grey, adj.
grey, n.
grisly, adj.
grizzle, n.
grizzled, adj.
gules, adj.
hazel, n.
heaven-hued, adj.
hell-black, adj.
high-coloured, adj.
hoar, adj.
hoary, adj.
hue, n.
impaint, vb.
incarnadine, vb.
inky, adj.
Kendal green, n.
lily-tincture, n.
lily-white, adj.
many-coloured, adj.
marble, n.
marble, vb.
milk-white, adj.

orange-tawny, adj.
over-dye, vb.
over-red, vb.
paint, vb.
parti-coloured, adj.
peach-coloured, adj.
pied, adj.
piedness, n.
proud-pied, adj.
purple, adj.
purple, n.
purple, vb.
purple-coloured, adj.
purple-hued, adj.
purple-in-grain, adj.
raven-coloured, adj.
red, adj.
red, n.
redness, n.
ripe-red, adj.
roan, adj.
rose, vb.
rosy, adj.
rubious, adj.
ruby, vb.
ruby-coloured, adj.
ruddiness, n.
ruddy, adj.
russet, adj.
sable, n.
sable-coloured, adj.
saffron, n.
sallow, adj.
sand, vb.
sanguine, adj.
scarlet, adj.
scarlet, n.
silver, vb.
silver-white, adj.
snow-white, adj.
snowy, adj.
stain, vb.
straw colour, n.
swart, adj.
swarth, adj.

swarthy, adj.
taint, vb.
tan, vb.
tanling, n.
tawny, adj.
tinct, n.
tincture, n.
umber, vb.
vermilion, n.
vert, fr. n.
wax-red, adj.
white, adj.
white, n.
whitely, adj.
whiteness, n.
yellow, adj.
yellow, n.
yellow, vb.
yellowness, n.
: 138

12.05
pale

blanch, vb.
blank, vb.
bleak, adj.
bloodless, adj.
cold-pale, adj.
cream-faced, adj.
maid-pale, adj.
pale, adj.
pale, n.
pale, vb.
pale-faced, adj.
paleness, n.
pale-visaged, adj.
pallid, adj.
paly, adj.
paper-faced, adj.
tallow-face, n.
wan, adj.
wan, vb.
wanny, adj.
whey-face, n.

white-faced, adj.
: 22

12.06
spotted

blood-bespotted, adj.
brinded, adj.
chequer, vb.
cinque-spotted, adj.
dapple, vb.
fleckled, adj.
freckle, n.
freckled, adj.
pied, adj.
piedness, n.
pinch-spotted, adj.
proud-pied, adj.
roan, adj.
spot, vb.
streak, vb.
toad-spotted, adj.
unspotted, adj.
: 17

12.07
hearing

attend, vb.
audible, adj.
audience, n.
audire, lat. vb.
auditor, n.
auditory, n.
auricular, adj.
deaf, adj.
deaf, vb.
deafen, vb.
deafness, n.
ear, n.
ear, vb.
ear-deafening, adj.
eavesdropper, n.
écouter, fr. vb.
hark, vb.

hear, vb.
hearer, n.
hearing, n.
hearken, vb.
inaudible, adj.
list, vb.
listen, vb.
mishear, vb.
never-heard-of, adj.
overhear, vb.
undeaf, vb.
unheard, adj.
: 29

12.08
sound

noise, n.
noisemaker, n.
organ, n.
organ-pipe, n.
son, fr. n.
sonance, n.
sound, n.
tune, n.
voice, n.
vox, lat. n.
: 10

12.09
clangour

bass, vb.
blow, vb.
chime, n.
clamorous, adj.
clamour, n.
clamour, vb.
clang, n.
clangour, n.
crack, n.
deep-mouthed, adj.
ding-dong, n.
echo, n.
echo, vb.

groan, n.
jangle, vb.
jingle, vb.
knell, n.
knoll, vb.
peal, n.
replication, n.
resound, vb.
respeak, vb.
reverb, vb.
reverberate, adj.
reverberate, vb.
reword, vb.
ring, vb.
rumble, vb.
sound, vb.
soundless, adj.
tang, n.
tang, vb.
thunder, vb.
toll, vb.
trumpet, vb.
trumpet-clangour, n.
trumpet-tongued, adj.
twang, vb.
twangle, vb.
: 39

12.10
din

berattle, vb.
bounce, n.
bounce, vb.
brawl, vb.
bray, n.
bray, vb.
bruit, vb.
burst, n.
clap, n.
clatter, n.
clink, n.
clink, vb.
crack, n.
crack, vb.

crash, n.
creak, vb.
din, n.
ear-deafening, adj.
ear-piercing, adj.
grate, vb.
harsh-resounding,
  adj.
harsh-sounding, adj.
hoarse, adj.
hoarsely, adv.
hubbub, n.
hurtle, vb.
ill-resounding, adj.
jar, n.
jar, vb.
noise, vb.
noisemaker, n.
percussion, n.
rattle, vb.
report, n.
rude, adj.
rumour, n.
strike, vb.
stroke, n.
swash, vb.
untuneable, adj.
volley, vb.
: 41

12.11
shout

alarm, n.
aloud, adv.
bawl, vb.
call, vb.
clamorous, adj.
clamour, n.
clamour, vb.
cry, n.
cry, vb.
exclaim, n.
exclaim, vb.
exclamation, n.

hallow, vb.
high, adj.
hollo, vb.
hoop, vb.
hoot, vb.
howl, n.
howl, vb.
hue, n.
hue and cry, n.
larum, n.
loud, adj.
loudest, n.
loudly, adv.
loudness, n.
night-shriek, n.
on high, adv.
outcry, n.
outroar, vb.
oyez, n.
roar, n.
roar, vb.
roarer, n.
rope, n.
scream, n.
scream, vb.
sharp, adj.
shout, n.
shout, vb.
shriek, n.
shriek, vb.
shrill, adj.
shrill, vb.
shrill-gorged, adj.
shrill-shrieking, adj.
shrill-sounding, adj.
shrill-tongued, adj.
shrill-voiced, adj.
shrilly, adv.
unshout, vb.
whistle, vb.
whoop, vb.
yell, n.
yell, vb.
: 55

12.12
whisper

buzz, n.
buzz, vb.
buzzer, n.
ear-bussing, adj.
hum, n.
hum, vb.
lisp, vb.
low, adj.
low-voiced, adj.
mammer, vb.
mellifluous, adj.
mumble, vb.
murmur, n.
murmur, vb.
murmurer, n.
pule, vb.
round, vb.
rustle, vb.
silver-voiced, adj.
small, adj.
soft, adj.
softly, adv.
squeak, vb.
squeal, vb.
stammer, vb.
sweet, adj.
sweetly, adv.
sweetness, n.
whirr, vb.
whisper, n.
whisper, vb.
whispering, n.
whizz, vb.
: 33

12.13
neigh

baa, vb.
bark, vb.
bay, n.
bay, vb.

behowl, vb.
bellow, vb.
bleat, n.
bleat, vb.
bray, n.
bray, vb.
buzz, vb.
cackle, vb.
caterwaul, vb.
caw, vb.
chirp, vb.
cluck, vb.
croak, vb.
crow, vb.
gabble, n.
gibber, vb.
gnarl, vb.
grunt, vb.
hiss, n.
hiss, vb.
hoot, vb.
howl, n.
howl, vb.
hum, n.
loud-howling, adj.
low, n.
low, vb.
mew, vb.
mewl, vb.
mouth, n.
neigh, n.
neigh, vb.
night-shriek, n.
purr, n.
quest, vb.
screech, vb.
shriek, n.
shriek, vb.
shrill-shrieking, adj.
snarl, vb.
snort, vb.
spend [the] mouth,
  vb.
whine, vb.
yellow, vb.

yelp, vb.
 : 49

12.14
bow-wow
———————

baa, vb.
bow-wow, int.
cockadoodledoo, n.
ding a ding ding, int.
mew, int.
R, n.
tereu, int.
tirra-lirra, int.
tu-whit, int.
tu-whoo, int.
week, int.
 : 11

12.15
touch
———————

benumb, vb.
dull, adj.
dull, vb.
feel, vb.
feeler, n.
feelingly, adv.
finger, vb.
graze, vb.
grope, vb.
hand, vb.
handle, vb.
insensible, adj.
mull, vb.
never-touched, adj.
numb, adj.
numb, vb.
numbness, n.
paddle, vb.
palpable, adj.
senseless, adj.
sensible, adj.
sensibly, adv.
starve, vb.

stupefy, vb.
tickle, vb.
touch, n.
touch, vb.
unfeeling, adj.
unfelt, adj.
unhandled, adj.
untouched, adj.
 : 31

12.16
smell
———————

balmy, adj.
court-odour, n.
fragrant, adj.
luscious, adj.
noisome, adj.
nose, vb.
odoriferous, adj.
odorous, adj.
odour, n.
overstink, vb.
perfume, n.
rank-scented, adj.
savour, n.
savour, vb.
scent, n.
scent, vb.
scent-snuffing, adj.
smell, n.
smell, vb.
smell-less, adj.
stench, n.
stink, vb.
stinkingly, adv.
sweet, adj.
sweeten, vb.
sweetly, adv.
sweetness, n.
sweet-smelling, adj.
tender-smelling, adj.
unsavoury, adj.
wind, vb.
 : 31

12.17
taste
———————

acerb, adj.
bitter, adj.
bitterest, n.
dainty, adj.
delicate, adj.
delicious, adj.
deliciousness, n.
distaste, vb.
eager, adj.
gall, n.
gust, n.
gust, vb.
honey, n.
honeyless, adj.
honey-sweet, adj.
liquorish, adj.
luscious, adj.
mouth, n.
outsweeten, vb.
palate, vb.
relish, n.
relish, vb.
salt, adj.
saltness, n.
savour, vb.
savoury, adj.
smack, n.
smack, vb.
smatch, n.
sour, adj.
sour, n.
sour, vb.
sugar, vb.
sweet, adj.
sweet, n.
sweeten, vb.
sweetly, adv.
sweetness, n.
sweet-savoured, adj.
tart, adj.
tartness, n.
taste, n.

taste, vb.
tasteful, adj.
unsavoury, adj.
untasted, adj.
 : 46

13.01
happiness

———————

bliss, n.
blissful, adj.
felicitate, adj.
felicity, n.
grace, n.
happily, adv.
happiness, n.
happy, adj.
happy, n.
happy, vb.
heureux, fr. adj.
over-happy, adj.
well, adj.
: 13

13.02
joy

———————

blithe, adj.
bonny, adj.
comic, adj.
enjoy, vb.
frolic, adj.
gaudere, lat. vb.
glad, adj.
glad, n.
glad, vb.
gladly, adv.
gladness, n.
gleeful, adj.
humour, n.
jest, n.
jest, vb.
jocund, adj.
jollity, n.
jolly, adj.
jovial, adj.
joy, n.
joy, vb.
joyful, adj.
joyfully, adv.
joyous, adj.

lustick, adj.
merriest, n.
merrily, adv.
merriment, n.
merriness, n.
merry, adj.
merry-hearted, adj.
mirth, n.
mirthful, adj.
overjoy, n.
overjoy, vb.
over-merry, adj.
play, n.
pleasance, n.
pleasant, adj.
pleasantly, adv.
pleasant-spirited, adj.
rejoice, vb.
rejoicer, n.
rejoicingly, adv.
: 44

13.03
smile

———————

fleer, vb.
grim-grinning, adj.
grin, vb.
laugh, vb.
laughable, adj.
laugher, n.
laughter, n.
ridiculous, adj.
simper, vb.
smile, n.
smile, vb.
smilet, n.
smilingly, adv.
: 13

13.04
revelry

———————

ale, n.
banquet, vb.

candle-waster, n.
domineer, vb.
entertain, vb.
entertainment, n.
feast, n.
feast, vb.
festival, n.
gossip, vb.
marriage-feast, n.
mask, vb.
masker, n.
masque, n.
May, vb.
maypole, n.
pledge, n.
pledge, vb.
revel, n.
revel, vb.
reveller, n.
revelry, n.
shearing, n.
sheep-shearing, n.
utas, n.
wake, n.
: 26

13.05
exult

———————

all-triumphant, adj.
exult, vb.
exultation, n.
glory, vb.
insult, vb.
insulter, n.
insultment, n.
overcrow, vb.
palmy, adj.
rejoice, vb.
rejoicingly, adv.
triumph, n.
triumph, vb.
triumphant, adj.
triumphantly, adv.
vaunt, vb.   : 16

13.06
rapture

———————

ecstasy, n.
enrapt, adj.
rap, vb.
rapt, adj.
rapture, n.
trance, n.
transport, vb.
: 7

13.07
(dis)pleasure

———————

accept, vb.
acceptable, adj.
acceptance, n.
apay, vb.
approve, vb.
coming-on, adj.
congratulate, vb.
content, adj.
content, fr. adj.
content, n.
content, vb.
contenta, vb.
contentless, adj.
contento, vb.
delectable, adj.
delicate, adj.
delight, n.
delight, vb.
delightful, adj.
discontent, n.
discontent, vb.
dislike, n.
dislike, vb.
displease, vb.
displeasure, n.
dulcet, adj.
enjoy, vb.
fain, adj.
fain, vb.
flattering-sweet, adj.

fruition, n.
grace, n.
grace, vb.
grateful, adj.
gratify, vb.
gratulate, adj.
gratulate, vb.
greet, vb.
grumble, vb.
grumbling, n.
ill-favouredly, adv.
joy, vb.
like, vb.
lust, n.
malcontent, adj.
malcontent, n.
mislike, vb.
murmur, vb.
murmurer, n.
perfect, adj.
plausible, adj.
plausibly, adv.
plausive, adj.
pleasant, adj.
pleasantly, adv.
please, vb.
pleasing, n.
pleasure, n.
pleasure, vb.
prettily, adv.
prettiness, n.
pretty, adj.
pretty, n.
relish, vb.
repine, n.
repine, vb.
satisfaction, n.
satisfice, vb.
satisfy, vb.
sightly, adj.
silver-sweet, adj.
suffice, vb.
sufficere, lat. vb.
suppliance, n.
supply, vb.

sweet, adj.
sweet, n.
sweeten, vb.
sweetly, adv.
sweetness, n.
unpleasant, adj.
unpleased, adj.
unpleasing, adj.
unsatisfied, adj.
well, adv.
well-contented, adj.
 : 86

13.08
cheer(less)
————————

all-cheering, adj.
barren, adj.
bright, adj.
cheer, n.
cheer, vb.
cheerer, n.
cheerful, adj.
cheerfully, adv.
cheerless, adj.
cheerly, adj.
clear-spirited, adj.
comfort, n.
comfort, vb.
comfortable, adj.
comforter, n.
dull, adj.
frosty-spirited, adj.
gaudy, adj.
gay, adj.
gayness, n.
in heart, adv.
leaden, adj.
light, adj.
lighten, vb.
lightly, adv.
livelihood, n.
lively, adj.
lumpish, adj.
lustihood, n.

lustily, adv.
lusty, adj.
muddy-mettled, adj.
out of heart, adv.
overlusty, adj.
phlegmatic, adj.
sprightful, adj.
sprightfully, adv.
sprightly, adj.
uncheerful, adj.
winterly, adj.
 : 40

13.09
seriousness
————————

deeply, adv.
demure, adj.
demure, vb.
demurely, adv.
earnest, adj.
earnest, n.
earnestly, adv.
earnestness, n.
grave, adj.
gravely, adv.
graveness, n.
graver, n.
gravity, n.
heavy, adj.
over-earnest, adj.
perpetual-sober, adj.
sad, adj.
sad-eyed, adj.
sad-hearted, adj.
sadly, adv.
sadness, n.
serious, adj.
seriously, adv.
seriousness, n.
sober, adj.
sober-blooded, adj.
soberly, adv.
sober-sad, adj.
sobriety, n.

solemn, adj.
solemnity, n.
solemnly, adv.
solemnness, n.
staid, adj.
ungravely, adv.
 : 35

13.10
sorrow
————————

afflict, vb.
affliction, n.
aggrieve, vb.
amort, adv.
bitterly, adv.
canker-sorrow, n.
careful, adj.
cloudy, adj.
comfortless, adj.
condolement, n.
crest-fallen, adj.
dark, adj.
darkly, adv.
dear, adj.
deject, adj.
deject, vb.
dern, adj.
desolate, adj.
desolation, n.
disanimate, vb.
discomfit, n.
discomfit, vb.
discomfort, n.
discomfort, vb.
discomfortable, adj.
disconsolate, adj.
dishearten, vb.
dismal, adj.
distress, n.
distress, vb.
dole, n.
doleful, adj.
dolorous, adj.
dolour, n.

61 13 emotions

down, adj.
down, adv.
dreary, adj.
dump, n.
earn, vb.
fee-grief, n.
forlorn, adj.
fortunate-unhappy, n.
gloom, vb.
gloomy, adj.
grief, n.
grievance, n.
grieve, vb.
grievingly, adv.
grievous, adj.
grievously, adv.
grim, adj.
grimly, adv.
groan, n.
groan, vb.
heart-ache, n.
heart-break, n.
heart-breaking, n.
heart-burn, vb.
heart-grief, n.
heart-heaviness, n.
heart-sick, adj.
heart-sore, adj.
heart-sorrowing, adj.
heavily, adv.
heaviness, n.
heavy, adj.
joyless, adj.
languish, n.
languishment, n.
languor, n.
leaden, adj.
melancholy, adj.
melancholy, n.
miser, n.
miserable, adj.
miserable, n.
miserably, adv.

misery, n.
new-sad, adj.
passion, n.
passion, vb.
passionate, adj.
passionate, vb.
pensive, adj.
pensive, vb.
pensiveness, n.
rue, vb.
sad, adj.
sad-faced, adj.
sad-hearted, adj.
sadly, adv.
sadness, n.
sea-sorrow, n.
sigh, n.
sigh, vb.
sigher, n.
sober-sad, adj.
solemn, adj.
solemnly, adv.
solemnness, n.
sore, adj.
sorely, adv.
sorrow, n.
sorrow, vb.
sorrowful, adj.
sorry, adj.
sour, adj.
sour, vb.
sour-eyed, adj.
sour-faced, adj.
sufferance, n.
sullen, adj.
sullen, n.
teen, n.
tristful, adj.
uncheerful, adj.
uncomfortable, adj.
unhappily, adv.
unhappiness, n.
unhappy, adj.

unhappy, vb.
widow-dolour, n.
woe-begone, adj.
woeful, adj.
wretched, adj.
wretched, n.
wretchedness, n.
yearn, vb.
: 128

13.11
lament

bemoan, vb.
bewail, vb.
complain, vb.
complainant, n.
complaining, n.
complaint, n.
condole, vb.
condolement, n.
deplore, vb.
dire-lamenting, adj.
fore-bemoaned, adj.
lament, n.
lament, vb.
lamentable, adj.
lamentably, adv.
lamentation, n.
lamenting, n.
mean, vb.
moan, n.
moan, vb.
mourn, vb.
mourner, n.
mournful, adj.
mournfully, adv.
mourning, n.
mourningly, adv.
muse, vb.
obsequious, adj.
obsequiously, adv.
plain, vb.

plaining, n.
plaint, n.
plaintful, adj.
repine, n.
repine, vb.
sigh, vb.
sweet-complaining,
  adj.
unbewailed, adj.
unmoaned, adj.
wail, vb.
wailful, adj.
whine, vb.
: 42

13.12
sob

beweep, vb.
blubber, vb.
cry, vb.
eye-drop, n.
heaving, n.
milch, adj.
onion-eyed, adj.
sob, n.
sob, vb.
tear, n.
tearful, adj.
unwept, adj.
wail, vb.
water, n.
water, vb.
waul, vb.
weep, vb.
weeper, n.
weeping, n.
weepingly, adv.
: 20

14.01
goodness

---

bene, lat. adv.
benefactor, n.
beneficial, adj.
benefit, n.
benevolence, n.
best, n.
bien, fr. adv.
bon, fr. adj.
bonus, lat. adj.
bounty, n.
buono, it. adj.
cardinal virtue, n.
charitable, adj.
charitably, adv.
charity, n.
curious-good, adj.
good, adj.
good, n.
goodness, n.
grace, n.
gracious, adj.
graciously, adv.
honest, adj.
honesty, n.
honour, n.
ill-well, adv.
self-charity, n.
self-gracious, adj.
unvirtuous, adj.
virtue, n.
virtuous, adj.
virtuous, n.
virtuously, adv.
well, adj.
well, adv.
: 35

14.02
love • hate

---

abhor, vb.
abominable, adj.
abominably, adv.
affect, vb.
affectedly, adv.
affection, n.
affection, vb.
affectionate, adj.
affectionately, adv.
after-love, n.
alder-liefest, adj.
all-abhorred, adj.
all-hating, adj.
amiable, adj.
amorous, adj.
amorously, adv.
amour, fr. n.
belove, vb.
bosom lover, n.
brother-love, n.
cher, fr. adj.
cherish, vb.
cherisher, n.
dear, adj.
dear, vb.
dear-beloved, adj.
dearest, n.
dearly, adv.
dearness, n.
desire, n.
detest, vb.
detestable, adj.
dislike, n.
dislike, vb.
disrelish, vb.
distaste, vb.
distasteful, adj.
dote, vb.
doter, n.
enamour, vb.
enmity, n.
execrable, adj.
fancy, n.
fancy, vb.
favour, n.
favour, vb.
fulsome, adj.

hate, n.
hate, vb.
hateful, adj.
hater, n.
hatred, n.
hell-hated, adj.
lack-love, n.
lief, adj.
like, vb.
liking, n.
loathe, vb.
love, n.
love, vb.
love-affair, n.
love-cause, n.
loveless, adj.
lovely, adj.
lover, n.
lover, vb.
love-spring, n.
lovingly, adv.
mislike, n.
mislike, vb.
new-beloved, n.
odious, adj.
paramour, n.
passion, n.
rancour, n.
rival-hating, adj.
self-affected, adj.
self-endeared, adj.
self-love, n.
self-loving, adj.
unloved, adj.
unloving, adj.
well-beloved, adj.
: 83

14.03
hope • despair

---

cooling-card, n.
despair, n.
despair, vb.
desperate, adj.

desperately, adv.
desperation, n.
esperance, n.
espérance, fr. n.
forlorn, adj.
hope, n.
hope, vb.
hoped-for, adj.
hopeful, adj.
hopeless, adj.
sperato, n.
spero, n.
spes, lat. n.
unhoped, adj.
unhopeful, adj.
: 19

14.04
comfort

---

cheer, vb.
cocker, vb.
comfort, n.
comfort, vb.
comfortable, adj.
comforter, n.
comfortless, adj.
consolate, vb.
consolation, n.
discomfit, n.
discomfit, vb.
discomfiture, n.
discomfort, n.
discomfort, vb.
pamper, vb.
recomfort, vb.
recomforture, n.
solace, n.
solace, vb.
widow-comfort, n.
: 20

14.05
(in)constancy

changeling, n.
constancy, n.
constant, adj.
constantly, adv.
fickle, adj.
fickleness, n.
firm, adj.
firmness, n.
fortitude, n.
giddily, adv.
giddiness, n.
giddy, adj.
halt, vb.
hover, vb.
inconstancy, n.
inconstant, adj.
infirm, adj.
irresolute, adj.
mammer, vb.
marble-constant, adj.
minute-jack, n.
moonish, adj.
mutability, n.
mutable, adj.
mutation, n.
never-changing, adj.
perseverance, n.
persevere, vb.
skittish, adj.
slippery, adj.
stable, adj.
stableness, n.
stagger, vb.
tickle, adj.
ticklish, adj.
triple-turned, adj.
unconstant, adj.
unfirm, adj.
unstable, adj.
unstaid, adj.
unsteadfast, adj.
wave, vb.

waver, vb.
waverer, n.
wind-changing, adj.
: 45

14.06
(im)patience

abide, vb.
abrook, vb.
bear, vb.
bearer, n.
bearing, n.
bide, vb.
brook, vb.
carry, vb.
endurance, n.
endure, vb.
impatience, n.
impatient, adj.
impatiently, adv.
insupportable, adj.
intolerable, adj.
last, vb.
martyr, n.
not-to-be-endured,
  adj.
patience, n.
patient, adj.
patient, n.
patient, vb.
patiently, adv.
portable, adj.
put up, phr. vb.
suffer, vb.
sufferance, n.
sufferer, n.
support, vb.
supportable, adj.
sustain, vb.
tolerable, adj.
underbear, vb.
undergo, vb.
: 34

14.07
humility

bashful, adj.
bashfulness, n.
coy, adj.
homely, adj.
humble, adj.
humble, vb.
humbleness, n.
humbly, adv.
humility, n.
low, adj.
lowliness, n.
lowly, adj.
lowness, n.
mean, adj.
meanly, adv.
meek, adj.
meekly, adv.
meekness, n.
nice, adj.
niceness, n.
nicety, n.
obscure, adj.
obscure, vb.
plume-plucked, adj.
poor, adj.
poorly, adv.
pudency, n.
shamefaced, adj.
shy, adj.
silly, adj.
simple, adj.
simpleness, n.
simplicity, n.
tame, adj.
tameness, n.
unbashful, adj.
: 36

14.08
(un)gentle

affability, n.

affable, adj.
benign, adj.
debonair, adj.
delicate, adj.
dolcezza, it. n.
ever-gentle, adj.
fondness, n.
gentility, n.
gentle, adj.
gentle-hearted, adj.
gentleness, n.
gently, adv.
good, adj.
graciously, adv.
heartily, adv.
heartiness, n.
heartly, adj.
hearty, adj.
incony, adj.
kind, adj.
kind-hearted, adj.
kindly, adj.
kindly, adv.
kindness, n.
maiden-hearted, adj.
mildness, n.
overkind, adj.
overkindness, n.
soft, adj.
soften, vb.
soft-hearted, adj.
sweet, adj.
tameness, n.
tender, adj.
tender-hearted, adj.
tender-hefted, adj.
tenderly, adv.
tenderness, n.
thrice-gentle, adj.
ungentle, adj.
ungentleness, n.
ungently, adv.
unkind, adj.
unkindly, adv.
unkindness, n.

untender, adj.
: 47

14.09
lenity

apology, n.
clemency, n.
clement, adj.
dismiss, vb.
dispense, vb.
excusable, adj.
excuse, n.
excuse, vb.
excuser, fr. vb.
favour, n.
forgive, vb.
forgiveness, n.
humour, vb.
indulgence, n.
indulgent, adj.
lenity, n.
loose, vb.
merciful, adj.
mercifully, adv.
mercy, n.
mild, adj.
mildly, adv.
mildness, n.
none-sparing, adj.
pardon, n.
pardon, vb.
pardon-me, n.
pardonner, fr. vb.
patience, n.
perdonare, it. vb.
relent, vb.
remission, n.
remit, vb.
save, vb.
spare, vb.
unpardonable, adj.
venial, adj.
: 37

14.10
moderation

abstain, vb.
abstemious, adj.
abstinence, n.
continence, n.
continency, n.
continent, adj.
desist, vb.
dispense, vb.
forbear, vb.
forbearance, n.
forgo, vb.
intemperance, n.
intemperate, adj.
let-alone, n.
mannerly-modest,
  adj.
measure, n.
moderate, adj.
moderate, vb.
moderately, adv.
moderation, n.
modest, adj.
modestly, adv.
modesty, n.
qualify, vb.
refrain, vb.
season, vb.
spare, vb.
sparingly, adv.
temper, n.
temper, vb.
temperance, n.
temperate, adj.
temperately, adv.
tub-fast, n.
untempering, adj.
: 35

14.11
liberality

bounteous, adj.
bounteously, adv.
bountiful, adj.
bountifully, adv.
bounty, n.
frank, adj.
frankly, adv.
free, adj.
free-hearted, adj.
freely, adv.
freeness, n.
fruitful, adj.
fruitfully, adv.
fruitfulness, n.
generosity, n.
generous, adj.
large, adj.
largess, n.
liberal, adj.
liberality, n.
self-bounty, n.
: 21

14.12
(un)worthiness

all-worthy, adj.
death-worthy, adj.
dignify, vb.
dignity, n.
far-unworthy, adj.
formal, adj.
grave, adj.
gravely, adv.
graveness, n.
gravity, n.
indignity, n.
merit, n.
portly, adj.
stately, adj.
thrice-worthy, adj.
unworthiness, n.
unworthy, adj.
unworthy, n.
valure, n.
worthily, adv.
worthiness, n.
worthless, adj.
worthy, adj.
worthy, vb.
: 24

14.13
(un)deserving

condign, adj.
demerit, n.
desert, n.
desertless, adj.
deserve, vb.
deservedly, adv.
deserver, n.
deserving, n.
earn, vb.
meed, n.
merit, n.
merit, vb.
meritorious, adj.
praise, n.
undeserved, adj.
undeserver, n.
undeserving, adj.
unearned, adj.
unmeritable, adj.
unmeriting, adj.
unworthily, adv.
unworthy, adj.
unworthy, n.
well-deserved, adj.
well-deserving, adj.
worth, adj.
worth, n.
worthier, n.
worthiest, n.
worthily, adv.
worthiness, n.
worthy, adj.
: 32

14.14
honesty

---

fair, adj.
fairly, adv.
fairness, n.
fair-play, n.
honest, adj.
honest-hearted, adj.
honestly, adv.
honest-natured, adj.
honesty, n.
plain, adj.
plain dealer, n.
plain-dealing, adj.
plain dealing, n.
plainly, adv.
righteous, adj.
righteously, adv.
sincere, adj.
sincerely, adv.
sincerity, n.
single, adj.
singleness, n.
true, adj.
true-hearted, adj.
truepenny, n.
uncoined, adj.
unfeigned, adj.
unfeignedly, adv.
upright, adj.
uprighteously, adv.
uprightness, n.
: 30

14.15
courtesy

---

bonnet, vb.
civil, adj.
civility, n.
civilly, adv.
compliment, n.
complimental, adj.
courteous, adj.
courteously, adv.
courtesy, n.
court-like, adj.
courtly, adj.
courtship, n.
humane, adj.
humanely, adv.
manner, n.
mannerly, adj.
: 16

14.16
honour

---

addition, n.
all-honoured, adj.
attribute, n.
credit, n.
credit, vb.
dignify, vb.
dignity, n.
estimation, n.
fame, n.
fame, vb.
famous, adj.
famous, vb.
famously, adv.
glory, n.
glory, vb.
grace, n.
grace, vb.
honneur, fr. n.
honorificabilitudini-
  tas, n.
honour, n.
honour, vb.
honourable, adj.
honourably, adv.
imputation, n.
ingeniously, adv.
integer, lat. adj.
integritas, lat. n.
integrity, n.
justly, adv.
mouth-honour, n.

name, n.
onorare, it. vb.
opinion, n.
praeclarus, lat. adj.
praise, n.
pride, n.
renown, n.
renown, vb.
reputation, n.
repute, n.
six-or-seven-times-
  honoured, adj.
thrice-famed, adj.
thrice-gracious, adj.
thrice-renowned, adj.
undishonoured, adj.
well-famed, adj.
well-graced, adj.
worship, n.
: 48

14.17
boldness

---

audacious, adj.
audaciously, adv.
audacity, n.
aweless, adj.
bold, adj.
bold, n.
bold, vb.
bolden, vb.
bold-faced, adj.
boldly, adv.
boldness, n.
brave, adj.
brave, fr. adj.
brave, n.
brave, vb.
bravely, adv.
bravery, n.
bravest, n.
chivalry, n.
courage, n.
courageous, adj.

courageously, adv.
dare, n.
dare, vb.
daring, adj.
daring-hardy, adj.
dauntless, adj.
doughty, adj.
doughty-handed, adj.
embolden, vb.
ever-valiant, adj.
fearless, adj.
fierceness, n.
full-hearted, adj.
gallant, adj.
gallantly, adv.
gallant-springing, adj.
hardiment, n.
hardiness, n.
hardy, adj.
haughty, adj.
heart, n.
hero, n.
heroic, adj.
heroical, adj.
lion-mettled, adj.
magnanimity, n.
magnanimous, adj.
magnanimous, n.
manfully, adv.
manly, adj.
never-daunted, adj.
not-fearing, adj.
prowess, n.
stout, adj.
stout-hearted, adj.
stoutly, adv.
strong-hearted, adj.
tall, adj.
taller, n.
thrice-valiant, adj.
undaunted, adj.
undoubted, adj.
vaillant, fr. adj.
valiant, adj.
valiant, n.

valiantly, adv.
valiantness, n.
valorous, adj.
valorously, adv.
valour, n.
valure, n.
virtue, n.
worthy, n.
: 74

14.18
purity
─────────────
clean, adj.
cleanly, adj.
cleanly, adv.
cleanse, vb.
clear, adj.
clear, vb.
clearness, n.
fine, vb.
immaculate, adj.
lave, vb.
laver, fr. vb.
pure, adj.
purely, adv.
purest, n.
purge, vb.
purify, vb.
purity, n.
purus, lat. adj.
refine, vb.
rinse, vb.
sheer, adj.
spotless, adj.
stainless, adj.
strain, vb.
thrice-repured, adj.
try, vb.
unattainted, adj.
unbraided, adj.
unpolluted, adj.
unsmirched, adj.
unsoiled, adj.
unspotted, adj.

unstained, adj.
unsullied, adj.
untainted, adj.
unviolated, adj.
wash, vb.
well-refined, adj.
wipe, vb.
: 39

14.19
chastity
─────────────
chaste, adj.
chaste, n.
chastely, adv.
chastity, n.
pure, adj.
purest, n.
purity, n.
stubborn-chaste, adj.
vestal, adj.
: 9

14.20
beauty
─────────────
beau, fr. adj.
beauteous, adj.
beautiful, adj.
beautify, vb.
beauty, n.
beauty, vb.
blessed-fair, adj.
clear, adj.
comeliness, n.
comely, adj.
decorum, n.
fair, adj.
fair, n.
fair, vb.
fairest, n.
fair-eyed, adj.
fair-faced, adj.
fairly, adv.
fairness, n.

good-faced, adj.
goodly, adj.
grace, n.
graceful, adj.
handsome, adj.
handsomely, adv.
handsomeness, n.
likely, adj.
loveliness, n.
lovely, adj.
proper, adj.
pulcher, lat. adj.
quaint, adj.
seemly, adj.
sweet-faced, adj.
thrice-fair, adj.
well-favoured, adj.
: 36

14.21
spruce
─────────────
brisk, adj.
brisky, adj.
elegancy, n.
elegant, adj.
feat, adj.
fine, adj.
neat, adj.
neatly, adv.
nice, adj.
pick, vb.
prettily, adv.
smug, adj.
spruce, adj.
trim, adj.
trimly, adv.
undressed, adj.
: 16

14.22
badness
─────────────
arch-villain, n.
bad, adj.

bad, n.
badly, adv.
badness, n.
bale, n.
baleful, adj.
base, adj.
base, n.
basely, adv.
baseness, n.
basest, n.
black, adj.
blackness, n.
crooked, adj.
deadly, adj.
deprave, vb.
evil, adj.
evil, n.
evil-eyed, adj.
evilly, adv.
facinerious, adj.
foul, adj.
foul, n.
foully, adv.
foulness, n.
foul play, n.
graceless, adj.
graceless, n.
harm, n.
harm-doing, n.
heinous, adj.
heinously, adv.
high-viced, adj.
ill, adj.
ill, n.
ill-doing, n.
illness, n.
ill-spirited, adj.
ill-well, adv.
incharitable, adj.
iniquity, n.
lewd, adj.
lewdly, adv.
lewdness, n.
mal, fr. adv.
malefaction, n.

malefactor, n.
malevolence, n.
malevolent, adj.
malice, n.
malicious, adj.
maliciously, adv.
malign, vb.
malignancy, n.
malignant, adj.
malignantly, adv.
malus, lat. adj.
mauvais, fr. adj.
méchant, fr. adj.
mischief, n.
mischievous, adj.
naught, n.
naughtily, adv.
naughty, adj.
nought, n.
out-villain, vb.
paltry, adj.
pernicious, adj.
perniciously, adv.
rancorous, adj.
rancour, n.
scelus, lat. n.
shrewd, adj.
sinister, adj.
soulless, adj.
spiteful, adj.
taking, n.
uncharitably, adv.
unvirtuous, adj.
venomously, adv.
vicious, adj.
viciousness, n.
vild, adj.
vild, n.
vildly, adv.
vile, adj.
vile, n.
vilely, adv.
vileness, n.
villain, n.
villain-like, adj.

villainous, adj.
villainous, n.
villainously, adv.
villainy, n.
viperous, adj.
wicked, adj.
wicked, n.
wickedly, adv.
wickedness, n.
worse, n.
worser, n.
worst, n.
 : 104

14.23
pride
————————

haught, adj.
haughtiness, n.
haughty, adj.
high-stomached, adj.
misproud, adj.
orgulous, adj.
over-proud, adj.
pride, n.
proud, adj.
proud, n.
proud, vb.
proudest, n.
proud-hearted, adj.
proudly, adv.
proud-minded, adj.
self-glorious, adj.
stomach, n.
stout, adj.
stoutness, n.
top-proud, adj.
vainness, n.
 : 21

14.24
ambition
————————

ambition, n.
ambitious, adj.

ambitious, n.
ambitiously, adv.
aspiration, n.
aspire, vb.
high-reaching, adj.
sky-aspiring, adj.
 : 8

14.25
braggardism
————————

Basilisco-like, adj.
blusterer, n.
boast, n.
boast, vb.
boastful, adj.
bombast, n.
bounce, vb.
brag, n.
brag, vb.
braggardism, n.
braggart, n.
bragless, adj.
crack, vb.
cracker, n.
cuttle, n.
fustian, adj.
fustian, n.
jet, vb.
mouth, vb.
out-brag, vb.
out-Herod, vb.
rant, vb.
roist, vb.
ruffian, n.
ruffian, vb.
ruffle, vb.
self-glorious, adj.
swagger, n.
swagger, vb.
swaggerer, n.
swash, vb.
swasher, n.
swingebuckler, n.
thrasonical, adj.

vainglory, n.
vainness, n.
vaunt, n.
vaunt, vb.
vaunter, n.
vauntingly, adv.
 : 40

14.26
insolence
————————

arrogance, n.
arrogancy, n.
arrogant, adj.
audacious, adj.
bold, adj.
boldness, n.
brazen-face, n.
brazen-faced, adj.
high-minded, adj.
high-sighted, adj.
impudence, n.
impudency, n.
impudent, adj.
impudently, adv.
impudique, fr. adj.
insolence, n.
insolent, adj.
malapert, adj.
over-bold, adj.
overboldly, adv.
overween, vb.
presume, vb.
presumption, n.
presumptuous, adj.
saucily, adv.
sauciness, n.
saucy, adj.
shameless, adj.
spite, n.
unbashful, adj.
 : 30

14.27
contempt

---

abject, adj.
abject, n.
abjectly, adv.
abomination, n.
a-scorn, adv.
blurt, vb.
contemn, vb.
contempt, n.
contemptible, adj.
contemptuous, adj.
contemptuously, adv.
contumelious, adj.
contumeliously, adv.
contumely, n.
court-contempt, n.
coy, adj.
coy, vb.
damnable, adj.
damnably, adv.
defiance, n.
despise, vb.
despiser, n.
despising, n.
despite, n.
despiteful, adj.
despitefully, adv.
dirty, adj.
disdain, n.
disdain, vb.
disdainful, adj.
disdainfully, adv.
filthy, adj.
late-despised, adj.
lousy, adj.
low-spirited, adj.
misprision, n.
misprize, vb.
obscene, adj.
outrage, n.
out-scorn, vb.
scorn, n.
scorn, vb.

scornful, adj.
scornfully, adv.
slight, vb.
spite, n.
spite, vb.
spiteful, adj.
spurn, n.
spurn, vb.
uncontemned, adj.
: 51

14.28
envy

---

envious, adj.
envious, n.
enviously, adv.
envy, n.
envy, vb.
green-eyed, adj.
jealous, adj.
jealousy, n.
loving-jealous, adj.
malign, vb.
yellowness, n.
: 11

14.29
anger

---

after wrath, n.
anger, n.
anger, vb.
angerly, adj.
angry, adj.
chafe, n.
chafe, vb.
choler, n.
choleric, adj.
enchafe, vb.
enrage, vb.
ever-angry, adj.
exasperate, adj.
exasperate, vb.
fume, n.

fume, vb.
furious, adj.
furor, lat. n.
fury, n.
heat, vb.
hot, adj.
incensement, n.
indignation, n.
ira, lat. n.
ire, n.
ireful, adj.
mood, n.
outrage, n.
provoke, vb.
rage, n.
rage, vb.
red-eyed, adj.
snuff, n.
stomach, n.
stomach, vb.
take on, phr. vb.
wrath, adj.
wrath, n.
wrathful, adj.
wrathfully, adv.
wrath-kindled, adj.
: 41

14.30
savageness

---

barbarism, n.
beastliness, n.
beastly, adj.
bestial, adj.
bloodthirsty, adj.
brute, adj.
brutish, adj.
carnal, adj.
fierceness, n.
immanity, n.
inhumanity, n.
rage, n.
savage, adj.
savage, n.

savagely, adv.
savageness, n.
savagery, n.
savage-wild, adj.
wild, adj.
wilderness, n.
wildest, n.
wildly, adv.
wildness, n.
: 23

14.31
cruelty

---

bloody-minded, adj.
cruel, adj.
cruel, n.
cruel-hearted, adj.
cruelly, adv.
cruelty, n.
dogged, adj.
dog-hearted, adj.
fell, adj.
fell-lurking, adj.
fierce, adj.
fiercely, adv.
fierceness, n.
flesh, vb.
force, n.
force, vb.
grim, adj.
grim-looked, adj.
grimly, adv.
grim-visaged, adj.
grisly, adj.
hard, adj.
hardness, n.
harsh, adj.
harshly, adv.
heartless, adj.
holy-cruel, adj.
immanity, n.
impiteous, adj.
inhuman, adj.
inhumanity, n.

none-sparing, adj.
outrageous, adj.
perforce, adv.
pitiless, adj.
remorseless, adj.
rough, adj.
roughly, adv.
rude, adj.
rudely, adv.
rudeness, n.
ruthless, adj.
tyrannical, adj.
tyrannically, adv.
tyrannize, vb.
tyrannous, adj.
tyranny, n.
tyrant, n.
unmerciful, adj.
unpitied, adj.
unpitifully, adv.
violence, n.
 : 52

14.32
hard-hearted
───────────────
cold, adj.
cold-blooded, adj.
cold-hearted, adj.
cold-moving, adj.
coldness, n.
empty-hearted, adj.
flint-hearted, adj.
flinty, adj.
hard-hearted, adj.
heart-hardening, adj.
heartless, adj.
insensible, adj.
iron-witted, adj.
marble, n.
marble-breasted, adj.
marble-hearted, adj.
obdurate, adj.
rocky, adj.
stockish, adj.

stony, adj.
stony-hearted, adj.
unfeeling, adj.
unfelt, adj.
 : 23

14.33
curstness
───────────────
bitter, adj.
crabbed, adj.
crusty, adj.
currish, adj.
curstness, n.
frampold, adj.
ill-tempered, adj.
melancholy, adj.
melancholy, n.
mistemper, vb.
moody, adj.
peevish, adj.
pout, vb.
pouting, n.
shrewd, adj.
shrewish, adj.
shrewishly, adv.
shrewishness, n.
sour, adj.
sour, vb.
sourly, adv.
sour-natured, adj.
sullen, adj.
sullen, n.
surly, adj.
tart, adj.
tartly, adv.
testiness, n.
testy, adj.
tetchy, adj.
 : 30

14.34
revenge
───────────────
avenge, vb.

revenge, n.
revenge, vb.
revengeful, adj.
revengement, n.
revenger, n.
revengingly, adv.
revengive, adj.
unrevenged, adj.
venge, vb.
vengeance, n.
vengeful, adj.
vindicative, adj.
wanion, n.
wreak, n.
wreak, vb.
wreakful, adj.
 : 17

14.35
sternness
───────────────
austere, adj.
austerely, adv.
austereness, n.
austerity, n.
dry, adj.
hard, adj.
hardly, adv.
hardness, n.
inexorable, adj.
precisian, n.
rigorous, adj.
rigorously, adv.
rigour, n.
severe, adj.
severely, adv.
severity, n.
sharp, adj.
sharply, adv.
sharpness, n.
shrewdly, adv.
sore, adj.
sorely, adv.
stern, adj.
sternness, n.

stiff, adj.
stoic, n.
strait, adj.
strait, n.
strait, vb.
straitly, adv.
straitness, n.
strict, adj.
strictly, adv.
stricture, n.
stubborn-hard, adj.
unrelenting, adj.
 : 36

14.36
stubbornness
───────────────
awkward, adj.
obstinacy, n.
obstinate, adj.
obstinately, adv.
opposite, adj.
perverse, adj.
perversely, adv.
perverseness, n.
refractory, adj.
self-willed, adj.
senseless-obstinate,
 adj.
stiff-borne, adj.
stubborn, adj.
stubborn-hard, adj.
stubbornly, adv.
stubbornness, n.
untoward, adj.
untowardly, adv.
wayward, adj.
waywardness, n.
wilful, adj.
wilfully, adv.
wilfulness, n.
wilful-opposite, adj.
 : 24

14 qualities

70

14.37
vehemence

ardent, adj.
ardently, adv.
ardour, n.
eager, adj.
eagerly, adv.
eagerness, n.
fervency, n.
fervour, n.
fierce, adj.
fiercely, adv.
fiery, adj.
fond, adj.
forward, adj.
forwardness, n.
fury, n.
greediness, n.
greedy, adj.
heat, n.
hot, adj.
hot-blood, n.
hot-bloodied, adj.
hotly, adv.
impetuosity, n.
impetuous, adj.
industrious, adj.
industriously, adv.
industry, n.
keen, adj.
officious, adj.
passion, n.
passion, vb.
passionate, adj.
rage, n.
rage, vb.
sharp, adj.
sharply, adv.
vehemence, n.
vehemency, n.
vehement, adj.
vehemently, adv.
violence, n.
violent, adj.
violent, vb.
violently, adv.
wrath, n.
zeal, n.
zealous, adj.
: 47

14.38
uncontrolled

broad, adj.
easy-held, adj.
give the rein, vb.
irregular, adj.
irregulous, adj.
libertine, n.
licence, n.
loose, adj.
ramp, vb.
stanchless, adj.
unbitted, adj.
unbridled, adj.
unchecked, adj.
unconfinable, adj.
unconstrained, adj.
uncontrolled, adj.
uncurbable, adj.
uncurbed, adj.
ungoverned, adj.
unguided, adj.
unimproved, adj.
unmastered, adj.
unreclaimed, adj.
unrestrained, adj.
unruly, adj.
unstanched, adj.
unswayable, adj.
unswayed, adj.
wanton, adj.
wildness, n.
: 30

14.39
rashness

brainish, adj.
desperate, adj.
desperately, adv.
desperation, n.
foolhardiness, n.
foolhardy, adj.
hare-brained, adj.
hasty, adj.
hasty-witted, adj.
headlong, adj.
headly, adj.
headstrong, adj.
heady, adj.
heady-rash, adj.
hot-blood, n.
hot-bloodied, adj.
hotspur, n.
impetuosity, n.
impetuous, adj.
inconsiderate, adj.
inconsiderate, n.
lines, n.
pettish, adj.
rash, adj.
rashly, adv.
rashness, n.
self-willed, adj.
spleen, n.
spleenful, adj.
spleeny, adj.
splenative, adj.
sudden, adj.
unadvised, adj.
unadvisedly, adv.
unscanned, adj.
untoward, adj.
untowardly, adv.
waspish-headed, adj.
wayward, adj.
waywardness, n.
wild, adj.
: 41

14.40
rudeness

barbarian, adj.
barbarism, n.
barbarous, adj.
barbarous, n.
blunt, adj.
bluntly, adv.
bluntness, n.
boisterous, adj.
boisterously, adv.
boisterous-rough, adj.
churlish, adj.
churlishly, adv.
coarse, adj.
coarsely, adv.
discourtesy, n.
earthy, adj.
fatness, n.
giant-rude, adj.
gros, fr. adj.
gross, adj.
grossly, adv.
grossness, n.
harsh, adj.
harshly, adv.
harshness, n.
incivil, adj.
incivility, n.
kill-courtesy, n.
over-rank, adj.
rank, adj.
rankly, adv.
robustious, adj.
roinish, adj.
rough, adj.
roughly, adv.
roughness, n.
rude, adj.
rudely, adv.
rudeness, n.
rudesby, n.
scald, adj.
scall, adj.

scurrile, adj.
scurrility, n.
scurrilous, adj.
scurvy, adj.
surly, adj.
swinish, adj.
uncivil, adj.
uncourteous, adj.
unmannered, adj.
unmannerly, adj.
unpolished, adj.
untaught, adj.
untutored, adj.
: 55

14.41
levity

dalliance, n.
dally, vb.
idle, adj.
idle, vb.
idleness, n.
idly, adv.
levity, n.
light, adj.
lightness, n.
player, n.
skipper, n.
sportful, adj.
sportive, adj.
toy, vb.
trifle, vb.
trifler, n.
waggish, adj.
wanton, adj.
wanton, n.
wanton, vb.
wantonly, adv.
wantonness, n.
: 22

14.42
negligence

balk, vb.
bed-presser, n.
careless, adj.
carelessly, adv.
drumble, vb.
dullness, n.
fail, vb.
forget, vb.
forgetful, adj.
forgetfulness, n.
heavy, adj.
heedless, adj.
idle, adj.
idle, vb.
idleness, n.
idly, adv.
improvident, adj.
in vain, adv.
John a-dreams
lazy, adj.
lethargy, n.
lethargy, vb.
loiter, vb.
loiterer, n.
loose, adj.
loosely, adv.
mope, vb.
neglect, n.
neglect, vb.
neglectingly, adv.
neglection, n.
negligence, n.
negligent, adj.
negligent, n.
omission, n.
omit, vb.
omittance, n.
overskip, vb.
pass, vb.
random, n.
remiss, adj.
remissness, n.

resty, adj.
scant, vb.
self-neglecting, n.
slack, adj.
slack, vb.
slackly, adv.
slackness, n.
sleepy, adj.
slightly, adv.
sloth, n.
slothful, adj.
slovenly, adj.
slovenry, n.
slug, n.
slug-a-bed, n.
sluggard, n.
sluggardize, vb.
sluggish, adj.
spiritless, adj.
truant, n.
truant, vb.
unactive, adj.
unchary, adj.
unheedful, adj.
unheedfully, adv.
unheedy, adj.
unminded, adj.
unmindful, adj.
unregarded, adj.
unrespected, adj.
unrespective, adj.
vain, adj.
vainly, adv.
wilful-negligent, adj.
: 76

14.43
avarice

avarice, n.
avaricious, adj.
covetous, adj.
covetously, adv.
covetousness, n.
greedily, adv.

greediness, n.
greedy, adj.
insatiate, adj.
lucre, n.
miser, n.
niggard, n.
niggard, vb.
niggardly, adj.
over-greedy, adj.
: 15

14.44
prodigality

costliness, n.
costly, adj.
lavish, adj.
lavishly, adv.
opulency, n.
opulent, adj.
prodigal, adj.
prodigal, n.
prodigality, n.
prodigally, adv.
spendthrift, n.
sumptuous, adj.
sumptuously, adv.
thriftless, adj.
unthrift, n.
unthrifty, adj.
waste, n.
waste, vb.
wasteful, adj.
: 19

14.45
corruption

corrupt, adj.
corrupt, vb.
corrupter, n.
corruptible, fr. adj.
corruptibly, adv.
corruption, n.
corruptly, adv.

debase, vb.
debauch, vb.
degenerate, adj.
derogate, adj.
taint, adj.
taint, vb.
vicious, adj.
viciousness, n.
vild, adj.
vild, n.
vildly, adv.
vile, adj.
vile, n.
vilely, adv.
vileness, n.
: 22

14.46
fault
———————

amiss, n.
blemish, n.
default, n.
defect, n.
defective, adj.
eyesore, n.
fault, n.
faultiness, n.
fellow-fault, n.
foil, n.
gap, n.
imperfect, adj.
imperfection, n.
imperfectly, adv.
lamely, adv.
slip, n.
slip, vb.
taint, n.
unperfect, adj.
unperfectness, n.
vice, n.
: 21

14.47
dishonour
———————

abash, vb.
all-disgraced, adj.
ashamed, adj.
attainder, n.
attaint, adj.
attaint, n.
attainture, n.
blot, n.
crest-wounding, adj.
defame, n.
defame, vb.
discredit, n.
discredit, vb.
disgrace, n.
disgrace, vb.
disgraceful, adj.
disgracious, adj.
dishonest, adj.
dishonesty, n.
dishonour, n.
dishonour, vb.
dishonourable, adj.
false, adj.
hollow, adj.
hollowly, adv.
hollowness, n.
honnir, fr. vb.
honour-flawed, adj.
ignoble, adj.
ignobly, adv.
ignominious, adj.
ignominy, n.
ignomy, n.
indign, adj.
indigne, fr. adj.
indignity, n.
infamonize, vb.
infamous, adj.
infamy, n.
inglorious, adj.
reputeless, adj.
scandal, n.

scandal, vb.
scandalize, vb.
scandalous, adj.
shame, n.
shame, vb.
shameful, adj.
shamefully, adv.
shameless, adj.
slander, n.
slander, vb.
slanderous, adj.
spot, n.
stain, n.
stain, vb.
taint, adj.
taint, n.
taint, vb.
traduce, vb.
traducement, n.
turpitude, n.
under-honest, adj.
unfamed, adj.
ungracious, adj.
unjust, adj.
unjustly, adv.
unnoble, adj.
unrighteous, adj.
: 69

14.48
desire
———————

appetite, n.
covet, vb.
coveting, n.
covetous, adj.
covetousness, n.
desire, n.
desire, vb.
desirer, n.
desirous, adj.
greediness, n.
heart-wished, adj.
itch, n.
itch, vb.

list, n.
list, vb.
long, vb.
longed-for, adj.
longing, n.
lust, n.
thirst, n.
thirst, vb.
unwish, vb.
unwished, adj.
well-wished, adj.
will, n.
will, vb.
willing, adj.
wish, n.
wish, vb.
wisher, n.
wishful, adj.
: 31

14.49
impurity
———————

attaint, n.
attaint, vb.
bedabble, vb.
bedash, vb.
bedaub, vb.
begrime, vb.
bemoil, vb.
beray, vb.
beslubber, vb.
besmear, vb.
besmirch, vb.
bestain, vb.
blemish, n.
blemish, vb.
blood-stained, adj.
blot, n.
blot, vb.
blow, vb.
blur, n.
blur, vb.
colly, vb.
contaminate, adj.

contaminate, vb.
daub, vb.
deface, vb.
defacer, n.
defeat, vb.
defeature, n.
defile, vb.
defiler, n.
dirt, n.
dirty, adj.
distain, vb.
enseam, vb.
file, vb.
filthy, adj.
fly-bitten, adj.
fly-blow, vb.
fly-blown, adj.
foul, adj.
foul, n.
foul, vb.
grease, vb.
greasy, adj.
grime, vb.
imbrue, vb.
impure, adj.
impurity, n.
liquor, vb.
lust-stained, adj.
maculate, adj.
maculation, n.
meal, vb.
mire, vb.
mole, n.
mud, vb.
muddy, adj.
muddy, vb.
nasty, adj.
neighbour-stained,
    adj.
over-stain, vb.
pollute, vb.
pollution, n.
puddle, vb.
ray, n.
ray, vb.

rust, n.
rust, vb.
rusty, adj.
slobbery, adj.
slubber, vb.
sluttish, adj.
sluttishness, n.
smear, vb.
smirch, vb.
smutch, vb.
soil, n.
soil, vb.
spot, n.
spot, vb.
stain, n.
stain, vb.
stigmatic, n.
stigmatical, adj.
sully, n.
sully, vb.
taint, adj.
taint, n.
taint, vb.
tainture, n.
tear-distained, adj.
tear-stained, adj.
travel-tainted, adj.
unclean, adj.
uncleanliness, n.
uncleanly, adj.
uncleanness, n.
unpurged, adj.
unscoured, adj.
unswept, adj.
unwashed, adj.
unwiped, adj.
    : 102

14.50
sensuality
————————

bawdry, n.
bawdy, adj.
carnal, adj.
carnally, adv.

codding, adj.
colt's tooth, n.
concupiscible, adj.
concupy, n.
country matters, n.
dishonest, adj.
dishonesty, n.
dissolute, adj.
dissolutely, adv.
folly, n.
fulsome, adj.
goatish, adj.
greasily, adv.
harlotry, n.
hot-bloodied, adj.
immodest, adj.
immodestly, adv.
incontinence, n.
incontinency, n.
incontinent, adj.
intemperance, n.
intemperate, adj.
lascivious, adj.
lecher, n.
lecher, vb.
lecherous, adj.
lechery, n.
lewd, adj.
lewdly, adv.
lewdness, n.
lewdster, n.
liberal, adj.
libertine, n.
liberty, n.
licentious, adj.
light, adj.
loose, adj.
lust, n.
lust, vb.
lust-dieted, adj.
lustful, adj.
luxurious, adj.
luxuriously, adv.
luxury, n.
naught, n.

naughtily, adv.
naughty, adj.
nice, adj.
potato finger, n.
pride, n.
prime, adj.
proud, adj.
rage, vb.
rank, adj.
ribald, adj.
ribaudred, adj.
riggish, adj.
riot, n.
riot, vb.
rioter, n.
riotous, adj.
rut, vb.
ruttish, adj.
salt, adj.
saucy, adj.
sense, n.
sensual, adj.
sensuality, n.
sensually, adv.
sluttery, n.
sluttish, adj.
sluttishness, n.
tickle, vb.
ticklish, adj.
unchaste, adj.
venereal, adj.
voluptuously, adv.
voluptuousness, n.
wanton, adj.
wanton, n.
wanton, vb.
wantonly, adv.
wantonness, n.
wild, adj.
    : 88

14.51
fornication
————————

adulterate, adj.

adulterate, vb.
adulterer, n.
adulteress, n.
adulterous, adj.
adultery, n.
bawd, n.
bawd-born, adj.
bawdry, n.
bed-swerver, n.
bewhore, vb.
broke, vb.
broker, n.
broker-between, n.
colt, vb.
commit, vb.
concubine, n.
cornuto, n.
cuckold, n.
cuckold, vb.
cuckoldly, adj.
cuckold-mad, adj.
cuckold-maker, n.
door-keeper, n.
drab, vb.
fishmonger, n.
fleshmonger, n.
fornication, n.
fornicatress, n.
go-between, n.
goer-between, n.
hold-door trade, n.
horn, vb.
horn-mad, adj.
horn-maker, n.
incest, n.
incestuous, adj.
love-broker, n.
occupy, vb.
out-paramour, vb.
pander, n.
pander, vb.
panderly, adj.
paramour, n.
parcel-bawd, n.
procure, vb.

ring-carrier, n.
strumpet, vb.
trader, n.
uncuckolded, adj.
wench, vb.
whore, vb.
whoremaster, n.
whoremasterly, adj.
whoremonger, n.
whoreson, n.
whorish, adj.
wittol, n.
wittolly, adj.
: 59

14.52
fear
——————————
afear, vb.
affray, vb.
affright, vb.
aghast, adj.
all-feared, adj.
appal, vb.
awe, n.
awe, vb.
aweless, adj.
awful, adj.
beggar-fear, n.
coward, n.
coward, vb.
cowardice, n.
coward-like, adj.
cowardly, adj.
cowardship, n.
cowish, adj.
craven, adj.
craven, n.
craven, vb.
dastard, n.
daunt, vb.
dismay, n.
dismay, vb.
doubt, n.
doubt, vb.

doubtful, adj.
doubtfully, adv.
doubtless, adj.
dread, adj.
dread, n.
dread, vb.
dreadful, adj.
dreadfully, adv.
faint-hearted, adj.
fear, n.
fear, vb.
fearful, adj.
fearfully, adv.
fearfulness, n.
fearless, adj.
fright, n.
fright, vb.
frightful, adj.
gally, vb.
goose-look, n.
lily-livered, adj.
meacock, n.
milk-livered, adj.
milksop, n.
misdread, n.
pale-hearted, adj.
poltroon, n.
pusillanimity, n.
recreant, adj.
recreant, n.
redoubt, vb.
scare, vb.
self-affrighted, adj.
soul-fearing, adj.
terrible, adj.
terribly, adv.
terror, n.
timor, lat. n.
timorous, adj.
timorously, adv.
unfeared, adj.
weak-hearted, adj.
white-livered, adj.
: 70

14.53
horror
——————————
affright, vb.
aghast, adj.
all-dreaded, adj.
dern, adj.
dire, adj.
direful, adj.
direness, n.
dread, adj.
dread, n.
dread, vb.
dreadful, adj.
dreadfully, adv.
fray, vb.
fright, n.
fright, vb.
frightful, adj.
gast, vb.
gastness, n.
ghastly, adj.
hideous, adj.
hideously, adv.
hideousness, n.
horrible, adj.
horribly, adv.
horrid, adj.
horridly, adv.
horror, n.
loathly, adj.
loathsome, adj.
loathsomeness, n.
misdread, n.
monstrosity, n.
monstrous, adj.
monstrously, adv.
monstrousness, n.
self-affrighted, adj.
terrible, adj.
terribly, adv.
terror, n.
: 39

75

14.54
ugliness
_____

foul, adj.
foul, n.

foul-faced, adj.
foulness, n.
hard-favoured, adj.
ill-faced, adj.
ill-favoured, adj.

sightless, adj.
ugly, adj.
uncomeliness, n.
unfair, vb.
unhandsome, adj.

unseemly, adj.
unsightly, adj.
: 14

15.01
cognition

apprehend, vb.
apprehension, n.
apprehensive, adj.
apprendre, fr. vb.
brain, vb.
cognition, n.
cognizance, n.
comprehend, vb.
conceive, vb.
digest, vb.
discern, vb.
discerner, n.
discerning, n.
discover, vb.
discretion, n.
distinguish, vb.
entendre, fr. vb.
feeling, n.
have, vb.
imperceiverant, adj.
incomprehensible,
  adj.
inexplicable, adj.
intellect, n.
intellectual, adj.
intelligence, n.
intelligere, lat. vb.
judgement, n.
ken, vb.
mental, adj.
misconceive, vb.
misconstruction, n.
misconstrue, vb.
perceive, vb.
read, vb.
receive, vb.
see, vb.
sense, n.
sharp, adj.
smell, vb.
spell, vb.
suppose, vb.

take, vb.
taste, n.
taste, vb.
uncomprehensive,
  adj.
understand, vb.
understanding, n.
undiscernible, adj.
undistinguished, adj.
unintelligent, adj.
unwit, vb.
unwitnessed, adj.
wit, n.
  : 53

15.02
notion

conceit, n.
conceit, vb.
conceive, vb.
conception, n.
conjecture, n.
contrive, vb.
device, n.
devise, vb.
entertain, vb.
fancy, n.
fantasy, n.
figure, n.
first-conceived, adj.
idea, n.
image, n.
imagination, n.
imagine, vb.
imagining, n.
inkling, n.
inspiration, n.
invent, vb.
invention, n.
inventor, n.
liberal-conceited, adj.
notion, n.
odd-conceited, adj.
presuppose, vb.

principle, n.
project, n.
quick-conceiving,
  adj.
quiddity, n.
quillet, n.
quillity, n.
quirk, n.
self-assumption, n.
supposal, n.
supposition, n.
theoric, n.
  : 38

15.03
mind

absurd, adj.
animus, lat. n.
common sense, n.
ingenious, adj.
invention, n.
mens, lat. n.
mind, n.
mother wit, n.
pate, n.
pregnancy, n.
pregnant, adj.
quick-witted, adj.
rational, adj.
reason, n.
reasonable, adj.
reasonably, adv.
reasonless, adj.
sense, n.
senseless, adj.
sensible, adj.
sensibly, adv.
unreasonable, adj.
unreasonably, adv.
unreasoned, adj.
wit, n.
witless, adj.
  : 26

15.04
thought

account, vb.
advise, vb.
advisedly, adv.
bethink, vb.
brain, n.
chew, vb.
cogitation, n.
comment, vb.
conscience, n.
conscionable, adj.
consider, vb.
considerance, n.
considerate, adj.
consideration, n.
considering, n.
contemplate, vb.
contemplation, n.
contemplative, adj.
counsel, n.
deem, n.
deem, vb.
deep-brained, adj.
deep-revolving, adj.
deliberate, adj.
deliberate, vb.
discourse, n.
esteem, n.
esteem, vb.
estimation, n.
estimer, vb.
feel, vb.
forethink, vb.
hold, vb.
inconsiderate, n.
judge, vb.
judgement, n.
lay-thought, n.
love-thought, n.
maintain, vb.
make, vb.
mean, vb.
meaning, n.

meditance, n.
meditate, vb.
meditation, n.
methinks, vb.
mind, n.
misthink, vb.
muse, vb.
musing, n.
penser, fr. vb.
pensive, adj.
perpend, vb.
ponder, vb.
premeditate, vb.
premeditation, n.
reason, vb.
reckon, vb.
reflect, vb.
regard, n.
repute, vb.
respect, n.
respect, vb.
revolve, vb.
ruminare, lat. vb.
ruminate, vb.
rumination, n.
sick-thoughted, adj.
soft-conscienced, adj.
study, n.
study, vb.
surmise, n.
think, vb.
thinking, n.
thought, n.
thoughtful, adj.
trow, vb.
unadvised, adj.
unadvisedly, adv.
unconsidered, adj.
unthink, vb.
unthought, adj.
unthought-of, adj.
unthought-on, adj.
unweighed, adj.
unweighing, adj.
war-thought, n.

ween, vb.
weigh, vb.
well-regarded, adj.
well-reputed, adj.
well-respected, adj.
: 92

15.05
logic

argument, n.
collection, n.
conclude, vb.
conclusion, n.
derive, vb.
donc, fr. adv.
ergo, adv.
false-derived, adj.
gather, vb.
illegitimate, adj.
infer, vb.
inference, n.
legitimate, adj.
logic, n.
major, n.
premise, n.
proposition, n.
prove, vb.
suppose, n.
suppose, vb.
supposition, n.
syllogism, n.
therefore, adv.
thereupon, adv.
thus, adv.
whereupon, adv.
: 26

15.06
knowledge

can, vb.
capacity, n.
conversant, adj.
experience, n.

experience, vb.
experimental, adj.
familiar, adj.
ignorance, n.
ignorant, adj.
ignorant, n.
know, vb.
knower, n.
knowing, n.
knowingly, adv.
knowledge, n.
light, n.
long-experienced,
  adj.
noscere, lat. vb.
note, n.
prove, vb.
science, n.
skill, n.
skilless, adj.
small-knowing, adj.
unacquainted, adj.
unexperienced, adj.
unexperient, n.
unknowing, adj.
unknown, adj.
unknown, n.
unlearned, adj.
unlettered, adj.
unread, adj.
weet, vb.
well-known, adj.
well-noted, adj.
wis, vb.
wisdom, n.
wit, vb.
wot, vb.
: 40

15.07
memory

all-oblivious, adj.
bethink, vb.
by heart, adv.

con, vb.
forget, vb.
forgetful, adj.
forgetfulness, n.
Lethied, adj.
lose, vb.
memento mori
memorable, adj.
memorial, adj.
memorial, n.
memorize, vb.
memory, n.
mind, n.
mind, vb.
monument, n.
monumental, adj.
note, n.
oblivion, n.
oblivious, adj.
oublier, fr. vb.
recollect, vb.
record, n.
recordation, n.
relic, n.
remember, vb.
remembrance, n.
remembrancer, n.
retention, n.
rote, n.
rote, vb.
souvenir, fr. vb.
study, n.
study, vb.
think, vb.
trophy, n.
well-remembered,
  adj.
without-book, n.
: 40

15.08
fantasy

capriccio, n.
capricious, adj.

conceit, n.
conceit, vb.
conceitless, adj.
crotchet, n.
dream, n.
dream, vb.
dreamer, n.
fable, n.
fable, vb.
fabulous, adj.
fancy, n.
fantastic, adj.
fantastical, adj.
fantastically, adv.
fantasy, n.
fantasy, vb.
fiction, n.
figure, vb.
humorous, adj.
humour, n.
imaginary, adj.
imagination, n.
imagine, vb.
imagining, n.
invention, n.
muse, vb.
musing, n.
odd, adj.
phantasma, n.
quirk, n.
shape, n.
subtlety, n.
toy, n.
undreamed, adj.
unreal, adj.
wit, n.
: 38

15.09
amazement
————————

admirable, adj.
admiration, n.
admire, vb.
admirer, n.

admiringly, adv.
agazed, adj.
all-admiring, adj.
amaze, n.
amaze, vb.
amazedly, adv.
amazedness, n.
amazement, n.
astonish, vb.
dare, vb.
extraordinary, adj.
marvel, n.
marvel, vb.
mate, vb.
maze, vb.
mirable, adj.
miracle, n.
miracle, vb.
miraculous, adj.
muse, vb.
stare, n.
staring, n.
stonish, vb.
wonder, n.
wonder, vb.
wonderful, adj.
wonderfully, adv.
wonderingly, adv.
wondrous, adj.
wondrously, adv.
: 34

15.10
wisdom
————————

sage, adj.
sage, n.
sapere, lat. vb.
sapient, adj.
wisdom, n.
wise, adj.
wise, n.
wisely, adv.
wise man, n.
wisest, n.

wit, n.
wittily, adv.
witty, adj.
: 13

15.11
(in)discretion
————————

discreet, adj.
discreetly, adv.
discretion, n.
indiscreet, adj.
indiscretion, n.
judicious, adj.
politic, adj.
politicly, adv.
prudent, adj.
prudent, n.
unskilful, adj.
unskilfully, adv.
unwise, adj.
unwisely, adv.
: 14

15.12
foolishness
————————

apish, adj.
asinego, n.
ass, n.
ass-head, n.
beef-witted, adj.
beetle-headed, adj.
besot, vb.
block, n.
blockhead, n.
blockish, adj.
blunt-witted, adj.
boiled-brain, n.
brainless, adj.
calf, n.
capocchia, it. n.
childish-foolish, adj.
clay-brained, adj.
clod-poll, n.

conceitless, adj.
dolt, n.
dotage, n.
dotant, n.
dotard, n.
dote, vb.
doter, n.
drivelling, adj.
dry, adj.
dull, adj.
dullard, n.
dull-brained, adj.
dull-eyed, adj.
dullness, n.
dunce, n.
fat, adj.
fat-brained, adj.
fatuus, lat, adj.
fat-witted, adj.
folly, n.
fond, adj.
fond, vb.
fondly, adv.
fool, n.
foolery, n.
foolish, adj.
foolishly, adv.
foolishness, n.
geck, n.
gosling, n.
gudgeon, n.
gull, n.
hobby-horse, n.
idiot, n.
idle-headed, adj.
ignorance, n.
ignorant, n.
innocent, adj.
innocent, n.
jolt head, n.
knotty-pated, adj.
lack-brain, n.
lean-witted, adj.
linsey-woolsey, n.
loggerhead, n.

loggerheaded, adj.
mome, n.
motley-minded, adj.
natural, adj.
natural, n.
ninny, n.
nod-ay, vb.
noddy, n.
over-fond, adj.
pantaloon, n.
peevish-fond, adj.
puppy-headed, adj.
shallow, adj.
shallowly, adv.
sillily, adv.
silliness, n.
silly, adj.
simple, adj.
simpleness, n.
simplicity, n.
snipe, n.
sodden-witted, adj.
sot, n.
sot, vb.
sottish, adj.
stock, n.
stupid, adj.
thickskin, n.
unfool, vb.
vain, adj.
want-wit, n.
weak, adj.
witless, adj.
wit-old, adj.
woodcock, n.
wooden, adj.
  : 99

15.13
attempt
───────────

assay, n.
assay, vb.
attempt, n.
attempt, vb.

attemptable, adj.
endeavour, n.
endeavour, vb.
enterprise, n.
essay, n.
experiment, n.
go about, phr. vb.
labour, vb.
offer, vb.
push, n.
seek, vb.
strife, n.
strive, vb.
struggle, vb.
try, vb.
undergo, vb.
undertake, vb.
undertaker, n.
undertaking, n.
venture, n.
venture, vb.
well-took, adj.
  : 26

15.14
examination
───────────

ague-proof, adj.
anatomize, vb.
approbation, n.
approof, n.
approve, vb.
approver, n.
assay, n.
bolt, vb.
cast, vb.
essay, n.
examination, n.
examination, vb.
examine, vb.
fan, vb.
high-proof, adj.
narrow-prying, adj.
overlook, vb.
perusal, n.

peruse, vb.
probation, n.
proof, n.
prove, vb.
prover, n.
pry, vb.
question, vb.
re-survey, vb.
scan, vb.
shame-proof, adj.
sift, vb.
sound, vb.
study, vb.
supervise, n.
supervise, vb.
survey, n.
survey, vb.
task, vb.
taste, n.
taste, vb.
tempt, vb.
temptation, n.
tempting, n.
test, n.
test, vb.
testimony, vb.
touch, n.
touch, vb.
touchstone, n.
trial, n.
trial-fire, n.
trier, n.
try, n.
try, vb.
unapproved, adj.
unexamined, adj.
unimproved, adj.
unquestioned, adj.
unscanned, adj.
unsifted, adj.
unsounded, adj.
untried, adj.
view, n.
viva voce
war-proof, n.

well-found, adj.
winnow, vb.
  : 65

15.15
search
───────────

after-inquiry, n.
arbitrament, n.
inquire, n.
inquire, vb.
inquiry, n.
inquisition, n.
inquisitive, adj.
look, vb.
quest, n.
questant, n.
questrist, n.
search, n.
search, vb.
seek, vb.
spy, vb.
unsearched, adj.
unsought, adj.
  : 17

15.16
surmise
───────────

aim, n.
aim, vb.
conject, vb.
conjectural, adj.
conjecture, n.
estimation, n.
guess, n.
guess, vb.
guessingly, adv.
harp, vb.
level, vb.
presume, vb.
presurmise, n.
read, vb.
suppose, vb.
supposition, n.

surmise, n.
surmise, vb.
ween, vb.
: 19

15.17
choice

———————

adopt, vb.
adoption, n.
choice, adj.
choice, n.
choose, vb.
chooser, n.
consent, n.
cull, vb.
elect, n.
elect, vb.
election, n.
name, vb.
nominate, vb.
nomination, n.
pick, vb.
prefer, vb.
preferment, n.
rather, adv.
select, vb.
set out, phr. vb.
single, vb.
sort, vb.
unelected, adj.
unsorted, adj.
voice, n.
voice, vb.
well-chosen, adj.
: 27

15.18
comparison

———————

comparative, adj.
comparative, n.
compare, n.
compare, vb.
comparison, n.

like, adj.
like, adv.
like, vb.
liken, vb.
match, vb.
paragon, vb.
self-comparison, n.
set off, phr. vb.
unlike, adj.
: 14

15.19
impartial

———————

cold, adj.
coldly, adv.
even-handed, adj.
impartial, adj.
indifferency, n.
indifferent, adj.
indifferently, adv.
neuter, adj.
neutral, adj.
neutral, n.
partial, adj.
partialize, vb.
partially, adv.
unpartial, adj.
: 14

15.20
error • truth

———————

amiss, adv.
aright, adv.
baseless, adj.
belie, vb.
err, vb.
erroneous, adj.
error, n.
fallacy, n.
fallible, adj.
false, adj.
false, n.
false, vb.

falsely, adv.
falsify, vb.
faux, fr. adj.
forsooth, adv.
illegitimate, adj.
ill-taken, adj.
just, adj.
lie, n.
lie, vb.
misprision, n.
misprize, vb.
mistake, vb.
mistaking, n.
never-erring, adj.
oversight, n.
right, adj.
right, n.
rightly, adv.
sooth, adj.
sooth, adv.
sooth, n.
troth, n.
true, adj.
true, n.
truly, adv.
truth, n.
unfallible, adj.
untrue, adj.
untruth, n.
vain, adj.
vainly, adv.
verily, adj.
verily, adv.
veritable, adj.
vérité, fr. n.
verity, n.
very, adj.
vraiment, fr. adv.
wrong, adj.
wrong, n.
: 52

15.21
(un)clear

———————

allusion, n.
ambiguity, n.
ambiguous, adj.
both-sides, n.
broad, adj.
clear, adj.
clear, vb.
clearly, adv.
darkly, adv.
dilemma, n.
direct, adj.
directly, adv.
distinctly, adv.
double-meaning, adj.
downright, adj.
enigma, n.
enigmatical, adj.
equivocal, adj.
equivocate, vb.
equivocation, n.
equivocator, n.
express, adj.
expressly, adv.
flat, adj.
flatly, adv.
flatness, n.
gravel, vb.
home, adv.
indistinct, adj.
indistinguishable,
  adj.
indistinguished, adj.
mystery, n.
obscure, adj.
obscurely, adv.
obscurity, n.
openly, adv.
overt, adj.
perplex, vb.
perplexity, n.
perspicuous, adj.
plain, adj.

plain-dealing, adj.
plainly, adv.
plainness, n.
pose, vb.
pregnant, adj.
puzzle, vb.
riddle, n.
riddle, vb.
riddle-like, adj.
round, adj.
round, adv.
roundly, adv.
simple, adj.
simply, adv.
undistinguishable,
  adj.
unvarnished, adj.
  : 57

15.22
(un)certainty

absolute, adj.
affirm, vb.
affirmation, n.
affirmative, n.
assurance, n.
assure, vb.
assuredly, adv.
at (in) any hand, adv.
boldness, n.
by all means, adv.
certain, adj.
certain, n.
certainest, n.
certainly, adv.
certainty, n.
certes, adv.
certify, vb.
cock-sure, adj.
confidence, n.
confident, adj.
confidently, adv.
confirmation, n.
confirmer, n.

doubt, n.
doubt, vb.
doubtful, adj.
doubtfully, adv.
doubtless, adj.
downright, adj.
evident, adj.
if, n.
improbable, adj.
incertain, adj.
incertainty, n.
indubitate, adj.
infallible, adj.
infallibly, adv.
iwis, adv.
like, adj.
likelihood, n.
likely, adj.
manifest, adj.
manifest, vb.
more or less, adv.
of all hands, adv.
out of question, adv.
peradventure, adv.
perchance, adv.
perfect, adj.
perhaps, adv.
positive, adj.
positively, adv.
probable, adj.
probal, adj.
questionless, adj.
resemblance, n.
resolve, vb.
resolvedly, adv.
scruple, n.
scrupulous, adj.
surance, n.
sure, adj.
surely, adv.
surety, n.
suspense, n.
uncertain, adj.
uncertainly, adv.
uncertainty, n.

undoubted, adj.
undoubtedly, adv.
undoubtful, adj.
unlike, adj.
unlikely, adj.
unsure, adj.
unsured, adj.
warrant, n.
warrant, vb.
well-warranted, adj.
with a witness, adv.
  : 79

15.23
interpretation

apology, n.
apply, vb.
cipher, vb.
construction, n.
construe, vb.
decipher, vb.
define, vb.
definement, n.
explication, n.
exposition, n.
expositor, n.
expound, vb.
gloze, vb.
illustrate, vb.
interpret, vb.
interpretation, n.
interpreter, n.
misinterpret, vb.
misquote, vb.
moral, vb.
moralize, vb.
scan, vb.
self-explication, n.
translate, vb.
translation, n.
  : 25

15.24
belief

belief, n.
believe, vb.
convince, vb.
credence, n.
credent, adj.
credere, lat. vb.
credible, adj.
credit, n.
credit, vb.
credulity, n.
credulous, adj.
discredit, vb.
doubt, n.
doubt, vb.
douter, fr. vb.
faith, n.
faith, vb.
hard-believing, adj.
incredible, adj.
incredulous, adj.
judge, vb.
mind, n.
opinion, n.
over-credulous, adj.
persuade, vb.
persuasion, n.
position, n.
soon-believing, adj.
supposal, n.
trow, vb.
trust, vb.
truster, n.
unbelieve, vb.
  : 33

15.25
attribution

ascribe, vb.
assign, vb.
attribute, vb.
attribution, n.

15 mind • thought

give, vb.
impute, vb.
reference, n.
: 7

15.26
discovery
_____

descry, vb.
detect, vb.
detection, n.
detector, n.
discover, vb.
discoverer, n.
discovery, n.
feast-finding, adj.
find, vb.
finder, n.
finder-out, n.
find-fault, n.
finding, n.
new-found, adj.
smell, vb.
smoke, vb.
undescried, adj.
undiscovered, adj.
well-found, adj.
: 19

15.27
resolution
_____

appoint, vb.
arbitrament, n.
arbitrate, vb.
arbitrator, n.
bethink, vb.
collect, vb.
conclude, vb.
decide, vb.
decider, n.
decision, n.
decree, vb.
definite, adj.
definitive, adj.

definitively, adv.
determinate, adj.
determinate, vb.
determination, n.
determine, vb.
devise, vb.
enact, vb.
high-resolved, adj.
limit, vb.
ordain, vb.
peremptorily, adv.
peremptory, adj.
point, vb.
pre-ordain, vb.
resolute, adj.
resolute, n.
resolutely, adv.
resolution, n.
resolve, n.
resolve, vb.
resolvedly, adv.
settle, vb.
sort, vb.
undetermined, adj.
unresolved, adj.
unsettle, vb.
unsettled, adj.
vile-concluded, adj.
wilful, adj.
will, vb.
: 43

15.28
intention
_____

address, vb.
aim, n.
aim, vb.
be about, phr. vb.
cause, n.
design, n.
design, vb.
designment, n.
direct, vb.
direction, n.

drift, n.
effect, n.
end, n.
for the nonce, adv.
goal, n.
hent, n.
imply, vb.
intend, vb.
intendment, n.
intent, n.
intention, n.
level, vb.
mean, vb.
meaning, n.
mind, n.
mind, vb.
moral, adj.
moral, n.
motion, n.
motive, adj.
motive, n.
platform, n.
point, vb.
pretence, n.
pretend, vb.
pretender, n.
pretext, n.
purport, n.
purpose, n.
purpose, vb.
purpose-changer, n.
purposely, adv.
regard, n.
scope, n.
signify, vb.
substance, n.
tenor, n.
think, vb.
true-meant, adj.
unpurposed, adj.
unwittingly, adv.
well-meaning, adj.
well-meant, adj.
wittingly, adv.
: 54

15.29
motive
_____

because, adv.
cause, n.
causeless, adj.
ground, n.
insomuch, adv.
instance, n.
long of, adj.
motive, adj.
motive, n.
occasion, n.
pourquoi, fr. adv.
quare, lat. adv.
reason, n.
what, adv.
whereabout, adv.
wherefore, adv.
wherefore, n.
why, adv.
why, n.
: 19

15.30
import
_____

carriage, n.
charge, n.
concern, vb.
concernancy, n.
effectual, adj.
heavy, adj.
import, n.
import, vb.
importance, n.
importancy, n.
important, adj.
importantly, adv.
importless, adj.
material, adj.
matter, n.
moment, n.
ponderous, adj.
pregnant, adj.

pregnantly, adv.
profound, adj.
sense, n.
skill, vb.
substance, n.
thereabout, adv.
thereabouts, adv.
weight, n.
weighty, adj.
: 27

15.31
affair

---

affair, n.
affaire, fr. n.
argument, n.

business, n.
cause, n.
circumstance, n.
concern, vb.
concernancy, n.
concerning, n.
condition, n.
event, n.
gear, n.
head, n.
interest, n.
love-affair, n.
love-cause, n.
matter, n.
present, n.
propose, n.
purpose, n.

question, n.
sake, n.
self-affair, n.
subject, n.
theme, n.
thing, n.
touch, vb.
: 27

15.32
circumstance

---

bested, adj.
case, n.
circumstance, n.
circumstance, vb.
circumstantial, adj.

condition, n.
condition, vb.
estate, n.
fare, n.
pass, n.
passage, n.
plight, n.
point, n.
predicament, n.
premise, n.
proviso, n.
situation, n.
sort, n.
state, n.
term, n.
: 20

16.01
commonwealth

---

archbishopric, n.
barony, n.
body of the weal, n.
body politic, n.
body public, n.
borough, n.
city, n.
common body, n.
common weal, n.
commonwealth, n.
community, n.
country, n.
county, n.
demesne, n.
dominion, n.
duchy, n.
dukedom, n.
earldom, n.
empery, n.
empire, n.
field, n.
kingdom, n.
kingdomed, adj.
land, n.
market town, n.
metropolis, n.
monarchy, n.
nation, n.
parish, n.
precinct, n.
principality, n.
province, n.
provincial, adj.
public body, n.
public weal, n.
realm, n.
shire, n.
signory, n.
state, n.
suburb, n.
territory, n.
tithing, n.

town, n.
village, n.
villagery, n.
ward, n.
weal, n.
: 47

16.02
government

---

administration, n.
authority, n.
chancellor, n.
civil, adj.
Commons, The
court, n.
court-like, adj.
courtly, adj.
courtship, n.
Earl Marshal, n.
foundation, n.
govern, vb.
government, n.
hell-governed, adj.
High Steward, n.
institution, n.
Lord Chamberlain, n.
ministration, n.
misgovern, vb.
office, n.
office, vb.
parliament, n.
policy, n.
politic, adj.
politicly, adv.
public, adj.
rectorship, n.
senate, n.
senator, n.
sit, vb.
speaker, n.
state, n.
state affairs, n.
state matters, n.
temporal, adj.

temporary, adj.
uncivil, adj.
ungoverned, adj.
well-governed, adj.
: 39

16.03
statesman

---

politician, n.
right-hand file, n.
statesman, n.
statist, n.
wealsman, n.
: 5

16.04
senator

---

aedile, n.
candidatus, lat. n.
censor, n.
consul, n.
consulship, n.
dictator, n.
lictor, n.
praetor, n.
proconsul, n.
senate, n.
senator, n.
tribune, n.
triumvirate, n.
triumviry, n.
: 14

16.05
mayor

---

alderman, n.
bailiff, n.
beadle, n.
blue-bottle, n.
bumbailiff, n.
burgomaster, n.
constable, n.

crowner, n.
Custa-lorum, n.
deputy of the ward,
 n.
Lord Mayor, n.
magistrate, n.
mayor, n.
nut-hook, n.
officer, n.
postmaster, n.
provost, n.
recorder, n.
searcher, n.
sergeant, n.
sheriff, n.
shrievalty, n.
thirdborough, n.
whiffler, n.
yeoman, n.
: 25

16.06
treasurer

---

cheater, n.
controller, n.
exchequer, n.
privy coffer, n.
publican, n.
tithe-woman, n.
treasurer, n.
: 7

16.07
council

---

board, n.
board of council, n.
commission, n.
commissioner, n.
council, n.
Council, The
Council-board, n.
councillor, n.
Privy Council, n. : 9

85   **16 socio-political structure**

16.08
assembly

---

after-meeting, n.
assemble, vb.
assembly, n.
board, n.
collect, vb.
college, n.
conclave, n.
congest, vb.
congregate, vb.
congregation, n.
consistory, n.
constellation, n.
convent, vb.
conventicle, n.
convocation, n.
council, n.
flock, vb.
gather, vb.
interview, n.
meeting, n.
presence, n.
resort, n.
school, n.
sitting, n.
synod, n.
table, n.
  : 26

16.09
council-house

Capitol
Council-house, n.
Guildhall
jewel-house, n.
parliament house, n.
senate-house, n.
treasure, n.
treasure house, n.
treasury, n.
  : 9

16.10
edict

---

act, n.
arrest, n.
bill, n.
blank charter, n.
canon, n.
case, n.
certificate, n.
charter, n.
civil law, n.
commission, n.
decree, n.
deed, n.
doctrine, n.
edict, n.
enact, vb.
establish, vb.
establishment, n.
label, n.
label, vb.
law, n.
law of nature, n.
livery, n.
martial law, n.
night-rule, n.
ordinance, n.
pie, n.
praemunire, n.
preordinance, n.
principle, n.
rule, n.
statute, n.
Ten Commandments
testament, n.
writ, n.
  : 34

16.11
ruler

---

domination, n.
dominator, n.
dominator, lat. n.

domineer, vb.
dominion, n.
duke, vb.
empery, n.
empire, n.
governess, n.
governor, n.
Grace, n.
hard-ruled, adj.
head of state, n.
imperator, n.
king, vb.
Lord Governor, n.
Lord Protector, n.
Lord's Protectorship,
n.
mightiness, n.
monarchize, vb.
potentate, n.
president, n.
prince, n.
prince, vb.
principality, n.
protector, n.
protectorship, n.
queen, vb.
regent, n.
regentship, n.
regiment, n.
reign, n.
reign, vb.
royalize, vb.
rule, n.
rule, vb.
ruler, n.
signory, n.
sir, n.
sway, n.
sway, vb.
tyrannize, vb.
tyrant, n.
unking, vb.
unkinglike, adj.
unqueen, vb.
  : 46

16.12
majesty

---

all-royal, adj.
imperial, adj.
imperious, adj.
imperiously, adv.
kingdom, n.
kingly, adj.
lordliness, n.
majestas, lat. n.
majestic, adj.
majestical, adj.
majestically, adv.
majesty, n.
prince-like, adj.
princely, adj.
regal, adj.
royal, adj.
royally, adv.
royalty, n.
self-sovereignty, n.
sovereign, adj.
sovereignly, adv.
sovereignty, n.
  : 22

16.13
enthrone

---

bench, vb.
coronation, n.
couronner, fr. vb.
crown, vb.
degrade, vb.
depose, vb.
displant, vb.
disseat, vb.
dub, vb.
emballing, n.
enthrone, vb.
install, vb.
instalment, n.
instate, vb.
institute, vb.

invest, vb.
kingly-crowned, adj.
new-crowned, adj.
ordain, vb.
plant, vb.
replant, vb.
stall, vb.
throne, vb.
uncrown, vb.
unking, vb.
unqueen, vb.
unstate, vb.
: 27

16.14
ceremony
----
celebrate, vb.
celebration, n.
ceremonial, adj.
ceremonious, adj.
ceremoniously, adv.
ceremony, n.
circumstance, n.
form, n.
mystery, n.
pomp, n.
pompa, lat. n.
pompous, adj.
procession, n.
rite, n.
solemn, adj.
solemnity, n.
solemnize, vb.
solemnly, adv.
triumph, n.
: 19

16.15
castle

Ampthill
Barkloughly
base court, n.
Baynard's

Berkeley
Bristol
castle, n.
Cawdor
citadel, n.
cour, fr. n.
court, n.
Crosby House
Crosby Place
Dover
Dunsinane
Elsinore
Eltham Place
Ely House
Esher House
Flint
Hames
Kenilworth
Kimbolton
Louvre
palace, n.
Pleshey
Pomfret
quadrangle, n.
regia, lat. n.
Rougemont
Sandal
Savoy
Westminster
Whitehall
Windsor
York Place
: 36

16.16
heraldry
----
achievement, n.
addition, n.
arm, n.
ball, n.
blazon, n.
bloody-sceptred, adj.
caduceus, n.
chivalry, n.

cognizance, n.
coronet, n.
crest, n.
crest, vb.
crestless, adj.
crown, n.
crownet, n.
difference, n.
emblaze, vb.
emblem, n.
field, n.
first, n.
fleur-de-lis, n.
garter, n.
Golden Fleece, n.
great seal, n.
gules, adj.
hatchment, n.
herald, n.
heraldry, n.
heraldy, n.
household coat, n.
impresa, n.
impress, n.
Lord Marshal, n.
luce, n.
mace, n.
marshal, n.
mot, n.
motto, n.
officer-at-arms, n.
[Order of] St.
    George, n.
[Order of] St.
    Michael, n.
passant, adj.
pillar, n.
pursuivant, n.
pursuivant-at-arms,
    n.
quarter, vb.
Red Rose, n. →
    Lancaster
rod, n.
sceptre, n.

sceptre, vb.
scutcheon, n.
seal, n.
seal-ring, n.
signet, n.
staff, n.
tincture, n.
trick, vb.
trident, n.
triple crown, n.
truncheon, n.
wand, n.
warder, n.
White Rose, n. →
    York
: 63

16.17
king

Austria
Bohemia
Caesar
Cham, n.
Dane, The
dauphin, n.
Denmark
Egypt
emperor, n.
England
excellence, n.
France
highness, n.
Hungary
imperator, n.
imperial, adj.
imperial, n.
kaiser, n.
king, n.
king, vb.
liege, n.
monarch, n.
monarcho, n.
Naples
Norway

Pharaoh, n.
Pheazar, n.
Pole, The
prince, n.
Prince of Wales
rex, lat. n.
roi, fr. n.
Russia
Sicilia
Solyman
Sophy, n.
sovereign, n.
Spain
Sultan, n.
supreme, n.
Turk, The
unkinglike, adj.
 : 42

16.18
queen

empress, n.
mother-queen, n.
princess, n.
queen, n.
queen-mother, n.
regina, lat. n.
 : 6

16.19
duke

baron, n.
count, n.
countess, n.
Count Palatine, n.
county, n.
County Palatine, n.
duchess, n.
duke, n.
dukedom, n.
earl, n.
earldom, n.
marchioness, n.

marquis, n.
thane, n.
viscount, n.
 : 15

16.20
deputy

agent, n.
attorney[1], n.
attorney[2], n.
attorney, vb.
attorneyship, n.
deputation, n.
depute, vb.
deputy, n.
factor, n.
great master, n.
Lord Protector, n.
Lord's Protectorship,
 n.
mediation, n.
mediator, n.
minister, n.
minister, vb.
organ, n.
procurator, n.
protect, vb.
protector, n.
protectorship, n.
regent, n.
regentship, n.
secondary, n.
substitute, n.
substitute, vb.
substitution, n.
vicegerent, n.
viceroy, n.
 : 29

16.21
lord • lady

country lord, n.
dame, n.

don, n.
ennoble, vb.
generosity, n.
generous, adj.
gentle, vb.
lady, n.
ladyship, n.
lord, n.
lord, vb.
lording, n.
lordly, adj.
lordship, n.
madam, n.
madame, fr. n.
madonna, n.
magnifico, n.
mistress, n.
mistress-ship, n.
nobility, n.
noble, adj.
noble, n.
nobleman, n.
nobleness, n.
noblesse, n.
noblest, n.
nobly, adv.
patrician, n.
peer, n.
seigneur, fr. n.
seignior, n.
signor, n.
thrice-noble, adj.
well-born, adj.
 : 35

16.22
knight

armigero, n.
bully-knight, n.
chevalier, n.
chevalier, fr. n.
chivalrous, adj.
chivalry, n.
esquire, n.

knight, n.
knight, vb.
knighthood, n.
knightly, adj.
mountain-squire, n.
order, n.
she knight-errant, n.
squire, n.
squire-like, adj.
 : 16

16.23
ambassador

ambassade, n.
ambassador, n.
ambassage, n.
embassy, n.
ledger, n.
legate, n.
legative, adj.
nuncio, n.
 : 8

16.24
gentry

country gentleman,
 n.
gentilhomme, fr. n.
gentle, adj.
gentle, n.
gentlefolk, n.
gentleman, n.
gentlemanlike, adj.
gentlewoman, n.
gentry, n.
sir, n.
 : 10

16.25
usher

chamberer, n.
chamberlain, n.

courtier, n.
gentleman, n.
gentlewoman, n.
pensioner, n.
steward, n.
stewardship, n.
surveyor, n.
usher, n.
waiting-gentle-
  woman, n.
waiting-woman, n.
yeoman of the
  wardrobe, n.
  : 13

16.26
attendant
───────────────
accompany, vb.
adjunct, n.
assist, vb.
assistance, n.
assistant, n.
associate, vb.
attend, vb.
attendance, n.
attendant, n.
consort, vb.
depend, vb.
dependant, n.
depender, n.
disciple, n.
dog, vb.
follow, vb.
follower, n.
henchman, n.
liege man, n.
man, n.
man, vb.
meinie, n.
observant, n.
officer, n.
page, n.
page, vb.
retain, vb.

retainer, n.
retinue, n.
sectary, n.
sequent, n.
serve, vb.
service, n.
servitor, n.
squire, n.
squire-like, adj.
stander-by, n.
suit, n.
tend, vb.
tendance, n.
train, n.
unaccompanied, adj.
unattended, adj.
wait, vb.
woman, n.
yeoman, n.
  : 46

16.27
household servant
───────────────
blue coat, n.
butler, n.
chambermaid, n.
cook, n.
devil-porter, vb.
footboy, n.
footman, n.
handmaid, n.
household servant, n.
kitchen maid, n.
kitchen malkin, n.
kitchen trull, n.
kitchen vestal, n.
kitchen wench, n.
lackey, n.
lackey, vb.
maid, n.
pantler, n.
perfumer, n.
porter, n.
purveyor, n.

scullion, n.
  : 22

16.28
bearer
───────────────
ape-bearer, n.
bearer, n.
candle-holder, n.
carrier, n.
cup-bearer, n.
log-man, n.
porter, n.
purse-bearer, n.
torch-bearer, n.
torcher, n.
  : 10

16.29
servant
───────────────
country servant maid,
  n.
creature, n.
domestic, n.
drudge, n.
drug, n.
feeder, n.
fellow-servant, n.
follower, n.
groom, n.
hind, n.
joint-servant, n.
knave, n.
land-service, n.
man, n.
man, vb.
market-maid, n.
minion, n.
servant, n.
servant-monster, n.
serve, vb.
service, n.
serviceable, adj.
serving-creature, n.

servingman, n.
serviteur, fr. n.
servitor, n.
superserviceable, adj.
unserviceable, adj.
varlet, n.
  : 29

16.30
citizen
───────────────
burgher, n.
citizen, n.
limb, n.
member, n.
subject, n.
Sunday-citizen, n.
  : 6

16.31
commoner
───────────────
base, adj.
base-born, adj.
baseness, n.
basest, n.
common, adj.
common, n.
commonalty, n.
commoner, n.
common-hackneyed,
  adj.
common people, n.
commons, n.
community, n.
country folk, n.
domestic, adj.
folk, n.
general, adj.
general, n.
gens, fr. n.
gens, lat. n.
hack, vb.
home, n.
home-bred, adj.

intestine, adj.
lag, n.
lay, adj.
low, adj.
low-born, adj.
lowly, adj.
lowly, adv.
mean, adj.
mean, n.
mean-born, adj.
meaner, n.
meanest, n.
meanly, adv.
modern, adj.
more and less, n.
multitude, n.
nation, n.
native, adj.

ordinary, adj.
ordinary, n.
peasantry, n.
people, n.
plebeian, n.
plebeii, lat. n.
plebs, n.
popular, adj.
popularity, n.
populous, adj.
public, adj.
publicly, adv.
rabble, n.
rabblement, n.
rout, n.
simple, adj.
tag, n.
tag-rag people, n.

varletry, n.
vulgar, adj.
vulgar, n.
vulgarly, adv.
workaday, n.
working-day, n.
 : 64

16.32
townsman

────────────

borderer, n.
city-wife, n.
city-woman, n.
cockney, n.
confiner, n.
country girl, n.
country maid, n.

countryman, n.
country-woman, n.
market folks, n.
market man, n.
mountaineer, n.
mountainer, n.
natif, fr. n.
neighbour, n.
parishioner, n.
subject, n.
town, n.
township, n.
townsman, n.
villager, n.
 : 21

17.01
attention

attent, adj.
attention, n.
attentive, adj.
attentiveness, n.
beware, vb.
blind, adj.
blindly, adv.
care, n.
care, vb.
careful, adj.
carefully, adv.
careless, adj.
carelessly, adv.
carelessness, n.
caution, n.
cavere, lat. vb.
chariness, n.
chary, adj.
circumspect, adj.
diligence, n.
diligent, adj.
hear, vb.
heed, n.
heed, vb.
heedful, adj.
heedfully, adv.
intentively, adv.
look, vb.
look after, phr. vb.
mark, n.
mark, vb.
mind, vb.
mindful, adj.
mindless, adj.
non-regardance, n.
note, n.
note, vb.
noteworthy, adj.
notice, n.
observance, n.
observancy, n.
observant, adj.

observation, n.
observe, vb.
observer, n.
observingly, adv.
over-careful, adj.
prick up, phr. vb.
quote, vb.
reck, vb.
reckless, adj.
regard, n.
regard, vb.
regardfully, adv.
remark, vb.
remarkable, adj.
respect, n.
respect, vb.
respective, adj.
respectively, adv.
studious, adj.
studiously, adv.
tend, vb.
tendance, n.
tender, n.
tender, vb.
think, vb.
thoughtful, adj.
unminded, adj.
unmindful, adj.
unregarded, adj.
unrespective, adj.
ware, vb.
warily, adv.
wary, adj.
well-advised, adj.
wistly, adv.
 : 77

17.02
support

back, n.
back, vb.
basis, n.
bear, vb.
countenance, vb.

entertain, vb.
entertainer, n.
entertainment, n.
escot, vb.
exhibition, n.
hold up, phr. vb.
maintain, vb.
maintenance, n.
nourish, vb.
pillar, n.
principal, n.
prop, n.
prop, vb.
second, n.
second, vb.
side, vb.
stand, vb.
stay, n.
stay, vb.
support, n.
support, vb.
supportance, n.
supporter, n.
sustain, vb.
underprop, vb.
unseconded, adj.
uphold, vb.
 : 32

17.03
counsel

admonish, vb.
admonishment, n.
admonition, n.
advertise, vb.
advertisement, n.
advice, n.
advise, vb.
advisedly, adv.
advising, n.
caution, n.
chamber-counsel, n.
consult, vb.
counsel, n.

counsel, vb.
counsel-keeper, n.
counsel-keeping, adj.
counsellor, n.
direction-giver, n.
exhortation, n.
fore-advise, vb.
forewarn, vb.
prewarn, vb.
rede, n.
sententious, adj.
sententious, n.
vizament, n.
warn, vb.
warning, n.
well-advised, adj.
 : 29

17.04
assistance

abet, vb.
accessary, adj.
accessary, n.
aid, n.
aid, vb.
aidance, n.
aidant, adj.
aidless, adj.
assist, vb.
assistance, n.
assistant, adj.
assistant, n.
back, vb.
beneficial, adj.
benefit, n.
benefit, vb.
boot, n.
boot, vb.
comfort, vb.
comfortable, adj.
ease, vb.
favourer, n.
friend, vb.
friendliness, n.

further, vb.
furtherance, n.
furtherer, n.
help, n.
help, vb.
helper, n.
helpful, adj.
helpless, adj.
inaidible, adj.
minister, vb.
prefer, vb.
preferment, n.
promotion, n.
redress, n.
relief, n.
relieve, vb.
speed, n.
speed, vb.
stand to, phr. vb.
stead, n.
stead, vb.
succour, n.
succour, vb.
suppliant, adj.
supply, n.
supplyment, n.
unassisting, adj.
unhelpful, adj.
  : 52

17.05
guide

---

bear, vb.
bell-wether, n.
bring, vb.
conduct, n.
conduct, vb.
direct, vb.
direction, n.
guide, n.
guide, vb.
guider, n.
lead, vb.
leader, n.

leading, n.
marshal, vb.
misguide, vb.
mislead, vb.
misleader, n.
reduce, vb.
ringleader, n.
unguided, adj.
usher, vb.
wing-led, adj.
  : 22

17.06
protection

---

buckler, vb.
conserve, vb.
coverture, n.
defence, n.
defend, vb.
defendant, adj.
defender, n.
defensible, adj.
defensive, adj.
empatron, vb.
enshelter, vb.
enshield, adj.
ever-preserved, adj.
fence, n.
fence, vb.
force, vb.
garder, fr. vb.
harbour, vb.
harbourage, n.
haven, n.
hold, n.
life-preserving, adj.
muniment, n.
nice-preserved, adj.
past-saving, n.
patron, n.
patronage, vb.
patroness, n.
pistol-proof, adj.
plot-proof, adj.

preservation, n.
preserve, vb.
preserver, n.
proof, adj.
propugnation, n.
protect, vb.
protection, n.
protector, n.
protectress, n.
refuge, n.
refuge, vb.
reinforce, vb.
reinforcement, n.
rendezvous, n.
rescue, n.
rescue, vb.
reservation, n.
reserve, vb.
retirement, n.
safe, adj.
safe, vb.
safe-conduct, n.
safe-conduct, vb.
safeguard, n.
safeguard, vb.
safely, adv.
safety, n.
sanctuarize, vb.
sanctuary, n.
save, vb.
secure, adj.
secure, vb.
securely, adv.
security, n.
shade, vb.
shadow, n.
shadow, vb.
shelter, n.
shelter, vb.
shield, vb.
shroud, n.
shroud, vb.
starting-hole, n.
sure, adj.
surely, adv.

tuition, n.
unassailable, adj.
unfenced, adj.
unfortified, adj.
unsafe, adj.
unsure, adj.
ward, vb.
warrant, vb.
weather-fend, vb.
well-defended, adj.
  : 85

17.07
amendment

---

amend, vb.
amendment, n.
amends, n.
better, vb.
botch, vb.
clout, vb.
compensation, n.
correct, vb.
corrector, n.
corrigible, adj.
incorrect, adj.
irreparable, adj.
mend, n.
mend, vb.
mender, n.
patch, vb.
piece, vb.
proficient, n.
reanswer, vb.
recover, vb.
recovery, n.
recreate, vb.
recreation, n.
rectifier, n.
rectify, vb.
redress, n.
redress, vb.
reform, vb.
reformation, n.
refresh, vb.

remedy, n.
remedy, vb.
renew, vb.
repair, n.
repair, vb.
restitution, n.
restoration, n.
restore, vb.
time-bettering, adj.
uncorrected, adj.
: 40

17.08
vigilance

all-watched, adj.
attend, vb.
court of guard, n.
custody, n.
enguard, vb.
espy, vb.
governor, n.
guard, n.
guard, vb.
guardage, n.
guardant, n.
guardian, n.
housekeeper, n.
Jack guardant, n.
keep, n.
keeper, n.
night-watch, n.
open-eyed, adj.
overwatch, vb.
scout, vb.
sentinel, n.
sentinel, vb.
spy, vb.
tennis-court-keeper,
n.
unaware, adv.
unawares, adv.
unguarded, adj.
unkept, adj.
unwares, adv.

unwarily, adv.
unwatched, adj.
vigilance, n.
vigilant, adj.
ward, n.
warder, n.
ware, adj.
wary, adj.
watch, n.
watch, vb.
watcher, n.
watchful, adj.
watching, n.
watchman, n.
: 43

17.09
agreement

accord, n.
accord, vb.
accordant, adj.
accordingly, adv.
adhere, vb.
admit, vb.
agree, vb.
agreement, n.
answer, vb.
answerable, adj.
appointment, n.
approbation, n.
assent, n.
atone, vb.
atonement, n.
bargain, vb.
clap hands, vb.
close, vb.
cohere, vb.
coherence, n.
coherent, adj.
comart, n.
combination, n.
comply, vb.
compose, vb.
composition, n.

composure, n.
compound, vb.
compromise, n.
compromise, vb.
concord, n.
concordant, adj.
concur, vb.
condescend, vb.
confirm, vb.
conform, vb.
conformable, adj.
congree, vb.
congruent, adj.
consent, n.
consent, vb.
consign, vb.
consonancy, n.
conspire, vb.
content, adj.
content, n.
correspond, vb.
correspondence, n.
correspondent, adj.
corresponsive, adj.
deign, vb.
fall in, phr. vb.
fit, vb.
go even, phr. vb.
grant, vb.
gree, vb.
harmonious, adj.
harmony, n.
hit, vb.
in a tale, adv.
interchangeably, adv.
irreconciled, adj.
jump, vb.
match, n.
mutual, adj.
mutually, adv.
oui, fr. adv.
proportion, n.
proportion, vb.
proportionable, adj.
ratifier, n.

ratify, vb.
reciprocal, adj.
reciprocally, adv.
reconcile, vb.
reconcilement, n.
reconciler, n.
reconciliation, n.
responsive, adj.
sortance, n.
soul-confirming, adj.
square, vb.
subscribe, vb.
suffrage, n.
suit, vb.
sympathize, vb.
sympathy, n.
temporize, vb.
temporizer, n.
time-pleaser, n.
together, adv.
underwrite, vb.
unity, n.
unreconciled, adj.
unreconciliable, adj.
unsquared, adj.
verify, vb.
vouchsafe, vb.
will, n.
yea-forsooth, adj.
yes, adv.
yield, vb.
yielding, n.
: 103

17.10
(un)willingness

against the grain,
adv.
against the hair, adv.
content, fr. adj.
fain, adj.
fain, vb.
goodwill, n.
grudge, n.

grudge, vb.
ill will, n.
invitus, lat. adj.
lief, adj.
loath, adj.
loathness, n.
nill, vb.
relier, n.
rely, vb.
self-will, n.
toward, adj.
towardly, adj.
unurged, adj.
unwilling, adj.
unwillingly, adv.
unwillingness, n.
voluntary, adj.
voluntary, n.
vouloir, fr. vb.
wilful, adj.
wilfully, adv.
wilfulness, n.
will, n.
will, vb.
willing, adj.
willingly, adv.
willingness, n.
    : 34

17.11
acknowledgement
─────────────
acknow, vb.
acknowledge, vb.
acknowledgement, n.
admit, vb.
agnize, vb.
allow, vb.
allowance, n.
avouch, n.
avouch, vb.
avouchment, n.
confess, vb.
submission, n.
subscribe, vb.   : 13

17.12
affirmation
─────────────
affeer, vb.
affirm, vb.
affirmation, n.
confirm, vb.
confirmation, n.
confirmer, n.
counter-seal, vb.
justify, vb.
seal, vb.
unconfirmed, adj.
unseal, vb.
unsealed, adj.
verify, vb.
    : 13

17.13
obligation
─────────────
accountant, adj.
affined, adj.
answerable, adj.
band, n.
beholding, adj.
beholding, n.
bind, vb.
bond, n.
bondage, n.
book-oath, n.
break-promise, n.
break-vow, n.
countable, adj.
debt, adj.
debted, adj.
deep-sworn, adj.
due, adj.
due, n.
duly, adv.
duteous, adj.
dutiful, adj.
duty, n.
endear, vb.
engage, vb.

engagement, n.
enjoin, vb.
enter, vb.
entitle, vb.
falloir, fr. vb.
forfeit, adj.
forfeit, n.
forfeit, vb.
forfeiter, n.
forfeiture, n.
indebted, adj.
injunction, n.
jurement, fr. n.
knot, n.
land-service, n.
marriage vow, n.
must, vb.
oath, n.
oathable, adj.
oath-breaking, n.
obligation, n.
oblige, vb.
office, n.
ought, vb.
owe, vb.
perjure, n.
perjure, vb.
promise, n.
promise-breach, n.
promise-breaker, n.
promise-keeping, n.
protest, n.
protest, vb.
service, n.
shall, n.
shall, vb.
strong-bonded, adj.
tie, vb.
unduteous, adj.
undutiful, adj.
unforfeited, adj.
vapour-vow, n.
votaress, n.
votarist, n.
votary, n.

vouch, vb.
vow, n.
vow, vb.
    : 72

17.14
(dis)loyalty
─────────────
allegiance, n.
allegiant, adj.
alliance, n.
betray, vb.
constancy, n.
constant, adj.
disloyal, adj.
disloyalty, n.
faith, n.
faith-breach, n.
faithful, adj.
faithfully, adv.
faithfulness, n.
faithless, adj.
false, adj.
falsehood, n.
falsely, adv.
falseness, n.
fealty, n.
fidelity, n.
fides, lat. n.
fore-betrayed, n.
homage, n.
honest-true, adj.
late-betrayed, adj.
loyal, adj.
loyally, adv.
loyalty, n.
master-leaver, n.
perfidious, adj.
perfidiously, adv.
recreant, adj.
recreant, n.
runagate, n.
runaway, n.
secret-false, adj.
traitor, n.

traitorly, adj.
traitorous, adj.
traitorously, adv.
traitress, n.
treacher, n.
treacherous, adj.
treacherously, adv.
treachery, n.
treason, n.
treasonable, adj.
treasonous, adj.
troth, n.
true, adj.
true-hearted, adj.
truepenny, n.
truly, adv.
trustless, adj.
trusty, adj.
truth, n.
turncoat, n.
unfaithful, n.
unjust, adj.
unjustly, adv.
untrue, adj.
untruth, n.
  : 62

17.15
(mis)trust

---

affiance, n.
affy, vb.
authentic, adj.
confidence, n.
confident, adj.
credence, n.
depend, vb.
depositary, n.
diffidence, n.
distrust, n.
distrust, vb.
distrustful, adj.
doubt, n.
doubt, vb.
douter, fr. vb.

false, adj.
gain-giving, n.
green-eyed, adj.
jealous, adj.
jealousy, n.
misdoubt, n.
misdoubt, vb.
misgive, vb.
mistrust, n.
mistrust, vb.
mistrustful, adj.
refer, vb.
reliance, n.
relier, n.
rely, vb.
repose, vb.
secure, adj.
secure, vb.
securely, adv.
security, n.
self-trust, n.
sound, adj.
stand on (upon), phr.
  vb.
suspect, n.
suspect, vb.
suspicion, n.
suspicious, adj.
trust, n.
trust, vb.
truster, n.
unsound, adj.
unsuspected, adj.
  : 47

17.16
embrace • kiss

---

arm, vb.
baiser, fr. vb.
bill, vb.
buss, n.
buss, vb.
clasp, n.
clasp, vb.

clasping, n.
clip, vb.
common-kissing, adj.
embrace, n.
embrace, vb.
embracement, n.
embrasure, n.
fold, n.
fold, vb.
hug, vb.
kiss, n.
kiss, vb.
lip, vb.
mouth, vb.
rash-embraced, adj.
smack, n.
strain, vb.
twine, vb.
unkiss, vb.
unkissed, adj.
  : 27

17.17
praise

---

acclamation, n.
admirable, adj.
all-praised, adj.
applaud, vb.
applause, n.
approbation, n.
approof, n.
approve, vb.
attribution, n.
commend, n.
commend, vb.
commendable, adj.
commendation, n.
cry up, phr. vb.
exalt, vb.
extol, vb.
extolment, n.
fame, n.
fame, vb.
famous, adj.

famous, vb.
famously, adv.
glorify, vb.
glorious, adj.
gloriously, adv.
glory, n.
grace, n.
grace, vb.
laud, n.
laud, vb.
laudable, adj.
laus, lat. n.
magnify, vb.
plausible, adj.
plausibly, adv.
plausive, adj.
praise, n.
praise, vb.
praiseworthy, adj.
recommend, vb.
renown, n.
renown, vb.
self-admission, n.
superpraise, vb.
thrice-renowned, adj.
  : 45

17.18
encounter

---

accost, vb.
affront, n.
affront, vb.
bemeet, vb.
cope, vb.
cross, vb.
encounter, n.
encounter, vb.
encounterer, n.
greet, vb.
meet, vb.
meeting, n.
stumble on, phr. vb.
take, vb.
  : 14

**17.19
salutation**

---

adieu, int.
all-hail, n.
all-hail, vb.
ave, n.
ben trovato
ben venuto
bon jour
bonos dies
commend, n.
commendation, n.
congratulate, vb.
congreet, vb.
Dieu vous garde
dig-you-den, vb.
fair (good) time of
   day
farewell, n.
give the time of day,
   vb.
God-a-mercy
God buy you
God-den, n.
God dig-you-den

God-i-goden
God save you
good-bye
good day, n.
good-en, n.
good even, n.
good morrow, n.
good night, n.
gratulate, vb.
greet, vb.
greeting, n.
hail, vb.
half-cap, n.
leave, n.
leave-taking, n.
lullaby, int.
receive, vb.
regreet, n.
regreet, vb.
resalute, vb.
rest you merry
salutation, n.
salute, vb.
salve, n.
unsaluted, adj.
welcome, n.

welcome, vb.
   : 48

**17.20
hospitality**

---

cheer, n.
cherish, vb.
entertain, vb.
entertainment, n.
hospitable, adj.
hospitality, n.
host, n.
hostess, n.
hostess-ship, n.
housekeeping, n.
inhospitable, adj.
receive, vb.
unhospitable, adj.
unwelcome, adj.
welcome, adj.
welcome, n.
welcome, vb.
welcomer, n.
   : 18

**17.21
(in)gratitude**

---

foxship, n.
God-a-mercy
God yield
grateful, adj.
gratitude, n.
ingrate, adj.
ingrateful, adj.
ingratitude, n.
remerciement, fr. n.
thank, n.
thank, vb.
thankful, adj.
thankfully, adv.
thankfulness, n.
thanking, n.
thankless, adj.
thanksgiving, n.
ungrateful, adj.
unthankful, adj.
unthankfulness, n.
   : 20

18.01
subjection

assubjugate, vb.
corrigible, adj.
cow, vb.
depress, vb.
easy-yielding, adj.
enfeoff, vb.
humble, adj.
humble, vb.
humbleness, n.
humble-visaged, adj.
humbly, adv.
insuppressive, adj.
liable, adj.
lie under, phr. vb.
life-rendering, adj.
meek, adj.
oppress, vb.
overawe, vb.
passive, adj.
pocket, vb.
prostrate, adj.
reclaim, vb.
remit, vb.
render, vb.
resign, vb.
resignation, n.
servant, vb.
servile, adj.
servilely, adv.
servility, n.
servitude, n.
slave-like, adj.
subdue, vb.
subject, adj.
subject, n.
subject, vb.
subjection, n.
submission, n.
submissive, adj.
submit, vb.
subscribe, vb.
subscription, n.

tributary, adj.
tribute, n.
underling, n.
unreclaimed, adj.
unyielding, adj.
yield, vb.
yielding, n.
yoke, vb.
: 50

18.02
compulsion

command, vb.
compel, vb.
compulsatory, adj.
compulsion, n.
compulsive, adj.
constrain, vb.
constraint, n.
enforce, vb.
enforcedly, adv.
enforcement, n.
force, n.
force, vb.
force perforce, adv.
hold, n.
strain, vb.
unforced, adj.
: 16

18.03
(dis)obedience

all-obeying, adj.
always-wind-
   obeying, adj.
awkward, adj.
bend, vb.
bow, vb.
comply, vb.
congee, vb.
curtsy, n.
curtsy, vb.
disobedience, n.

disobedient, adj.
disobey, vb.
duck, vb.
duty, n.
follow, vb.
froward, adj.
leg, n.
low-crooked, adj.
obedience, n.
obedient, adj.
obeisance, n.
obey, vb.
obsequious, adj.
obsequiously, adv.
officious, adj.
silly-ducking, adj.
spaniel-like, adj.
stoop, vb.
tractable, adj.
unbowed, adj.
: 30

18.04
supremacy

almighty, adj.
almighty, n.
command, n.
commander, n.
conductor, n.
control, n.
control, vb.
controlment, n.
domineer, vb.
imperious, adj.
imperiously, adv.
master, n.
master, vb.
masterdom, n.
masterly, adj.
mastery, n.
might, n.
mightiest, n.
mightiness, n.
mighty, n.

omnipotent, adj.
overawe, vb.
overmaster, vb.
overmatch, vb.
overrule, vb.
oversway, vb.
power, n.
predominance, n.
predominant, adj.
predominate, vb.
pre-eminence, n.
prevail, vb.
prevailment, n.
self-sovereignty, n.
sovereignty, n.
strength, n.
supremacy, n.
vantage, n.
: 38

18.05
commandment

accite, vb.
appointment, n.
beck, n.
beck, vb.
beckon, vb.
behest, n.
bid, vb.
bidding, n.
boon, n.
call, n.
call, vb.
charge, n.
charge, vb.
cite, vb.
command, n.
command, vb.
commander, fr. vb.
commandment, n.
commission, n.
conduct, vb.
direct, adj.
direct, vb.

direction, n.
directive, adj.
directly, adv.
employment, n.
enjoin, vb.
hest, n.
impose, n.
impose, vb.
imposition, n.
injunction, n.
lead, vb.
leading, n.
manage, n.
mandate, n.
order, n.
overlook, vb.
oversee, vb.
precept, n.
preceptial, adj.
prescribe, vb.
prescript, n.
prescription, n.
process, n.
recall, vb.
repeal, n.
repeal, vb.
rule the roast, vb.
summon, vb.
summons, n.
whistle, vb.
writ, n.
  : 53

18.06
controlment
_____

arrest, n.
attachment, n.
bind, vb.
bridle, vb.
buckle, vb.
cabin, vb.
cage, vb.
captivate, adj.
captivate, vb.

captive, adj.
captive, n.
captive, vb.
captivity, n.
chain, n.
check, vb.
close, adj.
closely, adv.
closeness, n.
commit, vb.
confine, n.
confine, vb.
contain, vb.
control, n.
control, vb.
controller, n.
controlment, n.
coop, vb.
curb, vb.
detain, vb.
detention, n.
durance, n.
encage, vb.
enclose, vb.
enfetter, vb.
enjail, vb.
enthrall, vb.
fetter, vb.
govern, vb.
governance, n.
government, n.
guide, vb.
gyve, vb.
handfast, n.
handle, vb.
hold, n.
hold, vb.
immure, vb.
impound, vb.
imprison, vb.
imprisonment, n.
jailer, n.
keep, vb.
lock, vb.
long-imprisoned, adj.

manacle, vb.
manage, n.
manage, vb.
mew, vb.
pen, vb.
pent-up, adj.
pinion, vb.
pound, vb.
prison, n.
prison, vb.
prisoner, n.
prisonment, n.
prisonnier, fr. n.
rebuke, n.
rein, vb.
restrain, vb.
restraint, n.
retention, n.
retentive, adj.
school, vb.
shackle, vb.
shut, vb.
smother, vb.
spar, vb.
stall, vb.
stanch, vb.
stock, vb.
strict, adj.
sty, vb.
suppress, vb.
tenable, adj.
thrall, vb.
tied-up, adj.
trash, vb.
ward, n.
wield, vb.
withhold, vb.
  : 91

18.07
(ab)use
_____

abuse, n.
abuse, vb.
abuser, n.

apply, vb.
bestow, vb.
dispose, n.
dispose, vb.
disposer, fr. n.
employ, vb.
employer, n.
employment, n.
extent, n.
function, n.
ill-used, adj.
instrumental, adj.
lay-to, vb.
madly-used, adj.
misapply, vb.
misuse, n.
misuse, vb.
ply, vb.
pre-employ, vb.
self-apply, vb.
self-misused, adj.
spend, vb.
true-disposing, adj.
unused, adj.
usage, n.
use, n.
use, vb.
useful, adj.
useless, adj.
user, n.
user, fr. vb.
utility, n.
  : 35

18.08
stifle
_____

choke, vb.
quench, vb.
smother, vb.
snuff, vb.
stifle, vb.
strangle, vb.
suffocate, adj.
suffocate, vb.

suffocation, n.
throttle, vb.
worry, vb.
: 11

18.09
tame
_____

break, vb.
entame, vb.
man, vb.
manage, n.
manage, vb.
pace, vb.
reclaim, vb.
ride, vb.
tame, adj.
tame, vb.
tamely, adv.
tameness, n.
unhandled, adj.
unman, vb.
unmanned, adj.
unreclaimed, adj.
: 16

18.10
permission
_____

admit, vb.
admittance, n.
all-licensed, adj.
allow, vb.
allowance, n.
beteem, vb.
certificate, n.
connive, vb.
countermand, n.
defend, vb.
disallow, vb.
dispensation, n.
favour, n.
forbid, vb.
forbiddenly, adv.
forfend, vb.

gainsay, vb.
give head, vb.
grant, n.
grant, vb.
head, n.
inhibit, vb.
inhibition, n.
interdict, vb.
interdiction, n.
laisser, fr. vb.
leave, n.
leave, vb.
let, vb.
licence, n.
licence, vb.
may, vb.
pardon, n.
pass, n.
pass, vb.
passport, n.
patience, n.
permission, n.
permissive, adj.
permit, vb.
please, vb.
prohibit, vb.
prohibition, n.
proscription, n.
suffer, vb.
sufferance, n.
unlicensed, adj.
vouchsafe, vb.
: 48

18.11
request
_____

appeal, n.
ask, vb.
asker, n.
beg, vb.
bepray, vb.
beseech, n.
beseech, vb.
beseecher, n.

bid, vb.
boon, n.
challenge, vb.
challenger, n.
conjuration, n.
conjure, vb.
conjuring, n.
consist on, phr. vb.
crave, vb.
craver, n.
cry, vb.
demand, n.
demand, vb.
entreat, n.
entreat, vb.
entreatment, n.
entreaty, n.
exact, vb.
exaction, n.
fool-begged, adj.
for the Lord's sake,
  adv.
implorator, n.
implore, vb.
importance, n.
important, adj.
importunacy, n.
importunate, adj.
importune, vb.
importunity, n.
insist, vb.
intercession, n.
intercessor, n.
invitation, n.
invite, vb.
inviting, n.
love-suit, n.
motion, n.
of all loves, adv.
petition, n.
petition, vb.
petitionary, adj.
petitioner, n.
pity-pleading, adj.
plea, n.

plead, vb.
pray, n.
pray, vb.
precari, lat. vb.
prier, fr. vb.
prithee, vb.
request, n.
request, vb.
require, vb.
solicit, n.
solicit, vb.
solicitation, n.
soliciting, n.
still-soliciting, adj.
sue, vb.
sued-for, adj.
suit, n.
suitor, n.
suppliant, adj.
suppliant, n.
supplicant, adj.
supplication, n.
supplier, fr. vb.
treaty, n.
unasked, adj.
unbid, adj.
unbidden, adj.
unsolicited, adj.
unurged, adj.
urge, vb.
woo, vb.
wooer, n.
wooingly, adv.
: 85

18.12
dependence
_____

accessary, adj.
by-dependence, n.
depend, vb.
dependant, n.
dependence, n.
dependency, n.
dependent, adj.   : 7

18.13
freedom
_____

absolve, vb.
at large, adv.
bail, vb.
bring off, phr. vb.
clear, adj.
clear, vb.
deliver, vb.
deliverance, n.
delivery, n.
discharge, vb.
elbow-room, n.
enfranch, vb.
enfranchise, vb.
enfranchisement, n.
enfree, vb.
enfreedom, vb.
enlarge, vb.
enlargement, n.
excuse, vb.
exempt, adj.
exempt, vb.
fancy-free, adj.
franchise, n.
franchise, vb.
franchisement, fr. n.
frank, adj.
frankly, adv.
frankness, n.
free, adj.
free, vb.
freedom, n.
freely, adv.
freeman, n.
liberal, adj.
liberté, fr. n.
liberty, n.
loose, vb.
new-delivered, adj.
quit, vb.
quittance, n.
ransom, n.
ransom, vb.

redeem, vb.
redemption, n.
redimere, lat. vb.
release, n.
release, vb.
relieve, vb.
reprieve, n.
reprieve, vb.
rescue, n.
rescue, vb.
rid, vb.
riddance, n.
slip, vb.
unchain, vb.
unfold, vb.
unhand, vb.
unkennel, vb.
unloose, vb.
unmuzzle, vb.
unmuzzled, adj.
unreprievable, adj.
unyoke, vb.
unyoked, adj.
  : 65

18.14
vassal
_____

bondage, n.
bondmaid, n.
bondman, n.
bondslave, n.
cringe, vb.
fawn, vb.
feudary, n.
foot-licker, n.
homager, n.
inferior, adj.
inferior, n.
jack, n.
Jack slave, n.
liege man, n.
slave, n.
slavery, n.
slavish, adj.

tenant, n.
thraldom, n.
thrall, n.
tributary, n.
vassal, n.
vassalage, n.
villain, n.
villain-slave, n.
waiting vassal, n.
  : 26

18.15
conspiracy
_____

compact, n.
complot, n.
complot, vb.
conspiracy, n.
conspirant, adj.
conspirator, n.
conspire, vb.
conspirer, n.
faction, n.
knot, n.
pack, n.
pack, vb.
packing, n.
  : 13

18.16
plot
_____

cautel, n.
circumvent, vb.
circumvention, n.
compass, vb.
conspire, vb.
contrive, vb.
contriver, n.
conveyance, n.
death-practised, adj.
device, n.
devise, vb.
drift, n.
engine, n.

engineer, n.
farfet, adj.
fatal-plotted, adj.
feign, vb.
fetch, n.
forge, vb.
forgery, n.
frame, n.
frame, vb.
hatch, vb.
ill-breeding, adj.
invent, vb.
invention, n.
inventor, n.
juggling trick, n.
Machiavelli
machination, n.
out-crafty, vb.
overreach, vb.
plot, n.
plot, vb.
plotter, n.
policy, n.
politician, n.
practice, n.
practisant, n.
practise, vb.
project, n.
projection, n.
ropery, n.
rope-trick, n.
shift, n.
shift, vb.
sleight, n.
starting-hole, n.
stratagem, n.
train, n.
trick, n.
tricksy, adj.
unpolicied, adj.
wile, n.
windlass, n.
  : 55

18.17
enticement

———————————

allure, vb.
allurement, n.
attract, vb.
attraction, n.
attractive, adj.
bait, vb.
draw, vb.
entice, vb.
enticement, n.
fine-baited, adj.
inveigle, vb.
lure, n.
lure, vb.
saint-seducing, adj.
seduce, vb.
seducer, n.
suggest, vb.
suggestion, n.
sweet-suggesting,
   adj.
tempt, vb.
temptation, n.
tempter, n.
tempting, n.
tice, vb.
train, n.
train, vb.
unattempted, adj.
unseduced, adj.
vile-drawing, adj.
   : 29

18.18
instigation

———————————

abet, vb.
abettor, n.
accite, vb.
attempt, vb.
cue, n.
dissuade, vb.
drive, vb.

encourage, vb.
encouragement, n.
enforce, vb.
enkindle, vb.
excite, vb.
excitement, n.
exhort, vb.
exhortation, n.
flesh, vb.
fleshment, n.
fluster, vb.
force, vb.
goad, vb.
hearten, vb.
heart-inflaming, adj.
heat, vb.
heaven-moving, adj.
high-wrought, adj.
hint, n.
incense, vb.
incite, vb.
induce, vb.
inducement, n.
infect, vb.
inflame, vb.
inflammation, n.
influence, n.
infuse, vb.
insinuate, vb.
insinuation, n.
inspiration, n.
inspire, vb.
instigate, vb.
instigation, n.
intimate, vb.
intimation, n.
kindle, vb.
lay about, phr. vb.
lay on, phr. vb.
lay to, phr. vb.
love-kindling, adj.
lust-breathed, adj.
mirth-moving, adj.
motion, n.
motion, vb.

move, vb.
movingly, adv.
pathetical, adj.
persuade, vb.
persuasively, adv.
pluck on, phr. vb.
ply, vb.
press, vb.
prick, vb.
prompt, vb.
prompture, n.
provehere, lat. vb.
provocation, n.
provoke, vb.
provoker, n.
push, vb.
put, vb.
put on (upon),
   phr. vb.
putter-on, n.
putting-on, n.
quicken, vb.
raise, vb.
requicken, vb.
rouse, vb.
ruffle, n.
ruffle, vb.
salutation, n.
salute, vb.
set, vb.
solicit, vb.
spirit-stirring, adj.
spur, n.
spur, vb.
stir, n.
stir, vb.
strain, vb.
suborn, vb.
subornation, n.
suggest, vb.
suggestion, n.
sweet-suggesting,
   adj.
tarre, vb.
teach, vb.

tempt, vb.
tingle, vb.
touch, vb.
unheart, vb.
unprovoke, vb.
unurged, adj.
urge, vb.
urgent, adj.
wake, vb.
warm, vb.
well-moving, adj.
whet, vb.
whetstone, n.
word, vb.
wrath-kindled, adj.
   : 110

18.19
deceit

———————————

abuse, n.
abuse, vb.
barefaced, adj.
bastard, n.
bear in hand, vb.
beguile, vb.
belie, vb.
betray, vb.
bob, vb.
boggle, vb.
boggler, n.
both-sides, n.
braid, adj.
bribe, n.
bribe, vb.
briber, n.
cautel, n.
cautelous, adj.
cheat, n.
cheat, vb.
cheater, n.
clipper, n.
cog, vb.
colour, vb.
colt, vb.

cony-catch, vb.
corruption, n.
counterfeit, adj.
counterfeit, vb.
counterfeitly, adv.
cozen, vb.
cozenage, n.
cozener, n.
craft, n.
craftily, adv.
crafty, adj.
cunning, adj.
cunning, n.
cunningly, adv.
daub, vb.
daubery, n.
death-counterfeiting,
  adj.
deceit, n.
deceitful, adj.
deceivable, adj.
deceive, vb.
deceiver, n.
deceptious, adj.
delude, vb.
disguise, n.
disguise, vb.
disguiser, n.
disliken, vb.
dissemble, vb.
dissembler, n.
dodge, vb.
double, adj.
double tongue, n.
double-dealer, n.
double-dealing, n.
evasion, n.
fable, n.
fable, vb.
fable, fr. n.
fabulous, adj.
face, vb.
faitour, n.
false, adj.
false-faced, adj.

false-heart, n.
false-hearted, adj.
falsehood, n.
falseness, n.
false-play, vb.
false-speaking, adj.
fashion, vb.
feign, vb.
flatter, vb.
fob, vb.
foist, vb.
fool, vb.
fop, vb.
foppery, n.
fore-betrayed, n.
forge, vb.
forgery, n.
fraud, n.
fraudful, adj.
gloss, n.
guile, n.
guile, vb.
guileful, adj.
gull, n.
gull, vb.
gull-catcher, n.
hedge, vb.
high-witted, adj.
hollow-hearted, adj.
hypocrisy, n.
hypocrite, n.
ignis fatuus
illusion, n.
impostor, n.
imposture, n.
indirect, adj.
indirection, n.
indirectly, adv.
intend, vb.
inveigle, vb.
invention, n.
jadery, n.
juggle, vb.
juggler, n.
knavery, n.

knavish, adj.
late-betrayed, adj.
lease, vb.
liar, n.
lie, n.
lie, vb.
mask, vb.
misuse, vb.
mock, vb.
mocker, n.
mockery, n.
mountebank, vb.
mouth-made, adj.
outface, vb.
oversee, vb.
paint, vb.
palter, vb.
patchery, n.
practise, vb.
pretence, n.
pretend, vb.
proper-false, n.
seemer, n.
seeming, adj.
seeming, n.
self-abuse, n.
sell a bargain, vb.
shift, n.
shift, vb.
shrewd, adj.
shrewdly, adv.
shrewdness, n.
shuffle, vb.
simular, adj.
simular, n.
simulation, n.
sly, adj.
slyly, adv.
subtile, adj.
subtile-witted, adj.
subtilly, adv.
subtilty, n.
subtle, adj.
subtle, n.
subtlety, n.

subtly, adv.
super-subtle, adj.
time-beguiling, adj.
tromperie, fr. n.
trumpery, n.
uncolt, vb.
underwork, vb.
well-painted, adj.
wittily, adv.
witty, adj.
  : 169

18.20
flattery

adulation, n.
cap-and-knee, n.
claw, vb.
court, vb.
curry, vb.
fawn, n.
fawn, vb.
flatter, vb.
flatterer, n.
flattery, n.
gloze, n.
gloze, vb.
humour, vb.
insinuate, vb.
insinuation, n.
parasite, n.
pickthank, n.
please-man, n.
smooth, vb.
soothe, vb.
soother, n.
spaniel, vb.
time-pleaser, n.
trencher-friend, n.
trencher-knight, n.
  : 25

18.21
rebellion

---

capital treason, n.
discord, n.
dissension, n.
dissentious, adj.
factious, adj.
fallen-off, adj.
fraction, n.
high treason, n.
innovation, n.
innovator, n.

insurrection, n.
master-leaver, n.
mutine, n.
mutine, vb.
mutineer, n.
mutiner, n.
mutinous, adj.
mutiny, n.
mutiny, vb.
plot, n.
plotter, n.
proditor, n.
rebel, n.

rebel, vb.
rebel-like, adj.
rebellion, n.
rebellious, adj.
revolt^1, n.
revolt^2, n.
revolt, vb.
rise, vb.
sedition, n.
seditious, adj.
still-discordant, adj.
traitor, n.
traitorly, adj.

traitorous, adj.
traitorously, adv.
traitress, n.
treacher, n.
treacherous, adj.
treacherously, adv.
treachery, n.
treason, n.
treasonable, adj.
treasonous, adj.
turncoat, n.
: 47

19.01
opposition

---

abide, vb.
adverse, adj.
adversely, adv.
breast, vb.
contrary, adj.
contrary, vb.
cross, vb.
crossing, n.
dispute, vb.
hostile, adj.
hostility, n.
impugn, vb.
in (into, to) [one's]
  teeth, adv.
in the mouth, adv.
make a stand, vb.
oppose, vb.
opposeless, adj.
opposite, adj.
opposite, n.
opposition, n.
oppugnancy, n.
peevish, adj.
peevishly, adv.
repugn, vb.
repugnancy, n.
repugnant, adj.
resist, vb.
resistance, n.
retrograde, adj.
stand, n.
stand, vb.
stand out, phr. vb.
stand up, phr. vb.
turn head, vb.
unresisted, adj.
withstand, vb.
  : 36

19.02
rival

---

competitor, n.
contend, vb.
contention, n.
contest, vb.
corrival, n.
corrival, vb.
debate, vb.
emulate, adj.
emulate, vb.
emulation, n.
emulator, n.
emulous, adj.
outvie, vb.
rival, n.
rival, vb.
skill-contending, adj.
strife, n.
strive, vb.
unrivalled, adj.
vie, vb.
  : 20

19.03
menace

---

menace, n.
menace, vb.
threat, n.
threat, vb.
threaten, vb.
threatener, n.
threateningly, adv.
wrack-threatening,
  adj.
  : 8

19.04
vexation

---

afflict, vb.
affliction, n.
anguish, n.

annoy, n.
annoy, vb.
annoyance, n.
bait, vb.
bitterly, adv.
bitterness, n.
contagious, adj.
cumber, vb.
despite, vb.
disease, n.
distress, n.
distress, vb.
distressful, adj.
earth-vexing, adj.
ever-harmless, adj.
exasperate, adj.
exasperate, vb.
eye-offending, adj.
fret, vb.
fretful, adj.
gall, vb.
grate, vb.
grief, n.
grievance, n.
grieve, vb.
grievous, adj.
gripe, vb.
harm, n.
harm, vb.
harmful, adj.
harmless, adj.
harrow, vb.
harry, vb.
heart-offending, adj.
heat-oppressed, adj.
heavy, adj.
hurt, n.
ill-doing, n.
importune, vb.
incense, vb.
inconvenience, n.
infest, vb.
inflict, vb.
infliction, n.
injure, vb.

injurer, n.
injurious, adj.
injury, n.
injury, vb.
irk, vb.
irksome, adj.
life-harming, adj.
lug, vb.
mischief, n.
mischievous, adj.
molest, vb.
molestation, n.
nettle, vb.
noisome, adj.
offence, n.
offenceful, adj.
offenceless, adj.
offend, vb.
offender, n.
offendress, n.
offensive, adj.
oppress, vb.
oppression, n.
oppressor, n.
overgall, vb.
pain, n.
pain, vb.
painful, adj.
painfully, adv.
persecute, vb.
persecution, n.
persecutor, n.
pester, vb.
plague, n.
plague, vb.
prejudice, n.
prejudice, vb.
prejudicial, adj.
ruffle, vb.
self-harming, adj.
self-offence, n.
self-wrong, n.
soul-vexed, adj.
still-vexed, adj.
sting, n.

sting, vb.
take in snuff, vb.
tarre, vb.
tart, adj.
tartly, adv.
tedious, adj.
tediousness, n.
teen, n.
tickle, vb.
trouble, n.
trouble, vb.
troublesome, adj.
unhurtful, adj.
unplagued, adj.
unvexed, adj.
vex, vb.
vexation, n.
visit, vb.
visitation, n.
visiting, n.
waspish, adj.
waspish-headed, adj.
wasp-stung, adj.
wrong, adj.
wrong, n.
wrong, vb.
wrongful, adj.
wrongfully, adj.
wrongfully, adv.
wrong-incensed, adj.
  : 123

19.05
rejection

abandon, vb.
abandoner, n.
abhor, vb.
abjure, vb.
cashier, vb.
castaway, n.
denial, n.
deny, n.
deny, vb.
desert, adj.

desolate, adj.
discard, vb.
discharge, vb.
dismiss, vb.
dismission, n.
displace, vb.
eject, vb.
forsake, vb.
forswear, vb.
lass-lorn, adj.
outcast, adj.
outcast, n.
put back, phr. vb.
refusal, n.
refuse, vb.
reject, vb.
relinquere, lat. vb.
relinquish, vb.
renegue, vb.
renounce, vb.
renouncement, n.
repel, vb.
repulse, n.
  : 33

19.06
contradiction

abjure, vb.
again, adv.
antipathy, n.
at six and seven,
  adv.
bite thumb at, vb.
but, n.
confutation, n.
confute, vb.
contradict, vb.
contradiction, n.
contrariety, n.
contrarious, adj.
contrariously, adv.
contrary, adj.
contrary, n.
countermand, vb.

crossly, adv.
crossness, n.
defiance, n.
defier, n.
defy, vb.
denial, n.
deny, n.
deny, vb.
disclaim, vb.
discord, n.
disprove, vb.
dissuade, vb.
disvouch, vb.
division, n.
except, vb.
exception, n.
for all, adv.
forspeak, vb.
forswear, vb.
gainsay, vb.
negation, n.
negative, adj.
negative, n.
nonsuit, vb.
object, vb.
oppose, vb.
paradox, n.
recant, vb.
recantation, n.
recanter, n.
refel, vb.
renegue, vb.
renounce, vb.
renouncement, n.
reproof, n.
reprove, vb.
repulse, n.
retort, vb.
  : 54

19.07
debate

argue, vb.
argument, n.

chop, vb.
chopped logic, n.
contention, n.
debate, n.
debate, vb.
debatement, n.
debater, n.
disputable, adj.
disputation, n.
dispute, n.
dispute, vb.
quarrel, n.
question, n.
question, vb.
reason, vb.
sophister, n.
  : 18

19.08
reproach

attask, vb.
blame, n.
blame, vb.
blameful, adj.
chastise, vb.
chastisement, n.
check, n.
check, vb.
chide, vb.
chider, n.
condemn, vb.
condemnation, n.
countercheck, n.
cynic, n.
discommend, vb.
dispraise, n.
dispraise, vb.
dispraisingly, adv.
exclamation, n.
find-fault, n.
imputation, n.
inveigh, vb.
note, n.
note, vb.

obloquy, n.
rail, vb.
railer, n.
rate, vb.
rebuke, n.
rebuke, vb.
rebukeable, adj.
reprehend, vb.
reproach, n.
reproach, vb.
reproachful, adj.
reproachfully, adv.
reproof, n.
reprovable, adj.
reprove, vb.
sauce, vb.
self-reproving, n.
shend, vb.
sneap, n.
take up, phr. vb.
tax, n.
tax, vb.
taxation, n.
twit, vb.
unplausive, adj.
upbraid, vb.
upbraiding, n.
wilful-blame, adj.
 : 52

19.09
mockery

arch-mock, n.
bemock, vb.
bemocked-at, adj.
bob, n.
carp, vb.
carper, n.
cavil, vb.
deride, vb.
derision, n.
fleer, n.
fleer, vb.
fling, n.

flirt, vb.
flout, n.
flout, vb.
flouting-stock, n.
gibe, n.
gibe, vb.
giber, n.
gibingly, adv.
gird, n.
gird, vb.
gleek, n.
gleek, vb.
grin, vb.
jade, vb.
jeer, vb.
laughing-stock, n.
lout, vb.
mock, n.
mock, vb.
mockable, adj.
mocker, n.
mockery, n.
pointing-stock, n.
quip, n.
satirical, adj.
scoff, n.
scoff, vb.
scoffer, n.
scorn, n.
scorn, vb.
scornful, adj.
scornfully, adv.
scout, vb.
taunt, n.
taunt, vb.
tauntingly, adv.
 : 48

19.10
disparagement

abuse, n.
abuse, vb.
accurse, vb.
backbite, vb.

baffle, vb.
ban, vb.
calumniate, vb.
calumnious, adj.
calumny, n.
curse, vb.
depravation, n.
deprave, vb.
derogate, vb.
derogately, adv.
derogation, n.
detract, vb.
detraction, n.
disable, vb.
disgrace, vb.
disparage, vb.
disparagement, n.
fico, n.
fig, n.
figo, n.
fig's-end, n.
foul-mouthed, adj.
hiss, vb.
invective, n.
invectively, adv.
land-damn, vb.
libel, n.
libel, vb.
misreport, vb.
misuse, n.
misuse, vb.
opprobriously, adv.
pelt, vb.
revile, vb.
slander, n.
slander, vb.
slanderer, n.
slanderous, adj.
substractor, n.
uncurse, vb.
 : 44

19.11
quarrel

at odds, adv.
bate, n.
bickering, n.
brabble, n.
brabbler, n.
brawl, n.
brawl, vb.
breed-bate, n.
broil, n.
by the ears, adv.
carp, vb.
carper, n.
cavil, n.
contention, n.
contestation, n.
controversy, n.
critic, adj.
critic, n.
critical, adj.
currish, adj.
debate, n.
debater, n.
difference, n.
disagree, vb.
dispute, n.
dissension, n.
dissentious, adj.
factionary, adj.
factious, adj.
fall out, phr. vb.
feud, n.
jangle, vb.
jar, n.
jar, vb.
litigious, adj.
night-brawler, n.
odd, adj.
odds, n.
outscold, vb.
quarrel, n.
quarrel, vb.
quarreller, n.

quarrellous, adj.
quarrelsome, adj.
scold, vb.
squabble, vb.
square, vb.
squarer, n.
strife, n.
strive, vb.
unpeaceable, adj.
variance, n.
wrangle, vb.
wrangler, n.
: 54

19.12
challenge

affront, vb.
air-braving, adj.
beard, vb.
brave, adj.
brave, vb.
bravely, adv.
bravery, n.
challenge, n.
challenge, vb.
confront, vb.
dare, n.
dare, vb.
dareful, adj.
defiance, n.
defy, vb.
engage, vb.
face, vb.
face to face, adv.
front, vb.
front to front, adv.
oppose, vb.
outbrave, vb.
outdare, vb.
outface, vb.
overdare, vb.
: 25

19.13
obstruction

arrest, n.
awkward, adj.
bar, n.
bar, vb.
barful, adj.
bound, n.
check, n.
choke, vb.
clog, n.
clog, vb.
control, vb.
controller, n.
counter, adj.
counter, adv.
cross, adj.
dam, vb.
detain, vb.
dreg, vb.
embargement, n.
enclog, vb.
forbid, vb.
forbidding, n.
forestall, vb.
hamper, vb.
hinder, vb.
house-clog, n.
impeachment, n.
impede, vb.
impediment, n.
inhibit, vb.
inhibition, n.
interpose, vb.
interposer, n.
keeper-back, n.
let, n.
let, vb.
obstacle, adj.
obstacle, n.
obstruction, n.
pester, vb.
prevent, vb.
prevention, n.

ram, vb.
rub, n.
rub, vb.
snatch, n.
spell-stopped, adj.
stay, n.
stay, vb.
stop, n.
stop, vb.
stopple, vb.
stumbling-block, n.
thwart, adj.
thwart, vb.
thwarting, n.
trash, vb.
unbar, vb.
unclog, vb.
uncrossed, adj.
unprevented, adj.
wall, vb.
: 62

19.14
negation

haud, lat. adv.
minime, lat. adv.
nay, adv.
nay, n.
nayward, adv.
ne, adv.
ne, lat. adv.
ne pas, fr. adv.
ne point, fr. adv.
negation, n.
negative, adj.
negative, n.
no, adj.
no^1, adv.
no^2, adv.
no, n.
non, fr. adv.
non, it. adv.
non, lat. adv.
none, adv.

not, adv.
: 22

19.15
however

howbeit, adv.
however, adv.
howsoever, adv.
néanmoins, fr. adv.
nevertheless, adv.
notwithstanding, adv.
still, adv.
though, adv.
whereas, adv.
yet, adv.
: 10

19.16
disorder

amaze, vb.
amazedly, adv.
amazedness, n.
amazement, n.
astonish, vb.
betumbled, vb.
chaos, n.
cock-a-hoop, adv.
coil, n.
combustion, n.
commotion, n.
confound, vb.
confuse, vb.
confusedly, adv.
confusion, n.
diffuse, vb.
dishevel, vb.
disorder, n.
disorder, vb.
disorderly, adj.
distemper, vb.
distemperature, n.
distract, adj.
distract, vb.

distractedly, adv.
distraction, n.
eruption, n.
fever, n.
frenzy, n.
fury, n.
garboil, n.
hubbub, n.
hurl, vb.
hurly, n.
hurly-burly, n.
hurry, n.
irregular, adj.
irregulous, adj.
maze, vb.
misorder, vb.
orderless, adj.
outbreak, n.
pell-mell, adj.
perplex, vb.
perturbation, n.
riot, n.
riot, vb.
rioter, n.
riotous, adj.
roar, n.
rummage, n.
skimble-skamble,
  adj.
stir, n.
topsy-turvy, adv.
tribulation, n.
troublous, adj.
tumult, n.
tumultuous, adj.
turbulence, n.
turbulent, adj.
turmoil, n.
turmoil, vb.
uproar, n.
uproar, vb.
upside down, adv.
wild, adj.
wildly, adv.
wildness, n.   : 68

19.17
(un)rest

agitation, n.
appease, vb.
assuage, vb.
busy, adj.
calm, adj.
calm, n.
calm, vb.
calmly, adv.
calmness, n.
coil, n.
collect, vb.
commotion, n.
disease, vb.
disquiet, adj.
disquiet, n.
disquiet, vb.
disquietly, adv.
distemper, vb.
disturb, vb.
disturbance, n.
disturber, n.
ease, n.
ease, vb.
easeful, adj.
easiness, n.
extenuate, vb.
extenuation, n.
heart-easing, adj.
heartsease, n.
implacable, adj.
late-disturbed, adj.
leisure, n.
lull, vb.
mitigate, vb.
mitigation, n.
molestation, n.
mollification, n.
never-resting, adj.
night-rest, n.
pacify, vb.
peace, n.
peaceable, adj.

peaceably, adv.
peaceful, adj.
perturb, vb.
perturbation, n.
pother, n.
quiet, adj.
quiet, n.
quiet, vb.
quietly, adv.
quietness, n.
relief, n.
repose, vb.
rest, n.
restful, adj.
restless, adj.
rout, n.
settle, vb.
sob, n.
softly, adv.
still, adj.
still, vb.
stillness, n.
stilly, adv.
storm, vb.
stormy, adj.
taking, n.
tranquil, adj.
tranquility, n.
trouble, n.
trouble, vb.
troubler, n.
troublesome, adj.
troublous, adj.
unappeased, adj.
uneasiness, n.
uneasy, adj.
unmitigable, adj.
unmitigated, adj.
unmoved, adj.
unpeaceable, adj.
unquiet, adj.
unquiet, n.
unquietly, adv.
unquietness, n.
unrest, n.

unsettle, vb.
unsettled, adj.
untroubled, adj.
  : 90

19.18
peril

adventure, n.
adventure, vb.
adventurous, adj.
adventurously, adv.
apperil, n.
break-neck, n.
danger, n.
danger, vb.
dangerous, adj.
dangerously, adv.
endanger, vb.
expose, vb.
exposture, n.
exposure, n.
hazard, n.
hazard, vb.
jeopardy, n.
jump, n.
jump, vb.
parlous, adj.
parlously, adv.
peril, n.
perilous, adj.
plight, n.
predicament, n.
self-danger, n.
unsafe, adj.
unsure, adj.
venture, n.
venture, vb.
venturous, adj.
  : 31

19.19
avoid

all-shunned, adj.

avoid, vb.
doff, vb.
échapper, fr. vb.
escape, vb.
eschew, vb.

evade, vb.
evasion, n.
evitate, vb.
forbear, vb.
inevitable, adj.

scape, vb.
shun, vb.
shunless, adj.
unavoided, adj.
unshunnable, adj.

unshunned, adj.
void, vb.
winch, vb.
: 19

20.01
combat
---
at half-sword, adv.
atilt, adv.
bataille, fr. n.
battle, n.
battle, vb.
bear out, phr. vb.
bear up, phr. vb.
bloodshed, n.
blood-shedding, n.
break a lance, vb.
broil, n.
brunt, n.
buckle with, phr. vb.
challenge, n.
champion, vb.
civil war, n.
close, n.
close, vb.
close with, phr. vb.
closet-war, n.
combat, n.
combat, vb.
conflict, n.
conflict, vb.
contend, vb.
contention, n.
contentious, adj.
defiance, n.
encounter, n.
encounter, vb.
exploit, n.
field, n.
fielded, adj.
fight, n.
fight, vb.
fray, n.
grapple, n.
grapple, vb.
guerra, it. n.
high-battled, adj.
hostility, n.
join, vb.

martial, adj.
match, vb.
military, adj.
odds, n.
opposition, n.
oppugnancy, n.
repel, vb.
repulse, n.
scamble, vb.
scuffle, n.
sea-fight, n.
shock, n.
skirmish, n.
skirmish, vb.
stand, vb.
stratagem, n.
strike, vb.
stroke, n.
struggle, vb.
to-and-fro-
   conflicting, adj.
tournament, n.
tourney, vb.
unfought, adj.
wage, vb.
war, n.
war, vb.
warlike, adj.
well-foughten, adj.
  : 70

20.02
assault
---
alarm, n.
ambuscado, n.
ambush, n.
assail, vb.
assailable, adj.
assailant, n.
assault, n.
assault, vb.
attempt, n.
battery, n.
besiege, vb.

board, vb.
brush, n.
charge, n.
charge, vb.
course, n.
escape, n.
expedition, n.
forage, vb.
incursion, n.
inroad, n.
intrude, vb.
invade, vb.
invasion, n.
invasive, adj.
onset, n.
push, n.
push, vb.
rattle, vb.
road, n.
sack, n.
sally, n.
sally, vb.
set, vb.
set down, phr. vb.
shock, vb.
siege, n.
sit down, phr. vb.
strong-besieged, adj.
surprise, vb.
unassailable, adj.
unassailed, adj.
uncharge, vb.
uncharged, adj.
waylay, vb.
  : 45

20.03
foe
---
adversary, n.
arch-enemy, n.
challenger, n.
enemy, n.
enmity, n.
foe, n.

foeman, n.
night-foe, n.
opposer, n.
opposite, n.
  : 10

20.04
fighter
---
champion, n.
combatant, n.
fighter, n.
truncheoner, n.
  : 4

20.05
army • navy
---
after fleet, n.
ambush, n.
armada, n.
army, n.
array, n.
back, n.
battalia, n.
battalion, n.
battle, n.
century, n.
charge, n.
cohort, n.
command, n.
company, n.
convoy, n.
cornet, n.
division, n.
fleet, n.
foot, n.
force, n.
foreward, n.
front, n.
garrison, n.
garrison, vb.
head, n.
host, n.
legion, n.

muster, n.
navy, n.
power, n.
preparation, n.
puissance, n.
rear, n.
rearward, n.
regiment, n.
squadron, n.
square, n.
strength, n.
supply, n.
troop, n.
vaunt, n.
vaward, n.
wing, vb.
: 43

20.06
officer

admiral, n.
ancient, n.
capitaine, fr. n.
captain, n.
captain-general, n.
captainship, n.
centurion, n.
chief, n.
commander, n.
constable, n.
corporal, n.
corporal of [the]
field, n.
ensign, n.
general, n.
gentleman, n.
Great Marshal, n.
guidon, n.
head, n.
headless, adj.
High Admiral, n.
High Constable, n.
leader, n.
lieutenant, n.

lieutenantry, n.
Lord High Constable,
n.
Lord Marshal, n.
marshal, n.
officer, n.
officer-at-arms, n.
petty officer, n.
ringleader, n.
sergeant, n.
standard, n.
superior, n.
: 34

20.07
soldier

Amazon, n.
Amazonian, adj.
Amazonian, n.
armourer, n.
blower-up, n.
cannoneer, n.
engineer, n.
espial, n.
footman, n.
full-manned, adj.
galloglass, n.
gunner, n.
horse, n.
horseman, n.
kern, n.
landman, n.
light horseman, n.
man, vb.
man-at-arms, n.
martialist, n.
master gunner, n.
mercenary, n.
militarist, n.
perdu, n.
pioneer, n.
private, adj.
scout, n.
sentinel, n.

shooter, n.
shot, n.
soldat, fr. n.
soldier, n.
soldieress, n.
soldierlike, adj.
soldiership, n.
spy, n.
underminer, n.
war-man, n.
warrior, n.
: 39

20.08
levy

draw, vb.
impress, n.
impress, vb.
levy, n.
levy, vb.
muster, n.
muster, vb.
muster-book, n.
muster-file, n.
poll, n.
press, n.
press, vb.
press-money, n.
quick-raised, adj.
raise, vb.
rash-levied, adj.
roll, n.
: 17

20.09
camp

camp, n.
leaguer, n.
pavilion, n.
pavilion, vb.
quarter, n.
tent, n.
tent-royal, n.

untent, vb.
watch-case, n.
: 9

20.10
fortification

barricado, n.
barricado, vb.
battlement, n.
bulwark, n.
countermine, n.
embattle, vb.
fort, n.
forted, adj.
fortification, n.
fortify, vb.
fortress, n.
fortressed, adj.
front, vb.
frontier, n.
hold, n.
line, vb.
mine, n.
munition, n.
palisado, n.
parapet, n.
pike, n.
portcullis, vb.
rampire, vb.
sconce, n.
tower, n.
turret, n.
unfortified, adj.
work, n.
: 28

20.11
moat

abbey ditch, n.
castle-ditch, n.
moat, n.
moat, vb.
: 4

20.12
armour

---

armour, n.
barbed, adj.
brace, n.
breast-plate, n.
buckler, n.
coat, n.
corslet, n.
corslet, vb.
cuisse, n.
field, n.
gauntlet, n.
gorget, n.
grand-guard, n.
greave, n.
harness, n.
harness, vb.
iron, n.
mail, n.
mailed, adj.
plate, vb.
proof, n.
scaly, adj.
shield, n.
shoulder-piece, n.
targe, n.
target, n.
unarm, vb.
unarmed, adj.
unbarbed, adj.
vambrace, n.
: 30

20.13
helmet

---

beaver, n.
burgonet, n.
casque, n.
crest, n.
head-piece, n.
helm, n.
helmet, n.

helmet, vb.
sallet, n.
sight, n.
tongue, n.
undercrest, vb.
visor, n.
vizard, n.
vizard, vb.
vizard-like, adj.
: 16

20.14
weapon

---

arm, n.
arm, vb.
ash, n.
battle-axe, n.
bilbo, n.
bill, n.
blade, n.
boar-spear, n.
bodkin, n.
brown bill, n.
charging-staff, n.
curtal-ax, n.
dagger, n.
dancing-rapier, n.
dart, n.
dart, vb.
disarm, vb.
endart, vb.
falchion, n.
foil, n.
fox, n.
halberd, n.
iaculum, lat. n.
iron, n.
javelin, n.
knife, n.
lance, n.
lath, n.
long sword, n.
morris-pike, n.
partisan, n.

Philippan, adj.
piece, n.
pike, n.
point, n.
pole-axe, n.
poniard, n.
rapier, n.
scimitar, n.
spear, n.
staff, n.
stave, n.
sword, n.
toasting-iron, n.
tool, n.
tuck, n.
two-hand sword, n.
unarm, vb.
unarmed, adj.
victor-sword, n.
weapon, n.
weapon, vb.
Welsh hook, n.
: 53

20.15
sword-hilt

---

basket-hilt, n.
blade, n.
carriage, n.
chape, n.
chapeless, adj.
dudgeon, n.
edge, n.
fiery-pointed, adj.
hanger, n.
hilt, n.
ill-sheathed, adj.
mis-sheathed, adj.
pilcher, n.
point, n.
pommel, n.
scabbard, n.
sheath, n.
sheathe, vb.

sword-hilt, n.
unsheathe, vb.
: 20

20.16
gun

---

arm, n.
arm, vb.
artillery, n.
basilisk, n.
birding-piece, n.
bore, n.
broadside, n.
bullet, n.
caliver, n.
cannon, n.
cannon-bullet, n.
cannon-fire, n.
cannon-shot, n.
chamber, n.
cock, n.
culverin, n.
demi-cannon, n.
disarm, vb.
discharge, n.
discharge, vb.
elder-gun, n.
fire, vb.
flask, n.
gun, n.
gunstone, n.
lead, n.
linstock, n.
mortar-piece, n.
munition, n.
murdering-piece, n.
musket, n.
ordnance, n.
overshoot, vb.
petard, n.
pistol, n.
pistol, vb.
sear, n.
shoot, n.

shoot, vb.
shot, n.
unarm, vb.
unarmed, adj.
volley, n.
volley, vb.
well-armed, adj.
: 45

20.17
gunpowder

brimstone, n.
gunpowder, n.
powder, n.
powder, vb.
saltpetre, n.
sulphur, n.
sulphurous, adj.
wild-fire, n.
: 8

20.18
flag

banner, n.
bannerette, n.
colour, n.
ensign, n.
flag, n.
guidon, n.
pennon, n.
scarf, n.
sign, n.
standard, n.
streamer, n.
: 11

20.19
booty

boot, n.
booty, n.
cry havoc, vb.
despoil, vb.

forage, n.
forager, n.
hunt, n.
late-sacked, adj.
pill, vb.
pillage, n.
prey, n.
prey, vb.
preyful, adj.
prize, n.
purchase, n.
ransack, vb.
rapture, n.
ravish, vb.
sack, n.
sack, vb.
spoil, n.
spoil, vb.
trophy, n.
: 23

20.20
retreat

buckler, vb.
flight, n.
flyer, n.
retire, n.
retire, vb.
retrait, n.
retreat, n.
rout, n.
rout, vb.
: 9

20.21
destruction

all-eating, adj.
bane, n.
blow down, phr. vb.
blow out, phr. vb.
blow up, phr. vb.
break down, phr. vb.
catastrophe, n.

confound, vb.
confusion, n.
consume, vb.
consumer, n.
crush, vb.
dash, vb.
decimation, n.
destroy, vb.
destroyer, n.
destruction, n.
devour, vb.
dissolution, n.
dissolve, vb.
do, vb.
doom, n.
end, vb.
ending, n.
extermine, vb.
extincture, n.
fall, n.
fall, vb.
fatal, adj.
fatally, adv.
fordo, vb.
havoc, n.
havoc, vb.
lose, vb.
loss, n.
love-devouring, adj.
out-burn, vb.
overthrow, n.
perdition, n.
perish, vb.
put down, phr. vb.
raze, vb.
rid, vb.
ruin, n.
ruin, vb.
ruinate, vb.
ruinous, adj.
sink, vb.
slaughter, n.
slaughter, vb.
slaughterer, n.
slaughterman, n.

slaughterous, adj.
spill, vb.
spoil, n.
spoil, vb.
star-blasting, n.
starve, vb.
strike, vb.
subversion, n.
subvert, vb.
to the pot, adv.
unbuild, vb.
unclew, vb.
undo, vb.
undone, adj.
unmake, vb.
unroof, vb.
waste, n.
waste, vb.
wasteful, adj.
wrack, n.
wrack, vb.
wrackful, adj.
: 74

20.22
victory • defeat

abate, vb.
all-triumphant, adj.
bear down, phr. vb.
beat, vb.
bring under, phr. vb.
captivate, vb.
captive, adj.
carry, vb.
come over, phr. vb.
conquer, vb.
conqueror, n.
conquest, n.
convict, vb.
convince, vb.
defeat, n.
defeat, vb.
deliver, vb.
delivery, n.

discomfit, vb.
discomfiture, n.
fetch off, phr. vb.
foil, n.
foil, vb.
frustrate, adj.
frustrate, vb.
give in, phr. vb.
give up, phr. vb.
invincible, adj.
master, vb.
mate, vb.
never-conquered, adj.
never-yet-beaten, adj.
oft-subdued, adj.
oppressor, n.
overbear, vb.
overbulk, vb.
overcome, vb.

overgo, vb.
overpower, vb.
overpress, vb.
overrun, vb.
overthrow, n.
overthrow, vb.
overturn, vb.
overwhelm, vb.
palm, n.
palmy, adj.
poop, vb.
prevail, vb.
quail, vb.
rebuke, vb.
render, n.
render, vb.
rout, n.
rout, vb.
self-subdued, adj.

subdue, vb.
subduement, n.
suppress, vb.
surrender, n.
surrender, vb.
take in, phr. vb.
thrice-victorious, adj.
triumph, n.
triumph, vb.
triumphant, adj.
triumphantly, adv.
triumpher, n.
unconquered, adj.
unvanquished, adj.
vanquish, vb.
vanquisher, n.
victor, n.
victoress, n.
victorious, adj.

victory, n.
vincere, lat. vb.
whelm, vb.
yield, vb.
: 79

20.23
peace

———————

make-peace, n.
olive, n.
olive-branch, n.
peace, n.
peaceable, adj.
peaceably, adv.
peaceful, adj.
peacemaker, n.
truce, n.
: 9

21.01
(un)justice
---

action, n.
action-taking, adj.
equity, n.
fas. lat. n.
injustice, n.
just, adj.
justice, n.
justification, n.
justify, vb.
justly, adv.
justness, n.
law, n.
lawful, adj.
lawfully, adv.
lawless, adj.
lawlessly, adv.
nefas, lat. n.
outlaw, n.
outlaw, vb.
outlawry, n.
right, adj.
right, n.
right, vb.
rightful, adj.
rightfully, adv.
rightly, adv.
unequal, adj.
unjust, adj.
unjustice, n.
unjustly, adv.
unlawful, adj.
unlawfully, adv.
unrightful, adj.
wrong, adj.
wrong, n.
wrong, vb.
wronger, n.
wrongful, adj.
wrongfully, adj.
wrongfully, adv.
wrongly, adv.
  : 41

21.02
guilt • innocence
---

blameless, adj.
crimeless, adj.
culpable, adj.
dishonest, adj.
dishonestly, adv.
dishonesty, n.
faithful, adj.
faithfully, adv.
falsely, adv.
faultful, adj.
faultless, adj.
faulty, adj.
free, adj.
free, vb.
freely, adv.
guilt, n.
guiltily, adv.
guiltiness, n.
guiltless, adj.
guilty, adj.
guilty, n.
guilty-like, adj.
honest-true, adj.
innocence, n.
innocency, n.
innocent, adj.
innocent, n.
under-honest, adj.
  : 28

21.03
judgement
---

adjudge, vb.
award, vb.
bench, vb.
censure, n.
censure, vb.
censurer, n.
condemn, vb.
condemnation, n.
consider, vb.
convict, adj.
convince, vb.
critic, adj.
critic, n.
critical, adj.
deem, n.
deem, vb.
doom, n.
doom, vb.
gauge, vb.
high-judging, adj.
judge, n.
judge, vb.
judgement, n.
Judgement Day, n.
judicious, adj.
measure, n.
measure, vb.
mete, vb.
party-verdict, n.
prejudicate, vb.
sentence, n.
sentence, vb.
unsentenced, adj.
verdict, n.
weigh, vb.
  : 35

21.04
accusation
---

accusation, n.
accuse, n.
accuse, vb.
accuser, n.
appeach, vb.
appeal, n.
appeal, vb.
appellant, n.
arraign, vb.
arraignment, n.
attainder, n.
attaint, adj.
attaint, n.
attaint, vb.
challenge, vb.
charge, n.
charge, vb.
complain, vb.
complainant, n.
complaining, n.
complaint, n.
count, n.
defendant, n.
denounce, vb.
impeach, n.
impeach, vb.
impeachment, n.
imposition, n.
indict, vb.
indictment, n.
objection, n.
peach, vb.
plaintiff, n.
plead, vb.
pleader, n.
prosecute, vb.
uncharge, vb.
  : 37

21.05
law court
---

advocate, n.
advocation, n.
attorney^2, n.
attorney, vb.
attorney-general, n.
bar, n.
bench, n.
bencher, n.
brother-justice, n.
case, n.
civil doctor, n.
Clement's Inn
client, n.
counsellor, n.
court, n.
empanel, vb.
grandjuror, n.

grand-juryman, n.
Gray's Inn
guest-justice, n.
high court, n.
Inns of Court, n.
judge, n.
judgement-place, n.
judicious, adj.
jure, vb.
jurisdiction, n.
juror, n.
jury, n.
justice, n.
Justice of (the)
  Peace, n.
justice-like, adj.
justicer, n.
king's attorney, n.
law-day, n.
lawyer, n.
leet, n.
Lord Chief Justice,
  n.
Lycurgus
Master of the Rolls,
  n.
notary, n.
paritor, n.
plea, n.
process-server, n.
quest, n.
register, n.
sentence, n.
session, n.
solicitor, n.
Star Chamber, n.
stickler-like, adj.
sue, vb.
suit, n.
summoner, n.
Sworn Twelve, The
tawny-coat, n.
Temple Garden, n.
Temple Hall, n.
trial, n.

trial day, n.
umpire, n.
  : 61

21.06
testimony
_____

able, vb.
argue, vb.
argument, n.
attest, n.
attest, vb.
authorize, vb.
cite, vb.
demonstrable, adj.
demonstrate, vb.
demonstration, n.
depose, vb.
evidence, n.
examination, n.
fore-vouched, adj.
persuasion, n.
probation, n.
proof, n.
record, n.
record, vb.
test, n.
testify, vb.
testimony, n.
testimony, vb.
vouch, n.
vouch, vb.
voucher, n.
witness, n.
witness, vb.
  : 28

21.07
privilegium
_____

authorize, vb.
benefit, n.
birthdom, n.
birthright, n.
challenge, n.

charter, n.
charter, vb.
claim, n.
claim, vb.
conveyance, n.
country rights, n.
droit, fr. adj.
egress and regress, n.
freedom, n.
in capite
interess, vb.
intitule, vb.
legitimate, adj.
legitimate, n.
legitimation, n.
liberty, n.
patent, n.
prerogative, n.
prerogatived, adj.
prescription, n.
primogenity, n.
privilege, n.
privilege, vb.
privilegium, lat. n.
right, n.
suum cuique
title, n.
titler, n.
unauthorized, adj.
unclaimed, adj.
unrightful, adj.
untitled, adj.
warrant, n.
warrant, vb.
warrantise, n.
warranty, n.
  : 41

21.08
legacy
_____

apparent, n.
bequeath, vb.
bequest, n.
birthdom, n.

birthright, n.
coheir, n.
demise, vb.
disinherit, vb.
entail, vb.
heir, n.
heir apparent, n.
heir general, n.
heirless, adj.
hereditary, adj.
heres, lat. n.
heritage, n.
héritier, fr. n.
inherit, vb.
inheritance, n.
inheritor, n.
inheritrix, n.
intestate, adj.
legacy, n.
one-trunk-inheriting,
  adj.
patrimony, n.
portion, n.
primogenity, n.
rich-left, adj.
succeed, vb.
succeeder, n.
succession, n.
successive, adj.
successively, adv.
successor, n.
widowhood, n.
  : 35

21.09
crime
_____

abuse, n.
breaker, n.
commit, vb.
crime, n.
crimeful, adj.
criminal, adj.
delinquent, n.
digress, vb.

digression, n.
disorder, n.
enormity, n.
enormous, adj.
escape, n.
evil, n.
fault, n.
felon, n.
felonious, adj.
felony, n.
forfeit, n.
grievously, adv.
hempseed, n.
infringe, vb.
law-breaker, n.
malefaction, n.
malefactor, n.
misdeed, n.
miss, n.
mistreading, n.
misuse, n.
offence, n.
offenceful, adj.
offend, vb.
offender, n.
offendress, n.
overstep, vb.
scape, n.
scelus, lat. n.
self-offence, n.
transgress, vb.
transgression, n.
trespass, n.
trespass, vb.
unviolated, adj.
vice, n.
violate, vb.
violation, n.
wrong, n.
wronger, n.
 : 48

21.10
murder
————————
assassination, n.
behead, vb.
birth-strangled, adj.
boy-queller, n.
brain, vb.
butcher, vb.
butcherly, adj.
butchery, n.
child-killer, n.
comfort-killing, adj.
cutthroat, n.
execute, vb.
execution, n.
hang, vb.
head, vb.
homicide, n.
kill, vb.
king-killer, n.
manqueller, n.
manslaughter, n.
martyr, vb.
massacre, n.
massacre, vb.
mortify, vb.
murder, n.
murder, vb.
murderer, n.
murderous, adj.
new-killed, adj.
parricide, n.
poisoner, n.
quell, n.
quell, vb.
self-killed, adj.
self-slaughter, n.
self-slaughtered, adj.
slaughter, n.
slaughter, vb.
slaughterer, n.
slaughterman, n.
slaughterous, adj.
slay, vb.

soul-killing, adj.
still-slaughtered, adj.
strangle, vb.
strangler, n.
taking-off, n.
widow-maker, n.
woman-queller, n.
 : 49

21.11
rape
————————
deflower, vb.
enforce, vb.
enforcement, n.
force, vb.
rape, n.
rapine, n.
ravish, vb.
ravisher, n.
ravishment, n.
stuprum, lat. n.
violate, vb.
violation, n.
virgin-violator, n.
 : 13

21.12
thievery
————————
bandetto, n.
bribe, n.
bribe, vb.
briber, n.
bung, n.
burglary, n.
convey, vb.
conveyer, n.
cutpurse, n.
extortion, n.
filch, vb.
fleece, vb.
foot land-raker, n.
horse-stealer, n.
land-thief, n.

laron, n.
lifter, n.
lurch, vb.
mainour, n.
pick, vb.
picker, n.
pickpurse, n.
pilfer, vb.
pilfering, n.
pirate, n.
prig, n.
purloin, vb.
purse-taking, n.
ransack, vb.
rifle, vb.
rob, vb.
robber, n.
robbery, n.
snatcher, n.
St. Nicholas' clerks,
 n.
steal, vb.
stealer, n.
stealth, n.
striker, n.
theft, n.
thief, n.
thief-stolen, adj.
thievery, n.
thievish, adj.
water-rat, n.
water-thief, n.
 : 46

21.13
punishment
————————
amerce, vb.
cart, vb.
castigate, vb.
castigation, n.
chastise, vb.
chastisement, n.
correct, vb.
correction, n.

correctioner, n.
decimation, n.
fine, n.
fine, vb.
forfeit, n.
martyr, vb.
pain, n.
penalty, n.
plague, n.
plague, vb.
punish, vb.
punishment, n.
rack, vb.
racker, n.
stock-punish, vb.
strappado, n.
torment, n.
tormentor, n.
torture, n.
torture, vb.
torturer, n.
wheel, n.
whipper, n.
 : 31

21.14
prison
———————
cage, n.

confine, n.
Counter
dark house, n.
dungeon, n.
encage, vb.
Fleet
hell, n.
jail, n.
Limbo Patrum
Marshalsea
Newgate
prison, n.
prison-house, n.
Tower, The
ward, n.
 : 16

21.15
manacle
———————
band, n.
bilbo, n.
chain, n.
chain, vb.
down-gyved, adj.
fetter, n.
gyve, n.
house-clog, n.
iron, n.

link, n.
manacle, n.
pillory, n.
rack, n.
shackle, n.
stock, vb.
stocks, n.
unchain, vb.
unlink, vb.
 : 18

21.16
cudgel
———————
ballow, n.
bat, n.
billet, n.
club, n.
cudgel, n.
ferula, n.
lash, n.
ram, n.
rod, n.
rope's end, n.
scourge, n.
stick, n.
truncheon, n.
whip, n.
whipstock, n.   : 15

21.17
gallows
———————
gallows, n.
gibbet, n.
halter, n.
scaffold, n.
 : 4

21.18
hangman
———————
deathsman, n.
executioner, n.
executor, n.
hangman, n.
headsman, n.
under-hangman, n.
 : 6

22 trade • possession

22.01
trade

buy, vb.
buyer, n.
chapman, n.
cheapen, vb.
client, n.
commerce, n.
commodity, n.
custom, vb.
customer, n.
custom-shrunk, adj.
engross, vb.
factor, n.
fee, vb.
hire, vb.
market, n.
marketable, adj.
mart, n.
mart, vb.
merchandise, n.
merchandise, vb.
monopoly, n.
negotiate, vb.
negotiation, n.
overbuy, vb.
purchase, n.
purchase, vb.
repurchase, vb.
retail, vb.
sale, n.
sale-work, n.
sell, vb.
seller, n.
sellingly, adv.
trade, n.
trade, vb.
traffic, n.
traffic, vb.
untraded, adj.
utter, vb.
vendible, adj.
ware, n.
: 41

22.02
creditor • debtor

after-debt, n.
bankrupt, adj.
bankrupt, n.
bankrupt, vb.
borrow, n.
borrow, vb.
borrower, n.
creditor, n.
debitor and creditor,
  n.
debt, adj.
debt, n.
debted, adj.
debtor, n.
easy-borrowed, adj.
excess, n.
interest, n.
lend, vb.
lender, n.
lending, n.
loan, n.
principal, n.
remainder, n.
truster, n.
usure, vb.
usurer, n.
usury, n.
: 26

22.03
market

fair, n.
Hinckley Fair
market, n.
market-place, n.
mart, n.
Stamford Fair
: 6

22.04
merchant

broker, n.
chapman, n.
dealer, n.
factor, n.
marcantant, n.
mercer, n.
merchant, n.
merchant-like, adj.
pedlar, n.
trader, n.
tradesman, n.
trafficker, n.
: 12

22.05
monger

ballad-monger, n.
barber-monger, n.
carpet-monger, n.
costermonger, n.
fancy-monger, n.
fashion-monger, n.
fashion-monging,
  adj.
faucet-seller, n.
fishmonger, n.
love-monger, n.
newsmonger, n.
woodmonger, n.
: 12

22.06
money

angel, n.
cardecu, n.
cash, n.
cashier, vb.
chequeen, n.
chink, n.
coin, n.
coin, vb.
coinage, n.
coiner, n.
copper, n.
counterfeit, n.
cross, n.
crown, n.
crusado, n.
current, adj.
denier, n.
doit, n.
dollar, n.
drachma, n.
ducat, n.
écu, fr. n.
Edward shovel-
  board, n.
eight-penny, n.
elevenpence, n.
eleven-pence-
  farthing, n.
face royal, n.
fairy gold, n.
farthing, n.
French crown, n.
gild, vb.
gilt, n.
gold, n.
groat, n.
guilder, n.
half-faced groat, n.
halfpence, n.
halfpenny, n.
halfpenny farthing, n.
Harry groat, n.
Harry ten shilling, n.
hundred-pound, n.
ingot, n.
mark, n.
mill-sixpence, n.
mint, n.
money, n.
money, vb.
noble, n.
obulus, n.

passable, adj.
penny, n.
piece, n.
plate, n.
pound, n.
press-money, n.
ready money, n.
shilling, n.
shove-groat shilling,
  n.
sicle, n.
silver, n.
sixpence, n.
sixpenny, n.
slip, n.
solidare, n.
stamp, vb.
sterling, adj.
talent, n.
tester, n.
testern, vb.
testril, n.
three-farthing, n.
three-farthings, n.
threepence, n.
twelvepence, n.
twopence, n.
uncoined, adj.
  : 77

22.07
price

charge, n.
chargeful, adj.
cheap, adj.
cheapest, n.
cheaply, adv.
cost, n.
cost, vb.
dear, adj.
dearly, adv.
dearth, n.
endear, vb.
expense, n.

gratis, adv.
market-price, n.
price, n.
rate, n.
shot-free, adj.
  : 17

22.08
payment

acquittance, n.
advantage, n.
advantage, vb.
benefice, n.
come off, phr. vb.
coming-in, n.
contribution, n.
contributor, n.
disburse, vb.
discharge, n.
discharge, vb.
dispurse, vb.
earn, vb.
earnest, n.
escot, vb.
exchange, n.
exhibition, n.
expend, vb.
expense, n.
fee, n.
fee, vb.
hire, n.
income, n.
lay out, phr. vb.
mercenary, adj.
non-payment, n.
overpay, vb.
pay, n.
pay, vb.
payment, n.
pension, n.
pitch and pay, vb.
putter-out, n.
quittance, n.
ransom, n.

ransomless, adj.
redeem, vb.
remuneration, n.
rent, n.
repay, vb.
return, n.
return, vb.
revenue, n.
salary, n.
satisfaction, n.
sauce, vb.
spend, vb.
tender, n.
tender, vb.
tribute, n.
unfeed, adj.
unpaid, adj.
unpaid-for, adj.
unpay, vb.
unsatisfied, adj.
untendered, adj.
usance, n.
use, n.
vail, n.
wage, n.
wage, vb.
well-paid, adj.
  : 62

22.09
account

account, n.
arrearage, n.
audit, n.
auditor, n.
bill, n.
call on (upon), phr.
  vb.
note, n.
quietus, n.
render, n.
score, n.
score, vb.
shot, n.

tavern-bill, n.
tavern-reckoning, n.
  : 14

22.10
tax

benevolence, n.
contribution, n.
levy, n.
levy, vb.
scot, n.
scot and lot, n.
subsidy, n.
task, vb.
tax, n.
tax, vb.
taxation, n.
tithe, vb.
toll, vb.
  : 13

22.11
pledge

administer, vb.
assurance, n.
assure, vb.
bail, n.
bind, vb.
broking pawn, n.
engage, vb.
engagement, n.
gage, n.
gage, vb.
hostage, n.
impawn, vb.
mortgage, vb.
pawn, n.
pawn, vb.
pledge, n.
pledge, vb.
plight, n.
plight, vb.
plighter, n.

promettre, fr. vb.
promise, vb.
recognizance, n.
security, n.
subscribe, vb.
surance, n.
surety, n.
surety, vb.
surety-like, adj.
swear, vb.
token, n.
troth-plight, n.
troth-plight, adj.
undertake, vb.
warrant, n.
warrant, vb.
word, n.
 : 37

22.12
contract
——————————
agreement, n.
article, n.
articulate, vb.
bargain, n.
bond, n.
bound, adj.
capitulate, vb.
clause, n.
comart, n.
compact, adj.
compact, n.
composition, n.
composure, n.
condition, n.
condition, vb.
conditionally, adv.
contract, adj.
contract, n.
contract, vb.
contraction, n.
covenant, n.
deed, n.
double voucher, n.

farm, vb.
fine, n.
forfeit, n.
handfast, n.
in farm, adv.
indent, vb.
indenture, n.
item, n.
lease, n.
lease, vb.
let, vb.
let out, phr. vb.
obligation, n.
paction, n.
pre-contract, n.
proviso, n.
rent, vb.
single bond, n.
specialty, n.
subcontract, vb.
term, n.
treaty, n.
 : 45

22.13
value
——————————
account, n.
account, vb.
all-too-precious, adj.
censure, vb.
cess, n.
count, vb.
count of, phr. vb.
dear, adj.
dear-valued, adj.
disvalue, vb.
esteem, n.
esteem, vb.
estimable, adj.
estimate, n.
estimation, n.
ever-esteemed, adj.
extenuate, vb.
golden, adj.

goldenly, adv.
hair-worth, n.
halfpennyworth, n.
hold, vb.
inestimable, adj.
judge, vb.
low-rated, adj.
misprision, n.
misprize, vb.
number, vb.
out-prize, vb.
outsell, vb.
outworth, vb.
overhold, vb.
overprize, vb.
overrate, vb.
overvalue, vb.
pass, n.
pennyworth, n.
place, vb.
praise, vb.
precious, adj.
precious-dear, adj.
preciously, adv.
precious-princely,
 adj.
prezzare, it. vb.
price, n.
price, vb.
priceless, adj.
prize, vb.
prizer, n.
rate, n.
rate, vb.
reckon, vb.
reckoning, n.
regard, n.
regard, vb.
repute, vb.
respect, n.
respect, vb.
rich, adj.
set, vb.
sterling, adj.
sweet, adj.

treasure, n.
uncurrent, adj.
underprize, vb.
undervalue, vb.
unprizable, adj.
unprized, adj.
unvalued, adj.
validity, n.
valuation, n.
value, n.
value, vb.
valueless, adj.
weigh, vb.
well-regarded, adj.
well-reputed, adj.
well-respected, adj.
worth, adj.
worth, n.
worthier, n.
worthiest, n.
worthless, adj.
worthy, adj.
worthy, n.
 : 85

22.14
trifle
——————————
bauble, n.
baubling, adj.
bubble, n.
cherry-stone, n.
drossy, adj.
dust, n.
easy, adj.
eight-penny, n.
fig, n.
figo, n.
fig's-end, n.
fond, adj.
foolish, adj.
frivolous, adj.
gaud, n.
idle, adj.
immaterial, adj.

immoment, adj.
light, adj.
lightly, adv.
nice, adj.
nothing-gift, n.
paltry, adj.
pelting, adj.
pettiness, n.
petty, adj.
pin, n.
poor, adj.
puisne, adj.
puny, adj.
rush, n.
shallow, adj.
shallow-hearted, adj.
slight, adj.
slight, vb.
slightly, adv.
slightness, n.
small beer, n.
straw, n.
superficial, adj.
superficially, adv.
toy, n.
trick, n.
trifle, n.
trifle, vb.
trifling, adj.
trivial, adj.
trumpery, n.
valueless, adj.
vanity, n.
worthless, adj.
: 51

22.15
possession
───────────
avoir, fr. vb.
bag and baggage, n.
bear, vb.
bearer, n.
belong, vb.
endowment, n.

enjoy, vb.
enjoyer, n.
estate, vb.
fortune, n.
have, vb.
haver, n.
having, n.
hold, vb.
honour-owing, adj.
in fee, adv.
in hand, adv.
interest, n.
keeping, n.
land, n.
landed, adj.
landless, adj.
lien, vb.
living, n.
master, n.
master, vb.
masterless, adj.
mean, n.
more-having, n.
owe, vb.
own, n.
own, vb.
owner, n.
pelf, n.
possess, vb.
possession, n.
possession, fr. n.
possessor, n.
property, n.
property, vb.
repossess, vb.
reversion, n.
scrip and scrippage,
n.
seize, vb.
seizure, n.
title, n.
unowed, adj.
unpossessed, adj.
unpossessing, adj.
wearer, n.

worth, n.
: 51

22.16
keeping
───────────
contain, vb.
counsel-keeper, n.
counsel-keeping, adj.
hard-a-keeping, adj.
hold, n.
hold, vb.
holdfast, vb.
intenible, adj.
keep, vb.
keeping, n.
maintain, vb.
promise-keeping, n.
reservation, n.
reserve, vb.
retain, vb.
retention, n.
save, vb.
tenable, adj.
: 18

22.17
chattel
───────────
accoutrement, n.
appointment, n.
bag and baggage, n.
baggage, n.
belonging, n.
chattel, n.
dower, n.
dower, vb.
dowerless, adj.
dowry, n.
equipage, n.
furnishing, n.
furniture, n.
good, n.
hoard, n.
household-stuff, n.

luggage, n.
marriage-dowry, n.
movable, n.
pelf, n.
riches, n.
scrip and scrippage,
n.
stuff, n.
substance, n.
tire, n.
treasure, n.
treasury, n.
wedding-dower, n.
: 28

22.18
estate
───────────
copy, n.
demesne, n.
entitle, vb.
estate, n.
farm, n.
fee, n.
fee-farm, n.
fee-simple, n.
jointure, n.
landlord, n.
manor, n.
recovery, n.
seat, n.
tenement, n.
tenure, n.
widow, vb.
: 16

22.19
rich • poor
───────────
ability, n.
able, adj.
beggary, n.
enrich, vb.
entreasure, vb.
hoard, n.

indigent, adj.
kingly-poor, adj.
money, vb.
needy, adj.
pauvre, fr. adj.
pelf, n.
penurious, adj.
penury, n.
poor, adj.
poor, n.
poorly, adv.
poverty, n.
rich, adj.
rich, n.
rich, vb.
riches, n.
richly, adv.
richness, n.
treasure, n.
treasure, vb.
untreasure, vb.
want, n.
want, vb.
wealth, n.
wealthily, adv.
wealthy, adj.
: 32

22.20
prosperity

flourish, vb.
fruit, n.
gain, n.
palmy, adj.
profit, n.
prosper, vb.
prosperity, n.
prosperous, adj.
prosperously, adv.
soon-speeding, adj.
speed, n.
speed, vb.
success, n.
successful, adj.

successfully, adv.
thrift, n.
thriftless, adj.
thrifty, adj.
thrive, vb.
thriver, n.
win, vb.
winner, n.
: 22

22.21
beggar

almsman, n.
beggar, n.
beggar, vb.
beggarly, adj.
beggar-maid, n.
beggar-man, n.
beggar-woman, n.
beggary, n.
Poor Tom   (LR)
she-beggar, n.
Turlygod
: 11

22.22
loss

after-loss, n.
fail, vb.
fast-lost, adj.
forfeit, adj.
forfeit, vb.
forfeiture, n.
irrecoverable, adj.
leese, vb.
lose, vb.
loser, n.
loss, n.
moult, vb.
perdre, fr. vb.
shed, vb.
well-lost, adj.
: 15

22.23
deprive

bar, vb.
bereave, vb.
confiscate, adj.
confiscation, n.
deprive, vb.
detract, vb.
disfurnish, vb.
dispossess, vb.
disproperty, vb.
divest, vb.
geld, vb.
reave, vb.
unfurnish, vb.
: 13

22.24
lack

carere, lat. vb.
dearth, n.
default, n.
defect, n.
defective, adj.
deficient, adj.
destitute, adj.
fail, vb.
fault, n.
imperfect, adj.
imperfection, n.
imperfectly, adv.
lack, n.
lack, vb.
love-lacking, adj.
mercy-lacking, adj.
miss, vb.
necessity, n.
need, n.
need, vb.
pity-wanting, adj.
unperfect, adj.
unperfectness, n.
want, n.

want, vb.
: 25

22.25
necessity

egere, lat. vb.
exigent, n.
force perforce, adv.
in default, adv.
necessarily, adv.
necessary, adj.
necessary, n.
necessitied, adj.
necessity, n.
need, n.
need, vb.
needer, n.
needful, adj.
needless, adj.
needly, adv.
needs, adv.
needy, adj.
never-needed, adj.
occasion, n.
of force, adv.
perforce, adv.
require, vb.
requisite, adj.
requisite, n.
unnecessarily, adv.
unnecessary, adj.
use, n.
want, n.
want, vb.
: 29

22.26
spare

bare, adj.
frugal, adj.
hardly, adv.
lean, adj.
leanness, n.

Lenten, adj.
meagre, adj.
scant, adj.
scant, vb.
scantly, adv.
scarce, adj.
scarcely, adv.
scarcity, n.
slender, adj.
slenderly, adv.
spare, adj.
spare, n.
spare, vb.
thinly, adv.
thrift, n.
thrifty, adj.
 : 21

22.27
acceptance
————————

accept, adj.
accept, vb.
acceptable, adj.
acceptance, n.
embrace, vb.
entertain, n.
entertain, vb.
entertainer, n.
entertainment, n.
pocket, vb.
receipt, n.
receive, vb.
receiver, n.
take, vb.
 : 14

22.28
acquisition
————————

accomplish, vb.
achieve, vb.
achievement, n.
achiever, n.
acquire, vb.

acquisition, n.
arrive at, phr. vb.
assume, vb.
attain, vb.
beget, vb.
capable, adj.
capacity, n.
captious, adj.
catch, vb.
come by, phr. vb.
compass, vb.
dear-bought, adj.
dear-purchased, adj.
derive, vb.
earn, vb.
encompass, vb.
engross, vb.
feast-won, adj.
fetch, vb.
find, vb.
fruition, n.
gagner, fr. vb.
gain, vb.
gainer, n.
gather, vb.
get, vb.
glean, vb.
have, vb.
having, n.
incapable, adj.
incur, vb.
inherit, vb.
lucre, n.
make, vb.
obtain, vb.
perceive, vb.
procure, vb.
purchase, n.
purchase, vb.
reap, vb.
receive, vb.
recover, vb.
recovery, n.
repurchase, vb.
strange-achieved, adj.

take, vb.
ungained, adj.
well-won, adj.
win, vb.
 : 54

22.29
give
————————

afford, vb.
allot, vb.
allow, vb.
bequeath, vb.
bestow, vb.
cast, vb.
commend, vb.
commit, vb.
confer, vb.
consign, vb.
deal, vb.
demise, vb.
direction-giver, n.
donation, n.
donner, fr. vb.
forespent, adj.
gift, n.
give, vb.
giver, n.
giving-back, n.
grant, n.
grant, vb.
health-giving, adj.
honour-giving, adj.
impart, vb.
lend, vb.
lie-giver, n.
life-rendering, adj.
offer, n.
offer, vb.
offerer, n.
present, vb.
recommend, vb.
refer, vb.
remit, vb.
render, vb.

restore, vb.
return, vb.
unprovide, vb.
unrestored, adj.
yield, vb.
yielder, n.
yielder-up, n.
 : 43

22.30
offer
————————

bid, vb.
exhibit, vb.
motion, vb.
offer, n.
offer, vb.
overture, n.
present, vb.
presentment, n.
pretend, vb.
proffer, n.
proffer, vb.
profferer, n.
project, vb.
propose, vb.
proposer, n.
proposition, n.
propound, vb.
serve, vb.
tender, n.
tender, vb.
 : 20

22.31
furnish
————————

accommodare, lat.
 vb.
accommodate, vb.
accommodation, n.
appoint, vb.
arm, vb.
disappoint, vb.
dress, vb.

due, vb.
endow, vb.
endue, vb.
fit, adj.
fit, vb.
fitness, n.
foresee, vb.
furnish, vb.
minister, vb.
preparation, n.
prepare, n.
prepare, vb.
preparedly, adv.
provide, vb.
provider, n.
provision, n.
rig, vb.
see, vb.
serve, vb.
sharp-provided, adj.
store, vb.
supply, vb.
trim, n.
trim, vb.
unaccommodated,
 adj.
unfurnish, vb.
unfurnished, adj.
unprepared, adj.
unprovide, vb.
unprovided, adj.
well-appointed, adj.
 : 38

22.32
recompense
───────────
acquit, adj.
acquit, vb.
acquittance, n.
acquittance, vb.
answer, vb.
consider, vb.
content, vb.
deserve, vb.

deserving, n.
gratify, vb.
gratility, n.
guerdon, n.
guerdon, vb.
meed, n.
pay, vb.
payment, n.
prize, n.
quit, adj.
quit, vb.
quittal, n.
quittance, n.
recompense, n.
recompense, vb.
reguerdon, n.
reguerdon, vb.
remunerate, vb.
remuneration, n.
repay, vb.
reprisal, n.
requital, n.
requite, vb.
retort, vb.
reward, n.
reward, vb.
rewarder, n.
testern, vb.
unrewarded, adj.
wage, vb.
 : 38

22.33
gift
───────────
bounty, n.
exhibition, n.
fairing, n.
gift, n.
meed, n.
nothing-gift, n.
present, n.
 : 7

22.34
(dis)advantage
───────────
advantage, n.
advantage, vb.
advantageable, adj.
advantageous, adj.
auspicious, adj.
auspiciously, adv.
avail, n.
avail, vb.
awkward, adj.
backwardly, adv.
behalf, n.
behoof, n.
behoofeful, adj.
behove, vb.
beneficial, adj.
benefit, n.
benefit, vb.
boot, n.
boot, vb.
bootless, adj.
commodious, adj.
commodity, n.
convenience, n.
conveniency, n.
convenient, adj.
conveniently, adv.
detriment, n.
disadvantage, n.
double-vantage, vb.
effectless, adj.
expedience, n.
expedient, adj.
fair, adj.
fairly, adv.
favourable, adj.
favourably, adv.
fit, adj.
fitly, adv.
forehand, n.
gain, n.
gain, vb.
gainer, n.

get (have) the start,
 vb.
good, adj.
grace, n.
improve, vb.
in (on) behalf of,
 adv.
odds, n.
on (upon) the hip,
 adv.
opportune, adj.
opportunity, n.
privilege, n.
prize, n.
profit, n.
profit, vb.
profitable, adj.
profitably, adv.
profitless, adj.
prosperous, adj.
serve, vb.
sinister, adj.
sleeveless, adj.
speed, n.
speed, vb.
start, n.
take the heat, vb.
take the time, vb.
thrift, n.
thrifty, adj.
unimproved, adj.
unprevailing, adj.
unprofitable, adj.
unprofited, adj.
use, n.
useful, adj.
useless, adj.
vain, adj.
vainly, adv.
vantage, n.
wholesome, adj.
wholesome-
 profitable, adj.
 : 81

23.01
vocation

apprentice, n.
apprenticehood, n.
apron-man, n.
artificer, n.
calling, n.
craft, n.
craft, vb.
craftsman, n.
half-worker, n.
handicraft, n.
handicraftsman, n.
handiwork, n.
joint-labourer, n.
journeyman, n.
labourer, n.
master, n.
mechanic, adj.
mechanic, n.
mechanical, adj.
mechanical, n.
mystery, n.
occupation, n.
profession, n.
quality, n.
trade, n.
vocation, n.
workman, n.
  : 27

23.02
innkeeper

ale-wife, n.
chamberlain, n.
drawer, n.
host, n.
hostess, n.
innkeeper, n.
tapster, n.
under-skinker, n.
victualler, n.
  : 9

23.03
victualler

baker, n.
brewer, n.
butcher, n.
butter-woman, n.
comfit-maker, n.
costermonger, n.
dey-woman, n.
fishmonger, n.
fruiterer, n.
herb-woman, n.
orange-wife, n.
oyster-wench, n.
poulter, n.
sutler, n.
victualler, n.
  : 15

23.04
goldsmith

armourer, n.
brazier, n.
cutler, n.
goldsmith, n.
jeweller, n.
pewterer, n.
smith, n.
stithy, vb.
tinker, n.
  : 9

23.05
clothier

baste, vb.
botcher, n.
carder, n.
card-maker, n.
clothier, n.
distaff, n.
distaff-woman, n.
dyer, n.

flax-wench, n.
fuller, n.
glover, n.
goose, n.
ill-weaved, adj.
knitter, n.
milliner, n.
poking-stick, n.
seam, n.
seamster, n.
sew, vb.
shearman, n.
shuttle, n.
silkman, n.
spin, vb.
spinster, n.
tailor, n.
unweave, vb.
weave, vb.
weaved-up, adj.
weaver, n.
wheel, n.
whitster, n.
  : 31

23.06
mason

bricklayer, n.
mason, n.
mason, vb.
masonry, n.
plasterer, n.
  : 5

23.07
carpenter

carpenter, n.
coachmaker, n.
gallows-maker, n.
gibbet-maker, n.
joiner, n.
shipwright, n.
  : 6

23.08
shoemaker

cobble, vb.
cobbler, n.
cozier, n.
Leg
shoemaker, n.
  : 5

23.09
laundress

batler, n.
buck, n.
buck, vb.
buck-basket, n.
buck-washing, n.
dishclout, n.
fuller, n.
goose, n.
launder, vb.
laundress, n.
laundry, n.
washer, n.
wringer, n.
  : 13

23.10
delver

channel, vb.
delve, vb.
delver, n.
dig, vb.
ditch, vb.
ditcher, n.
earth-delving, adj.
furrow, vb.
grub, vb.
mine, vb.
pioned, adj.
pioneer, n.
root, vb.
shovel, vb.

undermine, vb.
underminer, n.
unearth, vb.
unroot, vb.
: 18

23.11
other trades
___

barber, n.
bearherd, n.
bellman, n.
bellows-mender, n.
carman, n.
carter, n.
chandler, n.
chimney-sweeper, n.
clock-setter, n.
collier, n.
crier, n.
drayman, n.
grave-maker, n.
haberdasher, n.
miller, n.
muleteer, n.
ostler, n.
potter, n.
rat-catcher, n.
rope-maker, n.
saddler, n.
sailmaker, n.
surveyor, n.
tan, vb.
tanner, n.
tinker, n.
town-crier, n.
waggoner, n.
: 28

23.12
husbandry
___

compost, n.
composture, n.
coulter, n.

crop, n.
crop, vb.
crow-keeper, n.
dung, n.
ear, vb.
end, vb.
fallow, adj.
fallow, n.
fan, n.
feed, n.
feeding, n.
flail, n.
foison, n.
furrow, n.
furrow, vb.
harvest, n.
harvest-home, n.
hay, n.
hay-stack, n.
husband, n.
husband, vb.
husbandry, n.
in, vb.
lea, n.
manure, vb.
mow, vb.
new-planted, adj.
pike, n.
plant, vb.
plantage, n.
plough, n.
plough, vb.
plough-iron, n.
plough-torn, adj.
rake, n.
reap, vb.
replant, vb.
root, vb.
scarecrow, n.
scythe, n.
scythe, vb.
seedness, n.
shearing, n.
sheep-hook, n.
sheep-shearing, n.

sheep-whistling, adj.
sickle, n.
soil, vb.
sow, vb.
stubble-land, n.
summer, vb.
swath, n.
swine-keeping, n.
thrash, vb.
till, vb.
tillage, n.
tilth, n.
uneared, adj.
unraked, adj.
unset, adj.
unweeded, adj.
weed, vb.
weeder-out, n.
: 66

23.13
farmer • herdsman
___

boor, n.
drover, n.
farmer, n.
franklin, n.
gardener, n.
harvestman, n.
herdman, n.
herdsman, n.
milkmaid, n.
mower, n.
neatherd, n.
paysan, fr. n.
peasant, n.
peasantry, n.
ploughman, n.
ram-tender, n.
reaper, n.
rural, adj.
rustic, adj.
rustic, n.
rustically, adv.
seedsman, n.

shearer, n.
shepherd, n.
shepherdess, n.
sickleman, n.
swain, n.
swineherd, n.
thrasher, n.
yeoman, n.
: 30

23.14
fodder
___

chawed-grass, n.
draff, n.
feed, n.
feeding, n.
fodder, n.
hay, n.
mast, n.
pasture, n.
provand, n.
provender, n.
soil, vb.
stover, n.
wash, n.
: 13

23.15
work
___

a-work, adv.
bed-work, n.
behind-door-work, n.
chare, n.
chare, vb.
dark-working, adj.
drudgery, n.
employment, n.
exercise, n.
labour, n.
labour, vb.
labourer, n.
laboursome, adj.
occupation, n.

oeuvre, fr. n.
outwork, vb.
plod, vb.
plodder, n.
stair-work, n.
strain, n.
strain, vb.
sweat, vb.
sweaty, adj.
task, n.
task, vb.
tasker, n.
toil, n.
toil, vb.
travail, n.
travail, vb.
traveller, n.
trunk-work, n.
underwork, vb.
well-labouring, adj.
work, n.
work, vb.
 : 36

23.16
build

architect, n.
build, vb.
building, n.
bulk, n.
cast, n.
clean-timbered, adj.
composition, n.
constitution, n.
edifice, n.
erect, vb.
erection, n.
fabric, n.
forge, vb.
forgetive, adj.
frame, n.
frame, vb.
hard-timbered, adj.
ill-erected, adj.

machine, n.
model, n.
mould, n.
new-built, adj.
pitch, vb.
raise, vb.
re-edify, vb.
rich-built, adj.
strong-framed, adj.
timber, vb.
unbuild, vb.
weak-built, adj.
well-knit, adj.
 : 31

23.17
tool

engine, n.
implement, n.
instrument, n.
instrumental, adj.
iron, n.
mean, n.
property, n.
tool, n.
utensil, n.
 : 9

23.18
cement

adhere, vb.
bird-lime, n.
bitume, vb.
blood-sized, adj.
caulk, vb.
cement, n.
cement, vb.
chalky, adj.
cleave, vb.
glue, vb.
inherent, adj.
lime, n.
lime, vb.

mortar, n.
oversize, vb.
pitch, n.
pitch-ball, n.
plaster, n.
plaster, vb.
rough-cast, n.
solder, vb.
tar, n.
tar, vb.
unvarnished, adj.
varnish, n.
varnish, vb.
white-lime, vb.
 : 27

23.19
nail

clout, vb.
cock, n.
doornail, n.
hobnail, n.
nail, n.
peg, n.
peg, vb.
pike, n.
pin, n.
pin, vb.
rivet, n.
rivet, vb.
screw, vb.
spigot, n.
spout, n.
unpeg, vb.
unpin, vb.
unwedgeable, adj.
wedge, n.
wedge, vb.
 : 20

23.20
hinge

anchoring hook, n.

gimmaled, adj.
gimmer, n.
hinge, n.
hook, n.
hook, vb.
joint, n.
loop, n.
nut-hook, n.
sheep-hook, n.
staple, n.
unjointed, adj.
weak-hinged, adj.
 : 13

23.21
rope

cable, n.
halter, n.
halter, vb.
line, n.
packthread, n.
rope, n.
rope, vb.
string, n.
twine, n.
wain-rope, n.
wire, n.
wiry, adj.
 : 12

23.22
barrel

barrel, n.
beer-barrel, n.
butt, n.
cade, n.
fat, n.
hogshead, n.
hoop, n.
malmsey-butt, n.
three-hooped, adj.
ton, n.
tun, n.

tun-dish, n.
vat, n.
: 13

23.23
broom

besom, n.
broom, n.
brush, n.
brush, vb.
: 4

23.24
knife

axe, n.
cuttle, n.
hatchet, n.
knife, n.
paring-knife, n.
penknife, n.
razor, n.
scissors, n.
shear, n.
unscissored, adj.
whittle, n.
: 11

23.25
gad

auger, n.
awl, n.
bodkin, n.
dibble, n.
gad, n.
needle, n.
spit, n.
toasting-iron, n.
toothpick, n.
toothpicker, n.
: 10

23.26
staff

broomstaff, n.
cowl-staff, n.
fescue, n.
long-staff, n.
pole, n.
post, n.
rod, n.
staff, n.
stake, n.
stake, vb.
stave, n.
stick, n.
torch-staff, n.
walking-staff, n.
wand, n.
wand-like, adj.
: 16

23.27
other tools

anvil, n.
bellows, n.
chisel, n.
crow, n.
file, n.
forked, adj.
hammer, n.
hand-saw, n.
hawk, n.
last, n.
level, n.
lever, n.
line, n.
mallet, n.
mattock, n.
pickaxe, n.
saw, n.
shovel, n.
spade, n.

stamp, n.
three-man beetle, n.
trowel, n.
vice, n.
vice, vb.
wrenching iron, n.
: 25

23.28
tavern

ale, n.
alehouse, n.
bottle-ale house, n.
brew-house, n.
Castle
Centaur
Crown
Elephant
Garter
house, n.
inn, n.
Lubber's Head
Pegasus
Phoenix
Porpentine
Sagittary
St. Francis
tap-house, n.
tavern, n.
Tiger
White Hart
: 21

23.29
working-house

butchery, n.
shambles, n.
slaughter-house, n.
stithy, n.
working-house, n.
: 5

23.30
brothel

bawdy-house, n.
brothel, n.
brothel-house, n.
common house, n.
Corinth
hot-house, n.
house of profession,
  n.
house of resort, n.
house of sale, n.
ill house, n.
leaping-house, n.
naughty house, n.
stew, n.
Windmill
: 14

23.31
shop

barber's shop, n.
bulk, n.
frippery, n.
Leg
shop, n.
stall, n.
: 6

23.32
mill

mill, n.
millstone, n.
mill-wheel, n.
paper-mill, n.
quern, n.
windmill, n.
: 6

24.01
language

accent, n.
anglais, fr. n.
boorish, n.
dialect, n.
diction, n.
English, adj.
English, vb.
français, fr. n.
French, n.
Greek, n.
Irish, n.
Italian, n.
King's English, n.
langage, fr. n.
language, n.
langue, fr. n.
Latin, adj.
Latin, n.
linguist, n.
Spanish, n.
speech, n.
tongue, n.
vulgar, n.
vulgo
Welsh, n.
word, n.
: 26

24.02
word

accent, n.
ayword, n.
court-word, n.
epithet, n.
epitheton, n.
mot, fr. n.
nayword, n.
no-verb, n.
palabra, n.
phrase, n.
phraseless, adj.

syllable, n.
term, n.
termination, n.
verbal, adj.
watchword, n.
word, n.
word, vb.
: 18

24.03
book

absey book, n.
almanac, n.
annals, n.
bible, n.
book, n.
Book of Numbers
Book of Riddles
Book of Songs and
    Sonnets
calendar, n.
chronicle, n.
Commentaries
copy, n.
folio, n.
God's book, n.
grammar, n.
holy writ, n.
hornbook, n.
Hundred Merry Tales
library, n.
love-book, n.
Metamorphoses
opus, lat. n.
Orator
prayer-book, n.
scripture, n.
volume, n.
word, n.
writ, n.
: 28

24.04
writings

bill, n.
blank, adj.
blank, n.
brief, n.
brown paper, n.
epistle, n.
epitaph, n.
humour-letter, n.
inscription, n.
instrument, n.
label, n.
label, vb.
letter, n.
letters-patent, n.
libel, n.
line, n.
love-letter, n.
love-line, n.
memorandum, n.
note, n.
pamphlet, n.
paper, n.
parchment, n.
passport, n.
posied, adj.
postscript, n.
posy, n.
precedent, n.
present, n.
prose, n.
record, n.
rhapsody, n.
schedule, n.
scrip, n.
scripture, n.
scroll, n.
sheet, n.
superscript, n.
superscription, n.
testament, n.
text, n.
title, n.

will, n.
writ, n.
: 44

24.05
list

abstract, n.
bill, n.
catalogue, n.
file, n.
inventorially, adv.
inventory, n.
inventory, vb.
list, n.
muster-book, n.
muster-file, n.
register, n.
roll, n.
rotulus, lat. n.
unregistered, adj.
unroll, vb.
: 15

24.06
print

copy, n.
edition, n.
press, n.
print, n.
print, vb.
: 5

24.07
title-leaf

argument, n.
chapter, n.
index, n.
leaf, n.
title, n.
title-leaf, n.
title-page, n.
: 7

24.08
epitome
————————

abridgement, n.
abstract, n.
brief, n.
continent, n.
epitome, n.
map, n.
method, n.
sum, n.
summary, n.
: 9

24.09
pen
————————

gall, n.
goose-pen, n.
goose-quill, n.
ink, n.
ink-horn, n.
inky, adj.
pen, n.
quill, n.
: 8

24.10
note-book
————————

calendar, n.
copy-book, n.
note-book, n.
table, n.
table-book, n.
tablet, n.
: 6

24.11
read
————————

candle-waster, n.
legere, lat. vb.
overlook, vb.
over-read, vb.

perusal, n.
peruse, vb.
read, vb.
reader, n.
: 8

24.12
write
————————

author, n.
book, vb.
chalk, vb.
character, n.
character, vb.
characterless, adj.
charactery, n.
chronicle, vb.
chronicler, n.
clerk, n.
clerkly, adj.
compile, vb.
compose, vb.
copy, vb.
court-hand, n.
engross, vb.
enrol, vb.
enschedule, vb.
hand, n.
handwriting, n.
indite, vb.
ink-horn mate, n.
inscribe, vb.
inscroll, vb.
line, n.
paper, vb.
pen, vb.
quote, vb.
record, vb.
register, vb.
Roman hand, n.
scribble, vb.
scribe, n.
scrivener, n.
secretary, n.
set, vb.

sign, vb.
stroke, n.
subscribe, vb.
table, vb.
text, vb.
text B, n.
underwrite, vb.
unregistered, adj.
write, vb.
writer, n.
writing, n.
: 47

24.13
Latin
————————

absque, lat. prep.
accommodare, lat.
  vb.
accusativus, lat. n.
aconitum, lat. n.
ad, lat. prep.
adesse, lat. vb.
Aeacides (2H6), lat.
aer, lat. n.
aio, lat. vb.
alere, lat. vb.
alius, lat. n.
Anglia, lat.
animus, lat. n.
antiquus, lat. adj.
apex, lat. n.
Apollo, lat.
arcus, lat. n.
artus, lat. n.
audire, lat. vb.
aut, lat. conj.
bene, lat. adv.
benedicite, lat. int.
bis, lat. adv.
bonus, lat. adj.
brevis, lat. adj.
Brutus, lat.
caelestis, lat. adj.
caelum, lat. n.

candidatus, lat. n.
canis, lat. n.
capere, lat. vb.
carere, lat. vb.
cavere, lat. vb.
celsus, lat. adj.
citus, lat. adj.
coquere, lat. vb.
coram, lat. prep.
credere, lat. vb.
cucullus, lat. n.
cum, lat. prep.
dea, lat. n.
deus, lat. n.
dies, lat. n.
diluculum, lat. n.
dominator, lat. n.
dominus, lat. n.
ecce, lat. int.
egere, lat. vb.
ego, lat. pron.
eo, lat. adv.
erga, lat. prep.
esse, lat. vb.
et, lat. conj.
exigere, lat. vb.
extinguere, lat. vb.
facere, lat. vb.
facile, lat. adv.
fas, lat. n.
fatuus, lat. adj.
fides, lat. n.
filius, lat. n.
finis, lat. n.
Francia, lat.
frater, lat. n.
furor, lat. n.
gaudere, lat. vb.
gelidus, lat. adj.
genitivus, lat. n.
gens, lat. n.
haud, lat. adv.
heres, lat. n.
hic, lat. adv.
hic, lat. pron.

homo, lat. n.
iaculum, lat. n.
idem, lat. pron.
ignis, lat. n.
imitari, lat. vb.
imprimere, lat. vb.
in, lat. prep.
integer, lat. adj.
integritas, lat. n.
intelligere, lat. vb.
intrare, lat. vb.
invitus, lat. adj.
ipse, lat. pron.
ira, lat. n.
ire, lat. vb.
iste, lat. pron.
Iupiter, lat.
lapis, lat. n.
laus, lat. n.
legere, lat. vb.
lentus, lat. adj.
leo-natus, lat.
loqui, lat. vb.
lux, lat. n.
magnus, lat. adj.
majestas, lat. n.
malus, lat. adj.
manes, lat. n.
manus, lat. n.
Mars, lat.
Maurus, lat. n.
medicus, lat. n.
mehercle, lat. int.
mens, lat. n.
meus, lat. pron.
minime, lat. adv.
mollis, lat. adj.
monachus, lat. n.
mons, lat. n.
mulier, lat. n.
multi, lat. adj.
ne, lat. adv.
ne, lat. part.
nec, lat. conj.
nefas, lat. n.

nihil, lat. n.
nominativus, lat. n.
non, lat. adv.
nos, lat. pron.
noscere, lat. vb.
noster, lat. pron.
nubes, lat. n.
occupare, lat. vb.
omnis, lat. adj.
opus, lat. n.
ostentare, lat. vb.
paedagogus, lat. n.
paene, lat. adv.
parvus, lat. adj.
pater, lat. n.
paucus, lat. adj.
pecus, lat. n.
per, lat. prep.
pergere, lat. vb.
plebeii, lat. n.
polus, lat. n.
pompa, lat. n.
posse, lat. vb.
praeclarus, lat. adj.
precari, lat. vb.
Priamus, lat.
primo, lat. adv.
privilegium, lat. n.
pro, lat. prep.
provehere, lat. vb.
pueritia, lat. n.
pulcher, lat. adj.
purus, lat. adj.
quam, lat. adv.
quando, lat. conj.
quare, lat. adv.
que, lat. conj.
qui, lat. pron.
quire, lat. vb.
quis, lat. pron.
quo, lat. adv.
quoniam, lat. conj.
redimere, lat. vb.
regia, lat. n.
regina, lat. n.

relinquere, lat. vb.
respicere, lat. vb.
rex, lat. n.
Romanus, lat. n.
rotulus, lat. n.
ruminare, lat. vb.
salicus, lat. adj.
sanctus, lat. adj.
sanguis, lat. n.
sapere, lat. vb.
satis, lat. adv.
scelus, lat. n.
se, lat. pron.
secundo, lat. adv.
semper, lat. adv.
senex, lat. n.
serenissimus, lat. adj.
sic, lat. adv.
sigeius, lat. adj.
signum, lat. n.
singulariter, lat. adv.
solus, lat. adj.
spectare, lat. vb.
spes, lat. n.
stare, lat. vb.
stuprum, lat. n.
stygius, lat. adj.
sub, lat. prep.
succedere, lat. vb.
sufficere, lat. vb.
summa, lat. n.
surgere, lat. vb.
tam, lat. adv.
tamquam, lat. conj.
tandem, lat. adv.
tantus, lat. adj.
tellus, lat. n.
terra, lat. n.
tertio, lat. adv.
timor, lat. n.
tu, lat. pron.
tuus, lat. pron.
ubique, lat. adv.
umbra, lat. n.
usque, lat. adv.

vehere, lat. vb.
venire, lat. vb.
verbum, lat. n.
via, lat. n.
videre, lat. vb.
vincere, lat. vb.
vir, lat. n.
vita, lat. n.
vivere, lat. vb.
vivus, lat. adj.
vocare, lat. vb.
vocativus, lat. n.
vox, lat. n.
  : 221

24.14
French
─────────────
à, fr. prep.
abaisser, fr. vb.
affaire, fr. n.
ainsi, fr. adv.
air, fr. n.
aller, fr. vb.
amour, fr. n.
ange, fr. n.
anglais, fr. n.
Angleterre, fr.
appeler, fr. vb.
apprendre, fr. vb.
assez, fr. adv.
aucun, fr. pron.
aussi, fr. adv.
autre, fr. adj.
avoir, fr. vb.
bailler, fr. vb.
baiser, fr. vb.
bataille, fr. n.
beau, fr. adj.
bien, fr. adv.
boîte, fr. n.
bon, fr. adj.
bourbier, fr. n.
bras, fr. n.
brave, fr. adj.

ça, fr. adv.
capitaine, fr. n.
car, fr. conj.
ce, fr. pron.
chaud, fr. adj.
cher, fr. adj.
cheval, fr. n.
chevalier, fr. n.
chez, fr. prep.
chien, fr. n.
ciel, fr. n.
col, fr. n.
commander, fr. vb.
comme, fr. conj.
comment, fr. pron.
content, fr. adj.
contre, fr. prep.
corruptible, fr. adj.
coude, fr. n.
couper, fr. vb.
cour, fr. n.
couronner, fr. vb.
coutume, fr. n.
dame, fr. n.
de, fr. prep.
déesse, fr. n.
déjà, fr. adv.
demoiselle, fr. n.
dépècher, fr. vb.
dès, fr. prep.
deux, fr. num.
deux cents, fr. num.
devant, fr. prep.
diable, fr. n.
dieu, fr. n.
difficile, fr. adj.
diner, fr. vb.
dire, fr. vb.
disposer, fr. vb.
distingué, fr. adj.
divin, fr. adj.
doigt, fr. n.
donc, fr. adv.
donner, fr. vb.
douter, fr. vb.

droit, fr. adj.
eau, fr. n.
échapper, fr, vb.
écolier, fr. n.
écouter, fr. vb.
écu, fr. n.
elle, fr. pron.
en, fr. prep.
encore, fr. adv.
enseigner, fr. vb.
ensemble, fr. adv.
entendre, fr. vb.
entre, fr. prep.
espérance, fr. n.
estimer, vb.
et, fr. conj.
être, fr. vb.
excellent, fr. adj.
excuser, fr. vb.
fable, fr. n.
faire, fr. vb.
falloir, fr. vb.
faux, fr. adj.
feu, fr. n.
fils, fr. n.
fin, fr. n.
fois, fr. n.
force, fr. n.
fort, fr. adv.
fortune, fr. n.
français, fr. n.
France, fr.
franchisement, fr. n.
gagner, fr. vb.
garçon, fr. n.
garder, fr. vb.
genou, fr. n.
gens, fr. n.
gentilhomme, fr. n.
gorge, fr. n.
grace, fr. n.
grand, fr. adj.
grandeur, fr. n.
gros, fr. adj.
héritier, fr. n.

heure, fr. n.
heureux, fr. adj.
homme, fr. n.
honneur, fr. n.
honnir, fr. vb.
ici, fr. adv.
il, fr. pron.
impossible, fr. adj.
impudique, fr. adj.
indigne, fr. adj.
je, fr. pron.
jour, fr. n.
jurement, fr. n.
là, fr. adv.
la, fr. art.
laisser, fr. vb.
langage, fr. n.
langue, fr. n.
laver, fr. vb.
le, fr. art.
leçon, fr. n.
lequel, fr. pron.
leur, fr. pron.
liberté, fr. n.
madame, fr. n.
main, fr. n.
mais, fr. conj.
maison, fr. n.
mal, fr. adv.
mauvais, fr. adj.
méchant, fr. adj.
menton, fr. n.
mettre, fr. vb.
mien, fr. pron.
mille, fr. num.
miséricorde, fr. n.
mon, fr. pron.
monde, fr. n.
monsieur, fr. n.
monter, fr. vb.
mort, fr. n.
mot, fr. n.
narine, fr. n.
natif, fr. n.
néanmoins, fr. adv.

ne pas, fr. adv.
ne point, fr. adv.
noce, fr. n.
non, fr. adv.
notre, fr. pron.
nous, fr. pron.
O, fr. int.
oeuvre, fr. n.
ongle, fr. n.
oublier, fr. vb.
oui, fr. adv.
par, fr. prep.
pardonner, fr. vb.
parler, fr. vb.
pauvre, fr. adj.
paysan, fr. n.
penser, fr. vb.
perdre, fr. vb.
père, fr. n.
permafoy, fr. int.
petit, fr. adj.
peu, fr. n.
pied, fr. n.
pitié, fr. n.
plein, fr. adj.
plus, fr. adv.
possession, fr. n.
pour, fr. prep.
pourquoi, fr. adv.
prendre, fr. vb.
présent, fr. n.
prêt, fr. adj.
prier, fr. vb.
prisonnier, fr. n.
promettre, fr. vb.
promptement, fr. adv.
prononcer, fr. vb.
propre, fr. adj.
puis, fr. adv.
puissant, fr. adj.
qualité, fr. n.
quand, fr. conj.
que, fr. conj.
que, fr. pron.
question, fr. n.

qui, fr. pron.
réciter, fr. vb.
remerciement, fr. n.
répétition, fr. n.
retourner, fr. vb.
rien, fr. pron.
robe, fr. n.
roi, fr. n.
sans, fr. prep.
sauf, fr. prep.
seigneur, fr. n.
semblable, fr. adj.
serviteur, fr. n.
si, fr. conj.
soldat, fr. n.
son, fr. n.
son, fr. pron.
souvenir, fr. vb.
suivre, fr. vb.
supplier, fr. vb.
sur, fr. prep.
temps, fr. n.
terre, fr. n.
tomber, fr. vb.
ton, fr. pron.
tout, fr. adj.
tout, fr. pron.
très, fr. adv.
tromperie, fr. n.
trop, fr. adv.
truie, fr. n.
tu, fr. pron.
un, fr. art.
une, fr. art.
user, fr. vb.
vaillant, fr. adj.
vérité, fr. n.
vert, fr. n.
vie, fr. n.
vitement, fr. adv.
vivant, fr. adj.
vivre, fr. vb.
voir, fr. vb.
voler, fr. vb.
vomissement, fr. n.

votre, fr. pron.
vouloir, fr. vb.
vous, fr. pron.
vraiment, fr. adv.
y, fr. adv.
: 257

24.15
Italian

a, it. prep.
basta, it. int.
buono, it. adj.
canto, it. n.
capocchia, it. n.
casa, it. n.
che, it. conj.
chi, it. pron.
con, it. prep.
coraggio, it. int.
cuore, it. n.
de, it. prep.
diabolo, it. n.
dolcezza, it. n.
fortuna, it. n.
forza, it. n.
guerra, it. n.
il, it. art.
io, it. pron.
la, it. art.
mio, it. pron.
molto, it. adv.
non, it. adv.
nostro, it. pron.
onorare, it. vb.
per, it. prep.
perdonare, it. vb.
più, it. adv.
prezzare, it. vb.
signor, it. n.
tu, it. pron.
tutto, it. adj.
vedere, it. vb.
venire, it. vb.
: 34

24.16
foreign phrases

[ad] unguem
alla stoccata
ben trovato
ben venuto
bon jour
bonos dies
Chi passa
Dieu vous garde
et cetera
hic jacet
hysterica passio
ignis fatuus
in capite
ipso facto
limbo patrum
ma foi
medius fidius
memento mori
Non Nobis
per se
pia mater
pocas palabras
punto reverso
suum cuique
Te Deum
tremor cordis
viva voce
: 27

24.17
pseudo foreign

acordo
boblibindo
bosko
boskos
calen
cargo
castiliano
chicurmurco
chimurcho
contenta, vb.

contento, vb.
corbo
custure
ducdame
dulche
honorificabilitudini-
tas, n.
kerelybonto
linta
manka
me
movousus
O
oscorbidulchos
par
portotartarossa
revania
si, conj.
sperato, n.
spero, n.
throca
thromuldo
tormenta, vb.
tormente, vb.
vauvado
villianda
volivorco
vulgo
: 37

24.18
malapropism

aggravate
(MND 1.2.81), vb.
agitation
(MV 3.5.4), n.
auspicious
(ADO 3.5.46), adj.
benefactor
(MM 2.1.50), n.
calm
(2H4 2.4.36), n.
cannibal
(2H4 2.4.166), n.

cardinally
(MM 2.1.80), adv.
collusion
(LLL 4.2.42), n.
commonty
(SHR in.2.138), n.
comprehend
(ADO 3.5.25), vb.
conceal
(WIV 4.5.45), vb.
confidence
(ADO 3.5.2), n.
confirmity
(2H4 2.4.58), n.
confusion
(MV 2.2.37), n.
contempt
(LLL 1.1.190), n.
coram
(WIV 1.1.6), n.
corporate
(2H4 3.2.220), adj.
courageous
(WIV 4.1.4), adj.
decern
(ADO 3.5.3), vb.
decrease
(WIV 1.1.247), vb.
defect
(MV 2.2.143), n.
desolation
(LLL 1.2.160), n.
detest
(MM 2.1.69), vb.
disfigure
(MND 3.1.60), vb.
dissembly
(ADO 4.2.1), n.
dissolutely
(WIV 1.1.252), adv.
dissolve
(WIV 1.1.251), vb.
distant
(MM 2.1.92), adj.
erection

(WIV 3.5.40), n.
excepting
(ADO 3.5.30), prep.
exclamation
(ADO 3.5.25), n.
excommunication
(ADO 3.5.63), n.
exhibit
(MV 2.3.10), vb.
exhibition
(ADO 4.2.5), n.
exposition
(MND 4.1.39), n.
extraordinarily
(2H4 2.4.24), adv.
falliable
(ANT 5.2.257), adj.
fartuous
(WIV 2.2.97), adj.
frutify
(MV 2.2.134), vb.
gibbet-maker
(TIT 4.3.80), n.
hang-hog
(WIV 4.1.48), n.
Hannibal
(MM 2.1.175)
honeyseed
(2H4 2.1.52), n.
honeysuckle
(2H4 2.1.50), n.
immortal
(ANT 5.2.247), adj.
impertinent
(MV 2.2.137), adj.
incardinate
(TN 5.1.182), adj.
incarnation
(MV 2.2.27), n.
indite
(ROM 2.4.129), vb.
infection
(WIV 2.2.115), n.
Jinny
(WIV 4.1.62)

obscenely
(LLL 4.1.143,
MND 1.2.108), adv.
obstacle
(1H6 5.4.17), n.
odious
(MND 3.1.82), adj.
odorous
(ADO 3.5.16), adj.
opinion
(ADO 4.2.67), vb.
passionate
(R3 1.4.118), adj.
piety
(ADO 4.2.78), n.
pollution
(LLL 4.2.46), n.
Pompion
(LLL 5.2.502)
possitable
(WIV 1.1.236), adj.
preposterous
(WT 5.2.148), adj.
prodigious
(TGV 2.3.3), adj.
prohibit
(ADO 5.1.326), vb.
rebuse
(SHR 1.2.6), vb.
recover
(ADO 3.3.167), vb.
reform
(ADO 5.1.254), vb.
reprehend
(LLL 1.1.183), vb.
reproach
(MV 2.5.20), vb.
respect
(MM 2.1.162), vb.
se offendendo
(HAM 5.1.9)
statue
(ADO 3.3.79), n.
suffigance
(ADO 3.5.52), n.

suppose
(MM 2.1.155), vb.
suspect
(ADO 4.2.75), vb.
tolerable
(ADO 3.3.36), adj.
vigitant
(ADO 3.3.94), adj.
: 77

24.19
crux
─────────────

an-heires, n.
arm-gaunt, adj.
brake, n.
ducdame
Humphrey Hour
mastic, n.
mered, adj.
miching malicho, n.
mock-water, n.
oney'rs, n.
prenzie, adj.
pugging, adj.
scamel, n.
scarre, n.
Strachy
tirrit, n.
windring, adj.
: 17

24.20
conversation
─────────────

accent, n.
aforesaid, adj.
aio, lat. vb.
babble, n.
babble, vb.
bespeak, vb.
bibble-babble, n.
blab, vb.
break a word, vb.
breath, n.

breathe, vb.
bruit, vb.
carry-tale, n.
chat, n.
chat, vb.
chatter, vb.
comment, vb.
commune, vb.
communication, n.
confer, vb.
conference, n.
confession, n.
conversation, n.
converse, n.
crack, vb.
dialogue, n.
dialogue, vb.
dire, fr. vb.
discourse, n.
discourse, vb.
discourser, n.
discuss, vb.
disputation, n.
double, vb.
drawl, vb.
expostulate, vb.
expostulation, n.
express, vb.
false-speaking, adj.
forename, vb.
foresaid, adj.
gabble, vb.
gibber, vb.
gossip, vb.
grumble, vb.
grumbling, n.
honey, vb.
lip, n.
long-tongued, adj.
loqui, lat. vb.
love-discourse, n.
love-prate, n.
mention, n.
mention, vb.
mince, vb.

mis-speak, vb.
mouth, n.
mouth, vb.
mouth-honour, n.
mouth-made, adj.
mumble, vb.
mumble-news, n.
murmur, vb.
mutter, vb.
noise, n.
outspeak, vb.
out-talk, vb.
out-tongue, vb.
out-voice, vb.
parle, n.
parle, vb.
parler, fr. vb.
parley, n.
parley, vb.
pass, vb.
prate, n.
prate, vb.
prater, n.
prattle, n.
prattle, vb.
prattler, n.
pribble, n.
prononcer, fr. vb.
pronounce, vb.
quoth, vb.
rave, vb.
respeak, vb.
reword, vb.
say, vb.
smatter, vb.
sound, n.
sound, vb.
speak, vb.
speaker, n.
speech, n.
spend, vb.
table-talk, n.
talk, n.
talk, vb.
talker, n.

tattle, n.
tattle, vb.
tattling, n.
thou, vb.
throat, n.
tittle-tattle, n.
tittle-tattle, vb.
tongue, n.
tongue, vb.
tuner, n.
unsay, vb.
unspeak, vb.
unspeakable, adj.
untalked, adj.
urge, vb.
venomed-mouthed,
  adj.
vent, n.
verbal, adj.
verbatim, adv.
voice, n.
voice, vb.
word, vb.
word of mouth, n.
  : 123

24.21
question • answer
─────────────
answer, n.
answer, vb.
ask, vb.
catechize, vb.
demand, vb.
hearken, vb.
inquire, n.
inquire, vb.
inquiry, n.
inquisition, n.
inquisitive, adj.
interrogatory, n.
quest, n.
question, fr. n.
question, vb.
questionable, adj.

quick-answered, adj.
reanswer, vb.
replication, n.
reply, n.
reply, vb.
retort, n.
return, n.
return, vb.
simple-answered, adj.
unanswered, adj.
unquestionable, adj.
unquestioned, adj.
  : 28

24.22
message
─────────────
account, n.
advertisement, n.
ambassade, n.
ambassage, n.
bill, n.
blazon, n.
breath, n.
bruit, n.
cital, n.
commendation, n.
comment, n.
confession, n.
definement, n.
delivery, n.
denunciation, n.
description, n.
diction, n.
embassy, n.
errand, n.
expressure, n.
fame, n.
giving-out, n.
greeting, n.
hearsay, n.
history, n.
house of fame, n.
impartment, n.
information, n.

instruction, n.
intelligence, n.
intelligencer, n.
interjection, n.
jerk, n.
love-news, n.
message, n.
messenger, n.
murmur, n.
news, n.
noise, n.
notice, n.
oration, n.
orator, n.
oratory, n.
oyez, n.
peroration, n.
process, n.
proclamation, n.
publication, n.
recountment, n.
relation, n.
renown, n.
report, n.
rhetoric, n.
rumour, n.
rumourer, n.
speech, n.
spokesman, n.
story, n.
tale, n.
text, n.
theme, n.
tiding, n.
treatise, n.
utterance, n.
vent, n.
volley, n.
whispering, n.
wind, n.
word, n.
word, vb.
 : 70

24.23
messenger
————————
ambassade, n.
ambassador, n.
ambassage, n.
bearer, n.
carrier, n.
courier, n.
embassy, n.
forerunner, n.
fore-spurrer, n.
harbinger, n.
herald, n.
Iris
messenger, n.
missive, n.
nuncio, n.
post, n.
pursuivant, n.
vaunt-courier, n.
woman-post, n.
 : 19

24.24
verbal • silent
————————
bite the tongue (lip),
 vb.
chewet, n.
clamour, vb.
close-tongued, adj.
dumb, adj.
dumb, n.
dumb, vb.
dumb-discoursive,
 adj.
dumbly, adv.
dumbness, n.
fair-spoken, adj.
foul-spoken, adj.
gag, vb.
hold [one's] peace,
 vb.
honey-mouthed, adj.

honey-tongued, adj.
humble-mouthed,
 adj.
hush, adj.
hush, vb.
languageless, adj.
lewd-tongued, adj.
maiden-tongued, adj.
mum, adj.
mum, n.
mum, vb.
mute, adj.
mute, n.
noiseless, adj.
peace, vb.
phraseless, adj.
prolixity, n.
self-breath, n.
silence, n.
silence, vb.
silent, adj.
silently, adv.
smooth-tongue, n.
soundless, adj.
speechless, adj.
still, adj.
still, adv.
still, vb.
stillness, n.
stilly, adv.
stretch-mouthed, adj.
taciturnity, n.
termless, adj.
tongued, adj.
tongueless, adj.
tongue-tie, vb.
unexpressive, adj.
unquestionable, adj.
unspeak, vb.
unspeakable, adj.
unspeaking, adj.
verbal, adj.
verbosity, n.
volubility, n.
voluble, adj.

well-spoken, adj.
windy, adj.
wordless, adj.
 : 62

24.25
make known
————————
acknowledge, vb.
acquaint, vb.
advertise, vb.
advise, vb.
allegation, n.
allege, vb.
all-telling, adj.
assure, vb.
aver, vb.
avouch, vb.
avow, vb.
blaze, vb.
blazon, vb.
blurt, vb.
bruit, vb.
certify, vb.
cite, vb.
commend, vb.
communicate, vb.
confess, vb.
convey, vb.
couch, vb.
cry, vb.
declare, vb.
deliver, vb.
deliverance, n.
denounce, vb.
descant, n.
descant, vb.
describe, vb.
description, vb.
dilate, vb.
dilation, n.
discourse, vb.
divulge, vb.
expressive, adj.
fame, vb.

fore-recited, adj.
foretell, vb.
give, vb.
give out, phr. vb.
giver, n.
groan, vb.
herald, vb.
history, vb.
ill-uttering, adj.
impart, vb.
import, vb.
infer, vb.
inference, n.
inform, vb.
informer, n.
instruct, vb.
intelligencing, adj.
intelligent, adj.
learn, vb.
maintain, vb.
misreport, vb.
newsmonger, n.
noise, vb.
notify, vb.
object, vb.
open, vb.
outspeak, vb.
partake, vb.
perfect, vb.
phrase, vb.
plead, vb.
pleader, n.
possess, vb.
present, vb.
pretend, vb.
proclaim, vb.
profess, vb.
profession, n.
professor, n.
promise, vb.
pronounce, vb.
propose, n.
propose, vb.
protest, n.
protest, vb.

protestation, n.
protester, n.
protesting, n.
provulgate, vb.
publication, n.
publish, vb.
publisher, n.
put, vb.
reason, vb.
recite, vb.
réciter, fr. vb.
recommend, vb.
recount, vb.
rehearsal, n.
rehearse, vb.
reiterate, vb.
relate, vb.
render, vb.
repeat, vb.
repetition, n.
répétition, fr. n.
report, vb.
reporter, n.
reportingly, adv.
resolve, vb.
retail, vb.
retell, vb.
rumour, vb.
signify, vb.
speak, vb.
specify, vb.
spend, vb.
story, vb.
swear, vb.
tell, vb.
teller, n.
tell-tale, n.
true-telling, adj.
twice-told, adj.
unbreathed, adj.
unburden, vb.
undivulged, adj.
unload, vb.
unpack, vb.
unpublished, adj.

unrecounted, adj.
unspoken, adj.
untold, adj.
urge, vb.
utter, vb.
vent, vb.
voice, vb.
vouch, vb.
vow, vb.
word, vb.
yield, vb.
  : 138

24.26
gesture
————————

beck, n.
beck, vb.
beckon, vb.
bite thumb at, vb.
blink, vb.
blush, n.
blush, vb.
connive, vb.
eye-wink, n.
fico, n.
fig, n.
fig, vb.
figo, n.
frown, n.
frown, vb.
frowningly, adv.
gape, vb.
gesture, n.
headshake, n.
lour, vb.
make a mouth, vb.
mop, n.
mop, vb.
mow, n.
mow, vb.
nod, n.
nod, vb.
out-frown, vb.
pink, adj.

pout, vb.
pouting, n.
scowl, vb.
scrawl, vb.
shrug, n.
shrug, vb.
waft, vb.
wafture, n.
wave, vb.
wink, n.
wink, vb.
yawn, vb.
  : 41

24.27
sign
————————

badge, n.
badge, vb.
beacon, n.
brand, n.
brand, vb.
caract, n.
crest, n.
death-marked, adj.
death-token, n.
denote, vb.
denotement, n.
elvish-marked, adj.
emblem, n.
favour, n.
figure, vb.
impression, n.
impressure, n.
line, n.
love-token, n.
manual seal, n.
mark, n.
mark, vb.
note, n.
note, vb.
office-badge, n.
prick, n.
prick, vb.
recognizance, n.

seal, n.
seal manual, n.
sign, n.
sign, vb.
signal, n.
significant, n.
signum, lat. n.
star, n.
streak, n.
symbol, n.
token, n.
token, vb.
type, n.
unsealed, adj.
war-marked, adj.
watchword, n.
: 44

24.28
disclose
—————————
betray, vb.
bewray, vb.
break, vb.
cipher, vb.
decipher, vb.
discase, vb.

disclose, vb.
divulge, vb.
open, adj.
open, vb.
opener, n.
overture, n.
reveal, vb.
show, vb.
unbolt, vb.
unbosom, vb.
uncape, vb.
unclasp, vb.
uncover, vb.
unfold, vb.
unhidden, adj.
unmask, vb.
unsecret, adj.
unveil, vb.
: 24

24.29
conceal
—————————
all-hiding, adj.
bescreen, vb.
bosom, vb.
cave-keeping, adj.

cloak, vb.
close, adj.
closely, adv.
conceal, vb.
concealment, n.
couch, vb.
cover, vb.
covert, adj.
covertly, adv.
dark, adj.
darkly, adv.
disguise, vb.
ensconce, vb.
fell-lurking, adj.
hide, vb.
hood, vb.
hugger-mugger, n.
immask, vb.
inscrutable, adj.
inward, adj.
long-hid, adj.
lurch, vb.
lurk, vb.
lurking-place, n.
mask, vb.
mystery, n.
obscure, vb.

occult, vb.
pocket, vb.
privacy, n.
private, adj.
privily, adv.
privity, n.
privy, adj.
scarf, vb.
screen, vb.
secrecy, n.
secret, adj.
secret, n.
secretly, adv.
self-covered, adj.
shade, vb.
shadow, vb.
shroud, vb.
sin-concealing, adj.
skulk, vb.
stealth, n.
stealthy, adj.
underhand, adj.
undivulged, adj.
veil, vb.
vizard, vb.
: 56

25.01
education

---

art, n.
breed, vb.
breeding, n.
bring up, phr. vb.
bringing-up, n.
catechism, n.
catechize, vb.
commence, vb.
con, vb.
disciple, vb.
discipline, n.
discipline, vb.
doctrine, n.
document, n.
edify, vb.
educate, vb.
education, n.
enseigner, fr. vb.
erudition, n.
good letters, n.
illiterate, adj.
illiterate, n.
ill-nurtured, adj.
inform, vb.
instruct, vb.
instruction, n.
knowledge, n.
learn, vb.
learned, adj.
learnedly, adv.
learning, n.
leçon, fr. n.
lecture, n.
lesson, n.
lesson, vb.
lettered, adj.
letters, n.
liberal arts, n.
literatured, adj.
nurture, n.
nuzzle, vb.
practise, vb.

preach, vb.
read, vb.
reading, n.
rear, vb.
school, n.
school, vb.
school-doing, n.
sermon, vb.
studious, adj.
study, n.
teach, vb.
train, vb.
tutor, vb.
unbookish, adj.
uneducated, adj.
unlearned, adj.
unlessoned, adj.
unlettered, adj.
unread, adj.
unschooled, adj.
untaught, adj.
untrained, adj.
untutored, adj.
well-educated, adj.
well-entered, adj.
well-learned, adj.
 : 68

25.02
teacher

---

artist, n.
artsman, n.
bookish, adj.
bookman, n.
by the book, adv.
clerk, n.
clerk-like, adj.
clerkly, adj.
doctor, n.
doctor-like, adj.
domine, n.
master, n.
paedagogus, lat. n.
parrot-teacher, n.

pedant, n.
pedantical, adj.
pedascule, n.
scholar, n.
scholarly, adj.
schoolmaster, n.
teacher, n.
tutor, n.
unpractised, adj.
 : 23

25.03
student

---

book-mate, n.
breeching scholar, n.
disciple, n.
écolier, fr. n.
pupil, n.
pupil-like, adj.
scholar, n.
scholarly, adj.
schoolboy, n.
schoolfellow, n.
school-maid, n.
sectary, n.
student, n.
 : 13

25.04
school

---

academe, n.
charge-house, n.
dancing-school, n.
grammar school, n.
learning place, n.
Oxford
school, n.
taming-school, n.
university, n.
unschooled, adj.
Wittenberg
 : 11

25.05
science • philosophy

---

alchemist, n.
alchemy, n.
Aristotle
astronomer, n.
astronomical, adj.
astronomy, n.
element, n.
Epicurus
grand liquor, n.
mathematics, n.
medicine, n.
metaphysics, n.
moral, adj.
moral, vb.
moralize, vb.
moraller, n.
philosopher, n.
philosopher's stone,
    n.
philosophical, adj.
philosophy, n.
Pythagoras
science, n.
Socrates
star-gazer, n.
stoic, n.
tinct, n.
 : 26

25.06
maxim

---

adage, n.
ayword, n.
by-word, n.
country proverb, n.
doctrine, n.
instance, n.
instruction, n.
maxim, n.
moral, n.
nayword, n.

precept, n.
preceptial, adj.
principle, n.
proverb, n.
proverb, vb.
rule, n.
saw, n.
saying, n.
sentence, n.
sententious, adj.
word, n.
: 21

25.07
alphabet

A, n.
abc, n.
alphabet, n.
alphabetical, adj.
B, n.
C, n.
cross-row, n.
D, n.
dominical, n.
E, n.
figure, n.
G, n.
H, n.
I, n.
L, n.
letter, n.
M, n.
O, n.
P, n.
R, n.
red letter, n.
Roman letter, n.
T, n.
U, n.
zed, n.
: 25

25.08
grammar

accidence, n.
accusative, adj.
accusativus, lat. n.
apostrophus, n.
article, n.
case, n.
comma, n.
consonant, n.
dash, n.
declension, n.
decline, vb.
full point, n.
gender, n.
genitive, adj.
genitivus, lat. n.
grammar, n.
nominativus, lat. n.
noun, n.
no-verb, n.
number, n.
orthography, n.
period, n.
plural, n.
point, n.
Priscian
pronoun, n.
sentence, n.
singulariter, lat. adv.
spell, vb.
stop, n.
verb, n.
verbum, lat. n.
vocative, n.
vocativus, lat. n.
vowel, n.
: 35

25.09
rhetoric

Artemidorus
comparison, n.

eloquence, n.
eloquent, adj.
figure, n.
hyperbole, n.
hyperbolical, adj.
metaphor, n.
oration, n.
orator, n.
oratory, n.
peroration, n.
phrase, n.
rhetoric, n.
simile, n.
speaker, n.
Strato
style, n.
tropically, adv.
: 19

25.10
adverb

about, adv.
again, adv.
anyway, adv.
as, adv.
by, adv.
ça, fr. adv.
else, adv.
eo, lat. adv.
hereby, adv.
herein, adv.
hereof, adv.
hereupon, adv.
hob nob, adv.
in, adv.
in lieu, adv.
instead, adv.
more above, adv.
on, adv.
out, adv.
over, adv.
over and above, adv.
quam, lat. adv.
quo, lat. adv.

so, adv.
tam, lat. adv.
tandem, lat. adv.
the, adv.
then, adv.
there, adv.
thereat, adv.
thereby, adv.
therein, adv.
thereof, adv.
thereon, adv.
thereto, adv.
thereunto, adv.
therewith, adv.
therewithal, adv.
this, adv.
thorough, adv.
through, adv.
thus, adv.
to, adv.
toward, adv.
up^1, adv.
up^2, adv.
upon, adv.
usque, lat. adv.
well, adv.
what, adv.
whereat, adv.
whereby, adv.
wherein, adv.
whereinto, adv.
whereof, adv.
whereon, adv.
whereout, adv.
wherethrough, adv.
whereto, adv.
whereuntil, adv.
whereunto, adv.
whereupon, adv.
wherewith, adv.
wherewithal, adv.
withal, adv.
: 65

25.11
article

———————

a, art.
il, it. art.
la, fr. art.
la, it. art.
le, fr. art.
the, art.
un, fr. art.
une, fr. art.
: 8

25.12
conjunction

———————

afore, conj.
after, conj.
against, conj.
albeit, conj.
although, conj.
and[1], conj.
and[2], conj.
as, conj.
aut, lat. conj.
because, conj.
before, conj.
being, conj.
both, conj.
but, conj.
car, fr. conj.
che, it. conj.
comme, fr. conj.
either, conj.
ere, conj.
et, lat. conj.
et, fr. conj.
except, conj.
for, conj.
fore, conj.
for that, conj.
for why, conj.
if, conj.
in that, conj.
lest, conj.

like, conj.
mais, fr. conj.
nec, lat. conj.
neither, conj.
nor, conj.
notwithstanding,
conj.
or[1], conj.
or[2], conj.
quand, fr. conj.
quando, lat. conj.
que, lat. conj.
que, fr. conj.
quoniam, lat. conj.
save, conj.
seeing (that), conj.
si, conj.
si, fr. conj.
since, conj.
sith, conj.
sithence, conj.
so, conj.
tamquam, lat. conj.
than, conj.
that, conj.
though, conj.
till, conj.
unless, conj.
until, conj.
when, conj.
whensoever, conj.
where, conj.
whereas, conj.
whether, conj.
while, conj.
whiles, conj.
whilst, conj.
without, conj.
yet, conj.
: 67

25.13
interjection

———————

adieu, int.

ah, int.
alack, int.
alas, int.
amen, int.
avaunt, int.
ay, int.
aye, int.
backare, int.
basta, it. int.
benedicite, lat. int.
budget, int.
buzz, int.
by my faith, int.
by my fay, int.
clubs, int.
coraggio, it. int.
de, int.
do, int.
do de, int.
ecce, lat. int.
faith, int.
farewell, int.
faugh, int.
fe, int.
fie, int.
foutre, int.
fum, int.
fut, int.
God's me, int.
good now, int.
go to, int.
gramercy, int.
ha, int.
halloo, int.
he, int.
heigh, int.
heigh-ho, int.
hem, int.
hewgh, int.
hey, int.
hey-day, int.
hillo, int.
hist, int.
ho, int.
holla, int.

hollo, int.
hoo, int.
hum, int.
hush, int.
husht, int.
in faith, int.
la, int.
law, int.
lo, int.
loa, int.
loo, int.
lulla, int.
lullaby, int.
ma foi
marry, int.
medius fidius
mehercle, lat. int.
mun, int.
non, int.
nonny, int.
nonny-no, int.
O, int.
O, fr. int.
ods, int.
out, int.
out on (upon), int.
owgh, int.
pah, int.
pardie, int.
permafoy, fr. int.
pish, int.
pooh, int.
proface, int.
rah tah tah, int.
rivo, int.
sa sa, int.
soho, int.
sola, int.
soud, int.
suum, int.
thas, int.
tilly-vally, int.
tush, int.
tut, int.
via, int.

welladay, int.
well-anear, int.
westward-ho, int.
what the goodyear,
 int.
whew, int.
whist, int.
who, int.
whoa-ho-hoa, int.
whoop, int.
why, int.
woe, int.
yea, int.
 : 103

25.14
preposition

à, fr. prep.
a, it. prep.
aboard, prep.
about, prep.
above, prep.
absque, lat. prep.
according to, prep.
across, prep.
ad, lat. prep.
afore, prep.
after, prep.
against, prep.
aloft, prep.
along, prep.
amid, prep.
amidst, prep.
among, prep.
amongst, prep.
aside, prep.
askant, prep.
at, prep.
athwart, prep.
before, prep.
behind, prep.
below, prep.
beneath, prep.
beside, prep.

besides, prep.
between, prep.
betwixt, prep.
beyond, prep.
but, prep.
by, prep.
chez, fr. prep.
con, it. prep.
concerning, prep.
considering, prep.
contre, fr. prep.
coram, lat. prep.
cross, prep.
cum, lat. prep.
de, fr. prep.
de, it. prep.
dès, fr. prep.
despite, prep.
devant, fr. prep.
down, prep.
during, prep.
en, fr. prep.
entre, fr. prep.
ere, prep.
erga, lat. prep.
except, prep.
excepting, prep.
for, prep.
fore, prep.
forth, prep.
from, prep.
in, prep.
in, lat. prep.
into, prep.
maugre, prep.
midst, prep.
near, prep.
next, prep.
nigh, prep.
notwithstanding,
 prep.
of, prep.
off, prep.
on, prep.
or, prep.

out, prep.
over, prep.
par, fr. prep.
past, prep.
per, lat. prep.
per, it. prep.
pour, fr. prep.
pro, lat. prep.
respecting, prep.
round, prep.
sans, fr. prep.
sauf, fr. prep.
save, prep.
saving, prep.
since, prep.
sith, prep.
south, prep.
sub, lat. prep.
sur, fr. prep.
thorough, prep.
through, prep.
throughout, prep.
till, prep.
times, prep.
to, prep.
touching, prep.
toward, prep.
towards, prep.
under, prep.
underneath, prep.
until, prep.
unto, prep.
up, prep.
upon, prep.
up-till, prep.
while, prep.
with, prep.
withal, prep.
within, prep.
without, prep.
 : 111

25.15
pronoun
---

all-thing, pron.
another, pron.
any, pron.
anybody, pron.
anyone, pron.
anything, pron.
aucun, fr. pron.
both, pron.
ce, fr. pron.
che, pron.
chi, it. pron.
comment, fr. pron.
each, pron.
each other, pron.
ego, lat. pron.
either, pron.
elle, fr. pron.
everyone, pron.
everything, pron.
he, pron.
hem, pron.
her, pron.
hers, pron.
herself, pron.
hic, lat. pron.
himself, pron.
his[1], pron.
his[2], pron.
I, pron.
idem, lat. pron.
il, fr. pron.
io, it. pron.
ipse, lat. pron.
iste, lat. pron.
it, pron.
its, pron.
itself, pron.
je, fr. pron.
lequel, fr. pron.
leur, fr. pron.
meus, lat. pron.
mien, fr. pron.

143

mine, pron.
mio, it. pron.
mon, fr. pron.
my, pron.
myself, pron.
neither, pron.
nobody, pron.
none, pron.
nos, lat. pron.
noster, lat. pron.
nostro, it. pron.
nothing, pron.
notre, fr. pron.
nous, fr. pron.
one, pron.
one another, pron.
other, pron.
our, pron.
ours, pron.

ourself, pron.
ourselves, pron.
que, fr. pron.
qui, lat. pron.
qui, fr. pron.
quis, lat. pron.
rien, fr. pron.
same, pron.
se, lat. pron.
she, pron.
some, pron.
somebody, pron.
someone, pron.
something, pron.
son, fr. pron.
such, pron.
such-like, pron.
that[1], pron.
that[2], pron.

their, pron.
theirs, pron.
themselves, pron.
they, pron.
thine, pron.
this, pron.
thou, pron.
thy, pron.
thyself, pron.
ton, fr. pron.
tout, fr. pron.
tu, lat. pron.
tu, it. pron.
tu, fr. pron.
tuus, lat. pron.
votre, fr. pron.
vous, fr. pron.
we, pron.
what, pron.

whatever, pron.
whatsoever, pron.
whatsomever, pron.
whether, pron.
which, pron.
who, pron.
whoever, pron.
whoso, pron.
whosoever, pron.
whosomever, pron.
ye, pron.
yonder, pron.
you, pron.
your, pron.
yours, pron.
yourself, pron.
yourselves, pron.
  : 116

26.01
playhouse

cockpit, n.
playhouse, n.
Pompey's Theatre
show-place, n.
theatre, n.
tiring-house, n.
wooden O, n.
 : 7

26.02
theatre

act, n.
act, vb.
action, n.
actor, n.
argument, n.
audience, n.
Basilisco-like, adj.
boy, vb.
Calipolis
Cambyses
catastrophe, n.
chorus, n.
Chorus
chorus-like, adj.
comedian, n.
comedy, n.
cue, n.
drollery, n.
dumb show, n.
epilogue, n.
groundling, n.
Herod
Hiren
historical-pastoral, n.
history, n.
Iniquity
interlude, n.
Jeronimy
jig, n.
Justice

masque, n.
mimic, n.
mock, vb.
motion, n.
mummer, n.
Murder of Gonzago
Nine Worthies, n.
out-Herod, vb.
overpart, vb.
pageant, n.
pageant, vb.
pageantry, n.
part, n.
pastoral, n.
pastoral-comical, n.
performance, n.
Plautus
play, n.
play, vb.
player, n.
prologue, n.
prologue-like, adj.
prompter, n.
rehearsal, n.
rehearse, vb.
Roscius
scene, n.
Seneca
show, n.
Soto
spectacle, n.
spectator, n.
stage, n.
stage, vb.
Termagant
tragedian, n.
tragedy, n.
tragic, adj.
tragical, adj.
tragical-comical-his-
  torical-pastoral, n.
tragical-historical, n.
Vanity
vice, n.
Vice, The   : 74

26.03
music

accord, n.
broken music, n.
care-tuned, adj.
change, n.
concord, n.
discord, n.
division, n.
dulcet, adj.
fall, n.
flourish, n.
flourish, vb.
harmonious, adj.
harmony, n.
ill-tuned, adj.
instrument, n.
jar, n.
jar, vb.
melodious, adj.
minstrelsy, n.
mort, n.
music, n.
musical, adj.
new-tuned, adj.
noise, n.
organ, n.
point, n.
recheat, n.
sad-tuned, adj.
still-discordant, adj.
strain, n.
time, n.
time, vb.
tucket, n.
tune, vb.
tuneable, adj.
unmusical, adj.
untune, vb.
untuneable, adj.
untuned, adj.
well-tuned, adj.
 : 40

26.04
gamut

A, n.
b, n.
bass, n.
C, n.
clef, n.
close, n.
crotchet, n.
d, n.
diapason, n.
e, n.
fa, n.
fa, vb.
gamut, n.
key, n.
la, n.
mean, n.
measure, n.
mi, n.
minim rest, n.
mood, n.
motion, n.
note, n.
note, vb.
re, n.
re, vb.
rest, n.
sharp, n.
sol, n.
sol, vb.
treble, n.
triplex, n.
ut, n.
 : 32

26.05
wind instrument

bagpipe, n.
blast, n.
bugle, n.
drone, n.
eunuch, n.

fife, n.
flute, n.
hautboy, n.
horn, n.
hornpipe, n.
Lincolnshire bagpipe,
  n.
pipe, n.
pipe, vb.
recorder, n.
sackbut, n.
sheep-whistling, adj.
stop, n.
trump, n.
trumpet, n.
trumpet, vb.
ventage, n.
whistle, n.
whistle, vb.
wind instrument, n.
  : 24

26.06
fiddle
_____

bass-string, n.
bass-viol, n.
calves'-gut, n.
catling, n.
cittern-head, n.
fiddle, n.
fiddlestick, n.
fret, n.
fret, vb.
harp, n.
horsehair, n.
jack, n.
key, n.
lute, n.
lute-case, n.
lute-string, n.
peg, n.
psaltery, n.
sticking place, n.
stop, n.

string, n.
string, vb.
stringless, adj.
unstringed, adj.
viol, n.
viol da gamba, n.
wiry, adj.
wrest, n.
  : 28

26.07
bell
_____

alarm-bell, n.
bell, n.
bells of St. Bennet,
  n.
clapper, n.
curfew-bell, n.
funeral bell, n.
larum-bell, n.
market bell, n.
passing bell, n.
sacring-bell, n.
tongue, n.
warning bell, n.
  : 12

26.08
other instruments
_____

bone, n.
chip, n.
cymbal, n.
drum, n.
drum, vb.
kettle, n.
kettledrum, n.
rattle, n.
tabor, n.
taborin, n.
tongs, n.
virginal, n.
virginal, vb.
  : 13

26.09
musician
_____

bagpiper, n.
bard, n.
breast, n.
chant, vb.
choir, n.
choir, vb.
consort, n.
descant, vb.
Dowland
drummer, n.
feign, vb.
fiddle, vb.
fiddler, n.
harper, n.
jig, vb.
jig-maker, n.
leader, n.
minstrel, n.
minstrelsy, n.
music, n.
musician, n.
noise, n.
out-breast, vb.
piper, n.
play, vb.
record, vb.
relish, vb.
sing, vb.
singer, n.
singing-man, n.
song-man, n.
taborer, n.
troll, vb.
trumpet, n.
trumpeter, n.
tuner, n.
warble, vb.
  : 37

26.10
song
_____

adown, adv.
air, n.
anthem, n.
ballad, n.
burden, n.
burden-wise, adv.
canto, it. n.
canzonet, n.
carol, n.
catch, n.
chanson, n.
Chi passa
Concolinel
Cophetua
derry, n.
descant, n.
dildo, n.
dirge, n.
ditty, n.
down, adv.
down, n.
ducdame
dump, n.
fading, n.
fancy, n.
fit, n.
good night, n.
Green-sleeves
ground, n.
Heart's ease
holding, n.
hunt's-up, n.
hymn, n.
jig, n.
lady, n.
laud, n.
lay, n.
love-song, n.
lullaby, n.
madrigal, n.
measure, n.
melody, n.

Non Nobis
Peg-a-Ramsey
plainsong, n.
prick-song, n.
psalm, n.
requiem, n.
song, n.
Te Deum
threne, n.
tune, n.
warble, n.
wedlock-hymn, n.
: 54

26.11
dance

back-trick, n.
Bergamask, n.
Bergamask dance, n.
bout, n.
brawl, n.
canary, n.
canary, vb.
caper, n.
change, n.
cinquepace, n.
coranto, n.
cut a caper, vb.
dance, n.
dance, vb.
dancer, n.
dancing-rapier, n.
footing, n.
foot it, vb.
French brawl, n.
galliard, n.
hay, n.
heel, vb.
hobby-horse, n.
hornpipe, n.
jig, n.
jig, vb.
lavolta, n.
Light o' love

measure, n.
Morisco, n.
morris, n.
morris-dance, n.
passemeasure, n.
pavan, n.
ringlet, n.
round, n.
roundel, n.
Scotch jig, n.
tread a measure, vb.
up-spring, n.
walk, n.
: 41

26.12
poem

elegy, n.
epigram, n.
love-rhyme, n.
ode, n.
poem, n.
poesy, n.
poetical, adj.
poetry, n.
posy, n.
satire, n.
satirical, adj.
sonnet, n.
verse, n.
: 13

26.13
metre

accent, n.
blank verse, n.
cadence, n.
change, n.
eight and eight, n.
eight and six, n.
envoy, n.
foot, n.
measure, n.

metre, n.
number, n.
rhyme, n.
staff, n.
stanza, n.
verse, n.
: 15

26.14
poet

Aesop
author, n.
ballad, vb.
ballad-maker, n.
ballad-monger, n.
berhyme, vb.
Chaucer
compose, vb.
Gower (PER)
Horace
Ovid (Ovidius Naso)
Petrarch
poet, n.
psalmist, n.
rhyme, vb.
rhymer, n.
sonnet, vb.
Spenser
verse, vb.
write, vb.
writer, n.
: 21

26.15
painting

air-drawn, adj.
bepaint, vb.
chimney-piece, n.
draw, vb.
drollery, n.
effigies, n.
expressure, n.
form, n.

Giulio Romano
ground, n.
ground-piece, n.
image, n.
imagery, n.
impaint, vb.
limn, vb.
line, vb.
map, n.
map, vb.
mappery, n.
nose-painting, n.
over-picture, vb.
paint, vb.
painter, n.
painting, n.
pencil, n.
pencil, vb.
picture, n.
picture, vb.
picture-like, adj.
portrait, n.
portraiture, n.
presentment, n.
shadow, n.
stell, vb.
table, n.
water-colour, n.
waterwork, n.
well-painted, adj.
: 38

26.16
insculpture

carve, vb.
carver, n.
Colossus, n.
colossus-wise, adv.
cut, vb.
cutter, n.
engrave, vb.
grave, vb.
hatch, vb.
insculp, vb.

insculpture, n.
monument, n.
state-statue, n.
statue, n.
stone-cutter, n.
 : 15

27.01
pastime

---

abridgement, n.
country pastime, n.
country sport, n.
disport, n.
disport, vb.
exercise, vb.
gamesome, adj.
outsport, vb.
pastime, n.
play, vb.
recreate, vb.
recreation, n.
sport, n.
sport, vb.
table-sport, n.
: 15

27.02
fencer

---

backswordman, n.
blade, n.
dagger, n.
duellist, n.
escrimer, n.
fence, vb.
fencer, n.
foil, n.
rapier, n.
sword, n.
sword-and-buckler,
  n.
sworder, n.
swordman, n.
tuck, n.
: 14

27.03
stoccado

---

alla stoccata
answer, n.

at a guard, adv.
bout, n.
cause, n.
come in, phr. vb.
distance, n.
duello, n.
fall, n.
fence, n.
foin, n.
foin, vb.
hay, n.
montant, n.
out of guard, adv.
pass, n.
pass, vb.
passado, n.
passage, n.
punto reverso
reverse, n.
stoccado, n.
stock, n.
stroke, n.
stuck, n.
thrust, n.
thrust, vb.
traverse, vb.
venue, n.
ward, n.
washing, adj.
: 31

27.04
archery

Adam [Bell] (ADO)
archer, n.
archery, n.
arcus, lat. n.
arrow, n.
Arthur's show, n.
bird-bolt, n.
blank, n.
bolt, n.
bow, n.
bow-boy, n.

bowcase, n.
bow-hand, n.
bow-string, n.
butt, n.
butt-shaft, n.
clout, n.
cross-bow, n.
cry aim, vb.
dart, n.
dribble, vb.
flight, n.
forehand, adj.
forehand shaft, n.
forked, adj.
loose, n.
loose, vb.
love-shaft, n.
mark, n.
markman, n.
mete, vb.
pin, n.
point-blank, adj.
point-blank, n.
prick, n.
quiver, n.
shaft, n.
shoot, n.
shoot, vb.
shooter, n.
shot, n.
sling, n.
stone-bow, n.
upshoot, n.
white, n.
: 45

27.05
bear-baiting

---

baiting-place, n.
bear-baiting, n.
stake, n.
: 3

27.06
games

---

all hid, n.
atilt, adv.
barley-break, n.
base, n.
billiards, n.
bo-peep, n.
bowl, vb.
career, n.
chase, n.
cherry-pit, n.
country base, n.
course, n.
dice, vb.
Edward shovel-
  board, n.
fast and loose, adj.
game, n.
gaming, n.
handy-dandy, n.
hazard, n.
heat, n.
hid-fox, n.
high and low, adj.
hoodman-blind, n.
just, n.
just, vb.
leap-frog, n.
loggat, n.
lottery, n.
marry trap
match, n.
morris, n.
muss, n.
nine men's morris, n.
novum, n.
Olympian Games, n.
play, n.
primero, n.
prize, n.
push-pin, n.
race, n.
set, n.

shove-groat, n.
shovel-board, n.
span-counter, n.
sport, n.
stool-ball, n.
tables, n.
tennis, n.
tick-tack, n.
tilt, n.
tilt, vb.
tournament, n.
tourney, vb.
trey-trip, n.
troll-my-dames, n.
wild-goose chase, n.
wild-mare, n.
  : 57

27.07
gamester
─────────────
bowler, n.
dicer, n.
gamester, n.
juggler, n.
Milo
player, n.
playfellow, n.
play-fere, n.
prizer, n.
stickler-like, adj.
tilter, n.
tumbler, n.
wrestler, n.
  : 13

27.08
toy
─────────────
aglet-baby, n.
bauble, n.
demi-puppet, n.
gaud, n.
Jack-a-lent
kickshaws, n.

knack, n.
maumet, n.
puppet, n.
top, n.
toy, n.
trick, n.
  : 12

27.09
ball
─────────────
ball, n.
blank, n.
bowl, n.
card, n.
chase, n.
cockpit, n.
court, n.
cut, n.
deck, n.
die, n.
flap-dragon, n.
football, n.
fulham, n.
gig, n.
gourd, n.
lot, n.
mistress, n.
Paris ball, n.
parish-top, n.
quintain, n.
quoit, n.
quoit, vb.
racket, n.
rub, n.
sort, n.
sporting-place, n.
ten, n.
tennis-ball, n.
tennis-court, n.
tilt-yard, n.
top, n.
whirligig, n.
  : 32

27.10
sport terms
─────────────
ace, n.
ambs-ace, n.
bet, n.
bet, vb.
bias, n.
cast, n.
cast, vb.
deuce-ace, n.
fall, n.
foil, vb.
gage, vb.
hazard, vb.
hold, vb.
kiss, vb.
lay, n.
lay, vb.
lots and blanks, n.
main, n.
main chance, n.
odds, n.
pair-taunt-like, adj.
pawn, n.
pawn, vb.
pip, n.
purr, n.
rub, vb.
set, vb.
stake, n.
stake, vb.
swoopstake, adv.
throw, n.
throw, vb.
trey, n.
trip, n.
triumph, n.
tumbling-trick, n.
upcast, n.
wage, vb.
wager, n.
wager, vb.
  : 40

27.11
fisherman
─────────────
angle, vb.
angler, n.
fish, vb.
fisher, n.
fisherman, n.
hook, n.
line, n.
  : 7

27.12
falconer
─────────────
bat-fowl, vb.
bird, vb.
falconer, n.
fowler, n.
hawk, vb.
imp, vb.
  : 6

27.13
forester
─────────────
forester, n.
ranger, n.
warrener, n.
  : 3

27.14
hunter
─────────────
at (a) bay, adv.
at gaze, adv.
bay, n.
bay, vb.
bloody-hunting, adj.
boar-spear, n.
bugle, n.
chase, n.
dry-foot, adv.
emboss, vb.
fault, n.

ferret, vb.
forage, n.
forage, vb.
forager, n.
game, n.
gull-catcher, n.
hare-finder, n.
hunt, n.
hunt, vb.
hunter, n.
huntress, n.
huntsman, n.
hunt's-up, n.
mort, n.
mouse, vb.
mouse-hunt, n.
recheat, n.
stalk, vb.
stalking-horse, n.
venison, n.
woodman, n.
 : 32

27.15
snare
——————————
angle, n.
bait, n.
benet, vb.
bird-lime, n.
call, n.
enmesh, vb.
ensnare, vb.
entangle, vb.
entrap, vb.
gin, n.
lime, vb.
lime-twig, n.
lure, n.
mesh, n.
mousetrap, n.

net, n.
pitfall, n.
snare, n.
snare, vb.
springe, n.
stale, n.
tame cheater, n.
tangle, vb.
toil, n.
trap, n.
trap, vb.
 : 26

27.16
horseman
——————————
at hand, adv.
back, vb.
bestride, vb.
dismount, vb.
give head, vb.
horse, n.
horse, vb.
horseman, n.
horsemanship, n.
monter, fr. vb.
mount, vb.
ride, vb.
rider, n.
run, vb.
unbacked, adj.
uncolt, vb.
unhorse, vb.
 : 17

27.17
bridle
——————————
bit, n.
bow, n.
bridle, n.

bridle, vb.
calkin, n.
collar, n.
curb, n.
foot-cloth, n.
furniture, n.
goad, n.
half-cheeked, adj.
harness, n.
harness, vb.
head-stall, n.
heavenly-harnessed,
 adj.
hobnail, n.
horseshoe, n.
rein, n.
rein, vb.
riding-rod, n.
rowel, n.
rowel-head, n.
shoe, vb.
snaffle, n.
spur, n.
switch, n.
thong, n.
trace, n.
unbitted, adj.
unbridled, adj.
unyoke, vb.
unyoked, adj.
yoke, n.
yoke, vb.

 : 34

27.18
saddle
——————————
caparison, n.
caparison, vb.
crupper, n.

girth, n.
pack-saddle, n.
point, n.
saddle, n.
saddle, vb.
saddle-bow, n.
stirrup, n.
 : 10

27.19
curb
——————————
chain, n.
chain, vb.
couple, n.
curb, n.
curb, vb.
jess, n.
leash, n.
leash, vb.
muzzle, n.
muzzle, vb.
slip, n.
tether, n.
uncouple, vb.
uncurbable, adj.
uncurbed, adj.
unmuzzle, vb.
unmuzzled, adj.
 : 17

28.01
religions

Brownist, n.
Christendom, n.
Christian, adj.
Christian, n.
Christian-like, adj.
Christians-soul, n.
church, n.
even-Christian, n.
Hebrew, adj.
Hebrew, n.
Jew, n.
Jewess, n.
Jewish, adj.
Lutheran, n.
Nazarite, n.
papist, n.
puritan, n.
religion, n.
: 18

28.02
God

All-Seer, The
Christ
creator, n.
dea, lat. n.
déesse, fr. n.
deity, n.
deus, lat. n.
dieu, fr. n.
divinity, n.
Eternal, The
Everlasting, The
Father, The
god, n.
god, vb.
God almighty, n.
goddess, n.
goddess-like, adj.
godhead, n.
godlike, adj.

godliness, n.
godly, adj.
Highest, The
King of heaven, n.
King of kings, n.
King's King, n.
Lord, The
Lord of hosts, n.
maker, n.
providence, n.
Redeemer, n.
saviour, n.
ungodly, adj.
: 32

28.03
Abraham • Paul

Abel
Abraham
Achitophel
Adam
apostle, n.
Barabbas
Cain
Daniel
Deborah
Dives
Eve
Goliath
Hagar
Herod
Jacob
Japhet
Jephthah
Jesus
Jezebel
Job
John
Joshua
Judas Iscariot
Judas Maccabaeus
Jude
Laban
Lazarus

Lucifer
Luke
Maria
Mary
Nebuchadnezzar
Noah
Paul
Peter
Pilate
Prodigal Son
Saba
Samson
Satan
Solomon
: 41

28.04
Mars • Venus

Abraham Cupid
  (ROM)
Aeolus
Aesculapius
Alecto
Apollo, lat.
Apollo
Aquilon
Astraea
Ate
Atropos
Aurora
Bacchus
Bel
Bellona
blind bow-boy, n.
blind boy, n.
Boreas
Ceres
Circe
Cupid
Cynthia
Cytherea
demigod, n.
Destinies, The
Diana

Dictynna
Dis
Fates, The
Flora
Furies, The
Hecate
Hermes
Hymen
Hyperion
Iris
Isis
Iupiter, lat.
Janus
Jove
Jovial, adj.
Juno
Juno-like, adj.
Jupiter
Love
love-god, n.
Lucina
Luna
Mars
Mars, lat.
Martial, adj.
Mercurial, adj.
Mercury
Minerva
muse, n.
Nemesis
Neptune
Pallas
Parca
Phoebe
Phoebus
Pluto
Plutus
Priapus
Promethean, adj.
Prometheus
Proserpina
Proteus (3H6)
Saturn
she-Mercury, n.
Sisters Three, n.

Tellus
Thetis
thunder-bearer, n.
thunder-darter, n.
thunderer, n.
thunder-master, n.
Titan
Triton
Venus
Vulcan
  : 80

28.05
spirits

Amaimon
ange, fr. n.
angel, n.
angelical, adj.
angel-like, adj.
apparition, n.
Ariel
Asmath
Barbason
Beelzebub
black prince (AWW),
  n.
bug, n.
bugbear, n.
cacodemon, n.
cherub, n.
Cobweb
Cricket
demi-devil, n.
demon, n.
devil, n.
devilish, adj.
devilish-holy, adj.
diable, fr. n.
diabolo, it. n.
dickens, n.
double man, n.
elf, n.
fairy, n.
fairyland, n.

fairy-like, adj.
familiar, n.
fiend, n.
fiend-like, adj.
Flibbertigibbet
foul fiend, n.
Frateretto
genius, n.
ghost, n.
ghost, vb.
goblin, n.
goodyear, n.
Harpier
Hobbididence
Hobgoblin
Hoppedance
host of heaven, n.
Legion
Mab
Mahu
manes, lat. n.
man in the moon, n.
mare, n.
meadow-fairy, n.
Mephistopheles
Modo
Mote (MND)
Mustardseed
nightmare, n.
nymph, n.
Oberon
Obidicut
ouph, n.
Paddock
Peaseblossom
phantasma, n.
prince of darkness, n.
principality, n.
puck, n.
Puck
Robin Goodfellow →
  Puck
satyr, n.
Setebos
shade, n.

shadow, n.
she-angel, n.
Smulkin
soul, n.
soulless, adj.
spirit, n.
sprightly, adj.
sprite, n.
Titania
urchin, n.
vision, n.
yoke-devil, n.
  : 85

28.06
mermaid

mermaid, n.
mermaid-like, adj.
naiad, n.
Nereides, n.
sea-maid, n.
sea-nymph, n.
siren, n.
  : 7

28.07
heaven • hell

Arthur's bosom, n.
caelestis, lat. adj.
celestial, adj.
Deep, The
demi-paradise, n.
Eden
Elysium
Erebus
heaven, n.
heavenly, adj.
hell, n.
hellish, adj.
infernal, adj.
Jerusalem
limbo, n.
Limbo Patrum

paradise, n.
purgatory, n.
supernal, adj.
Tartarus
under, adj.
under ground, n.
unearthly, adj.
  : 23

28.08
worshipper

anchor, n.
beadsman, n.
convertite, n.
hermit, n.
idiot-worshipper, n.
palmer, n.
parishioner, n.
pew-fellow, n.
pilgrim, n.
pilgrimage, n.
proselyte, n.
sacrificer, n.
votaress, n.
votarist, n.
votary, n.
worshipper, n.
  : 16

28.09
clergy

abbess, n.
abbot, n.
archbishop, n.
archdeacon, n.
bishop, n.
brother, n.
cardinal, n.
celestial, n.
chaplain, n.
Chartreux
churchman, n.
clergy, n.

clergyman, n.
cloistress, n.
confessor, n.
count-cardinal, n.
curate, n.
dignity, n.
divine, n.
dominus, lat. n.
father, n.
flamen, n.
Franciscan, adj.
friar, n.
ghostly father, n.
hedge-priest, n.
Holy Father, n.
holy order, n.
initiate, adj.
Jack priest, n.
king-cardinal, n.
minister, n.
monachus, lat. n.
monastic, adj.
monk, n.
mother, n.
novice, n.
nun, n.
order, n.
pardoner, n.
parson, n.
pastor, n.
pontifical, adj.
pope, n.
popedom, n.
popish, adj.
preacher, n.
prelate, n.
prester, n.
priest, n.
priesthood, n.
priestlike, adj.
priestly, adj.
prioress, n.
rector, n.
sexton, n.
shriver, n.

sin-absolver, n.
sister, n.
sisterhood, n.
soul-curer, n.
spiritualty, n.
vestal, adj.
vestal, n.
vicar, n.
: 65

28.10
sermon
———————
catechism, n.
catechize, vb.
creed, n.
gospel, n.
homily, n.
parable, n.
preach, vb.
preachment, n.
sermon, n.
sermon, vb.
: 10

28.11
prayer
———————
anthem, n.
Ave-Mary, n.
exercise, n.
hymn, n.
invocate, vb.
invocation, n.
invoke, vb.
laud, n.
morn-prayer, n.
Non Nobis
orison, n.
outpray, vb.
petition, n.
pray, vb.
prayer^1, n.
prayer^2, n.
psalm, n.

requiem, n.
Te Deum
thanksgiving, n.
: 20

28.12
sacrament
———————
absolution, n.
absolve, vb.
anoint, vb.
banns, n.
baptism, n.
baptize, vb.
benediction, n.
benison, n.
bless, vb.
blessing, n.
canonize, vb.
christen, vb.
christendom, n.
christening, n.
confession, n.
consecrate, adj.
consecrate, vb.
consecration, n.
cross, vb.
enshrine, vb.
holy bread, n.
holy oil, n.
holy water, n.
indulgence, n.
marriage-blessing, n.
mass, n.
night-oblation, n.
oblation, n.
offering, n.
requiem, n.
sacrament, n.
sacrifice, n.
sacrifice, vb.
sacrificial, adj.
sacring-bell, n.
sanctify, vb.
shrift, n.

shrive, vb.
true-anointed, adj.
unaneled, adj.
unbless, vb.
unhouseled, adj.
: 42

28.13
holiness
———————
benedictus, n.
blessedly, adv.
blessedness, n.
church-like, adj.
cursed-blessed, adj.
devilish-holy, adj.
devotion, n.
devout, adj.
devoutly, adv.
divin, fr. adj.
divine, adj.
divinely, adv.
faith, n.
faithful, adj.
ghostly, adj.
godliness, n.
gospel, vb.
grace, n.
grace, fr. n.
graceful, adj.
graceless, adj.
graceless, n.
gracious, adj.
graciously, adv.
hallow, vb.
holily, adv.
holiness, n.
holy, adj.
holy-thoughted, adj.
metaphysical, adj.
outward-sainted, adj.
piety, n.
pious, adj.
religious, adj.
religiously, adv.

sacred, adj.
saint, adj.
saint, vb.
saintlike, adj.
salvation, n.
sanctimonious, adj.
sanctimony, n.
sanctity, n.
sanctus, lat. adj.
spiritual, adj.
state of grace, n.
supernatural, adj.
thrice-blessed, adj.
unhallowed, adj.
unholy, adj.
unsanctified, adj.
well-hallowed, adj.
: 52

28.14
saints
───────────
Alban
Anne
Bartholomew
Bennet
Charity
Clare
Crispian
Crispin
Cupid
Davy
Denis
Francis
George
Gis
Gregory
Helen
Jacob
Jamy
Jaques
Jeronimy
Lambert
Luke
Magnus

Martin
Mary
Michael
Nicholas
Our Lady
Patrick
Paul
Philip
saint, n.
Stephen
Swithold
Valentine
: 35

28.15
reverence
───────────
adoration, n.
adore, vb.
adorer, n.
awe, n.
awe, vb.
aweless, adj.
awful, adj.
ceremony, n.
dedicate, adj.
dedicate, vb.
dedication, n.
deify, vb.
devote, adj.
devote, vb.
devotion, n.
dread, n.
duty, n.
god, vb.
homage, n.
honour, vb.
obeisance, n.
observance, n.
observancy, n.
observe, vb.
off-cap, vb.
respect, n.
respect, vb.
respective, adj.

respectively, adv.
reverence, n.
reverence, vb.
reverend, adj.
reverent, adj.
reverently, adv.
sacred, adj.
saving your
  reverence, vb.
service, n.
sir-reverence, n.
time-honoured, adj.
true-devoted, adj.
unreverend, adj.
unreverent, adj.
unvenerable, adj.
vail, vb.
venerable, adj.
worship, n.
worship, vb.
worshipful, adj.
worshipfully, adv.
: 49

28.16
compassion
───────────
alms, n.
alms-basket, n.
alms-deed, n.
alms-drink, n.
commiseration, n.
compassion, n.
compassion, vb.
compassionate, adj.
dispiteous, adj.
forgiveness, n.
merciful, adj.
mercifully, adv.
merciless, adj.
mercy, n.
mercy-lacking, adj.
miséricorde, fr. n.
pardon, n.
piteous, adj.

piteously, adv.
pitie, fr. n.
pitiful, adj.
pitiful-hearted, adj.
pitifully, adv.
pitiless, adj.
pity, n.
pity, vb.
remission, n.
remorse, n.
remorseful, adj.
remorseless, adj.
rue, vb.
ruth, n.
ruthful, adj.
ruthless, adj.
to-be-pitied, adj.
uncompassionate,
  adj.
unmerciful, adj.
unpitied, adj.
unpitifully, adv.
yearn, vb.
: 40

28.17
penitence
───────────
abide, vb.
aby, vb.
atone, vb.
atonement, n.
compunctious, adj.
contrite, adj.
fast, n.
fast, vb.
high-repented, adj.
irreconciled, adj.
penance, n.
penitence, n.
penitent, adj.
penitent, n.
penitential, adj.
penitently, adv.
redeem, vb.

redemption, n.
remorse, n.
repent, vb.
repentance, n.
repentant, adj.
: 22

28.18
church
_____

Abbey, The
cathedral church, n.
church, n.
deanery, n.
fane, n.
holy church, n.
Holy See, n.
Pantheon
parish church, n.
See, n.
St. Bennet
St. Gregory's
St. Jaques le Grand
St. Katherine's
St. Luke's
St. Magnus'
St. Mary's Chapel
St. Paul's
St. Peter's
synagogue, n.
temple, n.
Westminster
: 22

28.19
monastery
_____

abbey, n.
Blackfriars
Chertsey
cloister, n.
convent, n.
hermitage, n.
monastery, n.
nunnery, n.

order, n.
priory, n.
: 10

28.20
chantry
_____

chantry, n.
chapel, n.
choir, n.
cloister, vb.
sanctuary, n.
St. Mary's Chapel
: 6

28.21
altar
_____

altar, n.
beads, n.
cross, n.
font, n.
high cross, n.
holy cross, n.
holy rood, n.
incense, n.
manna, n.
market cross, n.
pax, n.
rood, n.
shrine, n.
surplice, n.
: 14

28.22
pagan
_____

Bacchanal, n.
blood-sacrifice, n.
heathen, adj.
heathen, n.
heathenish, adj.
pagan, adj.
pagan, n.
Turk, n.   : 8

28.23
irreligion
_____

arch-heretic, n.
faithless, adj.
heresy, n.
heretic, n.
idol, n.
idolatrous, adj.
idolatry, n.
infidel, n.
irreligious, adj.
misbelieve, vb.
misbeliever, n.
miscreant, n.
renegado, n.
sectary, n.
superstition, n.
superstitious, adj.
superstitiously, adv.
: 17

28.24
impiety
_____

ban, n.
beshrew, vb.
blaspheme, vb.
blasphemous, adj.
blasphemy, n.
cardinal sin, n.
curse, n.
cursed-blessed, adj.
damn, vb.
damnable, adj.
damnation, n.
drug-damned, adj.
excommunicate, adj.
execration, n.
forbid, vb.
impiety, n.
impious, adj.
inexecrable, adj.
lapse, n.
lapse, vb.

malediction, n.
profanation, n.
profane, adj.
profane, vb.
profanely, adv.
profaneness, n.
profaner, n.
reprobance, n.
reprobate, adj.
reprobate, n.
sacrilegious, adj.
shrew, vb.
simony, n.
sin, n.
sin, vb.
sinful, adj.
sinfully, adv.
sinner, n.
swear, vb.
swearer, n.
transgress, vb.
transgression, n.
trespass, n.
trespass, vb.
unbless, vb.
unblessed, adj.
ungodly, adj.
unhallowed, adj.
unholy, adj.
unsanctified, adj.
vice, n.
: 51

28.25
oaths
_____

a' devil's name
afore God
a' God's name
be Chrish
before God
be-gar
be God's sonties
bodikins
by all that's holy

by all the saints in
  heaven
by Christ's dear
  blood
by Cock
by Cock and pie
by Gadslugs
by Gar
by Gis
by God
by God's grace
by God's holy
  mother
by God's lid
by God's liggens
by God's mother
by God's will
by Gogs-wouns
by good St. Albon
by holy Mary
by holy Paul
by Jesu
by mass
by my halidom
by my holidam
by my holidame
by my holy order
by'r lady
by'r lakin
by St. Anne
by St. Charity
by St. George
by St. Jamy
by St. Patrick
by St. Paul
by the apostle Paul
by the eternal God
by the grace of God
by the holy mother
  of our Lord
by the holy rood
by the Lord
by the mass
by the mess
by the rood

by th' mass
by th' rood
Cock's passion
Cox my passion
darkness and devils
divinity of hell
'fore God
for God's love
for God's sake
forswear, vb.
for the love of God
God
God almighty
God damn me
gods and devils
God's blest mother
God's bodkin
God's body
God's bread
God's lady
God's lid
God's light
good Lord
Got's lords and His
  ladies
heart
holy St. Francis
in God's name
in the devil's name
in the name of Jesu
  Christ
in th' other devil's
  name
i' th' name of
  Belzebub
Jesu
Jesu Maria
jurement, fr. n.
Lady
Lord
marry
mass
mort Dieu
mort du vinaigre
o all the devils

oath, n.
oathable, adj.
oath-breaking, n.
o bon Dieu
o Dieu vivant
'od's heartlings
'od's lifelings
'od's nouns
'od's pittikins
'od's plessed will
o God
o God's lady dear
o heavenly God
o hell
o Jesu
o Lord
o Seigneur Dieu
o the Lord
outswear, vb.
perdie
perdy
perjure, n.
perjure, vb.
py'r lady
'sblood
'sblud
'sdeath
'sfoot
'slid
'slight
St. Jeronimy
swear, vb.
swearer, n.
swearing, n.
'swounds
'ud's pity
unswear, vb.
unsworn, adj.
zounds
  : 130

28.26
destiny
_____

allot, vb.

bound, adj.
destine, vb.
destiny, n.
dole, n.
doom, n.
fatal, adj.
fate, n.
fate, vb.
fortuna, it. n.
fortune, fr. n.
lot, n.
predestinate, adj.
sort, n.
  : 14

28.27
prognostication
_____

abode, vb.
abodement, n.
augur, n.
augur, vb.
augurer, n.
augury, n.
auspicious, adj.
auspiciously, adv.
betoken, vb.
bode, vb.
bodement, n.
calculate, vb.
ceremony, n.
death-boding, adj.
death-divining, adj.
Delphos
divination, n.
divine, vb.
diviner, n.
fair-boding, adj.
false-boding, adj.
fatal, adj.
figure, n.
figure, vb.
forecast, n.
foreknow, vb.
foreknowledge, n.

fore-run, vb.
forerunner, n.
fore-say, vb.
foresee, vb.
foreshow, vb.
foresight, n.
foretell, vb.
forethink, vb.
forewarn, vb.
fortune-tell, vb.
fortune-teller, n.
harbinger, n.
ill-boding, adj.
ill-divining, adj.
inauspicious, adj.
misgive, vb.
omen, n.
ominous, adj.
oracle, n.
portend, vb.
portent, n.
portentous, adj.
predict, n.
prediction, n.
prefigure, vb.
prenominate, adj.
prenominate, vb.

presage, n.
presage, vb.
presager, n.
prescience, n.
prewarn, vb.
prodigious, adj.
prodigiously, adv.
prodigy, n.
prognosticate, vb.
prognostication, n.
prophecy, n.
prophesier, n.
prophesy, vb.
prophet, n.
prophetess, n.
prophetic, adj.
prophetically, adv.
prophet-like, adj.
providence, n.
provident, adj.
providently, adv.
Sibyl
sign, n.
sign, vb.
soothsay, vb.
soothsayer, n.
table, n.

true-divining, adj.
unauspicious, adj.
unprovident, adj.
well-boding, adj.
 : 85

**28.28
sorcery**
────────────

bewitch, vb.
bewitchment, n.
black magician, n.
charm, n.
charm, vb.
charmer, n.
charmingly, adv.
conjuration, n.
conjure, vb.
conjurer, n.
conjuring, n.
cunning man, n.
enchant, vb.
enchantingly, adv.
enchantment, n.
enchantress, n.
exorciser, n.
exorcism, n.

exorcist, n.
fairy, n.
hag, n.
haggish, adj.
incantation, n.
magic, adj.
magic, n.
magical, adj.
magician, n.
overlook, vb.
ravish, vb.
sorcerer, n.
sorceress, n.
sorcery, n.
spell, n.
spell, vb.
take, vb.
uncharmed, adj.
weird sisters
 (women), n.
wise woman, n.
witch[1], n.
witch[2], n.
witch, vb.
witchcraft, n.
wizard, n.
 : 43

29.01
essence • matter

being, n.
bodiless, adj.
bodily, adj.
body, n.
essence, n.
essential, adj.
essentially, adv.
heart, n.
heart-blood, n.
immaterial, adj.
incorporal, adj.
insubstantial, adj.
life, n.
making, n.
material, adj.
matter, n.
pith, n.
quintessence, n.
self-substantial, adj.
soul, n.
spirit, n.
stuff, n.
substance, n.
substantial, adj.
thing, n.
unbodied, adj.
unsubstantial, adj.
virtue, n.
virtuous, adj.
  : 29

29.02
being

adesse, lat. vb.
be, vb.
be-all, n.
being, n.
buy, vb.
consist, vb.
esse, lat. vb.
être, fr. vb.

exist, vb.
extant, adj.
live, vb.
living, n.
soul, n.
  : 13

29.03
(un)natural

abortive, adj.
abortive, n.
bemonster, vb.
bully-monster, n.
demi-natured, adj.
disnature, vb.
enormity, n.
enormous, adj.
in grain, adv.
inherent, adj.
kind, adj.
kindless, adj.
kindly, adj.
kindly, adv.
man-monster, n.
monster, n.
monster, vb.
monster-like, adj.
monstrosity, n.
monstrous, adj.
monstrously, adv.
monstrousness, n.
native, adj.
natural, adj.
naturally, adv.
nature, n.
preposterous, adj.
preposterously, adv.
prodigious, adj.
prodigiously, adv.
prodigy, n.
servant-monster, n.
supernatural, adj.
unfathered, adj.
unkind, adj.

unnatural, adj.
unnaturally, adv.
unnaturalness, n.
  : 38

29.04
thing

any, adj.
anything, n.
aught, n.
object, n.
piece, n.
something, n.
somewhat, n.
thing, n.
what, adj.
whatever, adj.
whatsoever, adj.
which, adj.
  : 12

29.05
indeed

good-deed, adv.
indeed, adv.
ipso facto
real, adj.
really, adv.
true, adj.
truly, adv.
unreal, adj.
verily, adj.
verily, adv.
  : 10

29.06
pertain

appertain, vb.
appertaining, n.
appurtenance, n.
appurtenant, adj.
appurtenant, n.

assign, n.
belong, vb.
concern, vb.
corresponsive, adj.
impertinency, n.
impertinent, adj.
long, vb.
pertain, vb.
pertinent, adj.
relate, vb.
relative, adj.
  : 16

29.07
proportion

disproportion, n.
disproportion, vb.
past-proportion, n.
proportion, n.
proportion, vb.
proportionable, adj.
quantity, n.
reference, n.
relation, n.
square, n.
unproportioned, adj.
well-proportioned,
  adj.
  : 12

29.08
pattern

calendar, n.
copy, n.
counterpart, n.
example, n.
example, vb.
instance, n.
mirror, n.
model, n.
mould, n.
paragon, n.
paragon, vb.

pattern, n.
pattern, vb.
precedent, n.
sample, n.
scantling, n.
self-example, n.
square, n.
: 18

29.09
rank

condition, n.
degree, n.
description, n.
estate, n.
fore-rank, n.
nature, n.
order, n.
place, n.
quality, n.
rank, n.
respect, n.
sect, n.
siege, n.
sort, n.
standing, n.
state, n.
station, n.
: 17

29.10
pre-eminence

addition, n.
admirable, adj.
all-noble, adj.
arrant, adj.
best, n.
better, n.
better, vb.
beyond, adv.
choice, adj.
choice, n.
come over, phr. vb.

complete, adj.
co-supreme, n.
distingué, fr. adj.
divineness, n.
egregious, adj.
egregiously, adv.
eminence, n.
eminent, adj.
exceed, vb.
excel, vb.
excellence, n.
excellency, n.
excellent, adj.
excellent, fr. adj.
excellently, adv.
exquisite, adj.
favourite, n.
flower, n.
foremost, adj.
glorify, vb.
glorious, adj.
gloriously, adv.
glory, n.
glory, vb.
gorgeous, adj.
grand, adj.
grand, fr. adj.
grandeur, fr. n.
great, adj.
great, n.
greater, n.
greatest, n.
greatly, adv.
greatness, n.
heavenly, adj.
high, n.
honourable, adj.
illustrate, adj.
illustrious, adj.
incomparable, adj.
lofty, adj.
made-up, adj.
magnificence, n.
magnificent, adj.
magnify, vb.

majority, n.
marvellous, adj.
marvellously, adv.
matchless, adj.
nobility, n.
noble, adj.
noble-minded, adj.
nobleness, n.
noblesse, n.
noblest, n.
nobly, adv.
nonpareil, n.
notable, adj.
notably, adv.
note, n.
noteworthy, adj.
notorious, adj.
notoriously, adv.
of note, adv.
outdo, vb.
outpeer, vb.
over-great, adj.
overreach, vb.
paragon, n.
paragon, vb.
pass, vb.
passing, adj.
passing, adv.
peerless, adj.
perfect, adj.
perfection, n.
pink, n.
pompous, adj.
pre-eminence, n.
prerogative, n.
pure, adj.
rare, adj.
rarely, adv.
rareness, n.
rarest, n.
rarity, n.
redoubt, vb.
remark, vb.
remarkable, adj.
select, adj.

serenissimus, lat. adj.
singular, adj.
sovereignty, n.
splendour, n.
state, n.
supreme, adj.
surmount, vb.
surpass, vb.
thrice-gorgeous, adj.
thrice-noble, adj.
top, vb.
transcend, vb.
transcendence, n.
unfellowed, adj.
unmatchable, adj.
unmatched, adj.
unparagoned, adj.
unparalleled, adj.
unrivalled, adj.
well-accomplished,
    adj.
: 121

29.11
foremost

arch, adj.
arch, n.
arch-one, n.
capital, adj.
captain, adj.
cardinal, adj.
chief, adj.
chiefest, n.
chiefly, adv.
first, adj.
first, n.
foremost, adj.
fundamental, adj.
grand, adj.
head, n.
head lady, n.
main, adj.
main, n.
mainly, adv.

major, adj.
master, n.
mistress, n.
only, adj.
prime, adj.
prime, n.
primest, n.
principal, adj.
principal, n.

select, adj.
superior, adj.
: 30

29.12
extreme
————————

extreme, adj.
extreme, n.

extremely, adv.
extremity, n.
mightily, adv.
out of all nick, adv.
utmost, adj.
utmost, n.
utter, adj.
utterance, n.
utterly, adv.

uttermost, adj.
uttermost, n.
: 13

30.01
manner

_____

ainsi, fr. adv.
anyway, adv.
at all, adv.
else, adv.
fashion, n.
fashionable, adj.
garb, n.
guise, n.
how, adv.
how, n.
however, adv.
howsoever, adv.
howsomever, adv.
in kind, adv.
instrument, n.
manner, n.
mean, n.
method, n.
order, n.
other, adv.
othergates, adv.
otherwise, adv.
quality, n.
sic, lat. adv.
so, adv.
soever, adv.
somever, adv.
sort, n.
style, n.
such, adj.
thus, adv.
way, n.
wise, n.
  : 33

30.02
disposition

_____

addict, adj.
addict, vb.
addiction, n.
affect, n.

affection, n.
air, n.
appropriation, n.
apt, adj.
aptly, adv.
aptness, n.
aspect, n.
attribute, n.
attributive, adj.
barren-spirited, adj.
beef-witted, adj.
belonging, n.
bend, n.
bent, n.
bias, n.
blood, n.
bloody-minded, adj.
blunt-witted, adj.
cheer, n.
clear-spirited, adj.
complexion, n.
composure, n.
condition, n.
condition, vb.
conduce, vb.
constitution, n.
courage, n.
dispose, n.
dispose, vb.
disposition, n.
distemper, n.
endowment, n.
faculty, n.
fat-witted, adj.
frosty-spirited, adj.
genius, n.
gift, n.
habitude, n.
hair, n.
hasty-witted, adj.
heart, n.
heat, n.
high-minded, adj.
high-witted, adj.
honest-natured, adj.

humour, n.
ill disposed, adj.
ill-spirited, adj.
ill-tempered, adj.
inclinable, adj.
inclination, n.
incline, vb.
inclining, n.
indisposition, n.
infusion, n.
instinct, adj.
instinct, n.
instinctively, adv.
intend, vb.
iron-witted, adj.
lean, vb.
lean-witted, adj.
like, n.
liking, n.
lion-mettled, adj.
liver-vein, n.
low-spirited, adj.
mettle, n.
minded, adj.
month's mind, n.
mood, n.
motley-minded, adj.
muddy-mettled, adj.
nature, n.
noble-minded, adj.
over-partial, adj.
part, n.
pleasant-spirited, adj.
posture, n.
prone, adj.
propend, vb.
propension, n.
property, n.
property, vb.
proud-minded, adj.
qualification, n.
qualify, vb.
qualité, fr. n.
quality, n.
quick-witted, adj.

race, n.
savour, n.
savour, vb.
self-mettle, n.
sodden-witted, adj.
softly-sprighted, adj.
sour-natured, adj.
spirit, n.
sprite, n.
stomach, n.
strain, n.
strange-disposed, adj.
subtile-witted, adj.
talent, n.
temper, n.
temperality, n.
tend, vb.
tender-feeling, adj.
tender-minded, adj.
touch, n.
trick, n.
tune, n.
undisposed, adj.
unqualitied, adj.
vein, n.
want-wit, n.
well-conditioned, adj.
well-disposed, adj.
well-minded, adj.
well-tempered, adj.
  : 124

30.03
behaviour

_____

bearing, n.
behave, vb.
behaviour, n.
bestow, vb.
carriage, n.
carry, vb.
compliment, n.
conversation, n.
countenance, n.
country manners, n.

demean, vb.
demeanour, n.
encounter, n.
form, n.
gesture, n.
government, n.
habit, n.
haviour, n.
maintenance, n.
manner, n.
mannered, adj.
misdemean, vb.
misdemeanour, n.
misgovernment, n.
mishave, vb.
port, n.
portance, n.
presence, n.
quarter, n.
rule, n.
usage, n.
use, n.
use, vb.
well-behaved, adj.
well-governed, adj.
  : 35

30.04
(im)possibility

---

impossibility, n.
impossible, adj.
impossible, fr. adj.
may, vb.
posse, lat. vb.
possibility, n.
possible, adj.
possibly, adv.
unpossible, adj.
  : 9

30.05
(un)able

---

ability, n.

able, adj.
all-unable, adj.
can, vb.
capability, n.
capable, adj.
capacity, n.
disability, n.
faculty, n.
fathom, n.
hand, n.
incapable, adj.
posse, lat. vb.
quire, lat. vb.
reach, n.
self-unable, adj.
talent, n.
unable, adj.
uncapable, adj.
  : 19

30.06
(un)skilful

---

art, n.
artificial, adj.
artless, adj.
botch, vb.
bungle, vb.
cleanly, adj.
craft, n.
cunning, adj.
cunning, n.
cunningly, adv.
curious, adj.
deftly, adv.
delicate, adj.
dexteriously, adv.
exercise, n.
expert, adj.
expertness, n.
feat, adj.
featly, adv.
fine, adj.
fineness, n.
fumble, vb.

greenly, adv.
industrious, adj.
ingenious, adj.
masterly, adj.
masterpiece, n.
mastership, n.
mystery, n.
perfectness, n.
practice, n.
prettily, adv.
pretty, adj.
profess, vb.
proficient, n.
profit, vb.
quaint, adj.
quaintly, adv.
skilful, adj.
skilful, n.
skilfully, adv.
skill, n.
skilless, adj.
unpractised, adj.
unskilful, adj.
unskilfully, adv.
well-experienced,
  adj.
well-practiced, adj.
well-skilled, adj.
wittily, adv.
witty, adj.
workmanly, adj.
workmanship, n.
  : 53

30.07
preciseness

---

acute, adj.
acutely, adv.
[ad] unguem
by the card, adv.
choicely, adv.
curiosity, n.
curious, adj.
curiously, adv.

daintiest, n.
daintily, adv.
daintiness, n.
dainty, adj.
even, adj.
even, adv.
even, n.
exact, adj.
exactly, adv.
exquisite, adj.
feelingly, adv.
fine, adj.
fineness, n.
gingerly, adj.
jump, adv.
just, adj.
just, adv.
justly, adv.
nice, adj.
nice, n.
nicely, adv.
niceness, n.
point-device, adj.
precise, adj.
precisely, adv.
preciseness, n.
precisian, n.
quaint, adj.
quaintly, adv.
queasy, adj.
right, adj.
right, adv.
rightly, adv.
scrupulous, adj.
strict, adj.
strictly, adv.
subtile, adj.
subtle, adj.
super-dainty, adj.
to the point, adv.
  : 48

30.08
readiness

---

about, adv.
address, vb.
alacrity, n.
at an inch, adv.
at point, adv.
betake, vb.
bound, adj.
extemporal, adj.
extemporally, adv.
extempore, adv.
fettle, vb.
high time, n.
like, adj.
preparation, n.
prepare, n.
prepare, vb.
preparedly, adv.
prêt, fr. adj.
prompt, adj.
prompt, vb.
promptement, fr. adv.
rawly, adv.
rawness, n.
readiness, n.
ready, adj.
ripe, adj.
ripely, adv.
sinking-ripe, adj.
slow, adj.
sudden, adj.
suddenly, adv.
unpremeditated, adj.
unprepared, adj.
unready, adj.
weeping-ripe, adj.
yare, adj.
 : 36

30.09
(un)aptness

---

agree, vb.

appropriate, adj.
apt, adj.
aptly, adv.
aptness, n.
become, vb.
becoming, n.
befit, vb.
behoof, n.
behoofeful, adj.
behove, vb.
belong, vb.
beseem, vb.
besort, vb.
capable, adj.
coherent, adj.
convenience, n.
conveniency, n.
convenient, adj.
conveniently, adv.
convent, vb.
decent, adj.
decently, adv.
decorum, n.
due, adj.
duly, adv.
eft, adj.
fadge, vb.
feat, vb.
fit, adj.
fit, vb.
fitly, adv.
fitment, n.
fitness, n.
handsome, adj.
handsomely, adv.
hit, vb.
ill-beseeming, adj.
impair, adj.
impertinency, n.
impertinent, adj.
improper, adj.
inconvenient, adj.
in good time, adv.
in happy time, adv.
king-becoming, adj.

liable, adj.
long, vb.
measurable, adj.
measure, n.
meet, adj.
meetly, adj.
meetness, n.
misbecome, vb.
misbecomingly, adv.
opportune, adj.
pat, adv.
pregnancy, n.
pregnant, adj.
proper, adj.
properly, adv.
property, vb.
qualify, vb.
ready, adj.
responsive, adj.
seemingly, adv.
serve, vb.
sit, vb.
sort, vb.
sortance, n.
square, adj.
suit, vb.
suitable, adj.
timeless, adj.
timely, adj.
unagreeable, adj.
unapt, adj.
unaptness, n.
unbecoming, adj.
unbefitting, adj.
uncomeliness, n.
unfit, adj.
unfitness, n.
unhandsome, adj.
unmeet, adj.
unpregnant, adj.
unproper, adj.
unproperly, adv.
unseasonable, adj.
unseasonably, adv.
unseasoned, adj.

unsquared, adj.
unstaid, adj.
unsuitable, adj.
unsuiting, adj.
untimely, adj.
well-beseeming, adj.
worthy, adj.
 : 98

30.10
easy • hard

---

difficile, fr. adj.
difficult, adj.
difficulty, n.
ease, n.
easily, adv.
easy, adj.
facile, adj.
facile, lat. adv.
facility, n.
hard, adj.
hardly, adv.
hardness, n.
light, adj.
lightly, adv.
readily, adv.
uneasy, adj.
uneath, adv.
 : 17

31.01
quantity

batch, n.
belly-ful, n.
by gross, adv.
contain, vb.
containing, n.
content, n.
dash, n.
deal, n.
disquantity, vb.
dram, n.
drop, vb.
glimpse, n.
handful, n.
heap, n.
mass, n.
measure, n.
mess, n.
modicum, n.
mouth-filling, adj.
mouthful, n.
number, n.
pailful, n.
quantity, n.
relish, n.
set, n.
size, n.
smack, n.
smatch, n.
some, adj.
sum, n.
sup, n.
swath, n.
taste, n.
thought, n.
touch, n.
trace, n.
trick, n.
  : 37

31.02
quantor

all
another
any
both
each
either
every
few
many
much
neither
no
none
several
some
  : 15

31.03
all • nothing

absolute, adj.
absolutely, adv.
all, adj.
all, adv.
all, n.
altogether, adv.
any, adj.
anything, n.
at leisure, adv.
bag and baggage, n.
barely, adv.
by leisure, adv.
by no means, adv.
cap-à-pie, adv.
clean, adj.
cleanly, adv.
clearly, adv.
complete, adj.
cut and long-tail, n.
ensemble, fr. adv.
entire, adj.
entirely, adv.

even, adv.
every, adj.
exceptless, adj.
flat, adj.
flatly, adv.
flatness, n.
flesh and fell, n.
full, adj.
full, n.
fullness, n.
fully, adv.
general, adj.
general, n.
generally, adv.
gross, adj.
gross, n.
in gross, adv.
mere, adj.
merely, adv.
never, adv.
nihil, lat. n.
no deal, adv.
none, adj.
no point, adv.
nothing, adv.
nothing, n.
nought, adv.
nought, n.
nullity, n.
omnis, lat. adj.
outright, adv.
peremptorily, adv.
peremptory, adj.
perfect, adj.
perfectly, adv.
quite, adv.
right, adv.
scot and lot, n.
stark, adj.
thorough, adj.
thoroughly, adv.
through, adv.
throughly, adv.
total, adj.
total, n.

totally, adv.
tout, fr. adj.
tutto, it. adj.
universal, adj.
up and down, adv.
utter, adj.
utterly, adv.
versal, adj.
very, adj.
whole, adj.
whole, n.
wholly, adv.
  : 79

31.04
full • empty

abound, vb.
abundance, n.
abundant, adj.
abundantly, adv.
ample, adj.
amply, adv.
blank, adj.
blank, n.
bookful, n.
brim, vb.
brimful, adj.
brimfulness, n.
copious, adj.
depopulate, vb.
desolate, adj.
destitute, adj.
devoid, adj.
embowel, vb.
emptiness, n.
empty, adj.
empty, vb.
eventful, adj.
fill, n.
fill, vb.
fulfil, vb.
full, adj.
full, n.
fullness, n.

gap, n.
hollow, adj.
hollowness, n.
largely, adv.
line, vb.
lining, n.
make up, phr. vb.
mouth-filling, adj.
old, adj.
overfull, adj.
plein, fr. adj.
plenitude, n.
plenteous, adj.
plenteously, adv.
plentiful, adj.
plentifully, adv.
plenty, n.
replenish, vb.
replete, adj.
stop, vb.
store, n.
top-full, adj.
unfilled, adj.
unpeople, vb.
unpeopled, adj.
up-fill, vb.
vacancy, n.
vacant, adj.
void, adj.
waste, adj.
: 58

31.05
enough

assez, fr. adv.
competence, n.
competency, n.
competent, adj.
do, vb.
enough, adj.
enough, adv.
insufficience, n.
insufficiency, n.
satis, lat. adv.

suffice, vb.
sufficere, lat. vb.
sufficiency, n.
sufficient, adj.
sufficient, n.
sufficiently, adv.
: 16

31.06
load

ballast, n.
ballast, vb.
burden, n.
burden, vb.
burdenous, adj.
carriage, n.
charge, n.
charge, vb.
clog, n.
clog, vb.
disburden, vb.
double-charge, vb.
ease, vb.
enclog, vb.
fraught, n.
fraught, vb.
fraughtage, n.
full-charged, adj.
full-fraught, adj.
lade, vb.
lading, n.
load, n.
load, vb.
loading, n.
luggage, n.
overcharge, vb.
overfreight, vb.
pack, vb.
peise, vb.
portage, n.
unburden, vb.
unclog, vb.
unload, vb.
unpack, vb.

weight, n.
: 35

31.07
count

account, n.
add, vb.
addition, n.
amount, vb.
arithmetic, n.
arithmetician, n.
bifold, adj.
bis, lat. adv.
calculate, vb.
cast, vb.
cipher, n.
computation, n.
count, n.
count, vb.
counter, n.
counter-caster, n.
countless, adj.
couple, n.
divide, vb.
double, adj.
double, vb.
doubleness, n.
doubly, adv.
either, adj.
even number, n.
fiftyfold, adj.
figure, n.
fivefold, adj.
fois, fr. n.
forty thousand fold,
  adj.
half, adj.
half, adv.
half, n.
half-part, n.
innumerable, adj.
legion, n.
make, vb.
manifold, adj.

manifoldly, adv.
millioned, adj.
moiety, n.
multiply, vb.
ninefold, adj.
number, n.
number, vb.
numberless, adj.
odd number, n.
once, adv.
overcount, vb.
pair, n.
pennyworth, n.
poll, n.
proportion, n.
quarter, vb.
reckon, vb.
reckoning, n.
redouble, vb.
score, n.
sevenfold, adj.
sum, n.
sum, vb.
sumless, adj.
tally, n.
tell, vb.
tenfold, adj.
thousandfold, adj.
threefold, adj.
thrice, adv.
thrice-double, adj.
times, prep.
total, n.
treble, adj.
treble, vb.
tripartite, adj.
triple, adj.
twice, adv.
twofold, adj.
uncounted, adj.
unnumbered, adj.
untold, adj.
well-divided, adj.
: 81

31.08
numbers

---

a fifteenth, num.
a (one) half, num.
a (one) quarter, num.
a sixth, num.
a tenth, num.
a third, num.
century, n.
deux, fr. num.
deux cents, fr. num.
dime, n.
dozen, n.
eight, num.
eighteen, num.
eighth, num.
eight hundred five,
  num.
eightscore, num.
eightscore eight,
  num.
eight thousand, num.
eight thousand and
  four hundred, num.
eighty, num.
eleven, num.
eleven and twenty,
  num.
eleventh, num.
fifteen, num.
fifteen hundred, num.
fifteen thousand,
  num.
fifth, num.
fifty, num.
fifty-five, num.
fifty thousand, num.
first, num.
five, num.
five and thirty, num.
five and twenty,
  num.
five and twenty
  thousand, num.

five hundred, num.
fivescore, num.
five thousand, num.
forty, num.
forty-eight, num.
forty thousand, num.
four, num.
four and twenty,
  num.
four dozen, num.
four hundred one and
  twenty, num.
four hundred
  twenty-six, num.
fourscore, num.
fourscore three, num.
fourteen, num.
fourteen and a half,
  num.
fourteen hundred,
  num.
fourth, num.
four thousand, num.
four times seven,
  num.
half a dozen, num.
half a hundred, num.
half a million, num.
half a score, num.
hundred, num.
hundred and fifty,
  num.
hundred and seven,
  num.
hundred forty, num.
hundred thousand,
  num.
hundred twenty-six,
  num.
L, n.
leash, n.
mille, fr. num.
million, num.
nine, num.
ninescore, num.

ninescore and
  seventeen, num.
nineteen, num.
nine thousand, num.
ninety, num.
ninth, num.
ninth part, num.
number, n.
O, num.
one, num.
one and twenty,
  num.
primo, lat. adv.
second, num.
secondarily, adv.
secundo, lat. adv.
seven, num.
seven and a half,
  num.
seven dozen, num.
seven hundred, num.
seventeen, num.
seventh, num.
seven thousand, num.
seventy, num.
seventy-five, num.
six, num.
six and thirty, num.
six and twenty, num.
six dozen, num.
six score, num.
sixteen, num.
sixteen hundred,
  num.
sixth, num.
six thousand, num.
six thousand and two
  hundred, num.
sixth part, num.
sixty, num.
sixty and nine, num.
ten, num.
ten hundred, num.
tenth, num.
ten thousand, num.

tenth part of one,
  num.
ten times treble,
  num.
tertio, lat. adv.
third, num.
third, vb.
thirdly, adv.
third part, num.
thirteen, num.
thirtieth, num.
thirty, num.
thirty and six, num.
thirty dozen, num.
thirty-one, num.
thirty thousand, num.
thirty-three, num.
thousand, num.
thousand part, num.
thousand thousand,
  num.
three, num.
three and fifty, num.
three and thirty,
  num.
three and twenty,
  num.
three and twenty
  thousand, num.
three hundred, num.
three-quarters, num.
threescore, num.
threescore and ten,
  num.
threescore and two,
  num.
threescore thousand,
  num.
three thirds, num.
three thousand, num.
three threes, num.
three times thrice,
  num.
thrice six, num.
thrice three, num.

thrice threefold, num.
thrice three times,
  num.
tithe, n.
tithe, num.
treble, n.
twain, num.
twelfth, num.
twelve, num.
twelve and a half,
  num.
twelve hundred,
  num.
twelve score, num.
twelve thirties, num.
twelve thousand,
  num.
twentieth part, num.
twenty, num.
twenty-five, num.
twenty hundred,
  num.
twenty hundred
  thousand, num.
twenty-nine, num.
twenty-one, num.
twenty-seven, num.
twenty thousand,
  num.
twenty-three, num.
twice fifteen
  thousand, num.
twice five, num.
twice five hundred,
  num.
twice six, num.
twice treble, num.
twice two, num.
two, num.
two and fifty, num.
two and forty, num.
two and thirty, num.
two and twenty,
  num.
two dozen, num.

two hundred, num.
two hundred fifty,
  num.
two score, num.
two tens, num.
two thousand, num.
  : 185

31.09
pair

───────────

brace, n.
couple, n.
couplement, n.
couplet, n.
gemini, n.
pair, n.
twain, n.
yoke, n.
  : 8

31.10
many • few

───────────

agood, adv.
at (in the) least, adv.
few, adj.
few, n.
fewness, n.
least, n.
legion, n.
less, n.
lesser, n.
little, adj.
many, adj.
many, n.
mickle, adj.
mo, adj.
mo, adv.
mo, n.
molto, it. adv.
more, adv.
more, n.
most, adv.
most, n.

much, adj.
much, adv.
much, n.
multi, lat. adj.
multitude, n.
paucus, lat. adj.
peu, fr. n.
più, it. adv.
plus, fr. adv.
populous, adj.
rareness, n.
rarest, n.
short-numbered, adj.
some, adj.
tantus, lat. adj.
  : 36

31.11
several

───────────

divers, adj.
divers, n.
plural, adj.
several, adj.
sundry, adj.
  : 5

31.12
increase

───────────

accrue, vb.
add, vb.
addition, n.
aggravate, vb.
amplify, vb.
annex, vb.
annexment, n.
appendix, n.
augment, vb.
augmentation, n.
branch, vb.
crescent, adj.
crescive, adj.
dilate, vb.
double, vb.

draw, vb.
draw out, phr. vb.
eke, vb.
engross, vb.
enlarge, vb.
extend, vb.
extent, n.
fast-growing, adj.
great-grown, adj.
grow, vb.
growth, n.
high-grown, adj.
ill-annexed, adj.
increase, n.
increase, vb.
increaseful, adj.
length, vb.
lengthen, vb.
long-grown, adj.
multiply, vb.
outgrow, vb.
over and above, adv.
overblow, vb.
overgrow, vb.
overgrowth, n.
piece, vb.
propagate, vb.
propagation, n.
raise, vb.
reach, vb.
rough-grown, adj.
rude-growing, adj.
stretch, vb.
thick-grown, adj.
wax, vb.
waxen, vb.
wide-enlarged, adj.
  : 52

31.13
decrease

───────────

abate, vb.
abatement, n.
abbreviate, vb.

abridge, vb.
abridgement, n.
allay, vb.
allayment, n.
bate, vb.
beauty-waning, adj.
constringe, vb.
contract, vb.
curtail, vb.
custom-shrunk, adj.
decrease, vb.
degrade, vb.
diminish, vb.
diminution, n.
disquantity, vb.
dwindle, vb.
ebb, vb.
extenuate, vb.
extenuation, n.
lessen, vb.
pare, vb.
peak, vb.
qualification, n.
qualify, vb.
recoil, vb.
scant, vb.
short, vb.
shorten, vb.
shrink, vb.
shrivel, vb.
slake, vb.
unbated, adj.
wane, n.
wane, vb.
: 37

31.14
swell

bell, vb.
belly, vb.
big, adj.
big-bellied, adj.
big-swollen, adj.
blister, vb.

bloat, adj.
blow, vb.
bottled, adj.
dropsied, adj.
emboss, vb.
exsufflicate, adj.
high-blown, adj.
high-swollen, adj.
impostume, n.
outswell, vb.
overswell, vb.
puff, vb.
rank, adj.
summer-swelling,
  adj.
surfeit-swelled, adj.
swell, vb.
swelling, n.
whelked, adj.
: 24

31.15
moreover

again, adv.
also, adv.
another, adj.
as well as, adv.
aussi, fr. adv.
autre, fr. adj.
beside, adv.
besides, adv.
eke, adv.
else, adv.
et cetera
for and, conj.
furthermore, adv.
item, adv.
likewise, adv.
more, adv.
more, n.
more above, adv.
moreover, adv.
odd, adj.

of (to the) vantage,
  adv.
over, adv.
over and above, adv.
puis, fr. adv.
so-forth, n.
thereto, adv.
thereunto, adv.
too, adv.
: 28

31.16
join

add, vb.
adhere, vb.
adjoin, vb.
adjunct, adj.
adjunct, n.
all-binding, adj.
ally, vb.
along, adv.
among, adv.
annex, vb.
annexion, n.
annexment, n.
band, vb.
bind, vb.
cement, vb.
chain, vb.
cheek by jowl, adv.
clasp, vb.
cleave, vb.
cling, vb.
close, n.
close, vb.
combination, n.
combine, vb.
common, adj.
commutual, adj.
compact, adj.
compact, vb.
company, n.
conjoin, vb.
conjointly, adv.

conjunct, adj.
conjunction, n.
conjunctive, adj.
corollary, n.
corporate, adj.
couple, vb.
couplement, n.
embody, vb.
enchain, vb.
engage, vb.
engraff, vb.
engraft, vb.
enlink, vb.
espouse, vb.
fasten, vb.
five-finger-tied, adj.
gimmaled, adj.
glue, vb.
graff, vb.
graft, vb.
gripple, vb.
hand in hand, adv.
hang, vb.
hook, vb.
ill-annexed, adj.
imp, vb.
incorporate, adj.
incorporate, vb.
incorpsed, adj.
indissoluble, adj.
individable, adj.
injoint, vb.
inoculate, vb.
inseparable, adj.
inseparate, adj.
insinew, vb.
interchain, vb.
interjoin, vb.
in the quill, adv.
join, vb.
joinder, n.
joint, adj.
joint, n.
joint, vb.
jointly, adv.

knit, vb.
lace, vb.
link, vb.
long-engraffed, adj.
marry, vb.
match, vb.
mingle, n.
mingle, vb.
misgraffed, adj.
mortise, vb.
mutuality, n.
mutually, adv.
nail, vb.
pair, vb.
peg, vb.
piece, vb.
pin, vb.
rejoindure, n.
reunite, vb.
rivet, vb.
sheaf, vb.
sinew, vb.
solder, vb.
splinter, vb.
strong-knit, adj.
tack, vb.
tie, n.
tie, vb.
together, adv.
unbind, vb.
undividable, adj.
undivided, adj.
union, n.
unite, vb.
unity, n.
unseparable, adj.
unsevered, adj.
yoke, vb.
 : 114

31.17
separation
————————

apart, adv.
asunder, adv.

a-twain, adv.
blood-boltered, adj.
bolt, vb.
bolter, n.
brokenly, adv.
deep-divorcing, adj.
disbranch, vb.
disjoin, vb.
disjoint, adj.
disjoint, vb.
disjunction, n.
dislocate, vb.
dismantle, vb.
dismember, vb.
dissever, vb.
dissolution, n.
dissolve, vb.
distinguish, vb.
distract, adj.
distract, vb.
distractedly, adv.
distraction, n.
disunite, vb.
dividable, adj.
divide, vb.
divident, adj.
dividual, adj.
division, n.
divorce, n.
divorce, vb.
divorcement, n.
glean, vb.
in twain, adv.
long-parted, adj.
part, vb.
partition, n.
segregation, n.
separable, adj.
separate, vb.
separation, n.
sequester, n.
sequester, vb.
sequestration, n.
sever, vb.
sieve, n.

sift, vb.
single, vb.
strain, vb.
sunder, adv.
sunder, vb.
toze, vb.
try, vb.
twain, vb.
unbolted, adj.
unbound, adj.
unseam, vb.
unsifted, adj.
wean, vb.
well-divided, adj.
winnow, vb.
 : 62

31.18
mixture
————————

blend, vb.
card, vb.
churn, vb.
co-meddle, vb.
commix, vb.
commixtion, n.
commixture, n.
compound, adj.
compound, n.
compound, vb.
confound, vb.
gallimaufry, n.
intermingle, vb.
intermix, vb.
meddle, vb.
mell, vb.
mingle, n.
mingle, vb.
mix, vb.
mixture, n.
sophisticate, vb.
temper, vb.
tinct, n.
unmingled, adj.
unmixed, adj.   : 25

31.19
stuff
————————

cram, vb.
farce, vb.
force, vb.
news-crammed, adj.
promise-crammed,
  adj.
stuff, vb.
stuffing, n.
truss, vb.
unstuffed, adj.
 : 9

31.20
excess
————————

cruelly, adv.
exceeding, adj.
exceeding, adv.
exceedingly, adv.
excess, n.
excessive, adj.
extreme, adj.
extreme, n.
fierce, adj.
fort, fr. adv.
greatly, adv.
grievous, adj.
grossly, adv.
high, adj.
highly, adv.
hyperbolical, adj.
immoderate, adj.
immoderately, adv.
immodest, adj.
inordinate, adj.
intolerable, adj.
large, adj.
largely, adv.
lavish, adj.
lavishly, adv.
mad, adj.
much, adv.

out-Herod, vb.
outrageous, adj.
overdo, vb.
over-measure, n.
overmuch, adv.
overplus, n.
passing, adj.
passing, adv.
rank, adj.
rankness, n.
rich, adj.
richly, adv.
right, adv.
superfluity, n.
superfluous, adj.
superfluously, adv.
superflux, n.
surplus, n.
too, adv.
très, fr. adv.
trop, fr. adv.
vengeance, adv.
very, adv.
 : 50

31.21
omission

abridge, vb.
bar, vb.
debar, vb.
dispensation, n.
embar, vb.
except, vb.
exclude, vb.
exempt, vb.
fail, n.
miss, vb.
missingly, adv.
omission, n.
omit, vb.
omittance, n.
 : 14

31.22
cancel

abrogate, vb.
avoid, vb.
blot, vb.
cancel, n.
cancel, vb.
clear, adj.
clear, vb.
countermand, n.
cut, vb.
deface, vb.
disannul, vb.
dislimn, vb.
dout, vb.
eat [one's] word, vb.
extinct, adj.
extinct, vb.
extincture, n.
extinguere, lat. vb.
extinguish, vb.
frustrate, adj.
frustrate, vb.
irrevocable, adj.
never-quenching, adj.
quench, vb.
quenchless, adj.
rasure, n.
raze, vb.
recall, vb.
repeal, vb.
retract, vb.
reverse, vb.
revoke, vb.
revokement, n.
scrape, vb.
strike, vb.
swallow, vb.
uncrossed, adj.
undo, vb.
unpay, vb.
unrecalling, adj.
unreversed, adj.
unsay, vb.

unspeak, vb.
unswear, vb.
void, adj.
withdraw, vb.
 : 46

31.23
equality

alike, adj.
alike, adv.
all one
as, adv.
balance, vb.
coequal, adj.
companion, vb.
compeer, vb.
cope, vb.
counterpoise, n.
counterpoise, vb.
countervail, vb.
egall, adj.
egally, adv.
equal, adj.
equal, n.
equal, vb.
equality, n.
equally, adv.
equalness, n.
equivalent, adj.
even, adj.
even, vb.
evenly, adv.
fellow, n.
level, adj.
level, n.
level, vb.
like, adj.
like, adv.
like, n.
match, n.
match, vb.
mate, vb.
meet, adj.
parallel, adj.

parallel, n.
parallel, vb.
peise, vb.
poise, vb.
quid for quo, adv.
same, adj.
self, adj.
selfsame, adj.
such-like, adj.
unfellowed, adj.
unmatchable, adj.
unmatched, adj.
unparalleled, adj.
weal-balanced, adj.
 : 50

31.24
namely

namely, adv.
quasi, adv.
to wit, adv.
videlicet, adv.
 : 4

31.25
difference

another, adj.
differ, vb.
difference, n.
differency, n.
different, adj.
disparity, n.
divers, adj.
diversely, adv.
diversity, n.
inequality, n.
odd, adj.
oddly, adv.
odds, n.
other, adj.
several, adj.
tother, adj.
unequal, adj.

unlike, adj.
variable, adj.
variation, n.
variations, n.
variety, n.
vary, n.
vary, vb.
: 24

31.26
portion

allottery, n.
apiece, adv.
branch, n.
cantle, n.
commune, vb.
depart, vb.
distribute, vb.
divide, vb.
dole, n.
element, n.
half-part, n.
ingredience, n.
ingredient, n.
interess, vb.
interest, n.
lottery, n.
mess, n.
moiety, n.
parcel, n.
parcel, vb.
paring, n.
part, n.
part, vb.
partake, vb.
partaker, n.
participate, adj.
participate, vb.
participation, n.
partly, adv.
piece, n.
pittance, n.
portion, n.
proportion, n.

share, n.
share, vb.
size, n.
world-sharer, n.
: 37

31.27
heap

accumulate, vb.
accumulation, n.
balk, vb.
barn, vb.
cake, n.
candle-mine, n.
cupboard, vb.
dunghill, n.
engross, vb.
engrossment, n.
garner, vb.
heap, n.
heap, vb.
hoard, vb.
huddle, vb.
in store, adv.
layer-up, n.
lump, n.
mass, n.
new-store, vb.
pile, n.
pile, vb.
quarry, n.
save, vb.
scrape, vb.
store, n.
store, vb.
stow, vb.
stowage, n.
uphoard, vb.
: 30

31.28
particle

atom, n.

atomy, n.
eye, n.
grain, n.
hair, n.
jot, n.
mite, n.
mote, n.
particle, n.
point, n.
prick, n.
syllable, n.
tittle, n.
whit, n.
: 14

31.29
drop

dewdrop, n.
distil, vb.
distillation, n.
distilment, n.
drop, n.
drop, vb.
droplet, n.
dropping, n.
gout, n.
honey-drop, n.
stillatory, n.
water-drop, n.
: 12

31.30
remnant

antiquities, n.
relic, n.
remain, vb.
remainder, n.
remains, n.
remnant, n.
residue, n.
rest, n.
rest, vb.
: 9

31.31
morsel

bit, n.
broken meat, n.
crumb, n.
crumble, vb.
dreg, n.
gobbet, n.
lee, n.
morsel, n.
ort, n.
scrap, n.
: 10

31.32
tatter

botch, n.
botchy, adj.
feaze, vb.
fritter, n.
patch, n.
patch, vb.
rag, n.
ragged, adj.
raggedness, n.
shred, n.
snip, n.
tatter, n.
tatter, vb.
: 13

31.33
fragment

a-pieces, adv.
cheese-paring, n.
end, n.
fillet, n.
flaw, n.
fraction, n.
fragment, n.
limb-meal, adv.
piece, n.

rasher, n.
shard, n.
shive, n.
shiver, n.
slice, n.
snatch, n.
splinter, n.
: 16

31.34
dreg

dreg, n.
dross, n.
drossy, adj.
garbage, n.
lee, n.
offal, n.
refuse, n.
rubbish, n.
scum, n.
trash, n.
: 10

31.35
bunch

bavin, n.
bottle, n.
bunch, n.
cluster, vb.
faggot, n.
fardel, n.
flake, n.
flaky, adj.
flock, n.
pack, n.
pack, vb.
packet, n.
parcel, n.
sheaf, n.
tuft, n.
wisp, n.
: 16

31.36
multitude

band, n.
bevy, n.
body, n.
cluster, n.
company, n.
confluence, n.
crew, n.
crowd, n.
crowd, vb.
cry, n.
faction, n.
file, n.
flight, n.
flock, n.
fry, n.
gender, n.
ging, n.
heap, n.
herd, n.
host, n.
kennel, n.
kind, n.
knot, n.
litter, n.
many, n.
meinie, n.
mess, n.
multitude, n.
multitudinous, adj.
number, n.
pack, n.
parcel, n.
party, n.
pester, vb.
press, n.
rabble, n.
rout, n.
sect, n.
sectary, n.
sort, n.
spawn, n.
swarm, n.

swarm, vb.
team, n.
throng, n.
throng, vb.
tribe, n.
troop, n.
upswarm, vb.
: 49

31.37
single

alone, adv.
bare, adj.
but, adv.
distinct, adj.
distinct, n.
distinction, n.
distinctly, adv.
distinguishment, n.
especial, adj.
especially, adv.
mere, adj.
merely, adv.
notedly, adv.
odd, adj.
oddly, adv.
one by one, adv.
only, adj.
only, adv.
parcel, vb.
particular, adj.
particular, n.
particularity, n.
particularize, vb.
particularly, adv.
peculiar, adj.
per se
proper, adj.
property, n.
several, adj.
several, n.
severally, adv.
simple, adj.
simply, adv.

single, adj.
singly, adv.
singular, adj.
singularity, n.
sole, adj.
solely, adv.
solus, adj.
solus, lat. adj.
special, adj.
specially, adv.
specialty, n.
speciously, adv.
: 45

31.38
almost

almost, adv.
in (a) manner, adv.
near, adv.
nearly, adv.
paene, lat. adv.
slightly, adv.
somedeal, adv.
something, adv.
somewhat, adv.
thereabout, adv.
thereabouts, adv.
well-nigh, adv.
: 12

31.39
weight

avoirdupois, n.
carat, n.
counterpoise, n.
counterpoise, vb.
grain, n.
ounce, n.
outweigh, vb.
overweigh, vb.
peise, vb.
poise, n.
poise, vb.

173

31 quantity

pound, n.
scale, vb.
scruple, n.
tod, n.
tod, vb.
troy weight, n.
unweighed, adj.
unweighing, adj.
weigh, vb.
weight, n.
  : 21

31.40
pint
———————

bushel, n.

dram, n.
gallon, n.
half-pint, n.
moy, n.
peck, n.
pint, n.
pottle, n.
quart, n.
stoup, n.
tun, n.
  : 11

31.41
scale
———————

balance, n.

beam, n.
bemete, vb.
gauge, vb.
measure, vb.
mete, vb.
scale, n.
ton, n.
  : 8

31.42
heavy • light
———————

heavily, adv.
heaviness, n.
heavy, adj.
honey-heavy, adj.

leaden, adj.
light, adj.
lighten, vb.
lightness, n.
ponderous, adj.
thick, adj.
unwieldy, adj.
weigh, vb.
weight, n.
weightless, adj.
weighty, adj.
well-weighing, adj.
  : 16

32 time

174

32.01
clock

clock, n.
dial, n.
dial hand, n.
German clock, n.
glass, n.
hand, n.
horologe, n.
hour-glass, n.
jack, n.
Jack of the clock, n.
jar, n.
jar, vb.
prick, n.
sands, n.
watch, n.
: 15

32.02
hour • day • year

after-hour, n.
annual, adj.
daily, adj.
daily, adv.
day, n.
dies, lat. n.
diurnal, adj.
fortnight, n.
half hour, n.
heure, fr. n.
hour, n.
hourly, adj.
jour, fr. n.
journal, adj.
minute, n.
minutely, adj.
sennight, n.
sun, n.
three-hours, n.
twelvemonth, n.
week, n.
weekly, adj.

year, n.
yearly, adj.
: 24

32.03
times

after-dinner, n.
after-supper, n.
a' (o') clock, adv.
bedtime, n.
birthday, n.
birth-hour, n.
bridal day, n.
coronation-day, n.
dancing days, n.
date, n.
day, n.
dinner-time, n.
doomsday, n.
eaning time, n.
fasting-day, n.
golden age, n.
golden world, n.
great morning, n.
hey-day, n.
hour, n.
instant, n.
Judgement Day
law-day, n.
leet, n.
loveday, n.
market day, n.
marriage-day, n.
May-morn, n.
milking-time, n.
moment, n.
now-a-days, adv.
peascod-time, n.
playing-day, n.
ring time, n.
rut-time, n.
salad days, n.
school-days, n.
sealing-day, n.

season, n.
session, n.
simple time, n.
sleeping-hour, n.
summer day, n.
summer's day, n.
supper-time, n.
time, n.
treble-dated, adj.
trial day, n.
unseasonable, adj.
unseasonably, adv.
unseasoned, adj.
utas, n.
vacation, n.
vigil, n.
wedding-day, n.
when, adv.
whenas, adv.
whenever, adv.
whensoever, adv.
whiting-time, n.
workaday, n.
working-day, n.
: 62

32.04
season

All-hallown summer,
n.
autumn, n.
dog-days, n.
equinox, n.
harvest, n.
harvest-home, n.
Hiems, n.
middle summer, n.
midsummer, n.
prime, n.
season, n.
spring, n.
spring-time, n.
St. Martin's summer,
n.

summer, n.
summer, vb.
sweet-seasoned, adj.
unseasonable, adj.
Ver, n.
winter, n.
wintered, adj.
winterly, adj.
winter-time, n.
: 23

32.05
holidays

All-hallond Eve
All-hallowmas, n.
All-Souls' Day
Ascension-Day
Ash Wednesday
Bartholomew-tide, n.
Black Monday
Christmas, n.
Crispin Crispian
Crispin's Day
Day of Crispin
  Crispian(us)
Easter, n.
Ember-eve, n.
Feast of St. Crispian
festival, n.
Good Friday
Hallowmas, n.
high-day, n.
high tide, n.
holiday, n.
holiday-time, n.
holy-ale, n.
holy-day, n.
Holy-rood Day
Lammas-eve, n.
Lammas-tide, n.
Lent, n.
Lenten, adj.
Lupercal, n.
Martlemas, n.

May-day, n.
Michaelmas
new-year, n.
Pentecost, n.
Philip and Jacob
Sabbath, n.
Shrove-tide, n.
Shrove Tuesday
St. Crispin's Day
St. Davy's Day
St. George's Feast
St. Lambert's Day
St. Valentine's Day
Whitsun, n.
: 44

32.06
month
─────────────
April, n.
August, n.
December, n.
February, n.
full moon, n.
January, n.
July, n.
June, n.
March, n.
May, n.
May, vb.
month, n.
monthly, adj.
monthly, adv.
moon, n.
moonshine, n.
new moon, n.
: 17

32.07
monday
─────────────
Friday, n.
ides, n.
Monday, n.
Sabbath, n.

Saturday, n.
Sunday, n.
Thursday, n.
Tuesday, n.
Wednesday, n.
: 9

32.08
morning • night
─────────────
afternoon, n.
anight, adv.
anights, adv.
break of day, n.
cocklight, n.
cock-shut time, n.
curfew, n.
dawn, n.
dawn, vb.
dawning, n.
diluculum, lat. n.
eve, n.
even, n.
evening, n.
first cock, n.
forenoon, n.
matin, n.
midday, n.
midnight, n.
mid season, n.
morn, n.
morning, n.
morning cock, n.
morrow, n.
night, n.
nightly, adj.
noon, n.
noonday, n.
noontide, n.
odd-even, adj.
out-night, vb.
overnight, adv.
overnight, n.
second cock, n.
sunrise, n.

sunrising, n.
sunset, n.
to-night, adv.
twilight, n.
vesper, n.
vigil, n.
watch, n.
yesternight, adv.
: 43

32.09
childhood • youth
─────────────
childhood, n.
childishness, n.
childness, n.
eight-year-old, adj.
infancy, n.
leaping time, n.
March-chick, n.
minority, n.
nonage, n.
pueritia, lat. n.
pupil age, n.
senior-junior, n.
young, adj.
young, n.
younger, n.
youngest, n.
young-eyed, adj.
youngly, adv.
youth, n.
youthful, adj.
: 20

32.10
maidhood
─────────────
girl, n.
lass, n.
maid, n.
maid-child, n.
maiden, n.
maidenhead, n.
maidenhood, n.

maidenly, adj.
maidhood, n.
pucelle, n.
virgin, n.
virgin, vb.
virginal, adj.
virginity, n.
virgin-like, adj.
wench, n.
: 16

32.11
old age
─────────────
age, n.
age, vb.
aged, n.
ancient, adj.
ancient, n.
ancientry, n.
antiquity, n.
antiquus, lat. adj.
chair-days, n.
crutch, n.
eld, n.
elder, n.
eldest, n.
grey, adj.
greybeard, n.
mature, adj.
maturely, adv.
maturity, n.
mid-age, n.
middle age, n.
old, adj.
old, n.
old age, n.
oldest, n.
old-faced, adj.
oldness, n.
pantaloon, n.
senex, lat. n.
senior, n.
senior-junior, n.
seniory, n.

white-bearded, adj.
winter, n.
: 33

32.12
(un)ripe
───────────────
bloom, vb.
blossom, vb.
blow, vb.
bud, vb.
flourish, vb.
flower, vb.
flush, adj.
fresh, adj.
full-grown, adj.
green, adj.
greenly, adv.
grow, vb.
half-blown, adj.
initiate, adj.
mature, adj.
maturely, adv.
maturity, n.
May-morn, n.
mellow, adj.
mellow, vb.
new-sprung, adj.
novice, n.
overflourish, vb.
over-ripen, vb.
perfect, adj.
perfectness, n.
primy, adj.
puny, adj.
raw, adj.
rawly, adv.
ripe, adj.
ripe, vb.
ripen, vb.
ripeness, n.
riper, n.
salad days, n.
scarce-bearded, adj.
season, vb.

seed, vb.
shoot, vb.
spring, vb.
sprout, vb.
unbaked, adj.
unblown, adj.
unconfirmed, adj.
unfledged, adj.
ungrown, adj.
unhatched, adj.
unlicked, adj.
unmellowed, adj.
unripe, adj.
unseasoned, adj.
up-spring, n.
upstart, n.
: 54

32.13
newness
───────────────
afresh, adv.
anew, adv.
fertile-fresh, adj.
fire-new, adj.
fresh, adj.
freshly, adv.
freshness, n.
green, adj.
innovation, n.
innovator, n.
new, adj.
newly, adv.
newness, n.
not-of-the-newest,
  adj.
novel, adj.
novelty, n.
primy, adj.
renew, vb.
: 18

32.14
period
───────────────
after-age, n.
after-time, n.
age, n.
ancient, adj.
antiquary, adj.
antique, adj.
antiquity, n.
generation, n.
golden age, n.
golden world, n.
lease, n.
life, n.
lifetime, n.
limit, n.
limitation, n.
living, n.
period, n.
quarter, n.
space, n.
span, n.
term, n.
tide, n.
time, n.
: 23

32.15
interim
───────────────
a little, adv.
among, adv.
awhile, adv.
between, n.
breath, n.
breathing, n.
breathing while, n.
gest, n.
interim, n.
intermission, n.
intermissive, adj.
intervallum, n.
leisure, n.
mean time, n.

mean while, n.
minute while, n.
nonce, n.
otherwhiles, adv.
pissing-while, n.
point, n.
time to time, adv.
vacancy, n.
watch, n.
while, n.
whilst, adv.
whilst, n.
: 26

32.16
continuance
───────────────
again, adv.
alway, adv.
always, adv.
ay, adv.
ceaseless, adj.
constantly, adv.
continual, adj.
continually, adv.
continuance, n.
continuantly, adv.
continuate, adj.
continue, vb.
continuer, n.
dateless, adj.
day by day, adv.
durance, n.
dure, vb.
encore, fr. adv.
endless, adj.
endure, vb.
eternal, adj.
eternally, adv.
eterne, adj.
eternity, n.
eternize, vb.
ever, adv.
ever among, adv.
ever and anon, adv.

ever-during, adj.
everlasting, adj.
everlasting, n.
everlastingly, adv.
ever-living, adj.
evermore, adj.
evermore, adv.
ever-remaining, adj.
ever-running, adj.
forever, adv.
harp, vb.
hold, vb.
holding, n.
immortal, adj.
immortality, n.
immortalize, vb.
immortally, adv.
incessant, adj.
incessantly, adv.
insist, vb.
insisture, n.
inveterate, adj.
iterance, n.
iteration, n.
keep, vb.
last, vb.
live, vb.
livelong, adj.
long, adj.
long-continued, adj.
long-during, adj.
long-lived, adj.
long-living, adj.
longly, adv.
minutely, adj.
never, adv.
never-dying, adj.
never-ending, adj.
nevermore, adv.
never-withering, adj.
old, adj.
on, adv.
out-dure, vb.
over, adv.
over and over, adv.

over-long, adj.
over-tedious, adj.
pass, vb.
perdurable, adj.
perdurably, adv.
permanent, adj.
perpetual, adj.
perpetually, adv.
perpetuity, n.
perseverance, n.
persevere, vb.
persist, vb.
persistency, n.
persistive, adj.
proceed, vb.
process, n.
progress, n.
progression, n.
prolixious, adj.
prolixity, n.
remain, vb.
rest, vb.
semper, lat. adv.
stand, vb.
standing, n.
stay, n.
still, adj.
still, adv.
still and anon, adv.
still an end, adv.
still-lasting, adj.
subsist, vb.
survive, vb.
survivor, n.
time, n.
together, adv.
unchanging, adj.
wear, vb.
world-without-end, n.
yet, adv.
: 113

32.17
sojourn

abide, vb.
abode, n.
bide, vb.
biding, n.
call on (upon), phr.
vb.
continuance, n.
contrive, vb.
dwell, vb.
entertain, vb.
entertainment, n.
frequent, vb.
gest, n.
guest, n.
guestwise, adv.
haunt, n.
haunt, vb.
here-remain, n.
home-keeping, adj.
linger, vb.
live, vb.
out-dwell, vb.
outstand, vb.
outstay, vb.
outwear, vb.
overpass, vb.
pass, vb.
remain, n.
remain, vb.
residence, n.
resort, n.
resorter, n.
rest, n.
rest, vb.
revisit, vb.
see, vb.
sit, vb.
sojourn, n.
sojourn, vb.
sojourner, n.
spend, vb.
stand, vb.

stay, n.
stay, vb.
strangely-visited, adj.
tarriance, n.
tarry, vb.
temple-haunting, adj.
unfrequented, adj.
unvisited, adj.
visit, vb.
visitate, vb.
visitation, n.
visitor, n.
: 53

32.18
past • present •
future

after-age, n.
after-hour, n.
after-time, n.
ago, adv.
agone, adv.
ancient, adj.
antiquity, n.
backward, n.
bygone, adj.
bypast, adj.
decease, vb.
ere, adv.
erewhile, adv.
extant, adj.
forego, vb.
forepassed, adj.
former, adj.
former, n.
formerly, adv.
future, adj.
future, n.
futurely, adv.
futurity, n.
hence, adv.
henceforth, adv.
henceforward, adv.
hereafter, adj.

hereafter, adv.
hereto, adv.
hitherto, adv.
last, adv.
late, adj.
lately, adv.
new, adj.
new-dated, adj.
newly, adv.
newness, n.
now, adv.
now, n.
now-a-days, adv.
old, adj.
olden, adj.
once, adv.
past, adj.
past, n.
present, adj.
present, n.
présent, fr. n.
pristine, adj.
quondam, adj.
shall, vb.
since, adv.
sith, adv.
sithence, adv.
sometime, adj.
sometime, adv.
sometimes, adj.
sometimes, adv.
still, adv.
succession, n.
then, adj.
then, adv.
then, n.
to-day, adv.
tofore, adv.
to-morrow, adv.
to-morrow, n.
whilere, adv.
yesterday, adv.
yesterday, n.
yet, adv.
yore, adv.   : 72

32.19
beginning • end
————————
all-ending, adj.
at first, adv.
at (in the) last, adv.
begin, vb.
beginner, n.
beginning, n.
break the ice, vb.
broach, vb.
catastrophe, n.
cease, vb.
cess, n.
closure, n.
commence, vb.
commencement, n.
conclude, vb.
conclusion, n.
consummate, adj.
consummate, vb.
consummation, n.
desist, vb.
determinate, adj.
determinate, vb.
determination, n.
determine, vb.
discontinue, vb.
do, vb.
end, n.
end, vb.
end-all, n.
ender, n.
ending, n.
enter, vb.
exigent, n.
expiate, adj.
expiate, vb.
expiration, n.
expire, vb.
fall to, phr. vb.
fin, fr. n.
fine, n.
fine, vb.
finis, lat. n.

finish, vb.
finisher, n.
first, n.
firstling, n.
fore-end, n.
gin, vb.
give off, phr. vb.
include, vb.
index, n.
induction, n.
leave, vb.
noble-ending, adj.
onset, n.
out, adv.
period, n.
period, vb.
preface, n.
quietus, n.
renew, vb.
seal, vb.
set about, phr. vb.
stand to, phr. vb.
stay, n.
stay, vb.
stint, vb.
stop, n.
stop, vb.
surcease, n.
surcease, vb.
unfinished, adj.
upshot, n.
vile-concluded, adj.
                          : 74

32.20
origin
————————
founder, n.
head, n.
native, n.
origin, n.
original, n.
primal, adj.
primitive, adj.
pristine, adj.

rudiment, n.
source, n.
spring, n.
spring, vb.
 : 12

32.21
delay
————————
adjourn, vb.
break up, phr. vb.
comma, n.
dalliance, n.
dally, vb.
defer, vb.
delay, n.
delay, vb.
dilate, vb.
dilation, n.
dilatory, adj.
forslow, vb.
intermission, n.
intermit, vb.
linger, vb.
pause, n.
pause, vb.
pauser, n.
pausingly, adv.
post off, phr. vb.
procrastinate, vb.
prolong, vb.
prorogue, vb.
protract, vb.
protractive, adj.
put off, phr. vb.
rejourn, vb.
respite, n.
respite, vb.
stay, n.
stay, vb.
stretch, vb.
suspend, vb.
tardy, vb.
tarriance, n.
tarry, vb.   : 36

32.22
interruption

---

abruption, n.
break, vb.
cutter-off, n.
intercept, vb.
intercepter, n.
interception, n.
interrupt, vb.
interrupter, n.
interruption, n.
meddle, vb.
meddler, n.
  : 11

32.23
occurrence

---

accident, n.
act, n.
case, n.
chance, n.
chance, vb.
circumstance, n.
event, n.
eventful, adj.
example, n.
example, vb.
happen, vb.
instance, n.
occasion, n.
occurrence, n.
occurrent, n.
proceed, vb.
tiding, n.
  : 17

32.24
mischance

---

adversity, n.
calamity, n.
disaster, n.
disastrous, adj.

dismal, adj.
fault, n.
hapless, adj.
hazard, n.
ill-starred, adj.
inauspicious, adj.
infortunate, adj.
luckless, adj.
misadventure, n.
misadventured, adj.
mischance, n.
mischief, n.
misfortune, n.
mishap, n.
star-crossed, adj.
tragedy, n.
tragic, adj.
tragical, adj.
unauspicious, adj.
unfortunate, adj.
unfortunately, adv.
unhappily, adv.
unhappiness, n.
unhappy, adj.
unhappy, vb.
unluckily, adv.
unlucky, adj.
  : 31

32.25
chance

---

accident, n.
accidental, adj.
accidentally, adv.
adventure, n.
bechance, vb.
become, vb.
befall, vb.
befortune, vb.
betide, vb.
casual, adj.
casually, adv.
casualty, n.
chance, adv.

chance, n.
chance, vb.
cheer, vb.
come, vb.
come about, phr. vb.
come off, phr. vb.
do, vb.
fall, vb.
fare, n.
fare, vb.
fortunate, adj.
fortunately, adv.
fortunate-unhappy, n.
fortune, n.
fortune, vb.
full-fortuned, adj.
get, vb.
go, vb.
grow, vb.
hap, n.
hap, vb.
haply, adv.
happen, vb.
happily, adv.
happiness, n.
happy, adj.
in (any) case, adv.
luck, n.
luckily, adv.
lucky, adj.
maybe, adv.
occasion, n.
peradventure, adv.
perchance, adv.
sort, vb.
starred, adj.
success, n.
tide, vb.
turn, n.
worth, vb.   : 53

32.26
(un)usual

---

accustom, vb.

commonly, adv.
course, n.
coutume, fr. n.
current, adj.
custom, n.
custom, vb.
customary, adj.
extraordinarily, adv.
extraordinary, adj.
familiar, adj.
familiarity, n.
fashion, n.
fashionable, adj.
form, n.
formal, adj.
formally, adv.
frequent, adj.
habit, n.
inure, vb.
lightly, adv.
manner, n.
naturalize, vb.
odd, adj.
ordinance, n.
ordinary, adj.
practice, n.
practise, vb.
rare, adj.
rarely, adv.
rate, n.
regular, adj.
strange, adj.
strangely, adv.
stranger, n.
trade, n.
tradition, n.
traditional, adj.
trick, n.
unaccustomed, adj.
untraded, adj.
unused, adj.
unusual, adj.
unwonted, adj.
use, n.
use, vb.

usual, adj.
usually, adv.
wont, adj.
wont, n.
wont, vb.
  : 51

**32.27
issue**

consequence, n.
effect, n.
end, n.
event, n.
fruit, n.
issue, n.
redound, vb.
success, n.
upshot, n.
  : 9

**32.28
often • seldom**

frequent, adj.
oft, adj.
oft, adv.
often, adj.
often, adv.
oftentimes, adv.
oft-times, adv.
rare, adj.
rarely, adv.
seld, adv.
seldom, adj.
seldom, adv.
  : 12

**32.29
early • late**

betime, adv.
betimes, adv.
earliest, n.
earliness, n.

early, adj.
farthest, n.
forward, adj.
in good time, adv.
lag, adj.
late, adj.
lated, adj.
rearly, adv.
tardiness, n.
timely, adj.
too-timely, adj.
untimely, adj.
  : 16

**32.30
brevity**

abrupt, adj.
abruptly, adv.
at a clap, adv.
at once, adv.
at (with) a word,
  adv.
brevis, lat. adj.
brevity, n.
brief, adj.
brief, n.
briefly, adv.
briefness, n.
by and by, adv.
extemporal, adj.
extemporally, adv.
extempore, adv.
forthwith, adv.
immediate, adj.
immediately, adv.
incontinent, adv.
incontinently, adv.
in few, adv.
instant, adj.
instant, n.
instantly, adv.
in the nick, adv.
in (with) a thought,
  adv.

little, adj.
momentany, adj.
momentary, adj.
nick, n.
out of hand, adv.
outright, adv.
present, adj.
presently, adv.
readily, adv.
short, adj.
short, n.
shortest, n.
short-lived, adj.
shortness, n.
small, adj.
straight, adj.
straightway, adv.
sudden, adj.
suddenly, adv.
swift, adj.
trice, n.
twink, n.
upon the gad, adv.
wink, n.
  : 50

**32.31
imminence**

anon, adv.
betime, adv.
betimes, adv.
depend, vb.
dependant, n.
eftsoons, adv.
imminence, n.
imminent, adj.
incidency, n.
incident, adj.
in time, adv.
shortly, adv.
soon, adj.
soon, adv.
toward, adv.
towards, adv.   : 16

**32.32
expectation**

abide, vb.
abode, n.
anticipate, vb.
anticipation, n.
await, vb.
bide, vb.
expect, n.
expect, vb.
expectance, n.
expectancy, n.
expectation, n.
expecter, n.
fear-surprised, adj.
forestall, vb.
hearken, vb.
hope, n.
hope, vb.
look, vb.
look for, phr. vb.
look forward to, phr.
  vb.
prevent, vb.
promettre, fr. vb.
promise, n.
promise, vb.
stay, vb.
sudden, adj.
suddenly, adv.
surprise, n.
surprise, vb.
tarriance, n.
tarry, vb.
tiptoe, adv.
unaware, adv.
unawares, adv.
unexpected, adj.
unlooked, adj.
unlooked-for, adj.
unwares, adv.
unwarily, adv.
wait, vb.
watch, vb.   : 41

33.01
place

---

about, adv.
anywhere, adv.
baiting-place, n.
bested, adj.
birthplace, n.
burying-place, n.
elbow-room, n.
element, n.
elsewhere, adv.
everywhere, adv.
field, n.
footing, n.
ground, n.
here, adv.
here, n.
hereabout, adv.
hereabouts, adv.
hereby, adv.
hic, lat. adv.
ici, fr. adv.
in lieu, adv.
instead, adv.
judgement-place, n.
là, fr. adv.
local, adj.
lurking-place, n.
meeting, n.
meeting-place, n.
nowhere, adv.
otherwhere, adv.
place, n.
rendezvous, n.
room, n.
scope, n.
sea-room, n.
show-place, n.
situate, adj.
situation, n.
somewhere, adv.
somewhither, adv.
space, n.
spot, n.

station, n.
stead, n.
thence, adv.
there, adv.
throughout, adv.
ubique, lat. adv.
whence, adv.
whencesoever, adv.
where, adv.
where, n.
whereabout, adv.
whereabout, n.
whereas, adv.
wheresoever, adv.
wheresomever, adv.
wherever, adv.
whither, adv.
y, fr. adv.
  : 60

33.02
region

---

aground, adv.
aland, adv.
ashore, adv.
climate, n.
climature, n.
clime, n.
coast, n.
confine, n.
corner, n.
country, n.
desert, n.
earth, n.
ground, n.
home, n.
inland, n.
land, n.
limit, n.
main, n.
overland, adv.
part, n.
quarter, n.
region, n.

rural, adj.
shore, n.
soil, n.
territory, n.
vast, n.
waste, n.
  : 28

33.03
station

---

bestride, vb.
dark-seated, adj.
deadly-standing, adj.
foot, n.
foot, vb.
footing, n.
grovel, vb.
grovelling, adv.
horse, vb.
lay, vb.
lie, vb.
loll, vb.
low-laid, adj.
motionless, adj.
perch, vb.
prostrate, adj.
repose, vb.
rest, n.
rest, vb.
seat, vb.
set, vb.
set foot, phr. vb.
sit, vb.
stand, n.
stand, vb.
stander, n.
stander-by, n.
stand-under, vb.
stare, lat. vb.
state, n.
station, n.
stay, vb.
still, adv.
still-stand, n.

stone-still, adj.
stride, vb.
understand, vb.
unmoving, adj.
water-standing, adj.
  : 39

33.04
set

---

bestow, vb.
clap, vb.
establish, vb.
firm-set, adj.
fix, vb.
fixture, n.
found, vb.
foundation, n.
get on, phr. vb.
ground, vb.
high-pitched, adj.
high-placed, adj.
impose, vb.
infix, vb.
insert, vb.
inset, vb.
institute, vb.
lay, vb.
lodge, vb.
mettre, fr. vb.
misplace, vb.
overset, vb.
pitch, vb.
place, vb.
plant, vb.
plantation, n.
position, n.
posture, n.
prefix, vb.
put, vb.
putter-on, n.
putting-by, n.
reposal, n.
repose, vb.
seat, vb.

set, vb.
setter, n.
setter-up, n.
settle, vb.
sky-planted, adj.
stead, vb.
stell, vb.
stow, vb.
straight-pight, adj.
thrust, vb.
unlaid, adj.
: 46

33.05
north • south

east, adv.
east, n.
eastern, adj.
eastward, adj.
north, adv.
north, n.
north-east, n.
northen, adj.
northerly, adj.
northern, adj.
north-north-east, adv.
north-north-west,
  adv.
northward, adj.
northward, adv.
occident, n.
occidental, adj.
orient, n.
septentrion, n.
south, adv.
south, n.
southerly, adj.
southern, adj.
southward, adj.
southward, adv.
south-west, adv.
south-west, n.
west, adv.
west, n.

westerly, adj.
western, adj.
westward, adv.
: 31

33.06
side

abut, vb.
afront, adv.
back, n.
backside, n.
backward, n.
beside, adv.
butt-end, n.
dexter, adj.
end, n.
forward, adj.
front, n.
hand, n.
haunch, n.
hind, adj.
lag-end, n.
left, adj.
left, n.
orchard-end, n.
part, n.
rear, n.
rearward, n.
right, adj.
side, n.
side, vb.
sinister, adj.
vaunt, n.
vaward, n.
wing, vb.
: 28

33.07
middle

between, adv.
between, n.
centre, n.
centry, n.

core, n.
deep, n.
mean, adj.
mean, n.
mid, adj.
mid, n.
middle, adj.
middle, n.
mids, n.
midst, n.
midway, adj.
midway, adv.
midway, n.
navel, n.
: 18

33.08
inside • outside

bosom, n.
bowel, n.
exterior, adj.
exterior, n.
exteriorly, adv.
extern, adj.
extern, n.
external, adj.
in, adv.
inly, adj.
inly, adv.
inmost, adj.
inside, n.
interior, adj.
interior, n.
inward, adj.
inward, adv.
inward, n.
inwardly, adv.
lining, n.
out, adv.
out of door, adv.
outside, adv.
outside, n.
out-wall, n.
outward, adj.

outward, adv.
outward, n.
outwardly, adv.
outwards, adv.
within, adv.
without, adv.
without door, n.
without doors, n.
: 34

33.09
border

abut, vb.
adjacent, adj.
border, n.
bound, n.
bound, vb.
boundless, adj.
bourne, n.
brim, n.
brink, n.
compass, n.
confineless, adj.
determine, vb.
edge, n.
embound, vb.
end, n.
fathomless, adj.
fineless, adj.
fringe, vb.
hem, n.
infinite, adj.
infinite, n.
infinitely, adv.
infinitive, adj.
limit, n.
limit, vb.
limitation, n.
limiter, n.
list, n.
march, n.
margent, n.
measure, n.
measureless, adj.

past-proportion, n.
prescribe, vb.
side, n.
skirt, n.
tip, n.
unbounded, adj.
unlimited, adj.
unmeasurable, adj.
verge, n.
wide-skirted, adj.
: 42

33.10
encompassment

bail, vb.
bark, vb.
beset, vb.
blanket, vb.
border, vb.
bosom, vb.
bound, n.
bound, vb.
bower, vb.
brow-bound, adj.
canopy, vb.
case, vb.
cere, vb.
chain, vb.
circle, n.
circle, vb.
circuit, n.
circumference, n.
circummure, vb.
circumscribe, vb.
circumscription, n.
circumvent, vb.
circumvention, n.
clip, vb.
close, n.
close, vb.
closure, n.
coffer, vb.
coffin, vb.
compass, vb.

comprise, vb.
contain, vb.
continent, n.
cover, n.
cover, vb.
covering, n.
coverture, n.
crust, n.
crust, vb.
crusty, adj.
curtain, vb.
ditch, vb.
embar, vb.
embay, vb.
embound, vb.
embrace, vb.
encave, vb.
encircle, vb.
enclose, vb.
encloud, vb.
encompass, vb.
enfold, vb.
engird, vb.
engirt, vb.
enhearse, vb.
enring, vb.
enround, vb.
enswathe, vb.
envelop, vb.
environ, vb.
enwheel, vb.
enwrap, vb.
fence, vb.
film, vb.
fold, vb.
gird, vb.
girdle, vb.
girt, vb.
glass, vb.
glaze, vb.
gold-bound, adj.
hearse, vb.
hedge, vb.
hem, vb.
hold, vb.

hoop, vb.
immure, vb.
impale, vb.
inclip, vb.
include, vb.
inclusive, adj.
inhoop, vb.
lap, vb.
mantle, vb.
moat, vb.
over-canopy, vb.
overcome, vb.
overcover, vb.
overspread, vb.
pale, n.
pale, vb.
park, vb.
pave, vb.
pole-clipped, adj.
recover, vb.
rib, n.
rib, vb.
ring, vb.
roof, vb.
round, vb.
sea-walled, adj.
sheet, vb.
skin, vb.
tent, vb.
thatch, vb.
truss, vb.
urn, vb.
wall, vb.
water-walled, adj.
winter-ground, vb.
womb, vb.
wrap, vb.
: 112

33.11
firm

anchor, vb.
belock, vb.
bolt, vb.

brace, vb.
buckle, vb.
button, vb.
clasp, vb.
compact, adj.
compound, adj.
confirm, vb.
confirmation, n.
confirmer, n.
confix, vb.
corroborate, adj.
double-lock, vb.
earth-bound, adj.
engraff, vb.
engraft, vb.
ever-fixed, adj.
fast, adj.
fasten, vb.
firm, adj.
firmness, n.
firm-set, adj.
five-finger-tied, adj.
fix, vb.
fixture, n.
fixure, n.
gripple, vb.
impregnable, adj.
infix, vb.
inviolable, adj.
irremovable, adj.
irrevocable, adj.
lock, vb.
locked-up, adj.
mortise, vb.
nail, vb.
peg, vb.
pin, vb.
prick, vb.
rivet, vb.
rootedly, adv.
screw, vb.
seal, vb.
sealed-up, adj.
set, vb.
settle, vb.

shut, vb.
solid, adj.
solidity, n.
stable, adj.
stableness, n.
stake, vb.
staunch, adj.
steadfast, adj.
steadfastly, adv.
steady, adj.
stick, vb.
stick off, phr. vb.
strong, adj.
strong-barred, adj.
strong-based, adj.
strong-knit, adj.
strongly, adv.
sure, adj.
surely, adv.
ten-times-barred-up,
 adj.
tie, vb.
tied-up, adj.
tight, adj.
tightly, adv.
true-fixed, adj.
unremovable, adj.
unremovably, adv.
unshaked, adj.
unshaken, adj.
unshrinking, adj.
unslipping, adj.
unyielding, adj.
up-locked, adj.
 : 81

33.12
loose
────────────

loose, adj.
loose-bodied, adj.
loosen, vb.
ravel out, phr. vb.
slack, vb.
unbar, vb.

unbend, vb.
unbind, vb.
unbolt, vb.
unbound, adj.
unbraced, adj.
unbraided, adj.
unbreeched, adj.
unbuckle, vb.
unbutton, vb.
unbuttoned, adj.
unclasp, vb.
unclew, vb.
uncouple, vb.
uncurl, vb.
unfasten, vb.
unfirm, adj.
unfix, vb.
unfold, vb.
ungartered, adj.
ungird, vb.
unjointed, adj.
unknit, vb.
unlace, vb.
unlink, vb.
unlock, vb.
unloose, vb.
unpeg, vb.
unpin, vb.
unseal, vb.
unsteadfast, adj.
untangle, vb.
untie, vb.
untied, adj.
untucked, adj.
untwind, vb.
untwine, vb.
unweave, vb.
unwind, vb.
unwrung, adj.
unyoke, vb.
 : 46

33.13
open • close
────────────

close, vb.
dispark, vb.
dup, vb.
fast-closed, adj.
hatch, vb.
mouth, n.
mouth, vb.
narrow-mouthed, adj.
ope, adj.
ope, vb.
open, adj.
open, vb.
opening, n.
seel, vb.
set, vb.
shut, vb.
still-closing, adj.
widen, vb.
wink, vb.
yawn, vb.
 : 20

33.14
presence • absence
────────────

absence, n.
absent, adj.
absent, vb.
appear, vb.
appearer, n.
long-vanished, adj.
presence, n.
present, adj.
present, vb.
present-absent, adj.
vanish, vb.
 : 11

33.15
distance
────────────

abroad, adv.

absence, n.
absent, adj.
absent, vb.
afar, adv.
aloof, adv.
apart, adv.
aside, adv.
at foot, adv.
at half-sword, adv.
at hand, adv.
at (on) [one's] heels,
 adv.
away, adv.
back, adv.
beyond, adv.
beyond, n.
by, adv.
closely, adv.
distance, n.
distant, adj.
far, adj.
far, adv.
far-off, adj.
farthest, n.
forth, adv.
half-way, adv.
hand to hand, adv.
hard, adj.
hard by, adv.
hence, adv.
immediacy, n.
immediate, adj.
immediate, n.
near, adj.
near, adv.
nearest, n.
nearly, adv.
nearness, n.
neighbour, n.
neighbour, vb.
next, adv.
nigh, adj.
nigh, adv.
off, adv.
out, adv.

over, adv.
overfar, adv.
propinquity, n.
remote, adj.
remove, vb.
removedness, n.
sister, vb.
thereby, adv.
utmost, adj.
utmost, n.
way, n.
whereby, adv.
wide, adj.
yon, adj.
yon, adv.
yond, adj.
yond, adv.
yonder, adv.
: 63

33.16
size

agate, n.
big, adj.
big, n.
bigger, n.
bigness, n.
bulk, n.
bulky, adj.
dimension, n.
diminutive, adj.
diminutive, n.
dwarfish, adj.
extent, n.
great, adj.
great, n.
greater, n.
greatest, n.
greatness, n.
great-sized, adj.
gross, adj.
grossness, n.
growth, n.
huge, adj.

huge, n.
hugely, adv.
hugeness, n.
large, adj.
largeness, n.
least, n.
less, n.
lesser, n.
little, adj.
little, n.
magnus, lat. adj.
massy, adj.
minikin, n.
minimus, n.
monstrous, adj.
mountainous, adj.
multitudinous, adj.
parvus, lat. adj.
petit, fr. adj.
proportion, n.
puisne, adj.
puny, adj.
round, adj.
size, n.
size, vb.
small, adj.
small, n.
smaller, n.
smallest, n.
smallness, n.
tine, adj.
tiny, adj.
vast, adj.
vastidity, n.
vastly, adv.
vasty, adj.
: 58

33.17
giant • dwarf

diminutive, n.
dwarf, n.
dwarfish, adj.
giant, n.

giant-dwarf, n.
giantess, n.
giant-like, adj.
minimus, n.
scrubbed, adj.
shrimp, n.
: 10

33.18
fat • thin

bacon-fed, adj.
bare-bone, n.
bareness, n.
bare-ribbed, adj.
corpulent, adj.
engross, vb.
enlard, vb.
fat, adj.
fat-already, adj.
fat-guts, n.
fat-kidneyed, adj.
fatness, n.
fulsome, adj.
gaunt, adj.
gorbellied, adj.
great-bellied, adj.
gross, adj.
grossness, n.
half-faced, adj.
lank, adj.
lank, vb.
lank-lean, adj.
lard, vb.
lean, adj.
leanness, n.
little, adj.
meagre, adj.
plump, adj.
plumpy, adj.
pursy, adj.
round, adj.
rump-fed, adj.
skinny, adj.
slender, adj.

small, adj.
small, n.
spare, adj.
swag-bellied, adj.
thin, adj.
thinly, adv.
tidy, adj.
woolsack, n.
: 42

33.19
shape

block, n.
body, vb.
carve, vb.
compact, adj.
compact, vb.
compose, vb.
compound, vb.
consist, vb.
create, adj.
create, vb.
creation, n.
cut, n.
defeat, vb.
deform, vb.
disfigure, vb.
fashion, n.
fashion, vb.
figure, n.
figure, vb.
foolish-compounded,
  adj.
forge, vb.
forgetive, adj.
form, n.
form, vb.
formless, adj.
frame, n.
frame, vb.
hammer, vb.
ill-composed, adj.
ill-shaped, adj.
indigest, adj.

indigest, n.
indigested, adj.
inform, vb.
making, n.
miscreate, adj.
mis-shapen, adj.
mistemper, vb.
mood, n.
mould, n.
mould, vb.
prefigure, vb.
preform, vb.
proportion, n.
self-figured, adj.
shape, n.
shape, vb.
shapeless, adj.
stithy, vb.
temper, vb.
turn, vb.
unfashionable, adj.
unshape, vb.
unshaped, adj.
: 54

33.20
round

about, adv.
circle, n.
circle, vb.
compass, n.
compass, vb.
encompass, vb.
encompassment, n.
globy, adj.
hoop, n.
inhoop, vb.
O, n.
orb, n.
orb, vb.
pellet, vb.
pelleted, adj.
rigol, n.
ring, n.

ringlet, n.
rondure, n.
rotundity, n.
round, adj.
round, adv.
round, n.
round, vb.
roundure, n.
semi-circle, n.
semicircled, adj.
sphere, vb.
spherical, adj.
turn, vb.
: 30

33.21
square

quadrangle, n.
square, adj.
square, n.
trigon, n.
: 4

33.22
hole • trench

auger-hole, n.
bench-hole, n.
bore, n.
breach, n.
bunghole, n.
button-hole, n.
chap, n.
chink, n.
crack, n.
crannied, adj.
cranny, n.
crevice, n.
den, n.
ditch, n.
dog-hole, n.
eye, n.
flaw, n.
furrow, n.

gap, n.
hole, n.
hollow, n.
keyhole, n.
leak, n.
loop, n.
looped, adj.
loop-hole, n.
mortise, n.
muset, n.
orifice, n.
rift, n.
rupture, n.
sawpit, n.
sight, n.
sight-hole, n.
starting-hole, n.
trench, n.
vent, n.
ventage, n.
window, vb.
windowed, adj.
worm-hole, n.
: 41

33.23
hollowness

concave, adj.
concavity, n.
hole, n.
hollow, adj.
hollow, n.
hollowness, n.
womb, n.
womby, adj.
: 8

33.24
jutting-out

beetle, vb.
bulk, n.
jutting-out, n.
jutty, n.

jutty, vb.
nook-shotten, adj.
shelve, vb.
: 7

33.25
corner

angle, n.
black-cornered, adj.
coign, n.
corner, n.
hedge-corner, n.
nook, n.
nook-shotten, adj.
park-corner, n.
St. Magnus' Corner
three-nooked, adj.
: 10

33.26
sharp • dull

abate, vb.
acute, adj.
acutely, adv.
bateless, adj.
blunt, adj.
blunt, vb.
disedge, vb.
dull, adj.
dull, vb.
eager, adj.
edge, n.
edge, vb.
edgeless, adj.
fiery-pointed, adj.
grind, vb.
keen, adj.
keen-edged, adj.
keenness, n.
point, vb.
rebate, vb.
sharp, adj.
sharp, n.

sharpen, vb.
sharp-ground, adj.
sharply, adv.
sharpness, n.
sharp-pointed, adj.
trenchant, adj.
unbated, adj.
whet, vb.
 : 30

33.27
smooth • rough

choppy, adj.
easy, adj.
file, vb.
glib, adj.
harsh, adj.
harshly, adv.
harshness, n.
plain, adj.
raw, adj.
rough, adj.
rough-grown, adj.
roughly, adv.
roughness, n.
rub, n.
rude-growing, adj.
rugged, adj.
rug-headed, adj.
silken, adj.
sleek, adj.
sleek, vb.
slickly, adv.
slipper, adj.
slippery, adj.
smooth, adj.
smooth, vb.
smoothly, adv.
smoothness, n.
smug, adj.
uneven, adj.
unrough, adj.
 : 30

33.28
hard • soft

bake, vb.
braze, vb.
bristle, vb.
buckram, n.
discandy, vb.
dissolution, n.
dissolve, vb.
distil, vb.
flower-soft, adj.
gum, vb.
hard, adj.
hard, n.
harden, vb.
harder, n.
hardness, n.
heart-hardening, adj.
limber, adj.
lither, adj.
malleable, adj.
marble, n.
melt, vb.
mollis, lat. adj.
obduracy, n.
pliant, adj.
relent, vb.
resolve, vb.
rocky-hard, adj.
soft, adj.
soften, vb.
softness, n.
spongy, adj.
stare, vb.
stark, adj.
starkly, adv.
steel, vb.
steely, adj.
stiff, adj.
stiffen, vb.
stiffly, adv.
stone, n.
stone, vb.
stone-hard, adj.

strong-tempered, adj.
stubborn, adj.
stubborn-hard, adj.
stubbornly, adv.
stubbornness, n.
supple, adj.
temper, n.
temper, vb.
thaw, n.
tough, adj.
toughness, n.
unhardened, adj.
unrelenting, adj.
untempering, adj.
up-staring, adj.
waxen, adj.
 : 58

33.29
straight

direct, adj.
directly, adv.
downright, adj.
due, adv.
even, adj.
even, vb.
evenly, adv.
flat, adj.
flatlong, adv.
forthright, n.
headlong, adj.
level, adj.
level, n.
parallel, n.
perpendicular, adj.
perpendicularly, adv.
plain, adj.
point-blank, adj.
right, adv.
rightly, adv.
straight, adj.
upright, adj.
 : 22

33.30
oblique

across, adv.
aside, adv.
askance, adv.
askance, vb.
asquint, adv.
athwart, adv.
awry, adv.
bevel, adj.
bias, adv.
cam, adj.
collateral, adj.
counter, adv.
crank, n.
crooked, adj.
cross, adj.
cross, vb.
indent, vb.
indirect, adj.
indirection, n.
indirectly, adv.
oblique, adj.
thwart, adj.
thwart, adv.
traverse, adj.
traverse, vb.
uneven, adj.
wry, vb.
 : 27

33.31
entangle

across, adv.
bottom, vb.
braid, vb.
crank, vb.
crisp, adj.
crisp, vb.
cross, vb.
curious-knotted, adj.
curl, vb.
elf, vb.

encumber, vb.
engage, vb.
enmesh, vb.
enroot, vb.
entangle, vb.
entwist, vb.
even-pleached, adj.
feaze, vb.
fold, n.
fold, vb.
gage, vb.
gnarl, vb.
Gordian knot, n.
ill-wresting, adj.
impleach, vb.
interlace, vb.
intertangle, vb.
intertissued, adj.
intricate, adj.
intrince, adj.
intrinsicate, adj.
knit, vb.
knot, n.
knot, vb.
knotty, adj.
labyrinth, n.
maze, n.
plat, n.
plat, vb.
pleach, vb.
pleat, n.
plight, vb.
purse, vb.
ravel, vb.
ravel out, phr. vb.
rivel, vb.
screw, vb.
sorrow-wreathen, adj.
tangle, vb.
thick, adj.
thicken, vb.
thick-grown, adj.
thick-pleached, adj.
tie, n.
tortive, adj.

trammel, vb.
traverse, vb.
true-love knot, n.
twilled, adj.
twine, vb.
twist, vb.
unbraided, adj.
unclew, vb.
uncurl, vb.
unknit, vb.
unroll, vb.
untangle, vb.
untucked, adj.
untwind, vb.
untwine, vb.
unweave, vb.
unwind, vb.
unwrung, adj.
warp, vb.
weave, vb.
weaved-up, adj.
whelked, adj.
wind, vb.
wreathe, vb.
wrench, n.
wrench, vb.
wrest, vb.
wring, vb.
wrinkle, n.
wrinkle, vb.
wrinkled, adj.
writhled, adj.
 : 87

33.32
spread

broad-spreading, adj.
dilate, vb.
extend, vb.
flare, vb.
outstretch, vb.
rack, vb.
sprawl, vb.
spread, vb.

strain, n.
strain, vb.
stretch, vb.
stretched-out, adj.
wide-enlarged, adj.
wide-stretched, adj.
 : 14

33.33
length

along, adv.
extent, n.
great, adj.
length, n.
lengthen, vb.
long, adj.
long, n.
short, adj.
stretch, vb.
tall, adj.
 : 10

33.34
span

acre, n.
bemete, vb.
cubit, n.
diameter, n.
ell, n.
ell and three
  quarters, n.
fathom, n.
finger, n.
foot, n.
four-inched, adj.
furlong, n.
half-yard, n.
inch, n.
inchmeal, adv.
inch-thick, adj.
league, n.
measure, vb.
mete, vb.

meteyard, n.
mile, n.
nail, n.
pace, n.
perch, n.
plummet, n.
rule, n.
span, n.
span, vb.
square, n.
square, vb.
three-inch, n.
yard, n.
 : 31

33.35
hang

dangle, vb.
depend, vb.
down-roping, adj.
droop, vb.
flag, vb.
gibbet, vb.
hang, vb.
hover, vb.
lob, vb.
loll, vb.
overhang, vb.
pendent, adj.
pendulous, adj.
unhanged, adj.
 : 14

33.36
breadth

breadth, n.
broad, adj.
bulky, adj.
hairbreadth, n.
inch-thick, adj.
narrow, adj.
narrowly, adv.
spacious, adj.

strait, adj.
thick, adj.
thickest, n.
wide, adj.
widen, vb.
: 13

33.37
height

above, adv.
a-height, adv.
a-high, adv.
aloft, adv.
altitude, n.
apex, lat. n.
celsus, lat. adj.
cloud-capped, adj.
cloud-kissing, adj.
cop, vb.
crest, n.
crest, vb.
crown, n.
eagle-winged, adj.
head, n.
heaven-kissing, adj.
height, n.
high, adj.
high, n.
highest, n.
highly, adv.
highmost, adj.
highness, n.
high-peering, adj.
high-pitched, adj.
high-placed, adj.
lofty, adj.
meridian, n.
Olympus-high, adj.
overhead, adv.
pitch, n.
point, n.
pride of place, n.
skyish, adj.
spire, n.

stature, n.
steep, adj.
steep-up, adj.
steepy, adj.
summa, lat. n.
summit, n.
tall, adj.
taller, n.
tip, vb.
top, n.
topless, adj.
up^2, adv.
up, n.
upmost, adj.
upper, adj.
upward, n.
: 51

33.38
depth

abysm, n.
adown, adv.
base, adj.
base, n.
basest, n.
below, adv.
beneath, adv.
bottom, n.
bottomless, adj.
breast-deep, adj.
deep, adj.
deep, n.
deeply, adv.
depth, n.
down, adj.
down, adv.
downward, adv.
downwards, adv.
draught, n.
foot, n.
ground, n.
heart-deep, adj.
knee-deep, adj.
low, adj.

low, n.
lowest, n.
lowness, n.
nether, adj.
pottle-deep, adj.
profound, adj.
sandy-bottomed, adj.
shallow, adj.
soundless, adj.
steep-down, adj.
under, adj.
under, adv.
underfoot, adv.
underneath, adv.
: 38

33.39
row

abreast, adv.
a-row, adv.
deraign, vb.
dispose, n.
dispose, vb.
disposer, fr. vb.
disposition, n.
embattle, vb.
enrank, vb.
file, n.
form, n.
gradation, n.
line, n.
order, vb.
orderly, adj.
ordinance, n.
ordinant, adj.
range, n.
range, vb.
rank, n.
rank, vb.
row, n.
well-ordered, adj.
: 23

33.40
sequence

afore, adv.
aforehand, adj.
after, adv.
afterward, adv.
afterwards, adv.
already, adv.
at length, adv.
before, adv.
beforehand, adj.
beforetime, adv.
behind, adv.
behindhand, adv.
cap, vb.
chase, n.
chaser, n.
consequence, n.
consequently, adv.
continue, vb.
déjà, fr. adv.
ensue, vb.
finally, adv.
first, adj.
first, adv.
follow, vb.
follower, n.
fore, adv.
forego, vb.
forehand, n.
foremost, adj.
fore-run, vb.
former, adj.
former, n.
have after, phr. vb.
hindmost, adj.
imprimis, adv.
last, adj.
last, adv.
last, n.
lastly, adv.
latest, n.
latter, n.
next, adj.

next, n.
or, adv.
order, n.
posterior, n.
precede, vb.
precedence, n.
precedent, adj.
precedent, n.
precurrer, n.
precurse, n.
precursor, n.
predecessor, n.
prevent, vb.
prevention, n.
priority, n.
prologue, vb.
prosecute, vb.
prosecution, n.
pursue, vb.
pursuer, n.
pursuit, n.
quest, n.
second, vb.
secondary, n.
sequel, n.
sequence, n.
sequent, adj.
sequent, n.
stage, n.
step, n.
subsequent, adj.
succedere, lat. vb.

succeed, vb.
succeeder, n.
success, n.
successantly, adv.
succession, n.
successive, adj.
successively, adv.
successor, n.
suivre, fr. vb.
thereafter, adv.
trace, vb.
: 85

**33.41
distribution**

bestrew, vb.
diffuse, vb.
digest, vb.
disperse, vb.
dissipation, n.
distribute, vb.
distribution, n.
ill-dispersing, adj.
overstrew, vb.
powder, vb.
scatter, vb.
squander, vb.
strew, vb.
strewing, n.
strewment, n.
: 15

**33.42
change**

all-changing, adj.
alter, vb.
alteration, n.
avert, vb.
barter, vb.
change, n.
change, vb.
changeable, adj.
changeful, adj.
changeling, n.
child-changed, adj.
conversion, n.
convert, vb.
counterchange, n.
displant, vb.
double, n.
exchange, n.
exchange, vb.
innovation, n.
innovator, n.
interchange, n.
interchange, vb.
interchangeably, adv.
interchangement, n.
invert, vb.
metamorphize, vb.
mutable, adj.
mutation, n.

new-transformed, adj.
overset, vb.
pervert, vb.
purpose-changer, n.
quick-shifting, adj.
reform, vb.
revolution, n.
sea-change, n.
shift, n.
shift, vb.
transfer, vb.
transfigure, vb.
transform, vb.
transformation, n.
translate, vb.
transmigrate, vb.
transmutation, n.
transpose, vb.
trans-shape, vb.
triple-turned, adj.
turn, n.
turn, vb.
unchanging, adj.
variable, adj.
variation, n.
variations, n.
variety, n.
vary, n.
vary, vb.
wind-changing, adj.
: 58

34.01
go
___

afoot, adv.
aller, fr. vb.
amble, vb.
betake, vb.
career, n.
course, vb.
dodge, vb.
double, n.
earth-treading, adj.
ever-running, adj.
fiery-footed, adj.
fling, vb.
foot, vb.
footfall, n.
footing, n.
footman, n.
footstep, n.
free-footed, adj.
gait, n.
gallop, n.
gallop, vb.
get, vb.
giddy-paced, adj.
glide, n.
glide, vb.
go, vb.
goer, n.
heat, vb.
hedge, vb.
ire, lat. vb.
jet, vb.
jog, vb.
late-walking, n.
march, n.
march, vb.
measure, vb.
mince, vb.
night-walking, adj.
outrun, vb.
overgo, vb.
overrun, vb.
overstep, vb.

overwalk, vb.
pace, n.
pace, vb.
pass, n.
path, vb.
plod, vb.
pop, vb.
preambulate, vb.
progress, vb.
ride, vb.
run, vb.
runner, n.
rush, vb.
scour, vb.
scud, vb.
shift, vb.
shog, vb.
shuffle, vb.
sight-outrunning, adj.
skirr, vb.
slide, vb.
slip, vb.
stalk, n.
stalk, vb.
stamp, n.
stamp, vb.
step, n.
step, vb.
stride, n.
stride, vb.
strut, vb.
sweep, n.
sweep, vb.
take, vb.
thwart, vb.
trace, vb.
traverse, vb.
tread, n.
tread, vb.
troop, vb.
trot, vb.
trudge, vb.
turn, n.
untread, vb.
untrodden, adj.

waddle, vb.
wade, vb.
wag, vb.
walk, n.
walk, vb.
wend, vb.
whip, vb.
wind, vb.
: 95

34.02
leap
___

bob, vb.
bounce, vb.
bound, n.
bound, vb.
caper, n.
caper, vb.
career, n.
curvet, n.
curvet, vb.
cut a caper, vb.
frisk, n.
frisk, vb.
gallant-springing, adj.
gambol, n.
gambol, vb.
hop, vb.
jaunce, n.
jaunce, vb.
jerk, n.
jump, vb.
leap, n.
leap, vb.
night-tripping, adj.
overleap, vb.
overtrip, vb.
prance, vb.
ramp, n.
ramp, vb.
rampant, adj.
skip, vb.
spirt, vb.

spring, vb.
trip, vb.
vault, vb.
: 34

34.03
crawl
___

crawl, vb.
creep, vb.
fell-lurking, adj.
grovel, vb.
grovelling, adv.
knee, vb.
lurch, vb.
lurk, vb.
peak, vb.
skulk, vb.
slink, vb.
sneak, vb.
steal, vb.
stealth, n.
: 14

34.04
here-approach
___

accessible, adj.
accost, vb.
approach, n.
approach, vb.
approacher, n.
arrival, n.
arrivance, n.
arrive, vb.
attain, vb.
back, adv.
back-return, n.
board, vb.
coast, vb.
come, vb.
comer, n.
coming-on, adj.
disembark, vb.
draw, vb.

draw on, phr. vb.
drop in, phr. vb.
egress and regress, n.
forthcoming, adj.
get, vb.
here-approach, n.
hither, adv.
hitherto, adv.
hitherward, adv.
hitherwards, adv.
income, n.
land, vb.
new-come, adj.
reach, vb.
rebound, n.
recover, vb.
recoverable, adj.
reduce, vb.
relapse, n.
repair, n.
repair, vb.
resort, vb.
return, n.
revert, vb.
set foot, phr. vb.
shore, vb.
thick-coming, adj.
touch, vb.
turn, vb.
venire, lat. vb.
venire, it. vb.
visit, vb.
: 50

34.05
enter

access, n.
accessible, adj.
admit, vb.
admittance, n.
board, vb.
break in, phr. vb.
enter, n.
enter, vb.

entrance, n.
impenetrable, adj.
impregnable, adj.
inaccessible, adj.
intrare, lat. vb.
intrude, vb.
intruder, n.
intrusion, n.
invade, vb.
jet, vb.
man-entered, adj.
penetrable, adj.
penetrate, vb.
recourse, n.
well-entered, adj.
: 23

34.06
hence-going

abandon, vb.
abandoner, n.
aroint, vb.
avaunt, n.
avoid, vb.
away, adv.
back, adv.
back-return, n.
backward, adj.
backward, adv.
backwards, adv.
break, vb.
break forth, phr. vb.
break out, phr. vb.
congee, vb.
depart, n.
depart, vb.
departure, n.
discharge, n.
draw, vb.
egress and regress, n.
escape, n.
escape, vb.
exit, n.
fall from, phr. vb.

falling-from, n.
flee, vb.
fleet, vb.
flight, n.
flux, n.
fly, vb.
forsake, vb.
fugitive, adj.
fugitive, n.
go, vb.
goer-back, n.
go whistle, vb.
hence, adv.
hence-going, n.
issue, vb.
leave, n.
leave, vb.
leave-taking, n.
master-leaver, n.
pack, vb.
part, vb.
pass, vb.
passage, n.
peace-parted, adj.
quit, vb.
recoil, vb.
remotion, n.
remove, n.
remover, n.
repulse, n.
retire, n.
retire, vb.
retirement, n.
retourner, fr. vb.
retrograde, adj.
return, n.
return, vb.
scape, n.
scape, vb.
shrink, vb.
snick up, phr. vb.
thither, adv.
thitherward, adv.
timely-parted, adj.
transmigrate, vb.

unshrinking, adj.
void, vb.
whistle off, phr. vb.
withdraw, vb.
: 74

34.07
ascend

arise, vb.
ascend, vb.
ascension, n.
ascent, n.
aspire, vb.
canvas-climber, n.
clamber, vb.
climb, vb.
climber-upward, n.
heighten, vb.
high-soaring, adj.
horse, vb.
monter, fr. vb.
mount, vb.
mountant, adj.
new-sprung, adj.
overmount, vb.
overpeer, vb.
overtop, vb.
peer, vb.
rise, n.
rise, vb.
scale, vb.
soar, vb.
start-up, n.
surgere, lat. vb.
swell, n.
swell, vb.
top, vb.
tower, vb.
unscalable, adj.
up^1, adv.
up, n.
uprise, n.
upward, adj.
upward, adv.

upwards, adv.
: 37

34.08
descend

---

abaisser, fr. vb.
abase, vb.
alight, vb.
below stairs, adv.
cadent, adj.
couch, vb.
decline, vb.
deep-sunken, adj.
deject, vb.
descend, vb.
descension, n.
descent, n.
dew-dropping, adj.
dismount, vb.
dive, vb.
diver, n.
down, adv.
downfall, n.
down stairs, adv.
downward, adj.
downward, adv.
downwards, adv.
droop, vb.
drop, vb.
duck, vb.
fall, n.
fall, vb.
fallen-off, adj.
falling-off, n.
fast-falling, adj.
folly-fallen, adj.
founder, vb.
green-dropping, adj.
lapse, n.
lapse, vb.
light, vb.
low-declined, adj.
lower, vb.
new-fallen, adj.

plunge, n.
plunge, vb.
precipitance, n.
precipitate, vb.
precipitation, n.
set, n.
set, vb.
sink, vb.
slide, vb.
slope, vb.
souse, vb.
stoop, vb.
strike, vb.
stumble, vb.
swoop, n.
tear-falling, adj.
tomber, fr. vb.
topple, vb.
trade-fallen, adj.
trip, vb.
tumble, vb.
vail, n.
vail, vb.
: 62

34.09
stray

---

amiss, adv.
astray, adv.
cross, vb.
digress, vb.
digression, n.
divert, vb.
err, vb.
errant, adj.
erroneous, adj.
error, n.
extravagancy, n.
extravagant, adj.
gad, vb.
lag, vb.
miscarry, vb.
night-wanderer, n.
night-wandering, adj.

range, vb.
roam, vb.
rogue, vb.
roguish, adj.
rove, vb.
rover, n.
runagate, n.
runaway, n.
runner, n.
scatter, vb.
straggle, vb.
straggler, n.
stray, n.
stray, vb.
swerve, vb.
vagabond, n.
vagary, n.
vagrant, adj.
wander, vb.
wanderer, n.
wheel, vb.
wry, vb.
: 39

34.10
stir

---

abroach, adv.
afoot, adv.
alarm, vb.
bate, vb.
bestir, vb.
blench, n.
blench, vb.
bubble, vb.
budge, vb.
budger, n.
bustle, vb.
cold-moving, adj.
fan, n.
fan, vb.
flinch, vb.
flutter, vb.
go, vb.
lay to, phr. vb.

make, vb.
motion, n.
move, vb.
mover, n.
off and on, adv.
rear, vb.
start, n.
start, vb.
startingly, adv.
startle, vb.
stir, n.
stir, vb.
stirrer, n.
to and fro, adv.
whip, vb.
: 33

34.11
reel

---

betumbled, vb.
falter, vb.
reel, n.
reel, vb.
roll, vb.
stagger, vb.
stumble, vb.
totter, vb.
tumble, vb.
wallow, vb.
wheel, vb.
whirl, vb.
: 12

34.12
bend

---

bend, vb.
bias-drawing, n.
bow, vb.
buckle, vb.
congee, vb.
couch, vb.
couching, n.
counter-reflect, n.

cower, vb.
cringe, vb.
crook, vb.
crooked, adj.
crouch, vb.
curb, vb.
curtsy, n.
curtsy, vb.
decline, vb.
duck, vb.
flexible, adj.
flexure, n.
grovel, vb.
hinge, vb.
incline, vb.
inclining, n.
knee, n.
knee, vb.
knee-crooking, adj.
kneel, vb.
lean, vb.
leg, n.
limber, adj.
lither, adj.
low-crooked, adj.
malleable, adj.
pervert, vb.
pliant, adj.
reflect, vb.
reflection, n.
reflex, n.
reflex, vb.
retort, vb.
return, vb.
ruck, vb.
silly-ducking, adj.
slope, vb.
stoop, vb.
supple, adj.
sway, vb.
tractable, adj.
turn, vb.
turning, n.
unbend, vb.
unbowed, adj.

unstooping, adj.
wheel, vb.
wind, vb.
  : 56

34.13
advance
----
advance, vb.
advancement, n.
along, adv.
course, n.
forth, adv.
forward, adv.
forward, vb.
forwards, adv.
front, vb.
keep on, phr. vb.
make, vb.
on, adv.
onward, adv.
onwards, adv.
overcome, vb.
pass, vb.
passable, adj.
pergere, lat. vb.
proceed, vb.
proceeder, n.
process, n.
progress, n.
progress, vb.
progression, n.
repass, vb.
rid way, phr. vb.
  : 26

34.14
chase
----
bay, vb.
chase, vb.
course, vb.
dog, vb.
follow, vb.
follower, n.

pursue, vb.
pursuer, n.
pursuit, n.
trace, vb.
wild-goose chase, n.
  : 11

34.15
overtake
----
cote, vb.
outgo, vb.
outride, vb.
outstrip, vb.
overreach, vb.
override, vb.
overshoot, vb.
overslip, vb.
overtake, vb.
passage, n.
  : 10

34.16
travel
----
journey, n.
journey, vb.
measure, vb.
passenger, n.
peregrinate, adj.
pilgrimage, n.
poster, n.
road, n.
sail, n.
travel, n.
travel, vb.
traveller, n.
voyage, n.
  : 13

34.17
raise
----
advance, vb.
araise, vb.

buoy, vb.
elevate, vb.
erect, vb.
exalt, vb.
heave, n.
heave, vb.
heaved-up, adj.
heaving, n.
heft, n.
high-reared, adj.
hoise, vb.
hoist, vb.
lift, vb.
lifter, n.
mount, vb.
pluck up, phr. vb.
raise, vb.
rear, vb.
relieve, vb.
rouse, vb.
unraised, adj.
upheave, vb.
uplift, vb.
up-pricked, adj.
uprear, vb.
upswarm, vb.
weigh, vb.
white-upturned, adj.
  : 30

34.18
toss
----
betoss, vb.
canvass, vb.
cast, vb.
dart, vb.
death-darting, adj.
endart, vb.
fling, vb.
heave, vb.
hurl, vb.
peck, vb.
pick, vb.
pitch, vb.

quoit, vb.
seas-tossed, adj.
slight, vb.
tempest-tossed, adj.
throw, n.
throw, vb.
thrower-out, n.
toss, vb.
: 20

34.19
shake
───────────
all-shaking, adj.
ashake, vb.
bate, vb.
brandish, vb.
dandle, vb.
earthquake, n.
fawn, vb.
flare, vb.
flourish, vb.
flutter, vb.
love-shaked, adj.
quake, vb.
quiver, vb.
rock, vb.
shake, n.
shake, vb.
shaker, n.
shiver, vb.
shrink, vb.
shudder, n.
shudder, vb.
stream, vb.
swing, vb.
thrill, vb.
throb, vb.
tingle, vb.
tremble, vb.
tremblingly, adv.
unshaked, adj.
unshaken, adj.
wag, vb.
waggle, vb.

wave, vb.
wind-shaked, adj.
wind-shaken, adj.
: 35

34.20
send
───────────
banish, vb.
banisher, n.
banishment, n.
cashier, vb.
deliver, vb.
discard, vb.
discharge, vb.
dishabit, vb.
dislodge, vb.
dismiss, vb.
dismission, n.
dispatch, n.
dispatch, vb.
displace, vb.
eject, vb.
exile[1], n.
exile[2], n.
exile, vb.
expel, vb.
expulse, vb.
expulsion, n.
John Drum's
    entertainment, n.
mission, n.
outcast, adj.
outlaw, n.
outlaw, vb.
premise, vb.
remove, vb.
re-send, vb.
rid, vb.
send, vb.
sender, n.
shuffle off, phr. vb.
sun-expelling, adj.
supplant, vb.
utter, vb.

vent, vb.
: 37

34.21
transport
───────────
cart, vb.
convey, n.
convey, vb.
conveyance, n.
conveyer, n.
convoy, n.
drift, n.
drive, vb.
livery, n.
port, vb.
ride, vb.
ship, vb.
shipping, n.
sledded, adj.
transfer, vb.
transport, vb.
transportance, n.
transportation, n.
vehere, lat. vb.
waft, vb.
waftage, n.
: 21

34.22
carry
───────────
bailler, fr. vb.
bear, vb.
bring, vb.
bringer, n.
bringing-forth, n.
bull-bearing, adj.
carrier, n.
carry, vb.
carry-tale, n.
convey, vb.
farfet, adj.
fet, vb.
fetch, vb.

just-borne, adj.
portable, adj.
redeliver, vb.
ride, vb.
self-borne, adj.
shard-borne, adj.
stiff-borne, adj.
take, vb.
transport, vb.
wear, vb.
: 23

34.23
fast • slow
───────────
amain, adv.
apace, adv.
briefness, n.
celerity, n.
citus, lat. adj.
cursitory, adj.
dépècher, fr. vb.
dilatory, adj.
dispatch, vb.
expedience, n.
expedient, adj.
expediently, adv.
expedition, n.
expeditious, adj.
fast, adj.
fastly, adv.
festinate, adj.
festinately, adv.
fleet, adj.
fleet, vb.
fleet-foot, n.
fleet-winged, adj.
flighty, adj.
forslow, vb.
haste, n.
haste, vb.
hasten, vb.
haste-post-haste, n.
hastily, adv.
hasty, adj.

hasty-footed, adj.
headlong, adj.
heavy-gaited, adj.
helter-skelter, adv.
hie, vb.
high-speeded, adj.
hurry, vb.
leaden-footed, adj.
leisurely, adj.
lentus, lat. adj.
momentary-swift, adj.
on the spur, adv.
over-hasty, adj.
overpost, vb.
post, adv.
post, vb.
post-haste
post-post-haste
presently, adv.
quick, adj.
quickly, adv.
quickness, n.
rash, adj.
rashly, adv.
rashness, n.
rather, adv.
run, vb.
rush, vb.
scud, vb.
slow, adj.
slow, vb.
slow-gaited, adj.
slowly, adv.
slowness, n.
snail-paced, adj.
snail-slow, adj.
snap, adv.
snip, adv.
softly, adv.
soon, adv.
soon, adj.
speed, n.
speed, vb.
speediest, n.

speedily, adv.
speediness, n.
speedy, adj.
sudden, adj.
swift, adj.
swift, n.
swift-footed, adj.
swiftly, adv.
swiftness, n.
take head, vb.
tardily, adv.
tardiness, n.
tardy, adj.
tardy, vb.
tardy-gaited, adj.
tediosity, n.
tedious, adj.
tediously, adv.
tediousness, n.
thick, adj.
tiger-footed, adj.
vitement, fr. adv.
whip, vb.
whirr, vb.
wilful-slow, adj.
wind-swift, adj.
  : 100

34.24
nimbleness
————————
agile, adj.
alacrity, n.
brisk, adj.
brisky, adj.
buxom, adj.
deliverly, adv.
dexterity, n.
featly, adv.
fresh, adj.
legerity, n.
light, adj.
lighten, vb.
lightfoot, adj.
light-heeled, adj.

lightly, adv.
livelihood, n.
lively, adj.
lively, adv.
mercurial, adj.
nimble, adj.
nimble-footed, adj.
nimbleness, n.
nimbly, adv.
pert, adj.
pertly, adv.
prompt, adj.
promptement, fr. adv.
quick, adj.
quiver, adj.
readiness, n.
smartly, adv.
sprag, adj.
trippingly, adv.
yare, adj.
yarely, adv.
  : 35

34.25
swim
————————
afloat, adv.
diver, n.
fleet, vb.
float, vb.
hull, vb.
swim, vb.
swimmer, n.
  : 7

34.26
fly
————————
flee, vb.
fleet-winged, adj.
flight, n.
fly, vb.
high-soaring, adj.
light-winged, adj.
nimble-pinioned, adj.

outfly, vb.
overfly, vb.
overperch, vb.
slow-winged, adj.
soar, vb.
swift-winged, adj.
tower, vb.
voler, fr. vb.
wing, n.
wing, vb.
  : 17

34.27
waggon
————————
axle-tree, n.
barrow, n.
car, n.
carriage, n.
cart, n.
chariot, n.
chariot-wheel, n.
coach, n.
felloe, n.
fill, n.
hurdle, n.
nave, n.
spoke, n.
waggon, n.
waggon-spoke, n.
waggon-wheel, n.
wain, n.
wain-rope, n.
wheel, n.
wheel, vb.
  : 20

34.28
road
————————
alley, n.
Bucklersbury
bypath, n.
career, n.
church-way, n.

conveyance, n.
course, n.
crank, n.
creek, n.
cross-way, n.
Datchet Lane
Eastcheap
Fish Street
foot-path, n.
foot-path way, n.
forthright, n.
highway, n.

horse-way, n.
king's highway, n.
lane, n.
Lombard Street
Long Lane
Marseilles road, n.
meander, n.
Old Windsor way, n.
pass, n.
passage, n.
path, n.
pathway, n.

Pie Corner
right, n.
road, n.
roadway, n.
run, n.
St. Magnus' Corner
strait, n.
street, n.
thoroughfare, n.
town's end, n.
town way, n.
trace, n.

track, n.
tract, n.
trail, n.
Turnbull Street
turning, n.
unpathed, adj.
via, lat. n.
walk, n.
way, n.
: 50

35.01
ship

aboard, adv.
admiral, n.
after fleet, n.
Andrew
Antoniad
argosy, n.
ark, n.
armada, n.
barge, n.
bark, n.
boat, n.
bottom, n.
carrack, n.
cock, n.
crayer, n.
Delay
Expedition
fleet, n.
galley, n.
galliass, n.
George Alow
gondola, n.
hoy, n.
hulk, n.
keel, n.
long-boat, n.
man-of-war, n.
merchant, n.
overboard, adv.
Phoenix
pinnace, n.
raft, n.
sail, n.
ship, n.
shipboard, n.
shipping, n.
Tiger
traject, n.
Veronesa, n.
vessel, n.
: 40

35.02
deck • oar

ballast, n.
beak, n.
cabin, n.
deck, n.
hatch, n.
helm, n.
hold, n.
keel, n.
oar, n.
poop, n.
portage, n.
rib, n.
rudder, n.
stem, n.
stern, n.
sternage, n.
waist, n.
: 17

35.03
sail

course, n.
main-course, n.
mainsail, n.
sail, n.
sea-wing, n.
top, n.
topgallant, n.
topsail, n.
: 8

35.04
mast

bowsprit, n.
mainmast, n.
main-top, n.
mast, n.
topmast, n.
yard, n.
: 6

35.05
anchor

anchor, n.
anchorage, n.
cable, n.
fathom-line, n.
holding-anchor, n.
: 5

35.06
tackle

bowline, n.
rig, vb.
shroud, n.
tackle, n.
tackling, n.
: 5

35.07
wrack

shipwreck, n.
shipwreck, vb.
wrack, n.
wrack, vb.
: 4

35.08
navigation

a-hold, adv.
anchor, vb.
bank, vb.
bear up, phr. vb.
belee, vb.
buoy, n.
card, n.
coast, vb.
compass, n.
disembark, vb.
embark, vb.
fetch about, phr. vb.
helm, vb.

land, vb.
launch, vb.
lay by, phr. vb.
lay off, phr. vb.
luff, vb.
mark, n.
navigation, n.
oar, vb.
point, n.
poop, vb.
put forth (out) to, phr. vb.
restem, vb.
ride out, phr. vb.
sail, n.
sail, vb.
sea-mark, n.
ship, vb.
shipping, n.
shore, vb.
skiff, vb.
steer, vb.
steerage, n.
stem, vb.
try, vb.
under sail, adv.
weather, n.
weigh, vb.
well-sailing, adj.
yaw, vb.
: 42

35.09
seaman

boatswain, n.
canvas-climber, n.
captain, n.
ferryman, n.
gondolier, n.
mariner, n.
master, n.
pilot, n.
sailor, n.
sea-boy, n.

199

seafarer, n.
sea-faring, adj.
seaman, n.
ship-boy, n.
shipman, n.
swabber, n.
 : 16

35.10
harbour
_____

bay, n.
dock, vb.
harbour, n.

harbour, vb.
harbourage, n.
haven, n.
pier, n.
port, n.
Port Le Blanc
road, n.
 : 10

35.11
flood-gate
_____

bridge, n.
draw-bridge, n.

ferry, n.
flood-gate, n.
London Bridge
sluice, n.
sluice, vb.
 : 7

36.01
name

---

addition, n.
alias, adv.
appeler, fr. vb.
call, vb.
calling, n.
clepe, vb.
dub, vb.
entitle, vb.
forename, vb.
hight, vb.
honour, n.
intitule, vb.
miscall, vb.
misterm, vb.
name, n.
name, vb.
nameless, adj.
nickname, n.
nickname, vb.
nominate, vb.
nomination, n.
over-name, vb.
style, n.
style, vb.
suraddition, n.
surname, n.
surname, vb.
term, vb.
title, n.
title, vb.
titleless, adj.
vocare, lat. vb.
what-do-ye-call
 : 33

36.02
continents

Africa
America
Asia
Europa
Europe
 : 5

36.03
British

Abergavenny
Albany
Albion
Alton
Ampthill
Angleterre, fr.
Anglia, lat.
Angus
Arundel
Ashford
Athol
Banbury
Barkloughly
Barnet
Barson
Basingstoke
Bedford
Berkeley
Berwick
Blackheath
Blackmere
blue-cap, n.
Bolingbroke
Bosworth
Brecon
Brentford
Bridgnorth
Bristol
Britain, adj.
Britain, n.
Britain
British, adj.
Brittany
Buckingham
Burton
Burton Heath
Bury
Caernarvonshire
Cambria

Cambridge
Camelot
Canterbury
Carlisle
Cawdor
Chatham
Chertsey
Chester
Cinque Ports
Cirencester
Cobham
Colmekill
Colnbrook
Cornish, adj.
Cornwall
Cotswold
Coventry
Cumberland
Datchet
Daventry
Derby
Devonshire
Doncaster
Dorset
Dorsetshire
Douglas
Dover
Downs, The
Dunsmore
Dunstable
Eltham
Ely
England
English, adj.
English, n.
Englishman, n.
Englishwoman, n.
Essex
Eton
Exeter
Exton
Fife
flannel, n.
Flint
Forres

Frogmore
Gadshill
Gallia
Galloway
Gaultree
Glamis
Gloucester
Gloucestershire
Goodrig
Goodwins
Goodwin Sands
Greenwich
Greet
Hampton
Hastings
Hatfield
Haverfordwest
Hereford
Herefordshire
Hinckley
Holmedon
Hungerford
Huntingdon
Inverness
Ipswich
Ireland
Irish, adj.
Irish, n.
Irishman, n.
Isle of Man
Kendal
Kenilworth
Kent
Kentish, adj.
Kentishman, n.
Kildare
Kimbolton
Lancaster
Langley
Leicester
Leicestershire
Lincoln
Lincolnshire
Lincoln Washes
Lipsbury

Ludlow
Lynn
Maidenhead
Manningtree
March
Masham
Melford
Menteith
Milford
Milford Haven
Monmouth
Murray
Norfolk
Northampton
Northamptonshire
Northumberland
Old Windsor
Oxford
Oxfordshire
Pembroke
Pleshey
Pomfret
Ravenspurgh
Reading
Richmond
Rochester
Rochford
Ross
Rutland
Salisbury
Sandal
Sarum
Sarum Plain
Scone
Scot, n.
Scotch, adj.
Scotland
Scots, adj.
Scottish, adj.
Sheffield
Shrewsbury
Somerset
Southam
Southampton
St. Albans

St. Colme's Inch
St. Edmundsbury
St. Lawrence
Poultney
Stafford
Staffordshire
Staines
Stamford
Stony Stratford
Suffolk
Surrey
Sutton Coldfield
Swineshead
Tamworth
Tewkesbury
Urchinfield
Wakefield
Wales
Ware
Warwick
Warwickshire
Washford
Waterford
Welsh, adj.
Welsh, n.
Welshman, n.
Welshwoman, n.
Western Isles
Westmorland
Willoughby
Wiltshire
Winchester
Wincot
Windsor
Wingfield
Wingham
Woodmancote
Woodstock
Worcester
York
Yorkshire
: 214

36.04
African
———————
Africa
African, n.
Alexandria
Alexandrian, adj.
Algiers
Anthropophagi, n.
Anthropophaginian,
  n.
Arabia
Arabian, adj.
Barbary, n.
Barbary
blackamoor, n.
Cannibal, n.
cannibally, adv.
Carthage
Egypt
Egyptian, adj.
Egyptian, n.
Ethiop, adj.
Ethiop, n.
Ethiopian, n.
gipsy, n.
Guinea
Libya
Mauritania
Maurus, lat. n.
Memphis
Moor, n.
moorship, n.
Morisco, n.
Morocco
Negro, n.
Pentapolis
Pygmy, n.
Saracen, n.
Tripoli
Tunis
: 37

36.05
Middle / Far
Eastern
———————
Aleppo
Antioch
Armenia
Asia
Assyrian, adj.
Babylon
Basan
Byzantium
Cappadocia
Cataian, n.
China
Cilicia
Cimmerian, n.
Colchis
Commagene
Constantinople
Damascus
Dardan, adj.
Dardanian, adj.
Dardan plains, n.
East Indies (Inde)
Ephesian, n.
Ephesus
Golgotha
Holy Land, n.
Hyrcan, adj.
Hyrcania
Hyrcanian, adj.
Ilion
Ilium
India
Indian, adj.
Indian, n.
Indian-like, adj.
Indies
Ionia
Ionian, adj.
Israel
Jerusalem
Jewry
Lycaonia

Lydia
Mede
Media
Mesopotamia
Nazarite, n.
Ottoman, n.
Ottomite, n.
Palestine
Paphlagonia
Parthia
Parthian, adj.
Parthian, n.
Persia
Persian, adj.
Phoenicia
Phoenician, n.
Phrygia
Phrygian, adj.
Pontus
Sardian, n.
Sardis
sigeius, lat. adj.
Syria
Tarsus
Tartar, n.
Trojan, adj.
Trojan, n.
Troy
Turk, n.
Turkey
Turkish, adj.
Tyre
Tyrian, adj.
Tyrus
: 75

36.06
American
———————
America
Antipodes, n.
barbarian, n.
barbarous, adj.
Bermudas
Guiana

Mexico
western Inde
West Indies (Inde)
: 9

36.07
London
———————
Bucklersbury
chamber, n.
Charing Cross
Cheapside
Eastcheap
Finsbury
Fish Street
Holborn
Limehouse
Lombard Street
London
London Bridge
Londoner, n.
London Stone
Lud's-Town
Mile End
Mile-end Green
Moorditch
Moorfields
Paris Garden
Pickt-hatch
Pie Corner
Pissing-conduit, n.
Smithfield
Southwark
St. George's Field
St. Magnus' Corner
Strand
Tilt-yard
Tower Hill
Turnbull Street
Tyburn
Westminster
Whitefriars
: 34

36.08
Italian
———————
Antiates, n.
Antium
Ardea
Belmont
Bergamask, n.
Bergamo
Brundisium
Calaber
Collatia
Corioli
Ferrara
Florence
Florentine, n.
Free-town
Genoa
Hybla
Italian, adj.
Italian, n.
Italy
Lombardy
Mantua
Messina
Milan
Misena
Modena
Montferrat
Naples
Neapolitan, adj.
Neapolitan, n.
Padua
Pisa
Rialto
Roman, adj.
Roman, n.
Romanus, lat. n.
Rome
Romish, adj.
Sardinia
Sicilia
Sicilian, adj.
Sicily
Siena

Sienese, n.
Syracusa
Syracuse
Syracusian, adj.
Syracusian, n.
Tarentum
Tuscan, adj.
Venetian, adj.
Venetian, n.
Venezia
Venice
Verona
Veronesa, n.
Volsce, n.
Volscian, adj.
Volscian, n.
: 58

36.09
Southern European
———————
Actium
Aragon
Athenian, adj.
Athenian, n.
Athens
Aulis
Calydon
Canary
Candy
Castiliano
Corinth
Corinthian, n.
Cretan, adj.
Crete
Cyprus
Dalmatian, n.
Delphos
Epidamnus
Epidaurus
Grecian, adj.
Grecian, n.
Greece
Greek, adj.
Greek, n.

Greekish, adj.
Illyria
Illyrian, adj.
Ithaca
Lacedaemon
Lisbon
Macedon
Messaline
Mytilene
Navarre
Nemean, adj.
Olympian, adj.
Pannonian, n.
Paphos
Peloponnesus
Pharsalia
Philippan, adj.
Philippi
Portugal
Rhodes
Sestos
Sicyon
Spain
Spaniard, n.
Spanish, adj.
Spanish, n.
Sparta
Spartan, adj.
Spartan, n.
Tenedos
Thasos
Theban, adj.
Theban, n.
Thebes
Thessalian, adj.
Thessaly
Thracian, adj.
Toledo
Toryne
: 63

36.10
Northern European
────────────
Almain, n.

Belgia
Brabant
Dane, n.
Danish, adj.
Dansker, n.
Denmark
Dutch, adj.
Dutch, n.
Dutchman, n.
Elsinore
Flanders
Fleming, n.
Flemish, adj.
Frankfort
German, adj.
German, n.
Germany
[Ghent] (Gaunt)
Goth, n.
Holland
Hollander, n.
Iceland
Lapland
Low Countries
Meissen
Nervii
Netherlands
Norway
Norweyan, adj.
Poperinge
Rhenish, adj.
Salic, adj.
salicus, lat. adj.
Saxon, n.
Saxony
Swisser, n.
Walloon, n.
Walloon
Wittenberg
: 40

36.11
French
────────────
Agincourt

Aire
Alençon
Amiens
Angers
Anjou
Aquitaine
Arc
Arden
Ardres
Armagnac
Artois
Aumerle
Auvergne
Bar
Bayonne
Beaumont
Berri
Blois
Bois
Bonville
Bordeaux
Bourbon
Bretagne
Brittany
Burgundy
Calais
Champaigne
Châtillon
Crécy
Foix
France
France, fr.
Francia, lat.
French, adj.
French, n.
Frenchman, n.
Frenchwoman, n.
Gallia
Gallian, adj.
Gaul
Gisors
Grandpré
Guines
Guyenne
Hames

Harfleur
Limoges
Longueville
Lorraine
Maine
Marle
Marseilles
Narbon
Norman, adj.
Norman, n.
Normandy
Orléans
Paris
Parisian, n.
Paris-ward, adv.
Perigort
Picardy
Poitiers
Port Le Blanc
Provincial, adj.
Rheims
Rouen
Roussi
Roussillon
Santrailles
Touraine
Tours
Troy
Valence
Vaudemont
Volquessen
: 77

36.12
Eastern European
────────────
Austria
Bohemia
Bohemian, n.
Bohemian-Tartar, n.
Hungarian, adj.
Hungary
Muscovite, n.
Muscovy
Musko

Polack, adj.
Polack, n.
Poland
Pole, n.
Prague
Russia
Russian, adj.
Russian, n.
Scythia
Scythian, adj.
Scythian, n.
Transylvanian, n.
Vienna
: 22

**36.13
medieval legend**
——————————
Arthur, [King] (2H4)
Bevis
Chanticleer
Colbrand
Cophetua
Dagonet
Fairy Queen
Faustus, Doctor
Florentius
Gargantua
Gorboduc
Grissel
Guinevere
Guy, Sir
Herne
Hood, Robin
[Little] John
Marian, Maid
Merlin
Oliver (1H6)
Partlet, Dame
Pendragon
Roland (1H6)
Rowland (LR)
Scarlet, [Will]
: 25

**36.14
pseudohistorical**
——————————
Albany, Duke of
Apemantus
Arviragus
Aufidius, Tullus
Banquo
Blithild
Brutus, Junius   (COR)
Burgundy (LR)
Cawdor,
   Thane of (MAC)
Censorinus
Cham, n.
Collatine
Cordelia
Coriolanus, Martius
   Caius
Cornwall, Duke of
Cymbeline
Falconbridge, Philip
   (Richard) (JN)
Fleance
France (LR)
Gloucester (LR)
Gloucester, Edmund,
   Earl of (LR)
Goneril
Guiderius
Hostilius (COR)
Lartius, Titus
Lear
Lingare
Lucrece
Lucretia
Lucretius
Martian
Martius, Caius ➔
   Coriolanus
Mulmutius
Numa
Pharamond
Prester John
Publicola (COR)

Publius (COR)
Quintus
Regan
Sicinius Velutus
Solyman
Tenantius
Timandra
Timon
Valeria
Virgilia
Virginius
Volumnia
: 49

**36.15
Trojan myth**
——————————
Achilles
Aeacides (SHR)
Aeneas
Agamemnon
Ajax
Amphimachus
Anchises
Andromache
Antenor
Antenorides
Calchas
Cassandra
Cedius
Chetas
Cressida
Dardan
Deiphobus
Diomedes (TRO)
Doreus
Epistrophus
Hector (TRO)
Hecuba
Helen (TRO)
Helenus
Helias
Margarelon
Menelaus
Menon

Myrmidon, n.
Nell ➔ Helen (TRO)
Neoptolemus
Nestor
Nestor-like, adj.
Palamedes
Pandarus
Paris (TRO)
Patroclus
Penelope
Polixenes (TRO)
Polydamas
Polyxena
Priam
Priamus, lat.
Pyrrhus
Rhesus
Sinon
Telamon
Telamonius
Thersites
Thoas
Timbria
Troien
Troilus
Ulysses
: 54

**36.16
classical myth**
——————————
Absyrtus
Actaeon
Adonis
Aeacides (2H6), lat.
Aegle
Aeson
Agenor
Alcides
Althaea
Amazon, n.
Amazonian, n.
Anna
Antiope
Arachne

Ariadne
Arion
Ascanius
Atalanta
Atlas
Cadmus
Capaneus
Castor
Cephalus
Charon
Creon
Cyclops
Daedalus
Damon
Daphne
demi-Atlas, n.
Deucalion
Dido
Echo
Enceladus
Endymion
Europa
Ganymede (TNK)
Grace
Herculean, adj.
Hercules
Hero
Hesperides
Hippolyta
Icarus
Io
Jason
Laertes (TIT)
Leander
Leda
Lichas
Medea
Meleager
Merops
Midas
Minos
Narcissus
Ninus
Niobe
Orpheus
Pandion
Pelops
Penthesilea
Perigenia
Perseus
Phaeton
Philemon (ADO)
Philomela
Pirithous
Procne
Procris
Pygmalion
Pyramus (TIT)
Rhodope
Semiramis
Sibyl
Tantalus
Tereus
Theseus
Thisbe (MV)
: 79

36.17
historical: English

Abergavenny
Alton ➛ Talbot, John (1H6)
Angus, Earl of
Anne, Duchess of Gloucester (R3)
Archibald
Arthur, Prince (H8)
Arundel, Earl of
Athol, Earl of
Aumerle, Edward, Duke of
Bagot
Banister
Bardolph, Lord (2H4)
Beaufort ➛ Somerset (1H6)
Beaumont (R3)
Bedford ➛ John of Lancaster
Berkeley (R2)
Berkeley (R3)
Bess ➛ Grey, Lady (3H6)
Bigot
Blackmere ➛ Talbot, John (1H6)
Black Prince ➛ Edward (R2)
Blunt (2H4)
Blunt (R2)
Blunt, Sir James (R3)
Blunt, Sir Walter (1H4)
Bohun, Edward ➛ Stafford (H8)
Boleyn, Anne (H8)
Boleyn, Sir Thomas (H8)
Bolingbroke ➛ Henry [IV]
Bolingbroke, Henry (R2)
Bolingbroke, Roger (2H6)
Bonville
Brackenbury, Robert
Brandon, Sir William
Brittany, Arthur, Duke of (JN)
Brocas
Buckingham ➛ Stafford (H8)
Buckingham, Henry, Duke of (H8)
Buckingham, Humphrey of (2H6)
Bulmer, William
Bushy
Butts
Cade, John (Jack)
Cambridge, Richard, Earl of
Canterbury (H5)
Canterbury (H8) ➛ Cranmer
Canterbury (JN) ➛ Langton
Canterbury, Archbishop of (R2)
Car, John
Carlisle
Cassado, Gregory de
Cassibelan (CYM)
Catesby
Christopher, Sir (R3)
Clarence, George, Duke of (3H6)
Clarence, Lionel, Duke of (1H6)
Clarence, Thomas, Duke of (2H4)
Clifford (2H6)
Clifford, Young (3H6)
Clifton
Cobham (3H6)
Cobham, Eleanor (2H6)
Cobham, Rainold, Lord (R2)
Coeur-de-lion ➛ Richard [I]
Coint, Francis
Coleville of the Dale, Sir John
Constance
Courtney, Edward
Cranmer
Cromer, James
Cromwell ➛ Talbot, John (1H6)
Cromwell, Thomas (H8)
Cumberland ➛ Clifford (2H6)
Denny

Surrey → Kent (R2)
Surrey, Earl of (2H4)
Surrey, Earl of (H8)
Surrey, Earl
  of (STM)
Surrey, Thomas, Earl
  of (R3)
Talbonite, n.
Talbot (H5)
Talbot, Gilbert (R3)
Talbot, John (1H6)
Talbot,
  John (1H6 4.3.35)
Thomas of
  Woodstock (2H6)
Thump, Peter
Tressel
Tyrrel, James
Urchinfield →
  Talbot, John
Valence → Talbot,
  John (1H6)
Vaughan, Thomas
Vaux (2H6)
Vaux, Nicholas (H8)
Verdun → Talbot,
  John (1H6)
Vere, Aubrey
Vernon (1H6)
Vernon,
  Richard (1H4)
Wales → Edward
  (Black Prince)
Wales → Edward
  [V] (R3)
Wales →
  Plantagenet (R3)
Wales, Henry, Prince
  of (1H4)
Warwick →
  Neville (2H4)
Warwick →
  Neville (2H6)
Warwick (R3)

Washford → Talbot,
  John (1H6)
Waterford → Talbot,
  John (1H6)
Waterton, Robert
Westminster, Abbot
  of
Westmorland, Earl
  of (1H4)
Westmorland, Earl
  of (3H6)
Whitmore, Walter
William of
  Hatfield (2H6)
William of
  Windsor (2H6)
Willoughby
Wiltshire →
  Scrope (1H4 1.3.271)
Wiltshire, Earl
  of (3H6)
Winchester (1H6) →
  Beaufort
Winchester (H8) →
  Gardiner
Wingfield → Talbot,
  John (1H6)
Wolsey, Cardinal
Woodville (1H6)
Woodville,
  Anthony (R3)
Worcester
York → Edward [IV]
York → Langley,
  Edmund
York →
  Scrope (1H4 5.5.37)
York (H5) →
  Aumerle
York (H8) →
  Wolsey
York, Archbishop
  of (3H6)
York,
  [Duchess of] (R3)

York, Richard, Duke
  of (R3)
  : 377

36.18
historical: French

Aire → Joan of Arc
Alençon, Duchess
  of (H8)
Alençon, Duke
  of (1H6)
Alençon, John (H5)
Anjou, Reignier,
  Duke of
Armagnac, Earl of
Auvergne,
  Countess of
Bar, Edward,
  Duke of
Baynard
Bayonne, Bishop of
Beaumont (H5)
Berri, Duke of
Bouciqualt
Bourbon (3H6)
Bourbon, John, Duke
  of (H5)
Brabant, Anthony,
  Duke of
Bretagne, Duke of
Brittany, Duke
  of (H5)
Brittany, Duke
  of (R2)
Burgundy, Charolois,
  Duke (H5)
Burgundy, Duchess
  of (3H6)
Burgundy, Duke
  of (3H6)
Calaber, Duke of
Capet, Hugh
Charles [VI] (H5)
Charles [VII] (1H6)

Charolois
Châtillon (JN)
Châtillon,
  Jacques (H5)
Dauphin, Guiscard
Delabret, Charles
Ermengare
Falconbridge (H5)
Foix
France, King of (H8)
Grandpré
Isabel, Queen
Joan de
  Pucelle (1H6)
Joan of Arc
  (Aire) (1H6)
Kate →
  Katherine (H5)
Katherine (H5)
Le Fer
Lestrelles
Lewis [VIII] (JN)
Lewis [IX] (H5)
Lewis [XI] (3H6)
Lorraine, Charles,
  Duke of
Marle, Earl of
Melun
Montjoy
Naples, King of →
  Anjou
Orléans (1H6)
Orléans (H8)
Orléans, Charles,
  Duke of (H5)
Pepin, King
Philip [II]
Ponton de
  Santrailles, Lord
Pucelle → Joan of
  Arc
Rambures
Roussi
Vaudemont
  : 61

36.19
historical: other names (1)

Austria → Limoges
Bajazeth
Blanch of Spain
Bona, Lady
Cadwallader
Campeius, Cardinal
Capucius
Cawdor, Thane of →
  Macbeth
Charlemain
Charles
  (Charlemain) (H5)
Charles [V,
  Emperor] (H8)
Childeric
Clothaire
Cumberland, Prince
  of → Malcolm
Donalbain
Duff → Macduff
Duncan
Ferdinand, King of
  Spain (H8)
Ferrara
Fife, Earl of →
  Mordake
Fife, Thane of →
  Macduff
Glamis, Thane of →
  Macbeth
Innocent, Pope
Lewis (H5 1.2.76)
Limoges
Macbeth
Macdonwald
Macduff
Malcolm
Menteith, Earl of →
  Mordake
Mohammed
Mordake

Norway → Sweno
Pandulph, Cardinal
Ross, Thane
  of (MAC)
Sinel
Sweno
Turk Gregory
  : 38

36.20
cultural: English

Chaucer
Dowland
Gower (PER)
Scoggin
Spenser
  : 5

36.21
cultural: other names (1)

Froissart
Giulio Romano
Machiavelli
Mantuan
Paracelsus
Petrarch
  : 6

36.22
historical: Greek

Alcibiades
Alexander
  the Great (H5)
Cleitus
Lycurgus
Philip of
  Macedon (H5)
Solon
  : 6

36.23
historical: Roman

Agrippa (ANT)
Agrippa (COR) →
  Menenius
Ancus Martius
Antonius, Marcus
Antony, Mark
Augustus → Caesar
Brutus, lat.
Brutus, Decius   (JC)
Brutus, Junius   (H5)
Brutus, Marcus   (JC)
Caelius
Caesar,
  Augustus (CYM)
Caesar, Julius   (JC)
Caesar,
  Octavius (ANT)
Caesarion
Calpurnia
Canidius
Casca
Cassius, Caius
Cato (JC)
Cato, Marcus   (JC)
Cicero (JC)
Cimber,
  Metellus (JC)
Cimber, Publius   (JC)
Cinna (JC)
Cinna the Poet (JC)
Clitus
Cominius
Constantine
Cornelia (TIT)
Crassus,
  Marcus (ANT)
Dardanius
Decretas
Diomede (ANT)
Dolabella
Enobarbus, Domitius
Flavio

Flavius (JC)
Fulvia
Gallus
Helen (1H6)
Herod
Hipparchus
Hirtius
Justeius, Marcus
Labeo
Labienus
Lena, Popilius
Lepidus
Ligarius, Caius
Livia (ANT)
Lucilius (JC)
Lucius (ANT)
Maecenas
Marcellus,
  Caius (ANT)
Menas
Menecrates
Menenius Agrippa
Messala
Murellus
Nero
Octavia
Octavius, Marcus
Pansa
Pella, Lucius
Pindarus
Pompeius
Pompey,
  Cneius (ANT)
Pompey,
  Sextus (ANT)
Portia
Proculeius
Publicola (ANT)
Sosius
Statilius
Sulla
Tarquin (COR)
Tarquin (LUC)
Taurus (ANT)
Thidias

Titinius
Trebonius
Ventidius (ANT)
Volumnius
 : 83

36.24
historical: other
names (2)
—————————————
Adallas
Alexander (ANT)
Alexander (TRO)
Alexas
Amurath
Amyntas
Apollodorus
Archelaus
Bargulus

Bocchus
Cambyses
Cassibelan (CYM)
Charmian
Cleopatra
Cyrus
Darius
Hannibal
Iras
Malchus
Mardian
Mithridates
Orodes
Pacorus
Philadelphos
Polemon
Pothinus
Ptolemies
Ptolemy[1] (ANT)

Ptolemy[2] (ANT)
Seleucus
Tomyris
 : 31

36.25
cultural: Greek
—————————————
Aesop
Aristotle
Artemidorus
Epicurus
Hippocrates
Milo
Pythagoras
Socrates
Strato
Xantippe
 : 10

36.26
cultural: other
names (2)
—————————————
Galen
Horace
Ovid (Ovidius Naso)
Plautus
Priscian
Roscius
Seneca
Tully [Cicero] (TIT)
 : 8

37.01
classical: male

Aemilius
Alarbus
Andronicus,
  Marcus (TIT)
Andronicus,
  Titus (TIT)
Antigonus
Antiochus
Antipholus [of
  Ephesus] (ERR)
Antipholus [of
  Syracuse] (ERR)
Arcas
Arcite
Artesius
Autolycus
Bassianus
Belarius
Caius (TIT)
Caphis
Cerimon
Chiron
Claudio (JC)
Cleomenes
Cleon
Corambus
Corin (AYL)
Corin (MND)
Cornelius (CYM)
Cornelius (HAM)
Corydon
Cotus
Crassus (MM)
Demetrius (MND)
Demetrius (TIT)
Dion
Egeon
Egeus
Eros
Escalus (AWW)
Escalus (MM)
Escanes

Flaminius
Flavius (MM)
Flavius (TIM)
Helicanus
Horatio
Hortensius
Hostilius (TIM)
Isidore
Laertes (HAM)
Leonatus →
  Posthumus
Leonine
Leontes
Lucianus
Lucilius (TIM)
Lucius (JC)
Lucius (TIM)
Lucius (TIM 3.4.2)
Lucius (TIT)
Lucius (TIT)
Lucius, Caius (CYM)
Lucullus
Lysander
Lysimachus
Mamillius
Marcellus (HAM)
Marcus
Menaphon
Muliteus
Mutius
Nedar
Nicander
Nicanor
Palamon
Paris (ROM)
Pericles
Philarmonus
Philemon (PER)
Philostrate
Philotus
Pius → Andronicus,
  Titus
Polixenes (WT)
Polonius
Posthumus Leonatus

Proteus [1] (TGV)
Proteus [2] (TGV)
Publius (JC)
Publius (TIT)
Quinapalus
Rycas
Saturninus
Sempronius (TIM)
Sempronius (TIT)
Servilius
Sicilius
Silius
Silvius
Simonides
Solinus
Thaliard
Titus (TIM)
Titus (TN)
Valentinus
Valentius
Valerius (TGV)
Valerius (TNK)
Varrius (ANT)
Varrius (MM)
Varro
Varrus
Ventidius (TIM)
Zenelophon
  : 109

37.02
classical: female

Aemilia
Cornelia (TIT)
Desdemona
Dionyza
Dorcas
Euriphile
Flavina
Helen (CYM)
Helena (AWW)
Helena (MND)
Helena (ROM)
Hermia

Hermione
Hero (ADO)
Hiren
Hisperia
Lavinia
Livia (ROM)
Luciana
Lychorida
Marina
Miranda
Mopsa
Ophelia
Paulina
Phillida
Philoten
Phoebe, vb.
Phoebe
Phrynia
Portia
Silvia
Tamora
Thaisa
  : 34

37.03
English: male

Abraham
  Cupid (ROM)
Abraham
  Slender (WIV)
Adam (AYL)
Adam (ERR)
Adam (SHR)
Adam [Bell] (ADO)
Adrian (COR)
Adrian (TMP)
Andrew Aguecheek,
  Sir
Anselme, County
Anthony (ROM)
Anthony Dull (LLL)
Balthasar (ADO)
Balthasar (ERR)
Balthasar (MV)

Balthasar (ROM)
Bartholomew
Benedick
Bertram
Charles (AYL)
Christopher
  Sly (SHR)
Clement Perkes o'
  th' Hill
Cloten
Davy (2H4)
Dennis
Dick (1H4)
Dick (COR)
Dick Surgeon (TN)
Dick the
  Butcher (2H6)
Dick the
  Shepherd (LLL)
Edgar
Edmund
Fabian
Ferdinand (SHR)
Ferdinand (TMP)
Francis (1H4)
Francis, Friar (ADO)
Francis Feeble (2H4)
Francis Flute (MND)
Francis
  Pickbone (2H4)
Francis
  Seacole (ADO)
Frank Ford
Frederick (MM)
Frederick,
  Duke (AYL)
Gabriel
George (JN)
Gerrold, Master
Gregory (ROM)
Gregory (SHR)
Henry
  Pimpernell (SHR)
Hob

Hugh Evans,
  Sir (WIV)
Hugh Oatcake (ADO)
Hugh Rebeck (ROM)
Jack
James Gurney (JN)
James
  Soundpost (ROM)
Jamy, Captain (H5)
John (WIV)
John, Don (ADO)
John, Friar (ROM)
John,
  Goodman (2H6)
John Bates (H5)
John Falstaff (WIV)
John Naps (SHR)
John Rugby (WIV)
Joseph
Lance
Lancelet Gobbo
Laurence, Friar
Lawrence, Friar
Michael
  Cassio (OTH)
Nathaniel (SHR)
Nathaniel, Sir (LLL)
Ned Poins (1H4)
Nicholas (SHR)
Nick Bottom
Nob, Sir (JN)
Oliver (AYL)
Oswald
Patrick, Friar
Peter (JN)
Peter (ROM)
Peter (SHR)
Peter, Friar (MM)
Peter Bullcalf (2H4)
Peter Quince (MND)
Peter Simple (WIV)
Peter Turf (SHR)
Philip (SHR)
Ralph (1H4)
Ralph (SHR)

Ralph Mouldy (2H4)
Richard du
  Champ (CYM)
Robert (WIV)
Robert
  Shallow (2H4)
Robert
  Shallow (WIV)
Robin (2H6)
Robin (TN)
Robin (WIV)
Robin
  Nightwork (2H6)
Robin Ostler (1H4)
Robin
  Starveling (MND)
Rowland (MM)
Rowland de Bois,
  Sir (AYL)
Samson
Sebastian (AWW)
Sebastian (TMP)
Sebastian (TN)
Simon
  Catling (ROM)
Simon
  Shadow (2H4)
Stephen Sly
Thomas
  Tapster (MM)
Thomas Wart (2H4)
Timothy
Toby Belch, Sir
Tom (1H4)
Tom (2H6)
Tom (LLL)
Tom Drum (AWW)
Tom Snout (MND)
Valentine (ROM)
Valentine (TGV)
Valentine (TIT)
Walter
Will (2H6)
Will (SON)
William (AYL)

William Cook (2H4)
William Page (WIV)
William Visor (2H4)
Will Squeal (2H4)
Yead Miller
  : 133

37.04
English: female
___

Alice (H5)
Alice (SHR)
Alice Ford (WIV)
Alice
  Shortcake (WIV)
Audrey
Bessy
Bridget (ERR)
Bridget (MM)
Bridget (WIV)
Cicely (ERR)
Cicely (TNK)
Cicely Hacket (SHR)
Claribel
Diana
  Capilet (AWW)
Doll Tearsheet
Dorothy (CYM)
Dorothy,
  Mistress (2H4)
Ellen
Emily
Frances
Gill
Gillian
Ginn
Imogen
Isbel (AWW)
Jane
  Nightwork (2H4)
Jane Smile (AYL)
Jenny
Jessica
Jill
Joan (JN)

Joan (LLL)
Joan (SHR)
Jug
Jule
Kate (LLL)
Kate (SHR)
Kate (TMP)
Kate
  Keepdown (MM)
Katherine (LLL)
Luce (ERR)
Luce (TNK)
Mall
Margaret (ADO)
Margery (MV)
Margery (TMP)
Margery, Lady (WT)
Marian →
  Maria (TN)
Marian (ERR)
Marian (LLL)
Marian (TMP)
Mary → Maria (TN)
Maud
Maudlin
Meg (ADO)
Meg (TMP)
Meg (WIV)
Nan (TGV)
Nan (WIV)
Nell (2H4)
Nell (ERR)
Nell (H5)
Nell (ROM)
Nell (TNK)
Nell (TRO)
Rosalind
Rosaline (LLL)
Rosaline (ROM)
Rose → Rosalind
Susan (ROM)
Susan
  Grindstone (ROM)
Tib (AWW)
Tib (PER)

Ursula (2H4)
Ursula (ADO)
Ursula (TGV)
  : 76

37.05
English: surnames
———————

Bardolph (2H4)
Bardolph (WIV)
Barnes, George
Bates, John
Best
Boult
Bracy, Sir John
Butler
Cook, William
Curan
Curtis
Double
Evans, Sir Hugh
Falconbridge (MV)
Falconbridge (ROM)
Falstaff, Sir
  John (WIV)
Fenton, Master
Fluellen, Captain
Ford, Master
  Frank (WIV)
Ford, Mistress (WIV)
Gadshill
Gilliams
Goodfellow, Robin
Gower, Captain (H5)
Gray
Gurney, James
Hacket,
  Cicely (SHR)
Hacket,
  Marian (SHR)
Kent (LR)
Macmorris, Captain
Miller, Yead
Morgan (AWW)
Ostler, Robin

Page, Anne (WIV)
Page, George (WIV)
Page,
  Mistress (WIV)
Page, William (WIV)
Perkes a' th' Hill,
  Clement
Peto
Poins, Ned
Rugby, John
Seyton
Smith the Weaver
Travers
Verges
Visor, William
Watchins, Arthur
  : 47

37.06
Romance: male
———————

Adriano de Armado,
  Don
Alonso
Alphonso, Don
Angelo (ERR)
Angelo (MM)
Angelo (OTH)
Antonio (ADO)
Antonio (AWW)
Antonio (MV)
Antonio (SHR)
Antonio (TGV)
Antonio (TMP)
Antonio (TN)
Baptista
  Minola (SHR)
Barnardine
Barnardo
Bassanio
Bellario
Biondello
Brabantio
Camillo
Charles (LLL)

Claudio (ADO)
Claudio (HAM)
Claudio (MM)
Conrade
Cosmo
Curio
Dromio [of
  Ephesus] (ERR)
Dromio [of
  Syracuse] (ERR)
Florizel
Fortinbras (HAM)
Fortinbras,
  Young (HAM)
France, King
  of (AWW)
Francisco (HAM)
Francisco (WIV)
Gerard de Narbon
Gonzago
Gonzalo
Gratiano (MV)
Gratiano (OTH)
Gremio
Grumio
Gualtier
Guiltian
Hortensio
Iago
Jachimo
Jaques (AWW)
Jaques [1] (AYL)
Jaques [2] (AYL)
Jaques
  Falconbridge (LLL)
Leonardo
Leonato
Lodovico
Lorenzo
Lucentio (ROM)
Lucentio (SHR)
Lucio (MM)
Lucio (ROM)
Malvolio
Martino, Signior

Mercatio
Montano
Orlando
Orsino
Othello
Panthino
Pedro of Aragon,
   Don
Petruchio (ROM)
Petruchio (SHR)
Philario
Pisanio
Placentio
Prospero
Reynaldo
Rinaldo
Roderigo (OTH)
Rogero
Romeo
Salerio
Samingo
Stephano (MV)
Stephano (TMP)
Thurio
Tiberio
Tranio
Tybalt
Valentio
Vincentio
Vitruvio
   : 91

37.07
Romance : female
––––––––––––––
Adriana
Angelica
Baptista (HAM)
Beatrice
Bianca (OTH)
Bianca (SHR)
Celia
Emilia (OTH)
Emilia (TNK)
Emilia (WT)

Isabella
Jaquenetta
Julia
Juliet
Julietta
Katherina
   Minola (SHR)
Laura
Lucetta
Maria (LLL)
Maria (TN)
Mariana
Nerissa
Olivia
Viola
   : 24

37.08
Germanic
––––––––––––––
Friz
Gertrude
Guildenstern
Hamlet,
   King (HAM)
Hamlet, Lord (HAM)
Lodowick (AWW)
Osric
Rosencrantz
Voltemand
Yorick
   : 10

37.09
other names
––––––––––––––
Aaron
Bentii
Caliban
Chitopher
Chus
Emmanuel
Gratii
Holofernes
Leah

Luccicos, Marcus
Morocco, Prince of
Moyses
Pigrogromitus
Queubus
Shylock
Smalus
Spinii
Sycorax
Tubal
Vapians
   : 20

37.10
Romance: surnames
––––––––––––––
Alençon, Duke
   of (LLL)
Amiens
Aragon, Don Pedro
   of (ADO)
Aragon, Prince
   of (MV)
Armado, Don
   Adriano de
Bentivolii
Berowne
Bois, Sir Rowland de
Boyet
Caius, Dr. (WIV)
Capulet (ROM)
Capulet,
   Cousin (ROM)
Capulet,
   Diana (AWW)
Capulet, Old (ROM)
Cassio, Michael
Du Champ, Richard
Dumaine (LLL)
Dumaine,
   Captain (AWW)
Falconbridge,
   Jaques (LLL)
Florence, Duke of

Gobbo,
   Lancelet (MV)
Gobbo, Old (MV)
La Far, Monsieur
Lamord
Longueville
Marcade
Milan, Duke of
Minola,
   Baptista (SHR)
Minola,
   Katherina (SHR)
Montague (ROM)
Montagues (ROM)
Montferrat, Marquis
   of
Narbon, Gerard de
Navarre
Perigort, Lord
Ragozine
Roussillon, Count →
   Bertram
Sennois
Umfreville, Sir John
Valdes
Vaumond
   : 41

37.11
telling: male (DP)
––––––––––––––
Abhorson
Aguecheek, Sir
   Andrew
Belch, Sir Toby
Benvolio
Borachio
Bottom, Nick
Bullcalf o' th' Green,
   Peter
Bum, Pompey
Catling, Simon
Costard
Dogberry
Dull, Anthony

Eglamour, Sir (TGV)
Elbow (MM)
Fang, Master
Feeble, Francis
fer, vb.
Feste
Flute, Francis
fool, n.
Froth, Master
Hiems, n.
Hotspur
Lafew, Lord
Lavatch, Master
Le Beau, Monsieur
Le Fer
Martext, Sir Oliver
Mercutio
Mote (LLL)
Mouldy, Ralph
Mugs
Nym, Corporal
Parolles
Patch-breech
Pinch, Doctor
Pistol
Quince, Peter
Rebeck, Hugh
Seacoal,
   George (ADO)
Shadow, Simon
Shallow, Robert
Silence, Master
Simple, Peter
Slender, Abraham
Sly,
   Christopher (SHR)
Snare, Master
Snout, Tom
Snug the Joiner
Soundpost, James
Starveling, Robin
Touchstone
Trinculo
Wart, Thomas
 : 54

37.12
telling: female (DP)
—————————
Overdone, Mistress
Perdita
Quickly,
   Mistress (1H4)
Quickly,
   Mistress (WIV)
Tearsheet, Doll
Ver, n.
 : 6

37.13
telling: male
   (mentioned)
—————————
Caper, Master
Charbon
Copper-spur, Master
Deep-vow, Master
Deformed
Dizzy, Young
Doit, John
Dommelton, Master
Drop-heir, Young
Dumb, Master
Eglamour, Sir (TGV)
Father Time
Forthlight, Master
Goodman, John
Half-can
Le Bon, Monsieur
Naps, John
Nightwork,
   Old (2H4)
Nightwork,
   Robin (2H4)
Nobody
Oatcake, Hugh
Peascod, Master
Pickbone, Francis
Pilch
Pillicock
Pimpernel, Henry

Potpan
Pots
Poysam
Pudding
Puff, Goodman
Puppy, Master
Rash, Master
Safe, Sergeant
Seacoal,
   Francis (ADO)
Shoetie, Master
Sly, Stephen (SHR)
Smile, Sir (WT)
Smooth, Master
Sneak
Spurio
Squeal, Will
Starve-lackey, Master
Stockfish, Samson
Such-a-One, Lord
Sugarsop
Surgeon, Dick
Three-pile, Master
Tisick, Master
Turf, Peter
Veroles
Worm, Don
 : 52

37.14
telling: female
   (mentioned)
—————————
Dowsabel
Elbow,
   Mistress (MM)
Grace
Grindstone, Susan
Keech
Keepdown, Kate
Nightwork,
   Jane (2H4)
Patience (PER)
Shortcake, Alice
Smile, Jane (AYL)

Squash, Mistress
Tale-porter, Mistress
Temperance
Worm, Lady
 : 14

37.15
nicknames
—————————
Accost, Mary
Adramadio, Dun
Agueface, Sir
   Andrew
Bald-pate, Goodman
Basimecu, Mounsieur
Coldspur
Comfect, Count
Dew, Seigneur
Disdain, Lady
Drum, Tom (AWW)
Fontibell
Guest, Master
Hoodman
Knight of the
   Burning Lamp
Lack-beard, Lord
Love,
   Monsieur (ADO)
Love, Signior (AYL)
Melancholy,
   Monsieur
Mitigation, Madam
Mock-water,
   Monsieur
Mountanto, Signior
Oracle, Sir
Paunch, Sir John
Prat, Mother
Prudence (ROM)
Prudence, Sir (TMP)
Remorse, Monsieur
Sack and Sugar, Sir
   John
She, Doctor
Sooth, Signior

Surecard, Master
Tapster, Thomas
thick-lips, n.
Tongue, Lady
Traveller, Monsieur
trot, n.
Valour, Sir
What-ye-call-it,
  Master
Wisdom, Lady
  : 39

**37.16
assumed names**
_____

Alexander (LLL)

Aliena (AYL)
Balthasar (MV)
Brentford, Woman
  of (WIV)
Brook, Master (WIV)
Cadwal (CYM)
Caius (LR)
Cambio (SHR)
Cesario (TN)
Doricles (WT)
Fairy Queen (WIV)
Fidele (CYM)
Ganymede (AYL)
Harry le Roy (H5)
Hector (LLL)
Hercules (LLL)

Herne (WIV)
Hobgoblin (WIV)
Judas
  Maccabaeus (LLL)
Licio (SHR)
Lion (MND)
Lodowick, Friar (MM)
Misanthropos (TIM)
Moonshine (MND)
Morgan (CYM)
Mortimer, John (2H6)
Polydore (CYM)
Pompey
  the Great (LLL)
Poor Tom (LR)
Prologue (MND)

Pyramus (MND)
Revenge (TIT)
Roderigo (TN)
Sebastian (TGV)
Thisbe (MND)
Tom o' Bedlam (LR)
Topas, Sir (TN)
Wall (MND)
  : 38

Index

A

01.06 wind · storm
airy, adj.
  01.06 wind · storm
Ajax
  36.15 Trojan myth
akin, adv.
  04.14 kindred
alabaster, n.
  01.25 stone
alack, int.
  25.13 interjection
alacrity, n.
  30.08 readiness
  34.24 nimbleness
aland, adv.
  01.21 fen · shore
  33.02 region
Alarbus
  37.01 classical: male
alarm, n.
  12.11 shout
  20.02 assault
alarm, vb.
  34.10 stir
alarm-bell, n.
  26.07 bell
alas, int.
  25.13 interjection
Alban
  28.14 saints
Albans → St. Albans
Albany
  36.03 British
Albany, Duke of
  36.14 pseudohistorical
albeit, conj.
  25.12 conjunction
Albion
  01.20 island
  36.03 British
alchemist, n.
  25.05 science · philosophy
alchemy, n.
  25.05 science · philosophy
Alcibiades
  36.22 historical: Greek
Alcides
  36.16 classical myth
alder-liefest, adj.
  14.02 love · hate
alderman, n.
  16.05 mayor
ale, n.
  09.15 beer · wine
  13.04 revelry

23.28 tavern
Alecto
  28.04 Mars · Venus
alehouse, n.
  23.28 tavern
alembic, n.
  08.33 bottle
Alençon
  36.11 French
Alençon, Duchess of (H8)
  36.18 historical: French
Alençon, Duke of (1H6)
  36.18 historical: French
Alençon, Duke of (LLL)
  37.10 Romance: surnames
Alençon, John (H5)
  36.18 historical: French
Aleppo
  36.05 Middle / Far Eastern
alere, lat. vb.
  09.02 feed
  24.13 Latin
ale-washed, adj.
  01.19 dip
  09.03 eat · drink
ale-wife, n.
  23.02 innkeeper
Alexander (ANT)
  36.24 historical: other
      names (2)
Alexander (LLL)
  37.16 assumed names
Alexander (TRO)
  36.24 historical: other
      names (2)
Alexander the Great (H5)
  36.22 historical: Greek
Alexandria
  36.04 African
Alexandrian, adj.
  36.04 African
Alexas
  36.24 historical: other
      names (2)
Algiers
  36.04 African
alias, adv.
  36.01 name
Alice (H5)
  37.04 English: female
Alice (SHR)
  37.04 English: female
Alice Ford (WIV)
  37.04 English: female
Alice Shortcake (WIV)

37.04 English: female
alien, adj.
  04.23 stranger
alien, n.
  04.23 stranger
Aliena (AYL)
  37.16 assumed names
a-life, adv.
  05.01 life · death
alight, vb.
  34.08 descend
alike, adj.
  31.23 equality
alike, adv.
  31.23 equality
a little, adv.
  32.15 interim
alius, lat. n.
  04.13 somebody
  24.13 Latin
alive, adv.
  05.01 life · death
all, adj.
  31.02 quantor
  31.03 all · nothing
all, adv.
  31.03 all · nothing
all, n.
  31.03 all · nothing
all-abhorred, adj.
  14.02 love · hate
all-admiring, adj.
  15.09 amazement
alla stoccata
  24.16 foreign phrases
  27.03 stoccado
allay, n.
  07.04 weakness
allay, vb.
  07.04 weakness
  31.13 decrease
allayment, n.
  31.13 decrease
all-binding, adj.
  31.16 join
all-changing, adj.
  33.42 change
all-cheering, adj.
  13.08 cheer(less)
all-disgraced, adj.
  14.47 dishonour
all-dreaded, adj.
  14.53 horror
all-eating, adj.
  09.03 eat · drink

Anchises
    36.15 Trojan myth
anchor, n.
    35.05 anchor
anchor, n.
    28.08 worshipper
anchor, vb.
    33.11 firm
    35.08 navigation
anchorage, n.
    35.05 anchor
anchoring hook, n.
    23.20 hinge
anchovy, n.
    03.26 fish
ancient, adj.
    32.11 old age
    32.14 period
    32.18 past · present · future
ancient, n.
    32.11 old age
ancient, n.
    20.06 officer
ancientry, n.
    32.11 old age
Ancus Martius
    36.23 historical: Roman
and¹, conj.
    25.12 conjunction
and², conj.
    25.12 conjunction
andiron, n.
    08.18 hearth
Andrew
    35.01 ship
Andrew Aguecheek, Sir
    37.03 English: male
Andromache
    36.15 Trojan myth
Andronicus, Marcus (TIT)
    37.01 classical: male
Andronicus, Titus (TIT)
    37.01 classical: male
anew, adv.
    32.13 newness
ange, fr. n.
    24.14 French
    28.05 spirits
angel, n.
    22.06 money
    28.05 spirits
Angelica
    37.07 Romance : female
angelical, adj.
    28.05 spirits

angel-like, adj.
    28.05 spirits
Angelo (ERR)
    37.06 Romance: male
Angelo (MM)
    37.06 Romance: male
Angelo (OTH)
    37.06 Romance: male
anger, n.
    14.29 anger
anger, vb.
    14.29 anger
angerly, adj.
    14.29 anger
Angers
    36.11 French
anglais, fr. n.
    24.01 language
    24.14 French
angle, n.
    27.15 snare
angle, n.
    33.25 corner
angle, vb.
    27.11 fisherman
angler, n.
    27.11 fisherman
Angleterre, fr.
    24.14 French
    36.03 British
Anglia, lat.
    24.13 Latin
    36.03 British
angry, adj.
    14.29 anger
anguish, n.
    19.04 vexation
Angus
    36.03 British
Angus, Earl of
    36.17 historical: English
an-heires, n.
    24.19 crux
anight, adv.
    32.08 morning · night
anights, adv.
    32.08 morning · night
animal, n.
    03.01 animal
animus, lat. n.
    15.03 mind
    24.13 Latin
Anjou
    36.11 French
Anjou, Reignier, Duke of

    36.18 historical: French
ankle, n.
    06.16 leg
Anna
    36.16 classical myth
annals, n.
    24.03 book
Anne
    28.14 saints
Anne, Duchess of Gloucester
            (R3)
    36.17 historical: English
annex, vb.
    31.12 increase
    31.16 join
annexion, n.
    31.16 join
annexment, n.
    31.12 increase
    31.16 join
annoy, n.
    19.04 vexation
annoy, vb.
    19.04 vexation
annoyance, n.
    19.04 vexation
annual, adj.
    32.02 hour · day · year
anoint, vb.
    11.09 rub
    28.12 sacrament
anon, adv.
    32.31 imminence
another, adj.
    04.13 somebody
    31.02 quantor
    31.15 moreover
    31.25 difference
another, pron.
    25.15 pronoun
Anselme, County
    37.03 English: male
answer, n.
    24.21 question · answer
    27.03 stoccado
answer, vb.
    17.09 agreement
    22.32 recompense
    24.21 question · answer
answerable, adj.
    17.09 agreement
    17.13 obligation
ant, n.
    03.31 fly · louse
Antenor

appal, vb.
   01.12 light · dark
   14.52 fear
apparel, n.
   10.01 attire
apparel, vb.
   10.01 attire
apparent, adj.
   12.02 show
   12.03 semblance
apparent, n.
   21.08 legacy
apparently, adv.
   12.02 show
apparition, n.
   12.03 semblance
   28.05 spirits
appeach, vb.
   21.04 accusation
appeal, n.
   18.11 request
   21.04 accusation
appeal, vb.
   21.04 accusation
appear, vb.
   12.01 sight
   12.03 semblance
   33.14 presence · absence
appearance, n.
   06.05 lineament
   12.01 sight
   12.02 show
   12.03 semblance
appearer, n.
   33.14 presence · absence
appease, vb.
   19.17 (un)rest
appeler, fr. vb.
   24.14 French
   36.01 name
appellant, n.
   21.04 accusation
appendix, n.
   31.12 increase
apperil, n.
   19.18 peril
appertain, vb.
   29.06 pertain
appertaining, n.
   29.06 pertain
appetite, n.
   09.01 appetite
   14.48 desire
applaud, vb.
   17.17 praise

applause, n.
   17.17 praise
apple, n.
   02.13 apple · grape
apple-john, n.
   02.13 apple · grape
apple of eye, n.
   06.04 face
apple-tart, n.
   09.13 bread · cake
appliance, n.
   07.24 medicine · cure
application, n.
   07.24 medicine · cure
apply, vb.
   15.23 interpretation
   18.07 (ab)use
appoint, vb.
   15.27 resolution
   22.31 furnish
appointment, n.
   17.09 agreement
   18.05 commandment
   22.17 chattel
apprehend, vb.
   11.02 grasp
   15.01 cognition
apprehension, n.
   11.02 grasp
   15.01 cognition
apprehensive, adj.
   15.01 cognition
apprendre, fr. vb.
   15.01 cognition
   24.14 French
apprentice, n.
   23.01 vocation
apprenticehood, n.
   23.01 vocation
approach, n.
   34.04 here-approach
approach, vb.
   34.04 here-approach
approacher, n.
   34.04 here-approach
approbation, n.
   15.14 examination
   17.09 agreement
   17.17 praise
approof, n.
   15.14 examination
   17.17 praise
appropriate, adj.
   30.09 (un)aptness
appropriation, n.

30.02 disposition
approve, vb.
   13.07 (dis)pleasure
   15.14 examination
   17.17 praise
approver, n.
   15.14 examination
appurtenance, n.
   29.06 pertain
appurtenant, adj.
   29.06 pertain
appurtenant, n.
   29.06 pertain
apricot, n.
   02.13 apple · grape
April, n.
   32.06 month
apron, n.
   10.07 petticoat
apron-man, n.
   23.01 vocation
apt, adj.
   30.02 disposition
   30.09 (un)aptness
aptly, adv.
   30.02 disposition
   30.09 (un)aptness
aptness, n.
   30.02 disposition
   30.09 (un)aptness
aqua-vitae, n.
   09.15 beer · wine
Aquilon
   01.06 wind · storm
   28.04 Mars · Venus
Aquitaine
   36.11 French
Arabia
   36.04 African
Arabian, adj.
   36.04 African
Arabian bird, n.
   03.32 unicorn
Arachne
   36.16 classical myth
Aragon
   36.09 Southern European
Aragon, Don Pedro of (ADO)
   37.10 Romance: surnames
Aragon, Prince of (MV)
   37.10 Romance: surnames
araise, vb.
   34.17 raise
arbitrament, n.
   15.15 search

attachment, n.
   18.06 controlment
attain, vb.
   22.28 acquisition
   34.04 here-approach
attainder, n.
   14.47 dishonour
   21.04 accusation
attaint, adj.
   07.06 sickness
   14.47 dishonour
   21.04 accusation
attaint, n.
   07.06 sickness
   14.47 dishonour
   14.49 impurity
   21.04 accusation
attaint, vb.
   07.06 sickness
   14.49 impurity
   21.04 accusation
attainture, n.
   14.47 dishonour
attask, vb.
   19.08 reproach
attempt, n.
   15.13 attempt
   20.02 assault
attempt, vb.
   15.13 attempt
   18.18 instigation
attemptable, adj.
   15.13 attempt
attend, vb.
   12.07 hearing
   16.26 attendant
   17.08 vigilance
attendance, n.
   16.26 attendant
attendant, n.
   16.26 attendant
attent, adj.
   17.01 attention
attention, n.
   17.01 attention
attentive, adj.
   17.01 attention
attentiveness, n.
   17.01 attention
attest, n.
   21.06 testimony
attest, vb.
   21.06 testimony
attire, n.
   10.01 attire

attire, vb.
   10.01 attire
attorney[1], n.
   16.20 deputy
attorney[2], n.
   16.20 deputy
   21.05 law court
attorney, vb.
   16.20 deputy
   21.05 law court
attorney-general, n.
   21.05 law court
attorneyship, n.
   16.20 deputy
attract, vb.
   11.07 pull
   18.17 enticement
attraction, n.
   11.07 pull
   18.17 enticement
attractive, adj.
   18.17 enticement
attribute, n.
   14.16 honour
   30.02 disposition
attribute, vb.
   15.25 attribution
attribution, n.
   15.25 attribution
   17.17 praise
attributive, adj.
   30.02 disposition
a-twain, adv.
   31.17 separation
at (with) a word, adv.
   32.30 brevity
auburn, adj.
   12.04 colour
auburn, n.
   12.04 colour
aucun, fr. pron.
   24.14 French
   25.15 pronoun
audacious, adj.
   14.17 boldness
   14.26 insolence
audaciously, adv.
   14.17 boldness
audacity, n.
   14.17 boldness
audible, adj.
   12.07 hearing
audience, n.
   12.07 hearing
   26.02 theatre

audire, lat. vb.
   12.07 hearing
   24.13 Latin
audit, n.
   22.09 account
auditor, n.
   12.07 hearing
   22.09 account
auditory, n.
   12.07 hearing
Audrey
   37.04 English: female
Aufidius, Tullus
   36.14 pseudohistorical
auger, n.
   23.25 gad
auger-hole, n.
   33.22 hole · trench
aught, n.
   29.04 thing
augment, vb.
   31.12 increase
augmentation, n.
   31.12 increase
augur, n.
   28.27 prognostication
augur, vb.
   28.27 prognostication
augurer, n.
   28.27 prognostication
augury, n.
   28.27 prognostication
August, n.
   32.06 month
Augustus → Caesar
   36.23 historical: Roman
Aulis
   36.09 Southern European
Aumerle
   36.11 French
Aumerle, Edward, Duke of
   36.17 historical: English
aunt, n.
   04.09 woman
   04.12 strumpet
   04.15 family
aunt-mother, n.
   04.15 family
auricular, adj.
   12.07 hearing
Aurora
   28.04 Mars · Venus
auspicious, adj.
   22.34 (dis)advantage
   28.27 prognostication

B

16.15 castle
baseless, adj.
  15.20 error · truth
basely, adv.
  14.22 badness
baseness, n.
  14.22 badness
  16.31 commoner
bases, n.
  10.07 petticoat
basest, n.
  14.22 badness
  16.31 commoner
  33.38 depth
bashful, adj.
  14.07 humility
bashfulness, n.
  14.07 humility
Basilisco-like, adj.
  14.25 braggardism
  26.02 theatre
basilisk, n.
  03.32 unicorn
  20.16 gun
Basimecu, Mounsieur
  37.15 nicknames
basin, n.
  08.35 tub
Basingstoke
  36.03 British
basis, n.
  08.13 floor
  17.02 support
bask, vb.
  01.11 hot · cold
basket, n.
  08.34 basket
basket-hilt, n.
  20.15 sword-hilt
bass, n.
  26.04 gamut
bass, vb.
  12.09 clangour
Bassanio
  37.06 Romance: male
Bassianus
  37.01 classical: male
bass-string, n.
  26.06 fiddle
bass-viol, n.
  26.06 fiddle
basta, it. int.
  24.15 Italian
  25.13 interjection
bastard, n.

04.15 family
09.15 beer · wine
18.19 deceit
bastardize, vb.
  05.03 procreation
bastardly, adj.
  04.15 family
bastardy, n.
  04.15 family
baste, vb.
  23.05 clothier
baste, vb.
  09.05 cookery
baste, vb.
  11.03 hit
bastinado, n.
  11.03 hit
bat, n.
  03.23 owl · bat
bat, n.
  21.16 cudgel
bataille, fr. n.
  20.01 combat
  24.14 French
batch, n.
  09.13 bread · cake
  31.01 quantity
bate, n.
  19.11 quarrel
bate, vb.
  07.04 weakness
  31.13 decrease
bate, vb.
  34.10 stir
  34.19 shake
bate-breeding, adj.
  05.03 procreation
bateless, adj.
  33.26 sharp · dull
Bates, John
  37.05 English: surnames
bat-fowl, vb.
  27.12 falconer
bath, n.
  01.16 pool
  01.19 dip
bathe, vb.
  01.19 dip
batler, n.
  23.09 laundress
battalia, n.
  20.05 army · navy
battalion, n.
  20.05 army · navy
batten, vb.

03.47 peck · graze
09.01 appetite
batter, vb.
  11.03 hit
battery, n.
  11.03 hit
  20.02 assault
battle, n.
  20.01 combat
  20.05 army · navy
battle, vb.
  20.01 combat
battle-axe, n.
  20.14 weapon
battlement, n.
  20.10 fortification
batty, adj.
  03.23 owl · bat
bauble, n.
  22.14 trifle
  27.08 toy
baubling, adj.
  22.14 trifle
bavin, n.
  01.13 fire
  02.01 tree · bush · twig
  31.35 bunch
bawcock, n.
  04.22 companion
bawd, vb.
  14.51 fornication
bawd, n.
  03.11 rat
bawd-born, adj.
  05.04 birth
  14.51 fornication
bawdry, n.
  14.50 sensuality
  14.51 fornication
bawdy, adj.
  14.50 sensuality
bawdy-house, n.
  23.30 brothel
bawl, vb.
  12.11 shout
bay, adj.
  12.04 colour
bay, n.
  02.02 oak · brier
bay, n.
  01.21 fen · shore
  35.10 harbour
bay, n.
  08.09 arch
bay, n.

10.05 needlework
33.38 depth
35.01 ship
bottom, vb.
  10.05 needlework
  33.31 entangle
Bottom, Nick
  37.11 telling: male (DP)
bottomless, adj.
  33.38 depth
Bouciqualt
  36.18 historical: French
bough, n.
  02.01 tree • bush • twig
Boult
  37.05 English: surnames
bounce, n.
  12.10 din
bounce, vb.
  12.10 din
  14.25 braggardism
  34.02 leap
bound, adj.
  28.26 destiny
  30.08 readiness
bound, adj.
  22.12 contract
bound, n.
  19.13 obstruction
  33.09 border
  33.10 encompassment
bound, n.
  34.02 leap
bound, vb.
  33.09 border
  33.10 encompassment
bound, vb.
  34.02 leap
boundless, adj.
  33.09 border
bounteous, adj.
  14.11 liberality
bounteously, adv.
  14.11 liberality
bountiful, adj.
  14.11 liberality
bountifully, adv.
  14.11 liberality
bounty, n.
  14.01 goodness
  14.11 liberality
  22.33 gift
bourbier, fr. n.
  01.24 mud
  24.14 French

Bourbon
  36.11 French
Bourbon (3H6)
  36.18 historical: French
Bourbon, John, Duke of (H5)
  36.18 historical: French
bourn, n.
  01.17 river
bourne, n.
  33.09 border
bout, n.
  26.11 dance
  27.03 stoccado
bow, n.
  01.08 rain • snow
  27.04 archery
  27.17 bridle
bow, vb.
  18.03 (dis)obedience
  34.12 bend
bow-back, n.
  06.10 back
  06.18 anatomy compounds
bow-boy, n.
  27.04 archery
bowcase, n.
  08.36 case
  27.04 archery
bowel, n.
  04.15 family
  06.17 blood • bone
  33.08 inside • outside
bower, n.
  08.02 lodge
bower, vb.
  08.02 lodge
  33.10 encompassment
bow-hand, n.
  06.15 arm
  06.18 anatomy compounds
  27.04 archery
bowl, n.
  08.31 cup
bowl, n.
  27.09 ball
bowl, vb.
  27.06 games
bowler, n.
  27.07 gamester
bowline, n.
  35.06 tackle
bowsprit, n.
  35.04 mast
bow-string, n.
  27.04 archery

bow-wow, int.
  12.14 bow-wow
box, n.
  08.36 case
box, n.
  11.03 hit
box-tree, n.
  02.02 oak • brier
boy, n.
  04.03 boy • youth
boy, vb.
  04.03 boy • youth
  26.02 theatre
Boyet
  37.10 Romance: surnames
boyish, adj.
  04.03 boy • youth
boy-queller, n.
  21.10 murder
Brabant
  36.10 Northern European
Brabant, Anthony, Duke of
  36.18 historical: French
Brabantio
  37.06 Romance: male
brabble, n.
  19.11 quarrel
brabbler, n.
  19.11 quarrel
Brabbler
  03.08 dog
brace, n.
  20.12 armour
  31.09 pair
brace, vb.
  33.11 firm
bracelet, n.
  10.21 brooch
brach, n.
  03.08 dog
Brackenbury, Robert
  36.17 historical: English
Bracy, Sir John
  37.05 English: surnames
brag, n.
  14.25 braggardism
brag, vb.
  14.25 braggardism
braggardism, n.
  14.25 braggardism
braggart, n.
  14.25 braggardism
bragless, adj.
  14.25 braggardism
braid, adj.

06.19 breath
breast, n.
  06.08 breast
  26.09 musician
breast, vb.
  19.01 opposition
breast-deep, adj.
  33.38 depth
breast-plate, n.
  20.12 armour
breath, n.
  06.19 breath
  24.20 conversation
  24.22 message
  32.15 interim
breathe, vb.
  05.01 life • death
  06.19 breath
  24.20 conversation
breather, n.
  06.19 breath
breathing, n.
  32.15 interim
breathing while, n.
  32.15 interim
breathless, adj.
  05.01 life • death
  06.19 breath
Brecon
  36.03 British
breech, n.
  10.09 shoe • hose
breech, vb.
  10.09 shoe • hose
  11.03 hit
breeching scholar, n.
  25.03 student
breed, n.
  04.14 kindred
breed, vb.
  05.03 procreation
  25.01 education
breed-bate, n.
  19.11 quarrel
breeder, n.
  03.02 horse
  05.03 procreation
breeding, n.
  04.14 kindred
  25.01 education
breeze, n.
  03.31 fly • louse
Brentford
  36.03 British
Brentford, Woman of (WIV)

37.16 assumed names
Bretagne
  36.11 French
Bretagne, Duke of
  36.18 historical: French
brevis, lat. adj.
  24.13 Latin
  32.30 brevity
brevity, n.
  32.30 brevity
brew, vb.
  09.05 cookery
brewage, n.
  09.15 beer • wine
brewer, n.
  23.03 victualler
brew-house, n.
  23.28 tavern
Briareus
  03.32 unicorn
bribe, n.
  18.19 deceit
  21.12 thievery
bribe, vb.
  18.19 deceit
  21.12 thievery
bribed-buck, n.
  03.13 deer
briber, n.
  18.19 deceit
  21.12 thievery
brick, n.
  08.08 wall
bricklayer, n.
  23.06 mason
brick-wall, n.
  08.08 wall
bridal, n.
  04.18 marriage
bridal bed, n.
  08.22 bed
bridal chamber, n.
  08.17 rooms
bridal day, n.
  32.03 times
bridal dinner, n.
  09.08 repast
bridal flowers, n.
  02.08 flower
bride, n.
  04.18 marriage
bride, vb.
  04.18 marriage
bride-bed, n.
  08.22 bed

bridegroom, n.
  04.18 marriage
bride-habited, adj.
  10.01 attire
bridehouse, n.
  08.01 house
bridge, n.
  06.04 face
  35.11 flood-gate
Bridget (ERR)
  37.04 English: female
Bridget (MM)
  37.04 English: female
Bridget (WIV)
  37.04 English: female
Bridgnorth
  36.03 British
bridle, n.
  27.17 bridle
bridle, vb.
  18.06 controlment
  27.17 bridle
brief, adj.
  32.30 brevity
brief, n.
  24.04 writings
  24.08 epitome
brief, n.
  32.30 brevity
briefly, adv.
  32.30 brevity
briefness, n.
  32.30 brevity
  34.23 fast • slow
brier, n.
  02.02 oak • brier
bright, adj.
  01.12 light • dark
  13.08 cheer(less)
bright-burning, adj.
  01.13 fire
brighten, vb.
  01.12 light • dark
brightest, n.
  01.12 light • dark
brightly, adv.
  01.12 light • dark
brightness, n.
  01.12 light • dark
bright-shining, adj.
  01.12 light • dark
brim, n.
  33.09 border
brim, vb.
  31.04 full • empty

brown, adj.
　　12.04　colour
brown, n.
　　12.04　colour
brown bastard, n.
　　09.15　beer · wine
brown bill, n.
　　20.14　weapon
brown bread, n.
　　09.13　bread · cake
Brownist, n.
　　28.01　religions
brown paper, n.
　　24.04　writings
browny, adj.
　　12.04　colour
browse, vb.
　　03.47　peck · graze
bruise, n.
　　07.18　wound
bruise, vb.
　　07.18　wound
bruit, n.
　　24.22　message
bruit, vb.
　　12.10　din
　　24.20　conversation
　　24.25　make known
Brundisium
　　36.08　Italian
brunt, n.
　　20.01　combat
brush, n.
　　20.02　assault
　　23.23　broom
brush, vb.
　　11.09　rub
　　23.23　broom
brute, adj.
　　14.30　savageness
brutish, adj.
　　14.30　savageness
Brutus, lat.
　　24.13　Latin
　　36.23　historical: Roman
Brutus, Decius (JC)
　　36.23　historical: Roman
Brutus, Junius (COR)
　　36.14　pseudohistorical
Brutus, Junius (H5)
　　36.23　historical: Roman
Brutus, Marcus (JC)
　　36.23　historical: Roman
bubble, n.
　　01.14　water

22.14　trifle
bubble, vb.
　　34.10　stir
bubukle, n.
　　07.16　sore
buck, n.
　　03.13　deer
buck, n.
　　10.03　cloth
　　23.09　laundress
buck, vb.
　　23.09　laundress
buck-basket, n.
　　08.34　basket
　　23.09　laundress
bucket, n.
　　08.35　tub
bucket, n.
　　08.29　receptacle
Buckingham
　　36.03　British
Buckingham → Stafford (H8)
　　36.17　historical: English
Buckingham, Henry, Duke of
　　(H8)
　　36.17　historical: English
Buckingham, Humphrey of
　　(2H6)
　　36.17　historical: English
buckle, n.
　　10.13　belt
buckle, vb.
　　18.06　controlment
　　33.11　firm
　　34.12　bend
buckler, n.
　　20.12　armour
buckler, vb.
　　17.06　protection
　　20.20　retreat
Bucklersbury
　　34.28　road
　　36.07　London
buckle with, phr. vb.
　　20.01　combat
buckram, n.
　　10.03　cloth
　　33.28　hard · soft
buck-washing, n.
　　23.09　laundress
bud, n.
　　02.06　bud · root
bud, vb.
　　32.12　(un)ripe
budge, vb.

34.10　stir
budger, n.
　　34.10　stir
budget, int.
　　25.13　interjection
budget, n.
　　08.37　bag
buff, n.
　　10.04　leather
buffet, n.
　　11.03　hit
buffet, vb.
　　11.03　hit
bug, n.
　　28.05　spirits
bugbear, n.
　　28.05　spirits
bugle, n.
　　26.05　wind instrument
　　27.14　hunter
bugle, n.
　　10.18　ornament
bugle-bracelet, n.
　　10.21　brooch
build, vb.
　　23.16　build
building, n.
　　08.01　house
　　23.16　build
bulk, n.
　　06.01　body
　　23.16　build
　　33.16　size
bulk, n.
　　23.31　shop
　　33.24　jutting-out
bulky, adj.
　　33.16　size
　　33.36　breadth
bull, n.
　　03.04　cattle
Bull
　　01.04　zodiac
bull-bearing, adj.
　　34.22　carry
bull-beef, n.
　　09.10　meat
bull-calf, n.
　　03.04　cattle
Bullcalf o' th' Green, Peter
　　37.11　telling: male (DP)
bullet, n.
　　20.16　gun
bullock, n.
　　03.04　cattle

by the ears, adv.
   19.11 quarrel
by the eternal God
   28.25 oaths
by the grace of God
   28.25 oaths
by the head and shoulders, adv.
   07.02 vigour
by the holy mother of our Lord
   28.25 oaths
by the holy rood
   28.25 oaths
by the Lord
   28.25 oaths
by the mass
   28.25 oaths
by the mess
   28.25 oaths
by the rood
   28.25 oaths
by th' mass
   28.25 oaths
by th' rood
   28.25 oaths
by-word, n.
   25.06 maxim
Byzantium
   36.05 Middle / Far Eastern

C

C, n.
   25.07 alphabet
   26.04 gamut
ça, fr. adv.
   24.14 French
   25.10 adverb
cabbage, n.
   02.14 cabbage
cabilero, n.
   04.08 cavalier
cabin, n.
   08.17 rooms
   35.02 deck • oar
cabin, vb.
   08.04 inhabit
   18.06 controlment
cabinet, n.
   03.46 nest • kennel
   08.17 rooms
cable, n.
   23.21 rope
   35.05 anchor
cackle, vb.
   12.13 neigh
cacodemon, n.
   28.05 spirits
caddis, n.
   10.09 shoe • hose
caddis-garter, n.
   10.09 shoe • hose
cade, n.
   23.22 barrel
Cade, John (Jack)
   36.17 historical: English
cadence, n.
   26.13 metre
cadent, adj.
   34.08 descend
Cadmus
   36.16 classical myth
caduceus, n.
   16.16 heraldry
Cadwal (CYM)
   37.16 assumed names
Cadwallader
   36.19 historical: other
          names (1)
caelestis, lat. adj.
   24.13 Latin
   28.07 heaven • hell

Caelius
   36.23 historical: Roman
caelum, lat. n.
   01.02 sky
   24.13 Latin
Caernarvonshire
   36.03 British
Caesar
   16.17 king
Caesar, Augustus (CYM)
   36.23 historical: Roman
Caesar, Julius (JC)
   36.23 historical: Roman
Caesar, Octavius (ANT)
   36.23 historical: Roman
Caesarion
   36.23 historical: Roman
cage, n.
   03.46 nest • kennel
   08.34 basket
   21.14 prison
cage, vb.
   18.06 controlment
Cain
   28.03 Abraham • Paul
cain-coloured, adj.
   12.04 colour
caitiff, adj.
   04.04 rogue
caitiff, n.
   04.04 rogue
Caius (LR)
   37.16 assumed names
Caius (TIT)
   37.01 classical: male
Caius, Dr. (WIV)
   37.10 Romance: surnames
cake, n.
   09.13 bread • cake
   31.27 heap
cake, vb.
   09.07 congeal
Calaber
   36.08 Italian
Calaber, Duke of
   36.18 historical: French
Calais
   36.11 French
calamity, n.
   32.24 mischance
Calchas
   36.15 Trojan myth
calculate, vb.
   28.27 prognostication
   31.07 count

calen
    24.17 pseudo foreign
calendar, n.
    24.03 book
    24.10 note-book
    29.08 pattern
calf, n.
    03.04 cattle
    04.10 darling
    15.12 foolishness
calf, n.
    06.16 leg
calf-like, adj.
    03.04 cattle
calf's-head, n.
    03.33 beak · horn
calf-skin, n.
    10.04 leather
Caliban
    37.09 other names
Calipolis
    26.02 theatre
caliver, n.
    20.16 gun
calkin, n.
    27.17 bridle
call, n.
    18.05 commandment
    27.15 snare
call, vb.
    12.11 shout
    18.05 commandment
    36.01 name
callet, n.
    04.12 strumpet
calling, n.
    23.01 vocation
    36.01 name
call on (upon), phr. vb.
    22.09 account
    32.17 sojourn
calm, adj.
    19.17 (un)rest
calm, n.
    19.17 (un)rest
calm, vb.
    19.17 (un)rest
calm (2H4 2.4.36), n.
    24.18 malapropism
calmly, adv.
    19.17 (un)rest
calmness, n.
    19.17 (un)rest
Calpurnia
    36.23 historical: Roman

calumniate, vb.
    19.10 disparagement
calumnious, adj.
    19.10 disparagement
calumny, n.
    19.10 disparagement
calve, vb.
    05.03 procreation
calves'-gut, n.
    03.41 tripe
    26.06 fiddle
Calydon
    36.09 Southern European
cam, adj.
    33.30 oblique
Cambio (SHR)
    37.16 assumed names
Cambria
    36.03 British
cambric, n.
    10.03 cloth
Cambridge
    36.03 British
Cambridge, Richard, Earl of
    36.17 historical: English
Cambyses
    26.02 theatre
    36.24 historical: other
                names (2)
camel, n.
    03.16 elephant · lion
Camelot
    36.03 British
Camillo
    37.06 Romance: male
camlet, n.
    10.03 cloth
camomile, n.
    02.17 mandragora
camp, n.
    20.09 camp
camp, vb.
    08.04 inhabit
Campeius, Cardinal
    36.19 historical: other
                names (1)
can, n.
    08.31 cup
can, vb.
    15.06 knowledge
    30.05 (un)able
canary, n.
    09.15 beer · wine
    26.11 dance
canary, vb.

    26.11 dance
Canary
    01.20 island
    36.09 Southern European
cancel, n.
    31.22 cancel
cancel, vb.
    31.22 cancel
Cancer
    01.04 zodiac
candidatus, lat. n.
    16.04 senator
    24.13 Latin
candle, n.
    08.27 torch
candle-case, n.
    08.27 torch
    08.36 case
candle-holder, n.
    16.28 bearer
candle-mine, n.
    08.27 torch
    31.27 heap
candlestick, n.
    08.27 torch
candle-waster, n.
    08.27 torch
    13.04 revelry
    24.11 read
candy, n.
    09.16 sweetmeat
candy, vb.
    09.07 congeal
    09.16 sweetmeat
Candy
    01.20 island
    36.09 Southern European
Canidius
    36.23 historical: Roman
canis, lat. n.
    03.08 dog
    24.13 Latin
canker, n.
    02.09 rose
    03.30 vermin · spider
    07.05 decay
    07.16 sore
canker, vb.
    07.05 decay
canker-bit, adj.
    03.47 peck · graze
    07.05 decay
canker-bloom, n.
    02.09 rose
canker-blossom, n.

26.16 insculpture
casa, it. n.
  08.01 house
  24.15 Italian
Casca
  36.23 historical: Roman
case, n.
  15.32 circumstance
  16.10 edict
  21.05 law court
  25.08 grammar
  32.23 occurrence
case, n.
  08.36 case
case, vb.
  08.36 case
  11.11 strip
  33.10 encompassment
casement, n.
  08.10 window
cash, n.
  22.06 money
cashier, vb.
  19.05 rejection
  22.06 money
  34.20 send
cask, n.
  08.36 case
casket, n.
  08.36 case
casket, vb.
  08.36 case
casque, n.
  20.13 helmet
Cassado, Gregory de
  36.17 historical: English
Cassandra
  36.15 Trojan myth
Cassibelan (CYM)
  36.17 historical: English
Cassibelan (CYM)
  36.24 historical: other
        names (2)
Cassio, Michael
  37.10 Romance: surnames
Cassius, Caius
  36.23 historical: Roman
cassock, n.
  10.06 mantle
cast, n.
  12.04 colour
  23.16 build
  27.10 sport terms
cast, vb.
  01.18 effusion

06.20 excrement
15.14 examination
22.29 give
27.10 sport terms
31.07 count
34.18 toss
Castalion-King-Urinal, n.
  07.22 physician
castaway, n.
  19.05 rejection
cast (heave) the gorge, vb.
  06.20 excrement
castigate, vb.
  21.13 punishment
castigation, n.
  21.13 punishment
castiliano
  24.17 pseudo foreign
  36.09 Southern European
castle, n.
  16.15 castle
Castle
  23.28 tavern
castle-ditch, n.
  20.11 moat
Castor
  36.16 classical myth
casual, adj.
  32.25 chance
casually, adv.
  32.25 chance
casualty, n.
  32.25 chance
cat, n.
  03.07 cat
Cataian, n.
  04.04 rogue
  36.05 Middle / Far Eastern
catalogue, n.
  24.05 list
catamountain, n.
  03.16 elephant · lion
cataplasm, n.
  07.24 medicine · cure
cataract, n.
  01.14 water
catarrh, n.
  07.12 rheum
catastrophe, n.
  20.21 destruction
  26.02 theatre
  32.19 beginning · end
catch, n.
  11.02 grasp
  26.10 song

catch, vb.
  11.02 grasp
  22.28 acquisition
cate, n.
  09.04 food · drink
catechism, n.
  25.01 education
  28.10 sermon
catechize, vb.
  24.21 question · answer
  25.01 education
  28.10 sermon
cater, vb.
  09.02 feed
cater-cousin, n.
  04.14 kindred
caterpillar, n.
  03.30 vermin · spider
caterwaul, vb.
  12.13 neigh
Catesby
  36.17 historical: English
cathedral church, n.
  28.18 church
cat-like, adj.
  03.07 cat
catling, n.
  03.41 tripe
  26.06 fiddle
Catling, Simon
  37.11 telling: male (DP)
Cato (JC)
  36.23 historical: Roman
Cato, Marcus (JC)
  36.23 historical: Roman
cattle, n.
  03.04 cattle
Caucasus
  01.27 hill · dale
caudle, n.
  09.15 beer · wine
caudle, vb.
  09.02 feed
  09.15 beer · wine
cauldron, n.
  08.32 pot
caulk, vb.
  23.18 cement
cause, n.
  15.28 intention
  15.29 motive
  15.31 affair
  27.03 stoccado
cause, vb.
  11.01 do

causeless, adj.
  15.29 motive
causer, n.
  11.01 do
cautel, n.
  18.16 plot
  18.19 deceit
cautelous, adj.
  18.19 deceit
cauterize, vb.
  01.13 fire
  07.24 medicine · cure
caution, n.
  17.01 attention
  17.03 counsel
cavaleiro, n.
  04.08 cavalier
cavalery, n.
  04.08 cavalier
cavalier, n.
  04.08 cavalier
cavalleria, n.
  04.08 cavalier
cave, n.
  01.29 cave
cave, vb.
  08.04 inhabit
cave-keeper, n.
  08.04 inhabit
cave-keeping, adj.
  08.04 inhabit
  24.29 conceal
cavere, lat. vb.
  17.01 attention
  24.13 Latin
cavern, n.
  01.29 cave
caviar, n.
  09.09 pickle-herring
cavil, n.
  19.11 quarrel
cavil, vb.
  19.09 mockery
caw, vb.
  12.13 neigh
Cawdor
  16.15 castle
  36.03 British
Cawdor, Thane of → Macbeth
  36.19 historical: other
      names (1)
Cawdor, Thane of (MAC)
  36.14 pseudohistorical
ce, fr. pron.
  24.14 French

  25.15 pronoun
cease, vb.
  05.01 life · death
  32.19 beginning · end
ceaseless, adj.
  32.16 continuance
cedar, n.
  02.02 oak · brier
Cedius
  36.15 Trojan myth
celebrate, vb.
  16.14 ceremony
celebration, n.
  16.14 ceremony
celerity, n.
  34.23 fast · slow
celestial, adj.
  01.02 sky
  28.07 heaven · hell
celestial, n.
  28.09 clergy
Celia
  37.07 Romance : female
cell, n.
  08.17 rooms
cellar, n.
  08.03 storehouse
cellarage, n.
  08.03 storehouse
celsus, lat. adj.
  24.13 Latin
  33.37 height
cement, n.
  23.18 cement
cement, vb.
  23.18 cement
  31.16 join
censer, n.
  08.29 receptacle
censor, n.
  16.04 senator
Censorinus
  36.14 pseudohistorical
censure, n.
  21.03 judgement
censure, vb.
  21.03 judgement
  22.13 value
censurer, n.
  21.03 judgement
Centaur, n.
  03.32 unicorn
Centaur
  23.28 tavern
centre, n.

  33.07 middle
centry, n.
  33.07 middle
centure, n.
  10.13 belt
centurion, n.
  20.06 officer
century, n.
  20.05 army · navy
  31.08 numbers
Cephalus
  36.16 classical myth
Cerberus
  03.32 unicorn
cere, vb.
  05.07 swathe · shroud
  33.10 encompassment
cerecloth, n.
  05.07 swathe · shroud
cerement, n.
  05.07 swathe · shroud
ceremonial, adj.
  16.14 ceremony
ceremonious, adj.
  16.14 ceremony
ceremoniously, adv.
  16.14 ceremony
ceremony, n.
  16.14 ceremony
  28.15 reverence
  28.27 prognostication
Ceres
  28.04 Mars · Venus
Cerimon
  37.01 classical: male
certain, adj.
  15.22 (un)certainty
certain, n.
  15.22 (un)certainty
certainest, n.
  15.22 (un)certainty
certainly, adv.
  15.22 (un)certainty
certainty, n.
  15.22 (un)certainty
certes, adv.
  15.22 (un)certainty
certificate, n.
  16.10 edict
  18.10 permission
certify, vb.
  15.22 (un)certainty
  24.25 make known
Cesario (TN)
  37.16 assumed names

clasp, n.
   10.13 belt
   17.16 embrace · kiss
clasp, vb.
   17.16 embrace · kiss
   31.16 join
   33.11 firm
clasping, n.
   17.16 embrace · kiss
clatter, n.
   12.10 din
Claudio (ADO)
   37.06 Romance: male
Claudio (HAM)
   37.06 Romance: male
Claudio (JC)
   37.01 classical: male
Claudio (MM)
   37.06 Romance: male
clause, n.
   22.12 contract
claw, n.
   03.40 claw · hoof · fin
claw, vb.
   11.02 grasp
   11.10 scratch
   18.20 flattery
clay, n.
   01.23 soil
clay-brained, adj.
   06.18 anatomy compounds
   15.12 foolishness
clean, adj.
   14.18 purity
   31.03 all · nothing
cleanly, adj.
   14.18 purity
   30.06 (un)skilful
cleanly, adv.
   14.18 purity
   31.03 all · nothing
cleanse, vb.
   14.18 purity
clean-timbered, adj.
   06.14 limb
   23.16 build
clear, adj.
   01.12 light · dark
   14.18 purity
   14.20 beauty
   15.21 (un)clear
   18.13 freedom
   31.22 cancel
clear, vb.
   01.12 light · dark

   14.18 purity
   15.21 (un)clear
   18.13 freedom
   31.22 cancel
clearly, adv.
   15.21 (un)clear
   31.03 all · nothing
clearness, n.
   01.12 light · dark
   14.18 purity
clear-shining, adj.
   01.12 light · dark
clear-spirited, adj.
   13.08 cheer(less)
   30.02 disposition
cleave, vb.
   11.05 cut
cleave, vb.
   23.18 cement
   31.16 join
clef, n.
   26.04 gamut
Cleitus
   36.22 historical: Greek
clemency, n.
   14.09 lenity
clement, adj.
   14.09 lenity
Clement Perkes o' th' Hill
   37.03 English: male
Clement's Inn
   21.05 law court
Cleomenes
   37.01 classical: male
Cleon
   37.01 classical: male
Cleopatra
   36.24 historical: other
               names (2)
clepe, vb.
   36.01 name
clerestory, n.
   08.10 window
clergy, n.
   28.09 clergy
clergyman, n.
   28.09 clergy
clerk, n.
   24.12 write
   25.02 teacher
clerk-like, adj.
   25.02 teacher
clerkly, adj.
   24.12 write
   25.02 teacher

clew, n.
   10.05 needlework
client, n.
   21.05 law court
   22.01 trade
cliff, n.
   01.21 fen · shore
   01.27 hill · dale
Clifford (2H6)
   36.17 historical: English
Clifford, Young (3H6)
   36.17 historical: English
Clifton
   36.17 historical: English
climate, n.
   01.05 weather
   33.02 region
climate, vb.
   01.05 weather
   08.04 inhabit
climature, n.
   33.02 region
climb, vb.
   34.07 ascend
climber-upward, n.
   34.07 ascend
clime, n.
   01.05 weather
   33.02 region
cling, vb.
   07.05 decay
   31.16 join
clink, n.
   12.10 din
clink, vb.
   12.10 din
clinquant, adj.
   01.12 light · dark
clip, vb.
   17.16 embrace · kiss
   33.10 encompassment
clip, vb.
   11.05 cut
clipper, n.
   11.05 cut
   18.19 deceit
clip-winged, adj.
   03.37 wing
   06.18 anatomy compounds
Clitus
   36.23 historical: Roman
cloak, n.
   10.06 mantle
cloak, vb.
   10.06 mantle

18.03   (dis)obedience
34.12   bend
curtsy, vb.
    18.03   (dis)obedience
    34.12   bend
curvet, n.
    34.02   leap
curvet, vb.
    34.02   leap
cushion, n.
    08.25   cushion
Custa-lorum, n.
    16.05   mayor
custard, n.
    09.16   sweetmeat
custard-coffin, n.
    09.13   bread · cake
    09.16   sweetmeat
custody, n.
    17.08   vigilance
custom, n.
    32.26   (un)usual
custom, vb.
    22.01   trade
    32.26   (un)usual
customary, adj.
    32.26   (un)usual
customer, n.
    04.12   strumpet
    22.01   trade
custom-shrunk, adj.
    22.01   trade
    31.13   decrease
custure
    24.17   pseudo foreign
cut, n.
    27.09   ball
cut, n.
    03.02   horse
    03.08   dog
    04.04   rogue
    10.01   attire
    11.05   cut
    33.19   shape
cut, vb.
    11.05   cut
    26.16   insculpture
    31.22   cancel
Cut
    03.02   horse
cut a caper, vb.
    26.11   dance
    34.02   leap
cut and long-tail, n.
    31.03   all · nothing

cutler, n.
    23.04   goldsmith
cutpurse, n.
    21.12   thievery
cutter, n.
    26.16   insculpture
cutter-off, n.
    32.22   interruption
cutthroat, n.
    21.10   murder
cuttle, n.
    14.25   braggardism
    23.24   knife
Cyclops
    36.16   classical myth
Cydnus
    01.17   river
cygnet, n.
    03.21   swan
cymbal, n.
    26.08   other instruments
Cymbeline
    36.14   pseudohistorical
cynic, n.
    19.08   reproach
Cynthia
    28.04   Mars · Venus
cypress, n.
    02.02   oak · brier
cypress, n.
    10.03   cloth
Cyprus
    01.20   island
    36.09   Southern European
Cyrus
    36.24   historical: other
            names (2)
Cytherea
    28.04   Mars · Venus

D

D, n.
    25.07   alphabet
    26.04   gamut
dabble, vb.
    01.19   dip
dace, n.
    03.26   fish
dad, n.
    04.15   family
Daedalus
    36.16   classical myth
daffodil, n.
    02.09   rose
dagger, n.
    20.14   weapon
    27.02   fencer
Dagonet
    36.13   medieval legend
daily, adj.
    32.02   hour · day · year
daily, adv.
    32.02   hour · day · year
daintiest, n.
    30.07   preciseness
daintily, adv.
    30.07   preciseness
daintiness, n.
    30.07   preciseness
dainty, adj.
    09.04   food · drink
    12.17   taste
    30.07   preciseness
dainty, n.
    09.04   food · drink
daisied, adj.
    02.09   rose
daisy, n.
    02.09   rose
Dale → Coleville of the Dale
dale, n.
    01.27   hill · dale
dalliance, n.
    14.41   levity
    32.21   delay
dally, vb.
    14.41   levity
    32.21   delay
Dalmatian, n.
    36.09   Southern European
dam, n.

01.21 fen • shore
dam, n.
  03.01 animal
  04.15 family
dam, vb.
  19.13 obstruction
damage, n.
  07.18 wound
damage, vb.
  07.18 wound
Damascus
  36.05 Middle / Far Eastern
damask, n.
  12.04 colour
damask, vb.
  12.04 colour
damask rose, n.
  02.09 rose
dame, n.
  04.09 woman
  04.15 family
  16.21 lord • lady
dame, fr. n.
  04.09 woman
  24.14 French
damn, vb.
  28.24 impiety
damnable, adj.
  14.27 contempt
  28.24 impiety
damnably, adv.
  14.27 contempt
damnation, n.
  28.24 impiety
Damon
  36.16 classical myth
damosella, n.
  04.09 woman
damp, n.
  01.09 cloud • vapour
  01.10 dry • wet
damsel, n.
  04.09 woman
damson, n.
  02.13 apple • grape
dan, n.
  04.02 man
dance, n.
  26.11 dance
dance, vb.
  26.11 dance
dancer, n.
  26.11 dance
dancing days, n.
  32.03 times

dancing-rapier, n.
  20.14 weapon
  26.11 dance
dancing-school, n.
  25.04 school
dancing shoe, n.
  10.09 shoe • hose
dandle, vb.
  34.19 shake
Dane, n.
  36.10 Northern European
Dane, The
  16.17 king
danger, n.
  19.18 peril
danger, vb.
  19.18 peril
dangerous, adj.
  19.18 peril
dangerously, adv.
  19.18 peril
dangle, vb.
  33.35 hang
Daniel
  28.03 Abraham • Paul
Danish, adj.
  36.10 Northern European
dank, adj.
  01.10 dry • wet
dankish, adj.
  01.10 dry • wet
Dansker, n.
  36.10 Northern European
Daphne
  36.16 classical myth
dapple, vb.
  12.06 spotted
Dardan, adj.
  36.05 Middle / Far Eastern
Dardan
  08.11 entry
  36.15 Trojan myth
Dardanian, adj.
  36.05 Middle / Far Eastern
Dardanius
  36.23 historical: Roman
Dardan plains, n.
  01.28 wood • field • garden
  36.05 Middle / Far Eastern
dare, n.
  14.17 boldness
  19.12 challenge
dare, vb.
  14.17 boldness
  19.12 challenge

dare, vb.
  12.01 sight
  15.09 amazement
dareful, adj.
  19.12 challenge
daring, adj.
  14.17 boldness
daring-hardy, adj.
  14.17 boldness
Darius
  36.24 historical: other
        names (2)
dark, adj.
  01.12 light • dark
  13.10 sorrow
  24.29 conceal
dark, n.
  01.12 light • dark
dark, vb.
  01.12 light • dark
darken, vb.
  01.12 light • dark
dark-eyed, adj.
  06.04 face
  06.18 anatomy compounds
dark house, n.
  21.14 prison
darkling, adv.
  01.12 light • dark
darkly, adv.
  01.12 light • dark
  13.10 sorrow
  15.21 (un)clear
  24.29 conceal
darkness, n.
  01.12 light • dark
  05.01 life • death
darkness and devils
  28.25 oaths
dark room, n.
  08.17 rooms
dark-seated, adj.
  33.03 station
darksome, adj.
  01.12 light • dark
dark-working, adj.
  23.15 work
darling, n.
  04.10 darling
darnel, n.
  02.04 nettle • rush
dart, n.
  20.14 weapon
  27.04 archery
dart, vb.

24.27 sign
death-practised, adj.
  18.16 plot
death's-bed, n.
  08.22 bed
death's face, n.
  06.02 head
  06.18 anatomy compounds
death's-head, n.
  06.02 head
  06.18 anatomy compounds
deathsman, n.
  21.18 hangman
death-token, n.
  07.16 sore
  24.27 sign
death-worthy, adj.
  14.12 (un)worthiness
debar, vb.
  31.21 omission
debase, vb.
  14.45 corruption
debate, n.
  19.07 debate
  19.11 quarrel
debate, vb.
  19.02 rival
  19.07 debate
debatement, n.
  19.07 debate
debater, n.
  19.07 debate
  19.11 quarrel
debauch, vb.
  14.45 corruption
debile, adj.
  07.04 weakness
debility, n.
  07.04 weakness
debitor and creditor, n.
  22.02 creditor · debtor
debonair, adj.
  14.08 (un)gentle
Deborah
  28.03 Abraham · Paul
debt, adj.
  17.13 obligation
  22.02 creditor · debtor
debt, n.
  22.02 creditor · debtor
debted, adj.
  17.13 obligation
  22.02 creditor · debtor
debtor, n.
  22.02 creditor · debtor

decay, n.
  07.05 decay
decay, vb.
  07.05 decay
decayer, n.
  07.05 decay
decease, n.
  05.01 life · death
decease, vb.
  05.01 life · death
  32.18 past · present · future
deceit, n.
  18.19 deceit
deceitful, adj.
  18.19 deceit
deceivable, adj.
  18.19 deceit
deceive, vb.
  18.19 deceit
deceiver, n.
  18.19 deceit
December, n.
  32.06 month
decent, adj.
  30.09 (un)aptness
decently, adv.
  30.09 (un)aptness
deceptious, adj.
  18.19 deceit
decern (ADO 3.5.3), vb.
  24.18 malapropism
decide, vb.
  15.27 resolution
decider, n.
  15.27 resolution
decimation, n.
  20.21 destruction
  21.13 punishment
decipher, vb.
  15.23 interpretation
  24.28 disclose
decision, n.
  15.27 resolution
Decius → Brutus, Decius
deck, n.
  27.09 ball
  35.02 deck · oar
deck, vb.
  10.01 attire
  10.18 ornament
declare, vb.
  24.25 make known
declension, n.
  07.05 decay
  25.08 grammar

decline, vb.
  07.05 decay
  25.08 grammar
  34.08 descend
  34.12 bend
decoct, vb.
  09.05 cookery
decorum, n.
  14.20 beauty
  30.09 (un)aptness
decrease, vb.
  31.13 decrease
decrease (WIV 1.1.247), vb.
  24.18 malapropism
decree, n.
  16.10 edict
decree, vb.
  15.27 resolution
decrepit, adj.
  07.05 decay
Decretas
  36.23 historical: Roman
dedicate, adj.
  28.15 reverence
dedicate, vb.
  28.15 reverence
dedication, n.
  28.15 reverence
deed, n.
  05.03 procreation
  11.01 do
  16.10 edict
  22.12 contract
deed-achieving, adj.
  11.01 do
deedless, adj.
  11.01 do
deem, n.
  15.04 thought
  21.03 judgement
deem, vb.
  15.04 thought
  21.03 judgement
deep, adj.
  33.38 depth
deep, n.
  01.15 sea
  33.07 middle
  33.38 depth
Deep, The
  28.07 heaven · hell
deep-brained, adj.
  06.18 anatomy compounds
  15.04 thought
deep-dark, adj.

despiser, n.
  14.27 contempt
despising, n.
  14.27 contempt
despite, n.
  14.27 contempt
despite, prep.
  25.14 preposition
despite, vb.
  19.04 vexation
despiteful, adj.
  14.27 contempt
despitefully, adv.
  14.27 contempt
despoil, vb.
  20.19 booty
destine, vb.
  28.26 destiny
Destinies, The
  28.04 Mars · Venus
destiny, n.
  28.26 destiny
destitute, adj.
  22.24 lack
  31.04 full · empty
destroy, vb.
  20.21 destruction
destroyer, n.
  20.21 destruction
destruction, n.
  20.21 destruction
detain, vb.
  18.06 controlment
  19.13 obstruction
detect, vb.
  15.26 discovery
detection, n.
  15.26 discovery
detector, n.
  15.26 discovery
detention, n.
  18.06 controlment
determinate, adj.
  15.27 resolution
  32.19 beginning · end
determinate, vb.
  15.27 resolution
  32.19 beginning · end
determination, n.
  15.27 resolution
  32.19 beginning · end
determine, vb.
  15.27 resolution
  32.19 beginning · end
  33.09 border

detest, vb.
  14.02 love · hate
detest (MM 2.1.69), vb.
  24.18 malapropism
detestable, adj.
  14.02 love · hate
detract, vb.
  19.10 disparagement
  22.23 deprive
detraction, n.
  19.10 disparagement
detriment, n.
  22.34 (dis)advantage
Deucalion
  36.16 classical myth
deuce-ace, n.
  27.10 sport terms
deus, lat. n.
  24.13 Latin
  28.02 God
deux, fr. num.
  24.14 French
  31.08 numbers
deux cents, fr. num.
  24.14 French
  31.08 numbers
devant, fr. prep.
  24.14 French
  25.14 preposition
device, n.
  10.18 ornament
  15.02 notion
  18.16 plot
devil, n.
  28.05 spirits
devilish, adj.
  28.05 spirits
devilish-holy, adj.
  28.05 spirits
  28.13 holiness
devil-porter, vb.
  16.27 household servant
devise, vb.
  15.02 notion
  15.27 resolution
  18.16 plot
devoid, adj.
  31.04 full · empty
Devonshire
  36.03 British
devote, adj.
  28.15 reverence
devote, vb.
  28.15 reverence
devotion, n.

  28.13 holiness
  28.15 reverence
devour, vb.
  09.03 eat · drink
  20.21 destruction
devourer, n.
  09.03 eat · drink
devout, adj.
  28.13 holiness
devoutly, adv.
  28.13 holiness
dew, n.
  01.09 cloud · vapour
dew, vb.
  01.09 cloud · vapour
Dew, Seigneur
  37.15 nicknames
dew-bedabbled, adj.
  01.19 dip
dew-berry, n.
  02.12 strawberry
dewdrop, n.
  01.09 cloud · vapour
  31.29 drop
dew-dropping, adj.
  01.09 cloud · vapour
  34.08 descend
dewlap, n.
  03.33 beak · horn
  06.07 neck
  06.18 anatomy compounds
dew-lapped, adj.
  03.33 beak · horn
  06.07 neck
  06.18 anatomy compounds
dewy, adj.
  01.09 cloud · vapour
dexter, adj.
  33.06 side
dexteriously, adv.
  30.06 (un)skilful
dexterity, n.
  34.24 nimbleness
dey-woman, n.
  23.03 victualler
diable, fr. n.
  24.14 French
  28.05 spirits
diabolo, it. n.
  24.15 Italian
  28.05 spirits
diadem, n.
  10.12 chaplet
dial, n.
  32.01 clock

disloyal, adj.
  17.14 (dis)loyalty
disloyalty, n.
  17.14 (dis)loyalty
dismal, adj.
  13.10 sorrow
  32.24 mischance
dismantle, vb.
  10.01 attire
  31.17 separation
dismask, vb.
  10.11 veil · mask
dismay, n.
  14.52 fear
dismay, vb.
  14.52 fear
dismember, vb.
  11.05 cut
  31.17 separation
dismiss, vb.
  14.09 lenity
  19.05 rejection
  34.20 send
dismission, n.
  19.05 rejection
  34.20 send
dismount, vb.
  27.16 horseman
  34.08 descend
disnature, vb.
  29.03 (un)natural
disobedience, n.
  18.03 (dis)obedience
disobedient, adj.
  18.03 (dis)obedience
disobey, vb.
  18.03 (dis)obedience
disorb, vb.
  01.03 planet
disorder, n.
  19.16 disorder
  21.09 crime
disorder, vb.
  19.16 disorder
disorderly, adj.
  19.16 disorder
disparage, vb.
  19.10 disparagement
disparagement, n.
  19.10 disparagement
disparity, n.
  31.25 difference
dispark, vb.
  01.28 wood · field · garden
  33.13 open · close

dispatch, n.
  11.01 do
  34.20 send
dispatch, vb.
  11.01 do
  34.20 send
  34.23 fast · slow
dispensation, n.
  18.10 permission
  31.21 omission
dispense, vb.
  14.09 lenity
  14.10 moderation
disperse, vb.
  33.41 distribution
dispiteous, adj.
  28.16 compassion
displace, vb.
  19.05 rejection
  34.20 send
displant, vb.
  11.07 pull
  16.13 enthrone
  33.42 change
display, vb.
  12.02 show
displease, vb.
  13.07 (dis)pleasure
displeasure, n.
  13.07 (dis)pleasure
disport, n.
  27.01 pastime
disport, vb.
  27.01 pastime
dispose, n.
  18.07 (ab)use
  30.02 disposition
  33.39 row
dispose, vb.
  18.07 (ab)use
  30.02 disposition
  33.39 row
disposer, n.
  18.07 (ab)use
disposer, fr. vb.
  24.14 French
  33.39 row
disposition, n.
  30.02 disposition
  33.39 row
dispossess, vb.
  22.23 deprive
dispraise, n.
  19.08 reproach
dispraise, vb.

  19.08 reproach
dispraisingly, adv.
  19.08 reproach
disproperty, vb.
  22.23 deprive
disproportion, n.
  29.07 proportion
disproportion, vb.
  29.07 proportion
disprove, vb.
  19.06 contradiction
dispunge, vb.
  01.18 effusion
dispurse, vb.
  22.08 payment
disputable, adj.
  19.07 debate
disputation, n.
  19.07 debate
  24.20 conversation
dispute, n.
  19.07 debate
  19.11 quarrel
dispute, vb.
  19.01 opposition
  19.07 debate
disquantity, vb.
  31.01 quantity
  31.13 decrease
disquiet, adj.
  19.17 (un)rest
disquiet, n.
  19.17 (un)rest
disquiet, vb.
  19.17 (un)rest
disquietly, adv.
  19.17 (un)rest
disrelish, vb.
  14.02 love · hate
disrobe, vb.
  10.01 attire
disroot, vb.
  11.07 pull
disseat, vb.
  08.21 chair
  16.13 enthrone
dissemble, vb.
  12.03 semblance
  18.19 deceit
dissembler, n.
  12.03 semblance
  18.19 deceit
dissembly (ADO 4.2.1), n.
  24.18 malapropism
dissension, n.

divert, vb.
    34.09 stray
Dives
    28.03 Abraham • Paul
divest, vb.
    10.01 attire
    22.23 deprive
dividable, adj.
    31.17 separation
divide, vb.
    31.07 count
    31.17 separation
    31.26 portion
divident, adj.
    31.17 separation
dividual, adj.
    31.17 separation
divin, fr. adj.
    24.14 French
    28.13 holiness
divination, n.
    28.27 prognostication
divine, adj.
    28.13 holiness
divine, n.
    28.09 clergy
divine, vb.
    28.27 prognostication
divinely, adv.
    28.13 holiness
divineness, n.
    29.10 pre-eminence
diviner, n.
    28.27 prognostication
divinity, n.
    28.02 God
divinity of hell
    28.25 oaths
division, n.
    19.06 contradiction
    20.05 army • navy
    26.03 music
    31.17 separation
divorce, n.
    04.18 marriage
    31.17 separation
divorce, vb.
    04.18 marriage
    31.17 separation
divorcement, n.
    04.18 marriage
    31.17 separation
divulge, vb.
    24.25 make known
    24.28 disclose

dizzy, adj.
    07.14 queasiness
dizzy, vb.
    07.14 queasiness
Dizzy, Young
    37.13 telling: male
           (mentioned)
dizzy-eyed, adj.
    06.18 anatomy compounds
    07.14 queasiness
    12.01 sight
do, int.
    25.13 interjection
do, vb.
    11.01 do
    20.21 destruction
    31.05 enough
    32.19 beginning • end
    32.25 chance
Dobbin
    03.02 horse
dock, n.
    02.04 nettle • rush
dock, vb.
    35.10 harbour
doctor, n.
    07.22 physician
    25.02 teacher
doctor-like, adj.
    25.02 teacher
doctor of physic, n.
    07.22 physician
doctrine, n.
    16.10 edict
    25.01 education
    25.06 maxim
document, n.
    25.01 education
do de, int.
    25.13 interjection
dodge, vb.
    18.19 deceit
    34.01 go
doe, n.
    03.13 deer
doer, n.
    11.01 do
doff, vb.
    10.01 attire
    19.19 avoid
dog, n.
    03.08 dog
dog, vb.
    16.26 attendant
    34.14 chase

dog-ape, n.
    03.15 monkey
Dogberry
    37.11 telling: male (DP)
dog-days, n.
    32.04 season
dog-fish, n.
    03.26 fish
dog-fox, n.
    03.10 fox
dogged, adj.
    03.08 dog
    14.31 cruelty
dog-hearted, adj.
    06.18 anatomy compounds
    14.31 cruelty
dog-hole, n.
    03.46 nest • kennel
    33.22 hole • trench
dog-skin, n.
    10.04 leather
dog's-leather, n.
    10.04 leather
dog-weary, adj.
    07.03 weariness
doigt, fr. n.
    06.15 arm
    24.14 French
doing, n.
    11.01 do
doit, n.
    22.06 money
Doit, John
    37.13 telling: male
           (mentioned)
Dolabella
    36.23 historical: Roman
dolcezza, it. n.
    14.08 (un)gentle
    24.15 Italian
dole, n.
    28.26 destiny
    31.26 portion
dole, n.
    13.10 sorrow
doleful, adj.
    13.10 sorrow
dollar, n.
    22.06 money
Doll Tearsheet
    37.04 English: female
dolorous, adj.
    13.10 sorrow
dolour, n.
    13.10 sorrow

E

excrement, n.
    06.03 hair
excusable, adj.
    14.09 lenity
excuse, n.
    14.09 lenity
excuse, vb.
    14.09 lenity
    18.13 freedom
excuser, fr. vb.
    14.09 lenity
    24.14 French
execrable, adj.
    14.02 love · hate
execration, n.
    28.24 impiety
execute, vb.
    11.01 do
    21.10 murder
execution, n.
    11.01 do
    21.10 murder
executioner, n.
    21.18 hangman
executor, n.
    11.01 do
    21.18 hangman
exempt, adj.
    18.13 freedom
exempt, vb.
    18.13 freedom
    31.21 omission
exequy, n.
    05.06 burial
exercise, n.
    11.01 do
    23.15 work
    28.11 prayer
    30.06 (un)skilful
exercise, vb.
    11.01 do
    27.01 pastime
Exeter
    36.03 British
Exeter (3H6)
    36.17 historical: English
Exeter (H5)
    36.17 historical: English
Exeter (R2)
    36.17 historical: English
Exeter, Bishop of (R3)
    36.17 historical: English
exhalation, n.
    01.03 planet
exhale, vb.

01.09 cloud · vapour
exhale, vb.
    11.07 pull
exhaust, vb.
    11.07 pull
exhibit, vb.
    12.02 show
    22.30 offer
exhibit (MV 2.3.10), vb.
    24.18 malapropism
exhibiter, n.
    12.02 show
exhibition, n.
    17.02 support
    22.08 payment
    22.33 gift
exhibition (ADO 4.2.5), n.
    24.18 malapropism
exhort, vb.
    18.18 instigation
exhortation, n.
    17.03 counsel
    18.18 instigation
exigent, n.
    22.25 necessity
    32.19 beginning · end
exigere, lat. vb.
    11.01 do
    24.13 Latin
exile¹, n.
    34.20 send
exile², n.
    34.20 send
exile, vb.
    34.20 send
exist, vb.
    29.02 being
exit, n.
    34.06 hence-going
exorciser, n.
    28.28 sorcery
exorcism, n.
    28.28 sorcery
exorcist, n.
    28.28 sorcery
expect, n.
    32.32 expectation
expect, vb.
    32.32 expectation
expectance, n.
    32.32 expectation
expectancy, n.
    32.32 expectation
expectation, n.
    32.32 expectation

expecter, n.
    32.32 expectation
expedience, n.
    22.34 (dis)advantage
    34.23 fast · slow
expedient, adj.
    22.34 (dis)advantage
    34.23 fast · slow
expediently, adv.
    34.23 fast · slow
expedition, n.
    20.02 assault
    34.23 fast · slow
Expedition
    35.01 ship
expeditious, adj.
    34.23 fast · slow
expel, vb.
    34.20 send
expend, vb.
    22.08 payment
expense, n.
    22.07 price
    22.08 payment
experience, n.
    15.06 knowledge
experience, vb.
    15.06 knowledge
experiment, n.
    15.13 attempt
experimental, adj.
    15.06 knowledge
expert, adj.
    30.06 (un)skilful
expertness, n.
    30.06 (un)skilful
expiate, adj.
    32.19 beginning · end
expiate, vb.
    32.19 beginning · end
expiration, n.
    32.19 beginning · end
expire, vb.
    05.01 life · death
    32.19 beginning · end
explication, n.
    15.23 interpretation
exploit, n.
    11.01 do
    20.01 combat
expose, vb.
    19.18 peril
exposition, n.
    15.23 interpretation
exposition (MND 4.1.39), n.

24.18 malapropism
expositor, n.
  15.23 interpretation
expostulate, vb.
  24.20 conversation
expostulation, n.
  24.20 conversation
exposture, n.
  19.18 peril
exposure, n.
  19.18 peril
expound, vb.
  15.23 interpretation
express, adj.
  15.21 (un)clear
express, vb.
  24.20 conversation
expressive, adj.
  24.25 make known
expressly, adv.
  15.21 (un)clear
expressure, n.
  24.22 message
  26.15 painting
expulse, vb.
  34.20 send
expulsion, n.
  34.20 send
exquisite, adj.
  29.10 pre-eminence
  30.07 preciseness
exsufflicate, adj.
  31.14 swell
extant, adj.
  29.02 being
  32.18 past · present · future
extemporal, adj.
  30.08 readiness
  32.30 brevity
extemporally, adv.
  30.08 readiness
  32.30 brevity
extempore, adv.
  30.08 readiness
  32.30 brevity
extend, vb.
  11.02 grasp
  31.12 increase
  33.32 spread
extent, n.
  11.02 grasp
  18.07 (ab)use
  31.12 increase
  33.16 size
  33.33 length

extenuate, vb.
  19.17 (un)rest
  22.13 value
  31.13 decrease
extenuation, n.
  19.17 (un)rest
  31.13 decrease
exterior, adj.
  33.08 inside · outside
exterior, n.
  33.08 inside · outside
exteriorly, adv.
  33.08 inside · outside
extermine, vb.
  20.21 destruction
extern, adj.
  33.08 inside · outside
extern, n.
  12.02 show
  33.08 inside · outside
external, adj.
  33.08 inside · outside
extinct, adj.
  31.22 cancel
extinct, vb.
  31.22 cancel
extincture, n.
  20.21 destruction
  31.22 cancel
extinguere, lat. vb.
  24.13 Latin
  31.22 cancel
extinguish, vb.
  31.22 cancel
extirp, vb.
  11.07 pull
extirpate, vb.
  11.07 pull
extol, vb.
  17.17 praise
extolment, n.
  17.17 praise
Exton
  36.03 British
extort, vb.
  11.07 pull
extortion, n.
  21.12 thievery
extract, adj.
  04.14 kindred
extract, vb.
  11.07 pull
extraordinarily, adv.
  32.26 (un)usual
extraordinarily (2H4 2.4.24),

adv.
  24.18 malapropism
extraordinary, adj.
  15.09 amazement
  32.26 (un)usual
extravagancy, n.
  34.09 stray
extravagant, adj.
  34.09 stray
extreme, adj.
  29.12 extreme
  31.20 excess
extreme, n.
  29.12 extreme
  31.20 excess
extremely, adv.
  29.12 extreme
extremity, n.
  29.12 extreme
exult, vb.
  13.05 exult
exultation, n.
  13.05 exult
eyas, n.
  03.22 hawk
eyas-musket, n.
  03.22 hawk
eye, n.
  06.04 face
  12.01 sight
  31.28 particle
  33.22 hole · trench
eye, vb.
  12.01 sight
eye-ball, n.
  06.04 face
eye-beam, n.
  12.01 sight
eyebrow, n.
  06.03 hair
  06.04 face
eye-drop, n.
  13.12 sob
eye-glance, n.
  12.01 sight
eye-glass, n.
  06.04 face
eyeless, adj.
  12.01 sight
eyelid, n.
  06.04 face
eye-offending, adj.
  19.04 vexation
eyesight, n.
  12.01 sight

eyesore, n.
    14.46 fault
eyestring, n.
    06.04 face
eye to eye, adv.
    12.01 sight
eye-wink, n.
    12.01 sight
    24.26 gesture

F

fa, n.
    26.04 gamut
fa, vb.
    26.04 gamut
Fabian
    37.03 English: male
fable, n.
    15.08 fantasy
    18.19 deceit
fable, fr. n.
    18.19 deceit
    24.14 French
fable, vb.
    15.08 fantasy
    18.19 deceit
fabric, n.
    08.01 house
    23.16 build
fabulous, adj.
    15.08 fantasy
    18.19 deceit
face, n.
    06.04 face
    06.05 lineament
face, vb.
    10.17 fringe
    18.19 deceit
    19.12 challenge
facere, lat. vb.
    11.01 do
    24.13 Latin
face royal, n.
    22.06 money
face to face, adv.
    19.12 challenge
facile, adj.
    30.10 easy · hard
facile, lat. adv.
    24.13 Latin
    30.10 easy · hard
facility, n.
    30.10 easy · hard
facinerious, adj.
    14.22 badness
facing, n.
    10.18 ornament
fact, n.
    11.01 do
faction, n.
    18.15 conspiracy
    31.36 multitude
factionary, adj.
    19.11 quarrel
factious, adj.
    18.21 rebellion
    19.11 quarrel
factor, n.
    16.20 deputy
    22.01 trade
    22.04 merchant
factum → ipso facto
faculty, n.
    30.02 disposition
    30.05 (un)able
fade, vb.
    01.12 light · dark
    07.05 decay
fadge, vb.
    30.09 (un)aptness
fading, n.
    26.10 song
faggot, n.
    02.01 tree · bush · twig
    31.35 bunch
fail, n.
    31.21 omission
fail, vb.
    05.01 life · death
    07.04 weakness
    14.42 negligence
    22.22 loss
    22.24 lack
fain, adj.
    13.07 (dis)pleasure
    17.10 (un)willingness
fain, vb.
    13.07 (dis)pleasure
    17.10 (un)willingness
faint, adj.
    07.04 weakness
    07.14 queasiness
faint, vb.
    07.04 weakness
    07.14 queasiness
faint-hearted, adj.
    06.18 anatomy compounds
    14.52 fear
faintly, adv.
    07.04 weakness
faintness, n.
    07.04 weakness
fair, adj.
    01.12 light · dark
    14.14 honesty
    14.20 beauty

felony, n.
   21.09 crime
felt, n.
   10.03 cloth
female, adj.
   04.09 woman
female, n.
   04.09 woman
feminine, adj.
   04.09 woman
fen, n.
   01.21 fen · shore
fence, n.
   17.06 protection
   27.03 stoccado
fence, vb.
   17.06 protection
   27.02 fencer
   33.10 encompassment
fencer, n.
   27.02 fencer
fennel, n.
   02.16 parsley
fenny, adj.
   01.21 fen · shore
fen-sucked, adj.
   11.07 pull
Fenton, Master
   37.05 English: surnames
Fer → Le Fer
fer, vb.
   37.11 telling: male (DP)
Ferdinand (SHR)
   37.03 English: male
Ferdinand (TMP)
   37.03 English: male
Ferdinand, King of Spain (H8)
   36.19 historical: other
           names (1)
fere, n.
   04.18 marriage
fern-seed, n.
   02.07 seed
Ferrara
   36.08 Italian
   36.19 historical: other
           names (1)
Ferrers, Walter, Lord
   36.17 historical: English
ferret, n.
   03.10 fox
ferret, vb.
   27.14 hunter
ferry, n.
   35.11 flood-gate

ferryman, n.
   35.09 seaman
fertile, adj.
   05.02 fertility · sterility
fertile-fresh, adj.
   32.13 newness
fertility, n.
   05.02 fertility · sterility
ferula, n.
   21.16 cudgel
fervency, n.
   14.37 vehemence
fervour, n.
   14.37 vehemence
fescue, n.
   23.26 staff
Feste
   37.11 telling: male (DP)
fester, vb.
   07.05 decay
   07.16 sore
festinate, adj.
   34.23 fast · slow
festinately, adv.
   34.23 fast · slow
festival, n.
   13.04 revelry
   32.05 holidays
fet, vb.
   34.22 carry
fetch, n.
   18.16 plot
fetch, vb.
   11.07 pull
   22.28 acquisition
   34.22 carry
fetch about, phr. vb.
   35.08 navigation
fetch in, phr. vb.
   11.02 grasp
fetch off, phr. vb.
   20.22 victory · defeat
fetlock, n.
   03.34 fleece
fetter, n.
   21.15 manacle
fetter, vb.
   18.06 controlment
fettle, vb.
   30.08 readiness
feu, fr. n.
   01.13 fire
   24.14 French
feud, n.
   19.11 quarrel

feudary, n.
   18.14 vassal
fever, n.
   07.09 fever
   19.16 disorder
fever, vb.
   07.09 fever
feverous, adj.
   07.09 fever
fever-weakened, adj.
   07.04 weakness
few, adj.
   31.02 quantor
   31.10 many · few
few, n.
   31.10 many · few
fewness, n.
   31.10 many · few
fickle, adj.
   14.05 (in)constancy
fickleness, n.
   14.05 (in)constancy
fico, n.
   02.13 apple · grape
   19.10 disparagement
   24.26 gesture
fiction, n.
   15.08 fantasy
fiddle, n.
   26.06 fiddle
fiddle, vb.
   26.09 musician
fiddler, n.
   26.09 musician
fiddlestick, n.
   26.06 fiddle
Fidele (CYM)
   37.16 assumed names
fidelity, n.
   17.14 (dis)loyalty
fides, lat. n.
   17.14 (dis)loyalty
   24.13 Latin
fidius → medius fidius
fidius, vb.
   11.03 hit
fie, int.
   25.13 interjection
field, n.
   01.28 wood · field · garden
   16.01 commonwealth
   16.16 heraldry
   20.01 combat
   20.12 armour
   33.01 place

field-bed, n.
    08.22 bed
field-dew, n.
    01.09 cloud · vapour
fielded, adj.
    01.28 wood · field · garden
    20.01 combat
fiend, n.
    28.05 spirits
fiend-like, adj.
    28.05 spirits
fierce, adj.
    14.31 cruelty
    14.37 vehemence
    31.20 excess
fiercely, adv.
    14.31 cruelty
    14.37 vehemence
fierceness, n.
    14.17 boldness
    14.30 savageness
    14.31 cruelty
fiery, adj.
    01.12 light · dark
    01.13 fire
    07.02 vigour
    14.37 vehemence
fiery-footed, adj.
    06.18 anatomy compounds
    34.01 go
fiery-pointed, adj.
    20.15 sword-hilt
    33.26 sharp · dull
fiery Trigon, n.
    01.04 zodiac
fife, n.
    26.05 wind instrument
Fife
    36.03 British
Fife, Earl of ⇥ Mordake
    36.19 historical: other
           names (1)
Fife, Thane of ⇥ Macduff
    36.19 historical: other
           names (1)
fifteen, num.
    31.08 numbers
fifteen hundred, num.
    31.08 numbers
fifteenth ⇥ a fifteenth
fifteen thousand, num.
    31.08 numbers
fifth, num.
    31.08 numbers
fifty, num.

31.08 numbers
fifty-five, num.
    31.08 numbers
fiftyfold, adj.
    31.07 count
fifty thousand, num.
    31.08 numbers
fig, n.
    02.13 apple · grape
    22.14 trifle
fig, n.
    19.10 disparagement
    24.26 gesture
fig, vb.
    24.26 gesture
fight, n.
    20.01 combat
fight, vb.
    20.01 combat
fighter, n.
    20.04 fighter
fights, n.
    08.08 wall
figo, n.
    19.10 disparagement
    22.14 trifle
    24.26 gesture
fig's-end, n.
    19.10 disparagement
    22.14 trifle
figure, n.
    15.02 notion
    25.07 alphabet
    25.09 rhetoric
    28.27 prognostication
    31.07 count
    33.19 shape
figure, vb.
    12.02 show
    15.08 fantasy
    24.27 sign
    28.27 prognostication
    33.19 shape
filbert, n.
    02.11 walnut
filch, vb.
    21.12 thievery
file, n.
    23.27 other tools
file, n.
    24.05 list
    31.36 multitude
    33.39 row
file, vb.
    11.09 rub

33.27 smooth · rough
file, vb.
    14.49 impurity
filial, adj.
    04.15 family
filius, lat. n.
    04.15 family
    24.13 Latin
fill, n.
    31.04 full · empty
fill, n.
    34.27 waggon
fill, vb.
    09.01 appetite
    31.04 full · empty
fillet, n.
    10.12 chaplet
    31.33 fragment
fill-horse, n.
    03.02 horse
fillip, vb.
    11.03 hit
filly, n.
    03.02 horse
filly foal, n.
    03.02 horse
film, n.
    03.45 cobweb
film, vb.
    03.45 cobweb
    33.10 encompassment
fils, fr. n.
    04.15 family
    24.14 French
filth, n.
    01.24 mud
    04.04 rogue
    04.12 strumpet
filthy, adj.
    14.27 contempt
    14.49 impurity
filthy-mantled, adj.
    10.06 mantle
fin, n.
    03.40 claw · hoof · fin
fin, fr. n.
    24.14 French
    32.19 beginning · end
finally, adv.
    33.40 sequence
finch, n.
    03.18 nightingale
finch-egg, n.
    03.44 egg
find, vb.

fleece, n.
  03.34 fleece
fleece, vb.
  21.12 thievery
fleer, n.
  19.09 mockery
fleer, vb.
  13.03 smile
  19.09 mockery
fleet, adj.
  34.23 fast · slow
fleet, n.
  20.05 army · navy
  35.01 ship
fleet, vb.
  01.14 water
  34.06 hence-going
  34.23 fast · slow
  34.25 swim
Fleet
  21.14 prison
fleet-foot, n.
  06.18 anatomy compounds
  34.23 fast · slow
fleet-winged, adj.
  06.18 anatomy compounds
  34.23 fast · slow
  34.26 fly
Fleming, n.
  36.10 Northern European
Flemish, adj.
  36.10 Northern European
flesh, n.
  04.01 mortal
  04.14 kindred
  06.01 body
  06.17 blood · bone
  09.10 meat
flesh, vb.
  09.03 eat · drink
  11.05 cut
  14.31 cruelty
  18.18 instigation
flesh and blood, n.
  04.01 mortal
  04.14 kindred
flesh and fell, n.
  31.03 all · nothing
flesh-fly, n.
  03.31 fly · louse
fleshly, adj.
  06.01 body
fleshment, n.
  11.05 cut
  18.18 instigation

fleshmonger, n.
  14.51 fornication
fleur-de-lis, n.
  02.09 rose
  16.16 heraldry
flewed, adj.
  06.06 jaw
flexible, adj.
  34.12 bend
flexure, n.
  34.12 bend
Flibbertigibbet
  28.05 spirits
flicker, vb.
  01.12 light · dark
flight, n.
  03.37 wing
  27.04 archery
  31.36 multitude
  34.26 fly
flight, n.
  20.20 retreat
  34.06 hence-going
flighty, adj.
  34.23 fast · slow
flinch, vb.
  34.10 stir
fling, n.
  19.09 mockery
fling, vb.
  34.01 go
  34.18 toss
flint, n.
  01.25 stone
Flint
  16.15 castle
  36.03 British
flint-hearted, adj.
  06.18 anatomy compounds
  14.32 hard-hearted
flinty, adj.
  01.25 stone
  14.32 hard-hearted
flirt, vb.
  19.09 mockery
flirt-gill, n.
  04.12 strumpet
float, n.
  01.15 sea
float, vb.
  01.14 water
  34.25 swim
flock, n.
  31.36 multitude

flock, n.
  31.35 bunch
flock, vb.
  16.08 assembly
flood, n.
  01.14 water
  01.15 sea
flood-gate, n.
  35.11 flood-gate
floor, n.
  08.13 floor
Flora
  28.04 Mars · Venus
Florence
  36.08 Italian
Florence, Duke of
  37.10 Romance: surnames
Florentine, n.
  36.08 Italian
Florentius
  36.13 medieval legend
Florizel
  37.06 Romance: male
flour, n.
  09.06 salt · sugar
flourish, n.
  10.18 ornament
  26.03 music
flourish, vb.
  10.18 ornament
  22.20 prosperity
  26.03 music
  32.12 (un)ripe
  34.19 shake
flout, n.
  19.09 mockery
flout, vb.
  19.09 mockery
flouting-stock, n.
  19.09 mockery
flow, n.
  01.14 water
flow, vb.
  01.14 water
flower, n.
  02.08 flower
  29.10 pre-eminence
flower, vb.
  02.08 flower
  32.12 (un)ripe
flowered, adj.
  02.08 flower
floweret, n.
  02.08 flower
flower-soft, adj.

01.16 pool
fountain, n.
  01.16 pool
four, num.
  31.08 numbers
four and twenty, num.
  31.08 numbers
four dozen, num.
  31.08 numbers
four hundred one and twenty,
    num.
  31.08 numbers
four hundred twenty-six, num.
  31.08 numbers
four-inched, adj.
  33.34 span
fourscore, num.
  31.08 numbers
fourscore three, num.
  31.08 numbers
fourteen, num.
  31.08 numbers
fourteen and a half, num.
  31.08 numbers
fourteen hundred, num.
  31.08 numbers
fourth, num.
  31.08 numbers
four thousand, num.
  31.08 numbers
four times seven, num.
  31.08 numbers
four winds, n.
  01.06 wind · storm
foutre, int.
  25.13 interjection
fowl, n.
  03.17 bird
fowler, n.
  27.12 falconer
fox, n.
  03.10 fox
  20.14 weapon
foxship, n.
  03.10 fox
  17.21 (in)gratitude
fox[-skin], n.
  10.04 leather
fracted, adj.
  11.08 break
fraction, n.
  18.21 rebellion
  31.33 fragment
fragile, adj.
  07.04 weakness

fragment, n.
  31.33 fragment
fragrant, adj.
  12.16 smell
frail, adj.
  07.04 weakness
frailty, n.
  07.04 weakness
frame, n.
  18.16 plot
  23.16 build
  33.19 shape
frame, vb.
  18.16 plot
  23.16 build
  33.19 shape
frampold, adj.
  14.33 curstness
français, fr. n.
  24.01 language
  24.14 French
France
  16.17 king
  36.11 French
France, fr.
  24.14 French
  36.11 French
France (LR)
  36.14 pseudohistorical
France, King of (AWW)
  37.06 Romance: male
France, King of (H8)
  36.18 historical: French
Frances
  37.04 English: female
franchise, n.
  18.13 freedom
franchise, vb.
  18.13 freedom
franchisement, fr. n.
  18.13 freedom
  24.14 French
Francia, lat.
  24.13 Latin
  36.11 French
Francis
  28.14 saints
Francis (1H4)
  37.03 English: male
Francis, Friar (ADO)
  37.03 English: male
Franciscan, adj.
  28.09 clergy
Francisco (HAM)
  37.06 Romance: male

Francisco (WIV)
  37.06 Romance: male
Francis Feeble (2H4)
  37.03 English: male
Francis Flute (MND)
  37.03 English: male
Francis Pickbone (2H4)
  37.03 English: male
Francis Seacole (ADO)
  37.03 English: male
frank, adj.
  14.11 liberality
  18.13 freedom
frank, n.
  03.46 nest · kennel
frank, vb.
  03.46 nest · kennel
Frank Ford
  37.03 English: male
Frankfort
  36.10 Northern European
franklin, n.
  23.13 farmer · herdsman
frankly, adv.
  14.11 liberality
  18.13 freedom
frankness, n.
  18.13 freedom
frantic, adj.
  07.20 madness
franticly, adv.
  07.20 madness
frater, lat. n.
  04.15 family
  24.13 Latin
Frateretto
  28.05 spirits
fraud, n.
  18.19 deceit
fraudful, adj.
  18.19 deceit
fraught, n.
  31.06 load
fraught, vb.
  31.06 load
fraughtage, n.
  31.06 load
fray, n.
  20.01 combat
fray, vb.
  14.53 horror
freckle, n.
  12.06 spotted
freckled, adj.
  12.06 spotted

fur, n.
   03.34 fleece
fur, vb.
   03.34 fleece
furbish, vb.
   10.18 ornament
   11.09 rub
Furies, The
   28.04 Mars · Venus
furious, adj.
   14.29 anger
furlong, n.
   33.34 span
furnace, n.
   08.18 hearth
furnace, vb.
   01.09 cloud · vapour
   08.18 hearth
furnace-burning, adj.
   01.13 fire
furnish, vb.
   22.31 furnish
furnishing, n.
   22.17 chattel
furniture, n.
   10.01 attire
   22.17 chattel
   27.17 bridle
Furnival → Talbot, John (1H6)
   36.17 historical: English
furor, lat. n.
   14.29 anger
   24.13 Latin
furrow, n.
   23.12 husbandry
   33.22 hole · trench
furrow, vb.
   11.05 cut
   23.10 delver
   23.12 husbandry
furrow-weed, n.
   02.04 nettle · rush
further, vb.
   17.04 assistance
furtherance, n.
   17.04 assistance
furtherer, n.
   17.04 assistance
furthermore, adv.
   31.15 moreover
fury, n.
   07.20 madness
   14.29 anger
   14.37 vehemence
   19.16 disorder

Fury
   03.08 dog
furze, n.
   02.02 oak · brier
fust, vb.
   07.05 decay
fustian, adj.
   14.25 braggardism
fustian, n.
   10.03 cloth
   14.25 braggardism
fustilarian, n.
   04.12 strumpet
fusty, adj.
   07.05 decay
fut, int.
   25.13 interjection
future, adj.
   32.18 past · present · future
future, n.
   32.18 past · present · future
futurely, adv.
   32.18 past · present · future
futurity, n.
   32.18 past · present · future

G, n.
   25.07 alphabet
gabble, n.
   12.13 neigh
gabble, vb.
   24.20 conversation
gaberdine, n.
   10.06 mantle
Gabriel
   37.03 English: male
gad, n.
   23.25 gad
gad, vb.
   34.09 stray
Gadshill
   36.03 British
   37.05 English: surnames
Gadslugs → by Gadslugs
gag, vb.
   24.24 verbal · silent
gage, n.
   22.11 pledge
gage, vb.
   22.11 pledge
   27.10 sport terms
   33.31 entangle
gagner, fr. vb.
   22.28 acquisition
   24.14 French
gain, n.
   22.20 prosperity
   22.34 (dis)advantage
gain, vb.
   22.28 acquisition
   22.34 (dis)advantage
gainer, n.
   22.28 acquisition
   22.34 (dis)advantage
gain-giving, n.
   17.15 (mis)trust
gainsay, vb.
   18.10 permission
   19.06 contradiction
gait, n.
   34.01 go
Galathe
   03.02 horse
gale, n.
   01.06 wind · storm
Galen

gast, vb.
   14.53 horror
gastness, n.
   14.53 horror
gate, n.
   08.11 entry
gather, vb.
   11.07 pull
   15.05 logic
   16.08 assembly
   22.28 acquisition
gaud, n.
   22.14 trifle
   27.08 toy
gaud, vb.
   10.18 ornament
gaudere, lat. vb.
   13.02 joy
   24.13 Latin
gaudy, adj.
   01.12 light · dark
   10.18 ornament
   13.08 cheer(less)
gauge, vb.
   21.03 judgement
   31.41 scale
Gaul
   36.11 French
Gaultree
   36.03 British
Gaultree Forest
   01.28 wood · field · garden
Gaunt → John of Gaunt
gaunt, adj.
   33.18 fat · thin
gauntlet, n.
   20.12 armour
Gawsey, Nicholas
   36.17 historical: English
gay, adj.
   13.08 cheer(less)
gayness, n.
   10.18 ornament
   13.08 cheer(less)
gaze, n.
   12.01 sight
gaze, vb.
   12.01 sight
gazer, n.
   12.01 sight
gear, n.
   10.01 attire
   15.31 affair
geck, n.
   15.12 foolishness

geld, vb.
   11.05 cut
   22.23 deprive
gelding, n.
   03.02 horse
gelidus, lat. adj.
   01.11 hot · cold
   24.13 Latin
gem, n.
   10.19 gem
gemini, n.
   31.09 pair
gender, n.
   25.08 grammar
   31.36 multitude
gender, vb.
   05.03 procreation
general, adj.
   16.31 commoner
   31.03 all · nothing
general, n.
   16.31 commoner
   20.06 officer
   31.03 all · nothing
generally, adv.
   31.03 all · nothing
generation, n.
   04.14 kindred
   05.03 procreation
   32.14 period
generative, adj.
   05.03 procreation
generosity, n.
   14.11 liberality
   16.21 lord · lady
generous, adj.
   14.11 liberality
   16.21 lord · lady
genitive, adj.
   25.08 grammar
genitivus, lat. n.
   24.13 Latin
   25.08 grammar
genius, n.
   28.05 spirits
   30.02 disposition
Genoa
   36.08 Italian
genou, fr. n.
   06.16 leg
   24.14 French
gens, fr. n.
   16.31 commoner
   24.14 French
gens, lat. n.

   16.31 commoner
   24.13 Latin
gentilhomme, fr. n.
   16.24 gentry
   24.14 French
gentility, n.
   14.08 (un)gentle
gentle, adj.
   14.08 (un)gentle
   16.24 gentry
gentle, n.
   16.24 gentry
gentle, vb.
   16.21 lord · lady
gentlefolk, n.
   16.24 gentry
gentle-hearted, adj.
   06.18 anatomy compounds
   14.08 (un)gentle
gentleman, n.
   16.24 gentry
   16.25 usher
   20.06 officer
gentlemanlike, adj.
   16.24 gentry
gentleness, n.
   14.08 (un)gentle
gentle-sleeping, adj.
   06.21 sleep
gentlewoman, n.
   16.24 gentry
   16.25 usher
gently, adv.
   14.08 (un)gentle
gentry, n.
   16.24 gentry
Geoffrey
   36.17 historical: English
George
   28.14 saints
George (JN)
   37.03 English: male
George Alow
   35.01 ship
Gerard de Narbon
   37.06 Romance: male
german, adj.
   04.14 kindred
German, adj.
   36.10 Northern European
german, n.
   04.14 kindred
German, n.
   36.10 Northern European
German clock, n.

22.29 give
24.25 make known
give head, vb.
  18.10 permission
  27.16 horseman
give in, phr. vb.
  20.22 victory · defeat
give off, phr. vb.
  32.19 beginning · end
give out, phr. vb.
  12.02 show
  24.25 make known
giver, n.
  22.29 give
  24.25 make known
give suck, vb.
  05.05 nurse
give the rein, vb.
  14.38 uncontrolled
give the time of day, vb.
  17.19 salutation
give up, phr. vb.
  20.22 victory · defeat
giving-back, n.
  22.29 give
giving-out, n.
  24.22 message
glad, adj.
  13.02 joy
glad, n.
  13.02 joy
glad, vb.
  13.02 joy
glade, n.
  01.28 wood · field · garden
gladly, adv.
  13.02 joy
gladness, n.
  13.02 joy
Glamis
  36.03 British
Glamis, Thane of → Macbeth
  36.19 historical: other
          names (1)
glance, n.
  12.01 sight
glance, vb.
  11.03 hit
  12.01 sight
glanders, n.
  07.19 glanders
Glansdale, William
  36.17 historical: English
glare, vb.
  12.01 sight

glass, n.
  01.25 stone
  06.04 face
  08.26 mirror
  08.31 cup
  32.01 clock
glass, vb.
  01.25 stone
  33.10 encompassment
glass eye, n.
  12.01 sight
glass-faced, adj.
  06.18 anatomy compounds
  08.26 mirror
glass-gazing, adj.
  12.01 sight
glassy, adj.
  01.25 stone
glaze, vb.
  01.25 stone
  33.10 encompassment
glaze, vb.
  12.01 sight
gleam, n.
  01.12 light · dark
gleam, vb.
  01.12 light · dark
glean, vb.
  11.11 strip
  22.28 acquisition
  31.17 separation
gleeful, adj.
  13.02 joy
gleek, n.
  19.09 mockery
gleek, vb.
  19.09 mockery
Glendower, Owen
  36.17 historical: English
glib, adj.
  33.27 smooth · rough
glib, vb.
  11.05 cut
glide, n.
  34.01 go
glide, vb.
  34.01 go
glimmer, n.
  01.12 light · dark
glimmer, vb.
  01.12 light · dark
glimpse, n.
  01.12 light · dark
  31.01 quantity
glister, vb.

01.12 light · dark
glitter, vb.
  01.12 light · dark
globe, n.
  01.03 planet
globy, adj.
  01.03 planet
  33.20 round
gloom, vb.
  01.12 light · dark
  13.10 sorrow
gloomy, adj.
  01.12 light · dark
  13.10 sorrow
glorify, vb.
  17.17 praise
  29.10 pre-eminence
glorious, adj.
  17.17 praise
  29.10 pre-eminence
gloriously, adv.
  17.17 praise
  29.10 pre-eminence
glory, n.
  14.16 honour
  17.17 praise
  29.10 pre-eminence
glory, vb.
  13.05 exult
  14.16 honour
  29.10 pre-eminence
gloss, n.
  01.12 light · dark
  12.03 semblance
  18.19 deceit
Gloucester
  36.03 British
Gloucester → Anne (R3)
  36.17 historical: English
Gloucester → Thomas
         Woodstock
  36.17 historical: English
Gloucester (LR)
  36.14 pseudohistorical
Gloucester, Duchess of (R2)
  36.17 historical: English
Gloucester, Edmund, Earl of
         (LR)
  36.14 pseudohistorical
Gloucester, Humphrey, Duke of
         (2H4)
  36.17 historical: English
Gloucester, Richard, Duke of
         (R3)
  36.17 historical: English

27.09 ball
gout, n.
    07.10 gout
    31.29 drop
gouty, adj.
    07.10 gout
govern, vb.
    16.02 government
    18.06 controlment
governance, n.
    18.06 controlment
governess, n.
    16.11 ruler
government, n.
    16.02 government
    18.06 controlment
    30.03 behaviour
governor, n.
    16.11 ruler
    17.08 vigilance
Gower (PER)
    26.14 poet
    36.20 cultural: English
Gower, Captain (H5)
    37.05 English: surnames
Gower, Master (2H4)
    36.17 historical: English
go whistle, vb.
    34.06 hence-going
gown, n.
    10.06 mantle
grace, n.
    13.01 happiness
    13.07 (dis)pleasure
    14.01 goodness
    14.16 honour
    14.20 beauty
    17.17 praise
    22.34 (dis)advantage
    28.13 holiness
Grace, n.
    16.11 ruler
grace, fr. n.
    24.14 French
    28.13 holiness
grace, vb.
    10.18 ornament
    13.07 (dis)pleasure
    14.16 honour
    17.17 praise
Grace
    36.16 classical myth
    37.14 telling: female
          (mentioned)
graceful, adj.

    14.20 beauty
    28.13 holiness
graceless, adj.
    14.22 badness
    28.13 holiness
graceless, n.
    14.22 badness
    28.13 holiness
gracious, adj.
    14.01 goodness
    28.13 holiness
graciously, adv.
    14.01 goodness
    14.08 (un)gentle
    28.13 holiness
gradation, n.
    33.39 row
graff, n.
    02.01 tree · bush · twig
graff, vb.
    31.16 join
graft, vb.
    31.16 join
grafter, n.
    02.01 tree · bush · twig
grain, n.
    02.15 grain
    31.28 particle
    31.39 weight
grain, vb.
    12.04 colour
grained, adj.
    02.15 grain
grained, adj.
    11.05 cut
gramercy, int.
    25.13 interjection
grammar, n.
    24.03 book
    25.08 grammar
grammar school, n.
    25.04 school
Grand → St. Jaques le Grand
grand, adj.
    29.10 pre-eminence
    29.11 foremost
grand, fr. adj.
    24.14 French
    29.10 pre-eminence
grandam, n.
    04.15 family
grandchild, n.
    04.15 family
grandeur, fr. n.
    24.14 French

    29.10 pre-eminence
grandfather, n.
    04.15 family
grand-guard, n.
    20.12 armour
grandjuror, n.
    21.05 law court
grand-juryman, n.
    21.05 law court
grand liquor, n.
    25.05 science · philosophy
grandmother, n.
    04.15 family
Grandpré
    36.11 French
    36.18 historical: French
grandsire, n.
    04.15 family
grange, n.
    08.01 house
grant, n.
    18.10 permission
    22.29 give
grant, vb.
    17.09 agreement
    18.10 permission
    22.29 give
grape, n.
    02.13 apple · grape
grapple, n.
    20.01 combat
grapple, vb.
    11.02 grasp
    20.01 combat
grasp, n.
    11.02 grasp
grasp, vb.
    11.02 grasp
grass, n.
    02.04 nettle · rush
grass-green, adj.
    12.04 colour
grasshopper, n.
    03.31 fly · louse
grass-plot, n.
    01.28 wood · field · garden
grassy, adj.
    02.05 plant
grate, n.
    08.10 window
grate, vb.
    11.10 scratch
    12.10 din
    19.04 vexation
grateful, adj.

31.03 all · nothing
grossly, adv.
    14.40 rudeness
    31.20 excess
grossness, n.
    14.40 rudeness
    33.16 size
    33.18 fat · thin
ground, n.
    01.22 earth
    01.23 soil
    15.29 motive
    26.10 song
    26.15 painting
    33.01 place
    33.02 region
    33.38 depth
ground, vb.
    33.04 set
groundling, n.
    26.02 theatre
ground-piece, n.
    26.15 painting
grove, n.
    01.28 wood · field · garden
grovel, vb.
    33.03 station
    34.03 crawl
    34.12 bend
grovelling, adv.
    33.03 station
    34.03 crawl
grow, vb.
    31.12 increase
    32.12 (un)ripe
    32.25 chance
growth, n.
    31.12 increase
    33.16 size
grub, n.
    03.30 vermin · spider
grub, vb.
    23.10 delver
grudge, n.
    17.10 (un)willingness
grudge, vb.
    17.10 (un)willingness
gruel, n.
    09.11 sauce · porridge
grumble, vb.
    13.07 (dis)pleasure
    24.20 conversation
grumbling, n.
    13.07 (dis)pleasure
    24.20 conversation

Grumio
    37.06 Romance: male
grunt, vb.
    12.13 neigh
Gualtier
    37.06 Romance: male
guard, n.
    10.17 fringe
    17.08 vigilance
guard, vb.
    10.17 fringe
    17.08 vigilance
guardage, n.
    17.08 vigilance
guardant, n.
    17.08 vigilance
guardian, n.
    17.08 vigilance
Guards, n.
    01.03 planet
gudgeon, n.
    03.26 fish
    15.12 foolishness
guerdon, n.
    22.32 recompense
guerdon, vb.
    22.32 recompense
guerra, it. n.
    20.01 combat
    24.15 Italian
guess, n.
    15.16 surmise
guess, vb.
    15.16 surmise
guessingly, adv.
    15.16 surmise
guest, n.
    04.23 stranger
    32.17 sojourn
Guest, Master
    37.15 nicknames
guest-cavalier, n.
    04.08 cavalier
guest-justice, n.
    21.05 law court
guestwise, adv.
    04.23 stranger
    32.17 sojourn
Guiana
    36.06 American
guide, n.
    17.05 guide
guide, vb.
    17.05 guide
    18.06 controlment

guider, n.
    17.05 guide
Guiderius
    36.14 pseudohistorical
guidon, n.
    20.06 officer
    20.18 flag
Guildenstern
    37.08 Germanic
guilder, n.
    22.06 money
Guildford, Henry
    36.17 historical: English
Guildfords
    36.17 historical: English
Guildhall
    16.09 council-house
guile, n.
    18.19 deceit
guile, vb.
    18.19 deceit
guileful, adj.
    18.19 deceit
guilt, n.
    21.02 guilt · innocence
Guiltian
    37.06 Romance: male
guiltily, adv.
    21.02 guilt · innocence
guiltiness, n.
    21.02 guilt · innocence
guiltless, adj.
    21.02 guilt · innocence
guilty, adj.
    21.02 guilt · innocence
guilty, n.
    21.02 guilt · innocence
guilty-like, adj.
    21.02 guilt · innocence
Guinea
    36.04 African
Guinea hen, n.
    03.20 pheasant
    04.12 strumpet
Guines
    36.11 French
Guinevere
    36.13 medieval legend
Guiscard ➤ Dauphin, Guiscard
guise, n.
    30.01 manner
gules, adj.
    12.04 colour
    16.16 heraldry
gulf, n.

hap, vb.
   32.25 chance
hapless, adj.
   32.24 mischance
haply, adv.
   32.25 chance
happen, vb.
   32.23 occurrence
   32.25 chance
happily, adv.
   13.01 happiness
   32.25 chance
happiness, n.
   13.01 happiness
   32.25 chance
happy, adj.
   13.01 happiness
   32.25 chance
happy, n.
   13.01 happiness
happy, vb.
   13.01 happiness
harbinger, n.
   24.23 messenger
   28.27 prognostication
harbour, n.
   08.04 inhabit
   35.10 harbour
harbour, vb.
   08.04 inhabit
   17.06 protection
   35.10 harbour
harbourage, n.
   17.06 protection
   35.10 harbour
hard, adj.
   14.31 cruelty
   14.35 sternness
   30.10 easy · hard
   33.15 distance
   33.28 hard · soft
hard, n.
   33.28 hard · soft
hard-a-keeping, adj.
   22.16 keeping
hard-believing, adj.
   15.24 belief
hard by, adv.
   33.15 distance
harden, vb.
   33.28 hard · soft
harder, n.
   33.28 hard · soft
hard-favoured, adj.
   06.05 lineament

   14.54 ugliness
hard-haired, adj.
   06.03 hair
   06.18 anatomy compounds
hard-handed, adj.
   06.15 arm
   06.18 anatomy compounds
hard-hearted, adj.
   06.18 anatomy compounds
   14.32 hard-hearted
hardiment, n.
   14.17 boldness
hardiness, n.
   14.17 boldness
hardly, adv.
   14.35 sternness
   22.26 spare
   30.10 easy · hard
hardness, n.
   14.31 cruelty
   14.35 sternness
   30.10 easy · hard
   33.28 hard · soft
hardock, n.
   02.04 nettle · rush
hard-ruled, adj.
   16.11 ruler
hard-timbered, adj.
   08.19 plank
   23.16 build
hardy, adj.
   14.17 boldness
hare, n.
   03.11 rat
   04.12 strumpet
harebell, n.
   02.09 rose
hare-brained, adj.
   06.18 anatomy compounds
   14.39 rashness
hare-finder, n.
   27.14 hunter
hare-lip, n.
   06.04 face
   06.18 anatomy compounds
Harfleur
   36.11 French
hark, vb.
   12.07 hearing
harlot, n.
   04.04 rogue
   04.12 strumpet
harlotry, n.
   04.12 strumpet
   14.50 sensuality

harm, n.
   14.22 badness
   19.04 vexation
harm, vb.
   19.04 vexation
harm-doing, n.
   11.01 do
   14.22 badness
harmful, adj.
   19.04 vexation
harmless, adj.
   19.04 vexation
harmonious, adj.
   17.09 agreement
   26.03 music
harmony, n.
   17.09 agreement
   26.03 music
harness, n.
   20.12 armour
   27.17 bridle
harness, vb.
   10.01 attire
   20.12 armour
   27.17 bridle
harp, n.
   26.06 fiddle
harp, vb.
   15.16 surmise
   32.16 continuance
harper, n.
   26.09 musician
Harpier
   28.05 spirits
harpy, n.
   03.32 unicorn
harrow, vb.
   19.04 vexation
harry, vb.
   19.04 vexation
Harry → Bolingbroke (R2)
   36.17 historical: English
Harry → Guildford, Henry
   36.17 historical: English
Harry → Henry [V]
   36.17 historical: English
Harry → Henry [VI]
   36.17 historical: English
Harry → Percy, Henry (R2)
   36.17 historical: English
Harry groat, n.
   22.06 money
Harry le Roy (H5)
   37.16 assumed names
Harry (of) England →

01.10   dry · wet
15.08   fantasy
humour, n.
  01.10   dry · wet
  06.17   blood · bone
  13.02   joy
  15.08   fantasy
  30.02   disposition
humour, vb.
  14.09   lenity
  18.20   flattery
humour-letter, n.
  24.04   writings
Humphrey Hour
  24.19   crux
hundred, num.
  31.08   numbers
hundred and fifty, num.
  31.08   numbers
hundred and seven, num.
  31.08   numbers
hundred forty, num.
  31.08   numbers
Hundred Merry Tales
  24.03   book
hundred-pound, n.
  22.06   money
hundred thousand, num.
  31.08   numbers
hundred twenty-six, num.
  31.08   numbers
Hungarian, adj.
  36.12   Eastern European
Hungary
  16.17   king
  36.12   Eastern European
hunger, n.
  09.01   appetite
hunger, vb.
  09.01   appetite
Hungerford
  36.03   British
Hungerford (1H6)
  36.17   historical: English
Hungerford (3H6)
  36.17   historical: English
hungerly, adj.
  09.01   appetite
hunger-starve, vb.
  09.01   appetite
hungry, adj.
  05.02   fertility · sterility
  09.01   appetite
hungry-starved, adj.
  09.01   appetite

hunt, n.
  20.19   booty
  27.14   hunter
hunt, vb.
  27.14   hunter
hunter, n.
  03.08   dog
  27.14   hunter
Huntingdon
  36.03   British
  36.17   historical: English
huntress, n.
  27.14   hunter
huntsman, n.
  27.14   hunter
hunt's-up, n.
  26.10   song
  27.14   hunter
hurdle, n.
  34.27   waggon
hurl, vb.
  19.16   disorder
  34.18   toss
hurly, n.
  19.16   disorder
hurly-burly, n.
  19.16   disorder
hurricano, n.
  01.06   wind · storm
hurry, n.
  19.16   disorder
hurry, vb.
  34.23   fast · slow
hurt, n.
  07.18   wound
  19.04   vexation
hurt, vb.
  07.18   wound
hurtle, vb.
  11.03   hit
  12.10   din
hurtless, adj.
  07.18   wound
husband, n.
  04.18   marriage
  23.12   husbandry
husband, vb.
  04.18   marriage
  23.12   husbandry
husbandless, adj.
  04.20   widow · orphan
husbandry, n.
  23.12   husbandry
hush, adj.
  24.24   verbal · silent

hush, int.
  25.13   interjection
hush, vb.
  24.24   verbal · silent
husht, int.
  25.13   interjection
husk, n.
  02.15   grain
Hybla
  36.08   Italian
Hydra
  03.32   unicorn
Hydra-headed, adj.
  03.32   unicorn
  06.02   head
  06.18   anatomy compounds
hyena, n.
  03.09   wolf
Hymen
  28.04   Mars · Venus
hymn, n.
  26.10   song
  28.11   prayer
hyperbole, n.
  25.09   rhetoric
hyperbolical, adj.
  25.09   rhetoric
  31.20   excess
Hyperion
  28.04   Mars · Venus
hypocrisy, n.
  18.19   deceit
hypocrite, n.
  18.19   deceit
Hyrcan, adj.
  36.05   Middle / Far Eastern
Hyrcania
  36.05   Middle / Far Eastern
Hyrcanian, adj.
  36.05   Middle / Far Eastern
hyssop, n.
  02.17   mandragora
hysterica passio
  07.20   madness
  24.16   foreign phrases

I

I, n.
    25.07 alphabet
I, pron.
    25.15 pronoun
iacere → hic jacet
iaculum, lat. n.
    20.14 weapon
    24.13 Latin
Iago
    37.06 Romance: male
Icarus
    36.16 classical myth
ice, n.
    01.11 hot · cold
ice-brook, n.
    01.17 river
Iceland
    01.20 island
    36.10 Northern European
Iceland dog, n.
    03.08 dog
ici, fr. adv.
    24.14 French
    33.01 place
icicle, n.
    01.11 hot · cold
icy, adj.
    01.11 hot · cold
idea, n.
    12.03 semblance
    15.02 notion
idem, lat. pron.
    24.13 Latin
    25.15 pronoun
Iden, Alexander
    36.17 historical: English
ides, n.
    32.07 monday
idiot, n.
    04.06 madcap
    15.12 foolishness
idiot-worshipper, n.
    28.08 worshipper
idle, adj.
    14.41 levity
    14.42 negligence
    22.14 trifle
idle, vb.
    14.41 levity
    14.42 negligence

idle-headed, adj.
    06.18 anatomy compounds
    15.12 foolishness
idleness, n.
    14.41 levity
    14.42 negligence
idly, adv.
    14.41 levity
    14.42 negligence
idol, n.
    28.23 irreligion
idolatrous, adj.
    28.23 irreligion
idolatry, n.
    28.23 irreligion
if, conj.
    25.12 conjunction
if, n.
    15.22 (un)certainty
ignis, lat. n.
    01.13 fire
    24.13 Latin
ignis fatuus
    01.13 fire
    18.19 deceit
    24.16 foreign phrases
ignoble, adj.
    14.47 dishonour
ignobly, adv.
    14.47 dishonour
ignominious, adj.
    14.47 dishonour
ignominy, n.
    14.47 dishonour
ignomy, n.
    14.47 dishonour
ignorance, n.
    15.06 knowledge
    15.12 foolishness
ignorant, adj.
    15.06 knowledge
ignorant, n.
    15.06 knowledge
    15.12 foolishness
il, it. art.
    24.15 Italian
    25.11 article
il, fr. pron.
    24.14 French
    25.15 pronoun
Ilion
    36.05 Middle / Far Eastern
Ilium
    36.05 Middle / Far Eastern
ill, adj.

07.06 sickness
    14.22 badness
ill, n.
    14.22 badness
ill-annexed, adj.
    31.12 increase
    31.16 join
ill-beseeming, adj.
    30.09 (un)aptness
ill-boding, adj.
    28.27 prognostication
ill-breeding, adj.
    05.03 procreation
    18.16 plot
ill-composed, adj.
    33.19 shape
ill-dealing, adj.
    11.01 do
ill-dispersing, adj.
    33.41 distribution
ill disposed, adj.
    30.02 disposition
ill-divining, adj.
    28.27 prognostication
ill-doing, n.
    11.01 do
    14.22 badness
    19.04 vexation
illegitimate, adj.
    05.03 procreation
    15.05 logic
    15.20 error · truth
ill-erected, adj.
    23.16 build
ill-faced, adj.
    06.18 anatomy compounds
    14.54 ugliness
ill-favoured, adj.
    06.05 lineament
    14.54 ugliness
ill-favouredly, adv.
    13.07 (dis)pleasure
ill-headed, adj.
    06.02 head
    06.18 anatomy compounds
ill house, n.
    23.30 brothel
ill-inhabited, adj.
    08.04 inhabit
illiterate, adj.
    25.01 education
illiterate, n.
    25.01 education
illness, n.
    14.22 badness

ill-nurtured, adj.
25.01 education
ill-resounding, adj.
12.10 din
ill-roasted, adj.
09.05 cookery
ill-seeming, adj.
12.03 semblance
ill-shaped, adj.
33.19 shape
ill-sheathed, adj.
20.15 sword-hilt
ill-spirited, adj.
14.22 badness
30.02 disposition
ill-starred, adj.
32.24 mischance
ill-taken, adj.
15.20 error • truth
ill-tempered, adj.
14.33 curstness
30.02 disposition
ill-tuned, adj.
26.03 music
illume, vb.
01.12 light • dark
illuminate, vb.
01.12 light • dark
illumine, vb.
01.12 light • dark
ill-used, adj.
18.07 (ab)use
illusion, n.
18.19 deceit
illustrate, adj.
29.10 pre-eminence
illustrate, vb.
15.23 interpretation
illustrious, adj.
01.12 light • dark
29.10 pre-eminence
ill-uttering, adj.
24.25 make known
ill-weaved, adj.
23.05 clothier
ill-well, adv.
14.01 goodness
14.22 badness
ill will, n.
17.10 (un)willingness
ill-wresting, adj.
33.31 entangle
Illyria
36.09 Southern European
Illyrian, adj.

36.09 Southern European
image, n.
12.03 semblance
15.02 notion
26.15 painting
imagery, n.
26.15 painting
imaginary, adj.
15.08 fantasy
imagination, n.
15.02 notion
15.08 fantasy
imagine, vb.
15.02 notion
15.08 fantasy
imagining, n.
15.02 notion
15.08 fantasy
imbecility, n.
07.04 weakness
imbrue, vb.
01.18 effusion
14.49 impurity
imitari, lat. vb.
12.03 semblance
24.13 Latin
imitate, vb.
12.03 semblance
imitation, n.
12.03 semblance
immaculate, adj.
14.18 purity
immanity, n.
14.30 savageness
14.31 cruelty
immask, vb.
10.11 veil • mask
24.29 conceal
immaterial, adj.
22.14 trifle
29.01 essence • matter
immediacy, n.
33.15 distance
immediate, adj.
32.30 brevity
33.15 distance
immediate, n.
33.15 distance
immediately, adv.
32.30 brevity
imminence, n.
32.31 imminence
imminent, adj.
32.31 imminence
immoderate, adj.

31.20 excess
immoderately, adv.
31.20 excess
immodest, adj.
14.50 sensuality
31.20 excess
immodestly, adv.
14.50 sensuality
immoment, adj.
22.14 trifle
immortal, adj.
32.16 continuance
immortal (ANT 5.2.247), adj.
24.18 malapropism
immortality, n.
32.16 continuance
immortalize, vb.
32.16 continuance
immortally, adv.
32.16 continuance
immure, n.
08.08 wall
immure, vb.
18.06 controlment
33.10 encompassment
Imogen
37.04 English: female
imp, n.
04.03 boy • youth
imp, vb.
27.12 falconer
31.16 join
impaint, vb.
12.04 colour
26.15 painting
impair, adj.
30.09 (un)aptness
impair, vb.
07.04 weakness
07.18 wound
impale, vb.
33.10 encompassment
impart, vb.
22.29 give
24.25 make known
impartial, adj.
15.19 impartial
impartment, n.
24.22 message
impaste, vb.
09.05 cookery
impatience, n.
14.06 (im)patience
impatient, adj.
14.06 (im)patience

improbable, adj.
15.22 (un)certainty
improper, adj.
30.09 (un)aptness
improve, vb.
22.34 (dis)advantage
improvident, adj.
14.42 negligence
impudence, n.
14.26 insolence
impudency, n.
14.26 insolence
impudent, adj.
14.26 insolence
impudently, adv.
14.26 insolence
impudique, fr. adj.
14.26 insolence
24.14 French
impugn, vb.
19.01 opposition
impure, adj.
14.49 impurity
impurity, n.
14.49 impurity
imputation, n.
14.16 honour
19.08 reproach
impute, vb.
15.25 attribution
in, adv.
25.10 adverb
33.08 inside · outside
in, prep.
25.14 preposition
in, lat. prep.
24.13 Latin
25.14 preposition
in, vb.
23.12 husbandry
inaccessible, adj.
34.05 enter
inaidible, adj.
17.04 assistance
in (a) manner, adv.
31.38 almost
in (any) case, adv.
32.25 chance
in a tale, adv.
17.09 agreement
inaudible, adj.
12.07 hearing
inauspicious, adj.
28.27 prognostication
32.24 mischance

in blood, adv.
07.02 vigour
incantation, n.
28.28 sorcery
incapable, adj.
22.28 acquisition
30.05 (un)able
in capite
21.07 privilegium
24.16 foreign phrases
incardinate (TN 5.1.182), adj.
24.18 malapropism
incarnadine, vb.
12.04 colour
incarnate, adj.
06.01 body
incarnation (MV 2.2.27), n.
24.18 malapropism
incense, n.
28.21 altar
incense, vb.
01.13 fire
18.18 instigation
19.04 vexation
incensement, n.
14.29 anger
incertain, adj.
15.22 (un)certainty
incertainty, n.
15.22 (un)certainty
incessant, adj.
32.16 continuance
incessantly, adv.
32.16 continuance
incest, n.
14.51 fornication
incestuous, adj.
14.51 fornication
inch, n.
33.34 span
inch, n.
01.20 island
incharitable, adj.
14.22 badness
inchmeal, adv.
33.34 span
inch-thick, adj.
33.34 span
33.36 breadth
incidency, n.
32.31 imminence
incident, adj.
32.31 imminence
incision, n.
07.24 medicine · cure

11.05 cut
incite, vb.
18.18 instigation
incivil, adj.
14.40 rudeness
incivility, n.
14.40 rudeness
inclinable, adj.
30.02 disposition
inclination, n.
30.02 disposition
incline, vb.
30.02 disposition
34.12 bend
inclining, n.
30.02 disposition
34.12 bend
inclip, vb.
33.10 encompassment
include, vb.
32.19 beginning · end
33.10 encompassment
inclusive, adj.
33.10 encompassment
income, n.
22.08 payment
34.04 here-approach
incomparable, adj.
29.10 pre-eminence
incomprehensible, adj.
15.01 cognition
inconsiderate, adj.
14.39 rashness
inconsiderate, n.
14.39 rashness
15.04 thought
inconstancy, n.
14.05 (in)constancy
inconstant, adj.
14.05 (in)constancy
incontinence, n.
14.50 sensuality
incontinency, n.
14.50 sensuality
incontinent, adj.
14.50 sensuality
incontinent, adv.
32.30 brevity
incontinently, adv.
32.30 brevity
inconvenience, n.
19.04 vexation
inconvenient, adj.
30.09 (un)aptness
incony, adj.

invite, vb.
  18.11 request
inviting, n.
  18.11 request
invitus, lat. adj.
  17.10 (un)willingness
  24.13 Latin
invocate, vb.
  28.11 prayer
invocation, n.
  28.11 prayer
invoke, vb.
  28.11 prayer
invulnerable, adj.
  07.18 wound
inward, adj.
  04.24 solitary
  24.29 conceal
  33.08 inside · outside
inward, adv.
  33.08 inside · outside
inward, n.
  04.24 solitary
  06.17 blood · bone
  33.08 inside · outside
inwardly, adv.
  33.08 inside · outside
inwardness, n.
  04.24 solitary
in (with) a thought, adv.
  32.30 brevity
io, it. pron.
  24.15 Italian
  25.15 pronoun
Io
  36.16 classical myth
Ionia
  36.05 Middle / Far Eastern
Ionian, adj.
  36.05 Middle / Far Eastern
Ionian Sea
  01.15 sea
ipse, lat. pron.
  24.13 Latin
  25.15 pronoun
ipso facto
  24.16 foreign phrases
  29.05 indeed
Ipswich
  36.03 British
ira, lat. n.
  14.29 anger
  24.13 Latin
Iras
  36.24 historical: other

names (2)
ire, n.
  14.29 anger
ire, lat. vb.
  24.13 Latin
  34.01 go
ireful, adj.
  14.29 anger
Ireland
  01.20 island
  36.03 British
iris, n.
  06.04 face
Iris
  01.08 rain · snow
  24.23 messenger
  28.04 Mars · Venus
Irish, adj.
  36.03 British
Irish, n.
  24.01 language
  36.03 British
Irishman, n.
  36.03 British
irk, vb.
  19.04 vexation
irksome, adj.
  19.04 vexation
iron, n.
  01.26 metal
  20.12 armour
  20.14 weapon
  21.15 manacle
  23.17 tool
iron-witted, adj.
  14.32 hard-hearted
  30.02 disposition
irreconciled, adj.
  17.09 agreement
  28.17 penitence
irrecoverable, adj.
  22.22 loss
irregular, adj.
  14.38 uncontrolled
  19.16 disorder
irregulous, adj.
  14.38 uncontrolled
  19.16 disorder
irreligious, adj.
  28.23 irreligion
irremovable, adj.
  33.11 firm
irreparable, adj.
  17.07 amendment
irresolute, adj.

  14.05 (in)constancy
irrevocable, adj.
  31.22 cancel
  33.11 firm
Isabel, Queen
  36.18 historical: French
Isabella
  37.07 Romance : female
Isbel (AWW)
  37.04 English: female
Iscariot → Judas Iscariot
Isidore
  37.01 classical: male
Isis
  28.04 Mars · Venus
island, n.
  01.20 island
islander, n.
  01.20 island
isle, n.
  01.20 island
Isle of Man
  01.20 island
  36.03 British
Israel
  36.05 Middle / Far Eastern
issue, n.
  04.14 kindred
  32.27 issue
issue, vb.
  01.18 effusion
  04.14 kindred
  34.06 hence-going
issueless, adj.
  05.02 fertility · sterility
iste, lat. pron.
  24.13 Latin
  25.15 pronoun
it, pron.
  25.15 pronoun
Italian, adj.
  36.08 Italian
Italian, n.
  24.01 language
  36.08 Italian
Italy
  36.08 Italian
itch, n.
  07.15 itch
  14.48 desire
itch, vb.
  07.15 itch
  14.48 desire
item, adv.
  31.15 moreover

item, n.
    22.12 contract
iterance, n.
    32.16 continuance
iteration, n.
    32.16 continuance
Ithaca
    01.20 island
    36.09 Southern European
i' th' name of Belzebub
    28.25 oaths
its, pron.
    25.15 pronoun
itself, pron.
    25.15 pronoun
Iupiter, lat.
    24.13 Latin
    28.04 Mars · Venus
ivory, n.
    10.19 gem
ivy, n.
    02.02 oak · brier
ivy-tod, n.
    02.02 oak · brier
iwis, adv.
    15.22 (un)certainty

J

Jachimo
    37.06 Romance: male
jack, n.
    04.04 rogue
    08.31 cup
    18.14 vassal
    26.06 fiddle
    32.01 clock
jack, n.
    10.06 mantle
Jack
    04.02 man
    37.03 English: male
Jack → Cade, John
    36.17 historical: English
Jack-a-lent
    27.08 toy
jackanapes, n.
    03.15 monkey
    04.04 rogue
Jack-dog, n.
    03.08 dog
    04.04 rogue
Jack guardant, n.
    17.08 vigilance
Jack of the clock, n.
    32.01 clock
Jack priest, n.
    28.09 clergy
Jack sauce, n.
    04.04 rogue
Jack slave, n.
    18.14 vassal
Jacob
    28.03 Abraham · Paul
    28.14 saints
jade, n.
    03.02 horse
    04.12 strumpet
jade, vb.
    07.03 weariness
    19.09 mockery
jadery, n.
    18.19 deceit
jail, n.
    21.14 prison
jailer, n.
    18.06 controlment
jakes, n.
    08.16 sewer

James Gurney (JN)
    37.03 English: male
James Soundpost (ROM)
    37.03 English: male
Jamy
    28.14 saints
Jamy, Captain (H5)
    37.03 English: male
Jane Nightwork (2H4)
    37.04 English: female
Jane Smile (AYL)
    37.04 English: female
jangle, vb.
    12.09 clangour
    19.11 quarrel
January, n.
    32.06 month
Janus
    28.04 Mars · Venus
Japhet
    28.03 Abraham · Paul
Jaquenetta
    37.07 Romance : female
Jaques
    28.14 saints
Jaques (AWW)
    37.06 Romance: male
Jaques[1] (AYL)
    37.06 Romance: male
Jaques[2] (AYL)
    37.06 Romance: male
Jaques Falconbridge (LLL)
    37.06 Romance: male
jar, n.
    12.10 din
    19.11 quarrel
    26.03 music
    32.01 clock
jar, vb.
    12.10 din
    19.11 quarrel
    26.03 music
    32.01 clock
Jason
    36.16 classical myth
jaunce, n.
    34.02 leap
jaunce, vb.
    34.02 leap
jaundice, n.
    07.10 gout
javelin, n.
    20.14 weapon
jaw, n.
    06.06 jaw

jaw, vb.
      06.06   jaw
jaw-bone, n.
      06.06   jaw
jay, n.
      03.24   crow
      04.12   strumpet
je, fr. pron.
      24.14   French
      25.15   pronoun
jealous, adj.
      14.28   envy
      17.15   (mis)trust
jealousy, n.
      14.28   envy
      17.15   (mis)trust
jean, n.
      10.03   cloth
jeer, vb.
      19.09   mockery
jelly, n.
      09.07   congeal
      09.16   sweetmeat
jennet, n.
      03.02   horse
Jenny
      37.04   English: female
jeopardy, n.
      19.18   peril
Jephthah
      28.03   Abraham · Paul
jerk, n.
      24.22   message
      34.02   leap
jerkin, n.
      10.06   mantle
Jeronimy
      26.02   theatre
      28.14   saints
Jerusalem
      08.17   rooms
      28.07   heaven · hell
      36.05   Middle / Far Eastern
jess, n.
      27.19   curb
Jessica
      37.04   English: female
jest, n.
      04.06   madcap
      13.02   joy
jest, vb.
      04.06   madcap
      13.02   joy
jester, n.
      04.06   madcap

jesting, n.
      04.06   madcap
Jesu
      28.25   oaths
Jesu Maria
      28.25   oaths
Jesus
      28.03   Abraham · Paul
jet, n.
      10.19   gem
jet, vb.
      14.25   braggardism
      34.01   go
jet, vb.
      34.05   enter
jetted, adj.
      10.19   gem
Jew, n.
      28.01   religions
jewel, n.
      10.19   gem
jewel-house, n.
      16.09   council-house
jeweller, n.
      23.04   goldsmith
jewel-like, adj.
      10.19   gem
Jewess, n.
      28.01   religions
Jewish, adj.
      28.01   religions
Jewry
      36.05   Middle / Far Eastern
Jezebel
      28.03   Abraham · Paul
jig, n.
      26.02   theatre
      26.10   song
      26.11   dance
jig, vb.
      26.09   musician
      26.11   dance
jig-maker, n.
      26.09   musician
Jill
      04.09   woman
      37.04   English: female
jingle, vb.
      12.09   clangour
Jinny (WIV 4.1.62)
      24.18   malapropism
Joan (2H6)
      03.22   hawk
Joan (JN)
      37.04   English: female

Joan (LLL)
      37.04   English: female
Joan (SHR)
      37.04   English: female
Joan de Pucelle (1H6)
      36.18   historical: French
Joan of Arc (Aire) (1H6)
      36.18   historical: French
Job
      28.03   Abraham · Paul
Jockey → Norfolk (R3)
      36.17   historical: English
jocund, adj.
      13.02   joy
jog, vb.
      34.01   go
John
      28.03   Abraham · Paul
John (WIV)
      37.03   English: male
John, Don (ADO)
      37.03   English: male
John, Friar (ROM)
      37.03   English: male
John, Goodman (2H6)
      37.03   English: male
John, King (JN)
      36.17   historical: English
John, Sir (R3)
      36.17   historical: English
John a-dreams
      14.42   negligence
John ape, n.
      03.15   monkey
John Bates (H5)
      37.03   English: male
John Drum's entertainment, n.
      34.20   send
John Falstaff (WIV)
      37.03   English: male
John Naps (SHR)
      37.03   English: male
John of Gaunt (R2)
      36.17   historical: English
John of Lancaster, Prince (1H4)
      36.17   historical: English
John Rugby (WIV)
      37.03   English: male
join, vb.
      20.01   combat
      31.16   join
joinder, n.
      31.16   join
joiner, n.
      23.07   carpenter

joint, adj.
  31.16 join
joint, n.
  06.14 limb
  23.20 hinge
  31.16 join
joint, vb.
  31.16 join
joint-labourer, n.
  23.01 vocation
jointly, adv.
  31.16 join
jointress, n.
  04.20 widow · orphan
joint-ring, n.
  10.20 ring
joint-servant, n.
  16.29 servant
joint-stool, n.
  08.21 chair
jointure, n.
  22.18 estate
jollity, n.
  10.01 attire
  13.02 joy
jolly, adj.
  13.02 joy
jolt head, n.
  06.18 anatomy compounds
  15.12 foolishness
jordan, n.
  08.32 pot
Jordan, Margery
  36.17 historical: English
Joseph
  37.03 English: male
Joshua
  28.03 Abraham · Paul
jostle, vb.
  11.03 hit
  11.06 push
jot, n.
  31.28 particle
jour, fr. n.
  24.14 French
  32.02 hour · day · year
journal, adj.
  32.02 hour · day · year
journey, n.
  34.16 travel
journey, vb.
  34.16 travel
journey-bated, adj.
  07.03 weariness
journeyman, n.

  23.01 vocation
Jove
  28.04 Mars · Venus
Jove's tree, n.
  02.02 oak · brier
jovial, adj.
  13.02 joy
  28.04 Mars · Venus
jowl, n.
  06.04 face
jowl, vb.
  11.03 hit
joy, n.
  04.10 darling
  13.02 joy
joy, vb.
  13.02 joy
  13.07 (dis)pleasure
joyful, adj.
  13.02 joy
joyfully, adv.
  13.02 joy
joyless, adj.
  13.10 sorrow
joyous, adj.
  13.02 joy
Judas Iscariot
  28.03 Abraham · Paul
Judas Maccabaeus
  28.03 Abraham · Paul
Judas Maccabaeus (LLL)
  37.16 assumed names
Jude
  28.03 Abraham · Paul
judge, n.
  21.03 judgement
  21.05 law court
judge, vb.
  15.04 thought
  15.24 belief
  21.03 judgement
  22.13 value
judgement, n.
  15.01 cognition
  15.04 thought
  21.03 judgement
Judgement Day
  21.03 judgement
  32.03 times
judgement-place, n.
  21.05 law court
  33.01 place
judicious, adj.
  15.11 (in)discretion
  21.03 judgement

  21.05 law court
jug, n.
  08.33 bottle
Jug
  37.04 English: female
juggle, vb.
  18.19 deceit
juggler, n.
  18.19 deceit
  27.07 gamester
juggling trick, n.
  18.16 plot
juice, n.
  02.03 sap
  06.17 blood · bone
Jule
  37.04 English: female
Julia
  37.07 Romance : female
Juliet
  37.07 Romance : female
Julietta
  37.07 Romance : female
Julius → Caesar, Julius
July, n.
  32.06 month
jump, adv.
  30.07 preciseness
jump, n.
  19.18 peril
jump, vb.
  17.09 agreement
  19.18 peril
  34.02 leap
June, n.
  32.06 month
Junius → Brutus, Junius
junket, n.
  09.16 sweetmeat
Juno
  28.04 Mars · Venus
Juno-like, adj.
  28.04 Mars · Venus
Jupiter
  28.04 Mars · Venus
jure, vb.
  21.05 law court
jurement, fr. n.
  17.13 obligation
  24.14 French
  28.25 oaths
jurisdiction, n.
  21.05 law court
juror, n.
  21.05 law court

02.07 seed
02.10 fruit · nut
kersey, n.
   10.03 cloth
Ketly, Richard
   36.17 historical: English
kettle, n.
   26.08 other instruments
kettledrum, n.
   26.08 other instruments
key, n.
   08.12 lock
   26.04 gamut
   26.06 fiddle
key-cold, adj.
   01.11 hot · cold
keyhole, n.
   08.12 lock
   33.22 hole · trench
kibe, n.
   07.16 sore
kick, vb.
   11.03 hit
kickie-wickie, n.
   04.09 woman
kickshaws, n.
   09.04 food · drink
   27.08 toy
kidney, n.
   06.17 blood · bone
Kildare
   36.03 British
   36.17 historical: English
kill, vb.
   21.10 murder
kill-courtesy, n.
   14.40 rudeness
kiln-hole, n.
   08.18 hearth
Kimbolton
   16.15 castle
   36.03 British
kin, n.
   04.14 kindred
kind, adj.
   14.08 (un)gentle
   29.03 (un)natural
kind, n.
   04.14 kindred
   31.36 multitude
kind-hearted, adj.
   06.18 anatomy compounds
   14.08 (un)gentle
kindle, vb.
   01.13 fire

18.18 instigation
kindle, vb.
   05.03 procreation
kindless, adj.
   29.03 (un)natural
kindly, adj.
   14.08 (un)gentle
   29.03 (un)natural
kindly, adv.
   14.08 (un)gentle
   29.03 (un)natural
kindness, n.
   14.08 (un)gentle
kindred, n.
   04.14 kindred
king, n.
   16.17 king
king, vb.
   16.11 ruler
   16.17 king
king-becoming, adj.
   30.09 (un)aptness
king-cardinal, n.
   28.09 clergy
kingdom, n.
   16.01 commonwealth
   16.12 majesty
kingdomed, adj.
   16.01 commonwealth
king-killer, n.
   21.10 murder
kingly, adj.
   16.12 majesty
kingly-crowned, adj.
   16.13 enthrone
kingly-poor, adj.
   22.19 rich · poor
king of beasts, n.
   03.16 elephant · lion
King of heaven, n.
   28.02 God
King of kings, n.
   28.02 God
king's attorney, n.
   21.05 law court
King's English, n.
   24.01 language
king's evil, n.
   07.10 gout
king's highway, n.
   34.28 road
King's King, n.
   28.02 God
kinsman, n.
   04.14 kindred

kinswoman, n.
   04.14 kindred
kirtle, n.
   10.07 petticoat
kiss, n.
   17.16 embrace · kiss
kiss, vb.
   17.16 embrace · kiss
   27.10 sport terms
kissing-comfit, n.
   09.16 sweetmeat
kitchen, n.
   08.17 rooms
kitchen, vb.
   09.02 feed
kitchen maid, n.
   16.27 household servant
kitchen malkin, n.
   16.27 household servant
kitchen trull, n.
   16.27 household servant
kitchen vestal, n.
   16.27 household servant
kitchen wench, n.
   16.27 household servant
kite, n.
   03.22 hawk
   04.12 strumpet
kitten, n.
   03.07 cat
kitten, vb.
   05.03 procreation
knack, n.
   27.08 toy
knap, vb.
   11.03 hit
knap, vb.
   03.47 peck · graze
knave, n.
   04.03 boy · youth
   04.04 rogue
   16.29 servant
knavery, n.
   04.04 rogue
   18.19 deceit
knavish, adj.
   04.04 rogue
   18.19 deceit
knead, vb.
   11.04 press
knee, n.
   06.16 leg
   34.12 bend
knee, vb.
   34.03 crawl

L

10.05 needlework
10.18 ornament
31.16 join
Lacedaemon
36.09 Southern European
laced mutton, n.
04.12 strumpet
lack, n.
22.24 lack
lack, vb.
22.24 lack
Lack-beard
06.03 hair
06.18 anatomy compounds
Lack-beard, Lord
37.15 nicknames
lack-brain, n.
06.18 anatomy compounds
15.12 foolishness
lackey, n.
16.27 household servant
lackey, vb.
16.27 household servant
lack-linen, n.
10.01 attire
10.03 cloth
lack-love, n.
14.02 love · hate
lack-lustre, n.
01.12 light · dark
Lacy
36.17 historical: English
lad, n.
04.03 boy · youth
04.22 companion
ladder, n.
08.15 stair
ladder-tackle, n.
08.15 stair
lade, vb.
01.18 effusion
31.06 load
lading, n.
31.06 load
lady, n.
04.09 woman
04.18 marriage
16.21 lord · lady
26.10 song
Lady
28.25 oaths
Lady
03.08 dog
lady-bird, n.
03.31 fly · louse

04.10 darling
Lady Brach
03.08 dog
ladyship, n.
04.09 woman
16.21 lord · lady
lady-smock, n.
02.09 rose
Laertes (HAM)
37.01 classical: male
Laertes (TIT)
36.16 classical myth
La Far, Monsieur
37.10 Romance: surnames
Lafew, Lord
37.11 telling: male (DP)
lag, adj.
32.29 early · late
lag, n.
16.31 commoner
lag, vb.
34.09 stray
lag-end, n.
33.06 side
laisser, fr. vb.
18.10 permission
.24.14 French
lake, n.
01.16 pool
lakin → by'r lakin
lamb, n.
03.05 sheep
04.10 darling
Lambert
28.14 saints
lambkin, n.
04.10 darling
lambskin, n.
10.04 leather
lame, adj.
07.21 cripple
lame, n.
07.21 cripple
lame, vb.
07.21 cripple
lamely, adv.
07.21 cripple
14.46 fault
lameness, n.
07.21 cripple
lament, n.
13.11 lament
lament, vb.
13.11 lament
lamentable, adj.

13.11 lament
lamentably, adv.
13.11 lament
lamentation, n.
13.11 lament
lamenting, n.
13.11 lament
Lammas-eve, n.
32.05 holidays
Lammas-tide, n.
32.05 holidays
Lamord
37.10 Romance: surnames
lamp, n.
01.12 light · dark
08.27 torch
lampas, n.
07.19 glanders
Lancaster
36.03 British
Lancaster → Bolingbroke (R2)
36.17 historical: English
Lancaster → Henry [VI]
36.17 historical: English
Lancaster → John of Gaunt
36.17 historical: English
Lancaster → Prince John of
36.17 historical: English
lance, n.
20.14 weapon
lance, vb.
11.05 cut
Lance
37.03 English: male
Lancelet Gobbo
37.03 English: male
land, n.
01.22 earth
01.23 soil
16.01 commonwealth
22.15 possession
33.02 region
land, vb.
34.04 here-approach
35.08 navigation
land carrack, n.
04.12 strumpet
land-damn, vb.
19.10 disparagement
landed, adj.
22.15 possession
land-fish, n.
03.32 unicorn
landless, adj.
22.15 possession

landlord, n.
    22.18 estate
landman, n.
    20.07 soldier
land-raker → foot land-raker
land-rat, n.
    03.11 rat
    04.04 rogue
land-service, n.
    16.29 servant
    17.13 obligation
land-thief, n.
    21.12 thievery
lane, n.
    34.28 road
langage, fr. n.
    24.01 language
    24.14 French
Langley
    36.03 British
Langley, Edmund
    36.17 historical: English
Langton, Stephen
    36.17 historical: English
language, n.
    24.01 language
languageless, adj.
    24.24 verbal · silent
langue, fr. n.
    24.01 language
    24.14 French
languish, n.
    07.05 decay
    13.10 sorrow
languish, vb.
    07.05 decay
languishing, n.
    07.05 decay
languishment, n.
    07.05 decay
    13.10 sorrow
languor, n.
    07.05 decay
    13.10 sorrow
lank, adj.
    33.18 fat · thin
lank, vb.
    33.18 fat · thin
lank-lean, adj.
    33.18 fat · thin
lantern, n.
    08.06 steeple
    08.27 torch
lap, n.
    06.09 belly

lap, vb.
    09.03 eat · drink
lap, vb.
    33.10 encompassment
lapis, lat. n.
    01.25 stone
    24.13 Latin
Lapland
    36.10 Northern European
lapse, n.
    28.24 impiety
    34.08 descend
lapse, vb.
    11.02 grasp
    28.24 impiety
    34.08 descend
lapwing, n.
    03.18 nightingale
lard, vb.
    33.18 fat · thin
larder, n.
    08.03 storehouse
large, adj.
    14.11 liberality
    31.20 excess
    33.16 size
large-handed, adj.
    06.18 anatomy compounds
    11.02 grasp
largely, adv.
    31.04 full · empty
    31.20 excess
largeness, n.
    33.16 size
largess, n.
    14.11 liberality
lark, n.
    03.18 nightingale
lark's-heel, n.
    02.09 rose
laron, n.
    21.12 thievery
Lartius, Titus
    36.14 pseudohistorical
larum, n.
    12.11 shout
larum-bell, n.
    26.07 bell
lascivious, adj.
    14.50 sensuality
lash, n.
    11.03 hit
    21.16 cudgel
lash, vb.
    11.03 hit

lass, n.
    32.10 maidhood
lass-lorn, adj.
    19.05 rejection
last, adj.
    33.40 sequence
last, adv.
    32.18 past · present · future
    33.40 sequence
last, n.
    23.27 other tools
last, n.
    33.40 sequence
last, vb.
    14.06 (im)patience
    32.16 continuance
lastly, adv.
    33.40 sequence
latch, n.
    08.12 lock
latch, vb.
    11.02 grasp
late, adj.
    32.18 past · present · future
    32.29 early · late
late-betrayed, adj.
    17.14 (dis)loyalty
    18.19 deceit
lated, adj.
    32.29 early · late
late-deceased, adj.
    05.01 life · death
late-despised, adj.
    14.27 contempt
late-disturbed, adj.
    19.17 (un)rest
lately, adv.
    32.18 past · present · future
late-sacked, adj.
    20.19 booty
latest, n.
    33.40 sequence
late-walking, n.
    34.01 go
lath, n.
    08.19 plank
    20.14 weapon
Latin, adj.
    24.01 language
Latin, n.
    24.01 language
latten, n.
    01.26 metal
latter, n.
    33.40 sequence

league, n.
 04.22 companion
league, vb.
 04.22 companion
leaguer, n.
 20.09 camp
Leah
 37.09 other names
leak, n.
 33.22 hole · trench
leak, vb.
 01.18 effusion
 06.20 excrement
leaky, adj.
 01.18 effusion
lean, adj.
 22.26 spare
 33.18 fat · thin
lean, vb.
 30.02 disposition
 34.12 bend
Leander
 36.16 classical myth
lean-faced, adj.
 06.04 face
 06.18 anatomy compounds
lean-looked, adj.
 06.05 lineament
leanness, n.
 22.26 spare
 33.18 fat · thin
lean-witted, adj.
 15.12 foolishness
 30.02 disposition
leap, n.
 34.02 leap
leap, vb.
 05.03 procreation
 34.02 leap
leap-frog, n.
 27.06 games
leaping-house, n.
 23.30 brothel
leaping time, n.
 32.09 childhood · youth
Lear
 36.14 pseudohistorical
learn, vb.
 24.25 make known
 25.01 education
learned, adj.
 25.01 education
learnedly, adv.
 25.01 education
learning, n.

 25.01 education
learning place, n.
 25.04 school
lease, n.
 22.12 contract
 32.14 period
lease, vb.
 18.19 deceit
lease, vb.
 22.12 contract
leash, n.
 27.19 curb
 31.08 numbers
leash, vb.
 27.19 curb
least, n.
 31.10 many · few
 33.16 size
leather, n.
 10.04 leather
leather-coat, n.
 02.13 apple · grape
leathern, adj.
 10.04 leather
leave, n.
 17.19 salutation
 18.10 permission
 34.06 hence-going
leave, vb.
 18.10 permission
 32.19 beginning · end
 34.06 hence-going
leaven, n.
 09.13 bread · cake
leaven, vb.
 09.05 cookery
leave-taking, n.
 17.19 salutation
 34.06 hence-going
leavy, adj.
 02.06 bud · root
Le Beau, Monsieur
 37.11 telling: male (DP)
Le Bon, Monsieur
 37.13 telling: male
            (mentioned)
lecher, n.
 14.50 sensuality
lecher, vb.
 14.50 sensuality
lecherous, adj.
 14.50 sensuality
lechery, n.
 14.50 sensuality
leçon, fr. n.

 24.14 French
 25.01 education
lecture, n.
 25.01 education
Leda
 36.16 classical myth
ledger, n.
 16.23 ambassador
lee, n.
 31.31 morsel
 31.34 dreg
leech, n.
 07.22 physician
leech, n.
 03.30 vermin · spider
leek, n.
 02.14 cabbage
leer, n.
 06.05 lineament
leer, n.
 12.01 sight
leer, vb.
 12.01 sight
leese, vb.
 22.22 loss
leet, n.
 21.05 law court
 32.03 times
Le Fer
 36.18 historical: French
 37.11 telling: male (DP)
left, adj.
 33.06 side
left, n.
 33.06 side
left hand, n.
 06.15 arm
leg, n.
 06.16 leg
 18.03 (dis)obedience
 34.12 bend
Leg
 23.08 shoemaker
 23.31 shop
legacy, n.
 21.08 legacy
legate, n.
 16.23 ambassador
legative, adj.
 16.23 ambassador
legere, lat. vb.
 24.11 read
 24.13 Latin
legerity, n.
 34.24 nimbleness

legged, adj.
  06.16 leg
legion, n.
  20.05 army · navy
  31.07 count
  31.10 many · few
Legion
  28.05 spirits
legitimate, adj.
  05.03 procreation
  15.05 logic
  21.07 privilegium
legitimate, n.
  05.03 procreation
  21.07 privilegium
legitimation, n.
  05.03 procreation
  21.07 privilegium
Leicester
  36.03 British
Leicestershire
  36.03 British
leisure, n.
  19.17 (un)rest
  32.15 interim
leisurely, adj.
  34.23 fast · slow
leman, n.
  04.10 darling
lemon, n.
  02.13 apple · grape
Lena, Popilius
  36.23 historical: Roman
lend, vb.
  22.02 creditor · debtor
  22.29 give
lender, n.
  22.02 creditor · debtor
lending, n.
  22.02 creditor · debtor
length, n.
  33.33 length
length, vb.
  31.12 increase
lengthen, vb.
  31.12 increase
  33.33 length
lenity, n.
  14.09 lenity
Lent, n.
  32.05 holidays
Lenten, adj.
  22.26 spare
  32.05 holidays
lentus, lat. adj.

24.13 Latin
34.23 fast · slow
Leonardo
  37.06 Romance: male
Leonato
  37.06 Romance: male
leo-natus, lat.
  24.13 Latin
Leonatus → Posthumus
  37.01 classical: male
Leonine
  37.01 classical: male
Leontes
  37.01 classical: male
leopard, n.
  03.16 elephant · lion
leper, n.
  07.11 leprosy
Lepidus
  36.23 historical: Roman
leprosy, n.
  07.11 leprosy
leprous, adj.
  07.11 leprosy
lequel, fr. pron.
  24.14 French
  25.15 pronoun
less, n.
  31.10 many · few
  33.16 size
lessen, vb.
  31.13 decrease
lesser, n.
  31.10 many · few
  33.16 size
lesson, n.
  25.01 education
lesson, vb.
  25.01 education
lest, conj.
  25.12 conjunction
Lestrelles
  36.18 historical: French
let, n.
  19.13 obstruction
let, vb.
  18.10 permission
  22.12 contract
let, vb.
  19.13 obstruction
let-alone, n.
  14.10 moderation
lethargy, n.
  14.42 negligence
lethargy, vb.

14.42 negligence
Lethe
  01.17 river
Lethied, adj.
  01.17 river
  15.07 memory
let out, phr. vb.
  22.12 contract
letter, n.
  24.04 writings
  25.07 alphabet
lettered, adj.
  25.01 education
letters, n.
  25.01 education
letters-patent, n.
  24.04 writings
lettuce, n.
  02.14 cabbage
leur, fr. pron.
  24.14 French
  25.15 pronoun
level, adj.
  31.23 equality
  33.29 straight
level, n.
  23.27 other tools
  31.23 equality
  33.29 straight
level, vb.
  15.16 surmise
  15.28 intention
  31.23 equality
lever, n.
  23.27 other tools
leviathan, n.
  03.32 unicorn
levity, n.
  14.41 levity
levy, n.
  20.08 levy
  22.10 tax
levy, vb.
  20.08 levy
  22.10 tax
lewd, adj.
  14.22 badness
  14.50 sensuality
lewdly, adv.
  14.22 badness
  14.50 sensuality
lewdness, n.
  14.22 badness
  14.50 sensuality
lewdster, n.

loathsomeness, n.
14.53 horror
lob, n.
04.05 rustic
lob, vb.
33.35 hang
lobby, n.
08.17 rooms
local, adj.
33.01 place
lock, n.
06.03 hair
lock, n.
08.12 lock
lock, vb.
08.12 lock
18.06 controlment
33.11 firm
locked-up, adj.
33.11 firm
lockram, n.
10.03 cloth
locust, n.
02.14 cabbage
lodestar, n.
01.03 planet
lodge, n.
08.02 lodge
lodge, vb.
08.04 inhabit
11.03 hit
33.04 set
lodger, n.
08.04 inhabit
lodging, n.
08.01 house
08.02 lodge
Lodovico
37.06 Romance: male
Lodowick (AWW)
37.08 Germanic
Lodowick, Friar (MM)
37.16 assumed names
lofty, adj.
29.10 pre-eminence
33.37 height
lofty-plumed, adj.
03.36 feather
06.18 anatomy compounds
log, n.
02.01 tree · bush · twig
loggat, n.
27.06 games
loggerhead, n.
06.18 anatomy compounds

15.12 foolishness
loggerheaded, adj.
06.18 anatomy compounds
15.12 foolishness
logic, n.
15.05 logic
log-man, n.
16.28 bearer
loin, n.
06.09 belly
loiter, vb.
14.42 negligence
loiterer, n.
14.42 negligence
loll, vb.
33.03 station
33.35 hang
Lombard Street
34.28 road
36.07 London
Lombardy
36.08 Italian
London
36.07 London
London Bridge
35.11 flood-gate
36.07 London
Londoner, n.
36.07 London
London Stone
36.07 London
lone, adj.
04.22 companion
04.24 solitary
loneliness, n.
04.24 solitary
lonely, adj.
04.24 solitary
long → long of
long, adj.
32.16 continuance
33.33 length
long, n.
33.33 length
long, vb.
14.48 desire
long, vb.
29.06 pertain
30.09 (un)aptness
long-boat, n.
35.01 ship
long-continued, adj.
32.16 continuance
long-during, adj.
32.16 continuance

longed-for, adj.
14.48 desire
long-engraffed, adj.
31.16 join
long-experienced, adj.
15.06 knowledge
long-grown, adj.
31.12 increase
long heath, n.
02.02 oak · brier
long-hid, adj.
24.29 conceal
long-imprisoned, adj.
18.06 controlment
longing, n.
14.48 desire
Long Lane
34.28 road
long-legged, adj.
06.16 leg
06.18 anatomy compounds
long-lived, adj.
05.01 life · death
32.16 continuance
long-living, adj.
05.01 life · death
32.16 continuance
longly, adv.
32.16 continuance
long of, adj.
15.29 motive
long-parted, adj.
31.17 separation
long purple, n.
02.09 rose
long-staff, n.
23.26 staff
long sword, n.
20.14 weapon
long-tail, n.
03.02 horse
03.08 dog
long-tongued, adj.
06.18 anatomy compounds
24.20 conversation
Longueville
36.11 French
37.10 Romance: surnames
long-usurped, adj.
11.02 grasp
long-vanished, adj.
33.14 presence · absence
long-winded, adj.
06.19 breath
loo, int.

Lucio (MM)
　37.06 Romance: male
Lucio (ROM)
　37.06 Romance: male
Lucius (ANT)
　36.23 historical: Roman
Lucius (JC)
　37.01 classical: male
Lucius (TIM)
　37.01 classical: male
Lucius (TIM 3.4.2)
　37.01 classical: male
Lucius[1] (TIT)
　37.01 classical: male
Lucius[2] (TIT)
　37.01 classical: male
Lucius, Caius (CYM)
　37.01 classical: male
luck, n.
　32.25 chance
luckily, adv.
　32.25 chance
luckless, adj.
　32.24 mischance
lucky, adj.
　32.25 chance
lucre, n.
　14.43 avarice
　22.28 acquisition
Lucrece
　36.14 pseudohistorical
Lucretia
　36.14 pseudohistorical
Lucretius
　36.14 pseudohistorical
Lucullus
　37.01 classical: male
Lucy, Lady (R3)
　36.17 historical: English
Lucy, William (1H6)
　36.17 historical: English
Ludlow
　36.03 British
Lud's-Town
　36.07 London
luff, vb.
　35.08 navigation
lug, vb.
　11.07 pull
　19.04 vexation
luggage, n.
　22.17 chattel
　31.06 load
Luke
　28.03 Abraham · Paul

28.14 saints
lukewarm, adj.
　01.11 hot · cold
lull, vb.
　19.17 (un)rest
lulla, int.
　25.13 interjection
lullaby, int.
　17.19 salutation
　25.13 interjection
lullaby, n.
　26.10 song
lump, n.
　31.27 heap
lumpish, adj.
　13.08 cheer(less)
Luna
　28.04 Mars · Venus
lunacy, n.
　07.20 madness
lunatic, adj.
　07.20 madness
lunatic, n.
　07.20 madness
lune, n.
　07.20 madness
lung, n.
　06.17 blood · bone
Lupercal, n.
　32.05 holidays
lurch, vb.
　21.12 thievery
　24.29 conceal
　34.03 crawl
lure, n.
　18.17 enticement
　27.15 snare
lure, vb.
　18.17 enticement
lurk, vb.
　24.29 conceal
　34.03 crawl
lurking-place, n.
　24.29 conceal
　33.01 place
luscious, adj.
　12.16 smell
　12.17 taste
lush, adj.
　05.02 fertility · sterility
lust, n.
　13.07 (dis)pleasure
　14.48 desire
　14.50 sensuality
lust, vb.

14.50 sensuality
lust-breathed, adj.
　06.19 breath
　18.18 instigation
lust-dieted, adj.
　09.01 appetite
　14.50 sensuality
lustful, adj.
　14.50 sensuality
lustick, adj.
　13.02 joy
lustihood, n.
　07.02 vigour
　13.08 cheer(less)
lustily, adv.
　13.08 cheer(less)
lustre, n.
　01.12 light · dark
lustrous, adj.
　01.12 light · dark
lust-stained, adj.
　14.49 impurity
lusty, adj.
　07.02 vigour
　13.08 cheer(less)
lute, n.
　26.06 fiddle
lute-case, n.
　08.36 case
　26.06 fiddle
lute-string, n.
　26.06 fiddle
Lutheran, n.
　28.01 religions
lux, lat. n.
　01.12 light · dark
　24.13 Latin
luxurious, adj.
　14.50 sensuality
luxuriously, adv.
　14.50 sensuality
luxury, n.
　14.50 sensuality
lyam, n.
　03.08 dog
Lycaonia
　36.05 Middle / Far Eastern
Lychorida
　37.02 classical: female
Lycurgus
　21.05 law court
　36.22 historical: Greek
Lydia
　36.05 Middle / Far Eastern
Lynn

36.03 British
Lysander
37.01 classical: male
Lysimachus
37.01 classical: male

M

M, n.
25.07 alphabet
Mab
28.05 spirits
Macbeth
36.19 historical: other
names (1)
Maccabaeus → Judas
Maccabaeus
Macdonwald
36.19 historical: other
names (1)
Macduff
36.19 historical: other
names (1)
mace, n.
16.16 heraldry
mace, n.
09.06 salt • sugar
Macedon
36.09 Southern European
Machiavelli
18.16 plot
36.21 cultural: other
names (1)
machination, n.
18.16 plot
machine, n.
23.16 build
mackerel, n.
03.26 fish
Macmorris, Captain
37.05 English: surnames
maculate, adj.
14.49 impurity
maculation, n.
14.49 impurity
mad, adj.
07.20 madness
31.20 excess
mad, n.
07.20 madness
mad, vb.
07.20 madness
madam, n.
04.09 woman
16.21 lord • lady
madame, fr. n.
04.09 woman
16.21 lord • lady

24.14 French
mad-brain, n.
06.18 anatomy compounds
07.20 madness
mad-brained, adj.
06.18 anatomy compounds
07.20 madness
mad-bred, adj.
05.03 procreation
madcap, n.
04.06 madcap
Madeira, n.
09.15 beer • wine
made-up, adj.
29.10 pre-eminence
mad-headed, adj.
06.18 anatomy compounds
07.20 madness
madly, adv.
07.20 madness
madly-used, adj.
18.07 (ab)use
madman, n.
07.20 madness
madness, n.
07.20 madness
madonna, n.
04.09 woman
16.21 lord • lady
madrigal, n.
26.10 song
madwoman, n.
07.20 madness
Maecenas
36.23 historical: Roman
ma foi
24.16 foreign phrases
25.13 interjection
maggot, n.
03.30 vermin • spider
maggot-pie, n.
03.24 crow
magic, adj.
28.28 sorcery
magic, n.
28.28 sorcery
magical, adj.
28.28 sorcery
magician, n.
28.28 sorcery
magistrate, n.
16.05 mayor
magnanimity, n.
14.17 boldness
magnanimous, adj.

14.17 boldness
magnanimous, n.
   14.17 boldness
magnificence, n.
   29.10 pre-eminence
magnificent, adj.
   29.10 pre-eminence
magnifico, n.
   16.21 lord · lady
magnify, vb.
   17.17 praise
   29.10 pre-eminence
magnus, lat. adj.
   24.13 Latin
   33.16 size
Magnus
   28.14 saints
Mahu
   28.05 spirits
maid, n.
   16.27 household servant
   32.10 maidhood
maid-child, n.
   04.15 family
   32.10 maidhood
maiden, n.
   32.10 maidhood
maidenhead, n.
   32.10 maidhood
Maidenhead
   36.03 British
maiden-hearted, adj.
   06.18 anatomy compounds
   14.08 (un)gentle
maidenhood, n.
   32.10 maidhood
maidenly, adj.
   32.10 maidhood
maiden-tongued, adj.
   06.18 anatomy compounds
   24.24 verbal · silent
maiden-widowed, adj.
   04.20 widow · orphan
maidhood, n.
   32.10 maidhood
maid-pale, adj.
   12.05 pale
mail, n.
   20.12 armour
mail, n.
   08.37 bag
mailed, adj.
   10.01 attire
   20.12 armour
maim, n.

07.18 wound
07.21 cripple
maim, vb.
   07.18 wound
   07.21 cripple
main, adj.
   29.11 foremost
main, n.
   01.15 sea
   29.11 foremost
   33.02 region
main, n.
   27.10 sport terms
main, fr. n.
   06.15 arm
   24.14 French
main chance, n.
   27.10 sport terms
main-course, n.
   35.03 sail
Maine
   36.11 French
main flood, n.
   01.14 water
mainly, adv.
   07.02 vigour
   29.11 foremost
mainmast, n.
   35.04 mast
mainour, n.
   21.12 thievery
mainsail, n.
   35.03 sail
maintain, vb.
   15.04 thought
   17.02 support
   22.16 keeping
   24.25 make known
maintenance, n.
   17.02 support
   30.03 behaviour
main-top, n.
   35.04 mast
mais, fr. conj.
   24.14 French
   25.12 conjunction
maison, fr. n.
   08.01 house
   24.14 French
majestas, lat. n.
   16.12 majesty
   24.13 Latin
majestic, adj.
   16.12 majesty
majestical, adj.

16.12 majesty
majestically, adv.
   16.12 majesty
majesty, n.
   16.12 majesty
major, adj.
   29.11 foremost
major, n.
   15.05 logic
majority, n.
   29.10 pre-eminence
make, n.
   04.18 marriage
   04.22 companion
make, vb.
   11.01 do
   15.04 thought
   22.28 acquisition
   31.07 count
   34.10 stir
   34.13 advance
make a mouth, vb.
   24.26 gesture
make a stand, vb.
   19.01 opposition
makeless, adj.
   04.20 widow · orphan
   04.22 companion
make-peace, n.
   20.23 peace
maker, n.
   11.01 do
   28.02 God
make up, phr. vb.
   31.04 full · empty
make water, vb.
   06.20 excrement
making, n.
   29.01 essence · matter
   33.19 shape
mal, fr. adv.
   14.22 badness
   24.14 French
malady, n.
   07.06 sickness
malapert, adj.
   14.26 insolence
Malchus
   36.24 historical: other
          names (2)
Malcolm
   36.19 historical: other
          names (1)
malcontent, adj.
   13.07 (dis)pleasure

minnow, n.
  03.26 fish
Minola, Baptista (SHR)
  37.10 Romance: surnames
Minola, Katherina (SHR)
  37.10 Romance: surnames
minority, n.
  32.09 childhood · youth
Minos
  36.16 classical myth
Minotaur, n.
  03.32 unicorn
minstrel, n.
  26.09 musician
minstrelsy, n.
  26.03 music
  26.09 musician
mint, n.
  22.06 money
mint, n.
  02.16 parsley
minute, n.
  32.02 hour · day · year
minute-jack, n.
  14.05 (in)constancy
minutely, adj.
  32.02 hour · day · year
  32.16 continuance
minute while, n.
  32.15 interim
minx, n.
  04.12 strumpet
mio, it. pron.
  24.15 Italian
  25.15 pronoun
mirable, adj.
  15.09 amazement
miracle, n.
  15.09 amazement
miracle, vb.
  15.09 amazement
miraculous, adj.
  15.09 amazement
Miranda
  37.02 classical: female
mire, n.
  01.24 mud
mire, vb.
  01.19 dip
  14.49 impurity
mirror, n.
  08.26 mirror
  29.08 pattern
mirror, vb.
  08.26 mirror

mirth, n.
  13.02 joy
mirthful, adj.
  13.02 joy
mirth-moving, adj.
  18.18 instigation
miry, adj.
  01.24 mud
misadventure, n.
  32.24 mischance
misadventured, adj.
  32.24 mischance
Misanthropos (TIM)
  37.16 assumed names
misapply, vb.
  18.07 (ab)use
misbecome, vb.
  30.09 (un)aptness
misbecomingly, adv.
  30.09 (un)aptness
misbeget, vb.
  05.03 procreation
misbelieve, vb.
  28.23 irreligion
misbeliever, n.
  28.23 irreligion
miscall, vb.
  36.01 name
miscarry, vb.
  34.09 stray
mischance, n.
  32.24 mischance
mischief, n.
  14.22 badness
  19.04 vexation
  32.24 mischance
mischievous, adj.
  14.22 badness
  19.04 vexation
misconceive, vb.
  15.01 cognition
misconstruction, n.
  15.01 cognition
misconstrue, vb.
  15.01 cognition
miscreant, n.
  04.04 rogue
  28.23 irreligion
miscreate, adj.
  33.19 shape
misdeed, n.
  21.09 crime
misdemean, vb.
  30.03 behaviour
misdemeanour, n.

  30.03 behaviour
misdoubt, n.
  17.15 (mis)trust
misdoubt, vb.
  17.15 (mis)trust
misdread, n.
  14.52 fear
  14.53 horror
Misena
  36.08 Italian
miser, n.
  04.04 rogue
  13.10 sorrow
  14.43 avarice
miserable, adj.
  13.10 sorrow
miserable, n.
  13.10 sorrow
miserably, adv.
  13.10 sorrow
miséricorde, fr. n.
  24.14 French
  28.16 compassion
misery, n.
  13.10 sorrow
misfortune, n.
  32.24 mischance
misgive, vb.
  17.15 (mis)trust
  28.27 prognostication
misgovern, vb.
  16.02 government
misgovernment, n.
  30.03 behaviour
misgraffed, adj.
  31.16 join
misguide, vb.
  17.05 guide
mishap, n.
  32.24 mischance
mishave, vb.
  30.03 behaviour
mishear, vb.
  12.07 hearing
misinterpret, vb.
  15.23 interpretation
mislead, vb.
  17.05 guide
misleader, n.
  17.05 guide
mislike, n.
  14.02 love · hate
mislike, vb.
  13.07 (dis)pleasure
  14.02 love · hate

misorder, vb.
  19.16 disorder
misplace, vb.
  33.04 set
misprision, n.
  15.20 error • truth
misprision, n.
  14.27 contempt
  22.13 value
misprize, vb.
  14.27 contempt
  22.13 value
misprize, vb.
  15.20 error • truth
misproud, adj.
  14.23 pride
misquote, vb.
  15.23 interpretation
misreport, vb.
  19.10 disparagement
  24.25 make known
miss, n.
  21.09 crime
miss, vb.
  22.24 lack
  31.21 omission
mis-shapen, adj.
  33.19 shape
mis-sheathed, adj.
  20.15 sword-hilt
missingly, adv.
  31.21 omission
mission, n.
  34.20 send
missive, n.
  24.23 messenger
mis-speak, vb.
  24.20 conversation
mist, n.
  01.09 cloud • vapour
mist, vb.
  01.09 cloud • vapour
mistake, vb.
  15.20 error • truth
mistaking, n.
  15.20 error • truth
mistemper, vb.
  14.33 curstness
  33.19 shape
misterm, vb.
  36.01 name
mistful, adj.
  01.09 cloud • vapour
misthink, vb.
  15.04 thought

mistletoe, n.
  02.02 oak • brier
mist-like, adj.
  01.09 cloud • vapour
mistreading, n.
  21.09 crime
mistress, n.
  04.09 woman
  16.21 lord • lady
  27.09 ball
  29.11 foremost
mistress-ship, n.
  04.09 woman
  16.21 lord • lady
mistrust, n.
  17.15 (mis)trust
mistrust, vb.
  17.15 (mis)trust
mistrustful, adj.
  17.15 (mis)trust
misty, adj.
  01.09 cloud • vapour
misuse, n.
  18.07 (ab)use
  19.10 disparagement
  21.09 crime
misuse, vb.
  18.07 (ab)use
  18.19 deceit
  19.10 disparagement
mite, n.
  03.31 fly • louse
mite, n.
  31.28 particle
Mithridates
  36.24 historical: other
         names (2)
mitigate, vb.
  19.17 (un)rest
mitigation, n.
  19.17 (un)rest
Mitigation, Madam
  37.15 nicknames
mix, vb.
  31.18 mixture
mixture, n.
  07.24 medicine • cure
  31.18 mixture
mo, adj.
  31.10 many • few
mo, adv.
  31.10 many • few
mo, n.
  31.10 many • few
moan, n.

  13.11 lament
moan, vb.
  13.11 lament
moat, n.
  20.11 moat
moat, vb.
  20.11 moat
  33.10 encompassment
moble, vb.
  10.11 veil • mask
mock, n.
  19.09 mockery
mock, vb.
  18.19 deceit
  19.09 mockery
  26.02 theatre
mockable, adj.
  19.09 mockery
mocker, n.
  18.19 deceit
  19.09 mockery
mockery, n.
  18.19 deceit
  19.09 mockery
mock-water, n.
  24.19 crux
Mock-water, Monsieur
  37.15 nicknames
model, n.
  12.03 semblance
  23.16 build
  29.08 pattern
Modena
  36.08 Italian
moderate, adj.
  14.10 moderation
moderate, vb.
  14.10 moderation
moderately, adv.
  14.10 moderation
moderation, n.
  14.10 moderation
modern, adj.
  16.31 commoner
modest, adj.
  14.10 moderation
modestly, adv.
  14.10 moderation
modesty, n.
  14.10 moderation
modicum, n.
  31.01 quantity
Modo
  28.05 spirits
module, n.

Murellus
   36.23 historical: Roman
murk, adj.
   01.12 light · dark
murk, n.
   01.12 light · dark
murky, adj.
   01.12 light · dark
murmur, n.
   12.12 whisper
   24.22 message
murmur, vb.
   12.12 whisper
   13.07 (dis)pleasure
   24.20 conversation
murmurer, n.
   12.12 whisper
   13.07 (dis)pleasure
murrain, n.
   07.19 glanders
Murray
   36.03 British
Murray, Earl of
   36.17 historical: English
muscatel, n.
   09.15 beer · wine
Muscovite, n.
   36.12 Eastern European
Muscovy
   36.12 Eastern European
muse, n.
   28.04 Mars · Venus
muse, vb.
   13.11 lament
   15.04 thought
   15.08 fantasy
   15.09 amazement
muset, n.
   33.22 hole · trench
mushroom, n.
   02.14 cabbage
music, n.
   26.03 music
   26.09 musician
musical, adj.
   26.03 music
musician, n.
   26.09 musician
musing, n.
   15.04 thought
   15.08 fantasy
musk, n.
   10.22 perfume
musk-cat, n.
   03.07 cat

musket, n.
   20.16 gun
Musko
   36.12 Eastern European
musk-rose, n.
   02.09 rose
muss, n.
   27.06 games
mussel, n.
   03.27 oyster
mussel-shell, n.
   03.39 shell
must, vb.
   17.13 obligation
mustachio, n.
   06.03 hair
mustard, n.
   02.16 parsley
Mustardseed
   28.05 spirits
muster, n.
   20.05 army · navy
   20.08 levy
muster, vb.
   12.02 show
   20.08 levy
muster-book, n.
   20.08 levy
   24.05 list
muster-file, n.
   20.08 levy
   24.05 list
musty, adj.
   07.05 decay
mutability, n.
   14.05 (in)constancy
mutable, adj.
   14.05 (in)constancy
   33.42 change
mutation, n.
   14.05 (in)constancy
   33.42 change
mute, adj.
   24.24 verbal · silent
mute, n.
   24.24 verbal · silent
mutine, n.
   18.21 rebellion
mutine, vb.
   18.21 rebellion
mutineer, n.
   18.21 rebellion
mutiner, n.
   18.21 rebellion
mutinous, adj.

   18.21 rebellion
mutiny, n.
   18.21 rebellion
mutiny, vb.
   18.21 rebellion
Mutius
   37.01 classical: male
mutter, vb.
   24.20 conversation
mutton, n.
   03.05 sheep
   09.10 meat
mutual, adj.
   17.09 agreement
mutuality, n.
   31.16 join
mutually, adv.
   17.09 agreement
   31.16 join
muzzle, n.
   27.19 curb
muzzle, vb.
   27.19 curb
my, pron.
   25.15 pronoun
Myrmidon, n.
   36.15 Trojan myth
myrtle, n.
   02.02 oak · brier
myself, pron.
   25.15 pronoun
mystery, n.
   15.21 (un)clear
   16.14 ceremony
   24.29 conceal
mystery, n.
   23.01 vocation
   30.06 (un)skilful
Mytilene
   36.09 Southern European

N

nag, n.
    03.02 horse
    04.12 strumpet
naiad, n.
    28.06 mermaid
nail, n.
    06.15 arm
    06.16 leg
    23.19 nail
    33.34 span
nail, vb.
    31.16 join
    33.11 firm
naked, adj.
    10.02 naked
nakedness, n.
    10.02 naked
name, n.
    04.14 kindred
    14.16 honour
    36.01 name
name, vb.
    15.17 choice
    36.01 name
nameless, adj.
    36.01 name
namely, adv.
    31.24 namely
Nan (TGV)
    37.04 English: female
Nan (WIV)
    37.04 English: female
nap, n.
    06.21 sleep
nap, n.
    10.03 cloth
nap, vb.
    06.21 sleep
nape, n.
    06.07 neck
napkin, n.
    10.15 handkerchief
Naples
    16.17 king
    36.08 Italian
Naples, King of → Anjou
    36.18 historical: French
napless, adj.
    07.05 decay
    10.03 cloth

Naps, John
    37.13 telling: male
             (mentioned)
Narbon
    36.11 French
Narbon, Gerard de
    37.10 Romance: surnames
narcissus, n.
    02.09 rose
Narcissus
    36.16 classical myth
narine, fr. n.
    06.04 face
    24.14 French
narrow, adj.
    33.36 breadth
narrowly, adv.
    33.36 breadth
narrow-mouthed, adj.
    06.18 anatomy compounds
    33.13 open · close
narrow-prying, adj.
    15.14 examination
Narrow Seas
    01.15 sea
Naso → Ovid
nasty, adj.
    14.49 impurity
Nathaniel (SHR)
    37.03 English: male
Nathaniel, Sir (LLL)
    37.03 English: male
natif, fr. n.
    16.32 townsman
    24.14 French
nation, n.
    16.01 commonwealth
    16.31 commoner
native, adj.
    16.31 commoner
    29.03 (un)natural
native, n.
    32.20 origin
nativity, n.
    05.04 birth
natural, adj.
    04.14 kindred
    15.12 foolishness
    29.03 (un)natural
natural, n.
    15.12 foolishness
naturalize, vb.
    32.26 (un)usual
naturally, adv.
    29.03 (un)natural

nature, n.
    01.01 universe
    07.02 vigour
    29.03 (un)natural
    29.09 rank
    30.02 disposition
naught, n.
    14.22 badness
    14.50 sensuality
naughtily, adv.
    14.22 badness
    14.50 sensuality
naughty, adj.
    14.22 badness
    14.50 sensuality
naughty house, n.
    23.30 brothel
Navarre
    36.09 Southern European
    37.10 Romance: surnames
nave, n.
    06.09 belly
    34.27 waggon
navel, n.
    06.09 belly
    33.07 middle
navigation, n.
    35.08 navigation
navy, n.
    20.05 army · navy
nay, adv.
    19.14 negation
nay, n.
    19.14 negation
nayward, adv.
    19.14 negation
nayword, n.
    24.02 word
    25.06 maxim
Nazarite, n.
    28.01 religions
    36.05 Middle / Far Eastern
ne, adv.
    19.14 negation
ne, lat. adv.
    19.14 negation
    24.13 Latin
ne, lat. part.
    24.13 Latin
néanmoins, fr. adv.
    19.15 however
    24.14 French
Neapolitan, adj.
    36.08 Italian
Neapolitan, n.

24.25 make known
new-sprung, adj.
   32.12 (un)ripe
   34.07 ascend
new-store, vb.
   31.27 heap
newt, n.
   03.28 frog
new-taken, adj.
   11.02 grasp
new-transformed, adj.
   33.42 change
new-trothed, adj.
   04.18 marriage
new-tuned, adj.
   26.03 music
new-year, n.
   32.05 holidays
next, adj.
   33.40 sequence
next, adv.
   33.15 distance
next, n.
   04.14 kindred
   33.40 sequence
next, prep.
   25.14 preposition
nibble, vb.
   03.47 peck · graze
nibbler, n.
   03.47 peck · graze
Nicander
   37.01 classical: male
Nicanor
   37.01 classical: male
nice, adj.
   14.07 humility
   14.21 spruce
   14.50 sensuality
   22.14 trifle
   30.07 preciseness
nice, n.
   30.07 preciseness
nicely, adv.
   30.07 preciseness
niceness, n.
   14.07 humility
   30.07 preciseness
nice-preserved, adj.
   17.06 protection
nicety, n.
   14.07 humility
Nicholas
   28.14 saints
Nicholas (SHR)

37.03 English: male
nick, n.
   32.30 brevity
nick, vb.
   11.05 cut
Nick Bottom
   37.03 English: male
nickname, n.
   36.01 name
nickname, vb.
   36.01 name
niece, n.
   04.15 family
nieve, n.
   06.15 arm
niggard, n.
   14.43 avarice
niggard, vb.
   14.43 avarice
niggardly, adj.
   14.43 avarice
nigh, adj.
   33.15 distance
nigh, adv.
   33.15 distance
nigh, prep.
   25.14 preposition
night, n.
   32.08 morning · night
night, vb.
   01.12 light · dark
night-bird, n.
   03.18 nightingale
night-brawler, n.
   19.11 quarrel
night-cap, n.
   10.10 hat
night-crow, n.
   03.24 crow
night-dog, n.
   03.08 dog
night-fly, n.
   03.31 fly · louse
night-foe, n.
   20.03 foe
night-gown, n.
   10.06 mantle
nightingale, n.
   03.18 nightingale
nightly, adj.
   32.08 morning · night
nightmare, n.
   28.05 spirits
night-oblation, n.
   28.12 sacrament

night-owl, n.
   03.23 owl · bat
night-raven, n.
   03.24 crow
night-rest, n.
   19.17 (un)rest
night-rule, n.
   16.10 edict
night-shriek, n.
   12.11 shout
   12.13 neigh
night-taper, n.
   08.27 torch
night-tripping, adj.
   34.02 leap
night-waking, adj.
   06.21 sleep
night-walking, adj.
   34.01 go
night-wanderer, n.
   34.09 stray
night-wandering, adj.
   34.09 stray
night-watch, n.
   17.08 vigilance
Nightwork, Jane (2H4)
   37.14 telling: female
       (mentioned)
Nightwork, Old (2H4)
   37.13 telling: male
       (mentioned)
Nightwork, Robin (2H4)
   37.13 telling: male
       (mentioned)
nihil, lat. n.
   24.13 Latin
   31.03 all · nothing
Nile
   01.17 river
nill, vb.
   17.10 (un)willingness
Nilus
   01.17 river
nimble, adj.
   34.24 nimbleness
nimble-footed, adj.
   06.18 anatomy compounds
   34.24 nimbleness
nimbleness, n.
   34.24 nimbleness
nimble-pinioned, adj.
   34.26 fly
   06.18 anatomy compounds
nimbly, adv.
   34.24 nimbleness

nonpareil, n.
   29.10 pre-eminence
non-payment, n.
   22.08 payment
non-performance, n.
   11.01 do
non-regardance, n.
   17.01 attention
nonsuit, vb.
   19.06 contradiction
nook, n.
   33.25 corner
nook-shotten, adj.
   33.24 jutting-out
   33.25 corner
noon, n.
   32.08 morning · night
noonday, n.
   32.08 morning · night
noontide, n.
   32.08 morning · night
no point, adv.
   31.03 all · nothing
nor, conj.
   25.12 conjunction
Norbury, John
   36.17 historical: English
Norfolk
   36.03 British
Norfolk → Mowbray, Thomas
   36.17 historical: English
Norfolk → Surrey, Thomas
   36.17 historical: English
Norfolk (3H6)
   36.17 historical: English
Norfolk, Duchess of (H8)
   36.17 historical: English
Norfolk, John, Duke of (R3)
   36.17 historical: English
Norman, adj.
   36.11 French
Norman, n.
   36.11 French
Normandy
   36.11 French
north, adv.
   33.05 north · south
north, n.
   33.05 north · south
Northampton
   36.03 British
Northampton → Stafford (H8)
   36.17 historical: English
Northamptonshire
   36.03 British

north-east, n.
   33.05 north · south
northeast wind, n.
   01.06 wind · storm
northen, adj.
   33.05 north · south
northerly, adj.
   33.05 north · south
northern, adj.
   33.05 north · south
northern star, n.
   01.03 planet
North gate, n.
   08.11 entry
north-north-east, adv.
   33.05 north · south
north-north-west, adv.
   33.05 north · south
north pole, n.
   01.03 planet
north star, n.
   01.03 planet
Northumberland
   36.03 British
Northumberland → Siward
      (MAC)
   36.17 historical: English
Northumberland[1], Earl of (3H6)
   36.17 historical: English
Northumberland[2], Earl of (3H6)
   36.17 historical: English
Northumberland, Earl of (H8)
   36.17 historical: English
Northumberland, Earl of (R2)
   36.17 historical: English
Northumberland, Earl of (R3)
   36.17 historical: English
northward, adj.
   33.05 north · south
northward, adv.
   33.05 north · south
north [wind], n.
   01.06 wind · storm
Norway
   16.17 king
   36.10 Northern European
Norway → Sweno
   36.19 historical: other
      names (1)
Norweyan, adj.
   36.10 Northern European
nos, lat. pron.
   24.13 Latin
   25.15 pronoun
noscere, lat. vb.

   15.06 knowledge
   24.13 Latin
nose, n.
   06.04 face
nose, vb.
   12.16 smell
nosegay, n.
   02.08 flower
nose-herb, n.
   02.08 flower
noseless, adj.
   06.04 face
nose-painting, n.
   26.15 painting
noster, lat. pron.
   24.13 Latin
   25.15 pronoun
nostril, n.
   06.04 face
nostro, it. pron.
   24.15 Italian
   25.15 pronoun
not, adv.
   19.14 negation
notable, adj.
   29.10 pre-eminence
notably, adv.
   29.10 pre-eminence
notary, n.
   21.05 law court
notch, vb.
   11.05 cut
note, n.
   15.06 knowledge
   15.07 memory
   17.01 attention
   19.08 reproach
   22.09 account
   24.04 writings
   24.27 sign
   26.04 gamut
   29.10 pre-eminence
note, vb.
   17.01 attention
   19.08 reproach
   24.27 sign
   26.04 gamut
note-book, n.
   24.10 note-book
notedly, adv.
   31.37 single
noteworthy, adj.
   17.01 attention
   29.10 pre-eminence
not-fearing, adj.

O

occupare, lat. vb.
    11.02 grasp
    24.13 Latin
occupation, n.
    23.01 vocation
    23.15 work
occupy, vb.
    11.01 do
    14.51 fornication
occurrence, n.
    32.23 occurrence
occurrent, n.
    32.23 occurrence
ocean, n.
    01.15 sea
Octavia
    36.23 historical: Roman
Octavius, Marcus
    36.23 historical: Roman
ocular, adj.
    12.01 sight
odd, adj.
    15.08 fantasy
    19.11 quarrel
    31.15 moreover
    31.25 difference
    31.37 single
    32.26 (un)usual
odd-conceited, adj.
    15.02 notion
odd-even, adj.
    32.08 morning · night
oddly, adv.
    31.25 difference
    31.37 single
odd number, n.
    31.07 count
odds, n.
    19.11 quarrel
    20.01 combat
    22.34 (dis)advantage
    27.10 sport terms
    31.25 difference
ode, n.
    26.12 poem
o Dieu vivant
    28.25 oaths
odious, adj.
    14.02 love · hate
odious (MND 3.1.82), adj.
    24.18 malapropism
odoriferous, adj.
    12.16 smell
odorous, adj.
    12.16 smell

odorous (ADO 3.5.16), adj.
    24.18 malapropism
odour, n.
    12.16 smell
ods, int.
    25.13 interjection
'od's heartlings
    28.25 oaths
'od's lifelings
    28.25 oaths
'od's nouns
    28.25 oaths
'od's pittikins
    28.25 oaths
'od's plessed will
    28.25 oaths
oeillade, n.
    12.01 sight
oeuvre, fr. n.
    23.15 work
    24.14 French
of, prep.
    25.14 preposition
of all hands, adv.
    15.22 (un)certainty
of all loves, adv.
    18.11 request
off, adv.
    33.15 distance
off, prep.
    25.14 preposition
offal, n.
    06.17 blood · bone
    31.34 dreg
off and on, adv.
    34.10 stir
off-cap, vb.
    10.10 hat
    28.15 reverence
offence, n.
    19.04 vexation
    21.09 crime
offenceful, adj.
    19.04 vexation
    21.09 crime
offenceless, adj.
    19.04 vexation
offend, vb.
    19.04 vexation
    21.09 crime
offender, n.
    19.04 vexation
    21.09 crime
offendere → se offendere
offendress, n.

    19.04 vexation
    21.09 crime
offensive, adj.
    19.04 vexation
offer, n.
    22.29 give
    22.30 offer
offer, vb.
    15.13 attempt
    22.29 give
    22.30 offer
offerer, n.
    22.29 give
offering, n.
    28.12 sacrament
office, n.
    08.17 rooms
    11.01 do
    16.02 government
    17.13 obligation
office, vb.
    11.01 do
    16.02 government
office-badge, n.
    24.27 sign
officer, n.
    16.05 mayor
    16.26 attendant
    20.06 officer
officer-at-arms, n.
    16.16 heraldry
    20.06 officer
official, adj.
    11.01 do
officious, adj.
    14.37 vehemence
    18.03 (dis)obedience
of force, adv.
    22.25 necessity
offspring, n.
    04.14 kindred
    04.15 family
of note, adv.
    29.10 pre-eminence
oft, adj.
    32.28 often · seldom
oft, adv.
    32.28 often · seldom
often, adj.
    32.28 often · seldom
often, adv.
    32.28 often · seldom
oftentimes, adv.
    32.28 often · seldom
of (to the) vantage, adv.

outfly, vb.
    34.26 fly
out-frown, vb.
    24.26 gesture
outgo, vb.
    34.15 overtake
outgrow, vb.
    31.12 increase
out-Herod, vb.
    14.25 braggardism
    26.02 theatre
    31.20 excess
out-jest, vb.
    04.06 madcap
outlaw, n.
    21.01 (un)justice
    34.20 send
outlaw, vb.
    21.01 (un)justice
    34.20 send
outlawry, n.
    21.01 (un)justice
outlive, vb.
    05.01 life · death
outlook, vb.
    12.01 sight
outlustre, vb.
    01.12 light · dark
out-night, vb.
    32.08 morning · night
out of all nick, adv.
    29.12 extreme
out of door, adv.
    33.08 inside · outside
out of guard, adv.
    27.03 stoccado
out of hand, adv.
    32.30 brevity
out of heart, adv.
    13.08 cheer(less)
out of question, adv.
    15.22 (un)certainty
out on (upon), int.
    25.13 interjection
out-paramour, vb.
    14.51 fornication
outpeer, vb.
    29.10 pre-eminence
outpray, vb.
    28.11 prayer
out-prize, vb.
    22.13 value
outrage, n.
    14.27 contempt
    14.29 anger

outrageous, adj.
    14.31 cruelty
    31.20 excess
outride, vb.
    34.15 overtake
outright, adv.
    31.03 all · nothing
    32.30 brevity
outroar, vb.
    12.11 shout
outrun, vb.
    34.01 go
outscold, vb.
    19.11 quarrel
out-scorn, vb.
    14.27 contempt
outsell, vb.
    22.13 value
outshine, vb.
    01.12 light · dark
outside, adv.
    33.08 inside · outside
outside, n.
    06.05 lineament
    33.08 inside · outside
outsleep, vb.
    06.21 sleep
outspeak, vb.
    24.20 conversation
    24.25 make known
outsport, vb.
    27.01 pastime
outstand, vb.
    32.17 sojourn
outstare, vb.
    12.01 sight
outstay, vb.
    32.17 sojourn
outstretch, vb.
    33.32 spread
outstrike, vb.
    11.03 hit
outstrip, vb.
    34.15 overtake
outswear, vb.
    28.25 oaths
outsweeten, vb.
    12.17 taste
outswell, vb.
    31.14 swell
out-talk, vb.
    24.20 conversation
out-tongue, vb.
    24.20 conversation
outvenom, vb.

    07.25 poison
outvie, vb.
    19.02 rival
out-villain, vb.
    14.22 badness
out-voice, vb.
    24.20 conversation
out-wall, n.
    08.08 wall
    33.08 inside · outside
outward, adj.
    33.08 inside · outside
outward, adv.
    33.08 inside · outside
outward, n.
    06.05 lineament
    33.08 inside · outside
outwardly, adv.
    33.08 inside · outside
outwards, adv.
    33.08 inside · outside
outward-sainted, adj.
    28.13 holiness
outwear, vb.
    07.05 decay
    32.17 sojourn
outweigh, vb.
    31.39 weight
outwork, vb.
    23.15 work
outworth, vb.
    22.13 value
ouzel, n.
    03.18 nightingale
ouzel cock, n.
    03.18 nightingale
oven, n.
    08.18 hearth
over, adv.
    25.10 adverb
    31.15 moreover
    32.16 continuance
    33.15 distance
over, prep.
    25.14 preposition
over and above, adv.
    25.10 adverb
    31.12 increase
    31.15 moreover
over and over, adv.
    32.16 continuance
overawe, vb.
    18.01 subjection
    18.04 supremacy
overbear, vb.

Oxford (R3)
   36.17 historical: English
Oxfordshire
   36.03 British
ox-head, n.
   03.33 beak · horn
oxlip, n.
   02.09 rose
oyez, n.
   12.11 shout
   24.22 message
oyster, n.
   03.27 oyster
oyster-wench, n.
   23.03 victualler

P

P, n.
   25.07 alphabet
pace, n.
   33.34 span
   34.01 go
pace, vb.
   18.09 tame
   34.01 go
Pace, Doctor
   36.17 historical: English
pacify, vb.
   19.17 (un)rest
pack, n.
   31.35 bunch
   31.36 multitude
pack, n.
   18.15 conspiracy
pack, vb.
   31.06 load
   31.35 bunch
   34.06 hence-going
pack, vb.
   18.15 conspiracy
packet, n.
   31.35 bunch
pack-horse, n.
   03.02 horse
packing, n.
   18.15 conspiracy
pack-saddle, n.
   27.18 saddle
packthread, n.
   23.21 rope
Pacorus
   36.24 historical: other
            names (2)
paction, n.
   22.12 contract
paddle, vb.
   12.15 touch
paddock, n.
   03.28 frog
Paddock
   28.05 spirits
Padua
   36.08 Italian
paedagogus, lat. n.
   24.13 Latin
   25.02 teacher
paene, lat. adv.

   24.13 Latin
   31.38 almost
pagan, adj.
   28.22 pagan
pagan, n.
   04.12 strumpet
   28.22 pagan
page, n.
   16.26 attendant
page, vb.
   16.26 attendant
Page, Anne (WIV)
   37.05 English: surnames
Page, George (WIV)
   37.05 English: surnames
Page, Mistress (WIV)
   37.05 English: surnames
Page, William (WIV)
   37.05 English: surnames
pageant, n.
   26.02 theatre
pageant, vb.
   26.02 theatre
pageantry, n.
   26.02 theatre
pah, int.
   25.13 interjection
pail, n.
   08.35 tub
pailful, n.
   31.01 quantity
pain, n.
   07.17 ache
   19.04 vexation
   21.13 punishment
pain, vb.
   07.17 ache
   19.04 vexation
painful, adj.
   07.17 ache
   19.04 vexation
painfully, adv.
   07.17 ache
   19.04 vexation
paint, vb.
   12.04 colour
   18.19 deceit
   26.15 painting
painted cloth, n.
   08.23 curtain
painter, n.
   26.15 painting
painting, n.
   26.15 painting
pair, n.

11.05 cut
34.05 enter
penetrative, adj.
11.05 cut
penitence, n.
28.17 penitence
penitent, adj.
28.17 penitence
penitent, n.
28.17 penitence
penitential, adj.
28.17 penitence
penitently, adv.
28.17 penitence
Penker, Friar
36.17 historical: English
penknife, n.
23.24 knife
penner, n.
08.36 case
pennon, n.
20.18 flag
penny, n.
22.06 money
pennyworth, n.
22.13 value
31.07 count
penser, fr. vb.
15.04 thought
24.14 French
pension, n.
22.08 payment
pensioner, n.
16.25 usher
pensive, adj.
13.10 sorrow
15.04 thought
pensive, vb.
13.10 sorrow
pensiveness, n.
13.10 sorrow
Pentapolis
36.04 African
Pentecost, n.
32.05 holidays
Penthesilea
36.16 classical myth
penthouse, n.
08.02 lodge
penthouse lid, n.
06.04 face
penthouse-like, adj.
08.02 lodge
pent-up, adj.
18.06 controlment

penurious, adj.
22.19 rich • poor
penury, n.
22.19 rich • poor
people, n.
16.31 commoner
people, vb.
08.04 inhabit
Pepin, King
36.18 historical: French
pepper, n.
02.16 parsley
pepper, vb.
11.03 hit
pepper-box, n.
08.36 case
peppercorn, n.
02.16 parsley
pepper-gingerbread, n.
09.13 bread • cake
per, lat. prep.
24.13 Latin
25.14 preposition
per, it. prep.
24.15 Italian
25.14 preposition
peradventure, adv.
15.22 (un)certainty
32.25 chance
perceive, vb.
12.01 sight
15.01 cognition
22.28 acquisition
perch, n.
03.46 nest • kennel
33.34 span
perch, vb.
33.03 station
perchance, adv.
15.22 (un)certainty
32.25 chance
percussion, n.
12.10 din
Percy, Earl Northumberland
(R2)
36.17 historical: English
Percy, Henry (R2)
36.17 historical: English
Percy, Lady (1H4)
36.17 historical: English
perdie
28.25 oaths
Perdita
37.12 telling: female (DP)
perdition, n.

20.21 destruction
perdonare, it. vb.
14.09 lenity
24.15 Italian
perdre, fr. vb.
22.22 loss
24.14 French
perdu, n.
20.07 soldier
perdurable, adj.
32.16 continuance
perdurably, adv.
32.16 continuance
perdy
28.25 oaths
père, fr. n.
04.15 family
24.14 French
peregrinate, adj.
04.23 stranger
34.16 travel
peremptorily, adv.
15.27 resolution
31.03 all • nothing
peremptory, adj.
15.27 resolution
31.03 all • nothing
perfect, adj.
07.01 health
13.07 (dis)pleasure
15.22 (un)certainty
29.10 pre-eminence
31.03 all • nothing
32.12 (un)ripe
perfect, vb.
11.01 do
24.25 make known
perfection, n.
11.01 do
29.10 pre-eminence
perfectly, adv.
31.03 all • nothing
perfectness, n.
30.06 (un)skilful
32.12 (un)ripe
perfidious, adj.
17.14 (dis)loyalty
perfidiously, adv.
17.14 (dis)loyalty
perforce, adv.
14.31 cruelty
22.25 necessity
perform, vb.
11.01 do
performance, n.

15.14 examination
24.11 read
perverse, adj.
14.36 stubbornness
perversely, adv.
14.36 stubbornness
perverseness, n.
14.36 stubbornness
pervert, vb.
33.42 change
34.12 bend
pester, vb.
19.04 vexation
19.13 obstruction
31.36 multitude
pestiferous, adj.
07.07 plague
pestilence, n.
07.07 plague
pestilent, adj.
07.07 plague
petard, n.
20.16 gun
Peter
28.03 Abraham · Paul
Peter (JN)
37.03 English: male
Peter (ROM)
37.03 English: male
Peter (SHR)
37.03 English: male
Peter, Friar (MM)
37.03 English: male
Peter Bullcalf (2H4)
37.03 English: male
Peter Quince (MND)
37.03 English: male
Peter Simple (WIV)
37.03 English: male
Peter Turf (SHR)
37.03 English: male
petit, fr. adj.
24.14 French
33.16 size
petition, n.
18.11 request
28.11 prayer
petition, vb.
18.11 request
petitionary, adj.
18.11 request
petitioner, n.
18.11 request
Peto
37.05 English: surnames

Petrarch
26.14 poet
36.21 cultural: other
names (1)
Petruchio (ROM)
37.06 Romance: male
Petruchio (SHR)
37.06 Romance: male
petticoat, n.
10.07 petticoat
pettiness, n.
22.14 trifle
pettish, adj.
14.39 rashness
pettitoes, n.
09.10 meat
petty, adj.
22.14 trifle
petty officer, n.
20.06 officer
petty-ward, adv.
01.28 wood · field · garden
peu, fr. n.
24.14 French
31.10 many · few
pew, n.
08.21 chair
pew-fellow, n.
04.22 companion
28.08 worshipper
pewter, n.
01.26 metal
pewterer, n.
23.04 goldsmith
Phaeton
36.16 classical myth
phantasime, n.
04.06 madcap
phantasma, n.
15.08 fantasy
28.05 spirits
Pharamond
36.14 pseudohistorical
Pharaoh, n.
16.17 king
Pharsalia
36.09 Southern European
pheasant, n.
03.20 pheasant
pheasant cock, n.
03.20 pheasant
Pheazar, n.
16.17 king
Philadelphos

36.24 historical: other
names (2)
Philario
37.06 Romance: male
Philarmonus
37.01 classical: male
Philemon (ADO)
36.16 classical myth
Philemon (PER)
37.01 classical: male
Philip
03.18 nightingale
28.14 saints
Philip (SHR)
37.03 English: male
Philip and Jacob
32.05 holidays
Philip [II]
36.18 historical: French
Philip of Macedon (H5)
36.22 historical: Greek
Philippan, adj.
20.14 weapon
36.09 Southern European
Philippe
36.17 historical: English
Philippi
36.09 Southern European
Phillida
37.02 classical: female
Philomela
03.18 nightingale
36.16 classical myth
philosopher, n.
25.05 science · philosophy
philosopher's stone, n.
25.05 science · philosophy
philosophical, adj.
25.05 science · philosophy
philosophy, n.
25.05 science · philosophy
Philostrate
37.01 classical: male
Philoten
37.02 classical: female
Philotus
37.01 classical: male
phlegmatic, adj.
13.08 cheer(less)
Phoebe, vb.
37.02 classical: female
Phoebe
28.04 Mars · Venus
37.02 classical: female
Phoebus

28.04   Mars · Venus
Phoenicia
   36.05   Middle / Far Eastern
Phoenician, n.
   36.05   Middle / Far Eastern
Phoenix
   03.32   unicorn
   23.28   tavern
   35.01   ship
Phoenix-like, adj.
   03.32   unicorn
phrase, n.
   24.02   word
   25.09   rhetoric
phrase, vb.
   24.25   make known
phraseless, adj.
   24.02   word
   24.24   verbal · silent
Phrygia
   36.05   Middle / Far Eastern
Phrygian, adj.
   36.05   Middle / Far Eastern
Phrynia
   37.02   classical: female
phthisic, n.
   07.12   rheum
physic, n.
   07.24   medicine · cure
physic, vb.
   07.24   medicine · cure
physical, adj.
   07.24   medicine · cure
physician, n.
   07.22   physician
physiognomy, n.
   06.05   lineament
pia mater
   06.17   blood · bone
   24.16   foreign phrases
Picardy
   36.11   French
pick, vb.
   11.05   cut
   11.07   pull
   14.21   spruce
   15.17   choice
   21.12   thievery
pick, vb.
   34.18   toss
pickaxe, n.
   23.27   other tools
Pickbone, Francis
   37.13   telling: male
          (mentioned)

picker, n.
   06.15   arm
   21.12   thievery
pickle, n.
   09.06   salt · sugar
pickle-herring, n.
   09.09   pickle-herring
picklock, n.
   08.12   lock
pickpurse, n.
   21.12   thievery
pickthank, n.
   18.20   flattery
Pickt-hatch
   36.07   London
picture, n.
   12.03   semblance
   26.15   painting
picture, vb.
   26.15   painting
picture-like, adj.
   26.15   painting
pie, n.
   16.10   edict
pie, n.
   03.24   crow
pie, n.
   09.13   bread · cake
piece, n.
   20.14   weapon
   22.06   money
   29.04   thing
   31.26   portion
   31.33   fragment
piece, vb.
   17.07   amendment
   31.12   increase
   31.16   join
Pie Corner
   34.28   road
   36.07   London
pied, adj.
   12.04   colour
   12.06   spotted
pied, fr. n.
   06.16   leg
   24.14   French
piedness, n.
   12.04   colour
   12.06   spotted
pier, n.
   35.10   harbour
pierce, vb.
   11.05   cut
Pierce of Exton

36.17   historical: English
piety, n.
   28.13   holiness
piety (ADO 4.2.78), n.
   24.18   malapropism
pig, n.
   03.06   swine
pigeon, n.
   03.20   pheasant
pigeon-egg, n.
   03.44   egg
pigeon-livered, adj.
   06.18   anatomy compounds
   07.04   weakness
pig-like, adj.
   03.06   swine
pig-nut, n.
   02.11   walnut
Pigrogromitus
   37.09   other names
pike, n.
   20.10   fortification
   20.14   weapon
   23.12   husbandry
   23.19   nail
pike, n.
   03.26   fish
Pilate
   28.03   Abraham · Paul
Pilch
   37.13   telling: male
          (mentioned)
pilchard, n.
   03.26   fish
pilcher, n.
   20.15   sword-hilt
pile, n.
   31.27   heap
pile, n.
   10.03   cloth
pile, vb.
   31.27   heap
pile, vb.
   10.03   cloth
pilfer, vb.
   21.12   thievery
pilfering, n.
   21.12   thievery
pilgrim, n.
   28.08   worshipper
pilgrimage, n.
   28.08   worshipper
   34.16   travel
pill, n.
   07.24   medicine · cure

plus, fr. adv.
   24.14 French
   31.10 many · few
Pluto
   28.04 Mars · Venus
Plutus
   28.04 Mars · Venus
ply, vb.
   18.07 (ab)use
   18.18 instigation
Po
   01.17 river
poach, vb.
   11.05 cut
pocas palabras
   24.16 foreign phrases
pocket, n.
   08.37 bag
pocket, vb.
   08.37 bag
   18.01 subjection
   22.27 acceptance
   24.29 conceal
pocky, adj.
   07.13 pox
poem, n.
   26.12 poem
poesy, n.
   26.12 poem
poet, n.
   26.14 poet
poetical, adj.
   26.12 poem
poetry, n.
   26.12 poem
Poins, Ned
   37.05 English: surnames
point → ne point
point, n.
   10.16 tape
   15.32 circumstance
   20.14 weapon
   20.15 sword-hilt
   25.08 grammar
   26.03 music
   27.18 saddle
   31.28 particle
   32.15 interim
   33.37 height
   35.08 navigation
point, vb.
   11.05 cut
   15.28 intention
   33.26 sharp · dull
point, vb.

   15.27 resolution
point-blank, adj.
   27.04 archery
   33.29 straight
point-blank, n.
   27.04 archery
point-device, adj.
   30.07 preciseness
pointing-stock, n.
   19.09 mockery
poise, n.
   31.39 weight
poise, vb.
   31.23 equality
   31.39 weight
poison, n.
   07.25 poison
poison, vb.
   07.25 poison
poisoner, n.
   21.10 murder
poisonous, adj.
   07.25 poison
Poitiers
   36.11 French
poke, n.
   08.37 bag
poking-stick, n.
   23.05 clothier
Polack, adj.
   36.12 Eastern European
Polack, n.
   36.12 Eastern European
Poland
   36.12 Eastern European
pole, n.
   23.26 staff
pole, n.
   01.03 planet
Pole, n.
   36.12 Eastern European
Pole, The
   16.17 king
Pole, William
   36.17 historical: English
pole-axe, n.
   20.14 weapon
polecat, n.
   03.10 fox
   04.12 strumpet
pole-clipped, adj.
   33.10 encompassment
Polemon
   36.24 historical: other
          names (2)

policy, n.
   16.02 government
   18.16 plot
polish, vb.
   01.12 light · dark
   10.18 ornament
   11.09 rub
politic, adj.
   15.11 (in)discretion
   16.02 government
politician, n.
   16.03 statesman
   18.16 plot
politicly, adv.
   15.11 (in)discretion
   16.02 government
Polixenes (TRO)
   36.15 Trojan myth
Polixenes (WT)
   37.01 classical: male
poll, n.
   06.02 head
   20.08 levy

   31.07 count
poll, vb.
   11.11 strip
pollute, vb.
   14.49 impurity
pollution, n.
   14.49 impurity
pollution (LLL 4.2.46), n.
   24.18 malapropism
Polonius
   37.01 classical: male
poltroon, n.
   14.52 fear
polus, lat. n.
   01.02 sky
   01.03 planet
   24.13 Latin
Polydamas
   36.15 Trojan myth
Polydore (CYM)
   37.16 assumed names
Polyxena
   36.15 Trojan myth
pomander, n.
   10.22 perfume
pomegranate, n.
   02.02 oak · brier
   02.13 apple · grape
Pomegranate
   08.17 rooms
pomewater, n.

17.04 assistance
prompt, adj.
    30.08 readiness
    34.24 nimbleness
prompt, vb.
    18.18 instigation
    30.08 readiness
promptement, fr. adv.
    24.14 French
    30.08 readiness
    34.24 nimbleness
prompter, n.
    26.02 theatre
prompture, n.
    18.18 instigation
prone, adj.
    30.02 disposition
prononcer, fr. vb.
    24.14 French
    24.20 conversation
pronoun, n.
    25.08 grammar
pronounce, vb.
    24.20 conversation
    24.25 make known
proof, adj.
    17.06 protection
proof, n.
    15.14 examination
    20.12 armour
    21.06 testimony
prop, n.
    17.02 support
prop, vb.
    17.02 support
propagate, vb.
    05.03 procreation
    31.12 increase
propagation, n.
    05.03 procreation
    31.12 increase
propend, vb.
    30.02 disposition
propension, n.
    30.02 disposition
proper, adj.
    04.13 somebody
    14.20 beauty
    30.09 (un)aptness
    31.37 single
proper-false, n.
    18.19 deceit
properly, adv.
    04.13 somebody
    30.09 (un)aptness

property, n.
    22.15 possession
    23.17 tool
    30.02 disposition
    31.37 single
property, vb.
    22.15 possession
    30.02 disposition
    30.09 (un)aptness
prophecy, n.
    28.27 prognostication
prophesier, n.
    28.27 prognostication
prophesy, vb.
    28.27 prognostication
prophet, n.
    28.27 prognostication
prophetess, n.
    28.27 prognostication
prophetic, adj.
    28.27 prognostication
prophetically, adv.
    28.27 prognostication
prophet-like, adj.
    28.27 prognostication
propinquity, n.
    04.14 kindred
    33.15 distance
Propontic [Sea]
    01.15 sea
proportion, n.
    17.09 agreement
    29.07 proportion
    31.07 count
    31.26 portion
    33.16 size
    33.19 shape
proportion, vb.
    17.09 agreement
    29.07 proportion
proportionable, adj.
    17.09 agreement
    29.07 proportion
propose, n.
    15.31 affair
    24.25 make known
propose, vb.
    22.30 offer
    24.25 make known
proposer, n.
    22.30 offer
proposition, n.
    15.05 logic
    22.30 offer
propound, vb.

    22.30 offer
propre, fr. adj.
    04.13 somebody
    24.14 French
propriety, n.
    04.13 somebody
propugnation, n.
    17.06 protection
prorogue, vb.
    32.21 delay
proscription, n.
    18.10 permission
prose, n.
    24.04 writings
prosecute, vb.
    21.04 accusation
    33.40 sequence
prosecution, n.
    33.40 sequence
proselyte, n.
    28.08 worshipper
Proserpina
    28.04 Mars · Venus
prospect, n.
    12.02 show
    12.03 semblance
prosper, vb.
    22.20 prosperity
prosperity, n.
    22.20 prosperity
Prospero
    37.06 Romance: male
prosperous, adj.
    22.20 prosperity
    22.34 (dis)advantage
prosperously, adv.
    22.20 prosperity
prostitute, vb.
    04.12 strumpet
prostrate, adj.
    18.01 subjection
    33.03 station
protect, vb.
    16.20 deputy
    17.06 protection
protection, n.
    17.06 protection
protector, n.
    16.11 ruler
    16.20 deputy
    17.06 protection
protectorship, n.
    16.11 ruler
    16.20 deputy
protectress, n.

Q

quadrangle, n.
  16.15 castle
  33.21 square
quaff, vb.
  09.03 eat · drink
quagmire, n.
  01.21 fen · shore
quail, n.
  03.20 pheasant
  04.12 strumpet
quail, vb.
  07.04 weakness
  20.22 victory · defeat
quaint, adj.
  14.20 beauty
  30.06 (un)skilful
  30.07 preciseness
quaintly, adv.
  30.06 (un)skilful
  30.07 preciseness
quake, vb.
  34.19 shake
qualification, n.
  30.02 disposition
  31.13 decrease
qualify, vb.
  14.10 moderation
  30.02 disposition
  30.09 (un)aptness
  31.13 decrease
qualité, fr. n.
  24.14 French
  30.02 disposition
quality, n.
  23.01 vocation
  29.09 rank
  30.01 manner
  30.02 disposition
qualm, n.
  07.14 queasiness
qualmish, adj.
  07.14 queasiness
quam, lat. adv.
  24.13 Latin
  25.10 adverb
quand, fr. conj.
  24.14 French
  25.12 conjunction
quando, lat. conj.
  24.13 Latin

  25.12 conjunction
quantity, n.
  29.07 proportion
  31.01 quantity
quare, lat. adv.
  15.29 motive
  24.13 Latin
quarrel, n.
  19.07 debate
  19.11 quarrel
quarrel, vb.
  19.11 quarrel
quarreller, n.
  19.11 quarrel
quarrellous, adj.
  19.11 quarrel
quarrelsome, adj.
  19.11 quarrel
quarry, n.
  31.27 heap
quarry, n.
  01.29 cave
quart, n.
  08.31 cup
  31.40 pint
quarter, n.
  20.09 camp
  30.03 behaviour
  32.14 period
  33.02 region
quarter, vb.
  08.04 inhabit
  11.05 cut
  16.16 heraldry
  31.07 count
quart pot, n.
  08.32 pot
quasi, adv.
  31.24 namely
quat, n.
  07.16 sore
quatch-buttock, n.
  06.12 buttock
  06.18 anatomy compounds
que, lat. conj.
  24.13 Latin
  25.12 conjunction
que, fr. conj.
  24.14 French
  25.12 conjunction
que, fr. pron.
  24.14 French
  25.15 pronoun
quean, n.
  04.12 strumpet

queasiness, n.
  07.14 queasiness
queasy, adj.
  07.14 queasiness
  30.07 preciseness
queen, n.
  16.18 queen
queen, vb.
  16.11 ruler
queen-mother, n.
  16.18 queen
quell, n.
  21.10 murder
quell, vb.
  21.10 murder
quench, vb.
  18.08 stifle
  31.22 cancel
quenchless, adj.
  31.22 cancel
quern, n.
  23.32 mill
quest, n.
  15.15 search
  21.05 law court
  24.21 question · answer
  33.40 sequence
quest, vb.
  12.13 neigh
questant, n.
  15.15 search
question, n.
  15.31 affair
  19.07 debate
  24.14 French
  24.21 question · answer
question, vb.
  15.14 examination
  19.07 debate
  24.21 question · answer
questionable, adj.
  24.21 question · answer
questionless, adj.
  15.22 (un)certainty
questrist, n.
  15.15 search
Queubus
  37.09 other names
qui, lat. pron.
  24.13 Latin
  25.15 pronoun
qui, fr. pron.
  24.14 French
  25.15 pronoun
quick, adj.

R

R, n.
    12.14 bow-wow
    25.07 alphabet
rabbit, n.
    03.11 rat
rabbit-sucker, n.
    03.11 rat
rabble, n.
    16.31 commoner
    31.36 multitude
rabblement, n.
    16.31 commoner
race, n.
    27.06 games
race, n.
    04.14 kindred
    30.02 disposition
race, n.
    02.06 bud · root
    02.16 parsley
rack, n.
    01.09 cloud · vapour
rack, n.
    21.15 manacle
rack, vb.
    11.06 push
rack, vb.
    21.13 punishment
    33.32 spread
racker, n.
    21.13 punishment
racket, n.
    27.09 ball
radiance, n.
    01.12 light · dark
radiant, adj.
    01.12 light · dark
radish, n.
    02.14 cabbage
raft, n.
    35.01 ship
rag, n.
    04.04 rogue
    10.01 attire
    31.32 tatter
ragamuffin, n.
    04.04 rogue
rage, n.
    07.20 madness
    14.29 anger

    14.30 savageness
    14.37 vehemence
rage, vb.
    14.29 anger
    14.37 vehemence
    14.50 sensuality
ragged, adj.
    31.32 tatter
raggedness, n.
    31.32 tatter
Ragozine
    37.10 Romance: surnames
rah tah tah, int.
    25.13 interjection
rail, n.
    08.19 plank
rail, vb.
    19.08 reproach
railer, n.
    19.08 reproach
raiment, n.
    10.01 attire
rain, n.
    01.08 rain · snow
rain, vb.
    01.08 rain · snow
rainbow, n.
    01.08 rain · snow
Rainold → Cobham, Rainold
rain-water, n.
    01.08 rain · snow
rainy, adj.
    01.08 rain · snow
raise, vb.
    18.18 instigation
    20.08 levy
    23.16 build
    31.12 increase
    34.17 raise
raisins of the sun, n.
    02.13 apple · grape
rake, n.
    23.12 husbandry
rake, vb.
    11.10 scratch
rake up, phr. vb.
    05.06 burial
Ralph (1H4)
    37.03 English: male
Ralph (SHR)
    37.03 English: male
Ralph Mouldy (2H4)
    37.03 English: male
ram, n.
    03.05 sheep

    21.16 cudgel
ram, vb.
    11.06 push
    19.13 obstruction
Ram
    01.04 zodiac
Rambures
    36.18 historical: French
ramp, n.
    34.02 leap
ramp, vb.
    14.38 uncontrolled
    34.02 leap
rampallion, n.
    04.04 rogue
    04.12 strumpet
rampant, adj.
    34.02 leap
rampire, vb.
    20.10 fortification
Ramston, John
    36.17 historical: English
ram-tender, n.
    23.13 farmer · herdsman
rancorous, adj.
    14.22 badness
rancour, n.
    14.02 love · hate
    14.22 badness
random, n.
    14.42 negligence
range, n.
    33.39 row
range, vb.
    33.39 row
    34.09 stray
ranger, n.
    27.13 forester
rank, adj.
    07.05 decay
    14.40 rudeness
    14.50 sensuality
    31.14 swell
    31.20 excess
rank, n.
    29.09 rank
    33.39 row
rank, vb.
    33.39 row
rankle, vb.
    07.16 sore
rankly, adv.
    07.05 decay
    14.40 rudeness
rankness, n.

ringleader, n.
 17.05 guide
 20.06 officer
ringlet, n.
 26.11 dance
 33.20 round
ring time, n.
 04.18 marriage
 32.03 times
Ringwood
 03.08 dog
rinse, vb.
 14.18 purity
riot, n.
 14.50 sensuality
 19.16 disorder
riot, vb.
 14.50 sensuality
 19.16 disorder
rioter, n.
 14.50 sensuality
 19.16 disorder
riotous, adj.
 14.50 sensuality
 19.16 disorder
rip, vb.
 11.05 cut
ripe, adj.
 30.08 readiness
 32.12 (un)ripe
ripe, vb.
 32.12 (un)ripe
ripely, adv.
 30.08 readiness
ripen, vb.
 32.12 (un)ripe
ripeness, n.
 32.12 (un)ripe
riper, n.
 32.12 (un)ripe
ripe-red, adj.
 12.04 colour
rise, n.
 34.07 ascend
rise, vb.
 18.21 rebellion
 34.07 ascend
rite, n.
 16.14 ceremony
rivage, n.
 01.21 fen · shore
rival, n.
 04.22 companion
 19.02 rival
rival, vb.

 19.02 rival
rival-hating, adj.
 14.02 love · hate
rivality, n.
 04.22 companion
rive, vb.
 11.05 cut
rivel, vb.
 33.31 entangle
river, n.
 01.17 river
Rivers → Woodville, Anthony
 36.17 historical: English
rivet, n.
 23.19 nail
rivet, vb.
 23.19 nail
 31.16 join
 33.11 firm
rivo, int.
 25.13 interjection
road, n.
 20.02 assault
 34.16 travel
 34.28 road
 35.10 harbour
roadway, n.
 34.28 road
roam, vb.
 34.09 stray
roan, adj.
 12.04 colour
 12.06 spotted
roan, n.
 03.02 horse
roar, n.
 12.11 shout
roar, n.
 19.16 disorder
roar, vb.
 12.11 shout
roarer, n.
 12.11 shout
roast, n.
 09.10 meat
roast, vb.
 09.05 cookery
roast meat, n.
 09.10 meat
rob, vb.
 21.12 thievery
roba → bona roba
robber, n.
 21.12 thievery
robbery, n.

 21.12 thievery
robe, n.
 10.01 attire
 10.06 mantle
robe, fr. n.
 10.06 mantle
 24.14 French
robe, vb.
 10.01 attire
 10.06 mantle
Robert (WIV)
 37.03 English: male
Robert Shallow (2H4)
 37.03 English: male
Robert Shallow (WIV)
 37.03 English: male
Robin (2H6)
 37.03 English: male
Robin (TN)
 37.03 English: male
Robin (WIV)
 37.03 English: male
Robin Goodfellow → Puck
 28.05 spirits
Robin Nightwork (2H6)
 37.03 English: male
Robin Ostler (1H4)
 37.03 English: male
robin redbreast, n.
 03.18 nightingale
Robin Starveling (MND)
 37.03 English: male
robustious, adj.
 07.02 vigour
 14.40 rudeness
Rochester
 36.03 British
Rochford
 36.03 British
Rochford → Boleyn, Thomas
 36.17 historical: English
rock, n.
 01.25 stone
rock, vb.
 34.19 shake
rocky, adj.
 01.25 stone
 14.32 hard-hearted
rocky-hard, adj.
 33.28 hard · soft
rod, n.
 16.16 heraldry
 21.16 cudgel
 23.26 staff
Roderigo (OTH)

S

Saale
    01.17 river
Saba
    28.03 Abraham · Paul
sabaoth ➤ Sabbath
Sabbath, n.
    32.05 holidays
    32.07 monday
sable, n.
    03.34 fleece
sable, n.
    12.04 colour
sable-coloured, adj.
    12.04 colour
sack, n.
    08.37 bag
sack, n.
    20.02 assault
    20.19 booty
sack, n.
    09.15 beer · wine
sack, vb.
    20.19 booty
Sack and Sugar, Sir John
    37.15 nicknames
sackbut, n.
    26.05 wind instrument
sackcloth, n.
    05.07 swathe · shroud
    10.03 cloth
Sackerson
    03.14 bear
sacrament, n.
    28.12 sacrament
sacred, adj.
    28.13 holiness
    28.15 reverence
sacrifice, n.
    28.12 sacrament
sacrifice, vb.
    28.12 sacrament
sacrificer, n.
    28.08 worshipper
sacrificial, adj.
    28.12 sacrament
sacrilegious, adj.
    28.24 impiety
sacring-bell, n.
    26.07 bell
    28.12 sacrament

sad, adj.
    13.09 seriousness
    13.10 sorrow
sad-beholding, adj.
    12.01 sight
    12.02 show
saddle, n.
    27.18 saddle
saddle, vb.
    27.18 saddle
saddle-bow, n.
    27.18 saddle
saddler, n.
    23.11 other trades
sad-eyed, adj.
    06.18 anatomy compounds
    13.09 seriousness
sad-faced, adj.
    06.18 anatomy compounds
    13.10 sorrow
sad-hearted, adj.
    06.18 anatomy compounds
    13.09 seriousness
    13.10 sorrow
sadly, adv.
    13.09 seriousness
    13.10 sorrow
sadness, n.
    13.09 seriousness
    13.10 sorrow
sad-tuned, adj.
    26.03 music
safe, adj.
    07.01 health
    17.06 protection
safe, vb.
    17.06 protection
Safe, Sergeant
    37.13 telling: male
            (mentioned)
safe-conduct, n.
    17.06 protection
safe-conduct, vb.
    17.06 protection
safeguard, n.
    17.06 protection
safeguard, vb.
    17.06 protection
safely, adv.
    17.06 protection
safety, n.
    17.06 protection
saffron, n.
    02.16 parsley
    12.04 colour

sag, vb.
    07.05 decay
sage, adj.
    15.10 wisdom
sage, n.
    15.10 wisdom
Sagittary
    03.32 unicorn
    23.28 tavern
sail, n.
    35.01 ship
    35.03 sail
sail, n.
    34.16 travel
    35.08 navigation
sail, vb.
    35.08 navigation
sailmaker, n.
    23.11 other trades
sailor, n.
    35.09 seaman
saint, adj.
    28.13 holiness
saint, n.
    28.14 saints
saint, vb.
    28.13 holiness
saintlike, adj.
    28.13 holiness
saint-seducing, adj.
    18.17 enticement
sake, n.
    15.31 affair
salad, n.
    02.14 cabbage
salad days, n.
    32.03 times
    32.12 (un)ripe
salamander, n.
    03.28 frog
salary, n.
    22.08 payment
sale, n.
    22.01 trade
Salerio
    37.06 Romance: male
sale-work, n.
    22.01 trade
Salic, adj.
    36.10 Northern European
salicus, lat. adj.
    24.13 Latin
    36.10 Northern European
Salisbury
    36.03 British

14.42 negligence
22.26 spare
31.13 decrease
scantling, n.
29.08 pattern
scantly, adv.
22.26 spare
scape, n.
21.09 crime
34.06 hence-going
scape, vb.
19.19 avoid
34.06 hence-going
scar, n.
07.18 wound
scar, vb.
07.18 wound
scarce, adj.
22.26 spare
scarce-bearded, adj.
06.03 hair
06.18 anatomy compounds
32.12 (un)ripe
scarce-cold, adj.
01.11 hot · cold
scarcely, adv.
22.26 spare
scarcity, n.
22.26 spare
scare, vb.
14.52 fear
scarecrow, n.
23.12 husbandry
scarf, n.
10.11 veil · mask
20.18 flag
scarf, vb.
24.29 conceal
scarf, vb.
10.11 veil · mask
scarlet, adj.
12.04 colour
scarlet, n.
12.04 colour
Scarlet, [Will]
36.13 medieval legend
scarre, n.
24.19 crux
scathe, n.
07.18 wound
scathe, vb.
07.18 wound
scatheful, adj.
07.18 wound
scatter, vb.

33.41 distribution
34.09 stray
scelus, lat. n.
14.22 badness
21.09 crime
24.13 Latin
scene, n.
08.14 platform
26.02 theatre
scent, n.
12.16 smell
scent, vb.
12.16 smell
scent-snuffing, adj.
12.16 smell
sceptre, n.
16.16 heraldry
sceptre, vb.
16.16 heraldry
schedule, n.
24.04 writings
scholar, n.
25.02 teacher
25.03 student
scholarly, adj.
25.02 teacher
25.03 student
school, n.
25.01 education
25.04 school
school, n.
16.08 assembly
school, vb.
18.06 controlment
25.01 education
schoolboy, n.
25.03 student
school-days, n.
32.03 times
school-doing, n.
25.01 education
schoolfellow, n.
04.22 companion
25.03 student
school-maid, n.
25.03 student
schoolmaster, n.
25.02 teacher
sciatica, n.
07.10 gout
science, n.
15.06 knowledge
25.05 science · philosophy
scimitar, n.
20.14 weapon

scion, n.
02.01 tree · bush · twig
scissor, vb.
11.05 cut
scissors, n.
23.24 knife
scoff, n.
19.09 mockery
scoff, vb.
19.09 mockery
scoffer, n.
19.09 mockery
Scoggin
36.20 cultural: English
scold, n.
04.11 crone
scold, vb.
19.11 quarrel
sconce, n.
06.02 head
sconce, n.
20.10 fortification
Scone
36.03 British
scope, n.
15.28 intention
33.01 place
scorch, vb.
01.13 fire
scorch, vb.
11.05 cut
score, n.
22.09 account
31.07 count
score, vb.
11.05 cut
22.09 account
scorn, n.
14.27 contempt
19.09 mockery
scorn, vb.
14.27 contempt
19.09 mockery
scornful, adj.
14.27 contempt
19.09 mockery
scornfully, adv.
14.27 contempt
19.09 mockery
scorpion, n.
03.30 vermin · spider
Scot, n.
36.03 British
scot, n.
22.10 tax

scot and lot, n.
  22.10 tax
  31.03 all · nothing
Scotch, adj.
  36.03 British
scotch, n.
  07.18 wound
  11.05 cut
scotch, vb.
  11.05 cut
Scotch jig, n.
  26.11 dance
Scotland
  36.03 British
Scots, adj.
  36.03 British
Scottish, adj.
  36.03 British
scoundrel, n.
  04.04 rogue
scour, vb.
  11.03 hit
  34.01 go
scour, vb.
  11.09 rub
scourge, n.
  21.16 cudgel
scourge, vb.
  11.03 hit
scout, n.
  20.07 soldier
scout, vb.
  17.08 vigilance
scout, vb.
  19.09 mockery
scowl, vb.
  24.26 gesture
scrap, n.
  31.31 morsel
scrape, vb.
  11.09 rub
  11.10 scratch
  31.22 cancel
  31.27 heap
scratch, n.
  07.18 wound
  11.10 scratch
scratch, vb.
  11.10 scratch
scrawl, vb.
  24.26 gesture
scream, n.
  12.11 shout
scream, vb.
  12.11 shout

screech, vb.
  12.13 neigh
screech-owl, n.
  03.23 owl · bat
screen, n.
  08.08 wall
screen, vb.
  24.29 conceal
screw, vb.
  23.19 nail
  33.11 firm
  33.31 entangle
scribble, vb.
  24.12 write
scribe, n.
  24.12 write
scrip, n.
  08.37 bag
scrip, n.
  24.04 writings
scrip and scrippage, n.
  22.15 possession
  22.17 chattel
scripture, n.
  24.03 book
  24.04 writings
scrivener, n.
  24.12 write
scroll, n.
  24.04 writings
Scrope (1H4 1.3.271)
  36.17 historical: English
Scrope (1H4 5.5.37)
  36.17 historical: English
Scrope, Henry (H5)
  36.17 historical: English
Scrope, Stephen (R2)
  36.17 historical: English
scroyle, n.
  04.04 rogue
scrubbed, adj.
  33.17 giant · dwarf
scruple, n.
  31.39 weight
scruple, n.
  15.22 (un)certainty
scrupulous, adj.
  15.22 (un)certainty
  30.07 preciseness
scud, vb.
  34.01 go
  34.23 fast · slow
scuffle, n.
  20.01 combat
scullion, n.

  16.27 household servant
scum, n.
  31.34 dreg
scurrile, adj.
  14.40 rudeness
scurrility, n.
  14.40 rudeness
scurrilous, adj.
  14.40 rudeness
scurvy, adj.
  07.16 sore
  14.40 rudeness
scut, n.
  03.35 tail
scutcheon, n.
  16.16 heraldry
Scylla
  01.21 fen · shore
scythe, n.
  23.12 husbandry
scythe, vb.
  11.05 cut
  23.12 husbandry
scythe-tusked, adj.
  03.33 beak · horn
  06.18 anatomy compounds
Scythia
  36.12 Eastern European
Scythian, adj.
  36.12 Eastern European
Scythian, n.
  36.12 Eastern European
'sdeath
  28.25 oaths
se, lat. pron.
  24.13 Latin
  25.15 pronoun
sea, n.
  01.15 sea
sea-bank, n.
  01.21 fen · shore
sea-boy, n.
  35.09 seaman
sea-cap, n.
  10.10 hat
sea-change, n.
  33.42 change
sea-coal, n.
  01.25 stone
Seacoal, Francis (ADO)
  37.13 telling: male
         (mentioned)
Seacoal, George (ADO)
  37.11 telling: male (DP)
seafarer, n.

35.09 seaman
sea-faring, adj.
  35.09 seaman
sea-fight, n.
  20.01 combat
sea-gown, n.
  10.06 mantle
seal, n.
  16.16 heraldry
  24.27 sign
seal, vb.
  11.04 press
  17.12 affirmation
  32.19 beginning · end
  33.11 firm
sealed-up, adj.
  33.11 firm
sea-like, adj.
  01.15 sea
sealing-day, n.
  32.03 times
seal manual, n.
  24.27 sign
seal-ring, n.
  10.20 ring
  16.16 heraldry
seam, n.
  23.05 clothier
seam, n.
  03.42 tallow
sea-maid, n.
  28.06 mermaid
seaman, n.
  35.09 seaman
sea-marge, n.
  01.21 fen · shore
sea-mark, n.
  35.08 navigation
sea-monster, n.
  03.32 unicorn
seamster, n.
  23.05 clothier
seamy, adj.
  10.05 needlework
sea-nymph, n.
  28.06 mermaid
sear, n.
  20.16 gun
sear, vb.
  01.10 dry · wet
  01.13 fire
search, n.
  15.15 search
search, vb.
  07.24 medicine · cure

11.05 cut
  15.15 search
searcher, n.
  16.05 mayor
sea-room, n.
  01.15 sea
  33.01 place
sea-salt, adj.
  01.25 stone
sea-sick, adj.
  07.06 sickness
sea-side, n.
  01.21 fen · shore
season, n.
  09.06 salt · sugar
  32.03 times
  32.04 season
season, vb.
  09.05 cookery
  14.10 moderation
  32.12 (un)ripe
sea-sorrow, n.
  13.10 sorrow
sea-storm, n.
  01.06 wind · storm
seas-tossed, adj.
  34.18 toss
sea-swallowed, adj.
  01.19 dip
seat, n.
  08.01 house
  08.21 chair
  22.18 estate
seat, vb.
  33.03 station
  33.04 set
sea-walled, adj.
  33.10 encompassment
sea-water, n.
  01.14 water
sea-wing, n.
  35.03 sail
Sebastian (AWW)
  37.03 English: male
Sebastian (TGV)
  37.16 assumed names
Sebastian (TMP)
  37.03 English: male
Sebastian (TN)
  37.03 English: male
second, n.
  17.02 support
second, num.
  31.08 numbers
second, vb.

17.02 support
  33.40 sequence
secondarily, adv.
  31.08 numbers
secondary, n.
  16.20 deputy
  33.40 sequence
second cock, n.
  32.08 morning · night
secrecy, n.
  24.29 conceal
secret, adj.
  04.24 solitary
  24.29 conceal
secret, n.
  04.24 solitary
  24.29 conceal
secretary, n.
  24.12 write
secret-false, adj.
  17.14 (dis)loyalty
secretly, adv.
  24.29 conceal
sect, n.
  02.01 tree · bush · twig
  29.09 rank
  31.36 multitude
sectary, n.
  16.26 attendant
  25.03 student
  28.23 irreligion
  31.36 multitude
secundo, lat. adv.
  24.13 Latin
  31.08 numbers
secure, adj.
  17.06 protection
  17.15 (mis)trust
secure, vb.
  17.06 protection
  17.15 (mis)trust
securely, adv.
  17.06 protection
  17.15 (mis)trust
security, n.
  17.06 protection
  17.15 (mis)trust
  22.11 pledge
sedge, n.
  02.04 nettle · rush
sedged, adj.
  02.04 nettle · rush
sedgy, adj.
  02.04 nettle · rush
sedition, n.

shearman, n.
23.05 clothier
sheath, n.
20.15 sword-hilt
sheathe, vb.
11.05 cut
20.15 sword-hilt
sheave, vb.
02.15 grain
she-bear, n.
03.14 bear
she-beggar, n.
22.21 beggar
shed, vb.
01.18 effusion
22.22 loss
sheel, vb.
11.11 strip
sheen, adj.
01.12 light · dark
sheen, n.
01.12 light · dark
sheep, n.
03.05 sheep
sheep-biter, n.
03.08 dog
04.04 rogue
sheep-biting, adj.
03.47 peck · graze
04.04 rogue
sheepcote, n.
03.46 nest · kennel
sheep-hook, n.
23.12 husbandry
23.20 hinge
sheep-shearing, n.
13.04 revelry
23.12 husbandry
sheepskin, n.
10.04 leather
sheep-whistling, adj.
23.12 husbandry
26.05 wind instrument
sheer, adj.
14.18 purity
sheet, n.
05.07 swathe · shroud
24.04 writings
sheet, vb.
08.24 blanket
33.10 encompassment
Sheffield
36.03 British
Sheffield → Talbot, John (1H6)
36.17 historical: English

she-fox, n.
03.10 fox
she knight-errant, n.
16.22 knight
she-lamb, n.
03.05 sheep
shelf, n.
08.19 plank
shelf, n.
01.21 fen · shore
shell, n.
03.39 shell
shelly, adj.
03.39 shell
shelter, n.
08.01 house
17.06 protection
shelter, vb.
17.06 protection
shelve, vb.
33.24 jutting-out
shelvy, adj.
01.21 fen · shore
she-Mercury, n.
28.04 Mars · Venus
shend, vb.
19.08 reproach
shepherd, n.
23.13 farmer · herdsman
shepherdess, n.
23.13 farmer · herdsman
sheriff, n.
16.05 mayor
sherris, n.
09.15 beer · wine
sherris-sack, n.
09.15 beer · wine
she-wolf, n.
03.09 wolf
shield, n.
20.12 armour
shield, vb.
17.06 protection
shift, n.
18.16 plot
18.19 deceit
33.42 change
shift, vb.
18.16 plot
18.19 deceit
33.42 change
34.01 go
shilling, n.
22.06 money
shin, n.

06.16 leg
shine, n.
01.12 light · dark
shine, vb.
01.12 light · dark
shiny, adj.
01.12 light · dark
ship, n.
35.01 ship
ship, vb.
34.21 transport
35.08 navigation
shipboard, n.
35.01 ship
ship-boy, n.
35.09 seaman
shipman, n.
35.09 seaman
shipping, n.
34.21 transport
35.01 ship
35.08 navigation
ship-tire, n.
10.10 hat
shipwreck, n.
35.07 wrack
shipwreck, vb.
35.07 wrack
shipwright, n.
23.07 carpenter
shire, n.
16.01 commonwealth
Shirley
36.17 historical: English
shirt, n.
10.07 petticoat
shive, n.
31.33 fragment
shiver, n.
31.33 fragment
shiver, vb.
11.08 break
shiver, vb.
34.19 shake
shoal, n.
01.21 fen · shore
shock, n.
20.01 combat
shock, vb.
20.02 assault
shoe, n.
10.09 shoe · hose
shoe, vb.
27.17 bridle
shoeing-horn, n.

33.27 smooth · rough
sleek, vb.
  33.27 smooth · rough
sleek-headed, adj.
  06.02 head
  06.18 anatomy compounds
sleep, n.
  06.21 sleep
sleep, vb.
  06.21 sleep
sleeper, n.
  06.21 sleep
sleeping-hour, n.
  32.03 times
sleeping potion, n.
  07.24 medicine · cure
sleepy, adj.
  06.21 sleep
  14.42 negligence
sleeve, n.
  10.08 sleeve
sleeve-hand, n.
  10.08 sleeve
sleeveless, adj.
  10.08 sleeve
  22.34 (dis)advantage
sleight, n.
  18.16 plot
slender, adj.
  22.26 spare
  33.18 fat · thin
Slender, Abraham
  37.11 telling: male (DP)
slenderly, adv.
  22.26 spare
slice, n.
  31.33 fragment
slice, vb.
  11.05 cut
slickly, adv.
  33.27 smooth · rough
'slid
  28.25 oaths
slide, vb.
  34.01 go
  34.08 descend
slight, adj.
  22.14 trifle
slight, vb.
  14.27 contempt
  22.14 trifle
  34.18 toss
'slight
  28.25 oaths
slightly, adv.

14.42 negligence
22.14 trifle
31.38 almost
slightness, n.
  22.14 trifle
slime, n.
  01.24 mud
slimy, adj.
  01.24 mud
sling, n.
  27.04 archery
slink, vb.
  34.03 crawl
slip, n.
  02.01 tree · bush · twig
slip, n.
  14.46 fault
  27.19 curb
slip, n.
  22.06 money
slip, vb.
  14.46 fault
  18.13 freedom
  34.01 go
slipper, adj.
  33.27 smooth · rough
slipper, n.
  10.09 shoe · hose
slippered, adj.
  10.09 shoe · hose
slippery, adj.
  14.05 (in)constancy
  33.27 smooth · rough
slipshod, adj.
  10.09 shoe · hose
slish, n.
  11.05 cut
slit, vb.
  11.05 cut
sliver, n.
  02.01 tree · bush · twig
sliver, vb.
  11.05 cut
slobbery, adj.
  14.49 impurity
slop, n.
  10.09 shoe · hose
slope, vb.
  34.08 descend
  34.12 bend
sloth, n.
  14.42 negligence
slothful, adj.
  14.42 negligence
slough, n.

01.21 fen · shore
slough, n.
  03.39 shell
slovenly, adj.
  14.42 negligence
slovenry, n.
  14.42 negligence
slow, adj.
  30.08 readiness
  34.23 fast · slow
slow, vb.
  34.23 fast · slow
slow-gaited, adj.
  34.23 fast · slow
slowly, adv.
  34.23 fast · slow
slowness, n.
  34.23 fast · slow
slow-winged, adj.
  06.18 anatomy compounds
  34.26 fly
slubber, vb.
  14.49 impurity
slug, n.
  03.30 vermin · spider
  14.42 negligence
slug-a-bed, n.
  14.42 negligence
sluggard, n.
  14.42 negligence
sluggardize, vb.
  14.42 negligence
sluggish, adj.
  14.42 negligence
sluice, n.
  35.11 flood-gate
sluice, vb.
  01.14 water
  01.18 effusion
  35.11 flood-gate
slumber, n.
  06.21 sleep
slumber, vb.
  06.21 sleep
slumbery, adj.
  06.21 sleep
slut, n.
  04.12 strumpet
sluttery, n.
  14.50 sensuality
sluttish, adj.
  14.49 impurity
  14.50 sensuality
sluttishness, n.

05.03 procreation
soldieress, n.
20.07 soldier
soldierlike, adj.
20.07 soldier
soldiership, n.
20.07 soldier
sole, adj.
31.37 single
sole, n.
06.16 leg
10.09 shoe · hose
solely, adv.
31.37 single
solemn, adj.
13.09 seriousness
13.10 sorrow
16.14 ceremony
solemnity, n.
13.09 seriousness
16.14 ceremony
solemnize, vb.
16.14 ceremony
solemnly, adv.
13.09 seriousness
13.10 sorrow
16.14 ceremony
solemnness, n.
13.09 seriousness
13.10 sorrow
solicit, n.
18.11 request
solicit, vb.
18.11 request
18.18 instigation
solicitation, n.
18.11 request
soliciting, n.
18.11 request
solicitor, n.
21.05 law court
solid, adj.
33.11 firm
solidare, n.
22.06 money
solidity, n.
33.11 firm
Solinus
37.01 classical: male
solitary, adj.
04.24 solitary
Solomon
28.03 Abraham · Paul
Solon
36.22 historical: Greek

solus, adj.
31.37 single
solus, lat. adj.
24.13 Latin
31.37 single
Solyman
16.17 king
36.14 pseudohistorical
some, adj.
31.01 quantity
31.02 quantor
31.10 many · few
some, pron.
25.15 pronoun
somebody, n.
04.13 somebody
somebody, pron.
25.15 pronoun
somedeal, adv.
31.38 almost
someone, n.
04.13 somebody
someone, pron.
25.15 pronoun
Somerset
36.03 British
Somerset (1H6)
36.17 historical: English
Somerset (3H6)
36.17 historical: English
Somerset, Edmund, Duke of
(2H6)
36.17 historical: English
Somerville
36.17 historical: English
something, adv.
31.38 almost
something, n.
29.04 thing
something, pron.
25.15 pronoun
sometime, adj.
32.18 past · present · future
sometime, adv.
32.18 past · present · future
sometimes, adj.
32.18 past · present · future
sometimes, adv.
32.18 past · present · future
somever, adv.
30.01 manner
somewhat, adv.
31.38 almost
somewhat, n.
29.04 thing

somewhere, adv.
33.01 place
somewhither, adv.
33.01 place
Somme
01.17 river
son, n.
04.03 boy · youth
04.14 kindred
04.15 family
son, fr. n.
12.08 sound
24.14 French
son, fr. pron.
24.14 French
25.15 pronoun
sonance, n.
12.08 sound
song, n.
26.10 song
song-man, n.
26.09 musician
son-in-law, n.
04.15 family
sonnet, n.
26.12 poem
sonnet, vb.
26.14 poet
soon, adj.
32.31 imminence
soon, adv.
32.31 imminence
34.23 fast · slow
soon, adj.
34.23 fast · slow
soon-believing, adj.
15.24 belief
soon-speeding, adj.
22.20 prosperity
sooth, adj.
15.20 error · truth
sooth, adv.
15.20 error · truth
sooth, n.
15.20 error · truth
Sooth, Signior
37.15 nicknames
soothe, vb.
18.20 flattery
soother, n.
18.20 flattery
soothsay, vb.
28.27 prognostication
soothsayer, n.
28.27 prognostication

T

T, n.
    25.07 alphabet
table, n.
    08.19 plank
    08.20 table
    16.08 assembly
    24.10 note-book
    26.15 painting
    28.27 prognostication
table, vb.
    24.12 write
table-book, n.
    24.10 note-book
tables, n.
    27.06 games
table-sport, n.
    27.01 pastime
tablet, n.
    24.10 note-book
table-talk, n.
    24.20 conversation
tabor, n.
    26.08 other instruments
taborer, n.
    26.09 musician
taborin, n.
    26.08 other instruments
taciturnity, n.
    24.24 verbal · silent
tack, vb.
    31.16 join
tackle, n.
    35.06 tackle
tackled stair, n.
    08.15 stair
tackling, n.
    35.06 tackle
tadpole, n.
    03.28 frog
taffeta, n.
    10.03 cloth
tag, n.
    16.31 commoner
tag-rag people, n.
    16.31 commoner
tail, n.
    03.35 tail
    06.12 buttock
tailor, n.
    23.05 clothier

taint, adj.
    14.45 corruption
    14.47 dishonour
    14.49 impurity
taint, n.
    14.46 fault
    14.47 dishonour
    14.49 impurity
taint, vb.
    12.04 colour
    14.45 corruption
    14.47 dishonour
    14.49 impurity
tainture, n.
    14.49 impurity
take, vb.
    11.02 grasp
    11.03 hit
    15.01 cognition
    17.18 encounter
    22.27 acceptance
    22.28 acquisition
    28.28 sorcery
    34.01 go
    34.22 carry
take head, vb.
    34.23 fast · slow
take in, phr. vb.
    20.22 victory · defeat
take in snuff, vb.
    19.04 vexation
take on, phr. vb.
    14.29 anger
taker, n.
    11.02 grasp
take the heat, vb.
    22.34 (dis)advantage
take the time, vb.
    22.34 (dis)advantage
take up, phr. vb.
    19.08 reproach
taking, n.
    11.02 grasp
    14.22 badness
    19.17 (un)rest
taking-off, n.
    21.10 murder
Talbonite, n.
    36.17 historical: English
Talbot (H5)
    36.17 historical: English
Talbot, Gilbert (R3)
    36.17 historical: English
Talbot, John (1H6)
    36.17 historical: English

Talbot, John (1H6 4.3.35)
    36.17 historical: English
tale, n.
    24.22 message
talent, n.
    22.06 money
    30.02 disposition
    30.05 (un)able
Tale-porter, Mistress
    37.14 telling: female
             (mentioned)
talk, n.
    24.20 conversation
talk, vb.
    24.20 conversation
talker, n.
    24.20 conversation
tall, adj.
    14.17 boldness
    33.33 length
    33.37 height
taller, n.
    14.17 boldness
    33.37 height
tallow, n.
    03.42 tallow
tallow-catch, n.
    08.35 tub
tallow-face, n.
    06.04 face
    06.18 anatomy compounds
    12.05 pale
tally, n.
    31.07 count
talon, n.
    03.40 claw · hoof · fin
tam, lat. adv.
    24.13 Latin
    25.10 adverb
tame, adj.
    14.07 humility
    18.09 tame
tame, vb.
    18.09 tame
tame, vb.
    11.05 cut
tame cheater, n.
    27.15 snare
tamely, adv.
    18.09 tame
tameness, n.
    14.07 humility
    14.08 (un)gentle
    18.09 tame
taming-school, n.

throca
24.17 pseudo foreign
throe, n.
07.17 ache
throe, vb.
05.04 birth
07.17 ache
thromuldo
24.17 pseudo foreign
throne, n.
08.21 chair
throne, vb.
16.13 enthrone
throng, n.
31.36 multitude
throng, vb.
31.36 multitude
throstle, n.
03.18 nightingale
throttle, vb.
18.08 stifle
through, adv.
25.10 adverb
31.03 all · nothing
through, prep.
25.14 preposition
throughly, adv.
31.03 all · nothing
throughout, adv.
33.01 place
throughout, prep.
25.14 preposition
throw, n.
27.10 sport terms
34.18 toss
throw, vb.
27.10 sport terms
34.18 toss
thrower-out, n.
34.18 toss
thrum, n.
10.05 needlework
thrum, vb.
10.05 needlework
thrush, n.
03.18 nightingale
thrust, n.
11.06 push
27.03 stoccado
thrust, vb.
11.06 push
27.03 stoccado
33.04 set
thumb, n.
06.15 arm

thumb-ring, n.
10.20 ring
thump, vb.
11.03 hit
Thump, Peter
36.17 historical: English
thunder, n.
01.07 thunder
thunder, vb.
01.07 thunder
12.09 clangour
thunder-bearer, n.
28.04 Mars · Venus
thunderbolt, n.
01.07 thunder
thunder-clap, n.
01.07 thunder
thunder-darter, n.
28.04 Mars · Venus
thunderer, n.
28.04 Mars · Venus
thunder-like, adj.
01.07 thunder
thunder-master, n.
28.04 Mars · Venus
thunder-stone, n.
01.07 thunder
thunderstroke, n.
01.07 thunder
Thurio
37.06 Romance: male
Thursday, n.
32.07 monday
thus, adv.
15.05 logic
25.10 adverb
30.01 manner
thwack, vb.
11.03 hit
thwart, adj.
19.13 obstruction
33.30 oblique
thwart, adv.
33.30 oblique
thwart, vb.
19.13 obstruction
34.01 go
thwarting, n.
19.13 obstruction
thy, pron.
25.15 pronoun
thyme, n.
02.16 parsley
thyself, pron.
25.15 pronoun

Tib
04.09 woman
04.12 strumpet
Tib (AWW)
37.04 English: female
Tib (PER)
37.04 English: female
Tiber
01.17 river
Tiberio
37.06 Romance: male
tice, vb.
18.17 enticement
tick, n.
03.31 fly · louse
tickle, adj.
14.05 (in)constancy
tickle, vb.
12.15 touch
14.50 sensuality
19.04 vexation
ticklebrain, n.
06.18 anatomy compounds
09.15 beer · wine
ticklish, adj.
14.05 (in)constancy
14.50 sensuality
tick-tack, n.
27.06 games
tide, n.
01.14 water
32.14 period
tide, vb.
32.25 chance
tiding, n.
24.22 message
32.23 occurrence
tidy, adj.
33.18 fat · thin
tie, n.
31.16 join
33.31 entangle
tie, vb.
17.13 obligation
31.16 join
33.11 firm
tied-up, adj.
18.06 controlment
33.11 firm
tiger, n.
03.16 elephant · lion
Tiger
23.28 tavern
35.01 ship
tiger-footed, adj.

06.06 jaw
toothache, n.
  07.17 ache
tooth-drawer, n.
  07.22 physician
toothpick, n.
  23.25 gad
toothpicker, n.
  23.25 gad
too-timely, adj.
  32.29 early · late
top, n.
  06.02 head
  06.03 hair
  33.37 height
  35.03 sail
top, n.
  27.08 toy
  27.09 ball
top, vb.
  05.03 procreation
  11.05 cut
  29.10 pre-eminence
top, vb.
  34.07 ascend
Topas, Sir (TN)
  37.16 assumed names
top-branch, n.
  02.01 tree · bush · twig
top-full, adj.
  31.04 full · empty
topgallant, n.
  35.03 sail
topless, adj.
  33.37 height
topmast, n.
  35.04 mast
topple, vb.
  34.08 descend
top-proud, adj.
  14.23 pride
topsail, n.
  35.03 sail
topsy-turvy, adv.
  19.16 disorder
torch, n.
  08.27 torch
torch-bearer, n.
  16.28 bearer
torcher, n.
  08.27 torch
  16.28 bearer
torch-light, n.
  01.12 light · dark
  08.27 torch

torch-staff, n.
  08.27 torch
  23.26 staff
torment, n.
  21.13 punishment
torment, vb.
  07.17 ache
tormenta, vb.
  07.17 ache
  24.17 pseudo foreign
tormente, vb.
  07.17 ache
  24.17 pseudo foreign
tormentor, n.
  21.13 punishment
torrent, n.
  01.14 water
tortive, adj.
  33.31 entangle
tortoise, n.
  03.29 serpent
torture, n.
  21.13 punishment
torture, vb.
  21.13 punishment
torturer, n.
  21.13 punishment
Toryne
  36.09 Southern European
toss, vb.
  34.18 toss
tosspot, n.
  09.03 eat · drink
total, adj.
  31.03 all · nothing
total, n.
  31.03 all · nothing
  31.07 count
totally, adv.
  31.03 all · nothing
to the point, adv.
  30.07 preciseness
to the pot, adv.
  20.21 destruction
tother, adj.
  31.25 difference
totter, vb.
  34.11 reel
touch, n.
  01.25 stone
  11.03 hit
  12.15 touch
  15.14 examination
  30.02 disposition
  31.01 quantity

touch, vb.
  09.03 eat · drink
  11.03 hit
  12.15 touch
  15.14 examination
  15.31 affair
  18.18 instigation
  34.04 here-approach
touching, prep.
  25.14 preposition
touchstone, n.
  01.25 stone
  15.14 examination
Touchstone
  37.11 telling: male (DP)
tough, adj.
  33.28 hard · soft
toughness, n.
  33.28 hard · soft
Touraine
  36.11 French
tournament, n.
  20.01 combat
  27.06 games
tourney, vb.
  20.01 combat
  27.06 games
Tours
  36.11 French
touse, vb.
  11.07 pull
tout, fr. adj.
  24.14 French
  31.03 all · nothing
tout, fr. pron.
  24.14 French
  25.15 pronoun
tow, vb.
  11.07 pull
toward, adj.
  17.10 (un)willingness
toward, adv.
  25.10 adverb
  32.31 imminence
toward, prep.
  25.14 preposition
towardly, adj.
  17.10 (un)willingness
towards, adv.
  32.31 imminence
towards, prep.
  25.14 preposition
tower, n.
  20.10 fortification
tower, vb.

transmutation, n.
  33.42 change
transparent, adj.
  01.12 light · dark
transport, vb.
  13.06 rapture
  34.21 transport
  34.22 carry
transportance, n.
  34.21 transport
transportation, n.
  34.21 transport
transpose, vb.
  33.42 change
trans-shape, vb.
  33.42 change
Transylvanian, n.
  36.12 Eastern European
trap, n.
  27.15 snare
trap, vb.
  27.15 snare
trap, vb.
  10.18 ornament
trapping, n.
  10.18 ornament
trash, n.
  04.04 rogue
  31.34 dreg
trash, vb.
  18.06 controlment
  19.13 obstruction
travail, n.
  23.15 work
travail, vb.
  23.15 work
travel, n.
  34.16 travel
travel, vb.
  34.16 travel
traveller, n.
  23.15 work
  34.16 travel
Traveller, Monsieur
  37.15 nicknames
travelling lamp, n.
  08.27 torch
travel-tainted, adj.
  14.49 impurity
Travers
  37.05 English: surnames
traverse, adj.
  33.30 oblique
traverse, vb.
  27.03 stoccado

33.30 oblique
33.31 entangle
34.01 go
treacher, n.
  17.14 (dis)loyalty
  18.21 rebellion
treacherous, adj.
  17.14 (dis)loyalty
  18.21 rebellion
treacherously, adv.
  17.14 (dis)loyalty
  18.21 rebellion
treachery, n.
  17.14 (dis)loyalty
  18.21 rebellion
tread, n.
  34.01 go
tread, vb.
  05.03 procreation
  34.01 go
tread a measure, vb.
  26.11 dance
treason, n.
  17.14 (dis)loyalty
  18.21 rebellion
treasonable, adj.
  17.14 (dis)loyalty
  18.21 rebellion
treasonous, adj.
  17.14 (dis)loyalty
  18.21 rebellion
treasure, n.
  16.09 council-house
  22.13 value
  22.17 chattel
  22.19 rich · poor
treasure, vb.
  22.19 rich · poor
treasure house, n.
  16.09 council-house
treasurer, n.
  16.06 treasurer
treasury, n.
  16.09 council-house
  22.17 chattel
treat, vb.
  11.01 do
treatise, n.
  24.22 message
treaty, n.
  18.11 request
  22.12 contract
treble, adj.
  31.07 count
treble, n.

26.04 gamut
31.08 numbers
treble, vb.
  31.07 count
treble-dated, adj.
  32.03 times
treble-sinewed, adj.
  06.18 anatomy compounds
  07.02 vigour
Trebonius
  36.23 historical: Roman
tree, n.
  02.01 tree · bush · twig
tremble, vb.
  34.19 shake
tremblingly, adv.
  34.19 shake
tremor cordis
  07.08 fit
  24.16 foreign phrases
trench, n.
  33.22 hole · trench
trench, vb.
  11.05 cut
trenchant, adj.
  11.05 cut
  33.26 sharp · dull
trencher, n.
  08.30 dish
trencher-friend, n.
  04.21 friend
  18.20 flattery
trenchering, n.
  08.30 dish
trencher-knight, n.
  18.20 flattery
trencher-man, n.
  09.03 eat · drink
Trent
  01.17 river
très, fr. adv.
  24.14 French
  31.20 excess
trespass, n.
  21.09 crime
  28.24 impiety
trespass, vb.
  21.09 crime
  28.24 impiety
tress, n.
  06.03 hair
Tressel
  36.17 historical: English
trey, n.
  27.10 sport terms

trot, n.
    04.11 crone
    37.15 nicknames
trot, vb.
    34.01 go
troth, n.
    15.20 error • truth
    17.14 (dis)loyalty
troth-plight, adj.
    04.18 marriage
    22.11 pledge
troth-plight, n.
    04.18 marriage
    22.11 pledge
trotting-horse, n.
    03.02 horse
trouble, n.
    19.04 vexation
    19.17 (un)rest
trouble, vb.
    19.04 vexation
    19.17 (un)rest
troubler, n.
    19.17 (un)rest
troublesome, adj.
    19.04 vexation
    19.17 (un)rest
troublous, adj.
    19.16 disorder
    19.17 (un)rest
trough, n.
    08.35 tub
trout, n.
    03.26 fish
trovare → ben trovato
trow, vb.
    15.04 thought
    15.24 belief
trowel, n.
    23.27 other tools
Troy
    36.05 Middle / Far Eastern
    36.11 French
troy weight, n.
    31.39 weight
truant, adj.
    04.04 rogue
truant, n.
    14.42 negligence
truant, vb.
    14.42 negligence
truce, n.
    20.23 peace
truckle-bed, n.
    08.22 bed

trudge, vb.
    34.01 go
true, adj.
    14.14 honesty
    15.20 error • truth
    17.14 (dis)loyalty
    29.05 indeed
true, n.
    15.20 error • truth
true-anointed, adj.
    28.12 sacrament
true-begotten, adj.
    05.03 procreation
true-born, adj.
    05.04 birth
true-bred, adj.
    04.14 kindred
    05.03 procreation
true-derived, adj.
    04.14 kindred
    05.03 procreation
true-devoted, adj.
    28.15 reverence
true-disposing, adj.
    18.07 (ab)use
true-divining, adj.
    28.27 prognostication
true-fixed, adj.
    33.11 firm
true-hearted, adj.
    06.18 anatomy compounds
    14.14 honesty
    17.14 (dis)loyalty
true-love, n.
    04.10 darling
true-love knot, n.
    33.31 entangle
true-meant, adj.
    15.28 intention
truepenny, n.
    14.14 honesty
    17.14 (dis)loyalty
true-telling, adj.
    24.25 make known
truie, fr. n.
    03.06 swine
    24.14 French
trull, n.
    04.12 strumpet
truly, adv.
    15.20 error • truth
    17.14 (dis)loyalty
    29.05 indeed
trump, n.
    26.05 wind instrument

trumpery, n.
    18.19 deceit
    22.14 trifle
trumpet, n.
    26.05 wind instrument
    26.09 musician
trumpet, vb.
    12.09 clangour
    26.05 wind instrument
trumpet-clangour, n.
    12.09 clangour
trumpeter, n.
    26.09 musician
trumpet-tongued, adj.
    06.18 anatomy compounds
    12.09 clangour
truncheon, n.
    16.16 heraldry
    21.16 cudgel
truncheon, vb.
    11.03 hit
truncheoner, n.
    20.04 fighter
trundle-tail, n.
    03.08 dog
trunk, n.
    02.01 tree • bush • twig
    06.01 body
    08.36 case
trunk sleeve, n.
    10.08 sleeve
trunk-work, n.
    23.15 work
truss, vb.
    31.19 stuff
    33.10 encompassment
trust, n.
    17.15 (mis)trust
trust, vb.
    15.24 belief
    17.15 (mis)trust
truster, n.
    15.24 belief
    17.15 (mis)trust
    22.02 creditor • debtor
trustless, adj.
    17.14 (dis)loyalty
trusty, adj.
    17.14 (dis)loyalty
truth, n.
    15.20 error • truth
    17.14 (dis)loyalty
try, n.
    15.14 examination
try, vb.

31.09 pair
twain, num.
   31.08 numbers
twain, vb.
   31.17 separation
twang, vb.
   12.09 clangour
twangle, vb.
   12.09 clangour
tweak, vb.
   11.07 pull
twelfth, num.
   31.08 numbers
twelve, num.
   31.08 numbers
twelve and a half, num.
   31.08 numbers
twelve hundred, num.
   31.08 numbers
twelvemonth, n.
   32.02 hour · day · year
twelvepence, n.
   22.06 money
twelve score, num.
   31.08 numbers
twelve thirties, num.
   31.08 numbers
twelve thousand, num.
   31.08 numbers
twentieth ➤ a twentieth
twentieth part, num.
   31.08 numbers
twenty, num.
   31.08 numbers
twenty-five, num.
   31.08 numbers
twenty hundred, num.
   31.08 numbers
twenty hundred thousand, num.
   31.08 numbers
twenty-nine, num.
   31.08 numbers
twenty-one, num.
   31.08 numbers
twenty-seven, num.
   31.08 numbers
twenty thousand, num.
   31.08 numbers
twenty-three, num.
   31.08 numbers
twice, adv.
   31.07 count
twice fifteen thousand, num.
   31.08 numbers
twice five, num.

31.08 numbers
twice five hundred, num.
   31.08 numbers
twice six, num.
   31.08 numbers
twice-told, adj.
   24.25 make known
twice treble, num.
   31.08 numbers
twice two, num.
   31.08 numbers
twig, n.
   02.01 tree · bush · twig
twiggen, adj.
   02.01 tree · bush · twig
twilight, n.
   01.12 light · dark
   32.08 morning · night
twilled, adj.
   33.31 entangle
twin, n.
   04.14 kindred
   12.03 semblance
twin, vb.
   04.14 kindred
   12.03 semblance
twin-born, adj.
   05.04 birth
twin-brother, n.
   04.15 family
twine, n.
   10.05 needlework
   23.21 rope
twine, vb.
   17.16 embrace · kiss
   33.31 entangle
twink, n.
   32.30 brevity
twinkle, vb.
   01.12 light · dark
twire, vb.
   01.12 light · dark
twist, n.
   10.16 tape
twist, vb.
   33.31 entangle
twit, vb.
   19.08 reproach
two, num.
   31.08 numbers
two and fifty, num.
   31.08 numbers
two and forty, num.
   31.08 numbers
two and thirty, num.

31.08 numbers
two and twenty, num.
   31.08 numbers
two dozen, num.
   31.08 numbers
twofold, adj.
   31.07 count
two-hand, n.
   06.15 arm
   06.18 anatomy compounds
two-hand sword, n.
   20.14 weapon
two-headed, adj.
   06.02 head
   06.18 anatomy compounds
two hundred, num.
   31.08 numbers
two hundred fifty, num.
   31.08 numbers
two-legged, adj.
   06.16 leg
   06.18 anatomy compounds
twopence, n.
   22.06 money
two score, num.
   31.08 numbers
two tens, num.
   31.08 numbers
two thousand, num.
   31.08 numbers
Tybalt
   37.06 Romance: male
Tyburn
   36.07 London
tyke, n.
   03.08 dog
   04.04 rogue
type, n.
   24.27 sign
Typhon
   03.32 unicorn
tyrannical, adj.
   14.31 cruelty
tyrannically, adv.
   14.31 cruelty
tyrannize, vb.
   14.31 cruelty
   16.11 ruler
tyrannous, adj.
   14.31 cruelty
tyranny, n.
   14.31 cruelty
tyrant, n.
   14.31 cruelty
   16.11 ruler

vambrace, n.
20.12 armour
vane, n.
08.07 vane
vanish, vb.
33.14 presence · absence
vanity, n.
22.14 trifle
Vanity
26.02 theatre
vanquish, vb.
20.22 victory · defeat
vanquisher, n.
20.22 victory · defeat
vantage, n.
18.04 supremacy
22.34 (dis)advantage
Vapians
37.09 other names
vaporous, adj.
01.09 cloud · vapour
vapour, n.
01.09 cloud · vapour
06.17 blood · bone
vapour-vow, n.
17.13 obligation
variable, adj.
31.25 difference
33.42 change
variance, n.
19.11 quarrel
variation, n.
31.25 difference
33.42 change
variations, n.
31.25 difference
33.42 change
variety, n.
31.25 difference
33.42 change
varlet, n.
04.04 rogue
16.29 servant
varletry, n.
16.31 commoner
varletto, n.
04.04 rogue
varnish, n.
10.18 ornament
23.18 cement
varnish, vb.
10.18 ornament
23.18 cement
Varrius (ANT)
37.01 classical: male

Varrius (MM)
37.01 classical: male
Varro
37.01 classical: male
Varrus
37.01 classical: male
vary, n.

31.25 difference
33.42 change
vary, vb.
31.25 difference
33.42 change
vassal, n.
18.14 vassal
vassalage, n.
18.14 vassal
vast, adj.
33.16 size
vast, n.
01.15 sea
33.02 region
vastidity, n.
33.16 size
vastly, adv.
33.16 size
vasty, adj.
33.16 size
vat, n.
23.22 barrel
Vaudemont
36.11 French
36.18 historical: French
Vaughan, Thomas
36.17 historical: English
vault, n.
08.09 arch
08.17 rooms
vault, vb.
34.02 leap
vaultage, n.
08.09 arch
08.17 rooms
vaulted, adj.
08.09 arch
vaulty, adj.
08.09 arch
Vaumond
37.10 Romance: surnames
vaunt, n.
14.25 braggardism
vaunt, n.
20.05 army · navy
33.06 side
vaunt, vb.

13.05 exult
14.25 braggardism
vaunt-courier, n.
24.23 messenger
vaunter, n.
14.25 braggardism
vauntingly, adv.
14.25 braggardism
vauvado
24.17 pseudo foreign
Vaux (2H6)
36.17 historical: English
Vaux, Nicholas (H8)
36.17 historical: English
vaward, n.
20.05 army · navy
33.06 side
veal, n.
09.10 meat
vedere, it. vb.
12.01 sight
24.15 Italian
vegetive, n.
02.05 plant
vehemence, n.
14.37 vehemence
vehemency, n.
14.37 vehemence
vehement, adj.
14.37 vehemence
vehemently, adv.
14.37 vehemence
vehere, lat. vb.
24.13 Latin
34.21 transport
veil, n.
10.11 veil · mask
veil, vb.
10.11 veil · mask
24.29 conceal
vein, n.
06.17 blood · bone
30.02 disposition
Velutus → Sicinius, Velutus
velure, n.
10.03 cloth
velvet, n.
10.03 cloth
velvet-guard, n.
10.17 fringe
vendible, adj.
22.01 trade
venerable, adj.
28.15 reverence
venereal, adj.

W

waddle, vb.
  34.01 go
wade, vb.
  34.01 go
wafer-cake, n.
  09.13 bread · cake
waft, vb.
  34.21 transport
waft, vb.
  24.26 gesture
waftage, n.
  34.21 transport
wafture, n.
  24.26 gesture
wag, n.
  04.06 madcap
wag, vb.
  34.01 go
  34.19 shake
wage, n.
  22.08 payment
wage, vb.
  20.01 combat
  22.08 payment
  22.32 recompense
  27.10 sport terms
wager, n.
  27.10 sport terms
wager, vb.
  27.10 sport terms
waggish, adj.
  14.41 levity
waggle, vb.
  34.19 shake
waggon, n.
  34.27 waggon
waggoner, n.
  23.11 other trades
waggon-spoke, n.
  34.27 waggon
waggon-wheel, n.
  34.27 waggon
wagtail, n.
  03.18 nightingale
  04.04 rogue
wail, vb.
  13.11 lament
  13.12 sob
wailful, adj.
  13.11 lament

wailing robe, n.
  10.06 mantle
wain, n.
  34.27 waggon
wain-rope, n.
  23.21 rope
  34.27 waggon
wainscot, n.
  08.19 plank
waist, n.
  06.09 belly
  10.13 belt
  35.02 deck · oar
wait, vb.
  16.26 attendant
  32.32 expectation
waiting-gentlewoman, n.
  16.25 usher
waiting vassal, n.
  18.14 vassal
waiting-woman, n.
  16.25 usher
wake, n.
  06.21 sleep
  13.04 revelry
wake, vb.
  06.21 sleep
  18.18 instigation
Wakefield
  36.03 British
waken, vb.
  06.21 sleep
Wales
  36.03 British
Wales ➤ Edward (Black Prince)
  36.17 historical: English
Wales ➤ Edward [V] (R3)
  36.17 historical: English
Wales ➤ Plantagenet (R3)
  36.17 historical: English
Wales, Henry, Prince of (1H4)
  36.17 historical: English
walk, n.
  26.11 dance
  34.01 go
  34.28 road
walk, vb.
  34.01 go
walking-staff, n.
  23.26 staff
wall, n.
  08.08 wall
wall, vb.
  08.08 wall
  19.13 obstruction

  33.10 encompassment
Wall (MND)
  37.16 assumed names
wallet, n.
  08.37 bag
wall-eyed, adj.
  06.04 face
  06.18 anatomy compounds
  12.01 sight
wall-newt, n.
  03.28 frog
Walloon, n.
  36.10 Northern European
Walloon
  36.10 Northern European
wallow, vb.
  34.11 reel
walnut, n.
  02.11 walnut
walnut-shell, n.
  02.11 walnut
Walter
  37.03 English: male
wan, adj.
  12.05 pale
wan, vb.
  12.05 pale
wand, n.
  16.16 heraldry
  23.26 staff
wander, vb.
  34.09 stray
wanderer, n.
  34.09 stray
wand-like, adj.
  23.26 staff
wane, n.
  31.13 decrease
wane, vb.
  31.13 decrease
wanion, n.
  14.34 revenge
wanny, adj.
  12.05 pale
want, n.
  22.19 rich · poor
  22.24 lack
  22.25 necessity
want, vb.
  22.19 rich · poor
  22.24 lack
  22.25 necessity
wanton, adj.
  14.38 uncontrolled
  14.41 levity

weal-balanced, adj.
   31.23 equality
weald, n.
   01.28 wood · field · garden
wealsman, n.
   16.03 statesman
wealth, n.
   22.19 rich · poor
wealthily, adv.
   22.19 rich · poor
wealthy, adj.
   22.19 rich · poor
wean, vb.
   05.05 nurse
   31.17 separation
weapon, n.
   20.14 weapon
weapon, vb.
   20.14 weapon
wear, n.
   10.01 attire
wear, vb.
   07.05 decay
   10.01 attire
   32.16 continuance
   34.22 carry
wearer, n.
   10.01 attire
   22.15 possession
wearily, adj.
   07.03 weariness
weariness, n.
   07.03 weariness
wearing, n.
   10.01 attire
wearing gown, n.
   10.06 mantle
wearisome, adj.
   07.03 weariness
weary, adj.
   07.03 weariness
weary, vb.
   07.03 weariness
weasand, n.
   06.07 neck
weasel, n.
   03.10 fox
weather, n.
   01.05 weather
   01.06 wind · storm
   35.08 navigation
weather-beaten, adj.
   11.03 hit
weather-bitten, adj.
   07.05 decay

weathercock, n.
   08.07 vane
weather-fend, vb.
   17.06 protection
weave, vb.
   23.05 clothier
   33.31 entangle
weaved-up, adj.
   23.05 clothier
   33.31 entangle
weaver, n.
   23.05 clothier
web, n.
   03.45 cobweb
   10.05 needlework
wed, vb.
   04.18 marriage
wedding, n.
   04.18 marriage
wedding-bed, n.
   08.22 bed
wedding-day, n.
   32.03 times
wedding-dower, n.
   22.17 chattel
wedding garment, n.
   10.01 attire
wedding gown, n.
   10.06 mantle
wedding-ring, n.
   10.20 ring
wedding-sheet, n.
   08.24 blanket
wedding torch, n.
   08.27 torch
wedge, n.
   23.19 nail
wedge, vb.
   11.05 cut
   11.06 push
   23.19 nail
wedlock, n.
   04.18 marriage
wedlock-hymn, n.
   26.10 song
Wednesday, n.
   32.07 monday
weed, n.
   02.04 nettle · rush
   03.02 horse
weed, n.
   10.01 attire
weed, vb.
   23.12 husbandry
weeder-out, n.

   11.07 pull
   23.12 husbandry
weeding, n.
   02.04 nettle · rush
weedy, adj.
   02.04 nettle · rush
week, int.
   12.14 bow-wow
week, n.
   32.02 hour · day · year
weekly, adj.
   32.02 hour · day · year
ween, vb.
   15.04 thought
   15.16 surmise
weep, vb.
   13.12 sob
weeper, n.
   13.12 sob
weeping, n.
   13.12 sob
weepingly, adv.
   13.12 sob
weeping-ripe, adj.
   30.08 readiness
weet, vb.
   15.06 knowledge
weigh, vb.
   15.04 thought
   21.03 judgement
   22.13 value
   31.39 weight
   31.42 heavy · light
   34.17 raise
   35.08 navigation
weight, n.
   15.30 import
   31.06 load
   31.39 weight
   31.42 heavy · light
weightless, adj.
   31.42 heavy · light
weighty, adj.
   15.30 import
   31.42 heavy · light
weird sisters (women), n.
   28.28 sorcery
welcome, adj.
   17.20 hospitality
welcome, n.
   17.19 salutation
   17.20 hospitality
welcome, vb.
   17.19 salutation
   17.20 hospitality

well-wished, adj.
  14.48 desire
well-won, adj.
  22.28 acquisition
Welsh, adj.
  36.03 British
Welsh, n.
  24.01 language
  36.03 British
Welsh hook, n.
  20.14 weapon
Welshman, n.
  36.03 British
Welshwoman, n.
  36.03 British
wen, n.
  04.04 rogue
  07.16 sore
wench, n.
  04.09 woman
  32.10 maidhood
wench, vb.
  14.51 fornication
wenchless, adj.
  04.09 woman
wench-like, adj.
  04.09 woman
wend, vb.
  34.01 go
west, adv.
  33.05 north · south
west, n.
  33.05 north · south
westerly, adj.
  33.05 north · south
western, adj.
  33.05 north · south
western Inde
  36.06 American
Western Isles
  01.20 island
  36.03 British
West Indies (Inde)
  36.06 American
Westminster
  16.15 castle
  28.18 church
  36.07 London
Westminster, Abbot of
  36.17 historical: English
[Westminster] Hall
  08.17 rooms
Westmorland
  36.03 British
Westmorland, Earl of (1H4)

36.17 historical: English
Westmorland, Earl of (3H6)
  36.17 historical: English
westward, adv.
  33.05 north · south
westward-ho, int.
  25.13 interjection
west wind, n.
  01.06 wind · storm
wet, adj.
  01.10 dry · wet
wet, n.
  01.10 dry · wet
wet, vb.
  01.10 dry · wet
wether, n.
  03.05 sheep
whale, n.
  03.26 fish
whale's bone, n.
  10.19 gem
wharf, n.
  01.21 fen · shore
what, adj.
  29.04 thing
what, adv.
  15.29 motive
  25.10 adverb
what, pron.
  25.15 pronoun
what-do-ye-call
  36.01 name
whatever, adj.
  04.13 somebody
  29.04 thing
whatever, pron.
  25.15 pronoun
whatsoever, adj.
  04.13 somebody
  29.04 thing
whatsoever, pron.
  25.15 pronoun
whatsomever, pron.
  25.15 pronoun
what the goodyear, int.
  25.13 interjection
What-ye-call-it, Master
  37.15 nicknames
wheat, n.
  02.15 grain
wheaten, adj.
  02.15 grain
wheel, n.
  21.13 punishment
  23.05 clothier

  34.27 waggon
wheel, vb.
  34.09 stray
  34.11 reel
  34.12 bend
  34.27 waggon
wheeze, vb.
  06.19 breath
whelk, n.
  07.16 sore
whelked, adj.
  31.14 swell
  33.31 entangle
whelm, vb.
  01.19 dip
  20.22 victory · defeat
whelp, n.
  03.01 animal
  04.15 family
whelp, vb.
  05.03 procreation
when, adv.
  32.03 times
when, conj.
  25.12 conjunction
whenas, adv.
  32.03 times
whence, adv.
  33.01 place
whencesoever, adv.
  33.01 place
whenever, adv.
  32.03 times
whensoever, adv.
  32.03 times
whensoever, conj.
  25.12 conjunction
where, adv.
  33.01 place
where, conj.
  25.12 conjunction
where, n.
  33.01 place
whereabout, adv.
  15.29 motive
  33.01 place
whereabout, n.
  33.01 place
whereas, adv.
  19.15 however
  33.01 place
whereas, conj.
  25.12 conjunction
whereat, adv.
  25.10 adverb

woeful, adj.
   13.10 sorrow
woe-wearied, adj.
   07.03 weariness
wold, n.
   01.28 wood · field · garden
wolf, n.
   03.09 wolf
wolfish, adj.
   03.09 wolf
Wolsey, Cardinal
   36.17 historical: English
woman, n.
   04.09 woman
   04.18 marriage
   16.26 attendant
woman, vb.
   04.09 woman
womanhood, n.
   04.09 woman
womanish, adj.
   04.09 woman
womankind, n.
   04.09 woman
womanly, adj.
   04.09 woman
woman-post, n.
   24.23 messenger
woman-queller, n.
   21.10 murder
woman-tired, adj.
   11.05 cut
womb, n.
   06.09 belly
   33.23 hollowness
womb, vb.
   06.09 belly
   33.10 encompassment
womby, adj.
   06.09 belly
   33.23 hollowness
womenkind, n.
   04.09 woman
wonder, n.
   15.09 amazement
wonder, vb.
   15.09 amazement
wonderful, adj.
   15.09 amazement
wonderfully, adv.
   15.09 amazement
wonderingly, adv.
   15.09 amazement
wonder-wounded, adj.
   07.18 wound

wondrous, adj.
   15.09 amazement
wondrously, adv.
   15.09 amazement
wont, adj.
   32.26 (un)usual
wont, n.
   32.26 (un)usual
wont, vb.
   32.26 (un)usual
woo, vb.
   04.18 marriage
   18.11 request
wood, adj.
   07.20 madness
wood, n.
   01.28 wood · field · garden
   02.01 tree · bush · twig
woodbine, n.
   02.09 rose
wood-bird, n.
   03.17 bird
woodcock, n.
   03.20 pheasant
   15.12 foolishness
wooden, adj.
   02.01 tree · bush · twig
   15.12 foolishness
wooden O, n.
   26.01 playhouse
woodland, n.
   01.28 wood · field · garden
wood-leaf, n.
   02.06 bud · root
woodman, n.
   27.14 hunter
Woodmancote
   36.03 British
woodmonger, n.
   22.05 monger
Woodstock
   36.03 British
Woodville (1H6)
   36.17 historical: English
Woodville, Anthony (R3)
   36.17 historical: English
wooer, n.
   04.18 marriage
   18.11 request
woof, n.
   10.05 needlework
wooingly, adv.
   04.18 marriage
   18.11 request
wool, n.

   03.34 fleece
woollen, adj.
   03.34 fleece
woollen, n.
   03.34 fleece
woolly, adj.
   03.34 fleece
woolsack, n.
   08.37 bag
   33.18 fat · thin
woolward, adj.
   10.03 cloth
Worcester
   36.03 British
   36.17 historical: English
word, n.
   22.11 pledge
   24.01 language
   24.02 word
   24.03 book
   24.22 message
   25.06 maxim
word, vb.
   18.18 instigation
   24.02 word
   24.20 conversation
   24.22 message
   24.25 make known
wordless, adj.
   24.24 verbal · silent
word of mouth, n.
   24.20 conversation
work, n.
   11.01 do
   20.10 fortification
   23.15 work
work, vb.
   11.01 do
   23.15 work
workaday, n.
   16.31 commoner
   32.03 times
working, n.
   11.01 do
working-day, n.
   16.31 commoner
   32.03 times
working-house, n.
   23.29 working-house
workman, n.
   23.01 vocation
workmanly, adj.
   30.06 (un)skilful
workmanship, n.
   30.06 (un)skilful

world, n.
01.01 universe
worldling, n.
04.01 mortal
worldly, adj.
01.01 universe
world-sharer, n.
31.26 portion
world-wearied, adj.
07.03 weariness
world-without-end, n.
32.16 continuance
worm, n.
03.29 serpent
03.30 vermin · spider
Worm, Don
37.13 telling: male
(mentioned)
Worm, Lady
37.14 telling: female
(mentioned)
worm-eaten, adj.
07.05 decay
worm-hole, n.
33.22 hole · trench
worm's-meat, n.
06.01 body
wormwood, n.
02.17 mandragora
wormy, adj.
03.30 vermin · spider
worn-out, adj.
07.05 decay
worry, vb.
11.05 cut
18.08 stifle
worse, n.
14.22 badness
worser, n.
14.22 badness
worship, n.
14.16 honour
28.15 reverence
worship, vb.
28.15 reverence
worshipful, adj.
28.15 reverence
worshipfully, adv.
28.15 reverence
worshipper, n.
28.08 worshipper
worst, n.
14.22 badness
worsted-stocking, n.
10.09 shoe · hose

wort, n.
02.14 cabbage
wort, n.
09.15 beer · wine
worth, adj.
14.13 (un)deserving
22.13 value
worth, n.
14.13 (un)deserving
22.13 value
22.15 possession
worth, vb.
32.25 chance
worthier, n.
14.13 (un)deserving
22.13 value
worthiest, n.
14.13 (un)deserving
22.13 value
worthily, adv.
14.12 (un)worthiness
14.13 (un)deserving
worthiness, n.
14.12 (un)worthiness
14.13 (un)deserving
worthless, adj.
14.12 (un)worthiness
22.13 value
22.14 trifle
worthy, adj.
14.12 (un)worthiness
14.13 (un)deserving
22.13 value
30.09 (un)aptness
worthy, n.
14.17 boldness
22.13 value
worthy, vb.
14.12 (un)worthiness
wot, vb.
15.06 knowledge
wound, n.
07.18 wound
wound, vb.
07.18 wound
wounding, n.
07.18 wound
woundless, adj.
07.18 wound
wrack, n.
20.21 destruction
wrack, n.
35.07 wrack
wrack, vb.
20.21 destruction

35.07 wrack
wrackful, adj.
20.21 destruction
wrack-threatening, adj.
19.03 menace
wrangle, vb.
19.11 quarrel
wrangler, n.
19.11 quarrel
wrap, vb.
33.10 encompassment
wrath, adj.
14.29 anger
wrath, n.
14.29 anger
14.37 vehemence
wrathful, adj.
14.29 anger
wrathfully, adv.
14.29 anger
wrath-kindled, adj.
14.29 anger
18.18 instigation
wreak, n.
14.34 revenge
wreak, vb.
14.34 revenge
wreakful, adj.
14.34 revenge
wreath, n.
10.12 chaplet
wreathe, vb.
33.31 entangle
wren, n.
03.18 nightingale
wrench, n.
11.07 pull
33.31 entangle
wrench, vb.
11.07 pull
33.31 entangle
wrenching iron, n.
23.27 other tools
wrest, n.
26.06 fiddle
wrest, vb.
11.07 pull
33.31 entangle
wrestle, vb.
11.02 grasp
wrestler, n.
27.07 gamester
wretch, n.
04.04 rogue
wretched, adj.

X

Y

Z